ALSO BY JEFFREY LIEBERMAN

Shrinks: The Untold Story of Psychiatry

MALADY
OF
THE MIND

SCHIZOPHRENIA

AND

THE PATH TO PREVENTION

Jeffrey Lieberman

SCRIBNER

New York   London   Toronto   Sydney   New Delhi

Scribner

An Imprint of Simon & Schuster, Inc.

1230 Avenue of the Americas

New York, NY 10020

First Scribner hardcover edition February 2023

SCRIBNER and design are registered trademarks of The Gale Group, Inc., used under license by Simon & Schuster, Inc., the publisher of this work.

For information about special discounts for bulk purchases, please contact Simon & Schuster Special Sales at 1-866-506-1949 or business@simonandschuster.com.

The Simon & Schuster Speakers Bureau can bring authors to your live event. For more information or to book an event, contact the Simon & Schuster Speakers Bureau at 1-866-248-3049 or visit our website at www.simonspeakers.com.

Interior design by Wendy Blum

Manufactured in the United States of America

1 3 5 7 9 10 8 6 4 2

Library of Congress Cataloging-in-Publication Data has been applied for.

ISBN 978-1-9821-3642-0

ISBN 978-1-9821-3644-4 (ebook)

For Michael Juman
1965–1994

It is a riddle, wrapped in a mystery, inside an enigma;
but perhaps there is a key.

—Winston Churchill

CONTENTS

PART 3
SEARCHING FOR SCHIZOPHRENIA

PART 4
THE PATH TO PREVENTION

PROLOGUE

Jonah was twenty years old when I met him: gifted, intelligent, prepossessed with lofty ambition and limitless potential. He was the youngest child in an orthodox Jewish family whose ancestors had emigrated from Poland after World War I and settled in Brooklyn. His family was considered religious elite, descended directly from the Kohanim—priests whose lineage could be traced to Aaron, the prophet Moses's brother. Jonah was an academic prodigy, a young man who radiated confidence, and his parents saw him as the worthy heir to the family's religious line—one of the intellectual "chosen." They had invested much in their son's future success: money, attention, aspirations. Rather than feeling burdened by the pressure of their expectations, Jonah reveled in his special status. Like many "good Jewish boys," he was going to be a doctor—and not just another doctor, but a great doctor, his mother would boast.

But in 1980, when Jonah was a freshman in college, his glorious future began to unravel. Always diligent, impeccably groomed, and well mannered, Jonah started missing classes, appearing disheveled, and acting in a strange and self-absorbed manner. He obsessed over obscure philosophical issues and constantly badgered others about them. Jonah's roommate, alarmed by the change, notified the dormitory supervisor, who called Jonah's parents to say that he was taking their son to the student health service. Jonah's parents instead insisted on coming to get him.

They brought Jonah to Mount Sinai Hospital in New York City, where I was a junior faculty member in psychiatry on night call. Jonah was experiencing his first episode of psychosis and, based on his history and symptoms, was likely developing schizophrenia. (Today it would be called schizophreniform disorder—a variant of schizophrenia in which symptoms have been present for less than six months.) He was admitted to the inpatient psychiatric service and treated with antipsychotic medication.

Jonah's symptoms receded, and, within four weeks, they had almost disappeared.

When he was discharged, I agreed to follow him for his aftercare treatment. But after a few weeks of sporadic attendance at his appointments, Jonah abruptly terminated treatment and, eager to retain his credits for the semester, returned to school.

Twelve weeks later, Jonah was sick again. Believing that the remission of his symptoms meant he didn't need the medicine any longer, he had simply stopped taking it. Predictably, his symptoms soon recurred, and by the time his parents called me, panic stricken, Jonah was on the verge of a full-blown psychotic relapse. Voices were telling him that the world was on the precipice of disaster. He saw portents of danger everywhere; he worried that God's will was being defeated, and the world would end.

We readmitted Jonah to the hospital and prescribed another antipsychotic with a different side effect profile, thinking that perhaps unpleasant side effects had contributed to his discontinuing his medication. Fortunately, his symptoms responded well to treatment, and he was given another chance to resume his life. But Jonah stumbled again. He felt that his ability to study was impaired by the mental fogginess and physical shakiness that the medication caused. And so, buoyed by his second dramatic recovery, and impelled by youthful imprudence, Jonah decided after six months to once again stop taking his medication. Two more relapses and hospitalizations later, Jonah finally had to drop out of college.

Feeling frustrated and helpless, I asked a former supervisor for advice. How could I help Jonah break this cycle of relapse and hospitalization? Rather than words of wisdom or empathy, he said blithely, "You just have to let some patients suffer and learn the hard way by having multiple relapses before they accept the need for treatment."

I was stunned. He was speaking about someone with schizophrenia the way people spoke of drug addicts or alcoholics who needed to hit rock bottom. Jonah's life was at stake, and the supervisor's attitude was shockingly callous. Imagine an oncologist saying something similar about a cancer patient who'd stopped chemotherapy because of the noxious side effects. "You just have to wait till the cancer spreads before they learn to accept chemotherapy." To my mind, my supervisor's comment was no different.

In fairness to Jonah, how could he have been expected to know about the potentially devastating consequences of schizophrenia? While most people have some understanding of cancer, heart disease, and diabetes, their knowledge of schizophrenia is likely vague or nonexistent. "Psychoeducation"—in which mental health staff educate patients and families about the nature of an illness and what they might expect for the future—was first introduced in the medical literature in 1980 but didn't become well known for another decade, and even now, it isn't widely practiced. When Jonah fell ill, psychiatry was just emerging from an era in which its doctors were proscribed from revealing diagnoses to patients or discussing them with their families. While Jonah and his family knew that he was sick, they didn't realize that his illness was recurrent and could cause irreparable damage, permanently impairing his ability to function, unless he received and stuck to the treatment he needed. Sadly, those of us treating Jonah did not take the initiative to explain this to them until it was too late. In fact, our training had actively discouraged us from doing so; educating patients and their families about an illness such as schizophrenia was thought to be inappropriate and even detrimental.

This withholding of information was due to a combination of tendencies. Doctors, at that time, adopted a demeanor and bearing that tended to be remote from the patient, and they had traditionally avoided telling patients their prognosis when it was exceptionally gloomy. My profession was also still infused with certain ideas imported from psychoanalysis, and informing someone in psychoanalytically oriented psychotherapy of the nature of their malady was thought to compromise the effectiveness of the treatment. Not telling our patients as much as we knew was the opposite of what they needed—especially those younger patients who were at the beginning of their illness, when a youthful sense of invulnerability inclined them to underestimate its seriousness and stop treatment at the first sign of remission.

I didn't realize it then, but Jonah and I were both learning hard lessons about this illness—lessons that would shape our lives in very different ways. For Jonah, it was the realization that he was not invulnerable and that there were aspects of life he couldn't control. He had been struck by the most malignant of mental illnesses—a disorder that, over time, often robbed people of cognitive functioning and left them disabled, and whose genetic and neurological complexity made it very challenging to treat—and he was learning the hard way what that meant. For me, it was seeing the current limits of the field of psychiatry and the tragic consequences of mental illness; I also experienced a generational clash between my own youthful idealism and the establishment views of what constituted an acceptable standard of clinical care.

Jonah's story was heartbreaking but not unique. In the early 1980s, the destructive cycle of relapses and hospital admissions—the so-called revolving door—was common for people with schizophrenia, a reality with which I was becoming painfully familiar. Unfortunately, the attitude reflected in my supervisor's comments was also common then and consistent with the prevailing therapeutic pessimism regarding schizophrenia. Outraged as I was at the indifference shown to patients with the illness, I was a psychiatric neophyte. Who was I to question the orthodoxy of the field I was only just entering? Yet something in me reacted viscerally to the inhumanity and injustice of a situation in which doctors failed to see the urgency of engaging their patients in treatment. Although it would be another decade before we learned that this hit-bottom approach resulted in irreversible damage, due to the progressive effects of the illness, it still struck me as a shameful standard of care. I believe that it was the day I heard my supervisor's comment that my commitment to study schizophrenia, and to find a better way to treat it, took root.

More than any other mental illness, schizophrenia is synonymous in the public's mind with madness: the homeless person standing barefoot in the cold shouting at no one, the family member who suddenly believes the neighbors are sending poison gas through the walls, the friend who is convinced that the government had planted cameras to spy on him, and the perpetrator of irrational acts of mass violence. To see someone in the midst of florid schizophrenic psychosis, someone who has lost the ability to distinguish between the real and the imagined, is to know that you are in the presence of insanity.

Schizophrenia is neither new nor rare. It has likely existed for centuries, if not millennia. It's one of the leading causes of disability in the world, with a lifetime prevalence of about 1 percent of the population. That's 3.3 million people in the United States and 78 million worldwide. Schizophrenia doesn't discriminate. It can strike the Ivy League–bound high school valedictorian or the star athlete as much as it can the impoverished kid from a broken home. Gender, race, ethnicity, affluence, education—none of these provides immunity. While schizophrenia may be an equal opportunity illness, epidemiologically speaking, socioeconomic and racial factors clearly influence on whom the diagnosis is conferred and what treatments they receive. A particularly cruel aspect of the illness is that it manifests in late adolescence and early adulthood, just as young people are coming into the prime of their lives.

From the extensive scientific progress made since the mid-twentieth century, we know that schizophrenia is a brain disorder that disrupts thought, perception, and emotion, and we have begun to identify its causal mechanisms. We can now see changes in brain structure, biochemical abnormalities, and genetic mutations in the deoxyribonucleic acid (DNA) of affected individuals and their family members. These findings have enabled us to map the biologic underpinnings of schizophrenia and have guided the search for new treatments.

The symptoms of schizophrenia manifest gradually before crystalizing in three distinct forms: "positive" (hallucinations and delusions), "negative" (apathy, or anhedonia, or the inability to experience pleasure; lack of emotionality; poverty of thought), and "cognitive" (limited attention span, memory impairments, loss of executive functions, e.g., lack of the ability to problem solve, strategically plan, and organize). Symptoms usually develop gradually before intensifying in the form of a psychotic episode. Timely, effective treatment can produce remission of symptoms and enable recovery in most patients. But if the illness goes untreated, or when sufferers experience repeated relapses, their mental faculties start to deteriorate until they are unable to function normally. Without treatment, they're defenseless against the ravages of schizophrenia, their lives often shortened by decades due to the medical complications and the societal neglect that the illness imposes.

The observation that schizophrenia tends to run in families implicated genes as causal factors. Since the advent of gene-sequencing technology, researchers have identified more than a hundred genes that conspire in myriad ways to induce the illness. Environmental factors that impact brain development during pregnancy and birth, such as physical trauma, can also increase the odds of developing schizophrenia. Certain recreational drugs can provoke psychotic symptoms, though they only induce enduring illness in people with genetic vulnerability or, in certain cases, through sustained, extensive use.

Despite its relative frequency and its enormous cost to society, schizophrenia has not received attention and funding on par with that of other scourges of humanity. There have been famous cases—legendary ballet dancer Vaslav Nijinsky and Nobel laureate mathematician John Nash, the subject of the powerful book by Sylvia Nasar and 2001 Academy Award–winning film *A Beautiful Mind*—that have captured the public's attention. But, unlike diabetes or Parkinson's disease or Alzheimer's disease, all of which have their well-known sufferers and spokespersons, schizophrenia has fallen prey to the phenomenon known as "hiding in plain sight." I imagine that most people would be hard-pressed to name someone in the public eye who suffered from schizophrenia, let alone who exemplifies recovery and speaks openly about it.

However, there are hopeful signs that things may be changing, such as Elyn Saks's memoir *The Center Cannot Hold: My Journey Through Madness* (2007), although the impression that people more commonly have is that depicted by the journalist Robert Kolker in *Hidden Valley Road: Inside the Mind of an Ameri-*

can Family (2020), an account of a mid-twentieth-century American family with twelve children, six of whom suffered the terrible consequences of schizophrenia.

Esmé Weijun Wang, a writer with lived experience of schizoaffective disorder, opens *The Collected Schizophrenias*, her book of essays, with an account of just how damning a diagnosis of schizophrenia can feel. The first sentence reads simply, "Schizophrenia terrifies."

Much of the inattention to schizophrenia has been due to stigma—the prejudice that culture creates in the absence of knowledge. In the course of history, the march of science and the progress of civilization have helped to lessen or eliminate the stigma attached to illnesses such as leprosy, smallpox, tuberculosis, cancer, and AIDS. Schizophrenia, however, has had a different fate, remaining bound by misconceptions and falsehoods. Schizophrenia does not mean a split personality. Nor does it mean swinging wildly between extremes or behaving inconsistently. Political parties aren't schizophrenic when they flip-flop on issues; rapidly changing weather is never schizophrenic. The illness is most certainly not, as psychiatrist R. D. Laing pithily insisted in the 1960s, "a perfectly rational response to an insane world." To add to the muddle, schizophrenia is often confused with other mental disorders, particularly severe forms of bipolar disorder and depression with psychotic symptoms (affective psychoses) and drug-induced psychoses. While all these conditions share psychotic symptoms, they have clear differences. The dominant symptoms in affective psychoses are extreme emotions. Drug-induced psychoses spontaneously subside after the drug is eliminated from the person's system. Other diagnoses such as schizoaffective disorder apply when psychotic and emotional symptoms co-occur equally, and schizoid personality disorder describes people who have many features of schizophrenia but without fully formed psychotic symptoms.

I have been fascinated by schizophrenia since before I knew its name. As a child, I loved stories of the ancient world. I read the creation myths of Marduk, Gilgamesh, Yahweh, and Odin; the Babylonian, Persian, and Greek histories; and narratives about people from the Roman Empire through the Dark Ages. I had a special fondness for Greek mythology and often wondered whether the frequent communication characters had with the gods in the *Iliad* and the *Odyssey* was a literary device or a realistic depiction of human behavior at that time.

I tried to imagine what the lives of the ancients were like compared with my own. While most stories described activities that had some parallel in the mid-twentieth century of my youth—domestic tasks, labor, preparing food, politics, religion, relationships, conflicts—other aspects of human behavior in ancient times were wholly unfamiliar and not readily understood. There were also figures who seemed "otherworldly."

One such character was a religious recluse called Symeon Salus, who lived in the sixth century AD. After years in the desert, Symeon heard a call from God to save human souls, and so he traveled to Emesa (what is now the city of Homs, in western Syria) to do God's bidding. On his way there, Symeon found a dead dog in a dunghill; he loosened the rope of his tunic, tied the dog's paw with it, and entered the gates of the city dragging the carcass behind him. Children chased and taunted him. At church, Symeon cracked nuts noisily and snuffed out the candles; when people ran after him, he pelted the women violently with nuts, then overturned tables of food. The crowd beat him nearly to death. He drank copiously in taverns, defecated publicly, appeared nude in the streets, and entered the baths of women.

At the time, I regarded Symeon as a historical anachronism; a figment of ancient superstitions and primitive beliefs, maybe a saint or semi-deity with no latter-day equivalent. I saw individuals such as Saint Francis of Assisi and Joan of Arc in a similar way: as apocryphal anomalies in the fog of history; supranormal figures whose type had become extinct, just as the Titans of Greek mythology were extinct, or the race of humans destroyed by the flood in the Old Testament. Only years later would I realize that these were ordinary people exhibiting the symptoms of schizophrenia: bizarre, irrational behavior; disconnected from reality; hearing voices and seeing visions.

It wasn't long after my literary encounters with Symeon, Saint Francis, and Joan of Arc that I saw up close what madness looked like. In 1961, when I was in the seventh grade, my class was taken on a field trip to—of all places—a mental institution. The outing was part of my school's health and hygiene course. I was twelve years old and knew next to nothing of mental illness, save what horror movies with crazed killers had (incorrectly) taught me, and certainly nothing of its causes or treatment.

The Cleveland State Hospital for the Insane was southeast of Cleveland, Ohio, where I grew up. Built in 1855, it was originally called the Northern Ohio Lunatic Asylum. On the day of our outing, my classmates and I were ferried in a school bus to the sprawling grounds. As we passed through the hospital gates, we seemed to be entering the wooded campus of a prep school or university rather than a mental institution. This illusion evaporated quickly, though, when we were deposited at the entrance to a cluster of dilapidated redbrick buildings.

A photograph of Cleveland State Hospital taken in 1927. Originally built in 1855, it was called the Northern Ohio Lunatic Asylum until the 1870s.

Entering the lobby, we were greeted by a nurse in a pristine white uniform and escorted through a long, dingy corridor and through wards of male and female patients, where we encountered a macabre mise-en-scène: what looked to me like grotesquely misshapen human beings loitered about the dismal hallways and dank bedrooms. A rank odor of excrement enveloped us like a fog, from which we escaped only when we were led through large steel-paneled doors into an industrial-scale kitchen, where staff tended huge pots of a colorless, treacly gruel.

I can still recall vividly the noxious sensory experience of that visit. The patients had strange postures and mannerisms, with elongated heads and limbs. Some made bizarre gestures, fidgeting and twitching, and one man seemed to be masturbating. Others had tucked themselves into corners or were perched on furniture or lying on the floor, wearing remote expressions. Though they were young or middle-aged men (the women were kept separately), they looked wizened and worn. When they walked, it was with the stiff, shuffling gait of the elderly. Periodically, someone would burst into laughter or unintelligible shouting, noises that punctuated the background institutional din.

At the end of our visit, we trundled out the door, eager to get away but half excited, half appalled by what we had seen, which felt as strange to us as a foreign country or alien planet. We had encountered a part of the world, and an aspect of human existence, that we could never have conceived of had we not seen it with our own eyes. I had no idea at the time of the role this institution had played in the lives of two members of my family—that I would only learn of in the course of writing this book.

My childhood brush with the world of the mentally ill might have deterred me from having anything to do with their troubles, but by the time I was in college, my interest in the brain and behavior—and in the causes of aberrant behavior—had deepened, so much so that by my third year of medical school, I had decided to go into psychiatry.

Following graduation from medical school in 1975, I moved to New York City and started my internship at St. Vincent's Hospital and Medical Center in Greenwich Village. It was a bleak time. Over the next few years, the city would struggle to stave off bankruptcy, emergency rooms would be filled with violently deranged people on the drug PCP, and Son of Sam—a serial killer named David Berkowitz, who was found to suffer from schizophrenia—would terrorize the city. In addition, we would soon begin to see patients turning up in the hospital with mysterious infections that we couldn't diagnose and for which we had no treatment. I watched skilled physicians and nurses stand by helplessly while their patients died. Later, we would understand that they had died of acquired immunodeficiency syndrome, or AIDS. I was greatly relieved when the time came for me to move on to my psychiatric training, an area of medicine where we at least knew what we were dealing with and had effective treatments—or so I thought.

What I would soon learn was that the prognoses for people with schizophrenia were almost as bleak as it was for those who were originally diagnosed with AIDS. The introduction of chlorpromazine (brand name Thorazine), the first antipsychotic drug, in the 1950s had enabled psychiatrists to quell psychotic symptoms—the hallucinations, delusions, scrambled thoughts, and bizarre behavior. But it was not believed to relieve the underlying causes of schizophrenia or prevent its progressive, destructive effects. This misconception was facilitated by the belief that schizophrenia stemmed from psychic conflicts (rather than genes, proteins, neurotransmitters, and neurons) and that the only way to expel those conflicts was through the "talking cure," based on psychoanalytic theory.

In the decades that followed, the wonders of psychopharmacology and the emergence of neuroscience loosened the grip that Freudian theory—with its emphasis on unconscious conflicts and early-life traumas as causes of mental disturbances—held on psychiatry for much of the twentieth century. Unfortunately, in a cruel irony, the same science that served to dispel psychiatry's spurious views of schizophrenia then replaced them with a new theory that, while scientifi-cally based, offered even less therapeutic optimism.

This neurodevelopmental theory, which was conceived and gained influence in the 1980s, postulated that genes and environmental factors that impacted gene expression, like physical trauma and exposure to toxins, caused abnormalities in brain development that later gave rise to schizophrenia. In this context, schizo-phrenia was considered a genetic neurodevelopmental disorder, along with au-tism, fragile X syndrome, Rett syndrome, and Down syndrome, and the prospects for those afflicted were grim. Even if treatment was able to suppress the symptoms of the illness temporarily, it did nothing to forestall the inevitable impairment of its victims' mental faculties. These ideas—that schizophrenia was genetic, caused by abnormal brain development, and led to inexorable disability—spurred an at-titude of therapeutic nihilism in which those who suffered from schizophrenia were, in the words of a prominent British psychiatrist, "doomed from the womb." Such was the pessimism that confronted Jonah and patients like him when they sought treatment, and the bad outcomes predicted by the neurodevelopmental theory became self-fulfilling.

As time wore on, and my own capacity for critical scientific thinking evolved, I began to question the dogma. My skepticism was prompted by the fact that there were too many aspects of schizophrenia that were not accounted for by effects on brain development. Why did the symptoms of the illness not manifest until people were in their mid-teens or early twenties? What caused the illness to be progressive, disabling, and seemingly irreversible for some, but not all, patients? And if people with schizophrenia rarely had children, why didn't the population frequency of the illness decline over time? The theory and the clinical reality of schizophrenia didn't match. Many of the people I saw had been functioning very well up to the point in their lives when they started to develop symptoms. More-over, treatment was able to alleviate their symptoms. Why, then, should we assume that the illness could not be held in check? Why assume disability was inevitable? These inconsistencies prompted me to wonder whether the timing and quality of the treatment people received could be key factors in determining their outcomes.

The problem was that there was little evidence to support more auspicious theories of schizophrenia, and no new better treatments since the advent of anti-psychotic drugs. All that would change over the next three decades, when a cadre of researchers conducted studies that focused on the early stages of schizophrenia and how early pharmacologic intervention, combined with psychosocial treatments (talk and rehabilitative therapies and support services), impacted patients' outcomes.

From these studies, we learned that the majority of patients (approximately 80 percent) in the early stages of schizophrenia responded well to antipsychotic drug treatment and experienced symptom relief. What the studies also showed was that the longer it took for patients to be treated after the onset of their symptoms, the slower their treatment response and the worse their long-term outcomes. Taken together, the findings implied that psychosis was bad for the brain. The upshot was that if we could, through early and effective treatment, reduce the duration of untreated psychosis and the number of relapses, perhaps we could not only quell the symptoms of the illness but also prevent its damaging effects on the brain, limit the disability it caused, and improve patients' chances for recovery. Finally, we had data that directly challenged the nihilism with which schizophrenia had always been regarded.

In my four decades as a psychiatrist, I have seen the full range of outcomes in people with schizophrenia: lives reclaimed that seemed headed for ruin, and the tragedy that results when the illness goes untreated. I've watched countless patients suffer through cycles of recovery and relapse, and witnessed the gamut of symptoms: paranoid suspicions and elaborate delusions; bizarre beliefs; auditory, olfactory, tactile, and visual hallucinations; disorganized thoughts; incoherent speech ("word salad"); bodily contortions and "waxy flexibility"; catatonia. While patients may be able to ignore mild symptoms, at their most severe, they form an individual's consuming reality and can dictate sufferers' behavior. I've talked patients out of killing themselves to escape their misery and knew one young man who took an electric drill to his chest. I knew a patient who tried to eviscerate himself because he believed there were snakes writhing inside his abdomen; others have sought surgery to remove the computer chips they insisted had been implanted in their brains. I've seen patients starve themselves because they believed their food was being poisoned and known others whose auditory hallucinations commanded them to violently attack, and sometimes kill, family members or total strangers.

In almost every case I have been a part of, including Jonah's, friends and family members were caught completely off guard when schizophrenia struck their loved ones. They had little or no understanding of the illness and, in the throes of the distress and turmoil it caused, were unable to navigate the maze of information or the health care system to find competent care. Consequently, they were often ill-advised or unsure how to help and ended up with their loved one poorly treated. I can't tell you how many times a parent has said to me, "If only I'd known," when it was already too late, and their son or daughter had passed a point of no return: a chance for education lost, a relapse from which they did not recover, suicide, or the perpetration of violence.

For a time, Jonah largely escaped the consequences of stopping his medication by responding well to retreatment and recovering from relapses. But his luck finally ran out. After his third relapse (and his fourth episode of illness), Jonah's symptoms no longer responded to antipsychotic medications. Persistent delusions, hallucinations, and disorganized thinking, combined with an inability to manage the tasks of daily life, rendered him a veritable invalid. Gone were his plans to complete his education, pursue a profession, marry and have a family, and extend his family's scholarly legacy. In a four-year span, his life had gone from one rich in potential and aspirations to one consigned to disability and dependence.

I was profoundly affected by Jonah's plight. It was a tragedy to witness a young man with tremendous potential and ambition become mentally disabled. But soon my feelings went beyond empathy: I identified with Jonah. We were both of the Jewish faith and were both drawn to the medical profession. We were also both descended from the Kohanim (my mother's maiden name was Kohn, and her father was a religious scholar in Austria in the early twentieth century before immigrating to the United States). The more I came to identify with Jonah, the stronger was my sense of *There but for the grace of God go I.*

When Jonah became ill, psychiatric medicine didn't yet have the knowledge or the treatment models to do better. Since then, we have acquired the capacity to change the fortunes of those afflicted by schizophrenia in a way and to a degree that was never possible before. What we now understand about the links between biology and clinical symptoms has informed the development of therapies that have, for the first time, enabled us to think realistically of symptom remission, recovery, and even the prospect (as you will see in later chapters) of prevention. The reality is that evidence-based, state-of-the-art treatments exist that enable physicians to control the symptoms of schizophrenia, prevent their recurrence, and preempt their destructive consequences.

The key to achieving better outcomes involves accurate diagnosis and competent treatment applied in an innovative, coordinated care model for young people in the early stages of the illness. Early-detection programs using novel interventions can halt the illness and prevent its progression. As I'm writing this book,

doctors are extending efforts at therapeutic intervention to what's called the prodromal stage of schizophrenia—before the first illness takes root and manifests its
full-blown psychotic symptoms—utilizing treatments to prevent the onset of the
illness. Increased surveillance and early intervention have reduced the frequency
and consequences of heart disease, stroke, diabetes, infectious diseases, breast
and prostate cancer; the same can be true for schizophrenia.

As a result of this progress, so much of the suffering and disability that have
afflicted people with schizophrenia can now be avoided. What once defined the
fate of those with this illness—the consuming torment of symptoms, the massive
disruption to their lives and families, the irreparable intellectual deterioration—is
no longer inevitable and should not be regarded as an acceptable outcome.

For millennia, we have been helpless against schizophrenia, whether societies regarded it as a spiritual, moral, psychic, or neurobiologic condition. Now, in
the first half of the twenty-first century, we have reached an inflection point in
the arc of history at which we can arrest the illness and prevent its devastating
consequences. While Jonah's illness fell short of this therapeutic milestone, future
generations are poised to inherit vastly more auspicious prognoses as a result. The
tragedy is that only a fraction of those affected by schizophrenia are even aware
of these developments, much less able to access treatments that can mean the
difference between a productive and meaningful life and one of distress and disability. Our failure to provide life-changing—even lifesaving—treatments to those
in need is not simply an unmet clinical need or a health care disparity; it's a social
injustice. The gap between what *we can* and what *we are* doing is the reason for
this book. No one should suffer like Jonah and so many others like him.

In the pages that follow, I tell the story of schizophrenia and our efforts to
understand its causes and treat it. My intent is to provide a scientifically informed,
clinically oriented treatise on the ne plus ultra of mental illnesses for patients,
families, and people interested in this mysterious malady. In doing so, I trace an
arc through history, looking at the illness through a succession of historical, cultural, and scientific lenses—from the magical beliefs and superstitions of the dis-
tant past to the cutting-edge, neuroscientific understandings of the present. (A
timeline of milestones in the evolution of our societal and scientific understanding
of schizophrenia is provided in appendix 1.)

In part 1, I describe the view of schizophrenia in the ancient world through
the Middle Ages, to the birth of the asylum movement and the emergence of the
first mental health care reformers in the eighteenth and nineteenth centuries.

Part 2 reviews the rise of medical specialization and the birth of psychiatry, the search for the roots of mental illness in the brain, and the ascendance of psychoanalysis. We see the desperate measures doctors employed to treat their psychotic patients before the advent of antipsychotic drugs. I describe the enormous clinical and social impact that antipsychotics had in alleviating suffering but also the disaster caused by deinstitutionalization, when patients were released en masse from mental hospitals beginning in the late 1950s—a noble idea gone badly wrong by failed implementation and the diversion of needed resources and social service programs to other purposes.

Part 3 delves into the brain itself, showing how scientists have been able to explore its workings at increasingly granular levels. I explain how early proto-neuroscientists of the nineteenth and early twentieth centuries mapped the brain's anatomy and discovered its fundamental elements—the neurons, circuits they formed and neurotransmitters by which they communicate—and, a century later, how the technological marvels of brain imaging enabled scientists to peer into the living brain noninvasively. Finally, I describe the astonishing role of genes and the way in which they choreograph and construct the brain's development and, in vulnerable individuals, sow the seeds of susceptibility to schizophrenia.

Part 4 presents the current state of diagnosis and treatment and the game-changing treatments and models of care—early diagnosis and intervention, combined with pharmacologic, psychotherapeutic, and rehabilitative therapies in a form of coordinated specialty care—that enable recovery from schizophrenia and have placed researchers on the path to prevention. This propitious possibility is sharply contrasted with our challenged mental health policies, how the system evolved, and what changes are required to offer people the full potential of the therapeutic capacities we now possess.

Patients are the essence of this story. They are the ones who endure the devastating effects of the illness, and whose sanity and very lives depend on our ability to understand and treat schizophrenia. They teach me about the illness, and they continually remind me that schizophrenia is not only about an excess neurotransmitter, a neuron misfiring, or a gene mutating; it is the derailing and eventual destruction of a life, the disruption of a family, and the disturbance and loss to society. To enable readers to understand the nature of the illness, what it looks and feels like for its victims, I have tried to share as many patients' stories as could reasonably be accommodated in the book—including, of course, stories of recovery. But ultimately, it is the story of how schizophrenia, which for far too long fascinated and frightened humankind, is, due to the progress and success of science, now and for the future, a malady of the mind no more.

Part 1

METAPHORS
OF
MADNESS

Chapter 1

From the Ancient World
to Father Amorth

There are more things in heaven and earth, Horatio,
Than are dreamt of in your philosophy.

—William Shakespeare, *Hamlet*

A Framework for Reality

On the afternoon of July 7, 2016, I received a call from William Friedkin, director of the 1973 supernatural thriller *The Exorcist*. The critically acclaimed film
earned ten Academy Award nominations and won two, including Best Screenplay.
It seemed that Billy, as he insisted I call him, had retained an interest in spiritual
possession since working on the movie, in which the young daughter of a film
star becomes ill and undergoes all manner of medical and psychiatric tests and
procedures to diagnose her condition. When all medical science's tests and treatments fail to reveal the reason for her increasingly bizarre and aggressive behavior,
including some bodily maneuvers that defy the natural laws of physics and biology, the desperate mother appeals to the Catholic Church and a wizened exorcist
is summoned, pitting the forces of evil against a mortal agent of God. In May of
2016, Billy told me, he had traveled to Rome, where the Vatican's ninety-one-year-
old chief exorcist, Father Gabriele Amorth, had allowed him to witness his first
real exorcism—a woman named Rosa. Not only had Billy attended the event, he
had filmed it. He was planning to produce a documentary sequel to *The Exorcist*.

Billy had already shown the footage to two physicians at UCLA Medical Center.
Neil Martin, the chief of neurosurgery, didn't think it looked like schizophrenia or

epilepsy, though it could be some form of delirium. He had performed thousands of brain surgeries—on tumors, traumatic injuries, ruptured aneurysms, none of which had produced symptoms like Rosa's. Itzhak Fried, an epilepsy specialist, was equally mystified, though he regarded what he was seeing as authentic: Rosa wasn't fabricating her symptoms. He'd mentioned hyper-religiosity and said he doubted you would see such behavior in someone with no religious background. "It's a physiological state . . . Can I characterize it? Maybe. Can I treat it? No."

Their reactions had surprised Billy. He'd expected these doctors to dismiss Rosa's behavior as insanity or fraud, but they were genuinely baffled. They left open the possibility of something that couldn't be explained medically or cured by medical treatment. Now Billy wanted psychiatrists to weigh in and asked if I'd review the case. But first he had to find out if I believed in the possibility of such things: spirits, demons, the supernatural. I thought for a moment and then offered, in a professorial tone, what I thought was a diplomatic answer. As a physician and scientist, I said, I always sought empirical evidence by which to understand clinical phenomena. On the other hand, I added, I tried to keep an open mind and didn't discount the existence of a spiritual plane or the possibility of its incursion into the natural world.

This was good enough for Billy. "When can I come see you?" he asked excitedly.

Billy arrived at the New York State Psychiatric Institute, part of Columbia University, around noon on a sunny September day. I had asked three members of my faculty who were experts in psychiatric diagnoses to join us. Dr. Michael First had played a key role in the development of the fourth and fifth edition of the *Diagnostic and Statistical Manual of Mental Disorders* (*DSM*)—the bible of psychiatric diagnoses—and was the most knowledgeable person I knew on the diagnosis of mental disorders. Dr. Roberto Lewis-Fernández, president of the World Association of Cultural Psychiatry, was an expert in transcultural psychiatry. And Dr. Ryan Lawrence had studied philosophy and religion at the University of Chicago before his medical training and thus straddled, epistemologically, the scientific and spiritual disciplines.

We settled in to watch the video. Rosa was a tall, dark-haired young woman who had traveled from her home in Alatri, a small and deeply religious mountain village about sixty miles from Rome, seeking relief from what she called "attacks," which tended to happen on dates related to Jesus' life (such as his birth, transfiguration, Passion Week, resurrection). She seemed certain she was in the grip of demonic possession. On Father Amorth's team were four middle-aged priests and two burly assistants. Ten or so relatives of Rosa's were crowded into the small room to watch. As the exorcism began, Rosa started to thrash. At various points during the exorcism, she appeared to lose consciousness. She foamed at the lips. It took all of Father Amorth's men to restrain her.

Father Amorth spoke to her throughout. *"Infer tibi libera,"* he would say, stroking her hair. "Set yourself free." *"Recede in nomini patris!"* "Leave in the name of the Father!"

"Mai!" Rosa would growl. "Never!"

"Cede! Cede!" "Surrender! Surrender!"

"Io sono Satana*!"* Rosa screamed. "I am *Satan!"*

Eventually, after much back-and-forth, and following Father Amorth's command *"Requie creatue* Dei" ("Rest, creature of *God"*), Rosa emerged from her trancelike state. She was briefly at ease, though when Father Amorth blessed her parents, she began to writhe and growl, before finally calming down again. After nearly an hour, the video ended, and Billy asked what we thought.

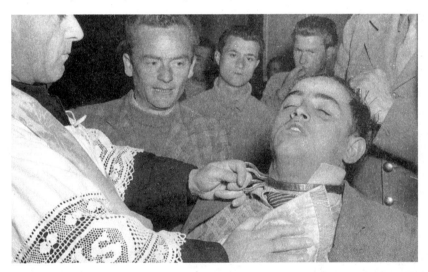

A photo of a priest performing an exorcism of a man
believed to be possessed.

Rosa was clearly suffering—none of us believed we were looking at a fraud—but nothing we saw in the video required the supernatural to explain it. Rosa's behavior didn't go beyond what we had all seen and treated in our mentally ill patients who were agitated, dissociated, or psychotic. We agreed that Rosa was most likely suffering from dissociative trance disorder, a variant of dissociative identity disorder (known previously as multiple personality disorder), a complex psychological condition that usually occurs in reaction to extreme or repeated physical, sexual, or emotional trauma in early life. The memory of this emotionally charged experience is so noxious that it cannot be processed neurobiologically or psychologically or stored in the usual way.

In adults, the effects manifest as post-traumatic stress disorder, or PTSD, but in children the cognitive and emotional residues of the experience are encapsulated and pushed out of conscious awareness. This compartmentalized experience is more than a painful memory; it is a segment of someone's life that is too hurtful and frightening to even acknowledge, and that he or she cannot assimilate into the conscious self. In the dissociation from the usual modes of behavior and sense of self, the sufferer has literally shut off, or dissociated from, the traumatic experience. This psychological coping mechanism suffices until the person matures into adulthood, when the repressed experience begins to seek expression through some new form of dissociation, including an emulation of psychosis or demon possession. In dissociative trance disorder, the particular form the dissociation takes is that of being possessed, usually by a demon, the devil, or a spiritual being.

Roberto remarked on the importance of culturally shared meanings in the scenario we'd just witnessed, saying, "What may work particularly well for some people in that setting is that everybody in the room actually believes that this is the framework for reality." Michael likened the situation and treatment to a kind of collective placebo response, with everyone "participating in a ritual that they all agree is the right way to look at the world." Ryan said that at that very moment, he had a patient who believed herself to be possessed by the devil. The woman came from a religious background and had a history of trauma. She was being treated with medications and psychotherapy. Ryan and his colleagues had seen her on the unit before: her "possession" would run its course, and she would get better and be discharged.

The most common antecedent to dissociative disorders is early-life trauma in the form of childhood abuse. These findings are highly consistent. We didn't have enough information about Rosa's background to know definitively, but based on what we had seen and been told, we believed that some psychological disturbance was at work, and speculated that, in order to cope, Rosa may have resorted to the only culturally acceptable expression of and way of seeking relief from her psychic trauma—religion, possession, and exorcism.

Medicine and religion have been intimately connected throughout history. In preliterate societies, there were few distinctions between religion, medicine, and magic. Illness was seen as the product of demons or spiritual forces that entered the person, and treatments were directed at these "causes," just as today's medical treatments address the germs or tumors that we believe produce the symptoms. For

Rosa, the treatment of choice was exorcism. We subsequently learned that this was not Rosa's first exorcism; it was her ninth. She had been receiving "exorcism therapy."

I expected Billy to question our diagnosis or at least express some disagreement, but he didn't protest. He asked several clarifying questions, then packed his gear, thanked us, and left.

I knew that Billy intended to make a documentary of the Vatican exorcism and interviews, including ours. Since our comments hadn't conformed to the script I assumed Billy might have envisioned, I wasn't sure how he would spin the story and represent our views. I didn't have long to wait. He wrote an article for *Vanity Fair*, published in November 2016, and the documentary premiered the following August. I was relieved and gratified that both reflected my views faithfully. Billy stuck to his word, but at the same time, the dramatic endings of the article and film shrewdly left open the possibility of spiritual possession.

MADNESS IMAGINED

Over the course of my career, I have become intimately familiar with the clinical manifestations of schizophrenia and their treatment. However, to those afflicted, the people around them, and the lay public, they remain as distressing and frightening as in the ancient past. Throughout human history, schizophrenia has been defined and redefined by a succession of pagan, religious, cultural, and secular environments. From ancient epochs governed by irrational beliefs and emotional reactions, to the modern age of rational thought and scientific enlightenment, schizophrenia has served as a behavioral totem straddling the boundaries between mysticism and madness, genius and insanity. Its victims have been viewed as diabolic or divine; cursed or blessed; miscreants, degenerates, and, finally, invalids.

Throughout history, our attitudes toward sickness have largely been shaped by what we understand of a given disease and our ability to treat it: that is, the less we know about the causes of an illness and the fewer treatments we have for it, the more our cultural attitudes and prejudices fill the gap in knowledge. This has been true of many of the most dreaded diseases. In her 1978 book, *Illness as Metaphor*, Susan Sontag explored how cultural distortions have framed various illnesses, and drew an analogy between the romanticized views of tuberculosis and insanity. "The melancholy character—or the tubercular—was a superior one: sensitive, creative, a being apart." But the myth of TB, Sontag writes, provided more than an account of creativity; it supplied a model of bohemian life, whether or not one had the artistic vocation. "The TB sufferer was a dropout, a wanderer in endless search of the healthy place."

The TB myth validated subversive longings and turned them into cultural pieties, which is what allowed it to survive both human experience and two centuries of accumulating medical knowledge. The power of the myth was dispelled only when the tubercle bacillus was isolated and effective treatments for TB were developed, in the form of antibiotics (streptomycin in 1944 and isoniazid in 1952).

Sontag then goes on to write, "If it is still difficult to imagine how the reality of such a dreadful disease could be transformed so preposterously, it may help to consider our own era's comparable act of distortion, under the pressure of the need to express romantic attitudes about the self. . . . In the twentieth century, the repellent, harrowing disease that is made the index of a superior sensitivity, the vehicle of 'spiritual' feelings and 'critical' discontent, is insanity."

A disease that suffered in a different way from culturally based attributions is HIV/AIDS. When the AIDS epidemic began in 1980, it was a mysterious, deadly illness for which we had no treatments, and which became an epidemic. Its victims were regarded as modern-day lepers. In the absence of information, and with the hardest-hit groups—homosexual men and intravenous drug users—being among society's most stigmatized, some people chose to attribute the illness to divine punishment for sinful behavior—a view that would have been right at home in the ancient world. It was only when LGBT activists exhorted the federal government, universities, and pharmaceutical companies to address the AIDS crisis that scientific research was mobilized, leading to breakthrough discoveries: isolation of the human immunodeficiency virus that caused the illness in 1984; AZT, the first medication for HIV, in 1987; and, subsequently, the invention of antiretroviral and protease inhibitor drugs, culminating in the pragmatic innovation of combining drugs, or triple therapy, in 1995. Eventually, the stigma surrounding the gay population lessened, and the hysteria that had greeted this plague-like illness in those early years abated. Now it is commonplace to see advertisements for its treatments on television.

Over the centuries, we have traced this arc from ignorance to knowledge for innumerable diseases. But progress in understanding schizophrenia has lagged behind, and false beliefs still linger. The scientific revolution that informed medicine and deepened our understanding of health and disease in the 1800s did not begin to impact mental illness until more than a century later. The suffering that accompanies madness was compounded by misunderstanding and mistreatment.

Only in the last several decades have technological advances in pharmacology, biochemistry, brain imaging, molecular biology, and genetics enabled us to elucidate the biological underpinnings of many mental disorders that in the past were attributed to demons, social deviance, or bad parenting.

This revelatory knowledge has been a long time coming and only recently come to light. While we need to be cautious about applying modern diagnoses to ancient figures and case histories, nevertheless we can recognize descriptions of behaviors in historical texts from as far back as 1550 BC that reflect symptoms characteristic of what we now associate with psychotic disorders, including schizophrenia. The "Book of Hearts" (contained in the ancient Egyptian medical text known as the *Ebers Papyrus*) describes a condition resembling schizophrenia, postulating that demons, fecal matter, poisons in the heart or uterus, or blood abnormalities caused madness. The Hindu Vedas, in about 1400 BC, contain descriptions of illnesses marked by bizarre behavior, absence of self-control, filthiness, and nudity. One of the earliest biographical descriptions we have of madness is that of Saul, first king of the Israelites, who reigned in the late eleventh century BC. According to the Old Testament's first book of Samuel, Saul was struck with insanity after disobeying the Lord. His torments included violent mood swings, rampant paranoia, fits of raving, and crushing despair. On one occasion, Saul stripped off his clothes and prophesied before Samuel, then lay naked all through the day and night. (In Hebrew, "prophesying" can mean "to rave" as well as "to behave like a prophet.") If Saul were alive today, he would mostly likely be diagnosed with psychotic depression or schizoaffective disorder. Interestingly, the story of Saul also contains an early depiction of "treatment." Saul suffers, and is soothed by music:

> But the Spirit of the LORD departed from Saul, and an evil spirit from the LORD troubled him. . . . And it came to pass, when the evil spirit from God was upon Saul, that David took a harp, and played with his hand: so Saul was refreshed, and was well, and the evil spirit departed from him.

A few centuries later, King Nebuchadnezzar of Babylon suffered a fate similar to Saul's. Nebuchadnezzar is described in the Book of Daniel as one who was punished by God for his pride and impiety, and compelled to "eat grass as oxen, and his body was wet with the dew of heaven, till his hairs were grown like eagles' *feathers*, and his nails like birds' *claws*."

In ancient societies, disease was understood as the result of divine displeasure at human conduct and indicated a state of disharmony. Given this link between religion and disease, it was logical that healers were priests who employed prayer, ritual, sacrifice, and magic as treatments.

As medical historian Andrew Scull puts it, in a world ordered by the divine, where God spoke routinely through human instruments and imposed severe penalties on those who defied him, misfortunes were invested with religious or supernatural meaning, and the transformations occasioned by madness were readily attributed to divine displeasure, spells, or possession by evil spirits.

Hunting in the Empty Air

Greek myth, drama, and poetry all drew frequent links between the machinations of the gods and human madness. Hera punished Heracles, the offspring of Zeus's adulterous affair, by "sending madness upon him." Agamemnon complained that "Zeus robbed me of my wits." The *Iliad* and the *Odyssey*—and the subsequent plays of Aeschylus, Sophocles, and Euripides—displayed a fascination with madness. The Greeks saw the gods everywhere, with their hands in all aspects of the natural world. Why should madness have been any different?

But Classical Greece's views of mental disturbances evolved beyond the cultural domains of myth and drama largely due to the influence of Hippocrates (c. 460–357 BC). Hippocrates, widely considered the father of medicine, and his followers produced a corpus of descriptive and theoretical knowledge and clinical practices based on his teachings that didn't rely on gods or supernatural explanations of diseases—including psychological disturbances. Hippocrates's practice of medicine was based on concepts developed through empirical observations and inference. He encouraged practitioners to obtain complete and detailed medical histories of patients. These thorough workups included patients' immediate environments—where they lived and what the climate was like—as well as age, diet, mood swings, sleep habits, menstruation patterns, dreams, and appetite; any symptom of physical illness was carefully assessed. A diagnosis was then made and a treatment devised. By declaring that the practice of medicine depended on detailed observation, inference of cause and effect, and reason rather than metaphysical explanations or religious beliefs, Hippocrates established the foundations of clinical medicine as it is now constructed and practiced. Numerous terms that we use today come directly from the Hippocratic corpus, such as symptom, diagnosis, therapy, trauma, and sepsis, as well as the physician's oath.

The Hippocratics were emphatically clear that even manic or melancholic troubles had naturalistic explanations, both due to social circumstances and physical ailments, and no more resulted from the whims of the gods than did physical ills: "Men ought to know that from the brain, and from the brain only, arise our pleasures, joys, laughter, and jests, as well as our sorrows, pains, griefs, and tears. . . . It is the same thing which makes us mad or delirious, inspires us with dread and fear."

Hippocratic physicians made sport of the beliefs of the temple healers who, with their notions of spiritual possession and arcane rituals, they regarded as little better than snake-oil salesmen. A key Hippocratic text, *On the Sacred Disease* (a title either ironic or just badly chosen, given its central argument that epilepsy results from pathological conditions of the body and not from the gods' displeasure), accuses these "charlatans and quacks" of having no treatment to offer and thus hiding behind the divine: "[They] called this illness sacred, in order that their utter ignorance might not be manifest."

So, what did madness look like to the ancients? And how can we relate the deluded thoughts and hallucinations of ancient figures to our contemporary notions of schizophrenia?

Hippocratic physicians were clearly familiar with hallucinations, in one instance attributing them to a brain illness in which "reason is disturbed and the victim goes about thinking and seeing alien things; one bears this kind of disease with grinning laughter and grotesque visions." And elsewhere: they "hunt in the empty air . . . snatch chaff from the walls—all these signs are bad, in fact, deadly." These symptoms were thought to indicate mental disorders with underlying physical causes. The Hippocratics also recognized what we might now call a predisposition or vulnerability to mental illness: The category of "half mad" was used to describe people regarded as susceptible to madness if stress or intoxicants came into play.

Medical explanations of what we now view as mental illnesses continued to be naturalistic into the first two centuries AD. Aulus Cornelius Celsus (25 BC–AD 50), an encyclopedist whose *On Medicine* (*De Medicina*) remains a key source of information in the Roman world, differentiated between acute and chronic psychosis. Celsus describes a form of insanity that was chronic and prolonged, in which patients remained physically healthy but mentally ill for the duration of their lives. This type of madness, in which patients were "duped . . . by phantoms," was very disabling and relatively resistant to treatment. Unfortunately, some of the treatments Celsus recommended were barbaric: these patients were "best treated by certain tortures" such as starvation, fetters (leg shackles), and flogging, while "untimely laughter" should be treated with "reproof and threats."

Celsus also held that an episode of insanity could be detected as it approached, with a patient becoming suddenly more talkative or speaking more quickly—almost certainly a description of what we now call "pressured speech" resulting from "flights of ideas" that can indicate the onset of a manic episode and may also be a feature of schizophrenia.

The prominent Roman physician Galen (AD 129–216) was influenced by the Hippocratics. He believed that all mental disorders arose not from demons or gods but were "the result of some lesion, some damage to the brain . . . that prevents it from functioning properly." As a child, he had high fevers, during which he experienced hallucinations; years later, he would deduce that mental disturbances can occur as temporary aspects of other medical conditions. When he served as physician to Roman gladiators, he saw injuries up close, giving him valuable knowledge about anatomy and physiology as well as experience in treatment.

Galen describes a patient named Theophilus, whose insanity took the form of hallucinating flute players who played in his house all through the day and night. Another patient of his was stricken by fear that the Titan Atlas, cursed to hold the world on his shoulders, would grow tired and drop the world. The man suffered insomnia, anguish, and melancholy because of this belief and was exhausted by his anxiety. Though it isn't clear how Galen treated him, we know that Galen was a creative physician. When faced with a delusional patient who believed she had a snake in her stomach, he "cured" her by inducing her to throw up and sneaking a snake into the vomit to convince her that she had expelled the creature.

While the Hippocratic school of medicine was conceptually advanced in its attempt to demystify disease, including attributing mental disturbances to natural rather than supernatural causes, the explanations and treatments that derived from its astute observations were grossly inaccurate. The Hippocratics believed that mental illnesses were the result of an imbalance of the body's four fluids, or humors, a theory extended by Galen that survived well into the eighteenth century. According to the humoral theory, the body contains blood, phlegm, yellow bile, and black bile. Health was the state in which these substances were in balance, and ill health, or pain, the state in which one of the humors was either excessive or deficient. Melancholy, for instance, arose from too much black bile (balance was restored through treatments such as special diets and bloodlettings), but the theory covered a range of mental disturbances, which went by the names of mania, melancholy, phrenitis, insanity, paranoia, panic, and epilepsy.

Apart from Galen, the Romans did little to advance medical science and the understanding of mental illness. However, they did leave behind an insightful legal text that touches on madness and presents practical approaches for dealing with it. *The Digest* (AD 530) focused on defining proper treatment under the law, rather than on identifying the causes of madness; "passive" conditions such as depression were thus of less concern than conditions that gave rise to violent acts. Romans understood that madness could come and go, and the law distinguished between a crime committed during a period of insanity and one committed when a formerly insane person was lucid—a distinction we still struggle with today. For the Romans, madness was principally a legal matter. The mad also had rights. They were entitled to be cared for by a "curator" and to retain their property and status. We can compare this pragmatic legalistic view to that of the seventeenth and eighteenth centuries, when madness was seen as a moral or social problem, and to the nineteenth and twentieth centuries and into the present, when we mostly view madness through a medical lens—a view that coexists and often conflicts with complex legal and social questions, and which science is still trying to free from the age-old vestiges of stigma.

Chapter 2

MADNESS IN
THE MIDDLE AGES

The candle flame gutters. Its little pool of light trembles.
Darkness gathers. The demons begin to stir.

—Carl Sagan,
The Demon-Haunted World: Science as a Candle in the Dark

SOME OTHER SPIRIT

With the collapse of the Roman Empire, Western civilization descended into the
Dark Ages. In Europe, the centuries that followed were characterized by poverty, disease, war, and intellectual and economic decline. The loss of the rational
tradition, coupled with the rise of Christianity, would shape medieval attitudes
to madness for the next thousand years. In Christianity, illness is understood in
the context of suffering and redemption, and illness was due to the lack of faith.
In this context priests and physicians were instruments of the divine and had
similar missions—to minister to the sick and provide comfort and relieve suffering using all means at their disposal, ranging from prayer to punishment and
religious relics.

An early sign of this regression in understanding of mental illness can
be seen in the work of the famed theologian Augustine (354–430), who wrote
that although visual hallucinations could result from fever, they might also
be brought on by "some other spirit, whether evil or good." As historian William V. Harris notes, the significance here is "the return to high intellectual

respectability of the view that a hallucinatory experience may be caused by an external being."

Few historical figures better illustrate the medieval blurring of ostensibly spiritual metaphysical states and mental illness than Saint Francis of Assisi. Born in 1181 to an affluent family, Francis enjoyed a privileged early life: he was "a lively young man, fond of music and parties, given to romantic tales, dreams of knighthood, fantastic treasure quests, and prayer in solitary chapels."

At the age of twenty, Francis was captured while on an expedition during the war between the Italian cities of Assisi and Perugia and imprisoned for a year. Two years later, while attempting to join the papal forces in Apulia, Francis had a vision in which he was called to return to Assisi to assume a special knighthood. Other visions of Christ followed, the most significant of which took place in the ruined chapel of San Damiano outside Assisi, where Francis heard God speaking to him from the crucifix above the altar: "Go, Francis, and repair my house which, as you see, is well nigh in ruins."

In the ensuing years, Francis wandered as a penitent, devoting himself to a life of poverty and attracting the first followers of what would become the Franciscan Order. According to one of Francis's biographers, Adrian House, his oddities were many. His tendency toward something close to pantheism made him revere fire so much that he refused to snuff out candles. He could erupt in mirth in the most unlikely situations, laughing at the mice infesting his bed or while being beaten by soldiers of the Crusade. He referred to his body as Brother Ass. But he was also obstinate, once removing the tiles from a roof so that his brethren would not become soft by sleeping in a dry shelter; on other occasions, he refused to have his bandages changed on a Friday because that was the day of the Crucifixion.

The bandages were, of course, those required by the stigmata: the wounds in his hands, feet, and side, which are said to have bled continually for the two years between his receipt of the wounds and his death. The stigmata had come to him following a vision while he was fasting and praying on Mount Alvernia: "As the vision disappeared, it left not only a greater ardour of love in the inner man but no less marvelously marked him outwardly with the stigmata of the Crucified." Francis died in 1226, aged forty-five, suffering from these stigmata and almost blind from a bacterial eye infection; two years later, he was canonized by Pope Gregory IX.

Saint Francis of Assisi receiving the stigmata of Christ
in an etching by William Unger.

I have no desire to impugn the religious significance of Saint Francis or to deny the basis of his sainthood, including the miracles and visions attributed to him. I can't state with certainty that the wounds of the stigmata were self-inflicted. Whether we take the supranormal events of his life literally, as apocryphal embellishments, or as manifestations of mental illness is a matter of how we interpret the stories that have come down to us through the ages, and our interpretations are shaped by the historical moment, social milieu, and cultural zeitgeist in which we're living. The content of psychotic symptoms likewise mirrors the culture of the times. In Francis's case, his behavior and beliefs, which seem strange to us now, were congruent with culturally acceptable themes of thirteenth-century Italy, and so were less likely to be viewed as abnormal—in much the same way that contemporary beliefs about being watched by the US National Security Agency (NSA) or seeing targeted, personal messages on the Internet might be extreme but would not be regarded as inconceivable.

I have seen the same pattern of messianic conviction, divergence from social norms, physical privations, and charismatic orations (characteristics and behaviors shared by mystics and the mentally ill) in many people I have treated for schizophrenia. Francis was a young man when his behavior became unusual and unpredictable, and his decline in his final years reflects a common scenario experienced by sufferers of schizophrenia, whose physical health often worsens as they age through personal neglect and self-injury.

OWT OF HIR MENDE

Sometime in the 1430s, an illiterate woman named Margery Kempe began dictating the narrative of her life to a scribe, creating a text now regarded as the first autobiography in English. The author was very religious, and possibly schizophrenic. *The Book of Margery Kempe* is a firsthand account of the inner workings of the mind of a woman who may have been mad, a mystic, or both. As Margery herself distinguished between what she saw as the mad and the mystical phases of her life, she offers us a unique picture of the relationship between the two states from the medieval perspective.

Margery was born in Norfolk, England, around 1373, and married at age twenty to John Kempe. She gave birth to the first of her fourteen children soon after. What followed was an eight-month period when, by her own account, she went *"owt of hir mende."* Margery describes symptoms that suggest postpartum psychosis or perhaps, given her age, the onset of schizophrenia: "And in this time she saw, as she thought, devils opening their mouths all alight with burning flames of fire, as if they would have swallowed her in, sometimes pawing at her, sometimes threatening her, sometimes pulling and hauling her both night and day." As a result of her agitated and bizarre behavior, Margery was isolated from her community and placed in physical restraints.

Those months of madness brought Margery to a spiritual crisis. When her milling and brewing businesses failed soon after, she turned to Jesus, who had appeared at her bedside: "In lyknesse of a man, most semly, most bewtyvows, and most amiable . . . clad in a mantyl of purpyl sylke, syttyng upon hir beddys syde."

The autobiography, rendered in the third person, recounts her life as a mystic over a twenty-five-year period. She describes conversations with God, Jesus, and Mary, and participates in biblical scenes, swaddling the infant Jesus, and consoling the Virgin with "a good cawdel" after the Crucifixion. She has auditory hallucinations, hearing "such sounds and melodies that she could not hear what anyone said to her at that time unless he spoke louder," and visual hallucinations, seeing "with her bodily eye many white things flying all about her on all sides, as thickly in a way as specks in a sunbeam." She is given to wailing, sobbing, and writhing in public; there are miracles and prophesies. She experienced God not only in the form of spiritual ravishment but as familiar and conversational, offering her practical advice on everyday matters. There are also times when God's voice is withdrawn, and Margery is prey to grotesque sexual and demonic visions ("horybyl syghtys and abhominabyl"), such as the devil mulling over which man she would prostitute herself with.

The book gives us a picture not only of Margery's mind but of how she was regarded by her contemporaries. Many rejected her and labeled her a devil worshipper; clerics and local officials charged her with heresy, put her in prison, and threatened to burn her to death. Others, however, thought her holy, and she attracted the support of prominent clerics and other religious people, such as the archbishop of Canterbury and Dame Julian of Norwich. She certainly didn't comply with conventional expectations of women. There is virtually no mention of her children in the autobiography, and she apparently abandoned her maternal role and lived apart from her husband. She did, however, return to care for him when he became ill and senile, and did so until his death.

Was Margery mad, as many contemporary clinicians have maintained, or was she, as scholar Alison Torn argues, communicating "a truly embodied spiritual experience, using the established religious metaphors" of the time? As Torn notes, much of what Margery reports in her autobiography would today be considered classically psychotic: visual and auditory hallucinations, delusions of grandiosity, and the negative symptoms of social withdrawal and passivity.

Symptoms alone, though, don't determine a diagnosis. Did Margery's visions and voices impede her ability to function? And if so, according to what criteria? It's unlikely that someone with Margery's set of behaviors would do well in secular twenty-first-century Manhattan. But in fifteenth-century England, where medieval spirituality accommodated intense emotional and physical expressions of faith, she gained supporters, apparently viewed her experiences positively, and produced an autobiography despite being illiterate.

From a distance of more than six hundred years, we cannot definitively diagnose Margery Kempe any more than we can Francis of Assisi. We cannot preclude the existence of real spiritual enlightenment and supernatural powers, and we must not fall into the trap of presentism (viewing the past through the lens of the present). What we know from the record she left is that she had a number of psychological experiences that are recognizable as psychotic symptoms, and whose nature, age of onset, and course align with schizophrenia. But within the confines of medieval society and the modes of expression available to her, she lived a life that incorporated those symptoms and made them meaningful.

WITCHES, DEMONS, AND THE UNEXPLAINED

The Renaissance changed Europe's social milieu and cultural paradigm, which in turn changed the conceptualization of mental illness. Religious, political, and economic transformations saw the demise of the feudal state, the growth of markets across Europe, and the loosening of the Catholic Church's grip on parts of the Continent. Classical learning underwent a revival, and the scientific revolution placed a new emphasis on empirical evidence.

At the same time, the witch hunts of Europe (the burning of the so-called heretics) continued through the fifteenth and sixteenth centuries. The victims often included people with psychotic illnesses. When Dutch physician Johann Weyer published *De Praestigiis Daemonum* (*On the Devil's Tricks*) in 1563, arguing that the madness of heretics and witches resulted from natural rather than supernatural causes, the Church proscribed the book and accused Weyer of being a sorcerer.

Exorcisms, meanwhile, continued. By the sixteenth century, the village of Geel, in present-day Belgium, had become something of a colony for the mad. Its economy was based on donations made by the families of those suffering the torments of insanity, and clerics oversaw their treatment. "Lunatics were placed in the church and chained by the ankle, and for eighteen days, efforts were made to exorcize the evil demons who had possessed them." If, after treatment, madness persisted, many of the afflicted would go to live with a local peasant family. (Interestingly, Geel still draws those with mental illnesses and mental disabilities, though the approach to their care has changed significantly; there are no more exorcisms but rather a program in which locals take them in as "boarders," with the aim of providing humane care in the community.) It is perhaps not surprising that exorcism had such a hold on the imagination of the Middle Ages. As Scull points out, the casting out of demons was perhaps the most powerful demonstration of God's omnipotence: "The drama of an exorcism was unmatched."

MEDICAL MISCHIEF

As Susan Sontag observed, behavioral disturbances due to mental illness are re-fracted through the culture in which they occur and interpreted through lenses of scientific knowledge and the prevailing politics. In the absence of the former, the latter often prevailed. Thus did societal views of mental illness progress from spiritual causation to moral deviance until the Enlightenment, when Western civilization began to understand insanity as being based on natural causes rather than spirits, superstition, and morality. Doctors reinterpreted the intense spirituality displayed by mystics of the past within a medical (if not scientific) framework. But it was difficult for mental illness to achieve clinical legitimacy and a scientific foundation: false medical theories, preposterous and barbaric treatments, and wholly inadequate services abounded. While mental illness had achieved a more enlightened conceptual status, sufferers were still considered a nuisance to society. Consequently, people with mental illnesses landed in poorhouses (called almshouses), asylums, jails, or on the streets. If they received any treatment at all, it was at best useless and at worst harmful.

The limitations, as well as the chicanery, of eighteenth-century medicine are epitomized by Franz Mesmer and Johann Joseph Gassner, whose paths once crossed in Bavaria. Mesmer was a German physician who might be called the first practitioner of what we'd later come to know as psychiatry. While studying in Austria, Mesmer proclaimed that he had discovered a vital force possessed by all people: animal magnetism. When the flow of this force around the body was obstructed or blocked, ill health occurred; fortunately, Mesmer possessed the ability to manipulate this force. His treatment involved sitting in front of a patient, holding his or her knees between his own, and touching and pressing around the body until the patient experienced a trance or perhaps something resembling an epileptic fit. This method, and Mesmer's considerable charisma, made him the most celebrated physician of his day.

Whatever Mesmer's clinical abilities, he was a gifted doctor of spin. On one occasion, he was asked to give an opinion of the controversial Catholic priest Johann Joseph Gassner at the Bavarian Academy of Sciences. The belief that physical and mental illnesses were caused by the devil had persisted well into the Enlightenment, and Gassner was something of a traveling exorcist in Germany. Mesmer cleverly explained that while Gassner's exorcisms might seem to be effective, that was only because he was endowed with an exceptional degree of animal magnetism. Thus did one dubious practitioner opine upon the dubious methods of another.

As Mesmer's renown grew, he was inundated with as many as two hundred patients a day, requiring him to modify his technique so that he could treat groups of patients simultaneously. Patients (usually women) frequently reacted to treatment with violent convulsions and fits of weeping or laughter, whereupon Mesmer would lead them to a "crisis room," which had mattresses on the floor. Mesmer disappeared for long periods of time to attend the women, inviting suspicion of sexual exploitation.

King Louis XVI of France appointed a commission to investigate Mesmer following allegations of quackery from his medical rivals. The committee, which included the American ambassador to France, Benjamin Franklin, found no evidence to support his theory of animal magnetism. Although disciples still flocked to Mesmer, gossip and scandal eventually drove him into exile in Switzerland, where he lived out the remainder of his days. As for Gassner, Pope Pius VI eventually censured him for promoting the idea that illnesses were caused by the devil and ordered him to cease his exorcisms—a prohibition that seems to have been rescinded, or at least not to have been applied to the Vatican's chief exorcist of our own era, Father Amorth.

A Clinical Mystery

I learned of the mystification and demonization of mental illness (and of medical quackery) in my history of medicine lectures in medical school, but I believed that such outlandish notions had long since been consigned to the dustbin. My views hadn't changed years later when I, and my colleagues, dispelled Billy Friedkin's illusion of Rosa's exorcism as evidence of spirit possession—but it revived an unsettling experience from early in my career that I never fully understood.

While completing a research fellowship as a young psychiatrist, I saw a number of patients in private practice to keep my clinical skills sharp and supplement my income. During my training, I had gained a reputation as an astute clinician and was accorded the privilege of having difficult patients referred to me. One such patient was unlike any I've ever encountered.

Ariana was seventeen years old and had been diagnosed with schizophrenia four years earlier. In that time, numerous antipsychotics and a lengthy course of electroconvulsive therapy had produced no improvement in her symptoms. It seemed I was Ariana's last chance before she faced the possibility of institutionalization.

Upon first meeting her, I was struck by her behavioral oddities. She entered my office cautiously, escorted by her parents, then froze abruptly, assuming a strange posture, before she resumed walking. Such motor symptoms would usually indicate catatonia, characteristic of a specific schizophrenia subtype. But there was something about Ariana's movements that made me resist the usual diagnosis. What was even more striking was how disconnected she seemed from her environment and the people in it; it was as though she were in a trance. Her demeanor and facial expression resembled that of people with locked-in syndrome, a neurologic condition in which consciousness remains intact but victims are unable to communicate due to bodily and facial paralysis. Ariana seemed to be attending to something other than the people in the room, possibly responding to internal stimuli, or so I thought. The other thing that struck me about Ariana was her childlike appearance. Her parents told me that she had not yet begun to menstruate, which explained her immature features.

Prior to her family's arrival, I had reviewed her history in the hospital records. She had been a normal child, cheerful, social, and affable, until age twelve. This surprised me, as patients with severe forms of mental illness frequently have some early (premorbid) deficits in their mental functioning. She'd undergone an elaborate medical workup, searching for an explanation for her appearance and symptoms, which ruled out conditions like polycystic ovary syndrome, acute intermittent porphyria, and Turner syndrome. All the tests and procedures had come back negative or within normal limits. Once all possible medical conditions had been ruled out, Ariana was diagnosed with schizophrenia, and given her motor symptoms, the most ominous catatonic subtype.

While I agreed with the diagnosis, I arranged to perform an Amytal interview on her just to cover all bases, something Ariana had not undergone with her previous doctors. This procedure involves the intravenous administration of a short-acting sedative—sodium amytal, known as "truth serum"—while asking the patient questions. In patients suffering from catatonia or dissociative states, the drug exerts a paradoxical effect, transiently awakening them and bringing them into contact with their surroundings, able to open up about what they are feeling and experiencing. The effect is dramatic but short lived, and they soon revert to their disconnected state.

With Ariana, however, there was no observable response. And unlike most patients, she didn't fall asleep at the end of the procedure. Sobered by this outcome and reluctant to repeat treatments Ariana had received already, I decided to take a different approach by asking a colleague to consult on the case.

Judith was finishing her doctorate in human development at Columbia and was a licensed counselor who specialized in family dynamics and transpersonal therapy. She was whip smart and had a quiet confidence and gentle demeanor. Before accepting the obvious diagnosis of treatment-refractory schizophrenia, I wanted to be sure that Ariana's condition wasn't the result of a toxic family dynamic, in which she'd become the designated sick family member, or some variant of Munchausen by proxy (a condition in which a caregiver, usually a parent, fabricates illness in another person, usually a child, for the purposes of gaining attention). Since my expertise was in psychopharmacology, I would feel more confident with Judith involved. Our strategy was to map the family relationships and dynamics and attempt to engage Ariana in that process.

Over the next few weeks, as Ariana's treatment continued, I began to feel out of sorts. I lacked energy and motivation, and my interest in the main pursuits of my life began to flag. I thought I might be getting sick or even depressed. I often became impatient and argued over trivial things with my girlfriend. Initially, I attached no special significance to these changes, as these fluctuations in mood, energy, and cognitive functions, often resulting from life circumstances, were within the range of normal human experience. But eventually something happened that I have never been able to explain and caused me to reexamine the preceding events and ultimately end my involvement with Ariana.

On the morning of what would be our last session, I overslept—which I never did. For some reason, my alarm had not gone off. I cursed while leaping out of bed, stubbing my toe in the process, and arrived late to the hospital. After finishing at the hospital, I headed to the office on the Upper West Side where I saw patients. Ariana and her parents were my second-to-last appointment of the evening. They were already seated in my office when Judith arrived, apologizing for being late. As she settled herself, she directed my attention to Ariana, who was rocking back and forth, turning her head side to side, and making occasional guttural sounds. While the young woman had exhibited abnormal motor symptoms before, these movements were new and signaled a different kind of agitation.

We attempted to proceed, but Ariana was clearly in too much distress. So, I suggested we end the session early. I wrote prescriptions for her medications and told her parents to call me if she didn't calm down. To cap off the day, my last patient didn't show.

Judith and I walked to the subway station on Eighty-Sixth Street and Broadway, where we parted. I was living in a prewar apartment building in Greenwich Village. Judith lived in a walk-up on East Ninety-Sixth Street, five miles away on the opposite side of the city.

I arrived home about seven o'clock. It was still dusk, and I could glimpse the sunset over the Hudson River from my apartment window. I decided to make a hamburger for dinner and had just put it in the frying pan when the lights went out, leaving me in the dark but for the glow of the gas flame on the stove. I suspected a fuse had blown and was cursing my day's run of bad luck. As I walked toward the fuse box in the hall, I spied a blue haze hovering in the corner of the living room ceiling. It was making a whirring sound that gradually grew louder as the blue light pulsated. Suddenly I felt a piercing pain, like a hot poker plunged into my forehead, over my left eye. I fell to the floor clutching my head, struggling to make sense of what was happening. As my thoughts cleared, I began to crawl away from the blue light and toward the bathroom. The pain ebbed and flowed in synchrony with the blue light's pulsations. I got to the bathroom, pulled myself up to the sink, and doused my face with cold water. Then, as I hesitantly walked back to see if it was still there, it suddenly stopped. The pain, the noise, the blue haze—all vanished, and the lights came back on. It couldn't have lasted more than a couple minutes but seemed an eternity.

Scared out of my wits, I wondered what I should do: Flee the building, call the superintendent or the police? But when I got to the phone, I instinctively dialed Judith. She picked up, and what she said alarmed me even more. Almost immediately, before I could speak, she said, "Did it happen to you?" and went on to describe a similar experience that she characterized as a hostile entity attacking her in the form of what she called "negative energy."

Shaken, we tried to make sense of what had happened. We didn't think we were going crazy or had suffered a folie à deux (a shared psychosis). Was it possible we had experienced a supernatural phenomenon? Some kind of spiritual encounter? Lacking any rational explanation for what had happened, we spontaneously connected it to Ariana. We had thought we were treating someone with a mental illness, but nothing about this patient had turned out to be typical: not her history, symptoms, or response to treatment. Even if she did have a severe and unusual variant of a brain disorder, no test we'd done had identified it. This was 1982, before technology enabled the identification of uncommon causes that could mimic mental illness, such as autoimmune conditions, infectious pathogens, and genetic mutations. While we talked, Judith and I were arriving at the same conclusion: that what we had jointly experienced was in some mysterious way related to our patient.

What made the events of that night so bizarre and ominous is that we hadn't merely had a strange experience; we'd felt attacked, as if in retaliation for something. Since the only thing that linked both of us was Ariana, we thought that our shared experience must be connected to her. The implication of this contradicted every rational and scientific belief I'd ever held, that we were assailed by something related to Ariana and that something was trying to drive us away. Ariana's parents had mentioned early on in her treatment something about curses and ancient feuds from Italy, which Judith and I had dismissed as superstition. Even now, the idea of a curse seemed to us like mumbo jumbo. Unable to think of a more plausible explanation, we eventually agreed that the evening's events were the culmination of a struggle for control of a young woman. On the one side, Judith and me—the agents for her family's desire to find a treatment for her affliction—and on the other, the affliction's source, whether it was a brain disorder, a psychological conflict, or a spiritual disturbance.

We decided to sleep on it and reconsider the matter the next day. But upon meeting, Judith and I felt more convinced that we had stumbled into something that was wholly foreign to our experience and way beyond our expertise. Moreover, we didn't know what could happen next if we continued in our efforts to treat Ariana. We didn't want to be too melodramatic but also didn't want to tempt fate. And then I made the decision that I still regard as the most ignoble act of my career, one I regret to this day: I decided to break off treatment.

I called Ariana's parents and told them that we were withdrawing from the case, because there was nothing more we could do for their daughter. They were surprised and disappointed, but they didn't protest or try to convince me to change my mind. When I hung up, I felt terrible—a combination of shame, relief, and fear—and I feel terrible remembering it now. Since then, I have occasionally thought about Ariana and that bizarre episode, but it would be almost four decades before I would reconnect with Judith and revisit it.

Chapter 3

THROUGH A GLASS, DARKLY

For now we see through a glass, darkly; but then face to face:
now I know in part; but then shall I know even as also I am known.

—1 Corinthians 13

TRAITEMENT MORAL

By the seventeenth century, the public's view of the insane had begun to shift from spiritually afflicted to morally deviant, and asylums for the mad and "morally disreputable" began to appear in many European countries. Their purpose was more to remove them from society than to minister to their infirmities. As the mad were incapable of behaving according to social or moral norms or performing productive labor, madness was seen as a form of deviance and depravity, and those who suffered from it were lumped in with vagrants, the impoverished, the disabled, and the elderly. Thus were the concepts of mental illness conflated with social conformity and convention and subordinated to political pressures. At the same time, a comingling of sociological prejudices and scientific theories would falsely attribute infirmity and inferiority to racial and socioeconomic factors.

The eighteenth century saw a growing middle class in Europe and the beginnings of consumer society. In England, those who could afford it often sought relief from the difficulties of managing a mentally ill family member in the home by placing them in private, for-profit madhouses. These institutions, which were not properly regulated, were often isolated and ominous looking. Along with the charitable asylums, they created a physical separation between the sane and the mad; with their high walls and barred windows, they served to intensify the fears of the people on the outside of those confined within. Conditions inside these facilities were generally appalling, with little or nothing in the way of decent living environments or facilities, much less therapy. Agitated and violent patients were regularly chained to the walls, sometimes naked.

It was about this time that Philippe Pinel (1745–1826) conceived a more humane model of mental health care—what became known as *traitement moral*, or "moral treatment." Mental institutions were not unlike prisons, sequestering people in squalid conditions in order to keep them from disturbing society. Pinel did not dispute the need for mentally ill persons to be kept apart, but he believed that they should, and could, reside in clean and compassionate therapeutic communities.

As a result of this innovation, Pinel became the most famous psychiatrist of his day. But he started his career in a very different way. As a young man, Pinel was content as a medical writer; his descriptions in 1809 of young patients showing signs of "premature dementia" are widely regarded as among the first thorough portraits of schizophrenia. But when a close friend, who'd become insane (his "mind elated"), committed suicide, he decided to study medicine. Pinel had seen the poor care that his friend received and wanted to develop a more humane treatment of mental illness. In time, he rose to head the Paris asylum for insane men at Bicêtre in 1793, where he implemented his new model of care, removing the iron chains long used to restrain patients. Two years later, he did the same at the Salpêtrière, the public hospital for women.

Others in Europe and the United States were simultaneously undertaking similar reforms and experimenting with unchaining asylum inmates, but it was Pinel who conceptualized the changes and produced the first published account of a new, more humane, and more optimistic way of caring for patients. Over the next two hundred years, medical science would reveal the full spectrum of schizophrenia's manifestations, course of illness, underlying causes, and effective treatments. Moral treatment and humane mental institutions were the first milestones on this path of discovery.

Central to Pinel's philosophy were two aspects of asylum life that he believed to have beneficial effects for patients. The first was the institutional setting itself. Pinel believed that madness arose from excessive irritation of the nerves and that a relaxing environment, orderly routines, and a communal spirit would soothe unsettled minds. Pinel's second tenet was that the routine of the asylum should encourage setting limits and instill a sense of self-mastery in patients. The patient's body and quarters were to be kept clean and a "well-timed variety" of amusements should be offered.

Philippe Pinel unchaining mental patients at Salpêtrière in 1795.
Painting by Tony Robert-Fleury.

The asylum movement quickly spread to the New World, but not through the influence of Pinel. While Pinel was lionized for this seminal innovation, other less celebrated figures shared in this conceptual leap. Principal among these was William Tuke who, with the Quaker Society of Friends, founded the York Retreat for the mentally ill in 1796. This new way of caring for the mentally ill inspired a fellow Quaker, Dr. Thomas Bond, and Benjamin Franklin to establish the Pennsylvania Hospital in 1751.

Years later, two prominent Philadelphia physicians on the hospital staff, Drs. Benjamin Rush and Thomas Kirkbride lobbied for a wing of the hospital to be designated for the care of the mentally ill. Over time this ward became inundated, so in 1841 a separate facility dedicated to the mentally ill, The Institute of the Pennsylvania Hospital, was built in West Philadelphia and Kirkbride was named the first superintendent. Three years later, Kirkbride established the Association of Medial Superintendents of American Institutions for the Insane, which in 1921 became the American Psychiatric Association.

Other institutions soon sprang up in the United States: the McLean Asylum for the Insane, in Boston; the Bloomingdale Asylum for the Insane, in New York; the Connecticut Retreat (later renamed the Institute of Living), in Hartford; and, outside of Baltimore, the Sheppard and Enoch Pratt Hospital. All aimed to operate according to Pinel's principles. Though the settings in which they were built may be less rural now, other reforms of the asylum movement are still visible. Most inpatient units, whether self-contained psychiatric hospitals or part of general hospitals, continue to employ the concept of a therapeutic community, with a routine schedule of activities that encourages structure, discipline, and personal hygiene. The self-mastery goal resembles the guiding principle of the contemporary "recovery movement" (discussed in chapter 21), which recognizes the capacity of people with mental illnesses for increased self-determination and greater participation in mainstream society.

But the poor could not afford these private mental asylums, and the need for public mental institutions was quickly appreciated by some states; others eventually followed. By the mid-nineteenth century, the demand was such that the expansion of public facilities couldn't keep pace, and the majority of mentally ill persons still resided in jails and almshouses, subject to abuse and neglect. The stage was set for an American Pinel. Rush and Kirkbride had established the model of care in the New World, but it needed to be scaled to meet the population's needs.

Patients in Bellevue Hospital, New York City, guarded by policemen, in about 1885.

A VOICE FOR THE MAD

Dorothea Dix was born in Hampden, Maine, in 1802. Evidence suggests that her childhood was unhappy and that her parents were negligent and abusive. At twelve, she moved to Boston to live with her wealthy grandmother, where for a time she flourished. By 1821, Dix had established an elementary school in her grandmother's home and written a popular book for schoolteachers. She went on to publish other works, including poetry, and started a secondary school in her own home. Her circle of friends included the poet and essayist Ralph Waldo Emerson. But Dix suffered frequently from ill health, especially during the cold Boston winters, and in time her workload and physical illnesses took their toll. Her biographer David Gollaher has suggested that Dix suffered bouts of depression and had some kind of mental breakdown in the 1830s.

Her doctor encouraged her to take a restorative trip to Europe, where she convalesced at the home of William Rathbone, an English politician and philanthropist. Rathbone introduced her to Samuel Tuke, a Quaker mental health reformer and grandson of the founder of Britain's York Retreat. The stay in England would be key to forming Dix's mission. Upon returning to Boston, she began teaching a Sunday school class to women kept at the East Cambridge Jail, where she saw the mentally ill incarcerated with criminals, locked in dingy, dirty, unheated cells. It was the push Dix needed to become a full-fledged reformer. She began to investigate the conditions in which the mentally ill were being kept throughout Massachusetts and was horrified. In 1843 she petitioned state legislators for better treatment, describing a situation in which people were being kept in cages and pens: "Chained, naked, beaten with rods, and lashed into obedience!"

It was around this same time that the first systematic effort was made in the United States to determine the population rates of brain disorders affecting mental functions and behavior. The 1840 census listed just two categories for mental infirmities: "insane" and "idiot," neither of which was clearly defined. Since the census takers received no clear guidance on how to identify mental illness or intellectual disabilities, they applied their own idiosyncratic diagnostic notions, and their judgments were excessively guided by ignorance and prejudice. Such was the atmosphere of inhumanity and confusion when, in 1855, Dix founded St. Elizabeths in Washington, DC, the first federally operated mental hospital in the country. Her hope was that the government would provide "the most humane care and enlightened curative treatment of the insane." She played a role in the establishment of thirty of the sixty mental asylums built in the United States during her lifetime. Her own declining years were spent in a suite specially designed for her use in the New Jersey State Lunatic Asylum, in Trenton, which she liked to refer to as her first-born child.

My career has taken me to many of the institutions that Dix established, where I have seen and felt her influence—as well as the influence of Rush, Kirkbride, and their European forebears—and thought about the passion and courage with which they pursued their cause on behalf of the mentally ill, despite their limited scientific knowledge. One of my first clinical rotations in medical school was at St. Elizabeths, the same institution where Richard Wyatt, who would play a seminal role in improving the treatment of schizophrenia, would establish a laboratory supported by the National Institute of Mental Health (NIMH) to investigate its causes. (John Hinckley Jr. was also remanded there after being found not guilty by reason of insanity for the attempted assassination of President Reagan.) I later became the director of research at the Dorothea Dix Hospital in Raleigh, North Carolina, while on the faculty of the University of North Carolina. The hospital had been named for her at the time of its founding, but Dix refused the honor. I would later learn of members of my own family who lived and died in the Ohio institutions inspired by Dix's mission.

The noble vision, promulgated by Pinel, Tuke, Rush, Kirkbride, and Dix, that aspired to liberate thousands of mentally ill people from their miserable plight was never fully realized. In large part, this was because the hoped-for treatments for mental illnesses did not materialize, and asylums remained relegated to the role of custodial care. Moreover, the fact that these were advertised as humane sites of therapy induced families eager for relief from the burden and stress of perpetual care of their loved ones to commit them to asylums, where they would receive compassionate care and possibly get better—or so they believed.

As the demand for admissions and the resident population increased, the adherence to the noble principles of "moral therapy" waned, turning mental hospitals into crowded bleak warehouses with abysmal conditions. This was epitomized by Dix's pride and joy, the nation's only federal mental institution (other than the Veteran's Administration Hospitals), St. Elizabeths Hospital.

Originally built for three hundred fifty patients, by the twentieth century, St. Elizabeths' population had swelled to eight thousand patients, creating intolerable conditions. Half a century later, antipsychotic drugs would be discovered—

but instead of being the remedy to the shameful state of the asylums, they led to another catastrophe: the emptying of patients from mental institutions to the communities under a policy of "deinstitutionalization." However, we are getting ahead of ourselves, as it would be some time before this calamity would befall people with schizophrenia, those who treated them, and society. In the interim, the field of psychiatric medicine would make other blunders as it continued to mature.

Part 2

THE
SCIENTIFIC
CIRCUS

Chapter 4

MEDICAL SPECIALIZATION

In some ways disease does not exist until we agree that it does—
by perceiving, naming, and responding to it.

—C. E. Rosenberg,
"Disease in History: Frames and Framers" (1989)

CURERS AND CARVERS

Prior to the nineteenth century and the growth of the asylum movement, the medical profession consisted of generalists who were either curers (physicians) or carvers (surgeons). These were journeymen practitioners who, with few exceptions (tooth extraction, eye ailments, midwives), were largely generalists who treated whatever kind of sickness afflicted their patients. But as ways of examining the body and its diseases improved through observational research, dissection of cadavers, examination of biologic specimens, and the advent of instrumentation (microscope, stethoscope, ophthalmoscope, laryngoscope), the volume of knowledge increased. This enabled the medical field to differentiate itself increasingly into areas of specialization.

In the nineteenth century, German-speaking countries were the intellectual centers of medicine. However, the process by which the field of medicine separated into specialties began in France.

At the time, Europe, including the Germanic countries, was constrained by traditional institutions and social structures, but the French Revolution of 1789 had dismantled the ancien régime, opening Paris to new and unconventional ideas and initiatives. The French Academy's network of educational and cultural institutions—including the Faculty of Medicine, the Sorbonne, and the Collège de France—along with a critical mass of intellectuals, fostered creative ferment.

As a consequence of these various currents, hospitals and practitioners concentrated on particular patient groups and diseases. A maternity hospital was established on the Boulevard Port Royal, and a hospital for children, the Enfants Malades, was set up. Patients with sexually transmitted diseases were transferred to the Vénériens Hospital on the Faubourg St. Jacques. Separate hospitals, or wards in general hospitals, were designated for the insane. Medical schools reconfigured their faculty into specialties, which allowed physicians to acquire a deeper knowledge of the growing medical literature in specific domains and gain greater clinical experience with particular illnesses, thus expanding the knowledge of their predecessors and developing canons of practice.

THE BRAIN DOCTORS

Brain doctors were among the first physicians to coalesce into a medical specialty. The earliest indication of this subspecialty occurred in 1808, when German physician Johann Reil proposed a branch of medicine dedicated to mental illness, which he called *"psychiaterie,"* a term derived from the Greek for "mind" (*psyche*) and "healing" (*iatreia*). Reil was a transitional figure, a physician who had an affinity for those conditions that were ostensibly medical but affected behavior. He believed in the continuity between psyche and soma, mind and body. Among his patients were the playwright and poet Johann Wolfgang von Goethe, and Jacob Grimm (of the brothers Grimm authors of *Grimms' Fairy Tales*).

While we now think of psychiatry and neurology as sibling specialties, originally the brain-focused specialty was called psychiatry, with neurology differentiating later. In 1841, the Association of Medical Officers of Asylums and Hospitals for the Insane was formed in the United Kingdom—the precursor to the Royal College of Psychiatrists—followed by the Association of Medical Superintendents of American Institutions for the Insane in 1844, which would later become the American Psychiatric Association. The neurological counterpart to the APA in the United States was the American Neurological Association, founded in 1875.

The divergence of these medical subspecialties was driven by scientific research into the brain and various diseases to which it was susceptible, a process that played out gradually. The first scientific stirrings to inform the as-yet inchoate disciplines of neurology and psychiatry can be seen in the work of Franz Joseph Gall (1758–1828). One of twelve children born into a wealthy German family, Gall became interested in the human brain as a boy, imagining a link between a classmate's oddly shaped head and his fluency with language. Later, while studying medicine at the University of Strasbourg, Gall observed that many of the brightest students in his class had prominent eyeballs, and he theorized that the feature must be linked to their intelligence. When Gall moved to Allgemeines Krankenhaus, the public hospital in Vienna, to continue his training, he undertook careful dissections of brains and drew two conclusions: first, that discrete anatomic areas orchestrated specific psychological functions; and second, that just as a muscle grows with exercise or atrophies from lack of use, brain regions increase or decrease in size depending on the activity of their associated mental functions.

Such observations laid the foundation for Gall's theory that personality and intelligence are related to the shape of the skull, which itself reflected underlying brain structures. Gall, calling his theory phrenology, cited twenty-seven mental functions and behaviors that he believed corresponded to cortical and cranial configurations, including the reproductive instinct, the love of offspring, affection, aggression, desire of possessions, wisdom, satire, wit, kindness, benevolence, mimicry, and religious belief.

Unfortunately, Gall's theory was exploited for nefarious purposes, such as offering a biologic basis for deviant behavior; because phrenology offered visual representation of deviance, it was ultimately linked to heritability and eugenic theories. Phrenology also provided the justification for subordination based on race and gender, which permeated the politics of the nineteenth and twentieth centuries, reaching its evil apotheosis in the German National Socialist (Nazi) ideology and policies implemented by the Third Reich.

Despite its misuses and ultimate discreditation, Gall's effort to link brain anatomy to behavior and mental functions represented a significant attempt at scientific thinking and provided an early foundation for the new cadre of brain doctors.

TWINS OF BRAIN MEDICINE

Over the course of the nineteenth century, four generations of physicians, most of whom were psychiatrists, would apply the cutting-edge scientific methodology of the time, anatomic pathology, to scour the brain in search of the tan-

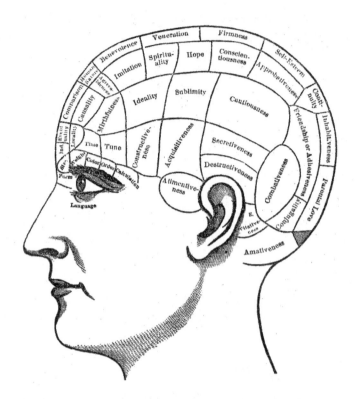

Diagram from *The New Illustrated Self-Instructor in Phrenology & Physiology*,
by Orson Squire and Lorenzo Niles Fowler, 1859.

gible basis for a host of mental disorders, including schizophrenia. These brain
doctors were among the scientific and clinical elite at the world's top institutions, and they made many remarkable discoveries. They were trained in what
became psychiatry and neurology and in the scientific disciplines of anatomy
and pathology through a system of apprenticeship. Moving from lab to lab,
like bees alighting on blossoms, these gifted young doctors learned from their
mentors. It was this cross-pollination that enabled synergies in mapping brain
anatomy, establishing relationships between anatomic regions and specific
mental and motor functions, and the identification of disorders that would fall
under the purview of neurology. (The relationships among this cadre of physicians are depicted in a pedagogical pedigree in appendix 2.)

The boundaries that would ultimately be drawn between psychiatry and neurology rested on an implied Cartesian dualism, the philosophy of René Descartes that
postulated a clear distinction between mental (intangible) and physical (tangible)

phenomena. Neurology would have dominion over brain disorders that had tangible and visible pathological signatures, while psychiatry inherited all the maladies that were invisible manifestations of the mind—as though emotion, thought, and consciousness itself could be divorced from the neurology underlying them. But for most of the nineteenth century, the boundaries between the two fields would be porous, and there was much overlap in patients and research. This crossover led to more than a few ironies, perhaps the greatest of which was that it was a neurologist named Sigmund Freud who came up with the psychoanalytic theory that would lead psychiatry away from scientific study of the brain and into the abstract realms of the mind.

The most visible maladies treated by brain doctors were those that caused physical and intellectual disabilities: amyotrophic lateral sclerosis (ALS), Parkinson's disease, multiple sclerosis, stroke, epilepsy, dementia, tumors. By the turn of the twentieth century, a trio of psychiatrists had defined distinct eponymous forms of dementia. Arnold Pick described frontotemporal dementia (Pick's disease), while Alois Alzheimer identified senile plaques and neurofibrillary tangles in the brain, the hallmarks of Alzheimer's disease. The Russian neuropsychiatrist Sergei Korsakoff described the brain atrophy and memory loss caused by excessive alcohol consumption, what we now call Korsakoff's syndrome.

Other psychiatrists trained in anatomy contributed to the understanding of the brain's structure. Karl Wernicke and Paul Broca mapped the brain's anatomy, revealing in the process the regions responsible for different forms of aphasia (expressive or Broca's aphasia involves the inability to speak coherently; receptive or Wernicke's aphasia is the inability to understand verbal communications, both usually due to strokes or head trauma). Korbinian Brodmann's monograph *Vergleichende Lokalisationslehre der Großhirnrinde* (*Localisation in the Cerebral Cortex*) presented a classification of cortical areas based on the organization of cells in specific brain regions. The fifty-two anatomic areas he identified, known as Brodmann areas, formed the basis of templates still used today by neurosurgeons, neurologists, and psychiatrists. Paul Emil Fleschig is remembered for his research on the formation of myelin, the lipidlike sheath wrapped around the long axons of neurons that facilitates transmission of nerve impulses. Theodor Meynert constructed an atlas of the various types of cells in different brain regions, discovering in the process a concentration of cells in the basal forebrain containing the neurotransmitter acetylcholine, which would lead, a century later, to the first effective treatment for the symptoms of Alzheimer's disease. Finally, Franz Nissl worked with Alzheimer and Emil Kraeplin, a prominent German psychiatrist, on the relationship of mental illness to glial cells, blood vessels, blood elements, and cerebrospinal fluid. Nissl popularized the use of spinal taps but is best known for the stain he developed to reveal the subcellular structures of neurons.

These breakthroughs contributed importantly to our knowledge of brain disorders and paved the way for advances in the early twentieth century: the discovery of microorganisms and the germ theory of infectious disease; anesthesia and sterile techniques for surgery; the identification of cellular pathology as the basis of disease; X-rays, insulin, antibiotics. Unfortunately, the scientists studying mental illness didn't find anything comparable to what they were able to discover about the brain's architecture and what were then called organic brain disorders— meaning that their symptoms had clear causes in the brain. The causes of mental illnesses, however, couldn't be observed, either by the naked eye or even under the light microscope.

Though these findings led to important advances in science and medicine, it should be acknowledged that this knowledge was disproportionately derived through the exploitation of people from lower socioeconomic classes, minority groups, and those with mental and physical infirmities. In addition, physicians conducted experiments on vulnerable populations (the poor, infirm, enslaved people, and prisoners) and collected human remains from the brutality of war and violence of slavery for anatomical dissection and collections. As with Gall's theory of phrenology, the results of these studies also served as a pseudoscientific basis for prejudicial theories of racial inferiority that would permeate the evolution of scientific explanations of the relationships among the brain, behavior, and mental functions. This practice was prevalent in Europe and the Americas, particularly in the antebellum south. In addition to generating medical knowledge about anatomy, physiology, and pathology, it also gave rise to radical theories of racial differences that prompted largely white professors to develop curricula that included the claim that people of African descent were anatomically and physiologically distinct.

The assignment of prejudicial racial characteristics extended to mental illness as well. For example, the wish to escape slavery was labelled "drapetomania." This medicalization was clearly meant to frame the desire to escape as pathological, rather than an assertion of the humanity, dignity, and right to freedom of enslaved people. Despite this racial fabrication, the prevailing belief among American psychiatrists was that black people were not susceptible to mental illness and therefore required less care in mental institutions.

Psychiatric researchers studying anatomic pathology in the Vogt Brain Collection, circa 1906. Left to right: Korbinian Brodmann, Cécile Vogt, Oskar Vogt, Louise Bosse, Max Borchert, Max Lewandowski.

THE BIRTH OF NEUROLOGY

If Gall was the first brain doctor and Reil the first psychiatrist, Jean-Martin Charcot (1825–1893) was the father of neurology. Born in Paris, Charcot trained in pathology and general medicine. He employed the cutting-edge research methodology of his day to amass extensive data through clinical observations, which he correlated with autopsy findings. Charcot certainly wasn't the first to engage in what we now know as neurology—by the time of Charcot's birth, James Parkinson had already published his "An Essay on the Shaking Palsy" (1817), the first clear medical description of what would become known as Parkinson's disease. Nor was he the only one of his era. John Hughlings Jackson wrote on the loss of speech after traumatic brain injury and stroke, for instance, and Silas Weir Mitchell, a Civil War–era surgeon, provided a detailed account of phantom limb syndrome (when amputees still feel the presence of their former appendage). But it was Charcot who would become one of the most influential physicians in the history of modern medicine, leaving behind him at least thirteen eponymous diseases. His students included Sigmund Freud, Georges Gilles de la Tourette, Pierre Janet, and Joseph Babinski, the latter of whom said that "to take away from neurology all the discoveries made by Charcot would be to render it unrecognizable."

Given the overlap between the twin disciplines, it's not surprising that the father of neurology devoted much of his practice to psychiatry. His first position was at the Salpêtrière, housing more than five thousand patients, which he called "that grand asylum of human misery." In 1862 Charcot became the chief physician and director of Salpêtrière and transformed the hospital into what was, for its time, a state-of-the-art center for neurology. Salpêtrière had its own pathology lab but also a farm, bakery, and photography studio—from which Charcot produced a large body of photographs of female hysterics (patients afflicted by emotional states causing abnormal, uncontrollable behaviors or physical symptoms for which there is no biologic basis). As professor of pathological anatomy, Charcot lectured on diseases of the organs, using cadavers and specimens. His Tuesday lectures were famous, and among the many physicians who came from around Europe to attend them was the young Austrian Freud, who took a special interest in Charcot's approach to hysteria.

Charcot saw legions of patients over the course of his career, and by connecting their clinical features to the pathological changes seen on autopsies after they had died, he was able to impose some descriptive and diagnostic order on an array of neurological disorders. At the time, only a small number of illnesses, such as epilepsy and neurosyphilis, had been differentiated from the mass of "nervous disorders." Charcot was the first to connect the clinical features of multiple sclerosis to the pathological changes seen postmortem, and the first to diagnose MS in a living patient. He was also the first to diagnose cases of amyotrophic lateral sclerosis, identifying it as a specific neurological disease with a distinct pathology.

But hysteria was the only discrete mental disorder Charcot was able to identify. From the time of Mesmer, who had attributed it to "animal magnetism," hysteria had been considered the "great neurosis"—a mysterious disorder that the leading experts of successive eras tried to explain through both physical and metaphysical theories. Charcot believed it to be a hereditary physiological disorder, due to its physical manifestations of paralysis, syncope (loss of consciousness caused by a drop in blood pressure), convulsions, and mutism. Freud speculated that hysteria reflected psychological conflicts caused by early sexual trauma. The contrasting views held by these two doctors were emblematic of the contrasting perspectives that would inform the views of neurology and psychiatry about mental illness for decades to come.

The Innovators

The people confined to insane asylums in the nineteenth century were a mix of patients with psychotic disorders, tertiary syphilis, developmental disabilities, and senile dementias, but the greatest proportion by far were thought to be suffering from what we know as schizophrenia—the mental illness that, though it would guide much of the seminal research of the time, had yet to be named. That would fall first to Emil Kraepelin, who distinguished schizophrenia from the mass of mental illness, and then to Eugen Bleuler, who revised Kraepelin's conception of the disorder and coined the term "schizophrenia."

Kraepelin was born in Germany in 1856 and trained in neuropathology and the nascent discipline of experimental psychology. By the time he became a professor of psychiatry at the University of Dorpat in modern-day Estonia, he'd grown frustrated by the jumble of imprecise diagnostic terminology and contradictory theories that characterized the field. One of the biggest problems in dividing insanity into discrete mental illnesses was the fact that many of the same symptoms could be observed in different disorders. Delusions, for example, appeared in a range of psychotic disorders and dementias, and anxiety was seen in depression, anxiety disorders, and psychoses.

Like his contemporaries, Kraepelin initially approached this problem via human autopsies and anatomic pathology. But while his colleagues in psychiatry had discovered the "footprints" of many neurological disorders, Kraepelin, like others before him, could find no trace of mental illness through these methods. So he changed his strategy. Instead of trying to dissect mental illness as a surgeon, he searched for historical and clinical patterns from which he could construct a taxonomy of different kinds of madness. He kept stacks of note cards, assembling his own classification system in a small book entitled *Compendium der Psychiatrie* (1883). What distinguished Kraepelin's system from others was that, in addition to symptoms, it included an illness's period of onset and its course over a person's lifetime. For example, some psychoses lifted spontaneously, and patients recovered, while others persisted and got worse, leaving people permanently impaired.

Focusing on the life history of mental illnesses, Kraepelin defined three types of psychoses: manic-depressive insanity, melancholia, and dementia praecox— what today we call schizophrenia. He used the term "praecox," meaning early or premature, to differentiate the illness from late-life or senile dementia. What

Kraepelin had observed in dementia praecox was not only psychotic symptoms but also a decline in cognitive capacity to the point of dementia; this was in contrast to manic-depressive illness and melancholia, where patients' cognitive functions returned intact once their symptoms subsided.

Kraepelin described, in exquisite detail, examples of each diagnosis. His portraits of dementia praecox are as compelling and dramatic today as when he wrote them more than a century ago:

> Delusions, either transitory or permanent, are developed with extraordinary frequency . . . the brain is burned, shrunken, as if completely gone to jelly, full of water, the mind is "drawn like rags from the brain," the patient "has only a little knuckle of brain left"; the nerves are teased out. . . .
>
> These delusions are frequently accompanied by ideas of sin. The patient has by a sinful life destroyed his health of body and mind, he is a wicked fellow, the greatest sinner. . . . God has forsaken him, he is eternally lost, he has been driven out of the church; is going to hell. . . .
>
> Ideas of persecution are invariably developed. . . . The patient notices that he is looked at in a peculiar way, laughed at, scoffed at, that people are jeering at him. . . . People spy on him; Jews, anarchists, spiritualists, persecute him, poison the atmosphere with poisonous powder, the beer with prussic acid. . . .
>
> [The patients] see mice, ants, the hound of hell . . . scythes, and axes. They hear cocks crowing, shooting, birds chirping, spirits knocking, bees humming, murmurings, screaming, scolding, voices from the cellar. . . . [The voices] say: "That man must be beheaded, hanged," "Swine, wicked wretch, you will be done for."

Kraepelin's newly defined diagnosis of dementia praecox was short lived. Swiss psychiatrist Eugen Bleuler proposed an alternative conception of dementia praecox at the 1908 German Psychiatric Association Meeting in Berlin. Bleuler was impressed by the unusual array of symptoms and behaviors exhibited by people with dementia praecox and less interested in the longitudinal course of the illness. Whereas Kraepelin had emphasized patients' intellectual decline and steadily worsening course, Bleuler believed that the central feature of the illness was the splitting of psychic function—for instance, in the lack of correspondence between thought and emotion, seen when patients exhibit what is termed "flat affect," which means that a patient experiencing bizarre delusions or hallucinations will not exhibit the expected emotional reaction but will instead remain seemingly oblivious or indifferent.

Bleuler's shift of emphasis inspired the term "schizophrenia," or "split mind," derived from the Greek *schizein*, indicating "splitting," and *phren*, originally meaning "diaphragm" but later "soul" or "spirit." (The word "schizophrenia" was never meant to indicate split or multiple personalities, a misunderstanding that persists to this day.) In addition to focusing on the schism, Bleuler emphasized the patient's manifest behavior and introduced the concept of primary and secondary symptoms. The four primary symptoms (the four As) were abnormal associations, autistic behavior and thinking (meaning self-absorbed), abnormal affect, and ambivalence. These mental aberrations could lead to secondary manifestations of hallucinations, delusions, social withdrawal, and diminished drive. In each case, as the disease progressed, the individual's personality lost its unity.

While well intended, Bleuler's revision and the field's embrace of it would have devastating consequences, as they shifted the target of treatment from preventing disease progression to reduction of the manifest symptoms. At the time this was moot, as there were no effective treatments for schizophrenia. However, this shift in therapeutic focus would later become hugely important. To appreciate the significance of the distinction, think of Alzheimer's and Parkinson's diseases. While we have treatments that can improve symptoms, we have nothing to alter the progression of these illnesses, and so patients continue to decline until death. In the case of schizophrenia, the emphasis was placed on the suppression of psychotic symptoms rather than on the prevention of intellectual deterioration that occurs over time in the context of successive psychotic episodes or sustained psychosis. Bleuler's revision suggested that the two conceptions of the illness were mutually exclusive; in fact, he and Kraepelin were simply emphasizing two different sides of the same coin: the longitudinal and the cross-sectional.

Both Bleuler and Kraepelin divided schizophrenia into subtypes based on the nature of their symptoms, a typology that was continued into the initial versions of the *DSM*. Kraepelin's turn away from anatomic pathology as a means to define schizophrenia and elucidate its underlying basis was the first sign that psychiatry was veering off in a new direction. In abandoning the dissection of cadavers in favor of the descriptive observation of living patients, he enabled a reconfiguration of the conceptual boundaries around how psychiatrists thought about this ancient malady. Now the question was not where in the brain the source of the problem might reside, but how a patient was thinking, feeling, behaving.

During his academic training, Kraepelin had worked in the lab of Wilhelm Wundt (1832–1920). It was a formative intellectual experience, but as Kraepelin worked on his taxonomy of mental illness, his mentor took his own intellectual pursuits in another direction. Wundt was an aspiring member of the generation of elite German psychiatrists trained by the leading scientific figures of the day. Like his forebears and colleagues, Wundt sought to uncover the roots of madness. Similarly frustrated by the inability of anatomical dissection to detect visible pathology in the brain, Wundt realized that a new approach for scientific inquiry was required: metaphysical rather than organic. Thus was the field of psychology created.

In his 1874 book *Principles of Physiological Psychology*, Wundt set down a vision for psychology as an independent discipline that, rather than employing the traditional philosophical or spiritual approaches to consciousness, would adhere to principles of the physical sciences and adopt the methods of an experimental, inductive science. Just as cardiology focused on the heart, ophthalmology the eyes, and neurology and psychiatry the brain, psychology would focus on the mind. Instead of using anatomic dissection and microscopic examination, this new discipline, which he termed experimental psychology, would combine physiology and psychology to interrogate the workings of the mind using controlled laboratory methodology.

The paradigm shift that Wundt set in motion—psychology as a means of extending our investigations into what lies behind normal and abnormal behavior—was an important contribution to science and medicine. Though his research ultimately did not have a major impact on our understanding of the brain, or the workings of the mind, he is credited with having founded a discipline whose many students have contributed much to our understanding of human behavior and mental functions.

Despite his seminal role in behavioral science, Wundt was quickly superseded, first by his star student Edward Titchener, and later by the American philosopher and psychologist William James. Titchener conceived of psychology's first major theory, structuralism, which sought to break consciousness down into its most basic components (for example, attention, memory, problem solving). James, influenced by the English naturalist and explorer Charles Darwin (creator of the theory of evolution and natural selection), developed a rival theory of functionalism, which focused on the *purpose* of consciousness and behavior. James regarded the scientific attempts of Titchener and others to chop up consciousness into discrete parts as misguided and wrote instead of consciousness as a continuous "stream."

But if Wundt's accomplishments were overshadowed by the work of Titchener and James, they would be utterly eclipsed by the next person who engaged in metaphysical speculations about the mind and its aberrations.

Chapter 5

The Freudians

Sigmund Freud was a novelist with a scientific background. He just didn't
know he was a novelist. All those damn psychiatrists afterward, they didn't
know he was a novelist either.

—John Irving,
Writers at Work: The Paris Review *Interviews* (1988)

The Takeover of Psychiatry

By the end of the nineteenth century, psychiatrists were frustrated. They hungered
for an intellectual framework that would explain mental illness and offer useful
methods for treating it: something that would legitimize their field and transform
their roles with living patients from wardens of the damned, and as scientists
studying cadavers into capable physicians and illuminating researchers.

Enter Freud. A brilliant and articulate physician who offered a comprehensive
theory of the mind that presumed to explain human behavior and the source of
mental illness, Freud looked like the savior for whom psychiatry had been waiting.
Over the next fifty years, psychiatrists and psychologists would embrace his dazzling
new ideas, which offered the chance to finally put psychiatry on equal footing with
the rest of medicine. Unfortunately, instead of securing psychiatry's place among
the medical specialties, Freud directed his psychiatric acolytes on a metaphysical
detour into the machinations of the mind that led to the margins of medicine.

Sigmund Freud was born in Freiburg, Austria, in 1856 and studied medicine
at the University of Vienna. Following graduation, he worked under the leading
figures in the brain sciences: first, the great psychiatrist and anatomist Theodor
Meynert, conducting research on brain anatomy; and then Charcot, the leading

neurologist of the day. Freud was enormously impressed by Charcot, and his studies with the renowned neurologist were instrumental in turning him away from a career in research neurology and toward one in clinical psychiatry. Freud subsequently studied with neuropsychiatrist Josef Breuer, who first used what became known as the "talking cure." Freud was trained as a neurologist, but his Vienna practice consisted largely of patients with nervous conditions—that is, mental disorders. His psychoanalytic theory would be based on his experience with these patients. His conception of mental illness deviated from the theories of his more anatomically focused German colleagues and was strikingly different from anything that had come before.

Freud understood mental disorders in terms of feelings, thoughts, the interplay between conscious and unconscious motivation, and conflicts between the psychic forces—not degenerate genes, stressed nerves, or physiological defects in the brain. These psychic elements were grouped in three mental constructs, the id, ego, and superego, formed through each individual's psychological and sexual development. The id is the source of drives and innate impulses, while the superego is the inhibiting, critical component and the source of conscience and moral behavior; the ego represents the individual's behavioral capacity and tendencies, and mediates between the id and superego. These psychodynamic forces aren't just at war with one another; they are also complementary, operating as a system of checks and balances, and psychoanalysis is meant to uncover their workings and modify them.

At the time Freud developed his theory, there was no comparable psychological model for how the mind worked. His model certainly wasn't correct in all respects, but it was conceptually brilliant and the first of its kind. There was something about it that rang true to human experience; people read Freud and saw their internal struggles and contradictory behaviors illuminated. Freud was also a clear, engaging writer and a brilliant communicator. Freud's theories would eventually capture the imagination not only of the medical field but also intellectuals of all disciplines.

Freud's view of the precise mechanisms underlying mental illness would change over time, but they were always situated within his id-ego-superego framework and explained through the tensions between those three structures. For example, he posited that psychosis erupted when the ego's allegiance to the external world dissolved, and it was overcome by the id, which then had free rein to define its own reality.

As innovative and profound as Freud's ideas were, they were limited in their application to mental conditions and more relevant to neuroses, such as anxiety, phobias, and obsessions, rather than psychoses such as schizophrenia. They also were the subject of much debate and considerable controversy at the time, as reflected by these comments by Kraepelin, a major adversary: "Here we meet everywhere the characteristic fundamental features of the Freudian trend of investigation, the representation of arbitrary assumptions and conjectures as assured facts, which are used without hesitation for the building up of always new castles in the air ever towering higher, and the tendency to generalization beyond measure from single observations. . . . As I am accustomed to walk on the sure foundation of direct experience, my Philistine conscience of natural science stumbles at every step on objections, considerations, and doubts, over which the lightly soaring power of imagination of Freud's disciples carries them without difficulty."

Over time, Freudians and neo-Freudians would adapt psychoanalytic theory in ways and for purposes—from schizophrenia to homosexuality—that the master neither sanctioned nor intended. It would take decades for the consequences of this to become clear, by which time Freudian psychoanalytic theory had ensnared American psychiatry.

COMING TO AMERICA

Freud made his first and only visit to the United States in 1909, when he crossed the Atlantic accompanied by his protégé, Carl Jung, to receive honorary doctorates from Clark University in Worcester, Massachusetts. In America, one of those captivated by Freud was James Jackson Putnam, the prominent neurologist and psychiatrist, and professor of nervous system diseases at Harvard Medical School, who invited Freud to his country retreat. After four days of intensive discussion, Putnam publicly endorsed Freud's theory. Soon after, he organized the first meeting of the American Psychoanalytic Association, of which he was elected president.

Despite his warm reception, Freud detested America. Many reasons have been given, among them the unbridled commerce and materialism of American culture; the contrast between Austria's austerity and America's vibrant economy and prosperity; and even American informality—he was particularly offended at being addressed as Sigmund instead of Professor Freud. The master, however, was not without his own flaws. He was described by his hosts as opinionated, closeminded, and prejudiced. William James attended his lecture and said that though brilliant, Freud impressed him as a man bound by his own ideas.

Over the next two decades, psychoanalytic theory gained followers, but it didn't immediately overtake American psychiatry. Somatic treatments such as hydrotherapy, heavy sedation, insulin coma, and, eventually, surgical lobotomies still dominated the care of patients with schizophrenia and other severe mental disturbances.

Though Freud generated his psychoanalytic theory from clinical observation and inspired scientific inference, shunning religious or spiritual influence, his ideas were inextricably linked to his Jewish identity and to Jewish culture at a time when anti-Semitism was increasing in Europe and America. Freud's inner circle was almost entirely Jewish, and the vast majority of the early psychiatrists who became analysts were Jewish. It was the rise of the Nazis that forced Freud and the most prominent psychoanalysts to flee Germany and Austria to other European countries, the United States, and other parts of the world (Hitler specifically denounced Freud and psychoanalysis), spreading Freudian theory and psychoanalytic practice.

As a result of this massive displacement of psychiatry's intellectual avant-garde, and despite the fact that Freud himself immigrated to London, the center of the psychoanalytic movement shifted to the United States—and to New York in particular. Having been analyzed or trained directly by Freud himself, the newcomers were welcomed like royalty by America's psychiatric community where they joined American acolytes of Freud and were offered plum positions in academic institutions. Starting in the 1940s, the best universities in the country—including Columbia, Harvard, Stanford, and Yale—saw analysts assume department chairs, and by 1960, psychoanalysts held the levers of power in American psychiatry. Virtually every psychiatrist in an important position, whether formally credentialed or not, was trained in psychoanalytic theory and treatment methods, and from 1940 to the 1970s, every American Psychiatric Association (APA) president was a psychoanalyst.

A psychiatry resident at Delaware State Hospital in the 1940s, quoted in Edward Shorter's *A History of Psychiatry: From the Era of the Asylum to the Age of Prozac*, recalled the sort of coercive hegemony that was imposed by the psychoanalysts. Residents were pressured to view institutional psychiatry and the treatment of severe mental illness as merely a transitional stage in their training, with the ideal professional goal instead being the practice of psychoanalysis. The somatic therapies used in hospitals and mental institutions were considered stopgaps that concealed rather than uncovered patients' pathology, and whoever expressed the slightest doubt about psychoanalytic interpretations or referenced other theories was viewed as unable to overcome his neurotic resistance. As the resident put it: "Ordering a sedative for even an agitated psychotic patient was not therapeutic for the patient but considered an anxiety reaction on the part of the doctor."

The impact of psychoanalytic theory on psychiatry was a truly unique moment in the history of medicine—one in which the theoretical framework of a medical specialty encouraged it to distance itself from the mainstream of medicine. Psychoanalytic theory was not the result of a body of scientific research, nor was its therapeutic application based on experimentally derived evidence. It was a speculative doctrine founded on clinical observation and inferential logic, neither scientifically proven nor experimentally tested. Moreover, psychoanalytic treatment was largely intended for the psychological needs of educated members of the middle and upper classes. With psychiatry's embrace of psychoanalysis, the original and most important part of its clinical mission—the care of severely ill and institutionalized patients—was deemphasized in favor of office-based treatment of the "worried well," people who were essentially mentally healthy but perhaps mildly neurotic or anxious.

For those tasked with treating mental illness and, more importantly, for the patients they treated, the shift of focus from the brain to the mind was disadvantageous. In fact, it would be hard to imagine a therapy less appropriate than psychoanalysis for people with schizophrenia. But in the absence of clinical explanations or the anatomical findings from postmortem studies done by his medical colleagues, Freud had little alternative but to formulate a psychological, rather than biological, hypothesis of schizophrenia.

Freud differentiated among various kinds of neuroses based on their responsiveness to psychoanalysis. The "transference" neuroses (for instance, hysteria, obsessions) were the proper objects of psychoanalysis. Such patients were able to form relationships—and thus to form transferences during analytic treatment—so they could potentially be helped by analysis. The "narcissistic" neuroses or psychoses (such as paranoia and schizophrenia) posed problems, however. These more severely disturbed patients were unable to invest "objects" (mental representations of other people) with libido—their libido was attached only to their own ego—and thus they could not be helped by psychoanalysis.

Freud's view of which disorders could and couldn't be treated by psychoanalysis and the boundaries for its use were, for a time, accepted by his followers. But in the mid-1950s, a shift occurred. American psychoanalyst Leo Stone argued that the "incapacity" of narcissistic patients to invest others with libido was not pervasive. Such patients could form transferences, albeit with greater difficulty, and could therefore be analyzed. Stone's view was endorsed by Anna Freud, the youngest of Sigmund's six children, who followed in her famous father's footsteps by becoming a psychoanalyst. With the guardrails on the talking cure breached, and the disciples of Freud in positions of power, it was *game on.*

THE NEO-FREUDIANS

Freud died in 1939, having never returned to America. But by the end of World War II, the seeds that had been planted by his 1909 visit and cultivated by the psychoanalytic refugees who'd fled the Nazis had germinated. Without the master to hold his theoretical empire together, Freud's teachings rapidly succumbed to the interpretations and adaptations of his European disciples and their American acolytes, who improvised their own forms of psychoanalysis. The consequences of this proliferation on the field of psychiatry would be profound, and nowhere were the effects more evident than in the United States.

Despite the creative brilliance of Freudian theory, it served psychiatry poorly in two fundamental ways. From the nineteenth to the early twentieth century, the most prominent role to which a psychiatrist could aspire was director of an asylum—an alienist overseeing a horde of incurables. (Neurologists, by contrast, had been treating minor nervous ailments such as hysteria and neurasthenia—a medical condition of emotional causation consisting of fatigue, low energy, and irritability—throughout the nineteenth century in lucrative office-based practices, and more severe conditions such as strokes and tumors in general hospitals.) Psychoanalysis offered psychiatrists a way out of the asylums. Now, psychiatrists could treat patients in the more civilized environs of the drawing room rather than in remote institutions separated from mainstream society. This was bad news for patients with schizophrenia and other psychotic disorders, who were mostly incapable of sitting calmly and engaging in intensive, coherent introspection. In 1917 only 8 percent of American psychiatrists saw patients in office-based private practice, but by 1933, this figure had increased to 31 percent.

The trend continued upward following World War II, particularly in the United States, as psychiatrists abandoned their commitment to serious mental illness and institutionally based mental health care in favor of more lucrative practices ministering to people with milder disorders and problems in living. Administrative and clinical responsibility for public mental health care and institutions were gradually assumed by allied health professionals (psychologists, social workers, nurses) and administrators.

The second disservice perpetrated by Freud's followers after his death was the wanton revision of psychoanalytic theory, adapting it for their own purposes to diagnose and treat severe mental illnesses such as schizophrenia—conditions for which it was never intended. Freud had clearly proscribed the use of psychoanalysis for certain conditions he felt it would be ineffective. His followers adhered to his views on this until the mid-1940s, when influential figures expanded its use to patients with schizophrenia.

Along with this broadening application of psychoanalytic theory came the formulation of new diagnoses. In 1942 Freud's colleague Helene Deutsch described the "as-if" personality: an individual whose "whole relationship to life has something about it which is lacking in genuineness and yet outwardly runs along 'as if' it were complete." Such a person seems normal—the intellect unimpaired and emotional responses appropriate—but one senses "something intangible and indefinable" at work that "invariably gives rise to the question 'What is wrong?'" Deutsch theorized that the as-if personality was a phase of the "schizophrenic process," before the illness built to its delusional form, though she left open the possibility that this as-if phase could imply either a "schizophrenic disposition" or rudimentary symptoms of schizophrenia. In 1949 Paul Hoch and Phillip Polatin described a condition they termed pseudoneurotic schizophrenia, which they viewed as a milder variant of schizophrenia, in which "an abundance of 'neurotic' (obsessive, phobic, depressive . . .) symptoms" were present.

The proliferation of these mild variants of, or precursors to, schizophrenia eventually coalesced into borderline personality disorder (BPD), though that diagnosis was ultimately dissociated from schizophrenia. BPD is now defined by instability in interpersonal relationships, emotional volatility, distortions in self-image, and impulsive behaviors.

From the 1930s to the 1970s, psychoanalytically inspired diagnoses and theories of causation for schizophrenia proliferated. These included theories and treatments with no empirical evidence or experimental verification to support them—little more than someone's opinion based on personal experience.

American psychoanalyst Harry Stack Sullivan, an early Freudian dissident, rejected Freud's theory of unconscious conflicts and developed an interpersonal theory of psychoanalysis that emphasized the pathology of relationships. Sullivan espoused a view of schizophrenia as a maladaptive reaction to anxiety, which he applied to patients at Sheppard Pratt Hospital, a private mental institution outside Baltimore. Frieda Fromm-Reichmann, an immigrant German analyst, soon supplanted Sullivan's notion of anxiety reactions to interpersonal relations, formally attributing the cause of schizophrenia to the "schizophrenogenic mother." This label, which would become notorious, described a mother ostensibly incapable of drawing a clear boundary between herself and her child, or of differentiating between her own needs and emotions and those of the child. Schizophrenia, in this formulation, was due to the psychological trauma in infancy and childhood.

Despite her far-fetched theories, Fromm-Reichmann was devoted to her patients. She believed that schizophrenia was curable, as long as one cared enough about the patient. It was the therapist's job to break through the delusions and save patients from themselves, and stories circulated of Fromm-Reichmann going to great lengths to do just that—at one point, it was said, keeping a daily vigil outside a patient's room for three months until he finally agreed to see her. (She was immortalized in the autobiographical novel *I Never Promised You a Rose Garden*, by Joanne Greenberg, one of her patients, under the pen name Hannah Green.) Fromm-Reichmann could be a resourceful and fearless companion, committed to therapy as a "mutual enterprise," with the patient often in the lead.

Though grounded in good intentions, Fromm-Reichmann's misguided theories were invalid and ineffective. The "schizophrenogenic mother" construct became the basis of psychiatrist Murray Bowen's family systems theory, which expanded the view of schizophrenia from an illness arising from the mother-child relationship to one related to the functioning of the entire family unit. Riffing on this in the mid-1950s, Gregory Bateson at the Mental Research Institute in Palo Alto, California, spun another fairy tale he called the double bind theory of schizophrenia. Bateson, an anthropologist and husband of the renowned cultural anthropologist Margaret Mead, undeterred by his lack of clinical psychiatric experience, posited that schizophrenia was an expression of social interactions in which someone was exposed repeatedly to contradictory directives or conflicting demands—for example, the parental assertions "Speak when you are spoken to!" and "Don't talk back!"

The absurdity of the era is perhaps epitomized best by Harold Searles, an influential member of the Washington Psychoanalytic Institute and a faculty member at Chestnut Lodge, a private psychiatric hospital in Rockville, Maryland.

Searles developed a form of transactional countertransference in which he would tell patients what he thought of them, sometimes describing his erotic or romantic longings. He gained a reputation for his flamboyant, outrageous style of interviewing patients, and clinicians flocked to see him give case conferences, which were as much entertainments as educational forums.

Searles's view of schizophrenia was that it resulted from a patient's "loving sacrifice of his very individuality for the welfare of a mother who is loved genuinely, altruistically, and with . . . wholehearted adoration." This intense love was mutual between mother and child, Searles explained, but both were afraid of it. Searles traced the conflict to the mother's own childhood experiences, which led her to believe that her love was destructive.

Videos of Searles's patient interviews can be found on YouTube. One, from 1973, in which Searles interviews a young woman, shows him in full flight: provocative, cavalier, supercilious, and lewd. A couple of minutes in, Searles interrupts what the woman is saying to announce: "I noticed that I suddenly had a fantasy of smashing you across the side of the head . . . with my fist." He asks the woman if that has ever happened to her, and when she says it has but with a hand rather than a fist, Searles suggests that she liked that. "Your tone implies that it was exciting."

This insinuation that the woman is desirous of physical pain—based apparently on nothing other than Searles's wish to sexualize the conversation—becomes a theme. When she says that getting close to people brings with it a fear of emotional hurt, Searles concludes: "Being hurt physically is sexual." When she tells him she was never strangled, he says, "You're still hoping, though."

Searles's body language conveys his ease and dominance. He puffs on a cigar, occasionally emitting great, put-upon sighs. When the woman challenges his interpretations of her behavior, he patronizes her. The gross power imbalance on display reflects the self-serving mentality that too often defined the doctor-patient relationship in mental health care during this era. At one point, Searles gives away his own game, revealing his cynical views both of women and of his chosen profession: "I chided my wife once for not being ethical, and she said women don't need ethics. And I suppose, similarly, psychotherapists can't be too concerned about ethics either."

As physicians from other disciplines became aware of the growing absurdity of psychiatric practice, they began to regard the field and its constituents with attitudes ranging from bemusement to scorn. The perception soon spread to the general public. The Russian-born novelist and poet Vladimir Nabokov, who famously referred to Freud as "the Viennese quack," was never shy about expressing his contempt for psychoanalysis and all it had wrought: "Freudism and all it has tainted with its grotesque implications and methods appears to me to be one of the vilest deceits practiced by people on themselves and on others."

By the second half of the twentieth century, psychiatry had distanced itself from mainstream medicine in virtually every way: intellectually, from medicine's commitment to research and the scientific method, and geographically, with the move out of the asylums and into private offices to treat the worried well. It had become a self-contained discipline, insulated against outside influence.

The hegemony that psychoanalytic theory held over American psychiatry was codified in a 1953 joint report of the American Psychiatric Association and the Association of American Medical Colleges (AAMC), the national body of medical educators. It stipulated that a competent psychiatrist has to understand "Freudian concepts" and the "principles of psychodynamics." Recently, I asked psychiatrist Darrell Kirch, a former researcher at the National Institutes of Health (NIH), dean of two medical schools, and the past president of the AAMC, about this. Kirch rolled his eyes and said ruefully, "What could we have been thinking?"

Chapter 6

DESPERATE MEASURES

My soul is sick . . . I am incurable.

—Vaslav Nijinsky

THE SNAKE PITS

From Philippe Pinel to the mid-twentieth century, society's solution to mental illness was institutionalization. In 1904 there were 150,000 people in mental hospitals in the United States. By 1955, the number had climbed to more than 558,000. The vast majority of these unfortunate souls were warehoused in cramped state institutions, many with more than 1,000 beds. Pilgrim State Hospital on Long Island at one point had in excess of 13,000 patients—a veritable city of the insane. With the exceptions of a few well-appointed havens for those who could afford them, the conditions of these facilities were hellish. In 1946 a former patient named Mary Jane Ward published an account from the inside of one such institution: Rockland State Hospital in New York. *The Snake Pit* took its title from the medieval practice of lowering the mentally ill into snake pits in the belief that the shock of such a terrifying experience, which might cause a sane person to become unhinged, would be therapeutic for an insane one. Ward's autobiographical novel, later made into an Oscar-winning film, detailed the horrors then all too common in mental hospitals: unsanitary conditions, overcrowding, physical restraints, abusive attendants, prolonged isolation, patients left to sit in their excrement.

One of the most famous denizens of the asylum during these decades was the virtuoso Russian ballet dancer and choreographer Vaslav Nijinsky. Born in Kiev in 1889 to Polish dancer parents, Nijinsky made his name dancing for Sergei Diaghilev's hugely influential company and is credited with having ushered classical ballet into modernism.

Despite his prodigious talent, by late adolescence it was clear there was something strange about Nijinsky. Confident and forceful when performing, he was, according to dance critic Joan Acocella, naive, remarkably introverted, and socially incompetent. A string of crises over a few years culminated in Nijinsky's descent into psychosis at the age of twenty-nine. He'd married Romola de Pulszky, a wealthy Hungarian he hardly knew, and been dismissed from the Ballets Russes after the end of a love affair with Diaghilev. His brother, Stanislav, had died, having spent much of his life in asylums. An attempt to mount a ballet season in London was canceled after two weeks. Nijinsky couldn't sleep and was beset by fears and prone to screaming rages. When World War I broke out, Nijinsky found himself a prisoner of war: the Hungarians placed him under house arrest for a year and a half.

Vaslav Nijinsky performing in Ballets Russes production of
Les Orientales by Michel Fokine in Paris, 1910.

It was not long after this that Nijinsky began to preach nonviolence, became a vegetarian, and attempted "marital chastity." He wore peasant shirts and told Romola that he wanted to forsake dancing and plow the land. And then, in early 1919, when he and Romola were in Switzerland, Nijinsky suffered a breakdown. He locked himself in his studio for entire nights, furiously drawing pictures of staring eyes. In fits of violence, he would steer his sleigh into oncoming traffic and, at one point, pushed Romola and their little girl down the stairs.

Romola consulted a doctor, Hans Curt Frenkel, who, as a medical trainee, had attended lectures by Eugen Bleuler. Frenkel's attempts to talk with his patient about his private thoughts only saw Nijinsky getting worse. (Romola and Frenkel, meanwhile, began an affair; the doctor, in his unhappiness over her refusal to divorce Nijinsky, attempted suicide and became addicted to morphine, remaining hooked until his death at age fifty-one.) Eventually Frenkel asked Bleuler to see Nijinsky. In Zurich, Bleuler listened to Romola's description of her husband's behavior and initially declared it "the case of an artist and a Russian," not proof of mental disturbance. But when he met with Nijinsky the following day, his assessment was starkly different: "a confused schizophrenic with mild manic excitement." Bleuler told Romola that her husband was incurably insane, and when she left the doctor's office and returned to the waiting room, Nijinsky reportedly looked at her and said, "*Femmka* [little wife], you are bringing me my death-warrant." Nijinsky was just thirty. His career over, his sanity gone forever.

During the six-week period in early 1919 in which Nijinsky was losing his hold on reality, he kept a diary. He may be the only major artist who has left a sustained account, written in real time, of the experience of psychosis, and the diary presents a remarkable record of his delusions, hallucinations, and thought and language disorder. As Acocella, who edited the diary for publication, describes it, "One feels a frantic struggle for control underlying much of the diary. . . . If he felt that eyes were watching him, they were—Romola's, Frenkel's—and he knew where this was leading. Apart from his campaign for feeling, no theme in the diary is more important than his fear of being hospitalized, as his brother was." Nijinsky mentions this on the night he begins the diary: "I will not be put in a lunatic asylum . . ." The former dancer's "campaign for feeling" was a battle he waged against the forces he believed were laying the world to waste—materialism, industrialism, opportunism. He is God now, and the diary will be his vehicle for bringing feeling back into the world.

The struggle is not only against those who believe he is going mad but also within himself. "I am standing in front of a precipice into which I may fall," he writes. Soon, however, he is God again. Acocella notes that this whiplash between grandiosity and the abyss is the most wrenching aspect of the diary.

"God is fire in the head. I am alive as long as I have a fire in my head. My pulse is an earthquake. I am an earthquake."

Nijinsky suffered nearly every kind of delusion typical of schizophrenia. He had delusions of grandeur and of persecution; he imagined that his actions were being controlled by an outside force and that events in the world were occurring with reference to himself. He thought the blood was draining from his head. He heard God speaking to him.

As Nijinsky spent the next thirty years of his life in and out of psychiatric hospitals and asylums—chronically ill, often mute, and largely helpless, unable to tie his shoes or brush his teeth—the Nijinsky myth was growing. But his own assessment, recorded in the diary, had been correct: "My soul is sick . . . I am incurable."

Barbaric Treatments

With the asylums full of the incurably mad, the conditions became intolerable. Faced with the inmates' cacophony of cries and moans and their bizarre and disturbing behavior, psychiatrists were desperate for better means of management, if not treatment. Their desperation led them to attempt a series of well-intentioned but highly invasive therapies that often did more harm than good and that in retrospect seem barbaric. In the latter half of the nineteenth century, psychiatrists injected disruptive patients with morphine to subdue them, which at least allowed them to avoid the use of physical restraints. But it also created addicts, as increasing doses of morphine were needed to achieve the same levels of sedation, and the practice was quickly terminated.

Chloral hydrate followed, a drug, as legend has it, that a nineteenth-century Chicago barkeep named Mickey Finn slipped into his customers' drinks so he could rob them (hence the phrase "slipping someone a Mickey"). The successors to chloral hydrate, Rohypnol ("roofies") and gamma hydroxy-butyric acid, are now associated with date rape. Chloral, a sedative, was preferable to morphine, as it was not addictive and could relieve insomnia in anxious and depressed patients, but it had an awful taste and left a characteristic odor on the breath.

At the start of the twentieth century, Scottish psychiatrist Neil Macleod attempted "deep sleep therapy," using the powerful sedative sodium bromide to render patients unconscious, sometimes for days or even weeks, in an effort to improve their symptoms. While Macleod claimed his patients were "cured," he provided very little evidence in the form of follow-up data. Nevertheless, bromide compounds spread rapidly in public asylums but were quickly abandoned when the dangers of the treatment became clear. Deep sedation was hard to control and could induce pneumonia, cardiovascular complications, or respiratory arrest.

Manfred Sakel, an Austrian psychiatrist, reasoned that the problem was not sleep therapy itself but the limitations or safety of the agents used to induce it. He began experimenting with a therapy even more dangerous than bromide. The doctor had already been treating drug addicts undergoing withdrawal with low doses of insulin, the hormone produced in the pancreas that regulates glucose levels in the blood. In 1927 Sakel noticed that an addict who had accidentally received an overdose of insulin and fallen into a coma had awoken in an improved mental state, with his more extreme behaviors mitigated. Sakel wondered if comas could also ease the symptoms of insanity. He began to experiment with injecting insulin into schizophrenic patients, causing their blood sugar to drop precipitously and sending them into hypoglycemic comas for hours at a time. Sakel would bring the patient out of the coma with a shot of glucose, then repeat the cycle, sometimes for six days in a row. Gradually, patients showed signs of improvement, their psychotic symptoms diminished. Sakel's insulin coma method was widely adopted and used in the 1940s and 1950s in the United States and Europe. Some patients received up to fifty or sixty treatments.

Insulin coma therapy came with significant risks, however, the most serious of which was permanent brain damage. The brain makes up only 2 percent of the body's total weight but consumes 20 percent of the body's total glucose. It is therefore acutely sensitive to fluctuations in blood glucose levels and can easily suffer damage if levels are too low for too long. Advocates of Sakel's method claimed that the therapy's risks were actually beneficial: if brain damage was incurred, it produced a "loss of tension and hostility." But insulin coma therapy was essentially the equivalent of a metabolic lobotomy, and it eventually went the way of morphine, chloral hydrate, and sodium bromide.

Pathogens and Pyrotherapy

At the start of the twentieth century, almost a third of patients in asylums suffered from general paresis of the insane (GPI), a stage of advanced syphilis. Left untreated, the spiral-shaped organism (*Treponema pallidum*) that causes this venereal disease burrows into the brain and produces symptoms easily mistaken for schizophrenia. Even if patients could be correctly diagnosed, psychiatrists were powerless to help.

In 1917 a Viennese professor of psychiatry named Julius Wagner-Jauregg observed a patient experiencing a transient remission of her psychosis when she developed a fever. Speculating that it was the hyperthermia (elevated body temperature) that improved her symptoms, Wagner-Jauregg conceived a bold experiment: intentionally inducing hyperthermia by administering infectious pathogens to psychotic patients. He began by inoculating them with streptococci or *Mycobacterium tuberculosis*. While these bacteria induced fever, which in turn improved the patients' symptoms, now they had a new ailment for which there were no treatments. He next used *Plasmodium vivax*, the most frequent—but not the most virulent—parasite that causes malaria. This approach produced dramatic improvements, and malaria became a standard treatment for individuals suffering from GPI. Whatever risks it entailed were regarded as acceptable, as the symptoms of malaria could be treated with quinine.

If syphilitic psychoses could be alleviated with fever, psychiatrists wondered if psychoses arising from different causes could be treated similarly. Wagner-Jauregg and other psychiatrists began to apply the "fever cure" to patients with schizophrenia. Some went so far as to inject malaria-infected blood through the skulls and directly into the brains of schizophrenic patients. Alas, "pyrotherapy" did not turn out to be the panacea that many had hoped for. While hyperthermia alleviated the psychotic symptoms of GPI by killing the heat-sensitive bacteria—thereby relieving patients' psychoses—it had no such effect in patients with schizophrenia.

Wagner-Jauregg's fever cure might strike us now as disturbing, but it represented the first effective treatment for mental illness. Never before had any biologic intervention been shown to alleviate psychosis. Its unexpected success punctured the therapeutic pessimism that had dominated psychiatry, and suggested, for the first time, that severe mental illness could be treated. For his pioneering work, Wagner-Jauregg received the Nobel Prize in Medicine in 1927, the first psychiatrist so honored.

THE STONE OF FOLLY

As barbaric as those treatments may seem to our modern minds, they were not the most notorious. That distinction is reserved for psychosurgery and the infamous frontal lobotomy. The earliest form of psychosurgery, trepanation, the drilling of holes in the skull, had been practiced for hundreds of years. Paintings from the fifteenth and sixteenth centuries depict the practice, including Hieronymus Bosch's *The Extraction of the Stone of Madness* and Pieter Huys's *A Surgeon Extracting the Stone of Folly*.

A surgeon extracting the Stone of Folly from an insane person, as depicted in
an oil painting by Pieter Huys, c. 1561.

The modern version of the procedure was pioneered by a Portuguese neurologist named António Egas Moniz. In 1935 Moniz attended a neurology conference in London, where he heard scientists from Yale describe how they had severed neural circuits in the frontal lobes of chimpanzees' brains, a surgical procedure that had rendered the normally frenetic apes tranquil. Moniz would say later that he had already been mulling over such methods by the time he saw the chimps; in any case, he returned to Lisbon ready to set in motion one of the most radical and troubling gambits in medicine's efforts to treat mental illness.

With the help of a young neurosurgeon, Pedro Almeida Lima, Moniz performed his first leucotomy—more commonly known now as a frontal lobotomy—at the Hospital de Santa Marta in Lisbon on November 12, 1935. After the patient was placed under general anesthesia, Lima drilled two holes in the front of the skull, just above each eye; he then inserted the needle of a special syringe-shaped instrument—a leucotome—through the orbit, or eye socket, into the intracranial cavity. Pressing the plunger on the syringe, which extended a wire loop into the brain, Lima was able to rotate the leucotome, carving out a small sphere of brain tissue, the way one would core an apple. The procedure targeted the brain region directly behind the forehead that is the most highly evolved and uniquely human part of the brain.

In 1936 Moniz and Lima published the results of their first twenty leucoto-mies. Nine patients had been diagnosed with depression, seven had schizophrenia, two had anxiety disorders, and two were manic-depressive. Moniz claimed that seven patients improved significantly, another seven were somewhat improved, and the remaining six were unchanged.

Moniz's treatment was quickly celebrated as a miracle cure, spreading through the asylums of Europe and America. The reasons for its embrace are obvious if unforgivable. One of the biggest problems for asylum psychiatrists was the management of disruptive patients; short of physical restraints, there had been no way to control those who were persistently agitated, noisy, violent, and self-destructive. (In 1939 Moniz himself was shot by a patient, leaving him partly paralyzed.) Now, after a relatively simple surgery, these patients could be rendered docile and obedient. The incessant din and commotion that had been so typical of mental institutions was replaced by a more agreeable hush. Patients who had smacked the walls, hurled their food or feces, and shouted at one another or at invisible specters now sat calmly and quietly. Moniz's leucotomy seemed an answer to the psychiatrists' prayers.

While most proponents of leucotomy were not oblivious to the dramatic changes in their subjects' personalities, they argued that Moniz's "cure" was more humane than putting people in straitjackets or padded cells for weeks on end; it was certainly preferable for hospital staff. The Nobel Prize committee recognized this and was convinced of its worth, and in 1949 Moniz was awarded the Nobel Prize for his discovery of "the therapeutic value of leucotomy in certain psychoses."

Walter Freeman was the director of research laboratories at St. Elizabeths Hospital in Washington, DC, the federal mental hospital inspired by Dorothea Dix more than a century earlier. He was impressed by Moniz's procedure and wanted to apply it to the abundant number of patients who had been at the facility for decades and for whom there were no prospects of effective treatment. Since Freeman wasn't trained in neurosurgery, he enlisted the services of a neurosurgeon, James Watts, and in 1936 the two men carried out the first prefrontal lobotomy in the United States at George Washington University Hospital.

The inaugural patient was a woman in her sixties who'd had several nervous breakdowns and had been diagnosed as suffering from "agitated depression." Prior to surgery, the woman had shown "uncontrollable apprehension, was unable to sleep, and by turns was laughing and weeping hysterically." A few hours after the anesthetic had worn off, she was placid and reported feeling much better. In fact, she could not remember what she had been so afraid of. "I seem to have forgotten," she said. "It doesn't seem important now."

Freeman was excited by the initial results of his surgeries. Of their first 623 cases, he and Watts reported "good" outcomes in 52 percent of the operations, "fair" in 32 percent, and "poor" in 13, with 3 percent having died from the surgery.

Not everyone was eager to embrace the new procedure, however. In 1937 Freeman proposed to William Alanson White, the superintendent of St. Elizabeths, that he lobotomize the hospital's more difficult patients. According to Freeman, White replied: "It will be a hell of a long time before I let you operate on any of *my* patients." After White's death later that same year, Freeman and Watts performed lobotomies on fifty patients at St. Elizabeths.

Over time, Freeman and Watts made deeper and ostensibly more accurate incisions. They also replaced general anesthesia with an injection of novocaine. Because the brain is the only organ in the body that does not feel pain (and the novocaine took care of any pain that cutting through the scalp caused), patients were able to remain awake during the procedure, and Freeman and Watts could more easily monitor the effects of the cuts they were making to the brain. Watts described the miraculous change in people who were suffering mental torments one minute, and the next, placid and free of distress. It also meant that the patient could hear the drill as it bore into his or her skull and could feel the movement of the scalpel on the brain tissue.

How Far to Cut . . .

Freeman and Watts's most famous patient was Rosemary Kennedy, daughter of Rose and Joseph, and sister to President John F. Kennedy. Rosemary was born in Boston on September 13, 1918, the third of nine children. The birth was traumatic. While Rose had birthed her first two babies at home without complications, when she went into labor with Rosemary, a flu epidemic was raging in the city, and the doctor was not immediately available. The nurse on the scene had obstetrical training, but instead of delivering the baby herself, she delayed the birth by two hours, first by holding Rose's legs together, then by holding the baby's head and forcing it back into the birth canal, causing trauma and a damaging loss of oxygen.

Rosemary seemed like a physically healthy baby, but by the time she was a toddler, her parents were concerned about her behavioral development, and by kindergarten, it was obvious she was suffering from mental disability. The experts the family consulted pronounced Rosemary mildly intellectually disabled (the terms used at the time would have included "feebleminded" and "moron"). Her parents retained a team of tutors, who enabled her eventually to achieve a fourth-grade level in math and a fifth-grade level in English. Along with the special educational arrangements, Rosemary's activities and information about her condition were managed carefully. Her disability was kept a secret from everyone outside of the immediate family. But as she grew older, she became more difficult to control, so her parents placed her in convents where, thanks to her father's largesse, they could be confident that she would be kept safe and out of the public eye.

In 1938, when Rosemary was nineteen years old, her father was named US ambassador to Great Britain, and she moved to London with her parents and siblings. In London, Rosemary thrived, briefly. She was apparently able to function socially, and was presented, along with her sister Kathleen, to King George VI and Queen Elizabeth at Buckingham Palace. Later, she went with her family to the investiture of Pope Pius XII in Rome. She did not live with her parents at the embassy in London but in a convent in Hertfordshire, northwest of the city, which trained Montessori schoolteachers and where she had a full-time companion to look after her.

When World War II broke out in the fall of 1939, her mother and siblings returned to New York. Her father remained for a time in London, and Rosemary stayed at Hertfordshire until May 1940. Her return to the States marked a significant worsening in her mental state. The mood swings the nuns had noticed when she was at Hertfordshire had given way to rages and violent tantrums. Doris Kearns Goodwin writes in *The Fitzgeralds and the Kennedys*, Rosemary paced "up and down the halls of her home . . . like a wild animal, given to screaming, cursing, and thrashing out at anyone who tried to thwart her will." At one point, she attacked her seventy-eight-year-old grandfather, hitting and kicking him until she was restrained. She shuttled from a summer camp in Massachusetts, to a Philadelphia boarding school, to a convent in Washington, DC, where things only grew worse. Rosemary took to sneaking out at night and wandering the streets. Such behavior posed the threat of illegitimate pregnancy, the sort of scandal that could derail her father's political ambitions for his other children. As E. Fuller Torrey, schizophrenia researcher and advocate, has pointed out, Rosemary's intellectual disability would have been a barrier to respectability, but to have a daughter who was seriously mentally ill or who became pregnant out of wedlock would be an unbearable disgrace.

Desperate for a solution, Joe Kennedy contacted Walter Freeman in the fall of 1941, and that November, at George Washington University Hospital, James Watts performed a prefrontal lobotomy on Rosemary, with Freeman supervising. Rosemary was mildly sedated but still awake. As Watts cut into Rosemary's brain, Freeman spoke to her—asking Rosemary to recite the Lord's Prayer or sing "God Bless America" or count backward. "We made an estimate on how far to cut based on how she responded," Watts told Ronald Kessler, author of *The Sins of the Father*. When Rosemary started to become incoherent, they stopped cutting.

The lobotomy was a disaster, and left Rosemary an invalid; she regressed to the level of a two-year-old, was unable to wash or dress herself, and lost most of her speech. The family first sent her to a private psychiatric hospital before permanently relocating her, in 1948, to St. Coletta's school and convent in rural Wisconsin, where they had a private house built for her and funded her full-time care. According to David Nasaw's biography of Joe Kennedy, *The Patriarch*, there is no evidence of anyone in the family visiting her for the first ten years or so that she was there. In 1961, Joe Kennedy suffered a stroke and was severely incapacitated for the last eight years of his life. In later years, after Joe's death in 1969, Rosemary joined the family for reunions in Hyannis Port, Massachusetts. By the time she died in 2005 at the age of eighty-six, members of her family had made disability and mental health central to their political platforms and advocacy work.

As for Walter Freeman, his correspondence and private writings are, perhaps not surprisingly, "silent on the question of [Rosemary's] surgery and its outcome."

What exactly did Rosemary suffer from? There had been the difficult birth. There had also been the flu epidemic; a wave of influenza swept through Boston when Rosemary's mother, Rose, was in the third and fourth months of pregnancy, and we know now that maternal exposure to influenza at that point in a pregnancy is a possible risk factor for developmental disabilities, lower IQ, and schizophrenia. In her autobiography, Rose Kennedy acknowledged that there were factors other than "retardation" affecting her daughter: "A neurological disturbance or disease of some sort seemingly had overtaken her, and it was becoming progressively worse." It seems reasonably certain that Rosemary developed a psychotic disorder, which would not be entirely surprising: numerous studies have reported that between 4 percent and 8 percent of children with intellectual disabilities go on to develop schizophrenia or other psychoses, a figure significantly above the population average.

In 2015 Kate Clifford Larson published *Rosemary: The Hidden Kennedy Daughter*. Larson was the first biographer to have access to all of Rosemary's known letters. In light of what Rosemary was ultimately subjected to, one line takes on an ominous air. In 1934, while a teenager away at boarding school, Rosemary wrote to her father: "I would do anything to make you so happy."

I HAVE A TOUCH OF SCHIZOPHRENIA IN ME . . .

Like the Kennedy siblings, playwright Tennessee Williams was haunted by what had happened to his own sister Rose, who had also undergone a lobotomy. Tennessee and Rose Williams were particularly close—"our love was, and is, the deepest in our lives," he wrote in his memoir—and some of the most powerful moments in Williams's plays arise from the dramatization of Rose's fragility, notably the character Laura in *The Glass Menagerie*, who falls apart when her "gentleman caller" rejects her. Rose, too, was abandoned by an "unscrupulously ambitious" boyfriend after her father created a scandal by losing his ear in a poker game. "Her heart broke, then, and it was after that that the mysterious stomach trouble began." Echoes of Rose can also be seen in the wounded Blanche DuBois, who comes to visit her sister Stella in *A Streetcar Named Desire* and loses her sanity following her brother-in-law's brutish assault.

Williams's notebooks, published in 2007, show the playwright attempting to grapple with his range of emotions about his sister's difficulties. "The house is wretched," he writes in October 1936. "Rose is on one of her neurotic sprees—fancies herself an invalid—talks in a silly dying-off way—trails around the house in negligees."

The following year, he describes the sensation of slowly losing someone to madness: "We have had no deaths in our family but slowly by degrees something was happening much uglier and more terrible than death." By May of that year, Rose was in an institution and had been diagnosed with schizophrenia.

A medical report from 1939 recorded that Rose suffered from delusions of persecution, auditory hallucinations, and impaired memory. Her speech was "free and irrelevant." She smiled and laughed while speaking of someone who was plotting to kill her. She masturbated frequently. Following a visit to his sister, Williams wrote of her continual laughter and obscenities, and of the doctor's assessment of her hopeless condition: "We could only expect a progressive deterioration."

In 1943 Rose's parents permitted doctors to perform a lobotomy. "A cord breaking," her brother wrote. "Rose. Her head cut open. A knife thrust in her brain. Me. Here. Smoking. My father, mean as a devil, snoring, 1,000 miles away." The event found its way into Williams's work, in *Suddenly Last Summer*, when an elderly socialite attempts to coerce doctors into lobotomizing her niece in order to prevent her from revealing that the woman's son was homosexual.

Williams was haunted by the fear of what his sister's infirmity might mean for his own mental health. As early as 1939, the playwright notes his fear that institutionalization will also be his fate. Williams *was* confined to a mental hospital in Saint Louis in 1969 for three months. A few years later, he said: "I've had a great deal of experience with madness; I have been locked up. My sister was institutionalized for most of her adult life. Both my sister and I need a lot of taking care of . . . I'm a lonely person, lonelier than most people. I have a touch of schizophrenia in me, and in order to avoid madness, I have to work."

Williams's dramatization of his sister's travails might easily have veered into exploitation. Instead, as writer Colm Tóibín argues, the playwright managed in his best work to enable the shadow of madness that threatened him and took possession of his sister to "appear almost normal, an unsettled striving within the soul. . . . He made its roots seem common to us all. But then, as he must have seen it develop in Rose, he dramatized its growth into a sort of poisonous power which slowly overcame and undid his characters."

An Ice Pick and a Grapefruit

As for Walter Freeman, he eventually soured on the standard lobotomy, not because he felt it wasn't a justifiable intervention—he remained a proponent of lobotomies long after they'd fallen into disrepute—but because he disliked the occasional side effects (epileptic convulsions or the loss of personality) and considered the procedure too slow and expensive. The operation, as developed by Moniz and Lima, required a neurosurgeon, anesthesiologist, and hospital operating room. Many more patients could benefit from the procedure, Freeman reasoned, if only it were cheaper and more convenient.

In 1945 Freeman parted ways with his neurosurgeon collaborator and began experimenting with an ice pick and a grapefruit. After perfecting his new procedure, Freeman performed the first-ever transorbital—or "ice pick"—lobotomy on January 17, 1946, in his Connecticut Avenue office in Washington, DC. The procedure, which could be performed using local anesthesia, involved placing the point of a thin surgical instrument (closely resembling an ice pick) under the patient's eyelid and against the top of the eye socket. Next, a mallet was used to drive the point through the thin layer of bone at the back of the socket and into the brain. As with Moniz's coring procedure using a leucotome, the tip of the ice pick was rotated to create a lesion in the frontal lobe. This method allowed for a quicker and less drastic cut to the frontal lobe and was therefore, Freeman believed, less likely to produce the vegetative state that Moniz's method often did. The operation took ten minutes. It could, Freeman insisted, be performed by psychiatrists without surgical training, in clinics and doctor's offices and even the occasional hotel room, making it ideal for dealing with the country's overcrowded wards. Freeman demonstrated this production-line efficiency in 1952 when he performed or supervised 228 transorbital lobotomies in twelve days at five state hospitals in West Virginia—an undertaking the press dubbed "Operation Ice Pick."

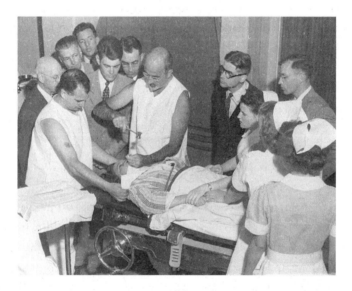

Dr. Walter Freeman performing a lobotomy at Western State Hospital, Washington State, in 1948.

While the lobotomy had initially been regarded as a last resort for chronically ill mental patients, Freeman began to advocate for earlier intervention, telling a group of doctors in Richmond, Virginia, in 1951 that a lobotomy should be considered for a patient "who fails to improve after six months of conservative therapy." While the lobotomy had initially been regarded as a last resort for chronically ill mental patients, Freeman began to advocate for earlier intervention, telling a group of doctors in Richmond, Virginia, in 1951 that a lobotomy should be considered for a patient "who fails to improve after six months of conservative therapy." Freeman also held bigoted beliefs about black and female patients. For example, he believed that black patients, especially women, were among the best candidates for lobotomy in part because of their "greater family solidarity"—meaning that black families were more likely to care for their relatives postoperatively if they survived. Agitated and boisterous behavior in women was less acceptable to doctors of that time than the same behavior in men, and many psychiatrists believed it was easier to return women to a life of domestic duties at home than it was to postoperatively rehabilitate men for a career as a wage earner. Consequently, women disproportionately became candidates for lobotomization.

In 1951 Freeman volunteered to treat black patients at the Veterans Administration hospital in Tuskegee, Alabama, with his transorbital lobotomy technique. However, when a neurosurgeon on staff protested, the Veterans Administration banned the use of the procedure at this hospital and the treatments were canceled. The next year, at the West Virginia state hospital, Freeman performed lobotomies on many black patients, later writing that when he returned a week or so later he found fifteen of these "very dangerous" people "sitting under the trees with only one guard in sight."

In 1967 Freeman performed his final transorbital lobotomy on a longtime patient, Helen Mortensen. Freeman had already performed two lobotomies on Mortensen, and, following the third, she died from a brain hemorrhage. As a result, Freeman was banned from operating, after having performed nearly 3,500 lobotomies from which 490 people died.

The lobotomy was arguably the most invasive and harmful treatment ever developed for mental illness and Freeman its most prolific proponent. Even to his death, he remained an ardent advocate for the procedure's usefulness despite the abundant evidence to the contrary.

Although they were no longer performed, I saw a patient who had undergone a lobotomy some years earlier when I rotated through St. Elizabeths Hospital as a medical student. He was a thin, elderly man; I can see him even now, sitting silently, staring at nothing in particular, as still as a statue. If you asked him a question, he responded in a quiet, uninflected tone. If you made a request, he complied robotically. Most disconcerting were his eyes, which were flat and lifeless. He was a shell of a person, without discernible emotion or animation. I was told that he had once been persistently aggressive and obstreperous. Now, he was a "model" patient: passive, compliant, indifferent—manageable in every way.

Chapter 7

LABORIT'S DRUG

"Hope" is the thing with feathers

That perches in the soul

And sings the tune without the words

And never stops at all.

—Emily Dickinson, "'Hope' Is the Thing with Feathers"

ELECTRIC ENCOUNTERS

Gloria Bruno was one of the most amusing and lovable patients that I have treated, and also one of the most challenging. But she stands out for me for another reason: she was the first patient I ever treated with electroconvulsive therapy (ECT).

I met Gloria in 1976, when I was a psychiatric resident. She was in the throes of a relapse, one of the many she'd suffered in her almost twenty-year history of what was called psychotic depression. At the time, the way we understood the condition empirically was as consisting of depressive symptoms (sadness, worry, fear, pessimism) co-occurring with delusions (false, frightening beliefs, such as having committed a terrible sin for which you would be punished or having some dreadful incurable illness) and/or hallucinations (voices saying you were a bad person and terrible things would happen to you). Conceptually, it was described in the old diagnostic schemas of the nineteenth century on a spectrum called the endogenous psychoses, which included depression without psychotic symptoms, manic-depressive illness (what is now called bipolar disorder), psychotic depression, schizoaffective disorders, and schizophrenia. The novelty of this approach was in the linkage of the various conditions in a sequence of increasing severity, but the concept was limited in that there was no evidence that they shared a common origin or pathology, other than having many symptoms in common.

Psychotic depression was also notable for its severity, high potential for suicidal behavior, and responsivity to ECT. Hence Gloria's arrival at the hospital with her husband, Giuseppe, an elegant and charming man in his sixties who had met the younger Gloria in her native Cuba, where he'd been managing a high-end Havana restaurant. After the Cuban Revolution, Giuseppe had brought Gloria to the United States. They were married in New York, and Giuseppe had risen in the restaurant world to become the maître d' of the finest Italian restaurant in the city.

Gloria was a vivacious person who suffered from a debilitating illness, and Giuseppe doted on her, alternating between the roles of adoring husband and father-protector. They both showed the effects of age—he from years of work in the restaurant business and she from the ravages of her illness—but they were a winsome couple. When I first met Gloria, I was struck by the contrast between the agitated dervish I saw before me and the petite, shy woman her husband described.

I looked over her records and learned that Gloria's relapses were associated with lapses in medication. She didn't like the side effects. This had led to the familiar revolving door pattern that resulted in her being well acquainted with the psychiatric unit staff. When Gloria was actively symptomatic, she could become so consumed by her psychotic experiences that she believed she was being chased by the devil and would shriek in terror. The staff would try to calm her with reassuring words—*cálmate, querida, mantente tranquila*—while stroking her hands and head. Sometimes their efforts allayed Gloria's fears, but other times she began to mimic what they were saying, a classic symptom of schizophrenia called echolalia, or to sing the words back to them nonsensically, so-called clang association, another symptom in which words are put together based on how they sound rather than what they mean.

My impressions of ECT up until then were limited to the same disturbing images that had shaped the public's impression of this apparently barbaric treatment—from movies such as *The Snake Pit* and *One Flew over the Cuckoo's Nest*, which depicted the practice as a physically traumatic form of mind control. But, whatever my initial misgivings, I had to admit that ECT might be the logical treatment for Gloria. She was uncontrollably agitated, shrieking in terror, hardly eating or drinking. Given the severity of her symptoms and the fragility of her condition, we didn't have the luxury of medicating her and waiting the two or more weeks usually required for the therapeutic effects to kick in. ECT could expedite her improvement and break the revolving door cycle.

REBOOTING THE BRAIN

The story of ECT began in the early 1930s when a Hungarian psychiatrist named Ladislas J. Meduna speculated that epilepsy might have a beneficial effect on schizophrenia—similar to the way that fever affected the course of general paresis of the insane (GPI). He had seen reports of patients who'd developed epileptic attacks during the acute phase of their schizophrenia and had been temporarily relieved of their psychotic symptoms. Meduna was intrigued. In his unpublished autobiography, he wrote that while he didn't dare to think of curing schizophrenia, which was then considered an endogenous hereditary disease, he wondered if this apparent antagonism between schizophrenia and epilepsy might be turned to a benefit: "With faint hope and trembling desire, the inexpressible feeling arose in me that perhaps I could use this antagonism, if not for curative purposes, at least to arrest or modify the course of schizophrenia."

In 1933 Meduna began to experiment on animals with various seizure-inducing compounds—strychnine, thebaine, nikethamide, caffeine, absinthe—finally settling on camphor, a scented wax used as embalming fluid, as the least toxic agent. On January 23, 1934, he administered the first injection of camphor to a patient who had been in a catatonic stupor for four years, never moving or taking care of his bodily needs, fed only through a tube. Meduna waited in a state of high anxiety for forty-five minutes, at which point the patient had a minute-long seizure. When the attack was over and the man regained consciousness, Meduna writes: "My legs suddenly gave out. My body began to tremble, a profuse sweat drenched me . . . my face became ashen gray. I went to the ward to observe the patient. He lay in bed, as he had before, like a wooden statue, oblivious to his surroundings."

After five camphor-induced seizures, however, the man rose, as though from the dead, and, for the first time in four years, got out of his bed, began to talk, asked for breakfast, and dressed himself. When he asked how long he'd been in the hospital and was told he'd spent four years in a catatonic stupor, the man did not believe it.

With that, a new era in psychiatry had dawned.

Meduna went on to induce seizures in twenty-six psychotic patients. First he used camphor to induce seizures, but later he found that a respiratory and circulatory stimulant, Metrazol, was a more effective and quick-acting agent. He achieved recovery in ten patients, good results in three, and no change in thirteen. He published these findings on January 18, 1935, concluding that the causes of schizophrenia and epilepsy must be inversely related, meaning that what caused seizures was protective of schizophrenia and vice versa. Therefore, the artificial induction of seizures in schizophrenia patients for therapeutic purposes was able to suppress psychotic symptoms. In a monograph two years later, Meduna reported data from 110 patients, which he said supported his hypothesis of an antagonism between the pathophysiology of schizophrenia and that of epilepsy. The overall rate of remission achieved by patients who had been ill from one week to ten years was 50 percent—a very good outcome in the age prior to antipsychotic medications. As for Meduna's first patient, six years after the initial treatment, he was reported to be doing well.

Meduna's novel Metrazol-seizure treatment quickly became known as convulsive therapy, and in 1937 the first international meeting on the new procedure was held in Switzerland. Within three years, it had joined insulin coma therapy as a standard treatment for severe mental illness in institutions around the world.

There were problems with Metrazol, however. First, before the convulsions actually started, the drug induced a feeling of impending doom in the patient, a morbid apprehension heightened by the awareness that he or she was about to experience uncontrollable seizures. This fearful anxiety must have been even worse for a psychotic patient already experiencing frightening delusions. In addition to the psychological effects, Metrazol provoked thrashing convulsions so violent they were sometimes literally backbreaking. In 1939 a study was conducted by the New York State Psychiatric Institute at Columbia University in which X-rays taken in patients undergoing Metrazol convulsive therapy found that 43 percent experienced spine fractures.

Seizures were clearly therapeutic in depression and psychosis, but the methods of inducing them were problematic. Physicians began looking for a better way to produce "fits." In the mid-1930s Ugo Cerletti, an Italian neurologist who had worked under Kraepelin and Alzheimer, was studying the effects of epilepsy on the brain by administering electrical shocks to dogs, when he thought of using electricity in humans. He got the idea when he saw pigs being anesthetized with electroshock before being butchered. While excited by the therapeutic possibilities, he was aware of the optics—"submitting a man to convulsant electric discharges was considered as utopian, barbaric, and dangerous," and conjured images of a person in the "electric chair."

While we might find the idea of medical professionals streaming electricity through a patient's brain appalling, we should bear in mind that, at the time Cerletti was working, there was no effective treatment for schizophrenia or other severe forms of mental illness besides coma therapy and Metrazol-induced seizures—both dangerous, volatile, and invasive interventions. For most patients, the only alternative to these therapies was permanent confinement in an asylum. We should also remember that electrical shock is used routinely now in cardioversion treatment to restore normal heartbeats in people with arrhythmia, not to mention the electric shocks used to reactivate the heart in cardiac arrests. Surgery itself can be pretty gruesome and invasive, but, when conducted properly, its benefits are more than worth it.

In April 1938 the first patient was treated with ECT at the Rome Royal University Clinic for Nervous and Mental Illnesses. The thirty-nine-year-old man, who had been found wandering in the railway station, behaving strangely, exhibited hallucinations and delusions and was given to murmuring in a strange jargon. The doctors diagnosed him with schizophrenia, and Cerletti and his colleague Lucio Bini prepared him for the treatment.

The results were dramatic. When the man awoke from his first seizure, he showed marked improvement and had no memory of the procedure. After eleven treatments, he had recovered fully and was discharged. One year later, he was living at home and working.

By the mid-1940s, ECT had been adopted by almost every major psychiatric institution in the world. It was less dangerous and frightening to patients than Metrazol therapy, as well as more convenient and more effective. Patients often showed dramatic improvements in their condition after just a few sessions. While there were some side effects to ECT—retrograde amnesia and, before the introduction of succinylcholine (an anesthetic agent that causes short-term muscle paralysis), possible bone fractures—they were still significantly less risky than those associated with comas, malaria, or psychosurgery. It was a significant advance and the first truly effective treatment. Cerletti and Bini didn't know how ECT worked, and to this day, its mechanism of action remains unknown. It is generally believed that ECT "reboots" the brain by synchronizing the electrochemical activity of its malfunctioning neural circuits.

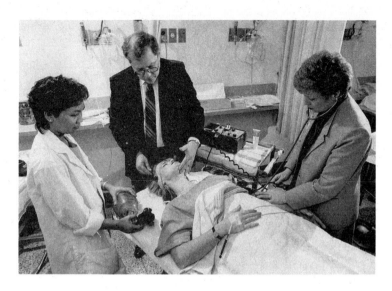

ECT being administered to a patient.

I was mentored in ECT by Lothar Kalinowsky, who was there the day we treated Gloria. The German-born psychiatrist was part of the ECT lineage that had developed in Europe prior to World War II and became one of the earliest practitioners of the therapy in the United States. By the time I met him, he was much sought after to train staff at New York hospitals in ECT and was then supervising its administration at St. Vincent's Hospital. My first day on the service, I arrived at the procedure room, changed into my scrubs, and introduced myself to Kalinowsky, a tall, slender man with silver-gray hair, dressed immaculately in a tailored three-piece suit.

We had eight patients that day who were to receive ECT, and it was my job to handle pre-procedure reviews of their cases and to ensure that they were properly cleared for treatment. After introducing me to the nurse and anesthetist, Kalinowsky directed me to the ECT device and asked me to calibrate it for the first patient. I had to inform him that as this was my first time administering ECT, I actually didn't know how. I expected a scolding, or at least a frown, but he only smiled faintly and, with gentle equanimity, explained how to adjust the current strength, duration, and wave form of the stimulus.

Gloria was the last of the day's patients. When it was her turn, I escorted her into the room and helped her onto the gurney. As I'd done with the seven patients before her, I inserted a butterfly needle into the antecubital vein in the crook of her elbow, to allow the anesthetic to flow and so that a line would be maintained during the procedure in case of any complications.

When Gloria had been positioned, Kalinowsky stepped to the head of the gurney and peered down at her. A nurse inserted the rubber bite plate in Gloria's mouth, and the anesthesiologist readied succinylcholine. Kalinowsky then applied a viscous gel to the sides of Gloria's forehead where the electrodes would be placed to conduct the electrical current. When she flinched at the touch of the cold gel on her skin, Kalinowsky gently reassured her with a soothing sound and a gentle stroke of her cheek. He told me where and how to put the electrodes, and I fastened them in place with an elastic rubber strap. Finally, we attached the wires from the ECT machine to the electrodes affixed to Gloria's scalp, and checked the voltage, pulse frequency, and duration of the current we were about to administer.

When all was ready, the anesthesiologist placed the oxygen mask over Gloria's face and injected the medications. Kalinowsky signaled me to flip the switch, which I did, with some trepidation. Less than ten seconds passed before Gloria's eyes opened in a grimace, and she began tensing and shaking in a tonic-clonic seizure (in which the person's muscles violently contract and their body shakes rapidly). The team kept her oxygenated, monitored her vital signs, and held her limbs to keep her from falling off the gurney. I watched, somewhat uncomfortable, wondering what we were doing to this petite woman.

In less than a minute, it was over, and Gloria was wheeled into the recovery room, where a nurse attended her. After thirty minutes, she was clear headed and alert, and in an hour, she returned to her room.

Gloria showed considerable improvement after just one treatment, but the beneficial effects had worn off by the time of her second procedure two days later. This was characteristic of how patients responded to ECT. With each successive treatment, the degree of improvement would increase and be sustained for a longer period, until the patient reached a plateau that ideally corresponded to the remission of all or most symptoms. For these reasons, the conventional frequency of treatment was three times per week: Monday, Wednesday, and Friday. Gloria reached our goal of 80 percent symptom remission after ten treatments and was discharged, to her and Giuseppe's delight, with an aftercare treatment plan.

The introduction of ECT in the late 1930s offered doctors the first truly effective treatment for schizophrenia, albeit one with serious side effects, including injury from convulsions and memory loss. Since then, the procedure's one-size-fits-all model has been refined and made more efficient and safer. Doctors are now able to individually calibrate the voltage and waveform of the current for each patient, so that the minimum amount needed to induce a seizure is used. Unilateral ECT, in which the electrodes are placed on one side of the head—typically the right, which is opposite the brain's learning and memory areas—has been found less likely to cause memory problems. The American Psychiatric Association, National Institutes of Health, and National Institute of Mental Health have investigated ECT over the past three decades and deemed it a reliable, safe, and highly beneficial treatment for patients with severe cases of depression, mania, or schizophrenia. It can work more quickly than medications and can be especially useful if a patient is suicidal, unresponsive to medications, or unable to tolerate a medication's side effects.

The advent of antipsychotic medications in the 1950s displaced ECT for treating schizophrenia, but it continues to play a role. In fact, electroconvulsive therapy is the only one of the "barbaric" treatments of the twentieth century that is still practiced. It is sadly ironic that Cerletti and Bini did not receive a Nobel Prize for their invention of ECT, unlike the doctors who infected patients with malaria and surgically destroyed unruly frontal lobes.

THE AGE OF PSYCHOPHARMACOLOGY

Psychiatry had finally scored a genuine victory for the first time in human history. But because ECT was invasive, expensive, and complicated, requiring an entire medical team to administer, its benefits weren't widely appreciated.

In the meantime, mental hospitals still overflowed with the miserable and the hopeless, and psychiatrists continued to yearn for more practical, less invasive treatments. In other areas of medicine, pharmaceuticals were at the forefront of therapeutic progress—antibiotics, insulin, medicines for the heart, and vaccines were working wonders. But not a single pharmaceutical company was researching drugs to treat schizophrenia. The reason was simple: nobody believed such medications could be developed. The discovery of antipsychotics was left to serendipity.

In the 1940s Henri Laborit, a French surgeon stationed at a military hospital in Tunisia, was seeking a way to reduce surgical shock in wounded soldiers. According to a hypothesis prevailing at the time, surgical shock was due to a patient's autonomic nervous system overreacting to the stress of physical injury. (The autonomic nervous system is a component of the peripheral nervous system composed of three divisions—sympathetic, parasympathetic, and enteric—that regulates involuntary physiologic processes, including heart rate, blood pressure, respiration, and digestion.) Laborit believed that if he could find a compound that suppressed this reaction, he could make surgical procedures safer.

While experimenting with antihistamines, now commonly used for allergies, Laborit noticed that when he gave patients a dose of one particular antihistamine compound, their attitude toward their impending surgery changed: they became calm, unconcerned, and downright uninterested. The drug was chlorpromazine, and it would trigger a revolution in the care of the mentally ill.

"Laborit's drug," as chlorpromazine came to be called, was developed by the French pharmaceutical company Rhône-Poulenc in 1952. At first, none of chlorpromazine's initial applications was related to mental illness; instead, it was tested in a wide range of medical conditions, including nausea, heart arrhythmias, and seizures, in addition to surgical shock—all to little avail. But Laborit recognized its potential use in psychiatry and believed that the drug's calming influence might be used to manage psychiatric disturbances. He first tested his hunch by administering chlorpromazine intravenously to a psychiatrist colleague who volunteered to serve as a guinea pig. All went well until the medicated doctor rose from his chair and collapsed due the drug's blood pressure–lowering effects. Outraged over this ad hoc experimentation, the director of the hospital's psychiatric service banned all further studies of chlorpromazine.

Laborit persevered. While dining in the canteen at Val-de-Grâce, the military hospital in Paris, he persuaded a group of psychiatrists to test the drug on one of its psychotic patients. On January 19, 1952, chlorpromazine was administered to a man known as Jacques Lh., an agitated, psychotic, and violent twenty-four-year-old with schizophrenia.

The effect was dramatic. A single dose of the drug made Jacques calm and rational. After three weeks of continued treatment, he was able to "resume normal life." He even played entire games of bridge. He recovered so well, in fact, that the astonished physicians discharged him from the hospital. It was nothing short of miraculous: a drug had reduced the symptoms of severe mental illness without significantly altering the patient's overall mental functioning or level of consciousness. News spread quickly, and psychiatrists across Europe began using chlorpromazine. Soon they were publishing dramatic results from clinical investigations with the drug, beginning with those of Jean Delay and Pierre Deniker at Sainte-Anne Hospital in Paris, two names linked indelibly with the advent of antipsychotics.

The following year, chlorpromazine was introduced to North America by European psychiatrists who had immigrated to Canada, chief among them Heinz Lehmann. Born in Berlin, Lehmann had fled Nazi Germany in 1937 and was now a staff physician at the Verdun Protestant Hospital in Montreal. Despite the dominance of psychoanalysis in psychiatry, Lehmann believed that the origin of mental illness had a biological basis that could be treated by chemical agents. He had already experimented on his patients using a variety of compounds, including high doses of caffeine, nitric oxide, insulin, pituitary extracts, typhoidal toxins—even turpentine—all without success.

One day a company representative from Rhône-Poulenc, the manufacturer of chlorpromazine in Europe, which had an office in French-speaking Montreal, dropped by Lehmann's office. Aware of the psychiatrist's predilection for pharmaceutical experimentation, the rep left him literature on the new drug. As Lehmann has told it, one Sunday morning three or four weeks later, he was reading a medical journal in the bath when he came to the article on chlorpromazine. He could hardly believe what he was reading, but if it was true, it would be a near-miraculous advance and an entirely new treatment strategy.

In the spring of 1953 Lehmann began the first North American trial of chlorpromazine. He selected patients with "psychomotor excitement" who had diagnoses such as manic depression and schizophrenia. The results were remarkable. Within weeks, the patients' delusions, hallucinations, and thought disorder had disappeared. A patient with mania said that the drug alleviated the feeling that she "had to live [her] whole life in one day." Another with chronic anxiety said it was "like a chairman taking control of a meeting where, previously, everybody had been shouting at once." The drug's effects were so striking that Lehmann thought initially it might be a fluke. But it wasn't.

As we know now, chlorpromazine was the first truly therapeutic drug for schizophrenia in history, a medical breakthrough that initiated a revolution in psychiatry on par with the leaps in general medicine occasioned by the discoveries of penicillin, insulin, and surgical anesthetics. Lehmann published his findings in 1954, and in 1955 chlorpromazine was approved by the US Food and Drug Administration (FDA) for the treatment of schizophrenia in the United States.

Meanwhile, in England, Joel and Charmian Elkes, a married couple who were both doctors in the Department of Experimental Psychiatry at the University of Birmingham, tested chlorpromazine against a placebo for people with schizophrenia. Their double-blind clinical trial—in which neither doctors nor patients knew who was receiving chlorpromazine and who was taking the placebo (a substance that has no active therapeutic effect)—was the first of its kind and introduced the methodology of randomized controlled trials and placebos into psychiatry. The results were astonishing. The Elkeses reported complete recovery in 26 percent of patients and substantial improvement in 41 percent. The publication of the first controlled study of chlorpromazine marked the birth of a new discipline that would dramatically alter the field of psychiatry: psychopharmacology.

The Elkeses stressed in their report that "in no case was the content of the psychosis changed. The schizophrenic . . . patients continued to be subject to delusions and hallucinations, though they appeared to be less affected by them." In other words, the drug was not curing people—it was simply damping down their symptoms, reducing their impact and the emotional agitation they caused, which allowed patients to behave and converse in a coherent fashion. But the drug also had downsides. Chlorpromazine has a narrow therapeutic index, meaning that the margin of safety between the dose that achieves a therapeutic effect and one that produces unwanted side effects is small. Consequently, if the dose wasn't calibrated carefully or if patients were hypersensitive, it caused stiffness, trembling, and emotionally restricted behavior.

Despite the dramatic results emerging from Canada and Europe, American psychiatrists were slow to embrace chlorpromazine. The pharmaceutical company SmithKline, which had licensed the drug from Rhône-Poulenc to market in the United States, encountered resistance from psychoanalytically oriented US psychiatrists skeptical that a drug could untangle the psychic conflicts they believed lay at the root of schizophrenia. Undaunted, SmithKline decided to target state governments rather than psychiatrists, presenting the drug as a way to save money. If state-funded mental institutions used chlorpromazine, the company explained, they would be able to discharge patients instead of keeping them indefinitely, thereby reducing costs.

For state governors and legislators, this was an appealing idea; they could save money while doing something humanitarian and politically popular. And, indeed, just as the discovery of the antibiotic streptomycin had emptied sanitariums of tuberculosis patients, chlorpromazine began to empty the asylums of schizophrenics. Some of those being discharged were able to live a normal life. Others, however, were incapable of adhering to their medications on their own or of living independently; thus, a drug that was so helpful to so many ironically played a significant role in the disaster that was deinstitutionalization. A century and a half after Philippe Pinel freed the inmates of Salpêtrière from their chains, psychiatrists were now releasing patients from the torment of confinement through an entirely different, and serendipitously discovered, treatment: Laborit's drug.

News outlets quickly picked up on the story, and reporters sometimes referred to the conflict between academic and practicing psychoanalysts and public mental institutions. A *Time* magazine article from March 7, 1955, commented scornfully: "The ivory-tower critics argue that the red-brick pragmatists [state hospitals] are not getting at the patients' 'underlying psychopathology,' and so there can be no cure. These doctors want to know whether [the patient] withdrew from the world because of unconscious conflict over incestuous urges or stealing from his brother's piggy bank at the age of five. In the world of red bricks, this is like arguing about the number of angels on the point of a pin."

As evidence emerged quickly that chlorpromazine was effective at treating the psychotic symptoms of schizophrenia, clinicians wondered how long they should continue medicating patients after symptoms had remitted. Early studies designed to determine this showed that discontinuing chlorpromazine once patients were stable resulted in the "reemergence or exacerbation of the acute symptoms of the illness."

Several well-designed, placebo-controlled relapse-prevention trials conducted in the late 1950s and 1960s demonstrated the benefits of maintenance medication among inpatients and outpatients. Nevertheless, the debate over the long-term use of antipsychotics among stable patients continues to this day. The persistent belief that schizophrenia was fundamentally a psychological or social problem rather than a biological disorder fueled a conviction that medication should be administered only as long as it took for psychodynamic factors to change. One study, for instance, concluded erroneously that patients who remained on medication long enough "to achieve ego reorganization were less likely to relapse when drugs were discontinued."

Despite these contentions, Thorazine, the American trade name for chlorpromazine, would eliminate the old crude treatments: lobotomies, insulin comas, sleep cures. The era of psychopharmacology had begun.

Three decades after introducing chlorpromazine to North America, Heinz Lehmann's feelings about the future of the field were nuanced. He acknowledged the major advances in neuroscience but worried that an overreliance on medication, and too much focus on diagnosing and prescribing—what he called "cookbook" psychiatry—was detrimental to the therapeutic relationship. His ideal psychiatrist was the science-minded physician who was still a healer, who knew "when to smile and when not to smile, what kind of tone to use and what not to." In other words, being able to explain something medically does not necessarily mean that one has understood a patient's needs or torments; those insights arise only after spending thousands of hours in the company of our patients, listening to what they tell us.

Chapter 8

The Anti-Psychiatry
Movement

Anyone who goes to see a psychiatrist ought to have his head examined.

—Samuel Goldwyn,
feature filmmaker and producer

An Inconvenient Myth

By 1970, the psychopharmacologic revolution, and the scientific pathway into the brain and its disorders that it opened, had begun to relax the grip that psychoanalytic theories and practice had held on psychiatry for more than half a century—a change that would ultimately relegate psychoanalysis to a discipline of great historical significance but a rarefied clinical specialty within psychiatric medicine. Freud's theory marked a seminal advance in the nascent field of psychology, but it was embraced and applied on faith, without experimental validation. As a result, it became a powerful, almost cultlike, ideology to which its psychiatric adherents had to swear allegiance; this was perhaps most eloquently expressed by the British poet W. H. Auden, who described Freud as "no more a person now but a whole climate of opinion."

Freud's influence also led psychiatry down a garden path that diverged from medicine's efforts to understand, through scientific research and experimentation, the brain and its susceptibility to disease. Psychiatry paid an enormous price for this dalliance in the form of damaged credibility and the relentless skepticism that spread through the general public and the medical profession.

Though psychoanalytic theory did not undergo experimental validation, other forms of psychotherapy developed in its wake—such as cognitive behavioral therapy and the treatments that would follow it, like interpersonal therapy, exposure therapy, and motivational interviewing—and underwent rigorous testing comparable to what governmental regulatory agencies require for approval of psychotropic drugs. The result, eventually, was a new, diverse, evidence-based therapeutic armamentarium for the treatment of mental illness.

But in the 1960s and early 1970s, just as psychiatry was establishing its scientific bona fides in an effort to regain public and professional confidence, a diverse coalition emerged—including families of mentally ill persons, legal advocates aiming to restore civil liberties to people with mental illness, dissident members of the psychiatric profession, and prominent intellectuals—that would shake the very foundations of the psychiatric profession.

The anti-psychiatry movement was buoyed by the deconstructionist spirit of the counterculture—which was challenging all establishment institutions—the goal of the more radical elements of this movement was not just to reform psychiatry but also to discredit and eliminate it. The first assault came from the French philosopher and historian Michel Foucault, whose *Madness and Civilization: A History of Insanity in the Age of Reason* (1961) argued that psychiatry's original mission of curing people of mental illness, or at least of relieving families of the burden of caring for the severely mentally ill, had been subverted: from the eighteenth century onward, the aim had been to protect society from undesirables by confining them to mental institutions.

Soon after, the sociologist Erving Goffman published a book of essays titled *Asylums*, in which he examined what he called "total institutions": closed worlds such as prisons and mental hospitals, including St. Elizabeths, where he'd spent a year doing fieldwork. Goffman rightly denounced the deplorable conditions in many such institutions. Unfortunately, his conclusions were unfounded. Goffman had no clinical experience yet felt qualified to insist that patients in mental institutions did not have genuine medical conditions but were instead victims of "contingencies" such as poverty or prejudice.

The sociologist Thomas J. Scheff took up Goffman's argument and, in his 1966 book *Being Mentally Ill: A Sociological Theory*, railed against the medical model of mental illness on the grounds that there was "no rigorous and explicit knowledge" of the cause or cure of mental disorders, or a coherent classification of their symptoms. While there was unquestionably less medical knowledge of schizophrenia than, say, tuberculosis, Goffman's and Scheff's argument ignored the fact that the absence of evidence is not evidence of absence. If it were true that a dearth of knowledge about an illness meant that it didn't exist at all, then many deadly diseases throughout history (the black plague, epilepsy, smallpox) were merely illusory.

Soon, a number of psychiatrists joined the assault on their own profession. Chief among these contrarians was Thomas Szasz, a Hungarian-born psychiatrist who was on the faculty of the State University of New York Upstate Medical University in Syracuse. In *The Myth of Mental Illness*, also published in 1961, Szasz argued that "mental illness" was nothing more than a "convenient myth," and that we should regard the phenomena rather as "expressions of man's struggle with the problem of *how* he should live." As for psychiatry, Szasz equated it with "pseudo-science" such as alchemy and astrology, because none had an empirical basis.

In a later book, *Schizophrenia: The Sacred Symbol of Psychiatry* (1976), Szasz wrote of the illness "that there is no such thing, that schizophrenia is a name and a metaphor" and that what psychiatrists call schizophrenia was simply the name given to "certain kinds of social deviance (or of behavior unacceptable to the speaker)." People get locked up in mental hospitals "because they annoy others and are then called 'schizophrenic.'" If we were to abolish institutional psychiatry, he contended, we would also abolish the category of "schizophrenic." Those individuals would still exist, but in Szasz's formulation, they would now be "persons who are incompetent, or self-absorbed, or who reject their 'real' roles, or who offend others in some other ways."

Szasz's final betrayal of his profession came in 1969 when he joined with L. Ron Hubbard and the Church of Scientology to found the Citizens Commission on Human Rights (CCHR). Drawing on Szasz's arguments, CCHR's position was—and remains—that psychiatric disorders are not medical diseases, and that psychiatric treatment is fraudulent and dangerous.

While anti-psychiatry arguments were being fomented in the United States, a Scottish psychiatrist emerged on the other side of the Atlantic who joined and expanded the movement. R. D. Laing believed that mental illness existed, but, like Goffman, he placed the source of illness, particularly schizophrenia, in a person's social environment, and especially in disruptions in the family network. If schizophrenia was an expression of distress prompted by intolerable social circumstances, then psychosis was a cry for help. Laing differed in ways from Szasz, however. While Szasz appeared to regard the schizophrenic as something like an annoying malingerer, Laing proclaimed the schizophrenic's superiority, describing the condition as "one of the forms in which . . . the light began to break through the cracks in our all-too-closed minds." In Laing's view, schizophrenia, with its tendency to violate social norms, was a state of authenticity. "We are all murderers and prostitutes," he wrote in the introduction to *The Politics of Experience*, a declaration of Western alienation that is now a refrigerator magnet available on Amazon.

Laing believed that a therapist could interpret the personal symbolism of a patient's psychosis (echoes of Freud's dream interpretations) and use this divination to identify the environmental issues that were the real source of the patient's schizophrenia. In order to decode a patient's psychotic symptomatology, Laing suggested that the therapist draw upon his or her own "psychotic possibilities." Only in that way could the schizophrenic's "existential position"— "his distinctiveness and differentness, his separateness and loneliness and despair"—be understood.

Laing applied his radical theory in the treatment of schizophrenia to people admitted to Kingsley Hall in London's East End. Laing's logic was that if schizophrenia was a special strategy a person invented to cope with an intolerable situation that required them to live in inauthentic ways, he would provide them with a place where they could exist authentically, without medication or restraint.

Laing was extremely charismatic, and the appeal of his theories came more from the power of his flamboyant personality than from their scientific plausibility. The basic premise was that people with schizophrenia must fully experience their psychosis to resolve the underlying psychic issues responsible for its eruption. If the psychosis was attenuated or interrupted by treatment, the recovery would be incomplete and the psychological outcome poor. People experiencing psychosis would come to Kingsley Hall, which had been adapted as a therapeutic safehouse, where therapists or minders would guide the patients (who were called clients) through the experience. If patients became violent or their symptoms persisted for too long, they were taken to a hospital emergency room.

Needless to say, this approach to a serious brain disorder was not therapeutic. (At least two people jumped off the roof of the building.) This ostensibly innovative practice was, in fact, the psychoanalytic approach—the Freudian talking cure used to exorcise the demon psychic conflicts supposedly causing psychosis—recast in a new formulation. The effect of both these so-called therapies was to withhold beneficial treatment from patients. In light of what we know now about the progressive nature of schizophrenia and the importance of timely, effective intervention, nothing could have been more detrimental than prolonging the duration of untreated illness.

One of the visitors to Kingsley Hall was Loren Mosher, a Harvard-trained psychiatrist who had arrived at London's Tavistock Clinic in 1966 with quite radical views. (Mosher would soon begin a twelve-year tenure as the first chief of the Center for Studies of Schizophrenia at the NIMH and go on to found a scientific journal devoted to schizophrenia: the *Schizophrenia Bulletin*.) Although Mosher was critical of what he saw as too little support for the residents of Kingsley Hall, he believed Laing's alternative methods had merit and subsequently founded a residential treatment program for patients with newly diagnosed schizophrenia in the United States that he called Soteria House. (Soteria was the name of the goddess of safety or refuge from harm in Greek mythology.) There were differences in the way Laing and Mosher approached treatment, but both Soteria House and Kingsley Hall embraced "a concept of schizophrenia as an existential crisis to be resolved at a personal and interpersonal level." Medications and medical models of illness were viewed as impediments to the creative resolution of psychotic episodes.

Amid of all this, *One Flew over the Cuckoo's Nest* came out—the 1975 Oscar-winning film based on Ken Kesey's 1962 novel. It was set in an Oregon State mental institution, where a charismatic and mischievous rogue named Randle Patrick McMurphy, played by Jack Nicholson, has been hospitalized for antisocial behavior. McMurphy leads a boisterous patient rebellion against the tyrannical Nurse Ratched, who forces him to take medication, then undergo electroshock treatment; when neither of these subdues McMurphy, she has him lobotomized. While the story was intended as a political allegory as much as an anti-psychiatry polemic, it seared into the public's mind the image of a morally and scientifically bankrupt profession.

By the 1980s, the gains of psychopharmacology and the influence of neuroscience had revealed the baseless and harmful nature of the experimental approaches of mavericks such as Laing and Mosher, just as it had done previously with the neo-Freudians and the old barbaric treatments. Soteria House and Kingsley Hall both shut down. Mosher was forced to resign from the NIMH as a result of continuing to espouse the view that the routine use of antipsychotics was unhelpful and potentially harmful. Laing's reputation ultimately suffered, in part, because of his personal life. Szasz quotes John Clay, Laing's biographer, who wrote that Laing's avoidance of responsibility for his first family was particularly "inde-

Kingsley Hall in London offered a radical, holistic, nonmedical approach to the treatment of psychosis. The photograph on the left shows the exterior of the building, and the top right shows R. D. Laing, Paul Zeal, and Leon Redler in Laing's consulting room in the 1960s. (Redler was an American psychiatrist who worked with Laing, and Zeal was a British psychoanalyst and New Age therapist.) Laing and his wife, Jutta, are featured in the photograph on the bottom right.

fensible since his line had been that the breakdown of children could be attributed to parents and families." His son Adrian has been more explicit. When Laing's daughter Fiona had a nervous breakdown and was taken to Gartnavel Mental Hospital in Glasgow, Adrian called his father for advice; he was worried that his sister could be subjected to ECT or other treatments Laing detested. At the time, the family was living in a house on Ruskin Place. Laing's cold response was: Gartnavel or Ruskin Place, what's the difference? "It was a double bind, you see," Adrian has said. "Either he had nothing to do with it [Fiona's breakdown], and his theories were shit, or he had everything to do with it, and he was shit."

E. Fuller Torrey, a major figure in the field of schizophrenia research and advocacy, believes that Laing became disillusioned with his own ideas when his daughter developed schizophrenia. Torrey knew all about the pain of watching a family member succumb to schizophrenia—and about the pain misplaced blame could cause. In 1957, when he was a third-year premed student at Princeton University and planning his future as a small-town family doctor, his eighteen-year-old sister, Rhoda, had a psychotic break, imagining that British soldiers were attacking the house. Torrey's father was dead, and so he became his mother's primary support, accompanying her and his sister to doctor appointments at the top hospitals in search of a diagnosis and treatment. Torrey came away from those consultations with the clear impression that no one had any idea what was causing his sister's schizophrenia. His mother blamed herself, as most parents did then. As Torrey has reminded me, "When the blame wasn't stated explicitly, it was implied in the literature."

Rhoda died in 2010 at age seventy. Throughout her life, she suffered from anosognosia: a lack of insight about the fact that she was ill. She had spent the greater part of her life in hospitals, group residences, and nursing homes. Her illness changed the direction of Torrey's medical career. And seeing his mother's attempts to understand the tragedy—she had only a high school education, and information was scant and unreliable—encouraged him, many years later, to write his seminal guidebook for families, *Surviving Schizophrenia: A Family Manual*.

In 1977 Torrey published a brief satiric piece in the magazine *Psychology Today* in which he imagined the many psychiatrists over the years who had blamed parents for their children's schizophrenia—Laing, Frieda Fromm-Reichmann, Harry Stack Sullivan, and others—tried in court for having caused unnecessary suffering. All are found guilty. The punishment? For a period of ten years, the convicted would be forced to read and reread their own writings.

Chapter 9

THE COST OF GOOD INTENTIONS

I thought how unpleasant it is to be locked out; and I thought how it is worse,
perhaps, to be locked in.

—Virginia Woolf, *The Essays of Virginia Woolf*, vol. 1, 1904–1912

D.P. 15

In the fall of 1968 I was studying for exams in my college dormitory when my
mother called to tell me that my grandmother had died suddenly of a heart attack.
Growing up, I had been very close to my paternal grandmother, and I prepared to
return home immediately. After the funeral, we came back to my parents' house,
and the family reminisced about my grandparents and their siblings. They had
both come from large families. I was preoccupied with the exams I had coming up
and only half listening to the conversation when my uncle Joe mentioned something about Great-Aunt Rose.

This startled me, as I had never heard of this relative. "Who's Aunt Rose?" I
asked.

Uncle Joe explained that she was his (and my late paternal grandfather's) sister. I had been close to my paternal grandfather and thought I knew all of his siblings, my great-aunts and great-uncles, but I had no recollection of Rose and asked
why I'd never met or even heard about her.

Rose, my father said, had been institutionalized. She was "mentally disabled."

I don't recall that anything more was explained to me, and with the self-
absorption of youth, I didn't press for details.

Flash forward fifty years. I'd begun writing this book, and I recalled the incident at my grandmother's funeral. I decided to ask my mother, then ninety-four,

what she knew about Rose. Her answer stunned me. She said that she had never met her aunt because Rose was in a mental hospital and that was not a place people visited. The institution, she added, was Cleveland State Hospital—the very place I'd been taken as a boy on the school field trip. But that wasn't the only surprising irony. My mother had also visited Cleveland State Hospital in another context, during which she may well have interacted with Aunt Rose without even knowing it.

She told me that in the early 1950s, when I was a child, she did charity work for the Council of Jewish Women. One of the places she volunteered was at Cleveland State Hospital. For two years, my mother and a small group of women would go weekly and visit a different female patient ward at the hospital (men and women patients were kept on separate units) and lay the table for the women's lunch: flowers and place mats and so on; nice little touches that the women never otherwise enjoyed. When the volunteers arrived, they would find the women in a cold, ugly room, huddled on long, iron benches. The patients never looked directly at the volunteers, and when the volunteers tried to engage them, they got little response. Still, it was clear that they appreciated the volunteers, and if my mother or any of the others missed a week, the patients would ask where they were. It was only years later that my mother put two and two together and realized that she may have served lunch to Aunt Rose during her visits.

Now I wanted to know more. I contacted a genealogy expert and asked for help. Six weeks later, she sent me an electronic zip file containing reams of family records from the first decades of the twentieth century. I learned that Rose was the sixth of seven children and that, in 1922, when she was eighteen years old, she came with one sister and her parents to America—the last of the Lieberman family to emigrate from Volozhin (then part of the Russian Empire [the USSR], but now in Belarus). From New York, they traveled on to Cleveland, where other members of the family had previously settled. Five years later, on December 28, Rose was admitted to Cleveland State Hospital as patient number 25904. The admission record didn't reveal whether Rose was admitted voluntarily or committed by the family or a court order.

At the time, Cleveland State Hospital did not write out the diagnoses for psychosis; instead, a coding system, the *Statistical Manual for the Use of Institutions for the Insane* (1918) (a forerunner of the *Diagnostic and Statistical Manual of Mental Disorders*), was used. Rose was designated in the admission book as "D.P. 15," the code that denoted dementia praecox, what we now call schizophrenia.

Rose remained a patient at Cleveland State Hospital for twenty-seven years. In 1955, with her condition recorded as "unimpr" (unimproved), she was transferred to Apple Creek Hospital, a former TB sanitarium, where she died in 1959.

My school field trip had just missed overlapping with Aunt Rose. Neverthe-less, I knew that conditions during her stay would hardly have been different from what I'd glimpsed there. (When I think about it now, I don't know which is more disturbing: that I had a relative who spent her life in that institution, or that my family had so completely disregarded her that I learned of her existence only by accident years after her death.) I was somewhat consoled in learning that rather than burying her at the mental hospital's cemetery, my grandfather's family had arranged for her to be laid to rest next to her parents and siblings. I had visited these family graves many times over the years to pay my respects. Strangely, until I learned of Rose's existence, I had never noticed her headstone.

Rose Lieberman's headstone in Bet Olam Cemetery, Beachwood, Ohio, 2019.

Some weeks after receiving the genealogy report, while delving into the his-tory of deinstitutionalization, I would see much more graphic evidence of the con-ditions in which my Aunt Rose had lived.

On May 6, 1946, an issue of *Life* magazine hit the newsstands that contained a searing exposé on the state of America's mental hospitals. It was written by Albert Maisel, who'd been a correspondent in both the South West Pacific and European theaters during World War II. Maisel had written about, among other things, com-bat medicine, and his testimony before a congressional committee had helped to bring about improvements in the Veterans Administration's own mental hospitals. His *Life* magazine piece, "Bedlam 1946: Most U.S. Mental Hospitals Are a Shame and a Disgrace," helped to kick-start the deinstitutionalization movement in America.

Deinstitutionalization was a government-mandated policy intended to enable patients to be released from state mental hospitals and cared for at community men-tal health centers; they could live with their families or in supervised residential facilities. Just as Philippe Pinel had liberated mental patients from their chains almost two centuries earlier, deinstitutionalization would liberate them from the institutions in which they were, for all practical purposes, incarcerated. Legislators, advocates for the mentally ill, and the general public were all enthusiastic about this dramatic new approach to care, and there were many reasons to support the idea. It looked more humane, therapeutically beneficial, and cost effective. And, as Maisel and others would show, conditions in state institutions were dire.

For his article, Maisel drew on his observations of a dozen hospitals, reams of court records and investigatory documents, and collated reports of more than three thousand conscientious objectors who had opted to spend their military service as mental hospital attendants. But he focused particularly on two state hospitals, the Philadelphia State Hospital at Byberry and the Cleveland State Hospital in Ohio—the hospital where my great-aunt Rose resided in 1946 and where, Maisel reported, "brutality was commonly practiced."

This wasn't the first time the dreadful state of American mental hospitals had been exposed. In 1887, in what was likely one of the earliest instances of immersion journalism, a writer for Joseph Pulitzer's *New York World* had feigned insanity to gain admission to the women's asylum on Blackwell's Island (now Roosevelt Island). Nellie Bly, whose real name was Elizabeth Cochran, brought attention to the brutality and neglect the institution's patients were subjected to, and published her report in the book *Ten Days in a Mad-House*. The book sometimes has the air of a tabloid about it (among the drawings included is one depicting the writer in front of a mirror, captioned: "Nellie practices insanity at home"), but Bly's outrage at what she found is undeniable. The book caused a sensation, making Bly one of the most famous journalists in the United States, and resulting in a $1 million increase in the budget of the New York City Department of Public Charities and Corrections.

More than three decades later, a photographer for the *Philadelphia Record* disguised himself as an attendant and took a series of photos showing disturbing conditions at Byberry. And in 1943 the *Cleveland Press* broke a story about conditions at the Cleveland State Hospital—the shackled patients, overcrowding and neglect, vile food. The journalist had been tipped off by a group of conscientious objectors working at the hospital and was tireless in pursuing the grisly story, at one point documenting that four female patients who arrived at the hospital were left unattended in "strong rooms" (used to isolate violent or agitated patients) until all four came down with pneumonia and were found dead. Elsewhere, in a makeshift basement morgue, rats ate the face of an elderly patient awaiting burial.

Despite the horrors uncovered by other journalists, it was Maisel's article that grabbed the public's attention. Its influence was no doubt partly a result of *Life* magazine's centrality in American culture, but the country was also particularly sensitive to images of horror. By then, Americans had seen photographs of Nazi concentration camps and atrocities, and some of the photos of mental patients that accompanied Maisel's article—thin, naked, huddling in distress—were eerily reminiscent of the images of concentration camp inmates. The preceding few decades had also seen compulsory sterilization in more than thirty states; it is estimated that by 1940, more than eighteen thousand mentally ill people in the United States had been surgically sterilized. This number would grow to seventy thousand by the time all states had repealed the laws allowing forced sterilization in 1981.

What Maisel found was that the vast majority of our state mental institutions were "dreary, dilapidated excuses for hospitals, costly monuments to the states' betrayal of the[ir] duty." Thousands slept on blankets or bare floors, and hundreds spent their days filthy and naked. Those well enough to work often labored twelve hours a day, seven days a week. People were left for weeks at a time in various kinds of restraints, including straps, "restraining sheets," and leather handcuffs. One ward had two bathtubs for sixty-five patients. Not surprisingly, tuberculosis was rife—in some hospitals, thirteen times what it was on the outside.

While the *Life* exposé may have galvanized the public's outrage at the conditions of mental institutions, which had been the cornerstone of mental health care policy for more than a century, it was two other events that fueled the seismic shift in mental health policy toward deinstitutionalization. First was the experience of successfully treating soldiers with psychiatric symptoms during World War II and returning them to their units instead of placing them in hospitals,

Photos of patients at Cleveland State Hospital by Jerry Cooke, featured in the *Life* magazine article "Bedlam 1946."

leading to the idea that outpatient treatment in the community could more effective than confinement in remote institutions. Second, was the introduction of chlorpromazine—the first medication for schizophrenia that was truly therapeutic, controlling sufferers' symptoms and enabling them to live outside of institutions. This, too, suggested the feasibility of community-based care.

As the pressure for change mounted, the federal government passed the National Mental Health Act of 1946 and created of the National Institute of Mental Health (NIMH) in 1949. The NIMH's mission was to conduct research on the causes and treatment of neuropsychiatric diseases and reduce the need for state mental hospitals, substituting a community-oriented policy.

Over the next three decades, additional legislation targeted the conditions experienced by mentally ill people. In 1955 Congress passed the Mental Health Study Act, which commissioned a comprehensive study of the nation's mental health situation. Its report, published in 1961, recommended emphatically that the role of state mental hospitals in the mental health care system be deemphasized in favor of community-based treatment. More specifically, the report recommended that two thousand community mental health centers be established that would deliver preventive and early treatment and provide ongoing care, thereby enabling patients to remain in their communities, close to their families and integrated into society. This recommendation became the central tenet of the Community Mental Health Act, which mandated deinstitutionalization and provided federal funding to create community mental health centers (CMHCs). President John F. Kennedy signed this landmark legislation in 1963. It would be Kennedy's last public bill-signing ceremony before his assassination three weeks later. Kennedy's ostensible motivation for this legislation was to improve the mental health care system. There was also a more personal reason: to dispel the haunting memory of his sister Rosemary's mental illness, disastrous lobotomy, and institutionalization.

Two years later, President Lyndon Johnson took up the baton, shepherding through two amendments to the Social Security Act of 1935: Medicare, which would provide health insurance for those over sixty-five, and Medicaid, which would provide federal matching funds to the states to finance health care, including mental health benefits, for low-income families—where most residents of public mental hospitals came from. Remarkably, Medicaid would *not* allow federal funds to go to states for services rendered in large hospitals solely for the mentally ill—the so-called IMD (institution for mental disease) exclusion. An IMD was a hospital, nursing facility, or other institution of more than sixteen beds that was engaged primarily in diagnosing, treating, or caring for people with mental illnesses. The exclusion provision was a blunt instrument designed to motivate states to keep patients out of hospitals, thereby reducing the number of hospitalized patients and, presumably, improving patients' quality of life while reducing expenses.

Despite the legislation's good intentions, deinstitutionalization lead to disastrous and enduring problems. The movement was predicated on three major assumptions: first, that there would be adequate living facilities in the community for patients discharged from mental hospitals, and second, that there would be sufficient clinical resources for their treatment. A third assumption was that the funds the federal government made available to the states would be utilized for the above purposes. Neither of the first two conditions was in place, and the third varied from state to state.

The result was that the vast majority of discharged patients didn't receive the intended treatment at community mental health centers. Of the two thousand centers that had been proposed in the legislation, less than half were established, and they were never fully funded. Paul Appelbaum, a Columbia University psychiatry professor and expert in the interactions of law, ethics, and medicine, has said that among the problems with the legislation was its failure to fund the centers long-term: "Having gotten them off the ground, the federal government left it to states and localities to support. That support never came through." Instead, the funds were diverted to other purposes. The community infrastructure, facilities, and workforce that was supposed to care for these patients simply didn't exist; workers were often inadequately trained to manage people suffering from severe mental illness or preferred caring for people with less complex mental disorders. In addition, the legislation failed to anticipate the massive deficiencies between institutionalized care (unsavory as it seemed) and community care, which lacked oversight, residential facilities, and assurance of treatment compliance. Left to their own devices, many patients simply stopped taking the medication that could enable them, with necessary psychosocial and residential adjunctive services, to function outside of the hospital. Around three quarters of people in mental hospitals were unmarried, widowed, or divorced, so it was unrealistic to assume that there were supportive families waiting to offer them housing and assume responsibility for them upon discharge.

In addition, the mission of the community mental health centers quickly got muddled. Were they social welfare agencies or were they health providers? Furthermore, which of a community's many mental health needs should they serve, and in what priority: people with severe psychotic disorders, or those with anxiety disorders, depression, substance abuse or stress disorders? There was also the matter of people whose problems didn't warrant a particular diagnosis, but who were nevertheless distressed—what some, perhaps somewhat dismissively, have called the "worried well."

Eventually, CMHCs broadened their mission and redirected their efforts to serve new and different populations, deemphasizing their focus on schizophrenia and related psychotic disorders (a segment of the patient population that became known as "severe mental illnesses," or SMIs). Mental health care providers even began referring to the people they served as clients instead of patients. Tellingly, while the total number of staff at these centers nearly tripled between 1970 and 1975, the number of full-time psychiatrists per center fell, from 6.8 to 4.3, reflecting the shifting orientation in populations and services.

Meanwhile, lacking the clinical care and residential facilities needed to support, and hopefully reintegrate, them into the community, patients released from state mental hospitals gravitated to other institutions (a phenomenon known as transinstitutionalization). This migration is reflected by the precipitous decline in the number of people from public psychiatric beds and the subsequent increase of mentally ill persons in prisons, nursing homes, and on the streets.

Between 1955 and 1994, 87 percent of the nation's 559,000 mentally ill patients in state hospitals were discharged. By 2016 it was 97 percent. A number of states downsized or permanently closed many of their hospitals, drastically reducing the availability of long-term, inpatient care facilities. The number of long-term hospital beds for the mentally ill has continued to decline, from more than three hundred beds per one hundred thousand people in 1955 to eleven beds per one hundred thousand in 2016. It would be a good thing if this decline was because people were receiving good community-based outpatient treatment, reducing the number needing hospitalization. But this wasn't the case.

The problem was exacerbated in 1980 when Ronald Reagan was elected president and converted the Community Mental Health Act's remaining funds into mental health block grants for the states. This gave states greater freedom to spend the funds earmarked for the mental health care of previously institutionalized SMI patients as they chose.

Appelbaum called this "a death knell" for the idea of community mental health centers fulfilling their intended purpose. This is because when state budgets are under pressure, it's often easiest to defund mental health programs, since the mentally ill tend not to form clear voting blocs or strong lobbies, and the mental health centers too often ended up focusing on people who had insurance or could pay out of pocket, leaving the indigent to their own devices.

By the 1990s, almost 37 percent of homeless people and 16 percent of people in jails were mentally ill. These numbers steadily increased over the next three decades.

This grand plan gone awry was the focus of a congressional hearing on "De-institutionalization, Mental Illness, and Medication" chaired by Daniel Patrick Moynihan, the eminent senator from New York, in May 1994. Moynihan opened the hearing by harkening back to the Community Mental Health Act, which he had worked on more than three decades earlier as assistant secretary of labor in the Kennedy administration, referring to a certain "pen certificate," which hung on his wall and commemorated the pen Kennedy had used to sign that act into law.

Reading Moynihan's statement now, you can hear the sorrow and frustration of a failed mission: "We keep this pen certificate hanging in our back room as a reminder of the cost of good intentions. To make great changes casually and not pay very rigorous attention to what follows is to invite large disturbances." It had become clear over time, Moynihan said, that discharging patients wasn't enough; they had to be looked after. "They had to have someone who knew who they were, where they were, how they were doing. Then a generation went by, and, lo and behold, we have a problem called 'the homeless,' which in my state, at least, is de-fined as a problem that arises from the lack of affordable housing. It is nothing of the kind. It arises from a decision based on research to follow a particular strategy with respect to a particular illness." More than any other illness, Moynihan's com-ments pertained to schizophrenia.

By the mid-2000s, there were more than three times as many seriously men-tally ill people in jails and prisons as there were in hospitals. In 2014, there were ten times as many. Today the three largest psychiatric facilities in the nation are the Cook County Jail in Chicago, Los Angeles County Jail, and Rikers Island in New York City. Ultimately, deinstitutionalization mostly shifted the burden of care from the state hospitals to other venues and agencies' budgets, namely transinstitutionalization.

While the Community Mental Health Act may have triggered this seismic transition, it was not the sole cause. Other legislation clearly contributed to shift-ing massive numbers of people from one institutional setting (state hospitals) to others (general medical hospitals, jails, prisons, nursing homes, shelters) by providing economic incentives. This included federal entitlements like Medicare and Medicaid in 1965 Social Security Disability Insurance (SSDI), Supplementary Security Income (SSI), food stamps, and housing supplements. This legislation encouraged the construction of nursing homes and provided a payment source for patients transferred from state mental hospitals to nursing homes and to general hospitals.

Previously the full cost for patients residing in state hospitals was borne by the states. With these legislative initiatives, they could now release them and have the federal government assume from half to three-quarters of the cost. The result was massive transinstitutionalization of long-term patients, primarily elderly patients with dementia who were housed in public mental hospitals for lack of other institutional alternatives.

The states' use of entitlement programs to shift costs to the national government was a reflection of a federal system of government that divided authority and sovereignty. The existence of three distinct levels of government—federal, state, and local—often encouraged efforts to shift fiscal burdens and, at the same time, ignored policy. Intergovernmental rivalries, in other words, shaped policies and priorities in unanticipated ways.

By the early 1970s, the states had continued to decant their state hospital populations by opening the proverbial back door for release and closing the front door for admission. But the states' decisions to reduce their public mental hospital populations and create obstacles to prevent the admission of patients, along with other changes in public attitudes, treatment ideologies, and social and economic factors, created a fragmented and confusing array of treatment settings for persons with mental illnesses including short-term general hospitals providing acute mental health care; a fast shrinking number of state and federal long-term hospital beds, nursing homes, residential care facilities, CMHCs, outpatient departments of general hospitals, community care programs, homeless shelters, and patient-run, and self-help services, among others. This diversity and the absence of any linkage or coordinating system for service integration combined with the lack of a unified structure of insurance coverage confronted patients (and their care providers) with a bewildering maze that would confuse even the most astute individuals let alone those with severe mental impairment. As a result mentally ill patients who had resided for years in custodial institutions were forced to seek refuge in nursing homes, homeless shelters, prisons, or on the streets.

The high cost of good intentions indeed.

Chapter 10

THE TAXONOMIST OF
MENTAL ILLNESS

Physicians think they do a lot for a patient when they give his disease a name.

—Immanuel Kant,
German philosopher (1724–1804)

BIBLE-O'-MADNESS

The advent of antipsychotic medications in the 1950s had provided a scientific lifeline and a window into the pathological basis of mental illness, but the policy of deinstitutionalization, which began in the 1960s, as well as revelations about snake pit institutions and harmful treatments, severely eroded psychiatry's credibility and reputation. With psychoanalytic theory's influence waning and biological psychiatry still in its nascent stage, a conceptual framework was needed to bolster psychiatry's bona fides and guide research and clinical practice. The final impetus for this framework would come from two very different but critically important studies conducted in the late 1960s and early 1970s. Each demonstrated the limitations and fallibility of psychiatric diagnoses—particularly when it came to schizophrenia.

The Cross-National Study of Diagnosis of Mental Disorders, which was carried out by researchers in the United States and Great Britain, aimed to determine the consistency of psychiatric diagnoses by psychiatrists on both sides of the Atlantic. We're used to such reproducibility in many aspects of our lives. If you measure your friend's height, for example, and then someone else measures your friend's height, the two of you should get the same result. Similarly, if your child has a fever and itchy blisters containing red fluid, different doctors should arrive at the same diagnosis: chicken pox. The Cross-National Study asked whether psychiatric diagnoses were similarly reliable.

The study, conducted from 1965 to 1969, examined admissions of psychiatric patients to hospitals in New York City and London. As mental illnesses were still diagnosed through a combination of what a patient reports and what a doctor observes, it was perhaps not surprising that patients with the same symptoms often received different diagnoses. The most glaring disparity between US and British psychiatrists occurred in the diagnosis of schizophrenia and affective disorders (also called mood disorders): Americans applied the diagnosis of schizophrenia to a much wider variety of clinical conditions than their British counterparts did. British psychiatrists diagnosed many patients with manic-depressive illness (what is now called bipolar disorder) who, in the United States, would have been labeled as having schizophrenia. These results revealed that existing methods of diagnosis were subject to distortion through practitioners' local biases and adherence to systematically different views of psychopathology. This also meant that estimates of population frequency of these illnesses were likely subject to these differences and thus inaccurate. A joke went around in the United States at the time that you could cure your patients from having schizophrenia simply by sending them across the Atlantic.

While the Cross-National Study was a legitimate research effort that used rigorous methodology, the same could not be said of a second study, published in 1973 in the normally staid pages of the prestigious journal *Science*. The author was David Rosenhan, a Stanford-trained lawyer with a degree in psychology but no clinical experience, and the title was "On Being Sane in Insane Places." Rosenhan opened with a question: "If sanity and insanity exist, how shall we know them?"

The article described the results of an experiment ostensibly to test the accuracy of psychiatric diagnoses. Rosenhan instructed eight collaborators—a graduate student, three psychologists, a pediatrician, a psychiatrist, a painter, and a housewife, none of whom had a history of mental illness—to feign psychotic symptoms in an attempt to gain admission to the psychiatric services of different hospitals. The "pseudopatients" used fake names and complained of hearing voices. Upon admission to the psychiatric ward, where all but one of them were diagnosed with schizophrenia (the other received a diagnosis of manic depression), the pseudopatients stopped simulating symptoms and behaved normally. Their behavior on the wards was variously recorded in their medical records by nurses as "friendly," "cooperative," and exhibiting "no abnormal indications." The pseudopatients took notes about their experience while they were there.

The pretense of Rosenhan's faux patients was never detected by hospital staff, and when they were discharged, after an average stay of nineteen days, all but the manic-depressive patient were labeled with "schizophrenia in remission." Rosenhan concluded that it was clear "we cannot distinguish the sane from the insane in psychiatric hospitals," and he condemned the entire profession for unreliable diagnoses and excessive labeling.

Upon learning of the ruse, the psychiatric community protested. A prestigious teaching hospital claimed that its staff could never be fooled by such a trick. Rosenhan decided to call its bluff and proposed a second experiment, the results of which were also reported in the 1973 *Science* paper. The hospital's staff would be told that in the coming months, one or more pseudopatients would try to gain admission to their hospital by the same means as in the first experiment.

After a period of time, the hospital staff were asked to rate each patient admitted to the psychiatric service according to the likelihood that the individual was a pseudopatient. Of 193 patients who were admitted in that time frame, 41 were identified as possible or likely impersonators by at least one member of the staff. The punch line was that Rosenhan hadn't sent any pseudopatients to the hospital.

This article reinforced the worst fears of the insurance companies and the government about psychiatry and provided them with the justification they needed to reduce mental health care benefits. In 1975 the vice president of Blue Cross told *Psychiatric News*, "Compared to other types of [medical] services, there is less clarity and uniformity of terminology concerning mental diagnoses, treatment modalities, and types of facilities providing care. . . . One dimension of this problem arises from the latent or private nature of many services; only the patient and therapist have direct knowledge of what services were provided and why."

Rosenhan's *Science* article resulted in public outrage and condemnation of psychiatry. In their defense, psychiatrists argued, quite reasonably, that if a person showed up at a mental hospital and complained of hearing voices, doctors were obligated to take him at his word unless an ulterior motive was apparent. This obligation held for all doctors: if someone faked illness by intentionally swallowing a vial of blood, then came to the ER coughing up blood, it would be extremely cynical, not to mention a dereliction of duty, for doctors to assume chicanery rather than admitting the patient for observation and tests to determine the source of the bleeding. Patients with Munchausen syndrome, who fabricate illnesses to gain attention, often are treated for false conditions. If psychiatrists didn't accept what their patients told them, not just psychiatry but also the entire medical profession would be at risk.

The renowned psychiatrist Robert Spitzer called the Rosenhan study "a sword plunged into the heart of psychiatry." The damage to its reputation caused by this study has remained part of the field's infamous legacy and only recently began to abate, thanks in part to a bestselling exposé of Rosenhan's notorious project written by a journalist, Susannah Cahalan. But more about that later in this chapter.

However, at the time, psychiatry didn't take this lying down. Spitzer composed a detailed rebuttal to Rosenhan's study in a piece published in 1975 in the *Journal of Abnormal Psychology*. Playing on Rosenhan's use of the term "pseudopatients," Spitzer charged that Rosenhan's work was "pseudoscience presented as science." He took particular issue with the author's failure to disclose his data and sources, noting that we actually knew very little about how the pseudopatients presented themselves.

It was against this backdrop that Spitzer was tapped to create a framework for diagnosing mental illness—what was to become the *DSM-III*, a radical revision of the APA's seminal diagnostic bible, the *Diagnostic and Statistical Manual*. The changes Spitzer oversaw in descriptive psychiatry would be comparable in their significance to those introduced by Emil Kraepelin almost a century earlier.

THE PROPHET OF PSYCHIATRY

Robert Spitzer had been an unusual child, hyper-attentive and methodical. A seeker of truth, and of explanations, from a young age, he was also abrasive, socially awkward, and a bit of a nerd. As Hannah S. Decker describes in her excellent history *The Making of DSM-III: A Diagnostic Manual's Conquest of American Psychiatry*, when Spitzer was about twelve years old, he went to summer camp. On the wall of his bedroom, he made a graph of his feelings toward five or six girls, including how his interest in each waxed and waned.

As a teenager, Spitzer snuck out of his parents' Manhattan apartment to attend therapy with a disciple of psychoanalyst Wilhelm Reich. In the 1930s the Austrian physician developed orgone therapy, which held that the achievement of "full orgastic potency" was the key to psychological well-being, and that the orgasm derives its power from a hypothetical cosmic force, orgone energy, which accounted for all life functions. The young Spitzer hoped that orgone therapy might help him become more at ease socially. He paid $5 a week for sessions of orgone therapy on the Lower East Side, where a therapist manipulated his body. When nothing much happened, Spitzer found another Reichian analyst, this one with an "orgone accumulator": a narrow wooden booth in which he sat for many hours, supposedly absorbing its stores of invisible orgone energy.

Spitzer's early desire for a framework to make sense of the world didn't come out of nowhere. His grandfather had "pitched his own wheelchair out of a window," killing himself, after being struck by a neurological illness. His mother struggled with depression, particularly after Spitzer's older sister died from encephalitis when Robert was four years old. Given his penchant for order, Spitzer, even at his young age, dealt with these painful incidents quantitatively, "translating feelings into some kind of a system."

After a year of orgone experiments, Spitzer grew disillusioned. He also became determined to expose orgone therapy as a fraud—which he did through a series of experiments he conducted as an undergraduate at Cornell University in 1953. He submitted his results (the data didn't even hint at the existence of orgone energy) to the *American Journal of Psychiatry* for publication. His submission was rejected, but months later, someone from the FDA showed up at his dorm. The agency was investigating Reich's claims of curing cancer, and it was looking for an expert witness to testify against him. The FDA didn't ordinarily seek out undergraduates for such tasks, but they'd gotten Spitzer's name from the APA, which published the *American Journal of Psychiatry*. In the end, Spitzer's testimony wasn't needed, but the incident was an early indicator that he was going to make his mark—and through the use of evidence and reason.

Spitzer graduated from the New York University School of Medicine, then moved to Columbia University for his postgraduate training in psychiatry at its New York State Psychiatric Institute. Once he'd completed his general psychiatry training, Spitzer began psychoanalytic training at the Columbia University Center for Psychoanalytic Training and Research, then the most influential psychoanalytic institute in America. By the time he'd finished his training in 1966, he was already becoming disillusioned with psychoanalysis: despite his earnest efforts to apply psychoanalytic therapy, his patients with serious illnesses showed little or no improvement. In time he began to wonder if he wasn't simply telling them what he wanted to believe was true. For the first time in his life, Spitzer found himself uncertain about his professional direction, and at a most inopportune time. After decades of education and training, and just when he was embarking on his career, Spitzer was losing faith in the intellectual foundations of his chosen field. He would soon find his footing, but it wouldn't be in psychoanalytic practice. Rather, Spitzer would oversee a project that created a scientifically oriented and empirically based foundation for psychiatry. This foundation would, at last, become the touchstone of clinical practice and research: the system of psychiatric diagnoses.

THE RIGHT ROAD

In 1973 the anti-psychiatry movement was at its peak, and the APA's board of trustees realized that fundamental changes were needed if the psychiatric profession was to survive. The field's practitioners would have to accept that a transformation was required in the way mental illness was conceptualized and diagnosed, one that moved away from unsubstantiated theory and was based instead on empirical science. The most compelling way to demonstrate a meaningful shift was through the APA's official compendium of mental illness: the *Diagnostic and Statistical Manual* (*DSM*).

Robert Spitzer was not an obvious choice to chair the *DSM-III* Task Force. While he'd been a member of the previous task force behind the *DSM-II*, published in 1968, he was not an expert in epidemiology, phenomenology, psychometrics, or biostatistics. His main qualifications were that he was a clinician, and, perhaps more importantly, that in 1973 he had steered the field of psychiatry through a heated controversy over homosexuality.

American psychiatry had long viewed homosexuality as a mental disorder, a view reflected in the *DSM-II*, which listed it within the category of "sexual deviations." But society was changing, and the gay-rights movement was active and growing. Because of psychiatry's history of willful pathologizing of diversity of sexual orientation, punitive treatment of gay people, and baseless intransigence to change, it became one of the movement's principal targets.

Spitzer didn't know any openly gay people at the time, nor had he questioned the designation of homosexuality as a mental disorder. It wasn't that he necessarily thought homosexuality was pathological, but rather that he didn't know enough to hold a strong opinion otherwise and hadn't yet bothered to learn more. However, he did believe that the issue should be given a fair and full hearing and settled by data and thoughtful debate. He arranged meetings with gay-rights advocates and convened an APA panel in which psychiatrists who believed that homosexuality resulted from flawed parenting debated those who saw no evidence to suggest that it was a mental illness. Spitzer soon found himself aligning with the latter camp, seeing no credible data suggesting that homosexuality impaired a person's emotional state or ability to function. The diagnosis should go.

But this left Spitzer in a bind. On the one hand, the anti-psychiatry movement was arguing that all mental illnesses were artificial social constructs, and Spitzer knew these arguments had contributed to the crisis of credibility in his profession. If he declared now that homosexuality was, after all, just such an artificially constructed "illness," wouldn't that bolster the arguments of the anti-psychiatrists about other illnesses—such as schizophrenia? On the other hand, if Spitzer maintained that homosexuality was a medical disorder to preserve psychiatry's credibility (and ensure that insurance companies continued to pay for care), it would perpetuate a social injustice and cause immeasurable harm to perfectly healthy and sane people who just happened to be gay. Psychoanalysis offered no way out, since its practitioners held that homosexuality arose from traumatic conflicts in childhood.

Spitzer resolved the dilemma rather ingeniously by introducing a new psychiatric concept that he called subjective distress, which could serve as a criterion for diagnosis and a way of gauging the severity of a patient's illness. Ultimately, this metric would be incorporated into the groundbreaking third edition of the *DSM*, but until then, it served to placate both gay-rights groups and liberally minded psychiatrists, and the psychoanalysts. Applying the concept of subjective distress to the issue of sexual orientation meant that if a person was content with his or her sexual orientation and was functioning adequately, a psychiatrist had no business labeling the behavior as a form of mental illness. (Other mental disorders could still justify a diagnosis: for example, a delusional patient might insist he was not distressed by his condition, but if his delusions prevented him from maintaining relationships or holding down a job, a diagnosis of schizophrenia might still be applied.) If, however, a person's sexual orientation—gay or straight—was a source of emotional distress or resulted in impaired functioning, then attempting to treat that person was warranted. Spitzer suggested a new category of diagnosis for such cases: sexual orientation disturbance.

The APA voted unanimously to approve the deletion of homosexuality disorder from the *DSM-II* and replace it with the more limited sexual orientation disturbance. (In 1987 the latter category was also eliminated from the *DSM*.) The change was officially incorporated in the sixth amendment to the *DSM-II*. Spitzer's adroit handling of the crisis had simultaneously fended off the anti-psychiatrists, proclaimed that homosexuality was not a disorder, and introduced a new way of thinking about mental illness. His reward was being asked to chair the *DSM-III* Task Force.

Spitzer recruited to his team data-oriented psychiatric researchers—people who were scientists as well as clinicians—and set about creating a diagnostic system that employed specific, concise, descriptive criteria instead of tradition, dogma, or general conceptual definitions. He quickly proposed a revolutionary idea: that the *DSM* should drop the one criterion that psychoanalysts had considered essential for diagnosing a patient's illness: the cause of the illness, or what physicians term etiology. Psychoanalysts believed that if you identified the unconscious conflicts causing mental illness, you would identify the illness. Spitzer and his team agreed that, apart from substance use disorders and what were then called organic brain disorders (such as dementia or delirium), there was no evidence whatsoever implicating any specific cause of any mental illness. They were unanimous: all references to causes not supported by data would be expunged.

In place of causes, Spitzer laid down two new criteria required for any diagnosis: (1) the symptoms must be distressing to the individual or impair his or her ability to function (subjective distress), and (2) the symptoms must be enduring. This was a radically different way of defining mental illness, worlds apart from the psychoanalytic view that a patient's mental illness could be hidden from patients themselves, but also a significant departure from Emil Kraepelin's definition of schizophrenia, which made no reference to subjective distress and included no duration requirement.

The clinician's task was now twofold: determine the presence or absence of specific symptoms, then compare the observed symptoms to a fixed set of criteria for each disorder, including level of subjective distress and duration. If the symptoms matched the criteria, a diagnosis was justified. Spitzer's team learned quickly that to remain faithful to the research data, it was often necessary to create rather complex sets of criteria. While the *DSM-II* had provided impressionistic descriptions of schizophrenia, the *DSM-III* presented several precisely defined sets and subsets of conditions that were required for a diagnosis. These changes are readily apparent when comparing the *DSM-II* and *DSM-III* side by side. (See appendix 3.)

Spitzer was not without his critics. While he and his team insisted that the complexity of the diagnostic system matched the data-informed reality of mental disorders far better than had the ambiguous generalities of the *DSM-II*, he was accused of having created an approach to diagnosis that resembled a "Chinese menu": select one item from criteria set A, select two from set B, and so on. Instead of taking careful patient histories, critics argued, doctors were now reduced to using checklists. The comment was a cheap shot, as this menu format was already used for defining diagnoses of nonpsychiatric diseases.

One important practical factor that influenced the new diagnostic criteria: ensuring that insurance companies would pay for treatments. Spitzer knew that insurers were already cutting back on mental health care benefits; psychiatry's credibility had declined in recent years, and the fiscal policies of the Reagan administration were no help. To combat this, in the *DSM-III* the task force stressed that the listed criteria were not the sole and ultimate word, but rather "clinical judgment is of paramount importance in making a diagnosis." They believed that this disclaimer would give psychiatrists protection against an insurance company intent on showing that a patient didn't conform precisely to the listed criteria.

The completion of the *DSM-III*, which established the contemporary system still used for diagnosing mental illness, was a revolutionary advance. It was empirical and atheoretical, neither psychodynamic nor biological, but able to incorporate new research from any ideological camp. No longer were diagnoses based on your relationship with your mother, your repressed sexual hang-ups, or your neurotic reaction to stressful life events. Nor were mental illnesses defined by lesions or hormonal imbalances. If we couldn't yet connect our diagnoses to the cause of illnesses, we could at least make them consistently reliable.

The *DSM-III* refocused psychiatry on the clinical treatment of serious mental illnesses. It provided a lingua franca for mental illness: insurance companies, universities, research funding agencies, pharmaceutical companies, federal and state legislatures, judicial systems, the military, Medicare, and Medicaid could now speak in a common language and could reasonably expect consistency in psychiatric diagnoses. But if the *DSM-III* was a declaration that mental illness exists, it still wasn't able to delineate a physiological basis for the mental disorders it described. For that, developments in technology were required, some of which were right around the corner.

Thirty-five years later, we honored Spitzer with a Festschrift (a celebration of a scholar's body of work) at Columbia University on the occasion of his retirement. I asked him if he'd realized at the time the enormous responsibility he'd taken on when he assumed leadership of the *DSM-III* mission, the success of which was so critical to the future of psychiatry. His reply was characteristically candid and curt: "I didn't have a clue."

THE GREAT PRETENDER

Spitzer didn't live to see the coda to his feud with Rosenhan and undertaking to redeem psychiatry by revamping its system of diagnoses. That came in 2019, when an investigative journalist with the *New York Post*, Susannah Cahalan, published *The Great Pretender: The Undercover Mission That Changed Our Understanding of Madness*, uncovering the fraud perpetrated by Rosenhan and proving Spitzer's allegations of pseudoscience prescient.

This was a strange turn of events in several respects. Cahalan did not start out to write the book reflected by the title. Her first book, *Brain on Fire: My Month of Madness*, chronicles her monthslong bout with autoimmune encephalitis, which was misdiagnosed as a mental disorder and treated with psychotropic drugs before an astute neurologist provided the correct diagnosis and treatment (described further in chapter 16). Fortunately, Cahalan recovered fully but understandably was left with questions about the clinical acumen of the psychiatric profession. This clearly played a role in her choice of the Rosenhan study as the topic of her next book. However, she did not expect to find in researching the story all manner of sloppiness, inaccuracies, and outright fabrications—including discrepancies between what Rosenhan said about his own admission to Pennsylvania's Haverford State Hospital and what appeared in the admitting physician's notes. For one thing, Rosenhan had reported not just hearing voices; he'd presented a much more disturbing pseudo-portrait of himself that included long-lasting delusions and suicidal ideation. In addition, the data Rosenhan reported in his paper—for instance, patients' daily contact time with doctors—didn't always line up with those contained in his notes.

Cahalan also found a ninth pseudopatient whose positive experiences in the hospital had been excluded from the data—ostensibly for his having falsified details of his personal history, but in reality, she learned, because he had reported that the experience and supportive environment of the mental hospital had been beneficial. As Cahalan notes, the takeaway *could* have been that there were institutions that really were doing things well, even for patients who gained admission under false pretenses. But Rosenhan considered these data from a satisfied customer of a mental hospital contrary to his agenda and thus omitted them. In revealing this, Cahalan didn't just correct an important historical falsehood but also provided some posthumous vindication for Spitzer.

Part 3

SEARCHING

FOR

SCHIZOPHRENIA

Chapter 11

THE ENCHANTED LOOM

The brain is waking, and with it the mind is returning. It is as if the Milky Way
entered upon some cosmic dance. Swiftly the head mass becomes an enchanted
loom where millions of flashing shuttles weave an evanescent, always a meaningful, motif though never an abiding one; a shifting tapestry of patterns.

—British physiologist Charles G. Sherrington, *Man on His Nature* (1946)

SCRATCHING THE SURFACE

The *DSM-III* set out a more reliable set of criteria by which we could recognize
and diagnose schizophrenia, a process guided by observing symptoms, listening to
patients' subjective reports, and tracing their history. More importantly, it established a framework that was empirically based on data—objective evidence rather
than subjective opinion or unsubstantiated theory. However, it still did not speak
to what was actually going on in the brain, at the most granular level, of someone
who suffered from this illness. By the time of *DSM-III*'s arrival, psychiatric luminaries trained in anatomy and pathology had been searching for an answer to
that question for well over a century. The results of their scrupulous efforts would
be both hugely successful and deeply disappointing. They created maps of brain
structure and function that are still used today, and they identified numerous neurological conditions. But while many such conditions would gradually reveal their
visible traces—lesions after strokes; tangled clumps of proteins in the gray matter
of Alzheimer's or Parkinson's victims; cancerous tumors—it seemed that psychiatric illnesses were, if not invisible, then certainly more elusive. This prompted an
eminent neurologist to gloat, "Schizophrenia is the graveyard of neuropathology."
Psychiatric researchers could see the forest, in the form of manifestly disturbed

behavior, but the trees, the neurobiological elements that gave rise to the behavior, were invisible.

Those who studied the brain began to believe that schizophrenia was either something in the metaphysical realm, which left no anatomic footprints, or it was a "functional disorder," meaning that the neural machinery might appear intact, but communication between neural circuits was, for some reason, going awry. If the latter, then schizophrenia was, in neurobiological parlance, a connectopathy—a disease rooted in how cells communicate with one another—and thus not readily discernable in slices or sections of postmortem brain tissue.

The questions that followed were myriad. What was the basis of the defective connectivity? Which cell types were functionally altered, and which molecular elements gave rise to these alterations? Which neurotransmitters mediated these errant messages? What was the timing of the onset and progression of the disturbances in neural circuits? Were common circuits altered in the same way by different genetic, physiological, and environmental risk factors? What was the quantitative logic of neural systems, and which activity patterns were responsible for these aberrant behaviors?

But examining the inert brains of dead people can only provide limited information about the workings of the brain. To learn more about the causes of schizophrenia—what gave rise to the observable symptoms—we needed to observe the brain in action, to witness the workings of the organ that is the most extraordinary animate structure of any living thing.

Making Neurons Visible

Popular culture has celebrated the heart over every organ in the body. There are numerous references attributing behaviors to the heart that clearly emanate from the brain. (A person is bighearted, warmhearted, hard-hearted, and coldhearted. We know it and feel it in our hearts, our hearts are bursting with happiness, or we are brokenhearted.) The fact is our essence as a person resides in the brain. This reality is bluntly signaled by the brain's sequestration in the bony structure of the skull. It's the only organ of the body to be so thoroughly contained and shielded. (The heart and lungs, vital to our survival, are protected only by the scaffold of the rib cage.) Moreover, it is the only organ or part of the body that does not feel pain. (The pain that you would feel from a penetrating blow to the head would be from piercing the scalp and skull, but not the brain.)

Unlike the rest of our organs, which are identical in structure and function to those of other mammals, the brain is distinctly human. It has evolved over millennia, growing in size, composition, functional diversity, and capacity, and is three times the size of the brains of our closest primate relatives and consumes disproportionate amounts of glucose, oxygen, and energy relative to the rest of the body. It is also the only organ of the body capable of supporting metastructures. The heart pumps, the kidneys filter, and the lungs bellow, and each serves its specific function. The brain is presumed to be the organ from which the mind emanates, the source of your personality and, depending on your religious inclinations, possibly the source of spirituality and seat of the soul.

Looking at the brain's exterior, a corrugated, doughlike mass with an opaque veneer, it would be hard to imagine how it accomplishes all its many functions. Its interior is composed of an elaborate, intricate circuitry—consisting of one hundred billion neurons, two hundred billion glial cells (which support neurons), and more than thirty trillion synaptic connections. Neurons are brain cells specially structured for communicating through junctions called synapses, where electrical and chemical signals are transmitted between cells. The chemical conduit of communication between neurons is the neurotransmitter, of which there are more than a hundred types. Long, thin filaments, called axons, extend from the neuron and carry impulses from the cell body to other cells. Arbors of dendrites, extending from the cell body, are coated with spines that serve as the points of contact for receiving electrical/chemical signals. The brain's bundle of cells is precisely positioned in designated anatomic locations with specialized functions and wired into neural circuits that course within and between the different regions of the brain. Cells fire and circuits emit their signals at specified frequencies, creating a resonating mosaic whose pulsing pattern can be erased, reconfigured, or repeated. With this level of complexity in constantly changing motion, it's a wonder that things don't go wrong more often—that mental disorders are the exception rather than the rule.

An intact postmortem human brain. This three-pound, corrugated, doughlike mass of tissue is composed of billions of cells knitted together by trillions of connections, which control all mental and many bodily functions.

To peer beneath the brain's surface and begin to explore this marvel of nature required the contributions of three people, whose critical work enabled the first steps to be taken in advancing our understanding of the all-important organ by making its elemental unit, the neuron, visible.

Generic Neurotransmitter System

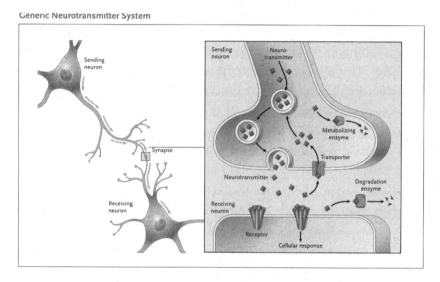

The left figure depicts a generic synapse connecting two neurons. The right is a close-up of the point of contact between the axon of the projecting neuron releasing neurotransmitters and the dendrite of the receiving neuron with receptors to which the neurotransmitter will bind, located on the surface of the membrane.

Antonie van Leeuwenhoek was born in 1632 to a family of tradesmen in the city of Delft, Holland. At age sixteen, he was sent to Amsterdam to apprentice at a linen draper's shop. When he returned to Delft six years later, he opened his own shop. Leeuwenhoek wanted to see the quality of the thread in the fabrics better than contemporary magnifying glasses allowed, and he began toying with lens making. Over time, Leeuwenhoek, who had no higher education or university degree, made more than four hundred optical lenses capable of magnification from fifty to three hundred times. The Dutchman was the first to observe bacteria and protozoa, and is regarded as the first microbiologist—a precursor to Louis Pasteur, who, with the aid of Leeuwenhoek's device, would formulate germ theory in the nineteenth century.

The microscope made deeper exploration of the brain possible, but it did not have the power to distinguish the brain's neurons from the surrounding tissue. Two centuries later, a pair of European physicians solved this problem. In 1873 the Italian pathologist Camillo Golgi (1843–1926) published the first image of a whole nerve cell, including its cell body, axon, and dendrites. Golgi had developed a chemical dye that made brain cells visible in postmortem tissue when they absorbed a staining ingredient, silver chromate. With the "black reaction" technique, the cells of the brain lit up, enabling researchers to visualize clearly the entities embedded in the brain's matrix. It was revelatory. Until then, looking at the brain had been a little like trying to peer into a deep, dark body of water. Golgi's technique made it possible to begin to see what was happening underneath the surface.

Santiago Ramón y Cajal (1852–1934), a Spanish anatomist, applied Golgi's innovation in a way that would transform the science of brain research, allowing him to demonstrate that the relationship between nerve cells was one of contiguity, or bordering each other, rather than of unbroken continuity. Although Cajal is now regarded as the father of neuroscience, his youth had hardly promised greatness. He was prone to getting into trouble at school because of truancy and poor grades, and was known for pranks, petty theft, and vandalism. As a teen, Cajal was interested in drawing and photography and had set his sights on becoming an artist, a path his father, a physician, very much opposed.

In the summer of 1868, desperate to redirect his wayward son's interests, Don Justo took his son to the local graveyard in an attempt to interest him in anatomy, which was his own field. There they were able to find human remains exhumed from burial plots whose leases had not been renewed. Cajal was intrigued; he began sketching bones, and soon changed course to follow his father into medicine. He entered medical school in Saragossa, where, he recalled in his autobiography, he "saw in the cadaver, not death, with its train of gloomy suggestions, but the marvellous workmanship of life."

In 1887, while a professor in Barcelona, Cajal made a series of meticulous and beautiful drawings of the brain cells that he surveyed under his microscope. The freehand drawings, which often combined in a single image his observations from successive viewings of different parts of the brain, depicted a universe unlike any other. Cajal's renderings of nerve cells represented the first genuine insight into the brain's composition and organization. On the basis of his observations, he developed the "neuron doctrine," the notion that the brain was not a seamless web of wiring but was composed of anatomically distinct processing units, or neurons, systematically organized and interconnected. The theory was controversial: when Golgi and Cajal shared the Nobel Prize in 1906, Golgi used part of his acceptance speech to present his points of disagreement with it. But in time Cajal's neuron doctrine was affirmed by newer technologies and subsequent studies. It proved to be one of the most significant scientific achievements in the history of medicine and a cornerstone of modern neuroscience.

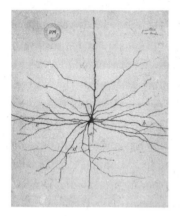
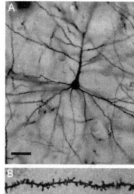
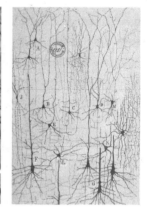

Ink and pencil drawings by Santiago Ramón y Cajal, c. 1904: The left panel is of a pyramidal cell (excitatory neuron found in the cerebral cortex, hippocampus, and amygdala). The right panel depicts microcircuits containing interneurons (cells that regulate the activity of pyramidal cells). These drawings show remarkable similarities to the middle panel A, a photomicrograph of pyramidal cells in postmortem brain tissue taken in 2013. The middle panel B shows magnification of a dendrite, with each spine representing a potential synaptic connection.

IMAGING THE BRAIN

But as previously stated, examination—no matter how detailed—of static structures in postmortem brains could only reveal so much. What was needed was a way to examine the structure and function of the living brain. This proved to be a formidable challenge. The brain is very complex, and it is also encased in the hard, thick skull, making exploration difficult. The X-ray, invented in 1895 by Wilhelm Röntgen, was the first method by which doctors were able to glimpse the brains of living patients without opening the skull. This was a major advance, but X-rays showed only rudimentary outlines of the skull, brain, and its fluid-containing compartments. X-rays could identify fractures caused by blunt trauma, penetrating wounds, or tumors, but their limited clarity and resolution yielded no clues to mental illness. What was needed for that were imaging techniques that could capture in much greater detail the brain's size, shape, composition, and function.

It would be seventy years before the next major brain imaging advance relevant to the search for schizophrenia occurred, and it came from an unlikely source: the British record company EMI. While its main focus was on music, the company had a small electronics division and allocated money out of the enormous profits it was raking in from the Beatles' recordings to its chief engineer Godfrey Hounsfield. On the basis of research conducted by South African physicist Allan MacLeod Cormack, Hounsfield developed a landmark innovation in diagnostic imaging technology: computer assisted tomography, or CT scans. (The two men would share the Nobel for this work.) CT scans acquire a series of X-ray images taken from different angles, then reconstruct these "slices" (just five millimeters thick) into a whole brain that can be examined from multiple perspectives. The three-dimensional images constructed by CT scans were more comprehensive and detailed than anything that came before. CT scans were also relatively noninvasive, involved limited radiation exposure, and produced no physical discomfort.

The first CT scan study of mental illness was published in 1976 by Scottish psychiatrist Eve Johnstone and her colleague Timothy Crow. Their findings were astonishing: *the brains of people with schizophrenia were different.* What Johnstone and her team saw was a noticeable enlargement of the lateral ventricles, a pair of chambers deep within the brain that contain cerebrospinal fluid, which cushions the brain, provides nutrients, and carries away waste products. The ventricular enlargement, along with corresponding increases in the space separating the brain's surface from the cranium, implied atrophy (shrinkage of the brain), as opposed to the brain having failed to grow to its normal size. Ventricular enlargement was a common feature of neurodegenerative diseases such as Alzheimer's and reflected the atrophy of surrounding brain structures. Psychiatrists were thunderstruck. It was the first time anyone could point to a concrete and readily identifiable physical abnormality in the brain associated with mental illness.

Even before the excitement over CT scans had died down, another imaging marvel arrived that would prove even more important for studying the brain and its disorders: magnetic resonance imaging, or MRI. While CT scans could show gross manifestations of atrophy or vascular accidents such as strokes or aneurysms, MRIs provided greater magnification and contrast of brain anatomy, enabling researchers to see the brain's individual component structures. MRIs concentrated a powerful magnetic field on the patient's body that temporarily realigned the body's water molecules. Radio waves were then emitted into the magnetic field, briefly perturbing the alignment of atoms, causing them to release faint signals, which were detected and reconstructed into cross-sectional images that could be assembled into a whole brain image; they were viewable from any angle and could be manipulated to allow for the visualization of any section or structure.

The vivid three-dimensional brain images produced by MRIs were of unprecedented clarity; the parameters of MRI could be adjusted to highlight different kinds of tissue, such as gray matter or white matter, or the flow of fluid or blood within the brain. MRI quickly replaced CT scans as the primary instrument of psychiatric research. Unlike CT scans, which use ionizing X-ray radiation that can accumulate over successive exposures and potentially cause adverse effects, MRI is harmless. This meant that the brains of people with mental disorders could be assessed repeatedly over time—critical in determining whether the structural abnormalities in the brain were static or progressed over the course of the illness.

The advent of MRI and the numerous refinements of its technology, magnetic strength, and applications that followed would produce a torrent of structural, chemical, and functional findings showing differences between the brains of healthy people and those with schizophrenia that were also distinct from people with other mental disorders.

THE PRUNING HYPOTHESIS

Just as these findings were emerging, an important article from an unexpected source captured the attention of schizophrenia researchers. One of the long-standing mysteries of schizophrenia is its emergence at a specific stage of life, a narrow window beginning after puberty and extending through adolescence to young adulthood. It occurs rarely in children prior to puberty or in people over age thirty. The timing of its appearance suggests that something happens during adolescence in brain development that unmasks the illness or triggers its manifestation; this usually occurs gradually over months or a few years but, less frequently, can seem to come out of nowhere, descending within a matter of weeks, or even days. In either case, schizophrenia changes a seemingly healthy young person into someone troubled by a disordered mind and beset by delusions and hallucinations.

In 1982 a little-known but scientifically imaginative psychiatrist published an article in an obscure academic journal that would have a huge impact on our understanding of the characteristic timing of schizophrenia's onset. Irwin Feinberg had received his medical degree in 1955 from NYU and begun his research career as a postdoctoral fellow at the NIMH. At that time, aspiring researchers didn't have much to choose from in terms of scientific disciplines. Since the advent of chlorpromazine, pharmacology had been the dominant area of research. Other modes of investigation yielded limited reliable results. Analytic chemistry, searching for toxic metabolites in the blood, had given researchers only false leads. CT and MRI hadn't yet been invented. Genetics was still only epidemiologic, and molecular biology had not yet emerged as a disruptive discipline of science. EEGs (or electroencephalograms), which measure brain waves via electrodes pasted to the scalp, were useful mainly in diagnosing epilepsy. Their most advanced application to mental illness was in sleep studies.

Sleep was what Feinberg focused on, diligently measuring and analyzing the electrical activity of the brains of people with schizophrenia during different sleep stages. Obtaining data from both patients and healthy subjects of various ages, he found that changes in sleep EEG patterns occurring in adolescence were dramatic compared with those seen in the later decades of life. Moreover, the magnitude of those changes over the adolescent years was greater in patients with schizophrenia than in healthy subjects. Colleagues of Feinberg's working in an adjacent lab at the NIMH had already identified measures of brain metabolic activity that corresponded to the brain electrical activity Feinberg had been measuring during sleep. While this was an interesting finding, it didn't provide Feinberg with any insight into the underlying causes of schizophrenia.

Feinberg moved to various institutions over the next twenty years, continuing his research but making little progress in understanding the relevance of his sleep findings to schizophrenia. Then, in 1979 a pediatric neurologist at the University of Chicago named Peter Huttenlocher published the results of a study in which he'd measured the density of synaptic connections (the number of synapses within a defined area) in the frontal cortex of twenty-one healthy human brains ranging in age from newborn to ninety years. He found that after birth, synaptic density shot up to a peak between ages two and three, after which it declined steeply through childhood and early adolescence, reaching a plateau, and then remaining largely stable through middle age. Huttenlocher's results suggested that the brain's early growth, beginning in gestation and extending through infancy, overshot the mark intentionally. This created excess neurons and connections, a surplus that was corrected in the course of normal brain development through synaptic pruning. This process, which eliminates extraneous cells and unnecessary or faulty connections, continues through childhood into adolescence before stabilizing until the aging process kicks in.

Imagine an orchestra. It begins with too many instruments and musicians who don't always follow the music or the conductor, creating discordance and confusion. Over time, the conductor weeds out those extraneous players and instruments to allow the composition's melody to emerge clearly. Similarly, the process of pruning eliminates the background noise resulting from extraneous synapses, allowing the brain to function more efficiently and the individual to think more clearly.

Huttenlocher speculated that this elimination of synapses altered the electrochemical signals that are transmitted between neurons. Upon reading Huttenlocher's paper, Feinberg was reminded of his earlier sleep EEG work, which had revealed that the highest rates of change in sleep patterns were in early infancy and adolescence. Inspired by Huttenlocher's research, he proposed a novel model of disrupted neurodevelopment in schizophrenia. His theory was based on a brilliant insight. Huttenlocher had suggested that the brain overproduced neural elements in its early development and then systematically eliminated the excess, redundant, or faulty ones, completing the process in adolescence. Feinberg extended this thesis to speculate that a disruption or abnormality in this normative pruning process—a defect in the mechanism for synaptic elimination active during adolescence; a "bug" in the genetic program—could result in too many, too few, or the wrong synapses being eliminated, allowing defects in neuronal integration to arise that caused the symptoms of schizophrenia.

Feinberg's synaptic pruning theory had the advantage of being able to link the age of illness onset with errors in synaptic remodeling that disrupted the wiring of neural circuits and led to dysregulated neurotransmission. While the research community took note of his clever hypothesis, it would be many years before any progress was made, either by Feinberg or other researchers, in experimentally verifying or extending it. Moreover, it was only a theory—a web of ideas and conjectures woven together into an elegant but wholly hypothetical story that, for the time being, would languish in the archives of the scientific literature.

THE EVIDENCE ACCUMULATES

The development of relatively noninvasive brain imaging methods revived the search for schizophrenia in the brain—as opposed to the mind—and soon yielded fruit. The detection of lateral ventricle enlargement in 1976 was followed by a plethora of MRI studies in the 1980s and 1990s. As the technical capacities of MRI systems improved, the diversity and specificity of anatomical findings increased.

Discoveries fell into three general categories: volume reductions in the gray matter of specific structures or regions (hippocampus, superior temporal gyrus, caudate nucleus); increased volume of structures containing cerebrospinal fluid (the lateral and third ventricles, and the subarachnoid space [the area between the inner surface of the skull and the outer surface of the brain]); and physiologic differences in the composition of brain white matter. The significance of these differences in white matter is still unknown.

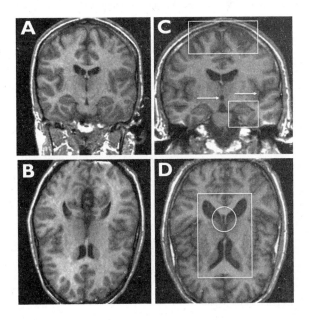

This set of MRI scans shows structural abnormalities in the brain of a young person with schizophrenia (panels C and D) in contrast to a healthy individual (panels A and B). The two rectangles in panel C outline atrophy in the cerebral cortex (top) and hippocampus (lower right). The two arrows point to enlargements of fluid-containing spaces, the ventricular system in the middle of the brain and the fissure separating the temporal and frontal/parietal lobes of the cerebral cortex. The rectangle in panel D outlines an enlargement of the ventricular system, and the circle within that rectangle highlights the septum pellucidum, the membrane dividing the two sides of the ventricular system, which has failed to come together as occurs in normal development.

As these findings began to emerge, they led to a startling realization: the structural brain abnormalities now being demonstrated by MRI studies in living patients were the same ones seen in the postmortem specimens by nineteenth-century psychiatrists. In 1915 Elmer Ernest Southard, a professor of neuropathology at Harvard, had published a paper in which he wrote that dementia praecox "must be conceded to be in some sense structural," as 90 percent of the fifty cases he'd examined over a four-year period showed evidence of brain atrophy when examined postmortem—even without the use of a microscope. Southard also found a high proportion of enlarged ventricles. The atrophy, or shrinkage, was usually moderate and didn't alter brain weight appreciably outside of normal variations. It also had a noticeable tendency to occur in the left hemisphere. (Given that most people are right-handed, the left tends to be the dominant hemisphere.)

The findings described in Southard's summary reprised perfectly the results of MRI studies conducted eighty years later in living patients, though initially their significance wasn't recognized. Researchers at the time were looking for qualitative rather than quantitative differences in the postmortem brains they examined: lesions that appeared distinct from the surrounding tissue (a tumor or clumps of material containing protein), or foreign organisms such as the bacterium that causes syphilis. In addition, when the psychiatric anatomists gave up the search for physical evidence of schizophrenia, and psychiatry embraced psychoanalytic theory, a false dichotomy was established. All brain diseases for which there was tangible, visible evidence were considered "organic," while those for which there were no known physical signs were called "functional"—shorthand for diseases of the mind. The latter became the province of psychology and psychoanalytic theory. Now those distinctions were being revisited.

THE TWIN STUDY

The growing and compelling body of evidence from the brain imaging studies complemented by the modern techniques of molecular biology and genetics would be the tipping point that convinced doubters that schizophrenia was indeed a brain disorder.

In March 1990 the *New England Journal of Medicine* published results of a landmark study by a team of NIMH investigators based at St. Elizabeths Hospital led by research psychiatrist E. Fuller Torrey. He and his colleagues had worked with the National Alliance on Mental Illness (NAMI), a nonprofit patient advocacy group, to identify twenty-seven sets of identical twins discordant for schizophrenia (meaning one twin had the illness but the co-twin did not) as study participants. Fifteen of these twin pairs agreed to have MRIs performed as part of their study participation.

Comparing sets of twins with identical genomes (the complete set of genes in a human) enabled the team to control for genetic effects. Any differences in their brain structure would be attributable to either environmental factors, such as birth trauma, or the effects of the disease following its onset. When the researchers examined the MRI scans on all the twins—not knowing beforehand which were the healthy individuals and which had schizophrenia—the differences between the brains of the two groups were so pronounced that, in every case, researchers were able to identify the ill twin simply by looking at the brain. (No such differences were found in seven pairs of healthy twins who served as comparison.) The features that distinguished the ill from the healthy twins were those seen previously in schizophrenia patients, including larger ventricles, wider cortical sulci (spaces in the folds at the surface of the cortex), smaller temporal lobes, and misshapen hippocampi.

The twin study added to the evidence that schizophrenia was a brain disease; it also indicated that factors apart from genes could contribute to the illness's effects on the brain. Beyond their scientific import, though, the MRI results of the twin study would, along with evidence from other brain imaging studies, help to dispel stigma about the disease and relieve families of the blame that psychoanalysts and the anti-psychiatry movement had wrongly directed at them. Torrey has said: "Almost all the drop in stigma is related to information we now have about what causes schizophrenia. Once we had MRI and CT scans, things changed quite dramatically." Torrey may have been the first person to utter the word "schizophrenia" on popular television, when he appeared on the *Phil Donahue* show in 1983. Since then, the changes in public perception have been enormous. While Torrey's mother had once believed she might have caused his sister's illness, his granddaughter was taught in her high school AP psychology class that schizophrenia is a brain disease. She was surprised to turn the page of her textbook one day to see a picture of her grandfather holding a brain in his hand.

THE LOSS OF BRAIN VOLUME

The renaissance in brain research on schizophrenia stimulated by the neuroimaging technologies prompted a new set of questions. When did the brain's structural anomalies occur? Did they precede the onset of schizophrenia? Did they remain static over its course, or were they progressive? Did they reflect the brain's failure to grow (hypoplasia) or shrinkage (atrophy) as a result of the illness? In the context of the neurodevelopmental theory, brain structural abnormalities were believed to predate the onset of symptoms and remain stable, apart from changes that occurred from the effects of aging. But this notion had not been confirmed.

With the advent of MRI, it was possible to cary out longitudinal studies, which involved repeated noninvasive scans in patients (e.g., weekly, monthly, yearly) to evaluate the presence of brain abnormalities and whether they change over time. Such studies were first carried out in the early 1990s and have been repeated many times since, including on patients in their first episode of psychosis or early in the course of schizophrenia. The findings showed volume changes in specific brain structures (including the frontal lobe, temporal lobe, hippocampus, and lateral and third ventricles) beginning in the prodromal stage, or the very beginning of symptoms, and continuing through the first psychotic episode and over the course of the illness. Most of the volume reduction was of gray matter. In one five-year study of first-episode patients, left frontal cortical density loss correlated with the number and duration of hospitalizations following relapses. These findings were consistent with an atrophic process due to the effects of psychosis on the brain. While these brain changes were demonstrable, they were relatively subtle compared with classic neurodegenerative diseases such as Alzheimer's. Whereas the latter is more aggressive and eventually devastates the whole brain, schizophrenia targets specific anatomic regions in a limited fashion.

The progressive loss of brain volume was thought to reflect the clinical deterioration associated with schizophrenia and was considered irreversible, though questions have been raised over the years about whether the degenerative effects could be due to antipsychotic medication. The main evidence for medication causing the reductions in brain volume comes from studies of rodents and monkeys. Animals given medication for sustained periods exhibited modest reductions in brain volume relative to those who had received a saline placebo.

But these were studies conducted on the brains of healthy animals, not the brains of people with schizophrenia. To address the question in humans, investigators examined the amount of medication patients received over the course of their illness and the magnitude of brain matter lost. They found significant correlations between the two: the greater the amount of medication, the larger the brain volume loss. However, because patients with more severe forms of the illness were likely to have taken more medication, it couldn't automatically be concluded that medication caused the loss of brain matter.

Evidence refuting the claim that medication is responsible for the decrease in brain volume has come from the fact that numerous studies of postmortem brains conducted *before* the invention of antipsychotic drugs (such as Southard's study) found structural abnormalities similar to those seen on more recent MRIs. If the same changes appear in both the brains of people never treated with drugs and the brains of those who've taken antipsychotics, we can't conclude that drugs are solely responsible for those changes.

INSIGHTS FROM DEVELOPMENTS IN IMAGING

Other MRI-based techniques have since been developed, each shedding light on the brains of people with schizophrenia. Magnetic resonance spectroscopy (MRS) uses an MRI scanner, but instead of generating an image, it uses special methods of data acquisition to determine the concentration of specific biochemical constituents of the brain. MRS is a powerful technique for measuring the presence and amount of a certain substance in response to disease, medication, or treatment. It is like doing a chemical biopsy of the specific anatomic region. MRS findings related to schizophrenia have included elevated glutamate, the brain's most common excitatory neurotransmitter, in the striatum (a cluster of neurons in the subcortical part of the forebrain involved with motor systems and aspects of cognition) and medial temporal lobe, and elevated gamma-aminobutyric acid (GABA, the main inhibitory neurotransmitter) in the medial prefrontal cortex. The specific roles these chemicals are believed to play in schizophrenia will be discussed in upcoming chapters.

Functional magnetic resonance imaging (fMRI) measures brain activity—underlying functional processes—in a specified area as reflected by blood flow. Observable alterations may be in response to a stimulus (such as seeing an image) or arise from changes in the brain at rest. In patients with schizophrenia, deficits have been found in several brain regions. These include the dorsolateral prefrontal cortex; anterior cingulate cortex, a structure in the inner part of the frontal cortex involved in mediating higher mental functions, including decision-making, attention focus, impulse control; and thalamus, a large bundle of neurons sitting on top of the brain stem and midbrain that branch out to the cerebral cortex, transmitting and receiving sensory and motor signals and involved in regulating sleep, arousal, and level of consciousness. During a memory task, people with schizophrenia often show changes in the strength of connections in the dorsolateral prefrontal region, the thalamus, and the limbic system. The limbic system consists of various structures, the most important being the hippocampus. The hippocampus is a seahorse-shaped structure critical for memory formation and located just in front of the amygdala, an almond-shaped structure that imbues memories with emotion. The hippocampus and amygdala are aligned along the medial side of the lower part of the temporal lobe around the thalamus.

Diffusion tensor imaging (DTI) is another MRI technique. Its measurements are based on the diffusion of water molecules. DTI provides information about the network, shape, and integrity of white matter. In patients with schizophrenia, DTI has revealed decreased fractional anisotropy (FA) throughout the entire known network of white matter. FA is a measure of connectivity in the brain and reflects the integrity and structure of white matter.

While radiologists, physicists, and biomedical engineers were developing the CT and MRI technologies, their colleagues in nuclear medicine were devising a complementary technique that provided yet another window onto the brain: positron emission tomography. PET imaging relies on the injection of a small amount of a radioactive substance called a radiotracer, which can mimic existing substances (glucose, for instance) or bind to existing sites, such as receptors for neurotransmitters. (Receptors are protein structures on the cell membranes of neurons that respond to a particular neurotransmitter, hormone, or other form of chemical stimulation, much as a lock will accommodate a particular key.)

Although resolution of PET scans is low, it is a robust tool for estimating the affinity of a substance to accumulate in an area of the brain and quantifying the amount. PET findings in schizophrenia have included elevated dopamine capacity and release in the striatum and reduced glucose uptake. Perhaps anticipating the use of PET scans by psychiatrists, James Robertson, the engineer who carried out the first PET scans at the Brookhaven National Laboratory in the mid-1970s, nicknamed the PET scanner the "head-shrinker."

REVISITING NEUROPATHOLOGY

By the late 1980s, the scientific understanding was that schizophrenia was a brain disorder caused by genes and/or environmental trauma, including social determinants of health, such as malnutrition, trauma, and poverty, that affected brain development and produced structural alterations. These changes were predominantly reductions of the size of brain structures and regions and could be observed and quantified on images of the whole brain. The basis for the abnormalities was still unknown, however. If parts of the brains of people with schizophrenia were smaller than those of healthy people, it was presumed that this had to be either because they had fewer cells or because shrinkage had resulted in smaller cells with shorter branches (axons and dendrites) and fewer connections. But what was causing these anomalies?

When researchers had probed beneath the surface to the brain's interior, they'd found no foreign bodies, signs of inflammation, clumps of toxic proteins, scarring, or infectious agents. Now, surprisingly, when they undertook the arduous task of counting neurons in postmortem specimens, they found that the brains of people with schizophrenia had no fewer neurons than those of people without mental illness. But just when it seemed the trail of pathology had gone cold, a new staining method called immunofluorescence was developed. Much as Golgi's black-reaction technique had made visible the previously invisible contours of neurons, immunofluorescence enabled researchers to distinguish pyramidal cells (large excitatory neurons found in the cerebral cortex, hippocampus, and amygdala) from a class of cells called interneurons. Such innovations made it possible to differentiate between different types of brain cells not only on the basis of their shape, but also according to which neurotransmitters they released when communicating with other neurons.

Interneurons serve two main functions: connecting circuits in different parts of the brain and regulating the activity of other neurons by releasing the neurotransmitter GABA, which blocks or inhibits certain brain signals. GABA interneurons compose 20 percent to 30 percent of brain neurons and play a vital role in maintaining brain function.

Two psychiatric anatomists, Francine Benes at Harvard and David Lewis of the University of Pittsburgh, seized on this new knowledge about interneurons. Reprising the efforts of the nineteenth-century brain researchers, they began investigating whether this class of cells might yield any clues to the basis of schizophrenia: Benes looking in the medial temporal lobe, and Lewis in the frontal lobes. Each made a unique finding involving the same phenomenon in the respective regions of the brain they examined. Using stereological methods to count the number of neurons, they found reduced numbers of interneurons. (Stereological counting involves standardizing the method of counting cells by ensuring that each brain section being assessed is of equivalent size.) Their findings confirmed a deficit in neuronal number found in patients with schizophrenia.

The reduction in GABA-secreting interneurons was significant. But the magnitude of the decrease in their numbers was modest and therefore couldn't account for the volume differences seen in the brains of people with schizophrenia. If it wasn't fewer numbers of cells, what was it?

An answer would come from the world of neuroscience, courtesy of Patricia Goldman-Rakic. Goldman-Rakic had attended Vassar College and then UCLA, where she received a PhD in 1963 in experimental psychology. She was tiny in stature, but like Supreme Court justice Ruth Bader Ginsburg, of whom she reminded me, she had a formidable intellect and could hold her own in any argument. During her time at the Massachusetts Institute of Technology (MIT) doing postdoctoral work, she met Pasko Rakic, a prominent neuroscientist then on the faculty of Harvard Medical School, and the two were married in 1979. She joined Rakic at Yale School of Medicine, where he had become head of the newly created Section of Neurobiology, and from that point on, they became an academic and scientific team from which great synergies emerged.

The main focus of Goldman-Rakic's research was linking the neurophysiology of the frontal cortex to cognitive functions, including working memory. Her elegant work would prove integral to our understanding of normative cognitive function, and throughout the 1990s, psychiatric researchers would try—unsuccessfully—to link it to schizophrenia. Other aspects of her work proved more illuminating. Goldman-Rakic's research on the role of the neurotransmitter dopamine in a uniquely human part of the brain (the prefrontal cortex) would inform the field's thinking about what brain disturbances were responsible for the cognitive impairment and negative symptoms of the illness. But it would be the incidental observations of a postdoctoral fellow in her lab that would constitute the most significant contribution to our understanding of schizophrenia.

By the 1990s, Goldman-Rakic was doing research on schizophrenia. She assigned a young scientist in her laboratory, Lynn Selemon, to examine postmortem brains from those who'd had the illness. What Selemon found was striking. While she confirmed that the cortex of someone with schizophrenia had normal numbers of neurons, she also found what she described as a lack of the "exuberance and redundancy of connections" that enable a brain to function normally and at full capacity. On closer inspection, she saw that this was due to a reduction in interneuronal neuropils (the branches extending from the cell bodies of neurons that form synaptic connections). This suggested that the neuropathology of schizophrenia was one of changes in cellular architecture and brain circuitry that, although subtle, have a devastating impact on cortical function. Her findings resonated with the field's understanding of schizophrenia and clarified long-standing questions about its neuropathological basis. They were quickly extended by other researchers, who found that many neurons in the brains of people with schizophrenia had shorter dendrites with fewer spines (the points of contact for synaptic connections) protruding from them.

Subsequent work by Goldman-Rakic's lab and other researchers integrated emerging findings on chemical neurotransmission into the neuropil hypothesis—theorizing that even small alterations in the dendritic branches, particularly at their vulnerable outermost tips where synapses form, would be detrimental to a neuron's ability to encode and respond to stimuli or to sustain activity in the absence of the stimulus or under resting conditions. Any or all of these component processes are presumed critical for the continuity of the thought process, and each could be desynchronized by slight neural alterations.

Goldman-Rakic was at the peak of her scientific powers when she died tragically in 2003 at the age of sixty-six. She was struck by a car in Hamden, Connecticut. Her death was a great loss to the scientific community, but one felt particularly by the many women whom she had mentored in neuroscience over the decades. I mourned her loss both professionally and personally; her work was outstanding and I had always found her to be a genuine, generous person. Because I'd always respected her work so deeply, I was surprised when a mutual friend, also a distinguished female scientist, revealed that Pat had once told her she wasn't sure she could "make it in a man's world"—meaning the male-dominated world of science. Once again I was reminded of the discrimination women have faced in the workplace, which we are only coming to terms with now.

Perhaps because of their resemblance (diminutive stature, dark hair, and oversized glasses), I sometimes thought of her as the Ruth Bader Ginsburg of neuroscience—and regarded her with similar reverence. After her death, Connie and Steve Lieber, the prominent mental illness philanthropists and sponsors of the prestigious Lieber Prize for Schizophrenia Research and the endowed chair that I now hold, would create the Goldman-Rakic Prize for Outstanding Achievement in Cognitive Neuroscience, to celebrate her memory and the groundbreaking body of work she left behind on the neurobiological basis of schizophrenia. After her death, Connie and Steve Lieber, the prominent mental illness philanthropists and sponsors of the prestigious Lieber Prize for Schizophrenia Research and the endowed chair that I now hold, would create the Goldman-Rakic Prize for Outstanding Achievement in Cognitive Neuroscience, to celebrate her memory and the groundbreaking body of work she left behind on the neurobiological basis of schizophrenia.

Progress Through Neuroscience

An important development in the midst of the proliferation of new imaging technologies and other scientific disciplines was their coalescence under the umbrella of neuroscience. This was more than just putting old wine in a new bottle. It was applying the techniques of physiology, pharmacology, genetics, anatomy, and molecular and computational biology to brain exploration—a unique, new multidisciplinary (involving different scientific methodologies) approach that has allowed scientists to study the brain's structure, development, functions, and malfunctions. It has become possible to understand, in great detail, the complex processes occurring within a single neuron. We now have a vocabulary to explain the neurons, axons, and dendrites Cajal depicted in his pencil-and-ink drawings. We're able to go beyond anatomical structures and physiologic functions to the component parts of cells, isolating and manipulating their molecular machinery.

We know that between human conception and maturity, neurons evolve, migrate to designated locations, and link up into circuits, all the while subject to various pressures placed on them by experiential demands, stress, and so on. Along the way, there are myriad possibilities for subtle alterations to occur that can give rise to dysfunction. In addition, most of the approximately twenty thousand protein-coding genes in the human genome are expressed in the brain—a far greater proportion than in any other organ. Neuroscience research is thus carried out at multiple levels: molecular, cellular, circuit, systems, and behavioral. It investigates everything from how neurons process signals physiologically and electrochemically, to programmed cell death and neurogenesis, to how circadian rhythms are produced.

Despite these astonishing scientific advances and the powerful technological tools now available to us, we're only just beginning to understand the way networks of neurons work together to create complex mental functions. Neuroscience has generated spectacular maps of the visual system, but these maps don't explain the neural processes that enable us to recognize a basketball, let alone those that orchestrate our ability to watch and understand a game, recognize the players and interpret their actions, and feel by turns thrilled, disappointed, and bored. Like so many prior instances in the march of progress, technology is the rate-limiting factor. To understand the workings of the brain, better tools were needed. Trying with our current tools was like trying to fly to the moon using Charles Lindbergh's *Spirit of St. Louis*.

It isn't surprising that we have not yet solved the mystery of schizophrenia. It's as if the closer we look into the brain's structure, composition, and functions, the further the pathology recedes. We can see structural abnormalities that suggest an underlying pathological process. We can detect at the chemical level (as we'll see in ensuing chapters) disturbances affecting neurotransmission and genes whose products are the sources of pathogenic consequences. But that's as far as we've been able to go. Still out of reach, or out of sight, are the subcellular and molecular underpinnings of the illness.

This is why I felt such excitement as I headed to San Diego in November 2013 for the annual meeting of the Society for Neuroscience, where big news was about to be announced. The society, founded in 1969, is now the world's largest organization of scientists and physicians devoted to understanding the brain, with tens of thousands of members in more than ninety countries, and its meetings bring together the best and brightest in the field of brain research. However, as I entered the main lecture hall of the convention center, I knew the limitations on what this army of thirty thousand neuroscientists could do. They could map the structure and functions of individual cells and isolated neural circuits, and they could measure the activity of whole structures or segments of the brain. But they could not examine the activity and connectivity of hundreds of thousands or millions of cells simultaneously and connect them to brain function—and, ultimately, to human behavior. Without new instruments and technological capabilities, neuroscientists would never be able to fully elucidate how the brain works; all of us would continue to function as if we were in a car we knew how to drive but whose motor and mechanisms we couldn't understand.

The lecture hall was thronged with people, all gathered to hear the director of the National Institutes of Health describe President Barack Obama's BRAIN Initiative (Brain Research Through Advancing Innovative Neurotechnologies). The initiative would accelerate the invention of new technologies to help researchers produce real-time pictures of complex neural circuits and visualize the rapid-fire interactions of thousands of cells that occur at the speed of thought. It would allow us to better understand how dynamic patterns of neural activity are transformed into thought, emotion, perception, and action in health *and* disease—and perhaps to modify these patterns when they malfunctioned. As I listened to the description of the BRAIN Initiative, I thought how, in its scope and the breadth of its ambition, it resembled Project Apollo, which landed the first humans on the moon, and the international project that sequenced the human genome.

Curiously, I felt that this bold scientific initiative held greater significance for the relatively small number of psychiatrists in the throng than it did for other doctors and scientists. This was because psychiatry had the potential to translate advances in brain science into reduced suffering and a better quality of life for huge numbers of people. What we were missing were the technological tools to understand the complex neural mechanisms underlying brain disorders and mental illnesses. Just as Galileo needed a telescope to prove heliocentrism and Pasteur a microscope to discover microorganisms and formulate germ theory, we awaited what the BRAIN initiative would hopefully provide.

As I left the lecture hall that day, I was full of enthusiasm about the possibility of gaining a greater understanding of the brain and illnesses like schizophrenia. We had come full circle since the nineteenth century, when the world's best medical practitioners were poring over human brains in search of the source of schizophrenia. What advances would this new initiative enable us to achieve, and how would they impact clinical care and the lives of people destined to develop schizophrenia?

Chapter 12

Am I My Genes?

"Survival of the luckiest" may be a better metaphor for the history of life than "survival of the fittest."

—Stephen Jay Gould, *Wonderful Life: The Burgess Shale and the Nature of History* (1989)

Stranger in a Strange Land

Brandon Staglin was about to turn fourteen when he lost track of what was real. His grandfather had leukemia, and the family knew that "Papa" wouldn't live much longer. Brandon had been thinking about him. He'd also been reading a lot of science fiction, recently Robert Heinlein's *Stranger in a Strange Land*, which had him ruminating on consciousness and what it would mean for Papa not to be conscious anymore. One night, while the family was on a vacation in Park City, Utah, Brandon drifted off to sleep. When he woke up a few minutes later, he couldn't tell the difference between fantasy and reality.

"It was very weird and scary," he says of what he now considers his first pre-psychotic episode. "I put on my Walkman and listened to one of my favorite songs, Springsteen's 'My Hometown,' but it didn't arouse any of the usual emotions. That scared me, too. I thought, *What's happened to my emotions?*"

Brandon woke his parents, and they managed to calm him down. He went back to sleep, and the next morning the disorientation was gone. But the fear lingered. What if the strange feeling came back again?

It did, though not until the summer of 1990, following Brandon's freshman year at Dartmouth College. He had worked hard that year, was on the ski patrol, had his first serious girlfriend. But he'd also begun feeling "a bit topsy-turvy" as he tried to define himself as an adult. He broke up with his girl and, when spring term ended, headed home to his parents' house in California. His father, Garen, was a former venture capitalist, and his mother, Shari, had worked in the medical field. A few years ago, they'd purchased a vineyard in Napa Valley, fifty-one acres of heaven.

But the week Brandon had his first psychotic break, his parents and younger sister happened to be away in France. He had opted to stay home to look for a summer job—but instead, he spiraled into psychosis. He felt a physical sensation of the right half of his awareness being "stripped away" and a "void" left in its place. Brandon believed that if he let any new thoughts or experiences into that side of his head, a new personality would form. Once again, his emotions had vanished. "I lay there trying to feel affection for my friends and family; none of it was there. I couldn't sleep. I was wandering around looking for a way to bring those feelings back."

Things went from bad to worse. He felt he was going to die. He spent a night in a jail cell after getting pulled over while driving with his eyes closed. Then he felt the other half of his awareness vanish. "The rest of my identity was gone," he explains. "I couldn't recognize any portion of my mind anymore."

A friend's mother took him to a psychiatric ward, where he was evaluated, told that he'd had a psychotic break, and put in an isolation room. He was given the option of committing himself or being committed. He knew "voluntary" would look better on his medical record, so he opted for that. Shari and Garen, who had rushed home from France, mystified by what could have struck their industrious and capable son, were told Brandon had schizophrenia. For years, no one would use that word around him. Brandon's problems were referred to by the more benign-sounding term "thought disorder."

What the Staglins didn't know back then, which could have helped them realize sooner that Brandon was at risk, was that their own family histories contained multiple instances of serious mental illness. A family history going back nine generations reveals several instances of manifestations of mental illness, including suicides, adjudications of insanity, and commitments to asylums. (See the family pedigree in appendix 5 or on the author's website at JeffreyLiebermanMD.com.)

In Brandon's case, the pattern of inheritance wasn't immediately obvious. Neither of his parents has serious mental illness, nor does his sister. But this reflects what is generally the case with schizophrenia and other mental illnesses: they aren't consistently transferred from an affected parent to his or her offspring (nor do they appear sex-linked in their transmission) and often skip generations.

In most cases, they occur sporadically, surfacing in individuals who have no affected relatives. In other words, they don't fit the basic model of genetic heritability mapped out by botanist Gregor Mendel in 1866. The Mendelian model, which Mendel developed after eight years of studying inheritance patterns in the common pea plant, illustrated single-gene-disease inheritance patterns and revealed the presence of dominant and recessive genes.

Mendel's studies, which essentially marked the founding of the field of genetics, were a first step to understanding genetic transmission. As researchers learned more, it became clear that genes contributed to the heritability of medical disorders in many different ways and to various degrees. We understand now that diseases may involve hundreds or even thousands of genes, and we have enough genomic data to identify which gene variants tend to be found more frequently in people with certain diseases.

A VIRILE CREED

We cannot talk about the role of heredity in mental illness without acknowledging its darkest chapter and the horrific uses to which genetic theories have been put. In the early twentieth century, Mendel's theories were co-opted by the eugenics movement, both in the United States and abroad. In France, the psychiatrist Benedict Morel articulated his theory of "degeneration" in *Treatise on the Degeneration of the Human Species* (1857), which purported to offer a biological explanation for how abnormal mental conditions came into being. Morel's ideas would dominate French psychiatry for decades and spread to other countries. The term "eugenics" was coined in 1883 by Darwin's half cousin, the British mathematician Francis Galton, who called it "a virile creed, full of hopefulness." Galton was convinced that the higher rates of reproduction among the poor were resulting in a decline of the quality of the race, and his proposition, advanced long before the discovery of chromosomes, DNA, or genes, rested upon the observation that "insanity" and "idiocy" (as they were then called) ran in families. He reasoned that the rational thing to do was to eliminate these heritable deficiencies from the population by preventing individuals who were seen as inferior from reproducing.

An American biologist and Harvard professor named Charles Davenport expanded on Galton's ideas in his book *Heredity in Relation to Eugenics* (1911), in which he argued that mentally disabled people should be prohibited from marrying or undergo sterilization. Davenport oversaw the influential Eugenics Record Office in Cold Spring Harbor, New York, the center of America's eugenics movement. (Davenport, who died in 1944, would become cozy with the Nazis in his final years.) Swayed by the scientific authority of Davenport and others, a number of US states established laws permitting compulsory sterilization of people with developmental disabilities and mental illness. In 1927 the practice gained the approval of the US Supreme Court, which ruled 8 to 1 in *Buck v. Bell* that government-mandated sterilization did not violate the due process clause of the Fourteenth Amendment. Justice Oliver Wendell Holmes Jr. wrote the opinion, and infamous lines from it are among the most widely known to people outside the world of jurisprudence. In reference to Carrie Buck's family, Holmes wrote: "Three generations of imbeciles are enough."

More than thirty US states would pass laws permitting eugenic sterilization. The practice of mandated sterilization began to wane after World War II, as American eugenicists sought to distance themselves from the Nazi agenda, though it was only in the civil rights era of the 1960s and 1970s that states started to repeal laws allowing forced sterilization. By that time, between sixty thousand and seventy thousand people had been sterilized.

The pseudoscience of eugenics, to rid society of people considered to be inferior—including people with disabilities and people of color—was a heinous, genocidal ideology whose application represents a shameful chapter in the scientific history of Western civilization.

A GENE'S-EYE VIEW

When we look at a disease such as schizophrenia, we're faced with an evolutionary puzzle. By rights, schizophrenia—a disease with such high heritability and so many reproductive and survival disadvantages—would be unable to perpetuate itself. And yet it has survived undiminished, snaking its way down the generations, sometimes clustering in a single generation, as it did with the Genain quadruplets, all four of whom developed schizophrenia, or with the Galvins, a family of twelve children, six of whom had schizophrenia, whose story was told in the recent book *Hidden Valley Road: Inside the Mind of an American Family.*

In 1976 evolutionary biologist Richard Dawkins published *The Selfish Gene*, which extended the principles of natural selection that Darwin set forth in *On the*

Origin of Species (1859). In the more than 3.5 billion years during which life has existed, 99 percent of all species that have ever lived have become extinct. In other words, the history of life on earth has been a story of perpetual winnowing. Darwin's work elucidated the mechanism underlying the survival of organisms: their ability to adapt to their physical and social environments.

Dawkins's book took a "gene's-eye view of evolution." The fundamental unit of selection, Dawkins wrote, and therefore of self-interest, was "not the species, nor the group, nor even, strictly, the individual. It is the gene, the unit of heredity."

We can think of our genes as blueprints that instruct cells to make special proteins that serve as building blocks for bodily structures (bones, organs, tissues) and perform specific biologic functions (growth, elimination of waste products, immune protection against toxins and disease). Genes are embedded in strands of DNA twisted in the shape of a helix. Each strand is made up of millions of small chemical units called bases that form nucleotides. (A nucleotide is the basic unit of genes embedded in the DNA, comprising chromosomes. It consists of four types of bases—adenine, cytosine, guanine, and thymine—attached to phosphate molecules.) Human genes vary in size from a few hundred bases to more than a million. Each of us has around twenty thousand protein-coding genes and three million bases. Your entire sequence of bases, and the genes they form, is your genome.

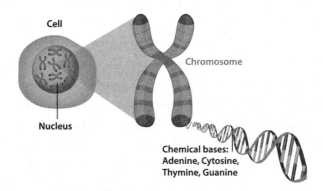

Cell

Chromosome

Nucleus

Chemical bases: Adenine, Cytosine, Thymine, Guanine

The nucleus of the body's trillions of cells holds a vast chemical information database contained in twenty-two chromosomes composed of two intertwined helixes of DNA made of four chemical units (bases) arranged in myriad sequences to form genes. These genetic sequences carry complete instructions for making all the proteins the human body will ever need.

There are genes that exist today that are identical to what they were tens of millions of years ago. As Dawkins explains, the genes that made it through have done so because they were good at things that perpetuated survival—whether building bodies or conferring certain advantageous behaviors or abilities. The coded information genes contain relies on the survival of the creature in which it resides. If a creature dies before reproduction, then the information is not passed on. What we term "negative selection" usually results in the elimination of genes and genetic variation that reduces reproductive fitness.

Despite the insistence with which genes prioritize their own survival and that of the bodies that house them, survival is a complex undertaking, and genes must sometimes choose between less than ideal options. One of the most widely cited examples of evolutionary adaptation is that of malaria and sickle cell disease, which illustrates the genetic compromises and biological trade-offs that evolution imposes on humans.

Sickle cell disease is a potentially fatal disorder of red blood cells in which the sickled, or distorted, cells become stuck in small blood vessels, causing pain, fever, swelling, and tissue damage. In the 1940s and 1950s British scientist John Burdon Sanderson Haldane and South African geneticist Anthony Clifford Allison demonstrated that the sickle cell genetic mutation correlated to tropical regions where malaria was endemic. Since sickle cell disease could be fatal, meaning the gene associated with it is consistently eliminated through deaths from anemia, Allison wondered how the gene could be maintained at such high frequency. The answer lay in the connection between the sickle cell trait and the protection from malaria that it conferred.

It was found that the red blood cells of those affected by a certain mutation in the beta hemoglobin gene lost oxygen and tended to warp into a crescent shape (sickle) when they were infected by malaria-carrying mosquitoes. The infected cells flowed through the spleen, where they were targeted and culled because of their abnormal shape; when the culling eliminated the sickle cells, it eliminated the malaria parasite, too. Scientists hypothesized that this genetic aberration was naturally selected in people in these regions because it protected its carriers against malaria and gave them a survival advantage.

The transmission of the genetic mutation that causes sickle cell disease works in a straightforward manner. If a person carries one copy of the mutated gene, he or she typically does not show signs and symptoms of the condition. However, if two people who carry the sickle cell trait mate, their child will have a 50 percent chance of having one copy of the sickle gene (a heterozygote) and being less susceptible to malaria; a 25 percent chance of no sickle gene; and a 25 percent chance of two copies of the gene (a homozygote). Homozygotes will develop sickle cell disease, while heterozygotes are less vulnerable to malaria and have less severe symptoms if they contract it, but they are carriers who can then pass the disease on to offspring. In other words, the immunity to malaria conferred by the mutation has become a selective advantage, even as the mutation simultaneously conferred the disadvantage of a higher risk of developing a different deadly disease.

In the case of schizophrenia, there is no apparent evolutionary trade-off (that has yet been discovered) of the kind that has allowed sickle cell to persist. And yet schizophrenia endures—the incidence may even be increasing due to rising substance abuse, older paternal age that can cause an increase in chromosomal fragility, and the frequency of genetic mutations—despite a range of reproductive disadvantages. One of the most significant of these is its age of onset. Schizophrenia arises from genes that render certain neural circuits essential to the performance of mental activities needed for social relations vulnerable to malfunction. These changes occur during a critical period of maturation, as the window of risk for developing the illness begins after puberty and extends through adolescence. The onset of symptoms thus coincides with rising levels of the hormones that stimulate secondary sex characteristics, as well as sexual and romantic interest that, in heterosexuals, tend to lead to procreation.

The symptoms of schizophrenia include a dampening of emotions (called blunted affect) and a loss of motivation, both of which can cause social withdrawal, not helpful for finding a mate. The illness also tends to cause a decline in hygiene and appearance. Add to this list of social and reproductive challenges the fact that people with schizophrenia have shorter life spans than people who are not mentally ill by an average of two decades due to their susceptibility to medical illnesses (abetted by poor primary health care), as well as to higher rates of self-injury and suicide.

Females with schizophrenia have slightly higher rates of intimate relationships and childbearing, in part because the illness strikes them at an older age. (On average, women experience the onset of symptoms three to five years later than men.) It is also believed that women are more discriminating in their choice of mates. Their selectivity in choosing a mate is believed to be due to the greater involvement and responsibility of women in carrying the unborn child, nursing, and raising their offspring. Therefore, they want to be sure that their mate is going to be up to the task of supporting and caring for her and their children.

Finally, there is stigma. In virtually all cultures, and especially those in which marriages are arranged, a man or woman known to be mentally ill is not viewed as a desirable mate, and families often attempt to hide the fact that their child has a mental illness. Even in developed countries, a diagnosis of mental illness, and particularly schizophrenia, can make it hard to find a partner—even when one is functioning relatively well with the illness.

Despite these impediments, schizophrenia has persisted in the gene pool. As is true with every other disease, we cannot say exactly what the frequency was hundreds or thousands of years ago, but we can see evidence of its existence in the historical literature. Since the mid-nineteenth century, when we began to compile epidemiological figures, the frequency has held steady at one in a hundred people, a fact that defies logic and raises interesting questions. Is schizophrenia a vestige of evolutionary biology, as the appendix is an anatomic remnant of the gastrointestinal system, or the supernumerary rib that one in five hundred people are born with? Is the illness the result of promiscuous genetic mutations—genes adapting to environmental pressures (the increasing complexity of our lives in the modern age, say, or exposure to environmental toxins), much as bacteria or viruses develop resistance to antibiotics? Might it simply be a manifestation of neurodiversity—a variant in brain wiring and its behavioral expression?

Mysteries remain, but over the last several decades, as we've gained a better understanding of the human genome and the role of genetics in disease, we've learned much more about the mechanisms underlying schizophrenia's surprising persistence.

Adoption Studies

Until the end of the twentieth century, genetic research was limited to epidemiologic and family studies: who inherited what from whom. While scientists were well aware that certain traits and diseases were frequently passed on to children, there were no means to prove that the mode of transmission was genetic—embedded in the DNA—rather than the result of environmental factors.

It had long been known that mental illness ran in families. But many features run in families—including wealth, good manners, food preferences, and languages—that clearly result from a shared environment rather than genetics. Freudian theory stressed the role of childhood experiences and parenting in shaping human behavior. The American psychologist and Harvard professor B. F. Skinner's behavioral theory of psychology, which built on the work of Russian physiologist Ivan Petrovich Pavlov, argued that environmental conditioning was the entire basis of learning, personality formation, and behavior, while R. D. Laing blamed family dynamics and environment for mental illness. In *The Politics of Experience*, Laing pronounced with great authority, "the experience and behaviour that gets labelled schizophrenic . . . is a special strategy that a person invents in order to live in an unlivable situation." Yale psychiatry professor Theodore Lidz argued a few years later in *The Origin and Treatment of Schizophrenic Disorders* that the illness was unlikely to be transmitted genetically rather than experientially: "the nature and origins of schizophrenic disorders are comprehensible without any unknown X-factor if we . . . examine the nature of the aberrant settings in which the patients grew up."

The task of challenging these views fell to a physician named Seymour Kety. Though he graduated from the University of Pennsylvania School of Medicine and completed an internship in medicine, Kety did not train in psychiatry. Nevertheless, he was interested in the biological basis of mental illness and became one of the first physicians to use brain imaging technology for research on mental disorders.

In the middle of his career, Kety switched abruptly to genetics and carried out a series of studies in the 1960s and 1970s that looked at whether schizophrenia had a genetic or environmental basis. He began working with Dr. David Rosenthal at the NIMH; Paul Wender, a psychiatrist at St. Elizabeths Hospital whose previous research identified minimal brain disorder (now called attention deficit/hyperactivity disorder); and a group of Danish scientists who had access to population health registries in Denmark going all the way back to the Middle Ages. The studies had two major goals: to determine the rate of schizophrenia in the general population and in the family members of affected individuals, and to disentangle the effects of environment and genetics on schizophrenia risk by examining rates of the illness in the biological and adopted families of people with schizophrenia. If Lidz and Laing were correct, the rate of schizophrenia in the adoptive and biological parents of people with schizophrenia should be the same.

Kety and his colleagues knew that 1 percent of the general population suffered from the illness, but what they found was that the probability of an individual having schizophrenia who had an affected family member was directly correlated with how closely the two people were related. If someone had a first-degree relative (family members who share 50 percent of their genes including parents, siblings, and children), the probability of their having it, too, was 10 percent. If they had an identical twin with schizophrenia, the probability rose to 50 percent. If both of their biological parents had schizophrenia, there was also a 50 percent chance of offspring being affected.

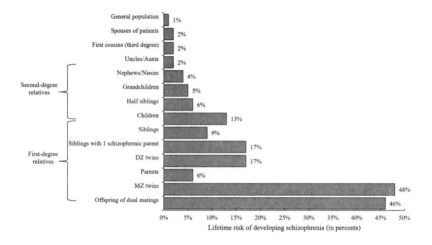

This table shows the average risk for developing schizophrenia in relation to relatives with schizophrenia, based on European family and twin studies conducted between 1920 and 1987. The level of risk is highly correlated with the level of genetic relatedness. The top bar shows the rate in the general population, 1 percent, as compared to the increased risk for relatives.

To address the nature-versus-nurture question, Kety examined children born to women with schizophrenia, both those reared in their family of origin and those reared in an adoptive family. He found that those who had been adopted developed schizophrenia at the same rate as those who remained with their biological mother. Finally, biological relatives of a person with schizophrenia who had been adopted and reared in another home had significantly elevated rates of schizophrenia, but the other members of the adoptive family had a rate no higher than that of the general population. These results clearly indicated that in the case of schizophrenia, nature was dominant over nurture.

IN MY HEART I AM ALWAYS AFRAID

In the mid-1980s I was asked to see a young man whose circumstances were a cruel validation of Kety's findings. Michael Juman was among the patients who, over the course of my career, have etched themselves indelibly in my memory; I think of him sometimes when I'm seeing a patient or reading a scientific article or occasionally out of nowhere at all. Schizophrenia has no shortage of tragic cases, and I have certainly seen my share, but the unrelenting suffering Michael endured and my utter failure to help him makes him emblematic in my mind of all the ways we have failed those who suffer from schizophrenia. For these reasons, I dedicated this book to Michael.

Michael, twenty-one years old when I first met him, was lively and engaging. With his thick, dark, curly hair and striking good looks, he resembled a young Mark Ruffalo. I liked him instantly. If you didn't know better, you'd think he had the world by the tail. But nothing would have been further from the truth.

Michael was born in 1965 and had been adopted and raised by Martin and Phyllis Juman, a middle-class couple living in suburban Long Island. He was the first of two children the Jumans would adopt through Louise Wise Services—the agency whose unethical practices would be the subject of the 2018 documentary *Three Identical Strangers*.

Martin and Phyllis had been rigorously vetted by the adoption agency: their work, medical and financial records, their living arrangements and family histories. In return, they were told certain things about the birth mother of the baby boy with whom they'd been matched. She'd won a scholarship to a well-known college and had completed two years of her education. But someone she had been dating seriously died suddenly of a heart attack, and, in her distress, she'd had a brief liaison that resulted in her pregnancy. These shocks led to some emotional difficulty, for which the woman sought professional help. That was pretty much it. The Jumans were sympathetic to the mother's travails, and not unduly alarmed by what they'd heard. Michael joined the Jumans when he was five months old.

As a child, Michael thrived. He was a gifted athlete, particularly good at baseball; he did well at school and had friends. He seemed self-conscious about the fact that he was adopted but otherwise showed no indications of psychiatric trouble. In high school, he played on the baseball team and continued to get good grades.

During his senior year, the bottom fell out. The Jumans received a phone call from one of Michael's teachers. Michael had been so conscientious, she said, she was wondering why he'd stopped attending class. The Jumans were puzzled, too, and thought maybe Michael had a case of senioritis. When their son got home later that day, they questioned him. Michael said he hadn't been going to class because he just didn't care anymore; he felt like walking into the ocean and never coming back.

The Jumans were stunned. This was entirely out of character. They wondered if the combined pressures of college looming and hidden, undiscussed feelings about his adoption might have caused their son to become depressed. They contacted a psychologist, who saw Michael, agreed that he was depressed, and said he thought he could help him.

The months leading up to his departure for college were shaky. Michael was often in bed. He was moody and had bouts of crying. But he was determined to start school at Eastern Michigan University as scheduled. His therapist gave the okay. He was going to room with his best friend, who would look out for him. So off he went.

In his second semester, Michael struggled; he was caught stealing. He transferred to the University of Florida, where he was soon in trouble again, this time for credit card theft. At this point, he came home. His parents watched him swing between manic and depressive states. His psychologist, after two years of seeing Michael, finally suggested that he see a psychiatrist. After evaluating Michael, the psychiatrist prescribed medication, which seemed initially to bring about some improvement. But Michael was soon symptomatic again—a pattern that would repeat itself through many years and many medications.

In 1985 Michael's psychiatrist wrote to Louise Wise Services, wondering if there was some family medical history that might shed light on his patient's condition. The agency said that Michael's mother had some depression at the time of Michael's birth. When Martin called them for clarification, he was told there was nothing more to know.

Over a two-year period, Michael's psychiatrist tried numerous medications, none of which helped him for very long. Finally, he said there was nothing more he could do. He told Martin and Phyllis that Michael had schizophrenia—although Michael had been suffering its symptoms since he was seventeen, this was the first time they'd heard that diagnosis—and that his brain was like a computer that was missing a chip. Maybe someday there would be help for someone like Michael, he added, but that was many years away.

Michael was hospitalized soon after. It would be the first of many hospital-izations, one of which lasted a full year. His symptoms had evolved from mood swings, exaggerated fears, and misperceptions to hallucinations and delusions. He thought people were following him, sometimes coming at him with an ax. Think-ing he needed to protect himself, he got a handgun, which his parents took away when they discovered it. And then, in 1986, Michael began to have seizures. His parents took away not only his car but also his bicycle, to keep him from hurting himself or others. The seizures were mysterious, as no increased electrical activity was found on EEG studies, which suggested a presumptive diagnosis of psycho-genic non-epileptic seizures (formerly called pseudo-seizures).

I came into the Jumans' lives in December 1986. At the time, I was a research psychiatrist at the Hillside Hospital of the Long Island Jewish Medical Center. While my main focus was research, I also saw patients and had a caseload of about forty. Martin Juman had found me through friends of his, and called me. Given my packed schedule and his urgency, we arranged to meet in the evening at my apart-ment. He came with Phyllis and Michael. They were clearly desperate. Michael told me that he was willing to do anything to help himself—and when the time came, he said, he wanted to donate his brain to science.

Later, Michael's previous psychiatrist sent me a letter. He noted three prob-lem areas: depression, including suicidal ideation; paranoid ideation; and socio-pathic behavior, including stealing and homicidal threats. Michael's insight and judgment were impaired. He had been on various combinations of medications with little benefit. "There has been no consistent improvement in the patient's condition since his treatment with me commenced," the doctor wrote.

Over the next two years, I tried everything that was rational and feasible in the way of indicated treatments: large doses of medications, combinations of an-tipsychotic drugs, ECT, and a new "atypical" that was effective in patients who did not respond to other antipsychotic drugs, clozapine, which would not be ap-proved in the United States until 1989 and so was considered experimental. One of the things that made Michael's case unusual was that his symptoms were very severe but, unlike most patients who are unresponsive to treatment, he did not seem to experience adverse effects. On the contrary, when not in the throes of his psychosis, he was engaging, empathetic, and personable, someone with whom I found it easy to establish a rapport. But I never knew which Michael would show up. He suffered extreme and precipitous mood swings, was tormented by threat-ening voices and delusional fears; he imagined demons were after him. Michael never managed more than a few weeks of stability at a time, but through it all, Martin and Phyllis remained hopeful, providing steadfast support and showing the patience of saints.

It eventually became clear that Michael could not be managed as an outpatient and required long-term hospitalization or residential care. His parents took him to High Point Hospital in Port Chester, New York, at which point I stopped treating him. Unfortunately, while the extended hospitalization may have given his parents some respite, the "treatment" in the hospital didn't help Michael. He was taken off all his medication and, for the first month, Martin and Phyllis were allowed no contact with him; apparently Michael either wasn't told this or didn't understand it, and he believed his parents had abandoned him. During the year he was at High Point, Michael escaped three times from locked wards, until finally he was discharged against medical advice. His diagnosis: schizophrenia paranoid type, axis II: borderline personality disorder.

In 1989 Michael began looking for his birth mother. He wanted to understand the source of his torments, and maybe she could provide some answers. (Michael's adopted sister, Marla, had already found her birth mother.) Louise Wise Services would give him no information. But Michael soon figured out that the ID number on his adoptive birth certificate was the same as the number on his original birth certificate; he went to the New York Public Library and combed through thousands of records until he found his own birth certificate. His mother's name was Florence Dayboch, and Michael began to call all the Daybochs listed in New York. Mostly his messages went unanswered or the Daybochs he reached claimed not to know anyone named Florence, but finally he reached Barry Dayboch. When Michael explained the reason for his call, Barry said, "Hey, cuz." Michael's mother was Barry's aunt.

Barry agreed to meet the Jumans, and in December 1990 the Juman family went to Barry's house. When Michael told Barry about his psychiatric problems, Barry said his aunt Florence had also had such problems. As a child, he had accompanied his parents to visit her in a psychiatric ward. Florence, he said, had had "some kind of operation" on her brain. When Martin asked if he meant a lobotomy, Barry said yes.

The Jumans were in shock. Michael was devastated. They did the math with Barry; Florence's lobotomy was before Michael's birth.

Back home that night, the family discussed whether to sue Louise Wise. Michael was insistent. He felt doomed to spend the rest of his life being sick, just like his birth mother. (He would later say of his own adoption that his parents got a "lemon . . . a deranged lunatic.") Phyllis was reluctant. She was worried about the effects of a grueling lawsuit on Martin, who'd already had three heart attacks, and on Michael, whose problems were ongoing. But the majority ruled, and in 1991 the Jumans filed suit for wrongful adoption—the intentional misrepresentation of the psychiatric history of Michael's mother—and subpoenaed records from Louise Wise.

Shortly after that, I heard from Michael again, under terrible circumstances. On the recommendation of a social worker, who'd felt it might help Michael to achieve some independence as well as offer his parents a respite from the stress of his illness, Michael had moved to an apartment close to Martin and Phyllis. He was there with a gun the day he called my home phone and told me he was going to kill himself. He said that he wanted to say good-bye. I immediately phoned Martin and Phyllis and then the police. Later, Martin would tell me that by the time he and Phyllis arrived at the apartment building—only two minutes from the Jumans' house—there were already several police cars and an ambulance parked outside. There were even police on the roof. Martin was hysterical, yelling over and over in the middle of the street, "Please don't kill my son, please don't kill him!" He wasn't allowed into the building but was told that Agnes, Michael's tireless caseworker—a woman Martin still refers to as "Agnes sent from God"—was inside with Michael.

At some point, Martin heard a loud crash and what sounded like a gunshot. He thought Michael was dead. He was worried about Agnes. He broke down and was lying on the ground, his heart pounding. But no one had been hurt. The police had smashed through the window and managed to grab Michael's arm. The gun went off, but the bullet went into the couch. Michael was brought out in handcuffs, with Agnes behind him. When Martin asked Agnes, who had nine children of her own, why she had stayed with Michael, she said she knew, she just knew, that he didn't want to harm anyone but himself.

That day was one of the more dramatic of the Jumans' lives, but Michael's illness created a daily grind of stress and uncertainty. Phyllis describes those years as an unending series of meetings with social workers, psychiatrists, pharmacologists, landlords, telephone company personnel, hospital workers, day program coordinators, clinic technicians, and many, many doctors and nurses. Sometimes Michael called her a dozen times a day. Once, she stood on a garbage can and crawled through his apartment window to see if he was still breathing. "His caseworker calls and thinks he's in trouble—I'm off and running again. In my heart, I am always afraid."

Over the years of Michael's struggle, he tried virtually everything he could to get better and get on with his life. But always the illness overcame him. He battled so many symptoms: anxiety, severe agitation, depression, mania, hallucinations, voices, paranoia, panic attacks, suicidal ideation, poor judgment and impulse control, inability to concentrate, mood swings, pacing, fainting spells, convulsions and seizures, nightmares, psychosis, emotional upsets, sleeplessness. He pulled out his hair. He forged scripts from pads stolen from his doctors and abused prescription drugs. He had surgeries and blood poisoning due to minor physical injuries he either didn't attend to or got because of accidents. He had a string of diagnoses from an array of different doctors, likely the result of their bewilderment at the severity of his illness.

More than once, he said to his parents, "I can't have the life I want, and I don't want the life I have."

The doctor who had treated Michael just before I did had told Martin that if Michael made it to age thirty, he just might have a chance. (His comment was based on the data indicating that the majority of suicides in people with schizophrenia occur in the earlier stages of the illness.) Michael died on March 11, 1994, aged twenty-nine. Phyllis and Martin were on a trip to Israel, which Michael had encouraged them to take, promising he wouldn't harm himself. They were nervous about going, but they knew that their son would be in constant contact with his extended family while they were away. He was also under the care of the Nassau County Mental Health Department and could call the agency any hour of the day or night. Martin knew the staff there and trusted them absolutely.

Martin and Phyllis were in their hotel room in Jerusalem when they got the phone call. Marla had discovered Michael's body. He was lying on the bed in his apartment, bags of groceries on the kitchen counter. He had kept his promise; he hadn't taken his own life. The Nassau County coroner's office determined that the cause of death was either seizure or a toxic accumulation of medications.

Florence Dayboch died nine months before her son. He never did get to meet her. He also didn't live to see the outcome of the court case. When the full records from Louise Wise Services were finally delivered to the Jumans in 1996, a few years after the lawsuit was filed, they showed that the agency had not only withheld what it knew about Florence and about Michael's birth father, but also had told the Jumans blatant lies. Staff at Louise Wise were aware that at the time of Florence's pregnancy with Michael, she had already spent a total of eleven years in Brooklyn State Hospital, had been diagnosed with schizophrenia, and had undergone a prefrontal lo-botomy in the mid-1940s following a period of worsening hallucinations and severe agitation. They also knew, because they'd handled the adoption, that she'd already given birth to a baby girl while a patient at Brooklyn State Hospital. When Florence came back to Louise Wise in 1964, she was five months pregnant with Michael. The social worker at Louise Wise noted that Florence was then disheveled, wearing ill-fitting clothes, and frequently laughing in an inappropriate manner.

Michael's father, also a patient, had met Florence either at the Brooklyn State Hospital or at an aftercare program called Fountain House and invited her to his apartment one day. According to the Bureau of Child Welfare's Referral for Adoption Placement, "Florence had difficulty expressing her feelings about this incident, which she does not completely understand."

The case went to trial in November 1999 after years of litigation. While the court recognized "wrongful adoption" as a new tort cause of action grounded in fraud and fraudulent misrepresentation, it disallowed damages for emotional distress, limiting compensation to money attributable directly to the alleged fraud—in other words, the cost of raising Michael. The court had already denied the Jumans' request for summary judgment (a verdict that the agency was liable to them for fraud), holding that it had yet to be proved that the Jumans would have declined the adoption had they been told the truth.

(Similar legal questions have arisen very recently with regard to the veracity of sperm donors. A Georgia sperm bank called Xytex was sued in 2017 by a couple after it had sold them sperm from a man it claimed was a PhD candidate with a high IQ and no history of mental health issues or criminal activity. Xytex had told the couple that it carefully screened donors for personal and family health history and criminal history, and that it confirmed the accuracy of any information provided. In fact, Xytex had done no such thing—never verifying the donor's answers, or asking him to supply medical records, or even to provide identification. The donor didn't have a college degree, had been arrested several times, and had been hospitalized for psychiatric treatment, with diagnoses of psychotic schizophrenia, narcissistic personality disorder, and grandiose delusions. The child went on to suffer numerous impairments, including an inheritable blood disorder, and also required multiple extended hospitalizations for suicidal and homicidal ideations. The donor had fathered thirty-six children with his sperm, and several other lawsuits were filed.)

Michael's life and death still weigh heavily on Martin and Phyllis. His illness tore through the fabric of a family, creating an environment of such uncertainty, pain, and fear that the rest of the Juman family suffered spin-off effects. Martin has had multiple heart attacks. He was diagnosed with major depression and chronic fatigue. In 1988 he took early retirement on his doctor's advice. Martin, Phyllis, and Marla all developed panic disorder in response to the upheaval. Michael's schizophrenia had become the hub around which the family functioned, and his death created what his father describes as a vacuum.

"We had lived with Michael's illness for so long," he said, "that we had to learn how to live without it. The adjustment was not easy. All three of us had to learn how to interact with each other without the unifying element of Michael."

The Jumans loved Michael beyond question; they put their lives into trying to help him get better. But as Phyllis says, "They put Michael in my arms, and I loved him for twenty-nine years. But I never would've considered this adoption had I known [the full psychiatric history]." The Jumans were a young couple just setting out in life. They wanted the sort of family that everyone wants: a happy and healthy one.

RARE GENETIC MUTATIONS

All parents are blindsided when a child develops schizophrenia, but in the Jumans' case, that state of ignorance was made worse because they had been actively lied to. And just when the information about Florence's diagnoses might have helped them, it was withheld once more. Michael was symptomatic with schizophrenia for two years before receiving a diagnosis or beginning medication. Had the Jumans known about Florence's history, they might have gotten him into treatment earlier.

In Michael's case, it is hard to say what the effects would have been. Not only did he have the genes of his mentally ill mother; he also had genes from a father who was a psychiatric patient. I don't know the psychiatric history on Michael's father's side, but a detailed family history of Florence Dayboch going back through her grandparents turned up something interesting: no apparent instances of serious mental illness. The fact that Florence, in the absence of such a history, had a severe form of schizophrenia that was unresponsive to treatment suggests that she had a de novo (new) genetic mutation—likely a rare mutation in a gene of significant biological importance that has high penetrance (meaning each of the genes individually is expressed in the phenotype—the set of observable characteristics of an individual, or traits—and in this case has high impact on mental functioning). It also suggests that Michael may either have inherited that mutation or had a different de novo mutation, making it not only very likely that he would develop schizophrenia, but also likely that he would have a severe form of it. Michael's case stands in contrast to Brandon Staglin's.

Brandon's background suggests that he may have a more polygenic form of schizophrenia, with many risk genes of low penetrance with fewer rare mutations that confer disease risk, which gives rise to a less severe and more treatable illness.

Michael was what is known as an extreme phenotype, which describes cases of unusual severity that respond poorly to treatment. In the 1980s we didn't know enough about the genetic architecture of schizophrenia to distinguish between polygenic common alleles (an allele is a variant form of a gene) with low penetrance and rare mutations with high penetrance. Had Michael lived, he might very well have ended up as a long-term resident of a state mental hospital on Long Island, not far from where his family resided—perhaps the Pilgrim Psychiatric Center. This was the hospital where, more than twenty years later, I would be part of a team studying extreme phenotypes among long-term psychiatric patients, which would confirm the role of rare genetic mutations in severe forms of treatment-resistant schizophrenia.

Today an optimal diagnostic workup for Michael would include whole genome sequencing to determine if he carried a rare mutation that might impact his treatment responsiveness. This kind of precision medicine is still in its early stages for mental disorders, but molecular profiling has become the standard of care in cancer treatment.

One well-known case of genetic profiling in mental illness was a study conducted almost ten years ago by Deborah Levy, then the director of the Psychology Research Laboratory at McLean Hospital outside Boston, which involved a mother and a son with diagnoses, respectively, of bipolar disorder with psychotic features, and schizoaffective disorder. Jessie Close and Calen Pick share a rare genetic mutation: a genomic copy number variant that results in extra copies of the gene for glycine decarboxylase. (Glycine decarboxylase encodes the enzyme that degrades the amino acid glycine, which acts to gently enhance the sensitivity of the NMDA receptor blocked by PCP.) These extra copies predicted that Jessie and Calen, the sister and nephew of actor and mental health advocate Glenn Close, might be deficient in glycine and D-serine, rendering their NMDA receptors understimulated.

When Dr. Levy and her colleagues gave Jessie and Calen glycine and D-cycloserine in consecutive clinical trials (both also remained on their usual psychotropic drugs), the results were remarkable. In the words of Thomas Insel, then director of the NIMH, it was "like giving insulin to a person with diabetes—their psychiatric symptoms largely resolved." Calen showed improvement in both positive psychotic and negative symptoms, while Jessie's positive symptoms and mood symptoms improved. When the drug was stopped, their symptoms returned. When they were given glycine again, this time as part of an open study, so all knew they were indeed receiving the two agents, they experienced the same improvements. These trials served as proof of concept for precision medicine using glycine as a treatment adjunct—a method that uses a second treatment to enhance the effect of the first—for schizophrenia. Glycine, however, is impractical for sustained general use, because it requires a large dose (60 grams per day) to produce therapeutic effects. We need to keep searching for alternative ways to produce similar benefits.

Jessie and Calen have different diagnostic labels, but they benefited from the same treatment, presumably because they share a certain genetic mutation. Levy's study illustrates the "genotype-first" approach, a kind of treatment that could become more prevalent as our ability to utilize precision medicine targeting genetic mutations for mental illnesses improves.

GENETIC BREAKTHROUGHS

Kety's adoption studies, the results of which have been replicated many times, proved that family dynamics were not responsible for schizophrenia but that familial biology played a very significant role. But there was still not any real understanding of what was being transmitted down the generations.

Psychiatrists collaborating with geneticists set out eagerly in search of "mental illness genes." As schizophrenia had the highest known heritability of any mental illness or developmental disorder at that time (now autism does), researchers regarded it as the low-hanging fruit of psychiatric genetics. The first researchers to strike genetic gold—or so they thought—were a team of British scientists led by Hugh Gurling of University College London. In a 1988 publication in the journal *Nature*, Gurling and his colleagues described a genetic locus (location where specific genes are) on chromosome 5 that they believed to be associated with schizophrenia. The *New York Times* trumpeted psychiatry's entry into the age of molecular medicine with a front-page story of the Gurling team's finding, which it deemed "the first concrete evidence for a genetic basis to schizophrenia." Alas, Gurling's discovery proved to be fool's gold. Scientists could not replicate it using the DNA from other schizophrenic patients.

Every few months, it seemed, news of a new gene associated with schizophrenia would appear in the scientific literature, only to be followed by reports of the failure to replicate the apparent breakthrough. It became a recurring and deeply frustrating pattern, and as the claims and failures piled up, skepticism grew about the viability of the search. Psychiatry experienced an unsettling sense of déjà vu: almost two centuries earlier, the discipline had split from neurology when neurologists had been unable to identify any clear anatomical basis for mental illness. Now, using near-miraculous molecular tools that nineteenth-century anatomists couldn't have imagined in their wildest dreams, scientists had identified specific genes for physical maladies such as cystic fibrosis and Huntington's disease—but were unable to identify any clear genetic basis for mental illness.

As it turned out, the difficulties they encountered were not unique to mental illness. Scientists had also been unable to pin down the genes involved in a variety of other medical conditions, including diabetes, hypertension, coronary artery disease, and even specific forms of cancer. Geneticists realized eventually that the failure resulted from the fact that these illnesses—including mental illnesses— were polygenic rather than monogenic, meaning they resulted from the effects of multiple, sometimes hundreds, of genes.

Just when prospects for finding the genetic basis for schizophrenia seemed hopelessly complex, three game-changing events occurred. In 2003 the Human Genome Project, led by Dr. Francis Collins at the NIH, completed the sequencing of the human genome, one of the most ambitious scientific projects ever undertaken. What Collins and his team discovered, to their surprise, was that the human genome contained only about twenty thousand genes that coded for proteins. However, these twenty thousand genes were composed of more than three million bases (the building blocks that can be rearranged to form different gene sequences). Thus, there were trillions of possible unique offspring—a seemingly enormous potential for variation. But perhaps the bigger surprise was how few differences there were between people in their genetic makeup (less than 1 percent of the total DNA). The fact that so little genetic variation accounts for the differences between people meant that genes must have numerous ways to express themselves. We can draw an analogy with musical notes that differ from each other only subtly but can be combined in an infinite number of ways by a composer altering the arrangement or by a performer changing the pacing, phrasing, or key of the musical piece.

These findings were hugely significant. It was known already that populations evolve and adapt through natural selection, and that in order for natural selection to operate, genetic variation must be present. Such variation leads to heterogeneity between generations: if evolution favors one variant—for example, the high concentrations of the skin pigment melanin in peoples living in sunny climates—then this advantageous variant will increase in frequency over generational time. If environmental conditions change, individuals migrate, or new predators or pathogens appear, genetic variation may allow a different variant to thrive in these new conditions. Genetic variation functions therefore as a kind of insurance for organisms against changing conditions, helping to guarantee that some offspring will survive. If the margin of variation in gene sequences was as constrained as the Human Genome Project had shown, the conclusion that had to be drawn was that there must be other ways for the genome to express itself that could account for greater diversity.

Through further study of the genome, we learned more about gene expression and the effect of mutations. There are many types of genetic mutations. The most common and smallest mutations are called single nucleotide polymorphisms (SNPs) and involve an error in a single base in the nucleotide of a gene. If a base (adenine, cytosine, guanine, thymine) is like the letter of a word, then an SNP is like one letter being changed in one word of a sentence on one page of a long book. Larger mutations involve a piece of DNA being removed (deletions), a new piece of DNA being added (insertions), a segment of DNA being duplicated, and various other types of alterations. Consequences of mutations include prematurely signaling a cell to stop building a protein, or producing too much of it, or causing a protein to function abnormally.

As the Human Genome Project was being completed, a cell biologist working at Cold Spring Harbor Laboratory on Long Island was uncovering another mechanism of variation in gene expression. Michael Wigler pioneered a new technique that would revolutionize our understanding of human genetics: representational oligonucleotide microarray analysis (ROMA). An oligonucleotide is a short molecule of DNA or RNA (ribonucleic acid). A microarray is a device used in large-scale genetic analysis to study how genes are expressed as messenger RNA and how cells control large numbers of genes simultaneously. Microarrays can look at which genes are producing what under a given set of conditions and can discover or investigate differences between the gene activity of healthy and diseased cells. Instead of the standard method of decoding the sequence of nucleotides in genes, ROMA revealed whether a particular gene had too many or too few copies in a genome. If there were excessive copies of a gene, it caused the gene to have an increased effect, or gain of function. A single copy or deletion of the gene caused it to have a loss of function.

ROMA was a very different way of thinking about genetic expression and, following the recognition of the polygenic nature of mental illnesses, represented the second paradigm-shifting view of the genetics of mental illness. Instead of saying, "Do you have the specific schizophrenia gene?" the model asked, "Could your schizophrenia be caused by possessing too many or too few copies of a certain gene or genes?" And instead of focusing exclusively on whether a particular gene for mental illness was inherited from a parent, it suggested that the genes responsible for mental illness could have developed spontaneously during conception and embryologic development through genetic errors that produced the over- or underrepresentation of genes. In other words, a person could be vulnerable to a mental illness because he had inherited certain genes from his parents—or because he had a certain number of mutations that had occurred spontaneously while still in the womb.

Wigler's primary focus was cancer research, but when he realized the technique's implications for understanding mental illness, he took a young genetics researcher, Jonathan Sebat, into his lab to apply ROMA to the DNA of patients with autism, schizophrenia, and bipolar disorder. Wigler and Sebat found that while both healthy and mentally ill people possessed varying numbers of the same genes, those with mental illnesses had more of certain genes involved with brain development and function. Copy number variants (CNVs) are common in the human genome, but it turned out that a certain kind of CNV—relatively rare and usually of recent origin within a family (arising during sperm or egg production or passed down for only a few generations)—is seen disproportionately in people with schizophrenia and with developmental disorders such as autism.

These findings added to our understanding of the ways the genetic blueprint could express itself and affect an individual's vulnerability to mental illness. For example, it had long been known that the children of older mothers had an increased risk for neurodevelopmental disorders such as Down syndrome. But molecular genetic studies showed that children of older fathers tended to have greater numbers of certain genes that increased the likelihood of autism and schizophrenia. The reason older fathers increase the probability of these genetic mutations is that sperm divide every fifteen days after first forming in male testes during puberty. Years and years of sperm division, with the continuous replicating of DNA, leads to the accumulation of errors. A twenty-year-old male has an average of twenty-five mutations in his sperm, whereas a forty-year-old has sixty-five mutations.

While copy number variations in genes demonstrate an ingenious way that nature produces diversity within human reproduction, environmental factors can also contribute to this variability, including with regard to disease vulnerability. For example, it was found that exposure of mothers and fetuses to toxic environmental effects could also alter genes in a way that increased the risk of schizophrenia. Women who became pregnant during the Dutch Hunger Winter of 1944–45, when Nazi Germany blocked food supplies during World War II, causing widespread famine in the Netherlands, gave birth to children who had higher rates of obesity, diabetes, and schizophrenia. Prenatal exposure to influenza during the first trimester has been associated with a significantly elevated risk of schizophrenia. And we know that certain drugs taken during pregnancy can cause fetal developmental abnormalities—for example, retinoids, a synthetic form of vitamin A found in the acne drug Accutane. Retinoic acid modulates gene expression and influences neuronal migration.

While the findings from ROMA did not provide a conclusive road map for detecting mental illness based on an individual's genome, they offered a new and more expansive way of thinking about the genetic basis of mental illness. Instead of searching for a "schizophrenia gene," psychiatrists now thought about too few or too many copies of dopamine receptor genes. Finally, a larger number of mutations, or copies of the gene, was found to have a strong correlation to the schizophrenia phenotype. This was in contrast to the weak associations found between schizophrenia and specific genes that had single nucleotide polymorphisms (differences in the individual nucleotides of genes), which are the most common type of genetic variations in humans.

The third advance in our understanding of the genetics of mental illness came from genome-wide association studies, or GWAS, which utilized microarray analyses. With the human genome sequenced, it was theoretically possible to compare all the genes, or at least those that coded for proteins, of people with and without specific illnesses. GWAS, observational scans of a person's whole genome, can detect genetic variants (typically SNPs) that may be associated with specific diseases. From individual samples of DNA, the technology reads millions of variants. If one type of variant is more frequent in people with the disease, that variant is said to be associated with the disease. The associated SNPs are then said to mark a region of the human genome that may influence the risk of disease.

While the great advantage of GWAS was their ability to examine the entire genome instead of a small number of prespecified genetic regions, there were disadvantages as well. Any two human genomes differ in millions of ways. There are small variations as well as many larger variations (deletions, insertions, duplications). Any of these may cause alterations in an individual's traits—anything from disease risk to a person's height. Most of the genes found using GWAS had weak associations to schizophrenia. The number of variants linked to schizophrenia was in the hundreds, many without plausible biologic relevance to the brain or illness. Nevertheless, GWAS have shed additional light on the complex, polygenic nature of schizophrenia—information that can't, at this point, determine diagnosis or treatment for individual patients, but which gives us a fuller picture of the genetics of the illness in the aggregate. As our ability to apply precision medicine for the treatment of mental illnesses increases, what we're learning from GWAS may guide us.

All of these developments in technology have provided deeper insights into the complex genetics of schizophrenia and enabled researchers to develop hypotheses about its evolutionary survival. The picture that has emerged from thousands of studies suggests that there are multiple genetic forms of schizophrenia, which can be broadly grouped into three categories.

1. The "common disease–common variant" form of the illness
    occurs when many genes, possibly one hundred to two
    hundred, combine to confer disease vulnerability. Each gene

is commonly found in the population and contributes a very small amount to overall disease liability (our degree of vulnerability to an illness). What determines the probability of developing the illness, as well as its severity, are the specific number and type of susceptibility genes (genes that confer risk) in an individual's genome. According to this theory, the illness has persisted in the gene pool due to the liability for developing it being spread across many different genes, each of which has such a small effect that it is below the threshold at which negative selection would eliminate it. The genetic culprit here is therefore not a single tile but a complex mosaic.

2. The "common disease–rare variant" form is caused by an inherited or de novo mutation that is rare in the population but exerts a large effect—that is, has high penetrance—resulting in the individual having a strong likelihood of developing the illness. Because de novo mutations are present for the first time in one family member, they are not subject to the same processes of negative selection that inherited mutations are.

3. The third genetic form is the genocopy of schizophrenia, which occurs when a genetic disorder is caused by a segment of DNA that contains schizophrenia-risk genes. The best example of this is DiGeorge syndrome, caused by the deletion of a small segment of DNA containing thirty to forty genes in the middle of chromosome 22. The syndrome, first described in 1965 by physician Angelo DiGeorge, occurs in about one in four thousand people. Symptoms vary but often include congenital heart malformations, facial and limb deformities, developmental delays, and learning disabilities. The phenotype is manifest at birth or in childhood, and almost 30 percent of those affected develop schizophrenia-like symptoms by adulthood. This rate of concurrence suggests that genes that confer risk of schizophrenia (or, conversely,

protect against it) are contained like stowaways within the affected segment of DNA.

These scientific developments have taught us much about the genetics of mental illness and the numerous means by which genes conspire to preserve and confer schizophrenia. They have also disabused us of many false beliefs. We know that no single gene causes schizophrenia, and that the genetic differences between affected and unaffected people are more quantitative than qualitative (with the exception of rare, highly penetrant mutations of critical genes). Indeed, if we analyzed the genetic constitution of you, me, and a group of our respective family members and friends, none of whom has a serious medical or mental condition, we would find that around 10 percent of our genes harbor genetic alterations of various types that do not bring about significant disease susceptibility.

There is another factor that, along with pathogenic genetic mechanisms and heritability and the various ways the genome can express itself, may have supported the persistence of schizophrenia: social evolution. While statistics for the incidence of schizophrenia do not go back very far, we can conjecture that the long process of civilization, in which societies have become increasingly inclined to care for those who cannot care for themselves, has worked against natural selection. It has also functioned as a kind of anti-eugenics. The development of principles and mechanisms supporting the survival of the sick or less able has meant that genes triggering vulnerability to schizophrenia have been to some extent protected from their own reproductive disadvantages. Some portion of people with the illness who were able to survive because of social systems (or, later, the asylums) would have procreated—a small number, perhaps, but more than would have been the case had they been left without any social support.

In very recent times, we have seen additional social changes and environmental effects that may be contributing to a rising frequency of schizophrenia. Longer life spans and changing economic and cultural conditions have encouraged older parenting, for instance, while cannabis and certain other drugs with psychotomimetic effects (meaning they produced an effect on the mind that mimicked the symptoms of psychosis) may be serving as triggers in individuals genetically predisposed to developing the illness.

Given the enormous magnitude of genetic range—the trillions of unique combinatorial possibilities to which the genome gives rise—procreation seems a game of roulette. Any number of genes can sufficiently impact critical neural systems and confer significant disease risk. Whether the effect on the system involves hundreds or thousands of genes or just a small number with large, rare mutations, the vulnerability is baked into the neural circuits regulated by the culpable neurotransmitters that course through the brain regions responsible for emotion, thought, and perception.

The question that naturally arises is: How can so many genetic combinations produce an illness like schizophrenia, which, despite its heterogeneity, has a consistent age of onset and clear groups of symptoms? The answer is fairly prosaic. While there are many trillions of possible combinations of genes in a person, the biological substrates and pathways that they build are much more limited in number. Think of a skyscraper. The owner may envision various purposes for its many spaces (retail, restaurants, health clubs, offices), and the architectural design could develop in a multitude of ways. But when it's time for construction, the fundamental materials and elemental structures will be the same ones that any building requires: bricks, steel, cement, glass, drywall, and so on.

The other question that comes to mind is why things don't go wrong more often. The answer to this is less clear. We may never fully understand the human brain. But we cannot doubt that it is a miracle of design, functionality, complexity, and durability.

Chapter 13

PSYCHOSIS, PSYCHEDELICS,
AND THE SEROTONIN THEORY

Explanations exist; they have existed for all time; there is always a well-known
solution to every human problem—neat, plausible, and wrong.

—H. L. Mencken,
Prejudices: Second Series (1920)

AN ACCIDENTAL VOYAGE

Midway through the twentieth century, scientists and physicians were still in the
dark about what caused schizophrenia. Genes had long been suspected, given how
frequently family members of someone with schizophrenia also suffered from mental illness. But that was as far as it went. The adoption and twin studies by Seymour
Kety and colleagues hadn't been done yet, so shared dysfunctional environments
had not been ruled out as causal factors. But beginning in the 1950s, researchers
began to make key observations that allowed them to move beyond the vague "it
runs in families" theory of degeneration and genetic causation, and to plumb the
pathological depths of the disease from another direction: that of neurochemistry.

The first drug that opened an ostensible window into the neurochemistry of
schizophrenia was lysergic acid diethylamide, or LSD. Its psychoactive properties
were discovered accidentally in 1938 by Dr. Albert Hofmann, a chemist working at
the Sandoz Laboratories in Basel, Switzerland. Hofmann was seeking a compound
to stimulate cardiac function and breathing; concocting a drug that would contribute to a countercultural revolution was the last thing on his mind.

After twenty-four unsuccessful iterations of ergot derivatives (ergot is a fungus that grows on plants and from which various pharmaceuticals are derived), and just when scientists at Sandoz were losing interest in his search for a cardio-respiratory stimulant, Hofmann formulated LSD. Further research was delayed, however, as just when Hofmann had completed his synthesis of LSD, he was assigned to another project. Five years later, nudged by a "strange feeling" that there was more to discover about this compound, he returned to studying LSD.

While preparing a batch one day, he accidentally absorbed some through his fingertips and soon sank into "a remarkable but not unpleasant state of intoxication." Hofmann found himself perceiving "a succession of fantastic, rapidly changing imagery of a striking reality and depth, alternating with a vivid, kaleidoscopic play of colors." The condition lasted about three hours.

Intrigued by the drug's unique properties, Hofmann decided to experiment on himself, ingesting 250 micrograms, or about a millionth of an ounce—too small a dose, he assumed, to have much of an effect. But as he bicycled home from his lab, he found his field of vision swaying; objects were distorted as though he were seeing them in curved mirrors. "I had the impression of being unable to move from the spot," he recounted, "although my assistant told me afterwards that we had cycled at a good pace."

The first intentional acid trip in history wasn't altogether pleasant. Having arrived home feeling nauseous, light-headed, and unsteady, Hofmann lay on the sofa as the room's familiar objects and furniture took on grotesque and threatening forms. When his next-door neighbor visited, she was no longer Mrs. R, but "a malevolent, insidious witch with a colored mask." He felt a demon had taken possession of him. "I was seized by the dreadful fear of going insane."

Hofmann was frightened enough to summon the family doctor, who found nothing out of the ordinary but dilated pupils. Eventually Hofmann's fears began to wane, and little by little he was able to enjoy the pageant of colors and shapes playing behind his closed eyes. As he described it: "Kaleidoscopic, fantastic images surged in on me, alternating, variegated, opening and then closing themselves in circles and spirals, exploding in colored fountains, rearranging and hybridizing themselves in constant flux . . ."

The glow was still with him the following morning: "Everything glistened and sparkled in a fresh light. The world was as if newly created. All my senses vibrated in a condition of highest sensitivity, which persisted for the entire day."

The events of what came to be known as "Bicycle Day" convinced Hofmann that he had stumbled on something of extraordinary potential. Here was a psychoactive substance of incredible potency, able to cause powerful changes in mental states and levels of consciousness. Although he would later refer to LSD as his "problem child," for the moment, Hofmann saw something that could be an important tool for studying how the mind works.

In 1947 LSD was introduced as a commercial medication under the trade name Delysid; by the mid-1950s, it had captured the interest of researchers in the United States and was being studied extensively. The vivid sensory distortions and disjointed thought process, by turns bizarre and profound, earned LSD the moniker "psychotomimetic." The drug was believed to be the first pharmacologic model for schizophrenia, and its seeming capacity to simulate the psychotic state raised researchers' hopes that it might provide insight into the pathologic mechanisms of the illness. They also believed that because LSD disrupted ingrained mental patterns and dredged up repressed thoughts and emotions, the drug might function as a kind of reboot for the brain and prove an effective treatment for other psychiatric conditions. It was tested initially as a treatment for anxiety, depression, psychosomatic disorders, and substance abuse. LSD showed such promise in treating alcoholism that Bill Wilson, the cofounder of Alcoholics Anonymous (AA), considered including it in the program. By the mid-1960s, LSD had been prescribed to more than forty thousand patients, and more than a thousand scientific papers and dozens of books on LSD were published. There were six international conferences on LSD research. Mainstream publications such as *Time* and *Life* sang the drug's praises.

At the same time, counterculture icons such as Timothy Leary, Richard Alpert (better known as Ram Dass), Ken Kesey, and novelist Aldous Huxley extolled the virtues of psychedelics and encouraged their use as instruments of mind expansion, spiritual growth, and liberation from oppressive social conventions. Psychedelics took on political connotations and were viewed as a threat to the status quo and existing societal norms.

The broad impact that LSD had on medical science and society intersected briefly with my personal and professional lives. In the late 1960s I was a college student at Miami University in the small college town of Oxford, Ohio. Even in such remote locations, the counterculture was in full swing: angry protests against the war in Vietnam, but also "free love" and lots of recreational drugs.

As a premed student, cautious by nature, I mostly observed the cultural landscape from a distance, systematically studying the pharmacopeia of intoxicants that were then popular, and carefully considering their risks and benefits. But then

I began dating a beautiful flower child, a fellow student far more experienced in hippie rituals than I was, and she introduced me to psychedelics. Ever the scholar, I prepared myself for the upcoming adventure by reading books that detailed the mind-bending journeys occasioned by psychedelic drugs: Huxley's *The Doors of Perception*, *The Varieties of Religious Experience* by William James, *The Varieties of Psychedelic Experience* by Robert Masters and Jean Houston, Carlos Castaneda's *The Teachings of Don Juan*, and, of course, *The Electric Kool-Aid Acid Test* by Tom Wolfe.

On a warm spring afternoon, my girlfriend and I each swallowed a square of blotter acid containing 50 micrograms of LSD, then headed out to the bucolic campus. Within fifteen minutes, I felt a slight tingling sensation in my abdomen, which soon spread throughout my body. My visual, auditory, and tactile perceptions intensified. My hands became objects of wonder, radiating kaleidoscopic patterns that oscillated in and out of focus. The grass and trees appeared brighter, the green spectacular in its vividness. The ambient noise of the field we were crossing twisted through beguiling arpeggios of sound.

We crossed the campus and arrived at a nearby church just as the sun was setting. We went inside and sat in a pew. I marveled at the light streaming through the stained glass and the majesty of the church's ambience and design. Until then, the effects of the LSD had been mostly sensory. Now, as I gazed at the altar and the image of Jesus in Crucifixion, I was filled with an overwhelming spiritual intensity, as if God were communicating a secret and divine message to me. A cascade of revelations tumbled through my consciousness, thrilling me with their profundity. Just as this flow of insights reached its climax, a voice whispered, "And no one will ever know." I interpreted this to mean that the real truths lay in the secret interstices of consciousness, which most people were never able to access.

I turned to my girlfriend and, assuming that she was having the same transcendent experience, said, "This is amazing! We need to come here more often!"

She looked at me querulously and snapped, "But you're Jewish!"

The following day, having returned to reality, I had another comedown. During my LSD trip, I had written copious notes about what I was thinking and feeling—I'd felt an urgency born of the fear that if I didn't record these precious insights, they would vanish when the drug's effects did. Expecting now, in the light of a clear consciousness, to find pearls of cosmic wisdom, I spread my crumpled notes on the desk and eagerly deciphered my scribbles. To my surprise, what I read was either painfully mundane ("Love is the essence") or nonsensical gibberish ("Leaves find green clouds"). What had conferred the sense of profundity and the ineffable was the emotional conviction associated with my prosaic revelations. In other words, my elation at the miraculous discovery that "the sun is bright" was more emotional intensity than cognitive insight.

Later, whenever I encountered Thomas Szasz, R. D. Laing, or others from the anti-psychiatry movement—either denying the pathological nature of schizophrenia or romanticizing it as a "journey"—I recalled my Great Thoughts of that day. I understood that just because someone believes he's having a cosmic insight doesn't mean he is. As exhilarating and revelatory as psychedelics seemed, they hadn't necessarily put me in touch with the Godhead or the life force.

But the LSD trip had given me a different insight—less profound, perhaps, but potentially more important. It had allowed me to see firsthand how a minuscule amount of a chemical—a fraction of a grain of salt! —could profoundly alter a person's thoughts, perceptions, and emotions. If tiny amounts of ingested substances could induce such powerful changes, how easily might the brain's fragile balance be perturbed by an aberration in the brain's neurochemistry?

Though I didn't know it at the time, the question that my LSD trip had left me with was already being taken up by scientists formulating an endotoxin theory of schizophrenia. The theory was as follows: minute doses of a drug could produce profound alterations in mental states. Human physiology involves an enormous range of chemical and metabolic reactions. Could an error in one of these reactions result in a psychosis-inducing substance instead of an enzyme, hormone, or neurotransmitter? It was already known that such genetically programmed inborn errors of metabolism occurred and caused serious diseases. The endotoxin theory sparked a frantic search for substances originating within the body that could give rise to psychosis. Bodily fluids were chemically analyzed for toxic agents, a futile quest that culminated in a study in which schizophrenia patients underwent kidney hemodialysis in an effort to "filter out" the offending agent from their blood.

In the meantime, a fractious dispute was brewing about whether LSD should actually be regarded as a good pharmacologic model for schizophrenia. Were the symptoms exhibited by people with the illness really so similar to what one saw in people tripping on LSD? It was true, for instance, that both people with schizophrenia and those on LSD were liable to experience hallucinations and delusions, but it was also true that the nature of the hallucinations was different—mainly visual in drug-induced states but primarily auditory in schizophrenia. And while the speech of someone on LSD was generally coherent, the speech of someone with schizophrenia could be extremely disorganized and illogical.

In an attempt to resolve the difference of opinion, researchers taped interviews with someone on LSD and someone in an acute phase of schizophrenia. When they played the recordings to a group of experienced psychiatrists, the psychiatrists were unable to distinguish the patient from the acid tripper.

The issue was hardly settled. Another dispute arose over differences in the ways in which people with schizophrenia and drug users interacted socially. Critics of the LSD model of psychosis pointed out that people with schizophrenia were characteristically withdrawn, whereas those on LSD preferred companionship. Proponents of the LSD model put this variance down not to differences in what was happening in the brain but to the fact that drug users chose to take LSD with friendly companions and had an idea of what to expect. If a person were surreptitiously given LSD, thus removing the bias of expectations, a more natural likeness to psychosis would emerge.

LSD was mired in far more nefarious controversies. In fact, it is hard to think of a substance that has been used for such sharply contrasting ends as LSD was in America during the 1950s and 1960s. On one side, medical researchers regarded psychedelics as a vehicle for exploring the mind-brain connection and saw multiple potential uses for them in the treatment of mental disorders, including as a tool to expedite the arduous and protracted process of psychotherapy. On the other side was the US Central Intelligence Agency. From 1953 until its official termination in 1973, the CIA conducted the infamous MK-Ultra program, in which LSD was tested as a potential mind control agent and aid to interrogation. The scope of the project was enormous, with activities carried out under the guise of research at more than eighty institutions, including universities, hospitals, and prisons. LSD was also administered to CIA employees, military personnel, doctors, other government agents, and members of the general public—often without the subjects' knowledge or consent. Ironically, one of the era's most enthusiastic acid trippers, Ken Kesey, volunteered for the MK-Ultra experiments while a graduate student at Stanford. Kesey reportedly stole hits of acid and invited friends to trip with him.

Details of MK-Ultra didn't emerge until after the program had been discontinued, and only through congressional hearings and the Freedom of Information Act. By that time, it was clear that LSD was never going to be the mind control weapon the CIA had hoped. If anything, the drug caused people to question authority rather than become more amenable to control. And MK-Ultra had had some disastrous results. Years after the program ended, I learned that a former Columbia University faculty member, Harold Abramson, had been, unbeknownst to the university or his colleagues, a key figure in MK-Ultra. It was Abramson, in fact, who treated the most famous victim of MK-Ultra: Frank Olson, a biochemist and research scientist at the US Army's biological warfare research center in Fort Detrick, Maryland. During the third week of November 1953, Olson attended a work retreat at nearby Deep Creek Lake. While there, he and several of his colleagues were unwittingly dosed with LSD by high-ranking CIA officials, including chemist Sidney Gottlieb.

Olson's family reported that he was a different person when he returned from the retreat. He became severely depressed and suffered what seemed to be a nervous breakdown, refusing to eat and withdrawing from his family. At work, he seemed agitated. Olson's emotional distress and erratic behavior worsened over the next few days. He was convinced to undergo treatment and flew to New York City accompanied by a colleague, where he met with Abramson for evaluation.

Abramson recommended inpatient treatment for what he diagnosed as psychosis and made arrangements for Olson to be admitted to Chestnut Lodge in Maryland. But before that could happen, Olson died—on November 28, he either fell or jumped from the tenth-story window of his room at the Statler Hotel in Manhattan. (Questions have persisted about Olson's cause of death, and in 1975 his family received a settlement from the US government and an apology from President Gerald Ford and CIA director William Colby.)

By the late 1960s, the media had soured on LSD. Reports came out about the association of psychedelics with notorious personalities like Charles Manson, the psychopathic leader of a murderous cult of disaffected youths steeped in the drug culture. Victims of bad trips had begun to show up in emergency rooms. In 1969 Diane, the twenty-year-old daughter of Art Linkletter, a popular television personality, jumped to her death from her sixth-floor apartment window in Hollywood. Her father called it murder rather than suicide—"She was murdered by the people who manufacture and sell LSD"—though his allegation was questionable, given that an autopsy would show no drugs in Diane's system.

Whatever the truth of Diane Linkletter's death, the perception that it was linked to LSD lingered and helped to fuel the growing public backlash against the drug. By 1970, LSD had been classed by the federal government as a Schedule I drug, the most restrictive category, reserved for substances regarded as having high potential for abuse and no currently accepted medical use.

The prospects for LSD and other psychedelics to inform medical science and psychiatry evaporated amid the social turmoil, controversies, negative press, and growing governmental aversion. As Michael Pollan wrote in *How to Change Your Mind*—his 2018 book on what psychedelics might yet teach us about consciousness, dying, and the treatment of mental disorders—the hopeful euphoria of the 1960s gave way to alarm, and soon "the whole project of psychedelic science had collapsed." (Pollan, who is in his sixties, refers to himself as "less a child of the psychedelic 1960s than of the moral panic that psychedelics provoked.") It is only now, decades later, that psychedelics have reemerged in biomedical research as legitimate substances for the study of potential therapeutic uses.

Before it was banned, though, research on LSD yielded important findings. In addition to the tantalizing glimmers noted in studies of its ability to aid in the treatment of specific mental disorders and facilitate psychotherapy, LSD also provided a clue about what did—or, more specifically, did not—cause schizophrenia. Analysis of the behavioral effects LSD induced had not, in the end, supported the claim that it produced a model psychosis. It turned out that LSD's pharmacology and mind-altering effects were not unique; it shared both with a group of naturally occurring substances (including psilocybin, mescaline, and ayahuasca) that had been used ritualistically by indigenous tribes in North, Central, and South America for centuries. These substances all brought on similar altered states of consciousness, which we would later learn were due to their molecular actions targeting the brain's receptors for serotonin, the neurotransmitter involved in regulating emotions and happiness.

While the mental states of an LSD trip might resemble elements of the psychotic experience, they did not mimic all the symptoms of schizophrenia or the qualitative state of mind that it induced. And the similarities seemed largely observational rather than what users were actually experiencing; when people with schizophrenia who had taken LSD were asked if the two states were comparable, they said no. Moreover, studies demonstrated that when schizophrenia patients ingested LSD, it did not exacerbate their symptoms—something that would have been expected if the drug were acting on the same neurochemical targets involved in the illness. Little evidence would be found in postmortem brains, imaging studies, or other pharmacologic studies that implicated the serotonin 2A receptors in schizophrenia.

Studies of LSD had shown just how fragile the brain systems are that mediate our mental functions. But they did not lead to a theory of causation for schizophrenia. Apparently, the brain had different neurochemical channels of psychosis, and psychedelics didn't tune into the schizophrenia channel. The search for schizophrenia's neurochemical cause would continue.

Chapter 14

DOPAMINE:
THE WIND IN THE PSYCHOTIC FIRE

Purple in the morning, blue in the afternoon, orange in the evening. . . .
And green at night. Just like that. One, two, three, four.

—Sara Goldfarb in *Requiem for a Dream* (2000)

SCHIZOPHRENIA BY ANY OTHER NAME

One of the most common questions I'm asked by family members of people with
schizophrenia is whether using recreational drugs can cause the illness. I used to
say no but my thinking has evolved over the years. In medical school and during
my postgraduate training in psychiatry, I had been taught that certain drugs—
psychedelics, PCP, stimulants—could induce a toxic psychosis that mimicked the
symptoms of schizophrenia, but that this was transient, the symptoms disappear-
ing when the drug's effects wore off and the drug was eliminated from the system.
I was also taught that recreational drug use could trigger the onset of psychotic illness in people who were constitutionally or genetically predisposed to it. (In such
instances, the onset of first psychotic episodes can be sudden and rapid rather
than gradual, as is usually the case.) But I hadn't been taught, nor had I seen evidence, that drug abuse could cause psychosis, except when people were under the
drug's influence.

My view began to change as more has been learned about the effects of certain drugs on the brain, their relationship to psychosis and usage patterns have
changed, and as I've encountered patients who provided me new insights. The
answer, I now believe, is more complex.

Sean was a junior in college when he arrived in the psychiatric unit of the Columbia University Medical Center, having taken an overdose of ibuprofen and the sleep medication Ambien. It was the latest in a string of drug-related problems Sean had suffered. Born in 1990 to a mother who worked in publishing and an emotionally remote father who was a senior executive at a major insurance company, Sean was diagnosed with ADHD when he was twelve and prescribed the stimulant medication Adderall. By the time he entered college in 2008, he was taking the maximum daily dose of Adderall. He breezed through his freshman year, but the following year began to suffer from anxiety. At the student mental health services, he was prescribed the antidepressant sertraline (the generic version of Zoloft). The drug temporarily eased his anxiety, but by spring semester, he was complaining that people were watching him and listening to his conversations. Finding it difficult to concentrate while studying for finals, Sean added Ritalin to the mix. Ritalin is a faster-acting stimulant used to manage ADHD, and Sean periodically took up to 60 milligrams a day, the maximum recommended dose, in addition to his Adderall.

Sean's paranoid thoughts intensified, and he had his first auditory hallucinations, hearing voices saying derogatory things about him. That summer, he was treated by a psychiatrist with an antipsychotic medication and resumed school in the fall. But by December, his symptoms had returned. He heard the voices of friends talking about him and believed that neighbors were trying to bore through his wall. He was treated with a different antipsychotic, one that controlled his paranoia but caused him to gain a significant amount of weight.

By the following summer, Sean's paranoid symptoms had come back even more floridly. He believed that his father had implanted a tracking device in his brain. In his distress, Sean threatened to take an overdose and was admitted to the hospital, this time receiving a diagnosis of schizoaffective disorder. His medication was switched to a third type of antipsychotic plus the mood stabilizer lithium.

Sean returned to school, somewhat improved, for his junior year, but in late November delusional thoughts and hallucinations recurred. He believed that his grade school friends were inserting thoughts into his mind. His mother withdrew him from college, hoping that a respite at home would allow him to stabilize. Instead, he took an overdose of Ritalin and lithium, which he immediately reported to his mother. She called 911, and Sean was admitted to the intensive care unit of a local hospital. When he was medically stable, he was transferred to the psychiatry unit at Columbia University Medical Center.

Because of the complexity of Sean's case and the dizzying array of drugs he'd been prescribed over the last several years, I was asked to see him. At our first meeting, I was struck by how personable and intelligent the young man was. His conversation was coherent, and his behavior appropriate. Despite the diagnosis, his demeanor and appearance didn't align with what I usually saw in someone with schizophrenia. I also didn't notice symptoms of ADHD, either due to his stimulant medication or because they weren't very prominent to begin with. (Such inconsistencies in cognitive disorder diagnoses weren't uncommon in New York City in the 1990s, as parents tried to gain academic advantages for their children through prescription drugs that promised cognitive enhancement or through extra time on standardized tests.) Adding to the mystery was the fact that Sean had been an excellent student. What became clear as I dug into Sean's history and talked with his family and friends was that, apart from the stimulants—which he'd gotten not only from doctors but also from dubious online sources and had stockpiled in large quantities—Sean had been notoriously noncompliant with his prescribed psychotropic medications, arbitrarily skipping doses of some and taking more of others than he should have.

As part of his evaluation, we ordered an EEG and an MRI. Sean's electroencephalogram showed no seizure-like abnormalities, and his MRI revealed none of the anomalies associated with schizophrenia, such as enlarged lateral ventricles, or increased or decreased blood flow or metabolic activity in the affected regions of the brain. In addition, a special analysis of his MRI depicting colorized maps of brain activity showed none of the hyperactivity in the anterior section of the hippocampus that we had found characteristic of schizophrenia.

Because of Sean's psychotic symptoms, we treated him with an antipsychotic, as well as naltrexone, a drug that addiction studies had shown prevented craving. Based on his history and the EEG and MRI results, I couldn't agree with his previous, provisional diagnoses of schizophrenia or schizoaffective disorder; I wasn't certain, but I believed that the weight of the evidence suggested that he was suffering from stimulant-induced psychosis. Sean's mother was grateful for the clarification in his diagnosis; she believed her son had dodged a bullet. But such a diagnosis did not necessarily mean that Sean's prognosis was any better, or that the course of his illness would differ markedly from that of schizophrenia, or that he would recover. Such diagnostic distinctions are not so clear cut. Should something that presents and persists like schizophrenia go by another name just because its cause is different from genetic forms of the illness? Or should we think of schizophrenia more like we do dementia or pneumonia: a syndrome that may have multiple causes but whose symptoms may respond to similar treatments regardless of the cause? (We shall return to this diagnostic dilemma in chapter 17.)

THE PHARMACOLOGIC PATH TO UNDERSTANDING SCHIZOPHRENIA

Drugs and schizophrenia have a long and tangled history. Much of what we've learned about the illness has been discovered through studying the ways that different drugs act on the brains of healthy people and those with schizophrenia. While drugs such as stimulants can wreak havoc in the brain, others (antipsychotics, to name one class) have provided a pathway out of the asylum and relief from the tortures of psychosis. The discovery of chlorpromazine in 1950 almost instantly changed the fate of millions of people with schizophrenia. Within a decade of its appearance, more than fifty million people around the world had taken it. In the seventy years since, upward of forty antipsychotic drugs have been developed based on chlorpromazine's biochemical profile, and virtually every person who develops schizophrenia is treated with one or another of these medications.

Despite their enthusiastic embrace of antipsychotics, however, for years psychiatrists actually had no idea how the drugs produced their therapeutic effects. The search for the answer to this question provided the first insight into the brain disturbance underlying schizophrenia, as well as the first scientifically credible and most enduring theory about what causes the illness—one involving the neurotransmitter dopamine.

Chemical communication between brain cells by neurotransmitters was first demonstrated in 1957 when Kathleen Montagu, a British scientist working at Runwell Hospital outside London, isolated dopamine in human brain tissue. Dopamine is the transmitter of several brain pathways and plays a critical role in facilitating motor activity, motivation, and reward signaling. Soon after Montagu's discovery, researchers would link diminished dopamine to Parkinson's disease, a finding that led to the development of the amino acid levodopa (L-dopa) as a treatment for the progressive brain disorder.

This was a pivotal moment for researchers studying schizophrenia. It was now plausible to imagine that the illness might also be caused by a disturbance in chemical communication between cells (the proverbial "chemical imbalance"), and dopamine looked like the most obvious culprit. After all, the telltale symptoms of Parkinson's—tremor, rigidity, slowness of movement—to which low levels of dopamine had been linked resembled closely the side effects produced by chlorpromazine, which implied that the drug was disrupting dopamine transmission. If chlorpromazine alleviated psychotic symptoms by blocking dopamine, then perhaps excess dopamine was causing the psychotic symptoms of schizophrenia.

In the 1960s researchers began to trace chlorpromazine's path once ingested and identify its target in the brain. (One of them, Arvid Carlsson, would win the Nobel Prize in 2000 for this work.) They found that once chlorpromazine makes its way to the brain, its molecules diffuse out of blood vessels and into the extracellular spaces between the brain's densely packed nerve cells; it then migrates to protein structures on the surface of neurons in particular parts of the brain areas, it turned out, where dopamine presides. Through a form of biologic attraction, chlorpromazine molecules home in on and bind to receptors. Instead of activating the receptor, and thus transmitting the nerve's electrical impulse from one neuron to the next, chlorpromazine blocks the effect, resulting in reduced neural activity in that circuit. Based on these findings, Dutch pharmacologist Jacques van Rossum speculated that schizophrenia (or at least its symptoms) must be caused by too much dopamine, and in 1967 the dopamine theory of schizophrenia was born.

Subsequent studies in the early 1970s by the laboratories of Solomon Snyder at Johns Hopkins University and Philip Seeman at the University of Toronto, using newly developed technology, confirmed the link and revealed that the clinical potency of chlorpromazine and similar antipsychotic drugs was directly correlated with the drug's affinity for dopamine receptors. In other words, the stronger the attraction of the molecule to dopamine receptors, the greater the inhibition of dopamine stimulation, and the lower the dose of the drug needed to alleviate psychotic symptoms. By the mid-1970s, the connection between dopamine, the psychotic symptoms of schizophrenia, and the therapeutic and side effects of chlorpromazine had been firmly established.

Carlsson, Solomon, and Seeman went on to trace the route dopamine usually travels through the brain, which also illuminated aspects of schizophrenia. Dopamine emanates from two clusters of neurons in the midbrain, called the ventral tegmental area (VTA) and substantia nigra (SN), and a third located in the hypothalamus. The first pathway extends from the midbrain VTA to the limbic region—a network of structures in the middle of the brain underneath the cerebral cortex and above the spinal cord, brain stem, and midbrain—and the frontal cortex, which is the front half and largest of the four components of the cerebral cortex (the outer layer of the brain). The limbic region assists in memory formation, learning, and emotional processing, while the frontal cortex performs numerous functions, including problem solving, planning, decision-making, abstract thinking, and creativity. The pathway from the midbrain neurons in the substantia nigra extends to the corpus striatum, a part of the brain involved in motor learning and coordination. In the hypothalamus, dopamine-releasing neurons reach into the pituitary gland and control the release of hormones like prolactin.

Their laboratories collectively demonstrated that disturbances in neurons located in the ventral tegmental area underlie the symptoms of the illness and were the sites of the therapeutic effects of antipsychotic drugs. Neurons in the substantia nigra and hypothalamus are innocent bystanders as far as the illness is concerned, but they are still subject to the effects of the drug; antipsychotics may cause movement and endocrine side effects, such as tremor, muscle rigidity, and elevated prolactin, causing enlargement and fluid leakage from the breast and disruption of the menstrual cycle.

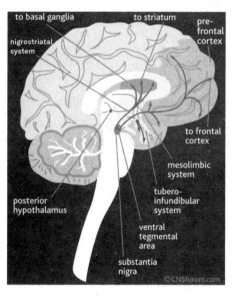

Imagine that you're looking sideways into the brain, through the ear, searching for the neural pathways that communicate using dopamine as their neurotransmitter. You would see that these pathways emanate from two clusters of cells (ventral tegmental area and substantia nigra) in the midbrain, which send branches to brain regions that control emotions, perception, and thought. Disturbances in these pathways are responsible for the symptoms of schizophrenia.

The Storming Tablet

Even before scientists elucidated dopamine's role and traced its neural pathways courtesy of chlorpromazine in schizophrenia, a second line of investigation was ongoing that bolstered the dopamine theory. This research involved the pharmacologic opposite of dopamine-blocking drugs such as chlorpromazine: drugs that stimulated the release of dopamine.

The first stimulant, methamphetamine, was synthesized in 1893 by the Japanese chemist Nagai Nagayoshi. But it wasn't until 1938 that the Berlin-based Temmler-Werke pharmaceutical company produced methamphetamine in a commercial tablet form under the brand name Pervitin. During the early years of World War II, tens of millions of Pervitin tablets were given to German Wehrmacht soldiers. The blitzkrieg invasions of Poland, the Netherlands, Belgium, Luxembourg, and France are said to have been fueled by "speed."

For most soldiers, the effects of the drug were much like those of the body's own adrenaline: increased concentration and a willingness to take risks, a reduced need for sleep, and decreased sensitivity to pain, hunger, and thirst. The results could be remarkable. In January 1942 hundreds of German soldiers found themselves surrounded by the Red Army on the eastern front. It was minus 22 degrees Fahrenheit, the snow waist high in places. A military doctor assigned to the unit reported that six hours into their ordeal the soldiers were so exhausted that they began to simply lie down in the snow. The commanding officers decided to give them Pervitin. "After half an hour," wrote the doctor, "the men began spontaneously reporting that they felt better. They began marching in orderly fashion again, their spirits improved, and they became more alert." Little wonder that Heinrich Boll, the German writer and future winner of the Nobel Prize in Literature, wrote letters to his family while stationed in occupied Poland, imploring them to send him more Pervitin.

The military leadership did notice, though, that the drug had some disturbing aftereffects, especially with repeated use, including cardiovascular problems, becoming accident-prone, and terrible drug hangovers that reduced soldiers to veritable zombies. Pervitin could also cause highly aggressive behavior, and these effects may have contributed to the massacre of civilians and to violence committed by soldiers against their own officers.

Despite Pervitin's downsides, after learning of its energizing effects on the Wehrmacht, Japanese military leaders began to produce and distribute methamphetamine to their forces to increase their "fighting spirits," or *senryoku zōkyō zai.*

Substantial quantities of the drug were combined with green tea powder to form tablets, which were branded with Emperor Hirohito's crest, and named *totsugekijō* or *tokkō-jō*—the "storming tablet." These were administered to pilots conducting the surprise attack on the US fleet anchored at Pearl Harbor on December 7, 1941. Later in the war, as Japan grew more desperate, kamikaze pilots—many of whom were only in their teens—resorted to injecting large doses of methamphetamine before their suicide missions.

By the late 1940s, postwar Japan was in shambles, its industrial and social infrastructure in ruins. To facilitate the rebuilding of the economy, Japanese industries distributed methamphetamine to civilian workers to increase productivity and reduce the need for sleep. The Dai-Nippon Seiyaku company marketed the drug under the name Philopon, based on the Greek words *philo* and *ponos*, which translated to "love of labor," and more than twenty Japanese companies began producing methamphetamine to meet the country's needs.

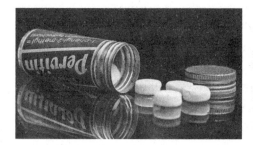 

The Temmler-Werke pharmaceutical company's Pervitin (left) was the stimulant given to German soldiers during World War II to increase their aggression. Philopon, the Japanese equivalent, was given to kamikaze pilots (right) in the ceremony prior to their mission.

In economic terms, this risky experiment succeeded. The Japanese economy began to expand in the 1950s, and, by the mid-1980s, it was the world's second-largest economic power after the United States. But the success had come at enormous human cost. It is estimated that by 1948, more than 5 percent of all Japanese people between the ages of sixteen and twenty-five abused stimulants. Some of them developed psychotic symptoms, including paranoid delusions, hallucinations, and agitated and occasionally violent behavior. These were among the first cases of drug-induced, or toxic, psychosis documented in the early 1950s. (The methamphetamine epidemic would prompt the Japanese government to restrict and later prohibit the use and sale of the drug.)

Initially, it was believed that after stopping drug use, people would experience psychotic symptoms for a few days at most (a transient psychosis). But an alternative explanation was that the symptoms—which closely resembled those of schizophrenia—were being provoked by the drug in people already vulnerable to developing the illness. However, methamphetamine-induced psychosis was occurring even in people who had no preexisting risk factors or were above the age of risk for schizophrenia. Moreover, it could persist after long periods of abstinence or recur in the context of stressful life events. Occasionally, patients exhibited recurrences of psychotic symptoms without any apparent trigger.

Against the backdrop of a second epidemic of methamphetamine abuse in Japan in the 1970s and 1980s, Japanese psychiatrist Mitsumoto Sato began studying the phenomenon of drug-induced psychosis. One of the cases he described occurred after the standard age of onset for schizophrenia—a forty-two-year-old man who had abused methamphetamine for the previous five years—but in all other respects mimicked the symptoms, course, and eventual worsening of the illness. The man's drug use had caused him persistent paranoia: he believed someone was hiding in his ceiling and that others were walking beneath the floor; he was under surveillance, and someone was trying to kill him; his wife was being prostituted by a drug dealer. When he finally went to the police asking for protection, his methamphetamine use stopped, and after several days, his symptoms disappeared. One month later, however, when he injected the drug again (less this time than his usual dose), he immediately experienced a psychotic episode. Another period of abstinence followed, and, for a while, he seemed fine. But the next time his psychosis returned—at this point he grew violent—he had not taken methamphetamine. He was admitted to the hospital for a brief stay and treated with antipsychotics before being released to outpatient care. Soon enough, a fourth episode occurred, again in the absence of any methamphetamine, and he was readmitted to the hospital suffering from paranoid delusions and auditory hallucinations. He no longer needed methamphetamine to trigger relapses; they occurred spontaneously, and even treatment could not bring about his recovery.

Meanwhile, researchers in other parts of the world had noted the relationship between amphetamine use and psychosis. The Australian researcher David S. Bell described a patient whose behavior and outcome were very similar to what had been seen in Japan with methamphetamine use. A young man of twenty-one had become addicted to amphetamines and experienced several short-lived psychotic episodes. He'd been admitted to the hospital numerous times and, on each occasion, had recovered fully within a week. But by the age of thirty-six, he'd undergone a permanent change. Repeated tests showed no amphetamine in his system, but the man had the formal thought disorder characteristic of schizophrenia, and he suffered various paranoid delusions. He believed the police were poisoning his food and asked to be castrated in order to avoid persecution. He assigned meaning to certain colors and insisted he was being brainwashed. The man remained in the hospital for years, and Bell noted that he had "the apathetic appearance of a chronic schizophrenic." Bell concluded that amphetamines could cause an illness that resembled paranoid schizophrenia but was distinct from it—a clinical entity unto itself.

This observation confirming the Japanese experience with chronic amphetamine use prompted a new series of studies that strengthened the case for dopamine's role in psychosis. In the late 1960s Bell experimented with reproducing amphetamine psychosis in voluntary subjects with no prior history of mental illness. His study involved sixteen patients, almost all of whom had drug addiction problems. All had recovered from their drug-induced psychotic disorders and were scheduled for discharge from a psychiatric hospital when they agreed to take part in the study. When researchers readministered amphetamine as per the study protocol, twelve of the sixteen experienced (mostly mild) psychotic symptoms lasting one to six days. A constant feature of their psychoses was paranoia, and almost all described auditory or visual hallucinations.

Bell's experiment replicated the fact that administering amphetamine could induce psychosis in people without schizophrenia and further demonstrated that in chronic amphetamine users, psychosis could be triggered by brief exposure to stimulants or even stress effects, indicating a greater susceptibility to develop psychosis. This research was being undertaken contemporaneously with research on LSD and psychedelics; Bell's findings indicated that the conditions provoked by stimulants resembled schizophrenia more closely than did the psychotic symptoms seen in LSD users.

By the mid-1970s, we knew that stimulants that caused the release of dopamine in the brain, if taken in large doses and/or repeatedly, could produce schizophrenia-like symptoms. We also knew that people with schizophrenia developed psychotic symptoms spontaneously—that is, without using stimulants—and that antipsychotic drugs could ameliorate them. It was seeming ever more likely that people with the illness either had too much dopamine or had an increased sensitivity to its stimulation. In an effort to find out which of these possibilities it was, Burt Angrist, a researcher at New York University Medical Center, conducted an experiment in which very low doses of amphetamine (too low to induce psychosis in healthy people) were given to patients with schizophrenia. He found that in the majority of patients, their symptoms were either provoked or exacerbated, which indicated that people with the illness had a greater sensitivity to the psychosis-inducing effects of dopamine stimulation.

The dopamine theory of schizophrenia was now supported by two powerful lines of evidence: chlorpromazine alleviated psychotic symptoms by blocking dopamine at the receptors on the postsynaptic neuron; and amphetamine and other stimulants activated psychotic symptoms by releasing dopamine from the presynaptic nerve terminal.

Despite the substantial evidence in support of the dopamine theory, it was still limited as an explanatory model of schizophrenia. It didn't tell us what caused the malfunction of dopamine neurotransmission, how or when it occurred, what dopamine's relationship was to the illness's adverse and cognitive symptoms, or how the dysregulation related to a person's prognosis. Beyond understanding that dopamine-blocking antipsychotic drugs were key to treating the psychosis of schizophrenia, we still had much to learn.

A DRUG HOLIDAY

By 1980, the majority of people with schizophrenia who had access to treatment had received or were receiving antipsychotic medications. The exceptions were, largely, people from underserved communities, including people of color, people from lower socioeconomic classes, and people living in developing countries. In addition to patients with schizophrenia, quite a few people with other diagnoses were also receiving them off-label (meaning the drug is prescribed for conditions in which there is a pharmacologic rationale but for which it does not have an FDA approval). However, the widespread benefits of having their psychotic symptoms alleviated came at a heavy price. People who took antipsychotics often suffered Parkinson's-like neurological side effects, including tremor, rigidity, and physical slowness. While these side effects can, to a degree, be counteracted by other medications, a related condition that sometimes developed in people taking antipsychotics could be irreversible. Tardive dyskinesia is an involuntary movement disorder characterized by writhing or flicking movements of the tongue, mouth, face, hands, or feet. Though the symptoms are disfiguring and naturally cause self-consciousness, they are usually not harmful.

However, the fact that tardive dyskinesia was irreversible suggested that it might reflect brain damage from antipsychotics' chronic blockade of dopamine receptors.

As a result, clinicians and patients found themselves between a rock and a hard place: either continue taking medication in order to sustain remission and prevent relapse, accepting the side effects, or decrease or stop medication, thereby avoiding side effects but risking relapse. We knew that some patients who discontinued medication could remain stable for months or even years before relapsing. The problem was that we did not know which ones. We needed to find a way to identify those patients who could take a "drug holiday" and still remain stable and not relapse, at least not for some time.

As a junior faculty member at the Mount Sinai School of Medicine in New York City in 1982, I helped to implement a study comparing the effectiveness of standard doses of antipsychotics with an ultralow dose over a two-year period. The hope was that while patients might require higher doses of medication when actively psychotic, once they were in remission, their symptoms under control, they could decrease the dosage and limit any unpleasant side effects.

The results of the study weren't as promising as had been hoped. The patients on low-dose treatment relapsed more often than those receiving the standard doses. They'd been spared the side effects, but at significant cost. At the same time, however, many study participants who received low-dose treatment did not relapse for months, and a small number didn't relapse at all. It was clear that a reliable measure or test that could predict who would relapse and who would remain stable after drug decrease or withdrawal would be very valuable to clinicians and patients. The challenge was identifying one.

I presented an idea for doing just that and began scouring the existing literature for clues from previous studies that might indicate which patients were likely to relapse and which were not. To my surprise, even patients who had been stable on medication for years could worsen soon after their antipsychotic drug was decreased or discontinued. I then came across a study published in 1976 in which the authors administered three stimulant drugs (levoamphetamine, dextroamphetamine, and methylphenidate) to schizophrenia patients and measured their responses. The aim was to understand better the role of neurotransmitters in schizophrenia.

All of the drugs stimulated dopamine release in the brain, but each had a different level of potency, and the first two also caused the release of another neurotransmitter, norepinephrine. As expected, the researchers found that the drugs evoked psychotic symptoms in patients. But what this study uniquely revealed was that the magnitude of the effect was related to the potency of the drug's effects on dopamine. Methylphenidate—the active ingredient in Ritalin, which was soon to become widespread as a treatment for ADHD—had the most powerful impact because it acted solely on dopamine, followed by dextroamphetamine and levoamphetamine, which also acted on other neurotransmitters. This provided further support for the dopamine theory of schizophrenia. But what was most exciting was the small follow-up study the researchers had conducted using levodopa (L-dopa)—the amino acid precursor to dopamine in brain cells that was the mainstay of treatment for Parkinson's disease.

L-dopa was made famous by Oliver Sacks's book *Awakenings*, which told the remarkable story of a group of patients who had survived the "sleepy-sickness," or encephalitis lethargica, pandemic of 1916 to 1927. In the late 1960s Sacks was a young neurologist working at Mount Carmel Hospital in Queens, where about eighty such patients lived. The sickness had left them in a strangely frozen state, often sitting motionless all day, without energy or initiative, and—most bizarrely—with their thoughts and feelings fixed at the point when they'd become ill: for many, it was still the 1920s. In 1969 Sacks administered the new wonder drug L-dopa and watched his patients "awaken" from their decades-long torpor. "I was seeing such things as had never, perhaps, been seen before," he wrote, "and which, in all probability, would never be seen again." Unfortunately, the benefits occasioned by L-dopa were short lived. They either wore off after several weeks, or the patients developed unintended adverse effects such as emotional volatility or involuntary movements that necessitated the medication be discontinued.

I had read Sacks's book with fascination. Now I was reading about L-dopa again, this time having activated patients' psychotic symptoms to a degree comparable to or exceeding that of the most potent stimulant. This was definitive confirmation that the effect of the drug on psychosis was being mediated by dopamine.

I pored over the paper, trying to fully absorb its significance. By that point, I had read numerous papers on stimulant-induced psychosis, but now I saw that the critical factor in determining someone's stability, particularly if he or she was to discontinue medication, was the person's sensitivity to dopamine. This was knowledge we could use to a patient's advantage.

I wrote a protocol for what is known as a "challenge" test. Such tests are procedures that intentionally try to induce symptoms of an illness and are used routinely in various areas of medicine, such as exercise stress tests in cardiology or glucose tolerance tests for diabetes. My study would serve as a "stress test" of the brain that would, hopefully, identify patients who would be candidates for drug holidays.

From the standpoint of the present, it may seem bizarre or unethical to intentionally induce these distressing symptoms. But seeing as how the symptoms were mild and would dissipate within an hour or two without serious adverse effects, it was reasonable to view them as much less damaging to the individual than a full-blown relapse. (In the early 1990s, when evidence had emerged that psychotic episodes might be toxic to the brain, I discontinued the use of the challenge test model, as did many people in my field. While the potential for neurotoxic effects was mainly associated with prolonged episodes of psychosis or psychotic relapses, it wasn't worth the risk of inducing even transient symptoms for even brief periods. Other researchers who continued to use this research paradigm finally stopped when they were subsequently criticized.) What we were sure of, because of tardive dyskinesia, was that the antipsychotics then in use could have a potentially irreversible effect on the brain—and yet studies had shown that without them, 60 percent to 80 percent of people relapsed within about two years. It was therefore imperative to figure out ways to limit patients' cumulative exposure to drugs without risking relapse, and to identify those 20 percent to 40 percent who could remain stable during that period without medication or on a low dose. My hypothesis, based on all the studies I'd read, was that patients who experienced activation of their psychotic symptoms by a stimulant would be more likely to relapse if they stopped the medication than those who did not see their symptoms worsen.

By the time the NIMH had awarded a grant for the study, it was the mid-1980s, and I had moved to the Hillside Hospital of Long Island Jewish Medical Center. I began evaluating patients from the schizophrenia clinic. The criteria for participating in the study were that the individuals had to have been stable at a certain level of remission for at least six months, were being treated with antipsychotics, were able to give informed consent, and wanted to try a drug holiday. Once enrolled, the patients were tapered off their medication (they would remain entirely drug free for fifty-two weeks, unless their symptoms returned). Each patient received two infusions one week apart: one of methylphenidate and the other of saline, a placebo. We randomized the order of the infusions, so that neither the investigators nor the patients knew which infusion anyone was receiving.

Thirty-four patients completed the study. On the one hand, their responses were as anticipated. Under the influence of methylphenidate, eleven showed an exacerbation of psychotic symptoms, varying in magnitude from moderate to extreme. In extreme cases, patients who had previously been stable and not experiencing delusions or hallucinations became almost as symptomatic as they had been during acute episodes of their illness. Fortunately, this intensification of symptoms subsided within one to two hours as the effects of the methylphenidate wore off.

Surprisingly, however, twenty-three patients had negative responses to methylphenidate, meaning they showed no signs of being affected by it—not even the increased energy, talkativeness, or euphoria one expects to see in healthy people. Their response to methylphenidate was indistinguishable from their response to the saline infusion. It was as if they lacked the brain sites on which the drug acted or as though their problems were due to something other than dopamine.

We saw the patients in weekly clinic visits and monitored them closely for a year after the infusions. Ten of the eleven patients who had responded to the methylphenidate relapsed in a median of eleven weeks (the median is the point in time by which 50 percent of subjects had relapsed); the remaining patient showed sufficient warning signs of relapse that we were able to reintroduce medication before he met the criteria for relapse. Of the twenty-three negative responders, fourteen relapsed in a median of thirty weeks, and nine did not relapse through the end of the study. These results confirmed my hypothesis that greater dopamine receptor sensitivity would be a predictor of relapse risk—with two caveats. First, the fact that fourteen of the negative responders relapsed only after a significant number of weeks of stability suggested that had they stayed on a very low dose of medication rather than stopping altogether, they might have remained in remission. The second was the marked diversity in patient responses to methylphenidate, which suggested there might be different forms of schizophrenia, or at least variations in the pathological disturbances that produced the symptoms of the illness which could be pharmacologically distinguished. This implied that treatments for patients would also vary and that one size fits all wasn't the best approach. Rather, treatments could be tailored for the individual patient's particular form of schizophrenia. This presumption foreshadowed the coming concept of precision medicine.

Soon after the results of my study were published, a parallel scientific initiative would introduce a second generation of antipsychotic drugs with a substantially lower risk of inducing neurologic side effects, thus reducing the need for drug holidays (and challenge tests to identify for which patients they were safe). This proved enormously fortuitous. Patients would benefit from more effective and safer medications. As for me, rather than obviating the need for the results of my research, it prompted me to redirect my efforts to what proved to be a more fruitful line of research: how to prevent schizophrenia or at least ameliorate its progressive course, and the pain and disability that it produces.

You Can't Measure Neurotransmitters in Living People

By the 1990s, scientists had clear evidence that inhibiting dopamine-mediated neurotransmission lessened psychotic symptoms and stimulating it exacerbated them. Studies of chlorpromazine and psychostimulants had provided compelling indirect evidence of overactive dopamine—that is, we could infer from the effects of those drugs that people with schizophrenia had more dopamine activity in their brains than did healthy people. But direct evidence of this variance was still needed to prove the dopamine theory. For that, researchers had to catch the biologic villain red-handed, not just rely on the chemical reverberations of drug effects. We had achieved this with other diseases. Increased glucose could be measured in the blood of people with diabetes, and viruses and bacteria had been isolated as the causes of infections. In the case of heart attacks, we can detect increased levels of troponin, a protein complex in cardiac muscle involved in muscle contraction.

Measuring chemicals in the brain, however, is not so easy. Once neurotransmitters have been released into synapses and have served their purpose of stimulating the targeted neurons, they are metabolized or inactivated before exiting the central nervous system via the cerebrospinal fluid surrounding the brain and the venous circulation. Unless we go into the brain itself, all we can readily measure are the chemical shadows of neurotransmitters in the form of metabolites in blood, urine, or cerebrospinal fluid. To complicate matters, dopamine is also made in the kidney, so the metabolites found in blood and urine come not only from the brain.

Researchers launched an intensive search for a way to measure increased levels of dopamine directly. They reasoned that dopamine hyperactivity could occur from increased numbers of dopamine receptors, which would amplify the neurotransmitter's impact, and they set out to measure levels of receptor binding in postmortem brain tissue and in PET scans of brains of living patients with schizophrenia. To their delight, they quickly struck paydirt, or so they thought. While they did indeed find increased numbers of dopamine receptors, it turned out that the increase was due to the antipsychotics patients had received and not to the illness itself. This was discovered by comparing PET and postmortem studies of drug-treated and drug-free patients, a result replicated in animal studies, where animals treated with drugs had many times more dopamine receptors than those not given drugs. Moreover, when the animals stopped receiving drugs, their dopamine receptor numbers declined to pretreatment levels.

These findings reflected the quality of plasticity, an ingenious aspect of mammalian biology that enables the brain to adapt to changing conditions. In the case of dopamine receptors, the brain compensated for fluctuations in the amount of dopamine stimulation: when a lot of dopamine is released into the synapse and stimulates the receptors, the number of receptors decreases to compensate—leaving the dopamine no choice but to either go back into the presynaptic neuron from which it came or be metabolized into inactive form. If too little dopamine is sent from the presynaptic neuron, the number of receptors increases in order to capture whatever dopamine is there. Likewise, when antipsychotic drugs are introduced into the system, blocking the dopamine receptors and preventing their stimulation by dopamine, the receptor number proliferates in an effort to compensate for the reduced stimulation. This is the neural system attempting to maintain its equilibrium.

Once again, researchers had been left frustrated and disappointed by another faux breakthrough. While the effects of antipsychotic drugs and psychostimulants implicated dopamine overactivity as causing psychotic symptoms, direct evidence of dopamine excess was still lacking. In the words of Yogi Berra, "It was like déjà vu all over again."

CONFIRMING THE DOPAMINE THEORY

In 1980 a young Lebanese American research fellow named Anissa Abi-Dargham arrived in Washington, DC, to work in the lab of Dan Weinberger, a researcher at the NIMH. She wanted to learn about the new brain imaging technologies. There she met another young researcher, a Belgian psychiatrist named Marc Laruelle. Abi-Dargham and Laruelle spent long hours together learning the nascent methodology of brain imaging as it applied to mental illness and, particularly, to schizophrenia—analyzing images and correlating findings with clinical features of the patients and postmortem tissue from laboratory brain specimens.

In 1989 Laruelle moved to Yale University Medical Center to work with Robert Innis, a talented psychiatrist who was pioneering the use of nuclear medicine techniques to measure neurotransmitter receptors in the brain. A year later, Abi-Dargham followed. Their professional relationship had become romantic, and in 1992 they married at the Yale chapel—becoming both a married couple and a dynamic scientific duo.

With Innis's help, they developed the idea of quantifying the amount of dopamine in the synapses of neurons by measuring changes in its binding to dopamine receptors under resting and activated conditions—that is, before and after subjects received a low dose of amphetamine. Laruelle and Abi-Dargham performed their investigations on schizophrenia patients using the single-photon emission computerized tomography (SPECT) system and a radiotracer called IBZM that binds to D-2 receptors. (A radiotracer is a sort of dye that is attracted to specific substances in the brain and emits a radioactive particle that the scanner detects and that a computer quantifies and assembles into colorized images.) To their delight and surprise, they found a massive difference between schizophrenia patients and healthy participants. If replicated, the finding could provide the critical piece of evidence to confirm the dopamine theory of schizophrenia.

In 1995 the couple was recruited to Columbia and the New York State Psychiatric Institute, where they were able to replicate their findings on excess dopamine release using a state-of-the-art PET scanner. PET scanning enables researchers to measure blood flow and chemical and metabolic activity in the brains of living patients. Along with their colleagues, Abi-Dargham and Laruelle would go on to show that patients experiencing acute psychotic symptoms during a first episode of schizophrenia and who had never received antipsychotic medications exhibited elevated brain dopamine. Moreover, the patients' dopamine levels were positively correlated with the severity of their hallucinations and delusions.

Other laboratories replicated their findings and proved that dopamine (over)stimulation of D-2 receptors gave rise to the psychotic symptoms of schizophrenia. Their results also indicated that the problem in regulating dopamine must be in the presynaptic neuron and necessarily involved synthesis, storage, release, or reabsorption of the neurotransmitter. It was the first *direct* evidence in support of the dopamine theory of schizophrenia. The theory was now confirmed.

POSITIVE TO NEGATIVE

While both Laruelle and Abi-Dargham contributed equally to this seminal research, as is often the case, the female's role on the team was undervalued. For Abi-Dargham, ensuing events would more than make up for this misperception, as she would go on to do important research in her own right and become a leader in the field of psychiatric neuroscience.

In keeping with the focus of schizophrenia research through the 1980s, Laruelle had concentrated on the psychotic symptoms of the illness, characterizing the overactivity of dopamine in the midbrain and limbic regions. But a seminal paper published in the early 1980s had put a new spin on the dopamine theory, showing a reciprocal but opposite relationship between the dopamine circuits projecting from the midbrain to the limbic region and those projecting from the midbrain to the frontal cortex. The work prompted an important revision to the dopamine theory, in which excess dopamine activity in the limbic region of the brain gave rise to psychotic symptoms, while too little dopamine stimulation of the frontal cortex could be the basis of negative symptoms and poor cognitive function.

At the same time, Abi-Dargham tackled the underexplored neurobiology of negative symptoms and cognitive impairment using a new PET radiotracer that labeled D-1 receptors. Her hypothesis was that since the frontal cortex was believed to be the site of higher mental functions and was predominantly activated by D-1 receptors (and only sparsely by D-2 receptors), there should be a deficit in dopamine stimulation of D-1 receptors in the frontal cortex. Much of this hypothesis stemmed from research done by the eminent neuroscientist Patricia Goldman-Rakic on the role of D-1 receptor mediation of working memory and other cognitive functions. Abi-Dargham had been influenced by Goldman-Rakic's work, and now she would carry out the clinical study that confirmed the role of the D-1 receptor and its importance as a target for drug development.

Abi-Dargham and Laruelle were still at Columbia in 2004 when I arrived as the newly appointed chair of Psychiatry. I was excited to work with this extraordinary research couple. Things quickly grew complicated, though, as they are wont to do in academia. In short, while Laruelle was a gifted scientist, he could be very difficult, and over time, alienated many of the people with whom he needed to work.

The hostile environment significantly impeded Laruelle and Abi-Dargham's research. Unfortunately, my interventions were too little, too late. Seeing the forces stacked against him, Laruelle accepted a prominent position with a major pharmaceutical company and departed Columbia. Unfortunately, their marriage also suffered during this tumultuous period. Apparently, the stress of the professional battles had placed a strain on their relationship, which eventually led to a decision to separate. Soon, an all too familiar scenario emerged. While both had contributed equally to their seminal body of research, the more gregarious and ostentatious Laruelle had sometimes overshadowed his more reserved wife and collaborator. Consequently, the question of how Abi-Dargham would fare on her own hovered over her. It didn't take long for Abi-Dargham to dispel any notions of her being the junior partner of the team. Her trajectory since has been gratifying to watch. She has developed an impressive body of work and earned an international reputation—reflected in her election as president of the American College of Neuropsychopharmacology in 2018 and to the National Academy of Medicine in 2020, the two most prestigious scientific organizations in the field of psychiatric neuroscience.

Sensitization

While Abi-Dargham and Laruelle were busy proving the dopamine theory, I had become fascinated by the question of what was actually happening in the brain when adolescents and young adults, who seemed to be functioning normally, would, often without warning or precipitating events, develop aberrations in their thoughts, behavior, and perception of reality—gradually becoming different people. And how, subsequently, recurrences and relapses eroded their intellectual capacity, often to the point that they eventually became shells of their former selves.

We had no explanation for why or how these changes occurred. The prevailing neurodevelopmental theory held that schizophrenia originates from disruptions in early brain development, when the circuitry that will support the adult brain is being established. These disruptions confer a vulnerability to subsequent stressors (such as traumatic life events or recreational drug use) that lead ultimately to the expression of schizophrenia symptoms. The strongest evidence for the neurodevelopmental hypothesis were studies implicating specific genes and/or environmental factors (examples include fetal exposure in the womb to infectious pathogens and the reactions of the maternal immune system; external toxins; nutritional deficiencies; and obstetric complications) that may increase the risk for schizophrenia.

While the neurodevelopmental theory was plausible and informative, in effect, it sentenced people with schizophrenia to a very bleak prognosis: regardless of treatment, they were "doomed from the womb," in a manner similar to children with genetic neurodevelopmental disorders such as autism, fragile X syndrome, and Down syndrome. But the defeatism the theory encouraged wasn't its only drawback; there were a number of aspects of schizophrenia that it didn't explain. While these other neurodevelopmental disorders were apparent at birth or in the early years of life, the symptoms of schizophrenia did not appear until the second or third decade. Moreover, the theory didn't account for schizophrenia's progressive course, patients' clinical deterioration, or the development of treatment resistance over successive episodes of the illness. Nor did it explain the variation among patients in the course of the illness or in their response to treatment.

The buzzword in brain science at the time was "plasticity"—such as we'd seen in the brain when the number of dopamine receptors fluctuated in response to changing levels of synaptic dopamine. The concept of plasticity was due in no small part to the work of my colleague at Columbia Eric Kandel. I had great admiration for him. In theory, as chair of the department, I was his boss, but the reality was the reverse. When colleagues from other departments asked how I got along with the Nobel laureate, I would say, "Great! Every Monday I go to his office and ask, 'Eric, what can I do for you this week?'" I used to call him the *other* psychiatrist from Vienna, because his family, like Freud's, had fled their home following Hitler's annexation of Austria.

Brain plasticity, or neuroplasticity, describes the brain's ability to change continuously over a person's lifetime through the formation or elimination, strengthening or weakening, of synapses in response to environmental or physiological stimulation. Kandel's research had shown how plasticity, in the form of what he called "sensitization," laid the cellular groundwork for memory formation—the discovery for which he would win the Nobel Prize in Medicine in 2000. Through the process of sensitization, the strength of a synapse is built up via repeated stimulation. When you memorize the words to a song or a speech or the digits of a phone number, you do so by strengthening the synapses, in much the same way a muscle is built up through exercise. This process induces a phenomenon called long-term potentiation, a persistent strengthening of synapses that produces a long-lasting increase in signal transmission between neurons and, by extension, circuits. (The opposite, a long-lasting decrease in synaptic strength called long-term depression, can also occur.) This modification of synaptic strength and the induction of long-term potentiation is widely considered one of the major cellular mechanisms underlying learning and memory.

While the ability of chemical synapses to change their strength is a specific form of synaptic plasticity, sensitization is a form of adaptive plasticity that enables cells to adjust to varying levels of stimulation in an effort to maintain equilibrium or build adaptive connections within their particular systems. However, depending on the nature and magnitude of the stimulus, plasticity could result in maladaptive consequences; it serves a useful purpose in learning and memory formation but is unhelpful in the case of drug abuse. People become addicted to opiates such as heroin, morphine, or oxycodone because repeated use of these drugs causes certain receptors in the brain to retreat into the cell membrane, becoming inaccessible to stimulation. The reduction in available receptors for the opiate to stimulate produces the condition of tolerance, in which a drug user needs progressively higher doses to achieve the same effect.

In reviewing the literature on stimulant-induced psychosis, I had come across another example of plasticity. Studies had demonstrated something called "behavioral sensitization," in which intermittent administration of stimulants produced progressively greater behavioral reaction with each successive drug exposure—that is, instead of the increased tolerance one saw in opiate addiction, stimulant users experienced increasing effects with lower doses. Moreover, once this sensitized condition developed, it could persist for a year or longer, even after the person had stopped using drugs.

Based on these studies, I speculated that sensitization might develop in patients predisposed to schizophrenia as a result of an excess release of dopamine. This excess, caused by a failure in neurotransmitter regulation, was mimicking what stimulants did when they released a surge of dopamine into the synapse, and the overstimulation resulted in the psychotic symptoms that signaled the onset of schizophrenia. Because dopamine neurons were clustered in the midbrain and projected their axons to limbic regions of the brain (involved in emotion, perception, and cognition), I focused on these structures specifically.

Many features of the course of schizophrenia bore a striking resemblance to the sensitization that took place with stimulants—including the marked contrast seen between patients at the onset of the illness and those in the chronic stages of it who had suffered multiple relapses over years or decades. New patients moved from normal behavior to active psychosis, but recovered with prompt treatment, and many saw their symptoms disappear. Chronic patients, on the other hand, were often disorganized and disconnected, their capacity to function impaired significantly, even when on medication. What happened between these stages was what Emil Kraepelin had called clinical deterioration. Though it was clear that the clinical picture of patients at advanced stages of schizophrenia resembled that of people who had been addicted to stimulants (as we saw in the Japanese methamphetamine epidemic), it still wasn't known what drove these changes in people with schizophrenia.

It was a seminal paper published by Richard Wyatt in 1991 that recognized the clues to this process. Wyatt came to the NIMH in 1967 as a research scientist and rose to become chief of the Neuropsychiatry Branch. His first assignment was studying sleep patterns, but his interest soon gravitated to schizophrenia. Over the next twenty years, Wyatt carried out an astonishing number of studies on the neurobiology and pharmacology of the disorder, while training a talented cadre of young scientists, but none of his findings resulted in major advances in the field. Then he decided to undertake a review of twenty-two studies in which similar groups of patients either received or did not receive antipsychotics in the early stages of their illnesses.

What Wyatt saw, refracted through the prism of those twenty-two studies, was that the earlier people were treated with antipsychotic medication after the onset of their psychotic symptoms, the more rapidly their symptoms remitted and the better the outcomes; the longer the duration of untreated psychosis, the poorer the patient's prognosis.

The results of the studies that Wyatt reviewed, and those of studies that would follow, cast a whole new light on the progressive nature of schizophrenia. The timing of treatment in first-episode patients was therefore a key factor in determining outcome. The findings also implied that active psychosis was bad for the brain. Psychosis, it seemed, reflected an underlying disease process that would advance unless alleviated by treatment. If this was true, it meant that preventing relapses and the development of treatment resistance was critical to improving long-term outcomes for patients by limiting the cumulative and progressive effects of active psychosis.

Over the course of his career, Wyatt published more than eight hundred papers in the scientific literature. But it was the 1991 paper on the duration of untreated psychosis that opened the door for other investigators and laid the groundwork for transformative research. It was his single greatest scientific contribution.

At the inaugural International Congress on Schizophrenia Research in April 1991, my colleagues and I presented data from our own study of first-episode schizophrenia that echoed Wyatt's paper: the duration of illness prior to treatment was associated with the likelihood and rapidity of remission. We concluded that acute psychotic symptoms could reflect an active morbid process, which, if not treated by antipsychotic drugs, might result in disease progression and worsening symptoms. This finding has since been replicated by countless other studies and echoed in review articles.

Interestingly, this clinical pattern seemed compatible with what we knew about the mechanism of sensitization: the longer and/or more frequently someone was acutely psychotic—with dopamine excessively stimulating dopamine receptors—the greater the degree of sensitization, meaning they were more susceptible to subsequent relapses and less responsive to treatment. Most importantly, it offered a glimmer of hope that countered the fatalistic prognoses of the neurodevelopmental theory.

How Does a Chemical Imbalance Cause a Delusion?

Applying the sensitization model to the study of dopamine allowed us to better understand dopamine's role in causing the symptoms and guiding the course of schizophrenia. Out of these insights, Shitij Kapur developed the model of "salience," which has become an influential tool for understanding how dopamine activity is related to hallucinations and delusions.

Kapur has long been one of the most popular members of the research community. With an imposing presence, often clad in tailored Nehru jackets, he's much sought after as a conference speaker because of his eloquence, wit, and imaginative way of explaining scientific concepts. Kapur was a professor of psychiatry at the University of Toronto when he published a paper about schizophrenia that attempted to provide a basis for uniting four aspects of the illness: the patient's internal experience, the clinical or behavioral presentation, the neurobiological theories, and the pharmacological interventions. In developing his salience model, Kapur was seeking a framework that would enable a psychiatrist to formulate an answer when a patient asked, "Doctor, how does my chemical imbalance cause my delusions?"

Salience refers to the process by which environmental stimuli and our thoughts combine to direct our attention and drive our motivation and behavior. The attribution of salience, in effect, assigns meaning to our perceptions and experiences. Dopamine plays a central role in this process, essentially managing the conversion of the neural representation of an external stimulus from a neutral piece of information into something attractive or aversive, meaningful or insignificant. Under normal circumstances, the release of dopamine is triggered by stimuli, and the attribution of salience is driven by context. In psychosis, however, excessive dopamine is released in response to, or even independent of, stimuli; the normal process of salience attribution is usurped, leading to aberrant assignment of salience to both external events and internal representations. Instead of mediating contextually relevant saliences, dopamine becomes, in the psychotic state, a creator of (aberrant) saliences.

For instance, suppose you're in a restaurant with friends. Your attention will be mainly focused on them, on the conversation, and on the food you're eating. You'll be aware of the ambience, décor, aromas, the waitstaff, and other diners, but—unless a waiter drops a tray, or another table launches into "Happy Birthday"—not to the extent that the surrounding environment distracts your attention from your own group. What's happening at your table is the stimuli to which you're attaching salience.

However, if you have schizophrenia, stimuli that wouldn't normally seem relevant or warrant salience are assigned importance. Conversation overheard from an adjacent table is interpreted as being about you. When you glance around the restaurant, you think that anyone who happens to glance back is watching you. The waiter serves your dessert last, and you think this is done to disparage you.

This aberrant attribution of salience is what gives rise to delusions and hallucinations. An inaccurately perceived premise leads to a false conclusion. Once this "explanation" is arrived at, things appear to fall into place; the explanation then serves as a guide for future thoughts and actions, driving the person to find additional confirmatory evidence in the comments of strangers, a message on a billboard, a news item relayed by a television announcer, and so on.

Delusions are essentially disorders of inferential logic. They begin as reasonable ideas (the government intrudes on individual privacy) that become overvalued and then turn into obsessions, progressing to questionable beliefs (the CIA or FBI might be monitoring me), and then to fixed beliefs for which there is no evidence (the government has spies and cameras watching me). In their extreme forms, these false beliefs can be so imbued with conviction that they drive behavior: I must flee my home to escape the surveillance and not tell anyone where I'm going.

Hallucinations, on the other hand, reflect a fabricated perception of sensory stimuli. Mild forms of sensory distortion occur as illusions, so that an actually occurring sound is perceived as something other than it really is, such as a vaguely perceived voice heard as someone calling your name. Fully formed hallucinations are when sounds, sights, smells, and so on are generated internally but are experienced as if they come from the external environment. Hallucinations are a direct experience of the aberrant salience of internal representations.

The aberrant salience caused by dopamine dysregulation doesn't happen overnight but is kindled like sparks that precede a flame. It helps to explain what so many patients describe experiencing during the prodromal stage of schizophrenia: perceptual abnormalities and heightened awareness or intensified emotions. Before having full-blown hallucinations or delusions, patients often report that their senses feel sharpened; sights and sounds are keener than ever before. Small things can acquire an overwhelming significance. The brain can feel more "awake" than it ever has.

CANNABIS AND PSYCHOSIS

For those of us who were part of the cannabis-fueled counterculture of the 1960s and 1970s, as well as for younger generations who've been the unwitting subjects in the recent social experiment of legalized marijuana, reading about Kapur's theory of salience may trigger some vaguely uncomfortable memories. I'm talking about the paranoid and self-referential feelings that many pot smokers experience when high.

Initially, that experience was regarded as simply an incidental effect of an otherwise benign recreational drug, much like the hangover that follows a night's drinking, or the feeling of being wired after too much coffee. Popular culture even made comedy out of it—think Cheech & Chong.

But from the late 1980s through the 2000s, data emerged from epidemiologic studies linking cannabis use to risk for developing psychoses, including schizophrenia. The first of these, which kick-started interest in the topic, was a longitudinal study from Sweden based on a registry of 45,570 men drafted for military service between 1969 and 1970. At that time, cannabis was used widely in Sweden, and a researcher named Sven Andréasson had heard reports from psychiatrists who were concerned about their patients with psychosis using cannabis; these doctors were noticing that their patients were returning to the hospital after being discharged. I would infer from this that the deterioration referred to in the paper resulted from the men continuing to smoke marijuana.

The conscription registry showed that 9.4 percent of the men reported using cannabis before entering the military. The researchers followed the men for the next fifteen years, until 1983, and found that the relative risk of developing schizophrenia was linked directly to the use of cannabis: as cannabis use increased, so did the risk of developing schizophrenia. Among those who had used cannabis at least once, the risk relative to nonusers was found to be more than double, while those who had used it more than fifty times had a risk six times that of nonusers. Based on these findings, the authors concluded that cannabis use could trigger psychosis in people with preexisting vulnerabilities to psychotic disorders.

Around the same time, experiments to examine the effects of cannabis on the brain were being conducted in rodents. Scientists isolated tetrahydrocannabinol (THC) as the psychoactive ingredient in cannabis producing intoxication and found that it acted through a class of cannabinoid receptors on neurons. Moreover, they identified naturally occurring neurochemicals in the brain (anandamide and arachidonoylglycerol) that mimic the action of cannabis ingredients and bind to the same cannabinoid receptors that THC does. These endocannabinoids serve as mediators in neuronal communication in a way that is distinct in range and function from neurotransmitters. Endocannabinoid transmission is more indirect and works by regulating the release of several neurotransmitters, including dopamine, and fine-tuning activity and plasticity in certain brain regions.

These findings complemented the dopamine theory of schizophrenia and prompted two psychologists to investigate further the link between cannabis and psychosis.

Avshalom Caspi and Terrie Moffitt are an unlikely couple. Caspi was born in Israel, raised on a kibbutz, and named for the talented but rebellious son of the biblical King David. Moffitt grew up on a farm in the Bible Belt of North Carolina. They met as postdoctoral fellows while attending a conference in Saint Louis. In one of the more memorable lines in the annals of academic romance, Caspi commented, upon seeing Moffitt's presentation, "You have the most beautiful data set." Thus began a decades-long personal and scientific love affair.

The stock-in-trade of this scientific duo was studying the psychologic features of people in large data sets. Seeing an opportunity to follow up on the emerging findings about cannabis, they approached Richie Poulton, the lead investigator on the Dunedin Study, about potential collaboration. The Dunedin Study is a longitudinal study that has tracked the health, development, and well-being of around a thousand people born in 1972 or 1973 in Dunedin, New Zealand. Every few years, a team of researchers conducts intensive cognitive, psychological, and health assessments, interviewing every participant as well as his or her families and friends.

The Dunedin Study is regarded as one of the world's richest sources of information about cannabis use. Approximately 80 percent of New Zealanders born in the 1970s reported using cannabis at least once, and enough reported using it with sufficient frequency over a long enough period to give a picture of the adverse effects of regular, sustained use. The Dunedin Study results have mirrored those of the Swedish Conscript study: for those who began using cannabis when young, the risk of developing a psychotic disorder by age twenty-six was approximately double that of nonusers. Between 5 percent and 10 percent of users were found to be at elevated risk because they had used cannabis on more days than not; had become dependent on cannabis; or had begun using it during mid-adolescence and continued well into adulthood. The increased risk for frequent users who begin using cannabis in early adolescence may be due to the fact that when the brain is still developing, it is most vulnerable to the harmful effects of cannabis. The results of the Swedish and New Zealand studies have been replicated in studies in Australia, Germany, the Netherlands, and the United Kingdom.

What the studies also made clear, however, was that the vast majority of young cannabis users were not developing psychotic symptoms or schizophrenia; this implied that some people might be genetically vulnerable to the drug's effects.

The Dunedin Study was beginning its fourth decade when Caspi and Moffitt contacted Poulton. Their hope was to leverage this population study to gather data on what demographic, clinical, and genetic factors were associated with the development of mental disorders, including schizophrenia. Because of the dopamine-stimulating effect of THC in cannabis, they were particularly interested in the catechol-O-methyl transferase (COMT) gene, which plays a critical role in metabolizing dopamine in the brain. Caspi and Moffitt hypothesized that the COMT gene would be a source of the selective vulnerability to psychosis among cannabis users. They had three reasons for this theory. First, the gene is located on chromosome 22q11, a region implicated in genome scans of schizophrenia. Second, a third of individuals with a microdeletion on 22q11, which causes velocardiofacial syndrome, also known as DiGeorge syndrome, develop symptoms of schizophrenia. And third, disturbances in dopamine function had been implicated in schizophrenia, so it was natural to look to a gene involved in dopamine's regulation.

Caspi and Moffitt's team genotyped 953 people from the Dunedin Study to try to determine why cannabis use was associated with the emergence of psychosis in a minority of users. What they found was that people with a particular variant of the COMT gene were more likely to develop psychotic symptoms if they used cannabis. This finding—that a gene involved in dopamine regulation affected people's responsiveness to cannabis—lent further weight to dopamine's role in schizophrenia. More broadly, the findings offered evidence of a gene/environment interaction and suggested that some susceptibility genes could influence vulnerability to environmental pathogens.

Subsequent studies have replicated the link between cannabis use and psychosis and the existence of selective genetic vulnerability. Certain people are more susceptible to the deleterious effects of cannabis use, but it is a genetic risk in the aggregate (rather than a single gene like COMT) that confers susceptibility to cannabis-induced psychosis.

We now have overwhelming evidence from numerous studies that cannabis increases the risk of developing schizophrenia. We also know that the greater the concentration of THC, the higher the high, the more potentially dangerous the drug. Depending on the frequency of use and the THC concentration, cannabis can produce psychotic symptoms in healthy people, including delusions, hallucinations, and cognitive impairment, all of which resemble schizophrenia. Cannabis can also exacerbate psychotic symptoms in schizophrenia patients, contribute to poor outcomes, increase the possibility of relapse, and decrease the effectiveness of antipsychotic drugs. The use of cannabis may also precipitate the onset of schizophrenia in individuals susceptible to psychosis.

In light of what's been learned about the endocannabinoid system and the actions of THC, it is believed that overactivity in this system caused by cannabis may lead to increased dopamine activity, which causes psychotic symptoms and can trigger the onset of schizophrenia. It is thought that cannabis use can cause changes in neurotransmitter functioning that, in susceptible people, may become permanent and lead to longer-term tendencies to developing a psychotic illness. The logical conclusion to draw, given the increasing availability and use of cannabis, along with its increased potency, is that rates of psychotic symptoms and schizophrenia will rise. Measuring the impact of cannabis use on rates of schizophrenia will take time if we're to assess anything more than acute symptomatology. A recent meta-analysis (a method to systematically merge data sets from single independent studies using statistical methods that can calculate a cumulative effect in a nonadditive fashion) of age at onset revealed that cannabis users had their first symptoms 2.7 years earlier than non–cannabis users.

In the meantime, in the absence of more complete scientific information, and with the potency of cannabis-based products rising, we're performing a social experiment that may have particularly serious consequences for young people. While advocates of legalization tend to underplay the risks of cannabis, conservatives exaggerate them. The fact is that the majority of people who use cannabis will not develop psychosis as a result. But any discussion about legalization that doesn't acknowledge an elevated risk for a minority of users is at best ill-informed and at worst dishonest.

So, Is It Schizophrenia?

In 2018, ten years after I'd first met Sean, the patient I'd diagnosed with stimulant-induced psychosis—a diagnosis his mother had wanted to believe gave her son a much better chance at recovery than schizophrenia—I received a call from her. I'd heard virtually nothing from the family in the decade since treating Sean, but it seemed that his parents, instead of following our recommendations when we'd revised his diagnosis and adjusted his treatment, had (understandably) acceded to his wishes and allowed him to investigate alternative forms of care, doctor shopping and dipping into everything from holistic remedies to wilderness programs. They'd spent vast sums of money to no avail. Sean, meanwhile, had continued to use stimulants surreptitiously and to take his prescribed medications erratically or not at all. Now he was in jail for forging prescriptions for stimulants and other drugs.

His parents were exhausted. I tried to suppress my own exasperation. There was no guarantee that Sean would have fared better had he continued in treatment with us, but I had firmly believed our treatment plan represented his best chance.

I helped his parents secure Sean's release from jail, and they brought him to our emergency room. When he refused to be admitted to the hospital voluntarily, he was civilly committed. The next day I met with him and his parents on the unit to discuss why he'd landed back in the hospital and what our next steps should be. But Sean had no interest in talking about anything other than leaving the hospital. He alternated between irate demands and pleading for my understanding. As to what he might do if released, he had an array of fantasies, such as moving in with an old girlfriend he hadn't seen in years and starting a new business for which he'd need a $100,000 loan from his mother. When I suggested that his plans didn't sound realistic, he became enraged and stormed out of the room. His parents were stunned.

It was obvious to me that Sean was not just symptomatic and mentally unstable, but that his brain was damaged. He was incapable of understanding our discussion or thinking rationally. His speech was disjointed, illogical, and at times incoherent. His mental state resembled the case descriptions of methamphetamine addicts in Japan after the war that I had read about in various studies. It was clear that the recommended care plan for Sean would have to be revised. He needed to enter a residential program for people with intellectual disabilities or mental illnesses that rendered them incapable of functioning independently. I told his parents that he might never be able to live on his own again. Whether in time he could recover his functioning to some degree wasn't clear, but for now, he needed a structured environment, supervision, and cognitive rehabilitation.

Sean was discharged to a rural residential program in North Carolina. As of now, he has not improved, much less recovered. His brain has likely sustained sufficient injury that is not amenable to rehabilitation and recovery. I fear the damage is permanent.

To return to the original question posed at the beginning of the chapter: Does Sean have schizophrenia? For decades, those in my profession, including me, had held that drugs cannot cause schizophrenia; they can only trigger an existing vulnerability. But what we've learned about dopamine, stimulant drugs, and cannabis—both through observing the effects of drug abuse and through controlled experiments—is that it's possible to induce a state of psychosis in healthy persons, and that chronic exposure to high doses of certain drugs can cause recurrent episodes or a persistent state of psychosis that simulates schizophrenia.

With time, we're learning more about the possible causal pathways of schizophrenia. Dysregulation of dopamine is one such route, maybe even a final common pathway by which all causes of schizophrenia express the disorder's symptoms. But dopamine doesn't account for everything. We know there must be other factors contributing to the cause and course of schizophrenia. It could be that the dopaminergic disturbance is an abnormality associated with the psychotic symptoms of schizophrenia but not the disease's fundamental cause or source. Dopamine may be, as Laruelle and Abi-Dargham have written, "the wind of the psychotic fire."

Chapter 15

Glutamate and GABA: The Accelerator and the Brake

Our real discoveries come from chaos, from going to
the place that looks wrong.

—Chuck Palahniuk, *Invisible Monsters*

The Devil's Dust

The dopamine hypothesis of schizophrenia had given us our first insight into the pathophysiology of the illness and highlighted the role of neurotransmitters. We had plausible models of dopamine that suggested how its dysfunction might lead to observable symptoms, offering an explanation at both neurobiological and clinical levels.

But there were aspects of schizophrenia for which dopamine was unable to account. Many patients didn't respond to the antipsychotic drugs that targeted the dopamine system. In addition, it was unclear how dopamine disturbances produced negative and cognitive symptoms, which for many people had debilitating effects on their daily lives comparable to hallucinations and delusions. While dopamine was clearly a contributor to schizophrenia, it was not plausible as the source. There had to be more than dopamine involved.

The suspected co-conspirator turned out to be the neurotransmitter glutamate. The discovery of its relevance to schizophrenia came about in the same way as dopamine: through serendipity, courtesy of a drug whose effects bore a remarkable resemblance to schizophrenia.

In the late 1970s an accidental and frightening "experiment" began to unfold that would afford us new insights into the illness. Anyone working in an emergency room in a large US city at that time remembers, with a shudder, patients who were "dusted." Dusters were high on angel dust, a street name for PCP, or phencyclidine. PCP had debuted as a street drug in the late 1960s. Although its powerful effects could be unpleasant or even lethal, use of the drug increased because of its availability and low price relative to other street drugs. Users were disconnected from reality and had bizarre thoughts, delusions, and hallucinations. But what was most frightening about them was their frenzied agitation, which could quickly turn to aggression. Because people on PCP often seemed to have inexhaustible energy and superhuman strength, they frequently had to be physically restrained and medicated before they could even be approached, let alone evaluated.

The PCP epidemic was well under way as I approached the end of my training in 1980. Initially, doctors in New York and elsewhere mistook PCP psychosis for schizophrenia and actually thought they were seeing an inexplicable increase in the incidence of the illness. In Washington, DC, admission rates for what appeared to be unusually severe and treatment-resistant schizophrenic psychoses suddenly tripled in emergency rooms and at community mental health centers. The patients had all used PCP prior to developing psychosis, and their clinical presentation seemed indistinguishable from a florid schizophrenic episode.

Unlike amphetamine psychosis, which was possible to treat with antipsychotic drugs, there was no antidote for PCP. All we could do was sedate someone and wait for the drug's effects to wear off. Some effects of phencyclidine, however, could persist for weeks or even months after it was eliminated from the body. To first responders and health care providers that had to deal with PCP's victims, it seemed like the devil's own drug.

MODELING PSYCHOSIS

For all the havoc it has wreaked, PCP's origins were innocent enough. Though synthesized in 1926, the drug was not developed until the 1950s, when the Parke-Davis Pharmaceutical Company in Detroit decided that it might be a promising surgical anesthetic. The company obtained FDA approval in 1957 and marketed it under the trade name Sernyl. Among those involved in the early studies was Edward Domino, a young professor of pharmacology at the University of Michigan who would become a pioneer in explorations into PCP and schizophrenia.

Domino joined a group of researchers at Detroit's Lafayette Clinic who were investigating schizophrenia as a brain disorder and had heard from Parke-Davis pharmacologists of PCP's psychosis-inducing effects. The Lafayette Clinic researchers had been trying to model psychosis using sensory isolation, sleep deprivation, and mind-altering drugs, including psychedelics, and were eager to test PCP. In their first study, they administered PCP to three groups of subjects: psychiatric residents, medical students, and schizophrenia patients, comparing their responses to a control group that received LSD or amobarbital, a sedative. The LSD subjects experienced altered mental states, including hallucinations, while the amobarbital subjects fell asleep after a brief period of garrulousness and giddiness. In contrast, PCP caused schizophrenia-like changes in mental states (perceptual distortions and cognitive deficits) in the residents and students; in the patients, a much more severe reaction was seen, with disorganized and bizarre thoughts and regressive behaviors that simulated the acute phase of their illness. PCP induced schizophrenia-like symptoms in healthy persons and greatly exacerbated the symptoms of schizophrenia patients.

The researchers also noticed something interesting about the way the patients responded to sensory input: they tolerated sensory isolation better than those without the illness. Perhaps, they reasoned, both PCP psychosis and schizophrenic psychosis produced a disturbance in the brain's capacity to filter and interpret normal sensory input—that is, a disruption in the *processing* of sensory information rather than in perception itself. If this was true, it could explain why many people with schizophrenia withdrew from the complex and dynamic flux of the everyday sensory environment: to compensate for an overwhelmed or distorted interpretative system.

The Lafayette Clinic investigators had seen firsthand that PCP heightened schizophrenic symptoms, and they'd concluded that the drug affected some fundamental aspect of the disorder, but they didn't know how or why these things happened. Perhaps PCP was producing a disruption that, in schizophrenia, existed already. However, it was still impossible to say, as PCP's pharmacology, or mode of action, wasn't understood yet, particularly its effect on neurotransmitters. But even before neuroscience caught up with their observations, the work in Detroit would prove useful. The group's finding that sensory isolation reduced PCP psychoses helped to shift the approach to treatment for schizophrenia in the 1960s; no longer was it considered helpful to subject patients to "total push" therapy, bombarding them with a series of different therapies, each of which involved some form of sensory stimulation. As Domino would write later, "We had come to respect withdrawal as the patient's only way of modulating intolerable sensory input."

By 1965, numerous cases of serious adverse side effects from phencyclidine—including anxiety, delirium, and postoperative psychosis—had led to the drug's withdrawal from the market and reclassification as a controlled substance. PCP research in humans was prohibited and its use restricted to veterinary purposes as an animal tranquilizer. But the work done by Domino and others would become a point of reference for doctors and researchers in the coming years as they tried to understand what was happening in America's inner-city hospitals. When the PCP epidemic was in full swing, Domino and his colleagues would express astonishment at PCP's reincarnation as a recreational drug: few of their volunteer subjects had been willing to take it a second time. As the *New York Times* would report, even in the 1970s PCP was known for "its extremely poor ratio of potential fun to potential risk."

Fortunately, Parke-Davis hadn't bet everything on phencyclidine, and when it failed as a safe anesthetic, company researchers focused on a less potent and shorter-acting derivative: ketamine. When Parke-Davis needed an academic partner to conduct research with, it turned again to Domino. Instead of going back to the Lafayette Clinic as a study site, Domino approached Jackson State Prison in Michigan. A human ethics committee composed of members from the University of Michigan, Parke-Davis, and the Upjohn Pharmaceutical Company was formed, which devised a detailed protocol for conducting clinical trials on prison volunteers under ketamine anesthesia.

This was necessary for two reasons. First, because prisoners were clearly a "vulnerable population" who could be subjected to research involuntarily or, because of their circumstances, coerced into participating in studies. Second, at the time of this research (the 1950s and 1960s), institutional review boards (IRBs) had not yet been formally established as mechanisms for ensuring the ethical nature of research involving human subjects and protecting their safety. This did not occur until 1974, when the National Commission for the Protection of Human Subjects of Biomedical and Behavioral Research was created as part of the National Research Act. This legislation required that all institutions conducting medical research on human subjects form an IRB to review and approve all studies to ensure their ethical nature and protection of the participants. Three foundational principles derived from the Belmont Report govern IRBs:

- Respect for persons. This principle includes both respect for the autonomy of human subjects and the importance of protecting vulnerable individuals.

- Beneficence. The duty of beneficence requires that research maximize the benefit-to-harm ratio for individual subjects and for the research program as a whole.
- Justice. Justice in research focuses on the duty to assign the burden and benefits of research fairly.

The National Research Act followed previous initiatives to establish a philosophical and legal framework for the conduct of ethical medical research—including the Nuremberg Code, which emerged from the Nuremberg Trials of Nazi war crimes following World War II, and the Declaration of Helsinki policy statement by the World Medical Association, first articulated in 1964 and amended seven times subsequently.

These actions to establish an ethical and protective framework for human subjects research was badly needed and long overdue given the extensive history of exploitative research on vulnerable people in the United States, such as the Willowbrook study of hepatitis transmission in a hospital for children impaired by developmental disabilities and the USPHS syphilis study at Tuskegee, in which hundreds of impoverished black men were intentionally left untreated for syphilis. The challenge for Domino and his colleagues was how to conduct this study ethically on prisoners at the Jackson State Penitentiary. They did so by establishing an ad hoc review process meant to protect the health and rights of the prisoner volunteers and ensured that the participation of subjects was voluntary.

Domino's study commenced in 1964 and led to successful results. An anesthetic dose of ketamine didn't depress breathing or blood pressure and was significantly safer than ether and other general anesthetics then in use. The main side effect was that subjects had residual sensory dissociation that was similar but milder than that caused by PCP. (Drugs such as diazepam, better known by its brand name, Valium, were found later to reduce the "emergence delirium" of ketamine.) In 1970 ketamine was approved by the FDA and sold by Parke-Davis under the trade name Ketalar. Although it did become famous as a club drug in the 1980s under the street name Special K, ketamine has had a much more salubrious history than PCP. It has been used widely as an anesthetic in hospitals for children, burn victims, and soldiers wounded in combat; recently a form of ketamine was approved for treatment-resistant depression.

I had my own ketamine experience in 1979, when I was chief resident at St. Vincent's Hospital. After my undergraduate years, I'd had little time or inclination during medical school and residency for dabbling in drugs. But on one occasion, I had a most unusual experience. At the invitation of a rather free-spirited and unconventional pastor whom I had met at a conference on alternative and complementary medicine—non-mainstream medical practices using naturopathic, neutraceutical, and nutritional treatments—I journeyed to a large Victorian residence in northern Westchester County that served as a site in an underground network for practitioners of the psychedelic arts. As a psychiatrist interested in psychopharmacology, I worked to keep abreast of new drug development in the medical field and by the lay public. In terms of the latter, following the legal prohibition of psychedelics in 1970, an underground network of self-styled practitioners of psychedelic therapies had emerged. Their rationale was that these drugs, which had been used by indigenous cultures ritualistically for centuries, were beneficial, even therapeutic, and therefore should continue to be administered, albeit surreptitiously. My experience was presided over by a renowned physician from Mexico who practiced in the *curandero* tradition, meaning that he acted more as a cultural healer than a medical doctor, and had developed a unique method of inducing altered states of consciousness.

I'd been instructed to fast (except for water) for eight hours prior to the event, wear loose clothes, and bring a tape of soft music, a cassette recorder, headphones, and five photos of meaningful people or events in my life. Along with seven others, I was to be guided through a night of psychic exploration and mind expansion under, ostensibly, controlled conditions by a skilled practitioner who happened to be a physician.

For the first six hours, I lay on a mattress, blindfolded, wearing headphones, plugged into my music, tripping on psilocybin. Events from my life paraded before my mind's eye in kaleidoscopic fashion. Some iterations were newsreel-like images; others played out like caricatures, as the images of people I knew said or did strange and funny things. There were no vivid colors, or beautiful images, or marvelous objects. Nor was there anything overly bizarre or any epiphanic insights. Just my mind stewing in its own juices.

Then the doctor injected me with ketamine, and, almost immediately, I was catapulted into a whole new state of consciousness, like my mind was shot out of a cannon. My sense of self felt shattered, in free fall, while my sensory perceptions were suddenly distorted. I lost perception of time and had no idea how many minutes or hours had passed when I felt a tap on my shoulder and was brought gently back to the here and now.

Still blindfolded I was led outside and seated at a picnic table. The fresh cool air and smell of the outdoors were bracing. As my blindfold was removed, I winced at the bright morning light and glimpsed the verdant, spacious backyard. My guide asked if I was ready. Instinctively, without knowing what I was agreeing to, I said, "Yes." He then slowly, deliberately placed in front of me on the table, one by one, the five photos I had brought with me. Throughout the night, even as the intensity, the strangeness of it all, had waxed and waned, I'd kept my composure and not uttered a word. But on seeing the photos (a mix of family members, living and dead, and past events), a surge of emotion suddenly welled up in me, and I burst into tears. For several minutes, I sobbed uncontrollably. It wasn't that the photos themselves were sad; they simply acted as a trigger that unleashed a torrent of pent-up emotions. When my sobbing finally subsided, a single thought crystalized in my mind: *How did we get so far away from these feelings?*

The question still strikes me as the perfect summation of my mental state. I had somehow been returned by the night's experience to a primordial and more innocent condition, and had felt a fleeting affinity with the world and sympathy with all that it contained. But upon surfacing, I realized immediately that this was a state from which we had all become alienated.

As with my experience of trying LSD in college, my nightlong voyage had reminded me of how a tiny amount of a chemical substance could so completely disrupt my normal state of mind. But I did not connect the trip with the psychoses of my patients until 1991, when I read of new research on schizophrenia and PCP, ketamine's forerunner. The knowledge that was then emerging about the disease and the drug allowed me to appreciate that the experience I'd had— the pervasive sense of dislocation, the sensory distortion, the dissolution of self, and the dysphoric emotional effects these engendered—might share certain elements with the psychoses my patients suffered. It was the beginning of an exciting new era in our understanding of schizophrenia.

ENTER GLUTAMATE

The saying "Success has many parents, while failure is an orphan" certainly applies to scientific discoveries. Numerous researchers can rightfully claim to have had input into the glutamate theory of schizophrenia, but if it began anywhere, beyond Domino and the Lafayette Clinic, it was in Solomon Snyder's laboratory at Johns Hopkins, the same place that had been a contributing source of the dopamine hypothesis. Snyder was focused on identifying receptors in the brain, protein structures on the membrane surfaces of neurons to which neurotransmitters and drugs attached themselves to modulate neurotransmission. Snyder's research on the neurobiology of mental illness and the development of psychotropic drugs was taking place just as American psychiatry was awakening from its decades-long enchantment with Freud and psychoanalytic theory. In 1980 Snyder founded one of the first departments of neuroscience in the country, where he oversaw the work of a cadre of talented protégés who studied the effects of the key neurotransmitters, glutamate and GABA, alongside PCP's mechanism of action. These researchers share much of the credit for the glutamate theory.

Glutamate hadn't previously been on the radar of schizophrenia researchers. It was considered relevant to stroke and epilepsy, but the focus of schizophrenia pathology had been on dopamine and serotonin. In fact, until the late 1970s, there was disagreement over whether glutamate was even a neurotransmitter. But as the field of neuroscience advanced, we learned that glutamate is not only a neurotransmitter but the most abundant excitatory neurotransmitter in our nervous system. (As the name suggests, "excitatory" neurotransmitters increase the likelihood that a neuron will send information.)

Most of the brain's eight key neurotransmitters (we have now identified more than forty in total) are localized, their functions limited to specific purposes. Dopamine cells are concentrated in the midbrain and regulate movement, motivation, reward, and, through the hypothalamus and pituitary, endocrine activity (a system of glands that secrete hormones as distinct from neurotransmitters). Cells that secrete serotonin are clustered in the brain stem and mediate appetite, sleep, and emotion. Norepinephrine cells, also found in brain stem structures, govern arousal and vigilance. But glutamate and GABA are all over the brain. Glutamate is so ubiquitous that it can potentially be involved in every brain function, from temperature regulation, to learning and memory formation, to body movement. GABA, which is similarly widespread, decreases the likelihood that a neuron will send information. Both neurotransmitters are amino acids, and it was logical to study them in relation to schizophrenia because of their global distribution in the brain and because they act as the opposing forces of excitation and inhibition.

The first time glutamate and schizophrenia were linked was in an Austrian study published in 1980, which showed that glutamate levels in the cerebrospinal fluid of schizophrenia patients were about half the normal amount, suggesting a possible dysfunction or degeneration of glutamatergic neurons in schizophrenia. But it was only when the PCP epidemic grabbed the attention of Dr. Snyder and others in the medical field, and their investigations into the drug's psychosis-mimicking effects converged with research on neurotransmitters, that the stage was set for the formulation of the glutamate theory.

Glutamate acts through more than a dozen receptors, differentiated by their physical structures. In order to better understand the mechanisms of action related to these receptors, Snyder assigned each of the trainees in his lab to study a different part of the glutamate system. The task of determining how PCP induced its psychosis-mimicking effects—trying to identify its binding site—was given to Steve Zukin, a medical student heading into psychiatry, and one of the youngest and least experienced of Snyder's coterie. This was ironic, as it was PCP that would turn out to be the most important line of inquiry. Zukin had not completed the project when he left Hopkins two years later and didn't resume work on it until he joined the faculty of the Downstate University of New York. His wife, Suzanne, was a faculty member in the Albert Einstein College of Medicine biochemistry department. Together the Zukins would continue the investigations begun at Johns Hopkins and ultimately arrive at a critical finding: that PCP blocked the N-methyl-D-aspartate (NMDA) receptor (a multifaceted ion channel complex stimulated by glutamate) by binding to a previously unknown site within the receptor that could recognize PCP and thus prevent the NMDA receptor from being activated. In other words, PCP is an NMDA receptor antagonist: it attenuates, or blocks, the action normally provoked by glutamate. It's like a key in a lock preventing the insertion of other keys, and thus affecting the normal transmission of chemical signals between nerve cells and other organs.

Glutamate's actions in the brain facilitate myriad functions, including complex planning, decision-making, predicting consequences of our actions, and anticipating events. Because of its critical role, glutamate activity is controlled carefully through various mechanisms that modulate neurotransmission. Its functions are mediated largely through the NMDA receptor, the same receptor the Zukins showed was blocked by PCP, and the one that would prove to be of greatest relevance to schizophrenia. The NMDA receptor has binding sites that can facilitate or inhibit activity, so that glutamate concentrations are modified subtly. These multiple mechanisms create a nuanced and redundant system regulating NMDA receptor stimulation and glutamate neurotransmission.

What makes glutamate important enough to warrant such a complex system? For one thing, there is little room for error in the functions it serves—most significantly, its unique responsibility for learning and memory. (Glutamate's repeated stimulation of NMDA receptors enables learning not just through inducing long-term potentiation—the means by which synaptic connections between neurons become stronger with frequent activation—but also by fostering neuroplasticity, when cells sprout new branches and make additional synaptic connections, thus strengthening circuits and neural pathways.) The second reason is that concentrations of glutamate must be maintained within a very narrow range. Too little, and functions fail to occur or are incompletely performed; too much causes damage to neurons in which glutamate comes into contact (a process called excitatory neurotoxicity). In this sense, glutamate is like the porridge in *Goldilocks and the Three Bears*, which must be not too hot, not too cold, but just right.

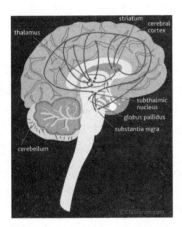 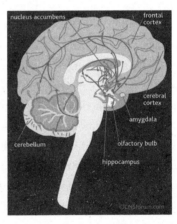

The image on the left shows the neuronal pathways of glutamate, the primary excitatory neurotransmitter, which are widely distributed in the brain. The image on the right shows the neuronal pathways of GABA-releasing neurons, which are also broadly distributed. GABA works to inhibit the activity of other neurotransmitters, particularly glutamate.

To ensure this precise trafficking of this all-important neurotransmitter, the glutamate synapses contain more regulatory mechanisms than other neurotransmitters (like dopamine, serotonin, norepinephrine). In addition to the numerous binding sites that can modulate the responsivity of the receptor to stimulation by glutamate, the synapse is bounded by an astrocyte (a glial cell that supports the functions of neurons) and an interneuron. The astrocyte absorbs glutamate from the synapse and metabolically inactivates it before returning the neurotransmitter to the presynaptic neuron for reuse. An interneuron that emits GABA as a neurotransmitter with inhibitory effects is also adjacent to the glutamate-releasing neurons and acts as a regulator of GABA activity.

The Birth of the Glutamate Theory

In the 1980s our knowledge of the distribution and functions of amino acid neu-rotransmitters such as glutamate was expanding. But research was in need of a good, strong push. In the mid-1980s a psychiatrist named Daniel Javitt started to look closely at PCP psychosis. Javitt was doing his residency at Albert Einstein College of Medicine when PCP was one of the most abused drugs in the country, and he saw a lot of "dusted" patients in his rotations at the Bronx Municipal Hospital Center. Doctors were still often unable to distinguish at first sight whether people showing up in emergency rooms and psych wards had schizophrenia or were high on PCP. Sometimes patients could report that they'd taken it, but often they didn't know—people unwittingly smoked PCP-laced joints—and it was only when they emerged from the psychosis and their histories were taken that doctors could learn more and check their blood for PCP.

Javitt wasn't intending to become a psychiatrist. His interest was in neuroscience. And the hardcore neuroscientists were an entirely different group compared to the doctors interested in possible parallels between PCP abuse and schizophrenia. He didn't even know much about schizophrenia at the time, but he knew that in PCP's effects, which mimicked the illness, he was witnessing something unique that could potentially illuminate the workings of the brain.

Steve and Suzanne Zukin's work with PCP had awakened Javitt's interest in PCP studies. The Zukins' findings had been crucial, but PCP is a "dirty" drug—meaning that it acts on many systems within the brain. Knowing that PCP acted on the NMDA receptor wasn't the same as being able to say that what happened at that particular receptor site was responsible for the drug's schizophrenia-like effects. Javitt, working with Steve Zukin—a medical doctor, and so assigned as his preceptor rather than Suzanne, who was a neuroscientist—was able to expand on the connection between glutamate and schizophrenia.

As had been done with antipsychotic drugs and dopamine, Javitt compared the potency of psychoactive drugs in inducing psychosis with their affinity for the PCP binding site on the receptor. He discovered that they were highly correlated, which meant that the effects of PCP could *only* be explained by its effects at the NMDA receptor. In an influential paper published in 1991, Javitt and Zukin proposed that dysfunctional neurotransmission at the NMDA receptor might cause schizophrenia—specifically, a malfunctioning NMDA receptor that isn't responding optimally to glutamate.

To get a sense of what's happening in such a scenario, imagine that you've been invited to a friend's party, only to arrive at the house and find the doorbell not working. Other guests arrive and ring the broken bell, but no one comes to open the door. The crowd on the doorstop begins to grow and starts milling around the yard, like so much glutamate swimming around in the synaptic cleft. Havoc ensues, as guests look for other access points and start to climb through windows. This is akin to what happens when the NMDA receptor isn't responding, causing glutamate to overstimulate other receptors and leading to toxic effects to the neurons.

Javitt and others also compared the behaviors induced by PCP to those brought about by other psychosis-inducing drugs such as amphetamine or LSD. They found that none mimicked the full spectrum of schizophrenia symptoms as well as inhibitors of NMDA stimulation, such as PCP and ketamine.

PCP psychosis offered an alternative conceptualization of schizophrenia. Although hallucinations, agitation, paranoia, and delusions occur when someone has taken PCP, its most striking and consistent behavioral effects are alterations in body image, thought disorganization, negativism, and apathy—effects remarkably similar to the "four As" proposed by Eugen Bleuler in the early twentieth century to indicate what he viewed as the primary symptoms of schizophrenia: abnormal associations, autistic behavior and thinking, abnormal affect, and ambivalence. PCP psychosis seemed to provide a neurochemical model that corresponded uniquely to Bleuler's conception of schizophrenia and that was distinct from the effects induced by dopamine hyperactivity.

Javitt and Zukin's 1991 paper brought together what we knew about glutamate and what they had learned about PCP's action in the brain to say something revolutionary about schizophrenia. Their work presented a whole new paradigm for thinking about the illness and an angle from which to explore potential targets for drug treatments. There was some initial skepticism about their glutamate theory, at least until 1994, when they took the next step. Administering large doses of glycine—a naturally occurring amino acid that gently stimulates the same NMDA receptor that PCP blocks—to patients with chronic schizophrenia, they found that it improved negative symptoms significantly. (Unfortunately, although glycine enhances NMDA receptor function, it isn't practical for schizophrenia patients to ingest every day the large quantities necessary for it to produce its therapeutic effects.) "Until 1994," Javitt recalls, "our theory was an interesting idea, but once we were able to show that we could reverse symptoms with glycine, we knew it was correct."

While their studies showing that modulators like glycine had therapeutic effects—presumably by bolstering the hypofunctioning NMDA receptor—and were strong indications of glutamate's role in schizophrenia, they didn't capture the whole picture of what was happening in the glutamate synapse in schizophrenia. Javitt and Zukin's original theory implied that the problem in schizophrenia was too little glutamate signaling because of the NMDA hypofunction, but the picture that would emerge soon suggested a more complex disturbance.

THE NEXT ITERATION

A key researcher in bringing the glutamate hypothesis to its next iteration was Bita Moghaddam. Born in Iran, Moghaddam left that country in the late 1970s to pursue her education in the United States. As a biochemist and neuroscientist, she began studying the mechanisms that controlled neural processes in mental disorders, focusing during her postdoctoral training at Yale on dopamine neurophysiology. By the mid-1990s, she had become a professor with her own laboratory and began a series of glutamate experiments in rodents in which she demonstrated that the effects of NMDA receptor antagonists such as PCP and ketamine blocked the NMDA receptor and produced a massive increase in synaptic concentrations of glutamate—which then substantially increased glutamate neurotransmission at non-NMDA receptors.

In other words, the drugs might be exerting their effect by increasing the release of glutamate into the synapse. Until then, the behaviors produced by ketamine and PCP had been attributed largely to the drugs' blocking effect at the NMDA receptor, which was believed to result in too little glutamate. The reality was that PCP-like drugs led to *too much* glutamate.

From these experiments, Javitt and Zukin's NMDA hypofunction theory was revised to one of glutamate hyperactivity. In essence, both theories were correct: NMDA hypofunction was the trigger, and a synaptic surge of glutamate was the response. With too much glutamate swimming in the synapses (remember all those locked-out party guests milling about the yard), the brain becomes overwhelmed and can't maintain its equilibrium. More ominously, if the surge in synaptic glutamate is not tamped down in a timely fashion, overstimulation of the receptors available to glutamate can produce neurotoxicity. It is now believed that glutamate hyperfunction initiates schizophrenia symptoms, and that treatments to prevent symptoms need to reduce synaptic glutamate levels.

A Two-Transmitter Theory

One of the strengths of the glutamate theory is that it can plausibly account for aspects of schizophrenia that the dopamine theory can't: the fact that some patients don't respond to dopamine-mediated antipsychotics, for instance, or the presence of negative and cognitive symptoms. Because glutamate is involved in so many brain functions and is spread so widely throughout the brain, even small disruptions in glutamate signaling could conceivably produce a wide variety of symptoms.

Glutamate also suggests a possible explanation for the progressive nature of schizophrenia. Since the mid-1980s, a small number of researchers, including myself, had believed that the progressive worsening of the illness corresponded to an active pathological process—one superimposed on the genetic effects on brain development that give rise to schizophrenia. Originally, the main driver of this pathology was thought to be dopamine. Genes were involved, needless to say, but they were upstream, causing the illness but not necessarily dictating its symptoms and course. Brain structural abnormalities were also present, but as consequences of the pathology, not a driver of it. Glutamate provided a more plausible and compelling suspect for why patients with schizophrenia grew progressively worse and lost brain volume. We theorized that the progression was due to the neurotoxic effects of excessive glutamate on the brain when the system went into overdrive while trying to stabilize itself. (Dopamine, by contrast, can become neurotoxic only under extreme conditions.) The brain's attempt to absorb, inactivate, and recycle glutamate overloads the metabolic machinery of cells and can't keep pace with the demands of glutamate metabolism. It's like being in a boat that's taking in water faster than you can bail it out. The inability to maintain a stable range of glutamate concentrations sets the stage for neurotoxicity, which erodes the dendrites and spines of neurons, causing loss of brain volume and progression of the illness.

The glutamate hypothesis has the potential to reconcile the apparent limitations of the dopamine hypothesis—the fact, for instance, that no single deficit in dopamine functioning can account for the spectrum of symptoms seen in schizophrenia (positive symptoms suggest dopaminergic hyperactivity, while the cognitive or negative symptoms suggest dopaminergic underactivity). But it isn't necessarily a question of either/or. The two neurotransmitter systems might be working—or malfunctioning—together. They may underlie different aspects of the disorder—a theory that could help to explain why some patients don't respond to dopamine-targeting antipsychotics, and why negative and cognitive symptoms aren't responsive, either.

Dopamine may account for schizophrenia's positive symptoms and glutamate for negative and cognitive symptoms. Or their effects could occur in sequence, with glutamate the primary source of dysfunction and dopamine dysfunction a secondary downstream effect.

One of the functions of the glutamate system is modulating the dopamine system. When you're very excited and motivated to do something—to buy that expensive, shiny, new sports car—it's dopamine that is stoking that desire. But when you step back and consider your bank account and your large family, this is where the frontal lobe steps in. It communicates via glutamate pathways to your dopamine cells and prevents you from acting on impulse. Seen in this light, it may be that glutamate dysfunction in schizophrenia is linked directly to core cognitive symptoms but is also involved indirectly in positive symptoms through its disinhibition of dopamine.

This new pathological model of schizophrenia, which integrated dopamine and glutamate, was articulated formally by the Swedish neuropharmacologist Arvid Carlsson and his daughter Maria, a neuroscientist. In 1997 Moghaddam published the results of a study in rodents that tested the hypothesis that ketamine increased dopamine neurotransmission and disrupted cognitive functions by activating glutamate neurotransmission at non-NMDA receptors. Her findings suggested that ketamine increased dopamine release by producing an initial rise in the release of an excitatory amino acid, such as glutamate, which in turn increased the release of dopamine by stimulating non-NMDA excitatory amino acid receptors. The finding was confirmed in humans by Alan Breier, a research psychiatrist, and his colleagues at the NIMH. Using PET scans on a group of healthy subjects given ketamine, they found a markedly increased release of dopamine in specific brain regions that correlated with the psychosis-like effects the participants were experiencing. These and other studies emphasized the fact that the glutamate and dopamine systems had reciprocal effects on each other.

THE YIN AND YANG: GLUTAMATE AND GABA

As the dominant neurotransmitters in the brain, the glutamate and GABA systems together establish and maintain an equilibrium between excitatory and inhibitory activity. Any disruption in their balance has broad and potentially serious consequences, including the dysregulation of glutamate by a hypofunctioning NMDA receptor.

As GABA's main role is inhibitory, it blocks or inhibits certain brain signals, and when it interacts with the receptors of a neuron, it makes that neuron less likely to fire an action potential or release neurotransmitters. GABA thus acts as a brake on the nervous system, holding the activity of excitatory neurons secreting glutamate in check. GABA works mostly through interneurons, which exert their effects on neighboring cells, as opposed to projecting their branches to other brain regions. As the name implies, interneurons are go-betweens. They can also communicate with one another, forming circuits of different levels of complexity.

Interestingly, the function of GABA changes over the course of neural development. In the immature brain in utero, it has an excitatory effect. But a switch occurs during infancy, when neurons secreting glutamate have been born and have migrated to their target locations and formed synaptic connections. At that point, there is a change in the direction of the flow of chemicals that control the neuron's activation, converting GABA's effects in the maturing brain from excitatory to inhibitory.

GABA interneurons have been found to play a key role in schizophrenia, both functionally and structurally. They perform a range of regulatory actions, and studies have shown that they are fewer in number in the brains of people with schizophrenia— a finding that provided additional evidence of the difficulty the brains of people with the illness may have in maintaining the excitatory/inhibitory equilibrium.

The deficiency of GABA interneurons was an important addition to the glutamate hypothesis. But the source of the deficiency was still unclear, posing a chicken-and-egg question: Were the reduced numbers of interneurons in the brains of people with schizophrenia collateral damage resulting from excess glutamate caused by faulty genetic encoding of the NMDA receptor? Or was something else knocking out the interneurons, leading to the excessive release of glutamate?

A possible explanation emerged from neuroscientists at Harvard who were studying the maturational process of GABA interneurons and found that their immature forms are surrounded by unique structures called perineuronal nets. These protective nets, which wrap around neurons during their development, are important for the onset and closure of critical periods of developmental plasticity that extend through adolescence into early adulthood—the period of onset for schizophrenia. The researchers demonstrated how this protective shell surrounding GABA interneurons could be eroded by a process of oxidative stress (a chemical reaction in a fetus or infant caused by exposure to toxins, viral infections, or trauma), leading to reduced inhibition of pyramidal cells, which in turn leads to excess glutamate release and neuronal stimulation. They also showed that antioxi-

dants (chemical agents that inhibit formation of free-radical molecules and oxidative stress) and substances that inhibited glutamate helped to protect maturing
cells and restore the integrity to the perineuronal nets, normalizing GABA inhibition and glutamate neurotransmission.

PIECING TOGETHER THE PUZZLE

With the understanding of the involvement of dopamine, glutamate, and GABA
in schizophrenia, the pieces of the puzzle were there; all that was needed was to
figure out how they fit together.

Enter Anthony Grace. When Grace joined the psychiatry and neuroscience
faculty at the University of Pittsburgh in 1985, there were few basic scientists—
meaning those who work in the lab but not with patients—in the psychiatry
departments of medical schools. Biomedical research utilized sophisticated laboratory methodology and numerous animal models (including fruit flies, round-
worms, rodents), but mental illness was seen as poorly understood and remote
from the application of basic science disciplines. The nervous systems of test organisms were too simple to shed much light on the human brain. While you could
create a valid animal model of diabetes, cancer, and infectious diseases, how do
you create schizophrenia in a rat?

Grace was a systems neuroscientist, meaning he made electrophysiologic recordings of the activity of neural circuits. His choice to study schizophrenia was an
outgrowth of his graduate student experience in the lab of Steve Bunney, then chair
of Psychiatry at Yale. Working with Bunney, Grace had published a series of papers
in the 1980s that provided the best evidence to date about how antipsychotic drugs
worked in people with schizophrenia. It had been established already that antipsychotic drugs exerted their therapeutic effects by blocking dopamine from overstimu-
lating D-2 receptors. It was also widely known that the drugs didn't alleviate psychotic
symptoms immediately but over a period of one to four weeks. This was puzzling, as
PET imaging, as well as animal studies, showed that antipsychotics bound to the D-2
receptors (thus blocking the actions of dopamine) within hours of being taken. In an
elegant series of experiments, Bunney and Grace demonstrated that the immediate
effects of blocking the D-2 receptors and silencing the neural circuit led to a feedback
signal being sent to release more dopamine. Thus, the initial effect of the medication
was to flood the synapse with dopamine. But Bunney and Grace observed that if they

continued to treat the animals and recorded the activity of the dopamine neurons, over time (seven to twenty-eight days) the presynaptic neuron gave up its futile attempt to overcome the drug-induced obstruction and stopped releasing dopamine. They called this phenomenon a "depolarization blockade."

After settling into his lab at Pittsburgh, and with the dopamine theory in ascendance, in the late 1990s Grace began investigating why and how dopamine became dysregulated and caused psychosis. He developed a model simulating the causal effects of schizophrenia, whether due to genes or environmental trauma, by injecting pregnant rats with a toxic substance that disrupted brain development in the unborn rats in a way that was believed to simulate what happens in utero to people who develop schizophrenia. When the rats exposed to this toxic substance had grown to adulthood, they showed behaviors regarded as the rodent equivalent of human psychosis: hyperactivity, such as running around their cages, and the avoidance of novel stimuli. By measuring the electrical activity and amounts of dopamine being released from the rats' neurons, Grace was able to track the source of the excessive dopamine to the hippocampus in the medial temporal lobe. It seemed that projections from the hippocampus involving both glutamate and GABA were enhancing dopamine activity in the midbrain neurons that is relevant to both salience and predicting errors—mental functions that enable us to assess situations accurately and choose appropriate behaviors based on predicted outcomes.

These findings offered several important new pieces of evidence, including illuminating the connection between the hippocampus and the dopamine neurons in the midbrain; this was significant because it aligned the relevant neurotransmitters (dopamine and glutamate) with anatomical findings related to schizophrenia. Despite the focus by researchers on other parts of the brain (such as the prefrontal cortex and the thalamus), the hippocampus was the structure affected most commonly in schizophrenia, and also the place where anatomic abnormalities first appear in the course of the illness.

Based on these results, Grace concluded that antipsychotic medications were targeting the downstream dopamine dysfunction associated with positive symptoms and not the upstream source of the problem. He and others in the field suggested that based on the increasing evidence for hippocampal dysfunction driving dopamine excesses, a more direct therapeutic approach would be to home in on the hippocampal dysfunction.

Two therapeutic strategies followed from this line of reasoning. The first was to restore the deficient GABA interneuron regulation of glutamate activity within the hippocampal circuits. This has been attempted, in a rudimentary way, by using high doses of benzodiazepine (Valium-like) drugs, which act through the GABA system. But at the doses required for therapeutic effect, the accompanying sedation and cognitive dulling were so great that they nullified the drug's benefits. It might seem that the solution to this would be to develop a regionally specific benzodiazepine that acted exclusively on the hippocampus and didn't affect the parts of the brain that gave rise to the side effects. But creating a drug that acts only on the part of the brain you want to target is difficult; drugs will go wherever their biochemical affinity attracts them, rather than remaining in the desired region. It was possible, however, to develop a drug that was selective for specific components of GABA receptors. One such receptor—the alpha-5 GABAA—was chosen because it was concentrated in the hippocampus but not widely distributed in other parts of the brain. David Lewis, a psychiatrist trained in anatomy and neuropathology who conducted postmortem brain research, tested this approach in a pilot study, and the initial results were positive, but they were not replicated in a larger, multisite study.

A second strategy for targeting hippocampal dysfunction would be to use drugs that inhibit the release or modulate the effects of glutamate. Given the complexity of the glutamate synapse, the question was for which molecular target to aim. The initial efforts involved amino acids (glycine and serine, among others) that acted to correct NMDA receptor hypofunction by facilitating the sensitivity of the postsynaptic receptor to stimulation. Another therapeutic approach involves inhibiting the release of glutamate from the presynaptic neuron. Studies of these drugs have produced mixed results. However, their failure could have been due to the ways in which they were administered (inaccurate drug dose, frequency and duration of administration) or the heterogeneity of the patients in the studies (people who had been ill for years, previously received extensive amounts of antipsychotic drugs or were not responsive to prior treatments) rather than the treatment being ineffective or hitting the wrong molecular target. Given these uncertainties, this therapeutic strategy remains among the most promising for novel drug discovery and warrants further investigation.

Both approaches offer potentially new ways to treat schizophrenia based on the most current understanding of its pathological underpinnings. If successful, the drugs developed wouldn't just powerfully validate the pathological model that was the rationale for their development, but also alleviate symptoms and suffering. And this is how it should be, for what good is knowledge or a theory of illness that doesn't lead to a treatment, prevention, or cure?

Part 4

THE PATH
TO
PREVENTION

Chapter 16

PEELING THE ONION

When all is said and done, they are stranger
to me than the birds in my garden.

—Eugen Bleuler (1857–1939)

I KNOW IT WHEN I SEE IT

On November 13, 1959, a new film by the young French auteur Louis Malle premiered at the Heights Art Theater on Coventry Road in Cleveland Heights, Ohio. Coventry Village, nested in a ring of suburbs that had formed after World War II around Cleveland proper, was already a Bohemian neighborhood, foreshadowing the counterculture movement that would soon sweep the country. It was also the suburb where I grew up.

Les Amants, or *The Lovers*, starred Jeanne Moreau as an adulterous wife. The film's content would be considered extremely tame by today's standards, but the police confiscated the film at the Heights Art Theater and arrested Nico Jacobellis, an Italian immigrant and film scholar who managed the movie house. Jacobellis was found guilty of possessing and exhibiting obscene content. His attorneys appealed the case all the way to the US Supreme Court, which overturned Jacobellis's conviction in 1964 in a 6-to-2 ruling. The majority opinion stated, among other things, that the definition of obscenity required objective standards that could be applied consistently across the country. What has stuck in the minds of Americans from the Jacobellis case is less Louis Malle's film than Justice Potter Stewart's comment in his concurring opinion that although he couldn't describe hard-core pornography, "I know it when I see it." And *The Lovers* wasn't it.

Following the court's decision, the film immediately reopened at the Heights

Art Theater. I was sixteen years old at the time and went with friends to check it out. Two hours later, we left the theater disappointed and wondering what all the fuss had been about.

It would be eight years before I was reminded of *The Lovers*, and in an unlikely setting. I was in medical school, attending a lecture on the diagnosis of mental illness, when the professor, a freshly minted neuropsychiatrist, launched into a pointed critique of the *DSM-II* definition of schizophrenia. (The transformational *DSM-III*, which standardized psychiatric diagnoses and established their empirical bases, was several years away.) As he read the description aloud, his tone grew increasingly derisive, until he stopped reading, looked up from his notes, and proceeded to paraphrase Justice Stewart's description of pornography. "Schizophrenia?" he said. "I can't tell you what it is, but I know it when I see it."

Peeling the Diagnostic Onion

When I examine the records of patients with long histories of schizophrenia, I often see a string of different psychiatric diagnoses from different doctors, which are either clinically contradictory or simply implausible. Apparently, we don't always "know it when we see it"—and this is all the more true in the absence of objective biological features, which can be measured by blood tests, imaging, or electrophysiologic procedures. The problem of diagnostic variability is due not just to differences in the subjective interpretation of patients' symptoms but also to the explicit and implicit sociocultural biases that permeate the population and to which health care professionals are also subject. These social and clinical sources of variation notwithstanding, and despite the lack of objective diagnostic tests, we have a system that, used properly, should enable us to arrive at diagnoses accurately and reliably. However, the aforementioned diagnostic limitations necessitate that clinicians diligently and rigorously evaluate each patient and arrive at their diagnosis with the utmost care, as this will guide their treatment, prognostic assessment, and the patient's identity in the future. Through this painstaking process—which has required much time, intense thought, acute perception, and great awareness—we *have* learned much about what schizophrenia is and isn't.

One might think that all medical diagnoses would be distinct and readily defined, even mental disorders. This is because all diagnoses of diseases have evolved in the same way, using three levels of validation pertaining to either manifestations or causes. The first is the phenomenological level and consists of signs (observable features such as a rash or swelling) and symptoms, as reported by the patient (pain, fatigue, sadness, and so on). The second level is the pathologic features of the illness, which can be measured with blood tests, tissue biopsies, imaging, and electrophysiologic procedures such as EEGs and EKGs (electrocardiograms). The third level is the cause, or etiology, of the illness, which identifies its source (bacterium or virus for infectious disease, cancer for a tumor, blood clot for a stroke) and is the final step in diagnostic validation. The three levels of diagnosis for a heart attack, for example, are (1) chest pain (phenomenological), (2) EKG abnormalities (pathologic), and (3) atherosclerotic plaques obstructing coronary arteries (etiologic). Asthma, on the other hand, has been validated at only two levels: (1) difficulty breathing (phenomenological) and (2) airway constriction of the lungs or bronchospasm (pathologic). Conditions such as headaches, fibromyalgia, and irritable bowel syndrome—along with virtually all mental disorders, including schizophrenia—are diagnosed only at the first level, on the basis of signs and symptoms.

Our diagnostic precision and certainty are less when we do not have measures of the pathology and cause to anchor our observations. To complicate the process further, we have learned that schizophrenia can be mimicked by other causes that are described in the next section. Consequently, diagnosing schizophrenia necessarily involves a process of first establishing a provisional diagnosis and then systematically ruling out other disorders or conditions that could be causing symptoms that mimic the illness. I use the metaphor of peeling the onion, layer by layer, until we reach the core, and the only remaining explanation for the symptoms is schizophrenia. This isn't to say that those layers of the onion are irrelevant. On the contrary, they provide pathologic or etiologic validation of other conditions, and point to alternative treatments. The three types of conditions that can mimic schizophrenia are genocopies, phenocopies, and facsimiles.

GENOCOPIES

The genetic forms of schizophrenia, as we saw in chapter 12, can be grouped into two broad categories: polygenic forms, involving multiple common genes with small causal effects; and rare mutations or copy number variants, in which large segments of DNA are either lost or repeated multiple times, that have large effects. (These can be either inherited or new, spontaneous mutations.) In some instances, patients have both, rare variants on a polygenic background. An example of a genocopy is DiGeorge syndrome, caused by a deletion of about thirty-five genes on chromosome 22 in the q11 region, in which a third of patients develop schizophrenia-like symptoms. However, this is not schizophrenia, because people with DiGeorge syndrome also have congenital heart malformations, facial and limb deformities, and developmental delays. Schizophrenia symptoms occur, presumably, because the loss of genes that have a significant effect on brain development allows other genes that confer vulnerability to schizophrenia to have a greater impact on brain development.

Phenocopies

Phenocopies of schizophrenia are caused by environmental factors that produce symptoms of the illness. Five sources of phenocopies have been identified: germs, seizures in the temporal lobe, chronic drug abuse, antibodies, and reproductive trauma.

Germs

In 1913 Hideyo Noguchi and Joseph Moore first recognized the *Treponema pallidum* microorganism as a source of madness in the form of general paresis of the insane, or tertiary syphilis. When treatments for syphilis (arsphenamine and penicillin) were developed, the number of cases of insanity caused by syphilis decreased precipitously. The schizophrenia-like symptoms were collateral damage that resulted from the spirochete (spiral-shaped bacterium that causes syphilis) penetrating the brain. Other infectious agents to which a developing fetus is exposed during gestation—such as influenza, Lyme disease, hepatitis C, and many of the viral encephalitides (particularly those caused by herpes viruses)—have also been associated with increased risk of developing schizophrenia or schizophrenia-like symptoms. None besides syphilis, however, has been definitively implicated as an imitator of schizophrenia.

Temporal Lobe Epilepsy

People with seizure disorders of the temporal lobe can experience psychotic symptoms, including auditory hallucinations and delusions. These symptoms usually follow seizures, sometimes after a period of years. In fact, a number of parallels have been found between temporal lobe epilepsy (TLE) and schizophrenia—related to memory impairments, loss of synaptic connectivity, and brain volume reduction. The overlap in symptoms of the two disorders seems related to the fact that the electrical overactivity that kicks off seizures occurs in the same brain regions where glutamate and GABA dysregulation occur in schizophrenia. We might say, therefore, that seizures are the electrophysiological equivalent of the neurochemical pathology of psychosis. Psychosis can also develop out of TLE from the neuropathological consequences of seizures: inflammation, sclerosis, and imbalance of inhibitory and excitatory systems of the brain.

Drug Abuse

We have already seen how drug abuse—particularly the use of stimulants and NMDA receptor antagonists such as PCP—can produce altered mental states that mimic schizophrenia. During the post–World War II methamphetamine epidemic in Japan and the PCP epidemic in the United States in the 1970s and 1980s, there were many cases of schizophrenia-like psychosis among users that persisted or recurred in the absence of drug intoxication. In such cases, the repeated use of methamphetamine and PCP, both of which target neurotransmitters implicated in schizophrenia, had sensitized the relevant systems, inducing and perpetuating symptoms. My former patient Sean, discussed in chapter 14, is a tragic example of such an outcome.

Antibodies

Among the most interesting phenocopies are those caused by the antibodies produced by autoimmune reactions. Prior to 1990, the brain was thought to be immunologically privileged, meaning that under normal physiological conditions, antibodies and immune cells were unable to penetrate it because of a blood-brain barrier composed of cells called pericytes that form "tight junctions" around the outer walls of blood vessels, restricting blood-borne substances of larger sizes or poor permeability from entering the brain. At the same time, it was known that psychotic symptoms could occur in the context of autoimmune disorders such as lupus and Hashimoto's thyroiditis. The fact that autoimmune diseases could result in psychotic symptoms suggested strongly that antibodies produced by the immune system *could* gain access to the brain and interfere with key mental functions. In the case of recently discovered immunologic phenocopies of schizophrenia, the antibodies attach to glutamate receptors, blocking their stimulation by glutamate. When the antibodies block the NMDA receptors, they mimic the actions of PCP and ketamine.

Initially, it was thought that the antibodies causing psychotomimetic effects were accidental byproducts of the body's reaction to tumors in other parts of the body stimulating the production of antibodies, which then gained entry to the brain. However, when these immune-mediated neuropsychiatric conditions were found to occur in the absence of tumors and were not associated with other known disorders, the term "autoimmune encephalitis" (or "limbic encephalitis") was applied. The name reflected the fact that the antibodies' effects were concentrated on the glutamate receptors in the limbic system, particularly the hippocampus and amygdala on the medial of the temporal lobe.

Autoimmune encephalitis targeting NMDA receptors was first identified in 2007 by the neurologist Josep Dalmau, then working at the University of Pennsylvania. Dalmau's findings gained attention, but the condition was neither common nor widely known, and clinicians didn't have extensive experience in diagnosing the disorder. Therefore, when Susannah Cahalan showed up at NYU Medical Center in 2009 with a range of psychotic symptoms—as well as migraines, memory loss, and numbness on her left side—no one thought of autoimmune encephalitis. (Only a couple hundred people had been diagnosed with it worldwide since 2007.) Instead, Cahalan was diagnosed with bipolar disorder and schizoaffective disorder and admitted to the hospital.

Cahalan recounts her experience in *Brain on Fire*. After a month of ineffective treatment with the gamut of psychotropic medications, a neurologist with a reputation for solving difficult cases was consulted. Souhel Najjar, a Syrian American doctor born and raised in Damascus, emigrated to the United States after finishing medical school to train in neurology. Najjar had, in Cahalan's telling, a bushy mustache, a booming voice, and a Syrian accent, and radiated warmth. His determination to never give up on his patients was grounded in his own experience. As a boy, he had done poorly in school, failing test after test ("Education is not for everyone," the principal told his parents), until one teacher took a special interest in him. Najjar eventually graduated at the top of his medical school class.

By the time he came on the scene, though, Cahalan had undergone virtually every imaginable test for all plausible causes of her symptoms (including epilepsy, Lyme disease, toxoplasmosis, cryptococcus, lupus, and multiple sclerosis), leaving a mental disorder as one of the few remaining possible culprits. Najjar began his assessment by doing something none of the other doctors had done: he spoke directly to Susannah, as though she were a friend instead of a patient. After taking her full history, he had her perform a series of simple but revealing tests, including drawing a clockface.

The clock drawing test is a simple screening tool used in neuropsychiatric assessments in which a patient's ability to remember and re-create the face of clock, with its circular shape, two hands, and twelve numbers placed accurately, can reveal cognitive dysfunction. The distorted image that Susannah produced—all the numbers were on the right side, with the left side left completely blank—suggested the possibility of brain dysfunction. Since other tests had already ruled out most of the other possible causes (trauma, infection, stroke, seizure), this suggested to Najjar that the problem must be either inflammatory, immunologic, or both. The question was which and from what? Other than disturbed behavior and mental function, Susannah had no objective signs of any illness. So Najjar decided to do something drastic: a brain biopsy, which requires drilling burr holes through the skull and taking small pieces of brain tissue from different locations. This is a highly invasive, rarely performed procedure, but they were running out of options, and even if they did not know it, time was of the essence.

Susannah's biopsy showed massive inflammation indicated by increased numbers of glial cells, the brain's equivalent of the white blood cells that fight foreign invaders. This was the smoking gun, but the clincher was the results of the cerebrospinal fluid they had sent to Dalmau's laboratory at Penn for analysis, which revealed elevated antibody levels. A diagnosis of autoimmune encephalitis was now confirmed.

Once Najjar had made the correct diagnosis, he treated Cahalan with a combination of immunosuppressant medication, immunoglobulin (a purified blood product containing healthy antibodies), and plasmapheresis (a procedure that filtered her blood to remove the offending antibodies, similar to what is done in hemodialysis for patients with kidney failure). The treatment was effective, and by the following year, Susannah was home with family and had returned to work and to her former self.

In May 2017 I was attending the annual meeting of the American Psychiatric Association in San Diego and noticed that Cahalan was delivering a keynote address. I contacted her, and we arranged to have dinner. I had first met her in 2014, when she'd interviewed me while researching her book *The Great Pretender*, about David Rosenhan's undercover experiment that discredited psychiatric diagnoses of mental illness.

Given Cahalan's harrowing experience of misdiagnosis and mistaken treatments with psychotropic drugs, I'd assumed that her prior experience with psychiatrists had left her skeptical of our field and been instrumental in her choice of topics for her next book. I was pleasantly surprised to learn that wasn't the case. She expressed little rancor. Susannah did recall how frightening it had been to lose control of her mind and have her fate rest in the hands of doctors she barely knew. She was grateful for the competent and compassionate care she'd received when her diagnosis was finally discovered. She laughed ruefully when I reminded her how her experience resembled the devil-possessed fictional character Regan MacNeil in *The Exorcist*. Both Regan, the young daughter on location with her movie star mother in Washington, DC, and Cahalan contracted a mysterious ailment that stumped the doctors and occasioned a seemingly endless battery of tests before the exotic causes of their maladies were finally identified and relieved. The only difference being that Susannah was saved by a neurologist and Regan by a priest.

When I wondered aloud how many other people were regularly misdiagnosed and, unlike Susannah, weren't lucky enough to live in a major city with top hospitals and knowledgeable doctors, Susannah told me that Dr. Najjar had estimated at the time of her illness in 2009 that 90 percent of people suffering from autoimmune encephalitis went undiagnosed. If you do the math, that is horrifying. If only 1 percent of the 2.6 million people who suffer from schizophrenia in the United States have this illness, by Najjar's account, it is possible that 26,000 have been misdiagnosed as having schizophrenia (or related mental illness) and treated improperly. This would mean that they are likely languishing in the back ward of state mental hospitals, or are in prison, or are dead.

REPRODUCTIVE TRAUMA

A number of factors related to pregnancy and birth are associated with increased risk for schizophrenia, including fetal exposure to infection, discussed above, and brain trauma sustained during pregnancy or delivery. Such complications occur either during pregnancy in the form of blunt trauma, intrauterine bleeding, nutritional deficiencies, or toxins (such as exposure to maternal drug abuse or environmental chemicals), or during delivery, due to oxygen deprivation, breech births, or a baby's head being too large to fit through the mother's pelvis (cephalopelvic disproportion).

But how does reproductive trauma, which can take so many forms and impact different parts of the brain, result two decades later in the development of a specific mental illness such as schizophrenia? The explanation lies in what is called the "two-hit hypothesis." Applied to complex genetic medical disorders such as schizophrenia, the two-hit hypothesis posits that a genetic or constitutional first "hit" disrupts some aspect of brain development, establishing a vulnerability to a specific illness. A second, subsequent "hit," which can occur in a variety of ways during pregnancy, delivery, or in the postnatal period, increases the person's vulnerability to the illness.

The 50 percent concordance rate for identical twins both being affected by schizophrenia first demonstrated this fact. This was subsequently confirmed in 1990 by the landmark study of identical twins led by E. Fuller Torrey, previously mentioned in chapter 11, which provided strong evidence of phenotypic differences in addition to the diagnosis of schizophrenia consistent with the two-hit principle. The team's findings indicated that although genes were clearly implicated in schizophrenia, factors other than genes must be involved in order for only one twin to become sick.

I have seen the two-hit principle at work in my own patients. I met Janice Lieber in 2006, though I had known her parents, Steve and Connie, for more than a decade because of their involvement in the National Association for Research in Schizophrenia and Affective Disorders. NARSAD had grown out of the American Schizophrenia Association, founded in 1981, and initially had engaged mainly in raising awareness rather than funding research. Steve had been an investor on Wall Street and then had founded his own financial services firm. Connie was educated as an architect but had given up her career to be a full-time mother—for reasons that will soon be apparent. Our relationship became much closer when I came to Columbia in 2004, as in addition to my role as chair of Psychiatry, I also became director of the Lieber Center for Schizophrenia Research, which they had generously supported.

I warmed to them immediately, not just because of their largesse but because they were genuinely gracious and humble people. Steve was voluble but dignified and unfailingly considerate of his wife. Connie was petite but tough and didn't suffer fools gladly. The Liebers had two children. Sam, the younger, was married with a family and was a partner in his father's investment firm. Janice, however, had been diagnosed with schizophrenia in 1978. Although she'd been treated with a series of medications and had gained some relief from her symptoms, she was far from well.

It was the combination of frustration over Janice's care and hope for improved treatments that had motivated the Liebers to join NARSAD in 1987. To say that Steve and Connie infused the organization with a new energy would be a gross understatement. They not only increased NARSAD's coffers, but also they shifted the foundation's emphasis from awareness to research on schizophrenia's causes and the development of better treatments. Within two years of joining NARSAD, Connie had become its president and Steve the chair of the board of trustees.

One evening when my wife and I were having dinner with them, I asked how their daughter was doing. Despite their usual discretion, they couldn't hide their distress. I didn't know what I could add to what numerous experts had already told them, but I offered to reevaluate Janice if they wanted another opinion. They readily accepted.

Janice was fifty-three years old when I met her and had spent most of her life debilitated by various symptoms, including delusions, hallucinations, and obsessional thoughts. She had a narrow range of interests, was socially very withdrawn, and had frequent compulsive behaviors. While she had symptoms, Janice did not have acute episodes of florid psychosis and had never been hospitalized. Apart from occasional spending sprees, she had no history of sustained elation or irritability, or other hypomanic or manic symptoms.

Determined to get the most detailed picture possible of Janice's condition, I invited other Columbia faculty members to assist me: a neurologist, a pediatric psychiatrist, and a neuropsychologist, the latter two specializing in developmental disabilities. I would later call in an expert in obsessive-compulsive disorder, too. During our consultation, Janice answered our questions courteously, coherently, and succinctly, but without any emotion. I never felt that I established a rapport with her. She was most animated when talking about her hobbies, which included collecting watches, perfumes, and CDs, but even then she spoke in a monotonic voice without inflection, as if she were reading from a catalogue. Janice's behavior wasn't bizarre or disorganized in any way, just disconnected. She was mostly un-aware of her surroundings and indifferent to social graces, given to yawning loudly or burping. At one point, I mentioned that she seemed distracted, and she said she'd been listening to "the voices." She apologized and asked me to repeat my question.

As we launched into Janice's history, Connie, who had accompanied her, began to reveal vital information that would shed light on Janice's condition and her limited response to treatment. Connie explained that her pregnancy with Janice had been difficult. She developed preeclampsia—a complication charac-terized by high blood pressure and damage to the liver and kidneys, as well as other organs—in her third trimester. This caused Janice to be born two months prematurely. At birth, Janice wasn't breathing properly and had to be rushed to the neonatal ICU, where she remained for two weeks before going home.

During her infancy and toddler years, Janice exhibited a number of worri-some behaviors: poor eye-to-eye gaze, impaired fine motor skills, delayed speech acquisition, repetitive movements, limited interests, and a stubborn adherence to specific routines. In nursery school, she had difficulty interacting and form-ing relationships with other children. Connie consulted their pediatrician about Janice's troubles, and was stunned when the doctor announced blithely that Janice was "probably retarded." Outraged, she took her daughter to see a renowned child psychiatrist at New York University, who assessed the four-year-old Janice and concluded that her developmental and behavioral abnormalities were most likely caused by brain injury resulting from the complicated pregnancy and traumatic delivery. Given Janice's behaviors, it's surprising that the psychiatrist didn't men-tion the possibility of autism. But this was 1957, and autism was barely acknowl-edged in the medical field.

While Janice had apparent social deficits, there was no evidence of low intel-ligence. In fact, tests showed her to be highly intelligent, results that would be borne out by her academic success in primary and secondary school. She excelled in most subjects and was a talented artist and voracious reader. After graduating from high school in 1972, Janice attended Manhattanville College, majoring in art and romance languages, learning to speak French, Spanish, and Italian near fluently. Following college, she enrolled at the State University of New York at Purchase to pursue a law degree.

Disaster struck during her first year of law school. Away from home for the first time, Janice's gradual behavior changes initially went unnoticed until one night, her roommates realized that she was confused and not making sense. The next day, she was nowhere to be found. Alarmed, her roommates called her parents, who immediately drove to the college to get her. By the time Connie and Steve arrived, Janice had been found wandering aimlessly around the campus, dazed and disoriented. She said she was getting messages from the radio and television telling her she was a criminal and was going to be killed.

The Liebers didn't take Janice to a hospital but arranged for her to be seen by a psychiatrist. Thus began the years of consultations with doctors and the succession of drug treatments—thioridazine, perphenazine, fluphenazine, trifluoperazine, molindone, thiothixene, and chlorpromazine—each of which had little benefit and caused varying degrees of neurologic side effects and sedation. Since leaving law school, Janice had lived in her parents' home, her psychotic symptoms and functional deficits seriously limiting her quality of life.

Almost ten years after the onset of Janice's symptoms, Connie and Steve heard about clozapine, a medication said to be effective for patients who had not responded to other antipsychotic medications and to have no neurologic effects. Although clozapine had not yet received FDA approval and therefore was still considered experimental, the Liebers accessed the drug for their daughter through what is called a compassionate-use protocol. To their delight, Janice showed considerable improvement, her delusions and hallucinations decreasing substantially. But she still had many residual symptoms (hearing voices, strange thoughts and obsessions, flat affect, lack of spontaneity, and robotic speech and movements), prompting her doctors to raise the dose to the maximum level, which brought on weight gain, borderline diabetes, and sedation. Regardless of these adverse effects and her diminutive stature, Janice was maintained on 700 milligrams of clozapine per day (the maximum recommended daily dose is 800 milligrams) and was on that dose when I saw her.

Despite her many limitations, Janice continued with a busy schedule of activities. She performed basic tasks at her father's office, worked with an art therapist, exercised, attended Weight Watchers, and went to Friday-evening services at her synagogue. But neither Janice nor her parents were happy about her condition. Connie estimated that her daughter spent about four hours per day obsessing, and an hour or two performing compulsive behaviors, such as taking repeated baths. She couldn't function independently and had no friends.

As part of our assessment, we had Janice undergo an EEG and an MRI. Her EEG was normal except for reduced electrical activity in the frontal cortex. But the MRI showed atrophy of the right frontal and parietal lobes, with asymmetrical enlargement of the lateral ventricles consistent with her history of prematurity and a traumatic delivery.

Surprisingly, Janice's psychiatric family history revealed little of significance. Her low genetic vulnerability, indicated by the absence of a family history of schizophrenia, along with her developmental history, gave me pause and redirected our thinking in an unanticipated way. Based on our evaluation, we came to a clear but surprising consensus: Janice did not have schizophrenia. We concluded that her primary diagnosis was what was then called Asperger's syndrome (it now comes under the umbrella of autism spectrum disorder, or ASD). This form of ASD has many of the characteristics of autism—difficulties in interpersonal relations and communication, along with restricted and repetitive patterns of behavior and interests—but is also often marked by high intelligence, high levels of functioning, and relatively unimpaired language skills. Signs usually begin before two years of age and typically last for a person's entire life. We also diagnosed Janice with obsessive-compulsive disorder (part of her autism, and exacerbated by high doses of clozapine), and psychotic symptoms. Those symptoms, which had led to the previous diagnosis of schizophrenia and been the primary reason for her parents' advocacy and philanthropic pursuits, were a secondary condition *complicating* her ASD. Although it's not a common occurrence, psychosis can occur later in life in those with autism. We therefore inferred that her birth traumas had placed her at risk for the psychotic symptoms that didn't develop until young adulthood when she entered law school.

Based on this new diagnostic formulation, we proposed an alternative treatment plan. In collaboration with Janice's psychiatrist, we eliminated all psychotropic medications, apart from clozapine. In addition, we lowered the dose to reduce the side effects, as Janice hadn't shown any additional benefit on doses above 450 milligrams per day, and her blood level of medication was well above the therapeutic threshold at that dose. We added an antidepressant, a selective serotonin reuptake inhibitor (SSRI), for Janice's OCD symptoms. The medications were important, but the main focus of Janice's treatment would be social and cognitive rehabilitation to address her autism and functional disabilities. Rehabilitation is labor intensive but, when implemented by skilled clinicians with specialized expertise, it is the most effective approach for functional and cognitive disabilities.

Janice began a rigorous course of cognitive remediation and social skills training four days a week in a rehabilitation and recovery program at Columbia directed by a recently recruited faculty member, the cognitive psychologist Alice Medalia. In addition to these therapies, Janice also received supportive psychotherapy and medication management.

Initially, Janice showed little improvement beyond acclimating to her new routine. Over the subsequent months and years, however, we saw a gradual but dramatic change. Instead of the slightly disheveled appearance we'd grown used to, Janice now appeared well groomed and appropriately—even stylishly—dressed. Where previously she had needed to be driven to the clinic, she now traveled alone on the train from her home to Grand Central Terminal, then walked to the midtown ColumbiaDoctors clinic. She began to socialize with people she met in the treatment program. Eventually she was able to travel alone to visit her favorite aunt in Florida.

By that point, my main contact with Janice was at the fund-raising events organized by the foundation. In 2011 NARSAD had changed its name to the Brain & Behavior Research Foundation and was the single most important source of philanthropic support for mental illness research. It's no exaggeration to say that during the twenty-five years of the Liebers' leadership, the foundation helped to launch the careers of virtually every major psychiatric researcher in the country and many more around the world. The fund-raising events were formal affairs held in fancy venues. In previous years, Janice had been part of the background, not an active participant. Now when I saw her—seated at one of the head tables greeting well-wishers and enjoying herself—I marveled at the change in her.

In 2016 Connie died. Three years later, Janice's brother, Sam, died. The family persevered. Steve stayed on as chair of the foundation's board of trustees, and Janice continued to attend the clinic that had by then been named in honor of her parents.

When the Covid-19 pandemic hit New York City in March 2020, I called Steve to check on him. He greeted me with warmth and enthusiasm. We talked about the Covid crisis, then I asked about Janice. Steve could hardly contain his excitement as he told me how well she was doing. Janice had been spending a lot of time at the offices of Steve's investment company. But rather than hanging around doing menial tasks, as she once had, his daughter was now investing her own portfolio. To Steve's surprise and delight, Janice's performance over the past year was better than those of some of the other traders in the office. I had never heard Steve so animated and happy. Before I could respond, he handed the phone to Janice, who repeated the good news. I told her I was delighted for her and hoped to see her at the clinic when on-site visits resumed. She handed the phone back to her father, and we said good-bye and hung up.

Three days later, Steve died. I hadn't known, when I was speaking with him, that he had been having trouble breathing for the previous two weeks. He was being treated for heart failure, and that, along with his age—Steve was ninety-four—put him at high risk for Covid's worst outcome. On top of that, Steve's housekeeper had tested positive two weeks before. Covid wasn't listed as Steve's cause of death, but it's what we suspected. Because of the pandemic, there was no funeral.

Within the span of a few years, Janice had lost her entire immediate family. But once again, she showed great resilience. She has weathered the string of painful losses admirably, without exacerbation of her symptoms or a relapse. She has kept up her treatment, continuing to attend the various programs in which she's involved. Her resilience has been greater than that of numerous people I know who are not living with mental disorders.

In many respects, Janice's life is a real success story. She overcame birth trauma and a developmental disorder to graduate from college and eventually create an active life for herself. These achievements are a testament both to Janice's perseverance and her family's tireless devotion. But they are also a result of Janice's having access to quality medical care and treatment resources. From the beginning of her life, she was in a rich educational and cultural environment, which helped to mitigate her infirmities and bolster her capacities. Later, when Janice was diagnosed and presented with new treatment options, she had the means to support this level of care and a family environment that could help and encourage her to do the hard work. The treatment that helped Janice should be available to all who need it, not only to those who can afford it or to those with ideal and loving parents. Everyone so afflicted deserves the same opportunities to get the best care to enable them to attain the highest level of recovery.

Imitating Schizophrenia

Facsimiles are "imitations" of schizophrenia, initiated either intentionally—as in David Rosenhan's experiment, when people feigned insanity to gain admission to mental hospitals—or unconsciously. The former state is called fabrication, or factitious disorder, while the latter occurs most commonly in dissociative disorders.

Dissociative disorders are among the most fascinating and frightening conditions in psychiatry. Characterized by involuntary alterations in consciousness, identity, awareness, and memory, and sometimes involving motor function impairment, they have fueled historical and literary imaginations with stories of amnesia, fugue states, paralysis, multiple personalities, and demon possession.

The *DSM-5* specifies three types of dissociative disorders, stemming from common causes and exhibiting related symptoms. Dissociative amnesia, as the name suggests, involves the selective loss of memory of events or periods of time. Dissociative depersonalization/derealization involves ongoing or recurring feelings of unreality or detachment from one's mind, self, body, or surroundings. Dissociative identity disorder is characterized by multiple personalities, or alternate identities, and can include a psychosis that mimics schizophrenia; sometimes it takes the form of dissociative possession disorder, in which an external entity—such as a dead person's spirit, a divine being or demon, or the devil himself—replaces someone's own identity. Some cultures induce or interpret dissociative states in the context of religious rituals: for example, ecstatic religious states such as those seen in the Pentecostal Church, the active meditation of whirling dervishes in the Sufi religion, or the kabbalists of Hasidic Judaism, among many others. In all of these conditions, this pervasion of "supranormal states" is often accompanied by a loss of awareness about or memory of the episode.

Genuine dissociative disorders usually develop as a reaction to extreme or repeated trauma occurring in childhood. The memory of the emotionally charged experience is so toxic that it can't be processed normatively, neurobiologically, or psychologically, or stored in the usual way. We see the effects of experiential trauma in adults as post-traumatic stress disorder, but children tend to isolate and push out of conscious awareness the cognitive and emotional elements of traumatic experience. This is why they so often seem virtually unfazed in the aftermath of something quite traumatic. The reality is that they have compartmentalized the experience, sealing it off outside of awareness. More than a painful memory, as in PTSD, it becomes a segment of their existence too disturbing to even acknowledge. This work-around mechanism can suffice until the child matures into adulthood, and the repressed experience finds expression through one of the forms of dissociation, including the emulation of psychosis.

The typical patient diagnosed with dissociative identity disorder is a female in her twenties or thirties with a history of early trauma from emotional, physical, or sexual abuse. By adulthood, she is manifesting dissociative phenomena, often taking the form of "alters," meaning altered states of consciousness or alternate identities. She may report "extrasensory" experiences that approximate hallucinations, as well as hearing voices, and periods of amnesia and depersonalization. She might also use the first-person plural ("we") when referring to herself. There may be periods of time of which she has no memory; she may meet people who know her but whom she doesn't recognize, and she may find objects or clothes in her possession that she doesn't recall purchasing and normally wouldn't use or wear.

Most such patients come to treatment because of severe behavioral disturbances involving memory loss, self-harm, or psychosis. Sexual promiscuity and emotional volatility often occur. Patients may not know, or be able to communicate, their names or backgrounds. In the absence of the sort of subjective report of symptoms and history that clinicians rely on to evaluate mental illness, it can be very challenging to diagnose someone with dissociative identity disorder correctly, and the bizarre and disconnected behavior is frequently misdiagnosed as schizophrenia.

I was presented with just such a challenge at a case conference while visiting the University of Pennsylvania. The case conference is a time-honored tradition of academic medicine, in which a young physician in training presents a patient to a senior doctor. The trainee gets to show what he or she knows before an audience while testing the professor's clinical acumen.

We took our seats for the case conference in a cramped room on the hospital's inpatient unit, and the resident began to present Sarah, a twenty-eight-year-old fitness instructor from a large working-class family in South Philadelphia. She'd been a model student with many friends, and involved in community activities, among them the church choir. There had been no instances of prior mental illness or substance abuse. But there was relevant family history. In addition to some of the male members of the family using alcohol to excess, the children had been subject to physical, and possibly sexual, abuse—particularly Sarah, who was the oldest of her siblings.

Sarah was an exceptional athlete and ran track in college. But during her sophomore year, she quit the team, then left school, got a job in a health club, and moved into an apartment with two roommates. One evening Sarah went out jogging and didn't return home. She was found by police hours later on the Schuylkill River Trail, dazed and disheveled. The police brought her to the ER at the Hospital of the University of Pennsylvania. An examination determined that she was not injured and had not been sexually assaulted. The psychiatrist on duty found Sarah disoriented, inattentive, appearing to respond to internal stimuli, and talking to herself. She explained that because she had sinned, the servants of the church wanted to punish her.

Sarah was diagnosed provisionally with paranoid schizophrenia, admitted to the hospital, and treated with antipsychotics. However, over a three-week period, her symptoms didn't budge in response to any of the medications she was prescribed.

When the resident had completed her presentation, she left the room and returned with Sarah. The young woman entered the room barefoot, attired in hospital garb, and had shoulder-length strawberry blond hair that appeared unwashed and uncombed. I introduced myself and offered her the chair beside me. I thanked her for agreeing to talk with me and asked why she was in the hospital. She said that she needed a place to hide because her pursuers wanted to punish and possibly kill her due to sins she'd committed. After inquiring about her family background, job, and living circumstances, I returned to her supposed misdeeds, and asked her to elaborate. But just then, it was as though a switch was turned off. Sarah didn't say another word. I tried for several minutes to draw her out, but to no avail. She stared blankly at the staff, withdrawn into herself.

With Sarah mute, I had to improvise and decided to perform a standard neurologic examination. I tested for motor and sensory functions and "defects of will" (passivity to the point of obedience to any direction given), the latter a typical feature of catatonic schizophrenia. Sarah did not show the passivity characteristic of catatonia or the paralysis or resistance seen in conversion reactions (neurological symptoms that can't be explained by a medical condition). There were no signs of echopraxia, another feature of schizophrenia in which the patient mimics another person's actions or movements.

Eventually I had no choice but to end the interview, and Sarah was led from the room. When the resident asked me to confirm the diagnosis of schizophrenia and recommend the next course of treatment (a combination of antipsychotic medications, including the possibility of clozapine, or electroconvulsive therapy), I hesitated. As the guest expert, I was in a bind. While Sarah's welfare didn't rest on my assessment—the staff here would make the ultimate decisions on her treatment—I felt that I was being forced to offer my opinion on the basis of insufficient information.

Nevertheless, I decided to go for it. My answer was not what they expected.

"I don't believe she has schizophrenia," I said.

Everyone looked at me quizzically, as I explained that my provisional diagnosis was dissociative identity disorder. Sarah had no family history of mental illness other than possible alcohol abuse and no premorbid risk factors for schizophrenia. Her clinical exam, though limited, was consistent with dissociative identity disorder. But the key information was her developmental history of trauma.

Diagnoses of dissociative disorders are difficult to prove. An old diagnostic technique entails administering the short-acting barbiturate amobarbital, which can dramatically "wake" people from catatonic or dissociative states and reconnect them with their environment and other people. The effects are transient, however: after thirty to sixty minutes, patients lapse back into their previous condition. But the main utility here is diagnostic rather than therapeutic.

The group responded eagerly to my suggestion of conducting an Amytal interview. A few members of the group who were involved in Sarah's care prepared a treatment room and escorted her in. I explained the procedure to her. Sarah signed an informed consent, and we began to administer the drug (the hospital pharmacy didn't carry Amytal so we used lorazepam, a short-acting benzodiazepine, instead), increasing the dose incrementally until, at 1.25 milligrams, she seemed to awaken magically. She recognized me as "the doctor from New York" and began to converse coherently. She told us that she was in the hospital because she needed protection. She repeated what she'd said earlier about being in danger because of "some very bad things" she'd done. I asked what had been so heinous as to warrant such punishment, and she said it was not her fault, she was the victim, not the perpetrator. This told me that she had a glimmer of insight into her plight but was tortured by shame about whatever had happened to her.

The procedure lasted about twenty minutes. Although none of her answers had provided much information, her dramatic reaction to the medication (she was still delusional but had become responsive and aware of her surroundings) supported my diagnosis of dissociative disorder. Still, I had no illusions that the procedure or the information we'd elicited would facilitate her recovery. I left the hospital that day feeling troubled, knowing that any path to recovery from what afflicted Sarah would be uncertain and arduous. If I had done her any good, it was in sparing her from misdiagnosis with schizophrenia and unnecessary treatment with antipsychotic medications, and indicating that instead she would be best served by trauma-informed psychotherapy.

Thirty years later, I cannot think of Sarah without also thinking of Ariana,￭

patient whose baffling array of symptoms I had attempted, unsuccessfully, to treat early in my career. Every physician who cares for patients has flashbulb memories of certain ones, usually those he or she has failed to help or whose outcome was especially tragic. Michael Juman, whom I discussed in chapter 12 and to whom this book is dedicated, is one. Ariana is another. I had largely put Ariana and that whole strange episode out of my mind, but while writing this book, I recalled what had occurred on the evening of our final session and wondered, Had I been party to a genuine supernatural encounter? Or was it a transient flight of fancy in which my imagination got the better of me? If the latter, the likely alternative was clearly dissociative identity disorder (or dissociative trance disorder, the diagnosis we had given Billy Friedkin's demon-possessed Rosa in chapter 1). As I turned it over and over in my mind, I became increasingly curious and decided to look for answers.

My first thought was to delve into Ariana's records. I searched my patient files, which had traveled with me over my moves, from New York City to Chapel Hill, and back to New York City. But while I have been able to find all the other charts of patients described in this book, I couldn't find a trace of Ariana's records anywhere. I had no more luck obtaining her hospital records. She had been hospitalized at St. Vincent's Hospital in New York City, which had been forced to close in 2006 for financial reasons. Its records had been transferred to a storage facility in Colorado. The facility, not surprisingly, couldn't release any information without patient consent; nor would it say whether it even had records for Ariana. I double-checked my old appointment books to make sure I was using the correct surname and called all the listed numbers under that name. Finally, I reached out to the professional identity tracker and genealogist I had used for Brandon Staglin, but she also came up empty-handed. It was as if Ariana and her family had never existed.

My last resort was to find Judith, the family therapist I had asked to work with me on Ariana's case and whom I hadn't seen since that collaboration. To my relief, she was easy to find, living in Connecticut and practicing psychotherapy.

Judith confirmed my recollection of Ariana and our efforts to treat her. In fact, she recalled more details than I did about our interaction with the seventeen-year-old, and specifically the "psychic variable" of her diagnosis. Judith reminded me that in addition to our joint sessions, she had seen Ariana on her own a few times, and clearly recalled three of what she called her "alters": the alternate mental states or identities that form as dissociative defense mechanisms to wall off the trauma of repeated sexual, physical, emotional, or spiritual assaults. One alter was a seductive young woman, another a scared child of about four, and the third an older, verbally abusive, and intimidating man. Alters are often associated with key points or ages in the trauma history; given the nature of Ariana's alters, Judith believed that she had experienced some kind of abuse—perhaps ritualized in nature—at a very young age.

Judith remembered our last appointment with Ariana, and how I'd called her later that evening, "freaked out," as she recounted, about the strange things that had happened to me in my apartment. Judith recounted her own "attack" that night, in which she, too, had felt threatened by an unknown presence. In the thirty-five years since we'd treated Ariana, Judith had treated other people provisionally diagnosed with dissociative identity disorder and had in some instances experienced similar "menacing dark energies," as she put it, that left her feeling strange and frightened.

When I put the question to her directly, Judith hedged. "Do you believe that Ariana was spiritually possessed?" I asked. She said she believed that Ariana's problems were occurring on two planes. At the psychological level, the young woman displayed signs of dissociative identity disorder and/or PTSD due to childhood trauma, but this made her vulnerable to being preyed upon by the spirit world. Judith reconciled these diagnoses by suggesting that people with severe mental disorders (including psychosis, dissociative identity disorder, and PTSD) have very porous boundaries of the self and are therefore more vulnerable to what Judith referred to as "spirit attachments": energetic entities that adhere to people, places, and things and can be at the root of a combination of physical, mental, emotional, and spiritual issues. These spirit attachments exist separately from mental illness and trauma but can contribute to them.

In dissociative identity disorder cases in which there has been repeated abuse, Judith said that if a therapist can gain the trust of the alters, they may begin to reveal details of the trauma. At that point, the threat of exposures for the abusers becomes real, and these energetic entities are invoked to frighten off those who are trying to help the victim.

Judith's recollections of Ariana and our experience working with her were generally consistent with mine. Though I thought she was trying to have it both ways in her explanations of Ariana's condition, she seemed utterly sincere. I persisted in trying to pin her down, but Judith would not give a categorical answer.

Eventually it dawned on me that she might be trying to protect me, either from the things that she herself had become aware of or vulnerable to or from any damage to my professional reputation. As a physician and researcher devoted to science and empiricism, how could I believe in spirits?

While I appreciated her consideration and magnanimity, I would have preferred a straight answer. Judith's professional orientation had clearly evolved from when she was in graduate school at Columbia. But rather than dismissing what she was saying, I tried to keep an open mind. If these things exist—supernatural phenomena, spirit attachments, and positive and negative energy—they would surely confound the diagnosis of schizophrenia. But then, so did phenocopies and facsimiles. We were far indeed from my comfort zone of genes, neurons, and neurotransmitters. But one thing was clear: I was no closer to understanding what had happened that night in my apartment than I'd been thirty-five years ago.

My diagnostic quest had reached an impasse. I had been stumped before, but this was particularly unsettling: accepting Judith's explanation suggesting a spiritual or paranormal experience required me to betray my scientific convictions. Stuck between the scientific Scylla and the spiritual Charybdis, I recalled an experience that I had on a trip to Israel many years ago. While visiting the Wailing Wall in the Old City of Jerusalem, one of the holiest places in the world to followers of Judaism, Christianity, and Islam, I had a momentary reverie in which I seemed to lose my sense of self and felt directed by external forces. The next thing I knew, I was standing in an alcove next to the wall, wearing a yarmulke, prayer shawl, and tefillin, a set of small black leather boxes containing parchment scrolls with passages from the Torah and attached with straps, beside a rabbi who was reading from a Torah scroll. Finally, my wife's voice pierced the rabbi's chanting: "Jeffrey, where were you? What are you doing and what are you wearing?" As my wife tugged at my arm, I recovered my awareness and presence of mind, removed the religious paraphernalia, and tried to flee the scene, but not before the rabbi's attendants demanded payment for the blessings that had been bestowed upon me.

Back at the hotel, I sought to make sense of what had happened and searched the Internet for information on something that I had been aware of but never experienced: Jerusalem syndrome. It was described as an altered state of consciousness in which a person experiences depersonalization, disorientation, and intense religiously themed ideas, delusions, or other psychosis-like encounters triggered by a visit to holy sites. It typically resolves in days or weeks, and more rapidly if one leaves the area. (Interestingly, it is not listed as a recognized condition in the *DSM* or the *International Classification of Diseases (ICD)*, the latter published by the World Health Organization.) Though this recollection did not necessarily shed light on Ariana's diagnosis, it reminded me that it was possible to occupy a philosophical middle ground, straddling both rational and irrational (or perhaps just spiritual) modes of understanding.

Ariana was a complicated case without an entirely clear diagnosis; given her symptoms, it was not implausible to believe that she suffered either from schizophrenia or from dissociative identity disorder, related wholly or in part to childhood trauma. Or perhaps it was something else. I cannot disavow what I experienced working with Ariana and Judith all those years ago, that frightening night in my apartment, any more than I could deny the unreality and vividness of what I had experienced at the Wailing Wall. Had we continued to work with her, we might have unraveled the mystery. As it is, I'll likely never know.

Chapter 17

Diagnosing Schizophrenia

To seize the true character of mental derangement in a given case,
and to pronounce an infallible prognosis of the event, is often a task of
particular delicacy, and requires the united exertion of great discernment, of
extensive knowledge, and of incorruptible integrity.

—Philippe Pinel,
A Treatise on Insanity (1801)

Looks Can Be Deceiving

While I never met my maternal grandfather, my mother told me that in the late 1930s, when he was fifty-seven years old, he developed a mysterious and agonizing illness from which he ultimately died. The baffling condition caused a searing pain in his head that was triggered by any noise. If he was lying in a bedroom in the back of their two-story house and heard someone ascending the front stairs, the sound would send him into a fit of tormented screams known as hyperacusis. My mother, who had just entered adolescence, remembers him beating his head and crying out, "The pressure! The pressure!" His pain was so excruciating that he grew agitated, and his thinking and behavior became deranged to the point that he appeared unhinged.

I grew up aware of this part of his story, but over the course of writing this book I learned of previously hidden aspects of my family's history. One was the outcome of my grandfather's illness. The doctors where he was ultimately hospitalized diagnosed him with a mental disorder, which infuriated my grandmother. She insisted that it was pain that had driven him, so to speak, "out of his mind"; he wasn't delusional, hallucinating, or thought disordered, and in the brief moments when the pain subsided he was perfectly lucid and coherent.

Throughout his illness, my grandmother never wavered in her belief that her husband was not mentally ill, and she was not afraid to voice her opinion to doctors. However, in 1942, despite my grandmother's protests, my grandfather was transferred to Cleveland State Hospital, where he died a month later. This was the same mental institution where my aunt Rose had been kept for so many years, which I visited as a boy on that school field trip, and where my mother had volunteered.

My grandmother was ultimately vindicated when an autopsy revealed that he died of encephalomyelitis, an inflammation of the brain and spinal cord. In his case, this was caused by a tear in the meninges, the protective membranes surrounding the brain and spinal cord. This allowed cerebrospinal fluid to leak out, causing his brain to dehydrate and excruciating symptoms. My grandmother was right. Her husband had not been mentally ill. His death certificate, which I retrieved, provided that proof. Today this condition would be diagnosed immediately and readily treated by surgically applying a patch to the source of the leak. The patient would be expected to recover completely.

FINDING THE CULPRIT

Diagnosing an illness is like solving a mystery, and even more so when the brain is the malfunctioning organ. The culprit is the illness, which cannot self-disclose but whose identity must be discovered. Its name is the diagnosis. The first step is to interview the victim, establishing what is called the chief complaint.

A complication of diagnosing people with schizophrenia is that when they are acutely symptomatic, they may not be reliable sources of information, so we must also consult people close to the patient. After establishing the chief complaint, the doctor should obtain complete histories (psychiatric, medical, social, and developmental) from the patient, informants, and other sources of information, such as medical records. In addition, the person's demographic, socioeconomic, and cultural circumstances should be assessed as part of the evaluation. Finally, in recent years, the Internet and social media have also become sources, albeit of uncertain accuracy. This is called the digital phenotype. Additional assessments follow as warranted. Pedigrees and genotyping provide information about possible inherited propensities or disorders, while mental status exams and lab tests can reveal medical or neurological problems. Brain imaging is useful, as corroborative evidence of a diagnosis of schizophrenia can yield information possibly relevant to a prognosis.

These steps should be undertaken systematically and comprehensively (the diagnostic process is described in appendix 6), but the answer we derive is not automatic; we don't input the information into a computer, which then spits out a diagnosis. Instead, we rely on a combination of scientific knowledge, medical experience, and clinical judgment. This is where the *art of medicine*—using knowledge and experience in a way that is intuitive rather than prescriptive—must complement the science, especially in psychiatry.

THE CHIEF COMPLAINT

A diagnostic interview begins with identifying the chief complaint: Why is this person seeking care? For physical ailments, chief complaints include pain, shortness of breath, fatigue, indigestion. Examples of chief complaints for mental ailments are anxiety, insomnia, sadness, deranged thoughts, inability to concentrate. In the case of schizophrenia, it usually involves strange behavior and mental changes—bizarre or disorganized thoughts, false beliefs, hearing voices—severe enough to be noticeable and distressing to the patient and/or loved ones.

Ideally, the patient would see a psychiatrist, but many people begin by consulting their primary care physician, who then refers them to a psychiatrist or other mental health professional. Because of a lack of awareness of the symptoms of mental illness, a denial of their significance, embarrassment, or not knowing how or where to seek help, the time lag between the onset of symptoms and accessing professional help is far too long.

An additional factor adds to the delay: mental illness corrupts the very organ that enables us to have insight into our condition. The person in need of care does not see her hallucinations and delusions as symptoms but is convinced they are real; therefore, she doesn't need treatment. It's like someone with a crushing chest pain that extends to his left shoulder and down the arm refusing to believe he's having a heart attack. But in the case of the heart attack, the brain can rationally evaluate the symptoms, which a brain whose function is compromised by schizophrenia is often unable to do.

This inability is different from denial and is thought to be due to a cognitive deficit, a neurological condition called anosognosia, which comes from the

Greek: *a*, meaning "without," *nosos* ("disease"), and *gnosis* ("knowledge"). In the case of strokes, it can manifest as lack of awareness about an affected part of the body. In the case of schizophrenia, it is lack of awareness of one's symptoms *as symptoms*, and it often leads to tragic consequences, as sufferers delay seeking help until a severe psychotic episode occurs, and they harm either themselves or others or are taken forcibly to the hospital. The dilemma is compounded by current legal statutes, which typically state that people over eighteen cannot be compelled to accept treatment against their will unless they can be proven to be imminent dangers to themselves or others. Bizarre and frightening behavior is not sufficient cause for mandatory medical evaluation or treatment, only violence or threats of violence.

The laws related to the right to refuse care have a long and complex history, which will be discussed in chapter 20. There are many good reasons for proceeding with caution when considering treating someone against his or her will—not least the history of abuses we've seen in previous chapters. But there is no doubt that in the case of schizophrenia, the basic premise of autonomy is complicated by this lack of awareness and the conviction sufferers have in the content of their hallucinations and delusions. I have seen this dilemma play out in numerous cases on which I've consulted, including one where a young man became convinced that his stepmother was trying to poison him—a belief that resulted in horrific consequences.

Growing up, Troy Hill loved sports. He was outgoing, had many friends, and was a good athlete. His parents had divorced when he was very young, and Troy was a caring big brother to his younger twin half brothers, often playing football or basketball with them. In 2006 he headed off to a small university in western Pennsylvania on a football scholarship.

He completed his freshman year, but problems began to surface in June after he'd returned to his father and stepmother's home in Pittsburgh for the summer. After smoking marijuana one night, Troy came into his parents' bedroom and told them he felt strange. He thought the pot might have been laced with something. His parents weren't happy, but they weren't unduly worried, either. Then, in early July Troy was at a family party and found himself feeling like an outsider. Over the rest of that summer, he isolated himself from his family and friends. During a visit to his biological mother in Virginia, he developed a delusion that he smelled bad and began taking long showers, sometimes three times a day. One day he tried to attack his mother's friend with a knife over a dispute about a washcloth.

His mother intervened and made him drop the knife. On another occasion, while asking his mother repeatedly if he smelled bad, he said to her, "Why don't you just take a knife and stab me with it?" He quit his job because he believed that his coworkers were talking about him and his (supposed) odor.

At the end of the summer, his father drove him back to college for football camp, but after two days, Troy wanted to come home. He told his father he no longer wanted to play football or attend college. His football coach remembers him simply walking off the field one day. This was completely out of character, because all his life, Troy had lived and breathed football.

After returning to his father's house, Troy would sit alone for long stretches in the basement, sometimes in total darkness, sometimes watching TV, which he imagined was communicating with him. He also believed that his parents were speaking about him in code.

His family became increasingly concerned, but Troy refused to see a doctor and did not believe anything was wrong with him. On August 27 Troy's grandmother called the Western Psychiatric Institute and Clinic (WPIC), part of the University of Pittsburgh, and a Mobile Crisis Team came to the house. Troy's father and grandmother met with the two crisis workers; when the team tried to interview Troy, he was largely unresponsive, insisting that he was fine and saying he didn't know why the medical team was there.

Here is where the stories start to vary. The crisis team, according to their subsequent deposition, described the options to the family: Troy could go voluntarily for evaluation at the hospital; they could make an appointment for a medical evaluation; or they could pursue a "302"—an involuntary admission to a hospital psychiatric unit. Later, the Hill family disputed this, saying the crisis team did not discuss involuntary hospitalization with them. Regardless of whose recollection was correct, the process of committing Troy would not have been easy, nor would it have guaranteed a hospital stay long enough to stabilize him. If Troy was hospitalized, he would immediately be visited by a mental health lawyer and granted a hearing within seventy-two hours; if a compelling case for his potential danger was not made, the presiding judge might order him to be released, after which Troy would be under no requirement to undergo treatment. This scenario illustrates the conundrum facing family members and mental health providers: Do you err on the side of caution and impose civil commitment over someone's wishes, or do you honor his or her civil liberties and refuse to petition for commitment, even if you feel it's needed? If you go the latter route, you are hoping that someone who is delusional or hallucinating won't tip into self-harm or lash out violently at others.

Given Troy's unwillingness to go to the hospital or speak with a doctor or, at the very least, make an appointment for an intake evaluation, there was nothing more the team members could do. They gave the family a pamphlet on an early-onset-psychosis program and asked the Hills to monitor Troy and call WPIC if his condition worsened. The following morning, one of the team made a routine follow-up call and was told Troy's condition was unchanged.

The next afternoon, tragedy struck. When the twins returned home from school, Troy brought them down to the basement and asked them repeatedly if their mother was putting something in his food, which they repeatedly denied. Troy was becoming angry. He went upstairs and got a butcher knife, which he concealed under his shirt. He returned downstairs, stabbed his brothers, then wrapped them in blankets and brought them up to the attic before fleeing the house.

The boys' grandfather, who lived across the street, discovered the horrific scene. His daughter—the twins' mother and Troy's stepmother—had called him out of concern when no one was answering the phone at home. When he went to the house to check, he saw blood everywhere. He found the boys and immediately called 911. Although one of the twins lived, the other could not be saved.

Troy was arrested the following day when he showed up at a woman's door asking her to call 911, as he wanted to turn himself in. He was charged with criminal homicide and attempted homicide but was deemed unfit to stand trial and transferred to a state mental hospital, where he was diagnosed with schizophrenia.

Two years after the killing, Troy's family filed a civil suit against WPIC and the crisis team members, arguing that the team failed to exercise reasonable care in providing services; the hospital argued that neither Troy nor his family had told it that Troy had made any specific threats of violence. I was asked to be an expert witness and testified that the failure was not on the part of the crisis team but with the laws to which they were subject, which prevented them from providing mental health care. Although Troy had clearly been psychotic and needed care, the team was constrained because of Troy's right to refuse treatment.

The Hill family settled with the Institute in 2015 for $3 million. Two years later, the prosecution dismissed the charges against Troy. He had been cooperative in his treatment and had moved from the hospital to a residential program and finally to his own apartment. He must remain in treatment, and the court will continue to have jurisdiction over his case.

Involuntary commitment to a psychiatric ward is not something to be undertaken lightly—either by a family or by those with the legal authority to compel it. But neither do we want this sort of senseless, often preventable tragedy.

PSYCHIATRIC, MEDICAL, DEVELOPMENTAL, AND SOCIAL HISTORIES

After the chief complaint is established and the patient's motivation for care is identified, the history of the patient's psychiatric illness should be fully established. This begins with the current episode and then includes past psychiatric history. A psychiatric history includes the following information: when the symptoms of the current episode of illness began and any precipitating or triggering events such as stress, recreational drug use, or forgetting to take antipsychotic medication; past episodes of active psychotic symptoms; circumstances surrounding previous episodes; past treatments, including names of drugs, doses, duration of administration; effectiveness and adherence to treatment; and consistency (or variability) of symptoms over time.

One of the most vexing things about reviewing the records of patients on whom I consult is the different diagnoses. It's not unusual to meet someone whose history includes diagnoses of schizophreniform disorder, bipolar disorder, schizoaffective disorder, depression with psychotic symptoms, and schizophrenia. Generally speaking, a diagnosis of schizophrenia is stable over a person's lifetime, so most of the variability in patient records is due to the unreliability of clinicians' diagnoses. To the extent that there is any evolution in symptoms over the course of schizophrenia, they should not be great enough to change the diagnosis. Over time, symptoms may shift from predominantly florid psychotic symptoms (delusional systems and rich hallucinations) to negative symptoms, like loss of emotionality, limited interest and initiative, and deteriorated intellect. It's as if the psychotic dimension of the illness burns itself out. The new variable, as we'll see in chapters 18 and 19, is state-of-the-art treatment, which can influence the course of schizophrenia and prevent its progression.

A medical history pertains to any serious medical conditions or chronic physical illnesses and tends to be more straightforward than the past psychiatric history, particularly if someone has been mentally ill for some time. I firmly believe, and have long taught my students, that patients with long-term illnesses should be approached in the same way as those who've only recently become ill: begin as if you know nothing and review the patient's entire history. Don't assume the accuracy of prior diagnoses and verify the details of previous treatments. This is obviously more difficult when you have a patient who has been ill for twenty or thirty years, has had numerous hospitalizations, and has volumes of medical records, but shortcuts risk perpetuating wrong diagnoses and mistakenly concluding that treatments weren't effective, when it may be the case that they weren't administered at the right dose or duration.

The course of a patient's physical, cognitive, and social development can be a rich source of information, as it reflects constitutional factors that may be related to schizophrenia risk and expression. A developmental history should include whether conception was natural or surgical, any complications during pregnancy or delivery, and details about the person's development (for instance, from the postnatal period, whether developmental milestones were reached on schedule through adolescence), academic performance, and any behavioral or learning difficulties. Among the strongest risk factors for developing schizophrenia are prematurity and low birth weight, which can be consequences of fetal exposure to toxic or traumatic insults that may complicate the illness. It should be noted that these hazards are not specific to schizophrenia but to behavioral brain disorders more generally.

Of course, socioeconomic and cultural factors play a significant role here. Other risk factors include poverty, malnutrition, unhygienic living conditions, exposure to violence, and rates of substance abuse. Racial and cultural bias within the medical system also impacts patients, leading to disparities in diagnosis: studies from North America and Europe have shown that the diagnostic rates of schizophrenia are markedly higher in black people and moderately higher in people of Hispanic heritage when compared to white people.

Immigration status also affects risk, with numerous studies finding that schizophrenia rates are higher among immigrants to countries—possibly related to, in addition to cultural or racial bias, the stress associated with being in a foreign culture.

Gender is also an issue for diagnosis, as men are more often diagnosed with schizophrenia than women.

A social history assesses a patient's interpersonal and recreational activities: friendships, romantic partners, and any children (and the health of those relationships); use of recreational drugs; education and employment history; legal trouble;

and any abrupt changes in the pattern of social activities. This last topic is important, as the onset of schizophrenia so commonly involves a young person showing marked changes in behavior and interests: withdrawing from former friends, for instance, and taking up with new and often different kinds of people, or avoiding social contact and becoming isolated. It's important to be aware, when doing this assessment, that the standards against which a person's activities should be judged are relative, and should be considered in relation to their demographic peer group.

PEDIGREES, GENOTYPING, AND GENEALOGY

Given that genes play such a key role in schizophrenia, a family history is crucial to uncovering the presence of the schizophrenia phenotype in a patient's biological relatives. The best way to do this is to construct a family tree, also called a pedigree—a schematic representation of a family across generations that displays patterns of inheritance regarding illnesses (schizophrenia, diabetes, autism, hypertension, and so on). Pedigrees can indicate which members express or silently carry the gene(s) for a given trait or disease, and can be complemented by genotyping, performed by extracting DNA from a blood sample, a mouth swab, or saliva sample, and sequencing some or all of the person's genome. All the better if DNA can be obtained from the parents and as many family members as possible to verify the pattern of transmission through generations and whether any mutations are inherited or spontaneous (de novo).

Pedigrees can reveal three patterns of familial illness: (1) family members affected by schizophrenia or traits associated with the illness (schizotypal personality); (2) family members affected by other serious mental disorders; and (3) an absence of mental illness. For a number of reasons, even the most thorough family history will likely underrepresent the presence of mental illness. In previous generations, people were less likely to be aware that strange behavior might indicate mental disturbance (and so many people were misdiagnosed or went undiagnosed), and more reluctant to expose the family to the stigma that would come from seeking diagnosis and treatment for psychotic or mood disorders.

The accuracy and completeness of pedigrees can be enhanced by genealogical information about previous generations, including birth and death certificates, and hospital, census, immigration, and legal records. The combination of genealogically enhanced pedigrees with genotyping is the current gold standard for creating family histories, and contributes important information to the diagnostic process, but this level of information is rarely obtained, as genealogies are expensive and labor intensive.

While pedigrees can show familial patterns of illness, genotyping can reveal which genes may be associated with the individual patient's schizophrenia. Genotyping will soon become more affordable, and research has demonstrated its clinical utility for diagnosis and treatment selection. We saw the possible use of genotyping to indicate the preferred treatment of a mental illness in chapter 12 with Jessie Close and Calen Pick, whose cases illustrate the powerful potential of precision medicine.

Mental Status and Other Examinations

The mental status examination (MSE) is the equivalent of the physical exam for mental disorders. If the patient isn't able to follow a systematic line of questioning, the doctor can talk and interact with the patient in a more free-form manner, while observing his or her speech, behavior, and mental acuity. Patients with paranoid delusions, on the other hand, may be perfectly coherent and lucid but guarded and unwilling to be forthcoming. In these instances, the doctor observes behavior and makes inferences that can be corroborated and expanded upon by other sources of information.

The structure of an MSE works through a number of categories, including a patient's level of consciousness, appearance and general behavior, speech and motor activity, affect and mood, thought organization and content, perception, and cognition. Because schizophrenia has been associated with minor physical and neurologic anomalies, physical and neurological exams should be performed. (This can also reveal medical problems from which people with schizophrenia are commonly known to suffer.) Soft neurologic signs such as lack of dexterity or imprecise sensory perception indicate the presence of brain developmental anomalies and are often signs of severe illness. As schizophrenia is usually not associated with any characteristic laboratory abnormalities, standard lab tests are generally not diagnostic; they are routinely performed, however, largely to identify medical disorders and to rule out diagnoses that can mimic schizophrenia. Lab tests, antibody screening, and certain diagnostic screening tools such as MRI, PET (for reasons described in the next section), and EEG (to rule out seizures) should be performed on all patients at the beginning of the illness; some tests should be repeated periodically to track any changes. The MSE and a list of relevant tests can be found in appendix 6.

BRAIN IMAGING

MRIs and PET scans are not in themselves diagnostic of schizophrenia, but the structural abnormalities they reveal (described in chapter 11) can offer corroborating evidence. For example, if I see a young person with psychotic symptoms showing on an MRI enlarged symmetrical ventricles and reduced volume in the hippocampus, I take this as strengthening the case for a diagnosis of schizophrenia. Conversely, a patient whose MRI shows neither of these abnormalities is less likely to be suffering from schizophrenia. PET scanning has yielded one of the most promising measures for a biomarker of schizophrenia. Akin to a stress test for the brain, the procedure measures the concentration of dopamine released into the synapses of critical neural circuits. People with schizophrenia will have concentrations that are two to three times greater than those without the illness.

One of the most notorious instances of brain structural abnormalities offered as evidence of schizophrenia was in the trial of John Hinckley Jr., the young man who attempted to assassinate President Ronald Reagan in 1981 as he was leaving the Hilton Hotel in Washington, DC. Hinckley had experienced intermittent psychiatric problems and had developed an obsession with actress Jodie Foster after seeing the movie *Taxi Driver*, in which Robert De Niro plays a Vietnam vet who plans to assassinate a presidential candidate and attempts to rescue Jodie Foster's character from prostitution. In attempting to assassinate Reagan, Hinckley was trying to impress Foster. His legal defense was that he was mentally ill, couldn't distinguish reality from fiction, and didn't understand the illegality of his actions.

Two psychiatrists, William Carpenter and David Bear, served as expert witnesses for the defense. Both diagnosed Hinckley with schizophrenia. Bear wanted to introduce CT scan images of Hinckley's brain and infuriated the judge by refusing to proceed with his testimony unless this was allowed as proof of the diagnosis. Prosecutors ultimately waived their objection, and images of Hinckley's brain were shown on a slide projector. There was general agreement that the scans showed some brain volume shrinkage, but various experts debated the significance of the changes to Hinckley's mental state, as not every person with schizophrenia exhibits these changes.

Ultimately, the jury found Hinckley not guilty by reason of insanity, and he was remanded to St. Elizabeths Hospital in Washington, DC, where he remained until 2021, when a federal judge ruled that he was no longer a threat to himself or others and granted his unconditional release.

Since the Hinckley trial, much progress has been made in developing imaging procedures that capture the pathologic features of schizophrenia. Although these techniques have not been wholly validated and incorporated into current diagnostic criteria, they still provide useful information. In my own practice, I have relied on brain imaging in different ways, such as with my patient Sean, discussed in chapter 14, who abused amphetamines; in his case, brain imaging helped to disprove a diagnosis of schizophrenia.

ALTERNATIVE DIAGNOSES

Advances in medical science are often slow to impact psychiatry; this includes precision medicine. However, when the renowned geneticist David Goldstein was recruited to Columbia to become director of the Institute for Genomic Medicine, I saw an opportunity to tap into his expertise. Given the enormity of the challenge in pinpointing the cause(s) of schizophrenia, Goldstein's recommendation was to focus on what he called "extreme phenotypes." These were unusual cases of schizophrenia in which the patients had distinct features in terms of illness severity, dysmorphia (deformity or abnormality in the shape or size of certain parts of the body), lack of treatment response, and poor outcomes reflected in persistent symptoms and cognitive decline. Goldstein speculated that while most schizophrenia patients had polygenic forms of the illness—meaning the involvement of tens or hundreds of common genes, each with low penetrance but contributing additively to a person's disease risk—the most severely ill patients (extreme phenotypes) had higher rates of rare mutations of individual genes with high penetrance, meaning genes that by themselves conferred a strong likelihood of developing the disease.

Goldstein had proven the utility of examining extreme phenotypes in neurological disorders such as epilepsy. If his hunch that the strategy could be applied to patients with schizophrenia was correct, it would show that the illness could take yet another genetic form. The product (the biochemical material resulting from the gene expression) of a given genetic mutation could yield critical clues about which treatment would target the aberrant protein most effectively and have the best chance of relieving patients' symptoms after standard antipsychotics had failed. This approach of using drugs that target mutated gene products has been studied extensively and proven successful in experiments with rodents. For extreme phenotypes, the most effective treatments may not be among those ordinarily considered for treating mental illness.

We decided to apply Goldstein's strategy by studying New York State mental hospital inpatients. As the policy of deinstitutionalization had pared down the state hospitals' population from a high of more than 558,000 in 1955 to just 52,000 in 2018, it was reasonable to suspect that among the remaining patients were the sickest of the sick, with a high proportion exhibiting extreme phenotypes. At the same time, we could also screen long-term patients for autoimmunity to see if any of them had been misdiagnosed, as Susannah Cahalan had been initially.

Along with three other faculty, I met with David to plan the study. Anthony Zoghbi was a trainee in our department with an interest in psychiatric genetics, Sander Markx was a psychiatrist who had worked with Josep Dalmau in characterizing the clinical syndrome of limbic encephalitis from which Susannah had suffered, and Terry Goldberg was a neuropsychologist whose research had focused on the cognitive deficits associated with schizophrenia.

We began by assessing the symptoms and cognitive functions of all inpatients diagnosed with schizophrenia who met criteria for extreme forms of the illness, and then taking blood samples from them to extract DNA for genotyping and antibody analyses. We considered a patient to have an "extreme phenotype" if he or she had been resident in an inpatient facility for five or more years and was treatment resistant, meaning that he or she was suffering continued psychotic symptoms despite adequate trials of at least two antipsychotic medications for six weeks or more—and had either dysmorphic features (slightly unusual or abnormal physical appearance) or significant cognitive impairment. The results would show what proportion of the extreme phenotype patients had rare genetic mutations or autoimmune reactions. What we would learn from this study might offer these patients a chance to be treated effectively.

New York State's commissioner of the Office of Mental Health, Anne Sullivan, and Chief Medical Officer Tom Smith were excited about the project. They said that even if only one patient could be rescued from lifelong illness and institutionalization, it would be worth it. We likened the undertaking to the Innocence Project, the nonprofit organization that uses DNA testing to exonerate prisoners wrongly convicted of crimes.

The first phase of the study was implemented at the Pilgrim Psychiatric Center on Long Island. The center, which opened in 1929 as Pilgrim State Hospital, was then the largest facility of its kind in the world. Though it now has fewer than three hundred inpatients, at its peak, in 1954, it housed almost fourteen thousand patients; it was like a self-contained city, with its own waterworks, sewage system, fire and police departments, courts, cemetery, and farm.

Zoghbi, Markx, and Goldberg examined each of the 268 patients at Pilgrim who'd been diagnosed with schizophrenia. Among them was a forty-two-year-old African American woman named Jamie. She'd been the valedictorian of her high school class and had made the dean's list every year of college. Three years after graduation, by then a successful saleswoman at a hospital supply company, she developed florid psychotic symptoms that didn't respond to any treatments—including various antipsychotics, mood stabilizers, and ECT. Eventually Jamie was admitted to Pilgrim State Hospital, where she remained for the next twenty-plus years, with persistent symptoms and marked deterioration in her functioning. Jamie didn't know what year it was and, while hospitalized, often believed she was in her own home. She was also incontinent.

Jamie's blood samples showed elevated antibodies indicative of an autoimmune encephalopathy. She was transferred to the New York State Psychiatric Institute for further evaluation and treatment. After consulting with colleagues in immunology and neurology, the team agreed to proceed on the assumption that Jamie likely had an autoimmune encephalitis; we treated it with medications to suppress her immune system, and Jamie responded well—so well, in fact, that when she was transferred back to Pilgrim, the staff and her family were taken by surprise. She was less prone to psychotic disorganized behavior and better able to attend to her own needs. On cognitive tests, her dementia scores, which had been severe, now showed moderate impairment.

The change in Jamie's mental state is evident in two images she produced before and after treatment, when she was asked to draw a clock face from memory. But while the improvement was significant, she was not well enough to be discharged from the institution. Sadly, after several weeks, she slid back toward the condition in which we had found her. Jamie's capacity for sustained recovery was limited, given how long she'd been ill. Had she been diagnosed and treated properly two decades earlier, she might have been able to sustain her recovery, as Susannah Cahalan had. It may be impossible to untangle everything that lead to her misdiagnosis—whether it was due to disparities in mental health care services, like those often faced by African American patients seeking treatment, or the lack of knowledge about autoimmune encephalitis at the time of her diagnosis or a range of other factors—but any misdiagnosis of this kind is a tragedy.

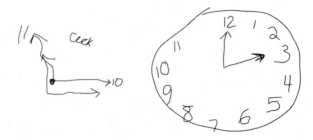

Two re-creations of clock drawings, done as part of the Montreal Cognitive Assessment (MoCA), show Jamie's level of impairment pretreatment (left side) and post-treatment (right side). Jamie's post-treatment drawing was much improved, though not perfect.

As this project progressed in parallel with writing this book, I wondered whether patients like Jamie, or even Ariana might be embedded among the residuum of state mental hospital patients. While it was an outlandish idea, so were the prospects of general paresis of the insane in the early 1900s when the microorganism that caused syphilis was found in the brain; as were the enduring consequences of methamphetamine when first realized in Japan and Germany during and after World War II; as well as the 22q11 deletion (DiGeorge) syndrome when its genetic basis was discovered in 1981; and autoimmune (limbic) encephalitis when antibodies to glutamate receptors in the brain were discovered in 2007.

The results of our study of extreme phenotypes, along with those of other studies, have revealed that some patients diagnosed with schizophrenia really had other identifiable illnesses that could have been detected by genotyping and laboratory analysis of blood samples. This could have been used to inform the choice of treatments. We don't know how common these distinct causes that mimic schizophrenia are, but, as Anne Sullivan and Tom Smith said, if such diagnostic workups spare even one patient from years of ineffective treatment and unnecessary institutionalization it would be worth it.

Chapter 18

The Importance of
Early Intervention

An ounce of prevention is worth a pound of cure.

—Benjamin Franklin

The Patient

In 1981, after having completed my training, I was starting my first job working at Mount Sinai Hospital and School of Medicine. I arrived home late one evening, exhausted after a long day of work, and crawled into bed. I was intending to read myself to sleep, as I normally did. I reached for the stack of *New Yorker* magazines on the nightstand and opened a copy to an article by Susan Sheehan called "The Patient." It told the story of Sylvia Frumkin, a pseudonym for a thirty-year-old woman with schizophrenia. I was hooked from the opening scene, which read like a tragic burlesque:

> Shortly after midnight on Friday, June 16, 1978, Sylvia Frumkin decided to take a bath. Miss Frumkin, a heavy, ungainly young woman who lived in a two-story yellow brick building in Queens Village, New York, walked from her bedroom on the second floor to the bathroom next door and filled the tub with warm water. A few days earlier, she had had her hair cut and shaped in a bowl style, which she found especially becoming, and her spirits were high. She washed her brown hair with shampoo and also with red mouthwash. Some years earlier, she had tinted her hair red and had liked the way it looked. She had given up wearing her hair red

only because she had found coloring it every six weeks too much of a bother. She imagined that the red mouthwash would somehow be absorbed into her scalp and make her hair red permanently. Miss Frumkin felt so cheerful about her new haircut that she suddenly thought she was Lori Lemaris, the mermaid whom Clark Kent had met in college and had fallen in love with in the old *Superman* comics. She blew bubbles into the water.

After a few minutes of contented frolicking, Miss Frumkin stepped out of the tub. She slipped on the bathroom floor—it was wet from her bubble-blowing and splashing—and cut the back of her head as she fell.

Sylvia poured some perfume on the cut. She knew perfume would be antiseptic, but she also now believed that she was Jesus Christ and that the bleeding on her head was the beginning of a crown of thorns. When the bleeding didn't stop, she eventually contacted the supervisor of her building, who drove her to the ER at Long Island Jewish–Hillside Medical Center. Sylvia's behavior was bizarre enough that the doctor stitching her head called for a psychiatric resident to evaluate her. By that time, Sylvia was repeatedly taking off her clothes and alternating between accusing the super of kidnapping her and asking him and the security guard to have sex with her.

By about five in the morning, Sylvia had been admitted to Creedmoor Psychiatric Center, the huge mental hospital on the eastern edge of Queens County. It was not her first admission to Creedmoor; nor would it be her last.

Creedmoor, which Sheehan describes as smelling of "coffee, stale cigarette smoke, and unwashed and incontinent patients," was a case study in how not to treat a psychiatric patient, though it was hardly unique in the annals of mental hospitals. Sylvia spent weeks in a straitjacket and was subjected to insulin coma therapy. Creedmoor's "seclusion rooms" had no pads on the walls, despite the fact that patients often banged their heads against them. The medical charts were riddled with errors. There were cultural barriers, too. A foreign doctor who didn't know that Mary Poppins (whom Sylvia insisted she knew) was a fictional character misdiagnosed Sylvia with bipolar disorder, and for months she was given the wrong medication, causing her to get worse. One of Sylvia's psychiatrists wound up being indicted for illegally selling thousands of prescriptions of Valium and another sedative-hypnotic, Tuinal. None of the psychiatrists Sylvia encountered in her many hospitalizations spent enough time with her or her chart to understand her case properly. They prescribed medications that had already been shown not to work or that worked only at much higher doses than they were giving.

After I finished the first installment, I dug out the other three in Sheehan's series and devoured them. The third part was called "Is There No Place on Earth for Me?," which would become the title of the Pulitzer Prize–winning book Shee-han published about Sylvia, based on the *New Yorker* series. The question was one Sylvia asked her mother repeatedly, the first time when she was sixteen years old and being transferred from a private psychiatric facility to a state mental hospital.

Sheehan's four articles did everything a piece of journalism on mental illness should do. First, it allowed us to see Sylvia not only during her most psychotic pe-riods (Mick Jagger wanted to marry her, she was pregnant with the son of God, she wore a bandanna on her head with a spoon lodged in it, and painted her whole face with bright red lipstick), but also when she was lucid and could remember the person she'd dreamed of being. "I once thought, when I was about to finish medical-secretarial school, before I had a breakdown on the last day of school, that I'd gradu-ate and get a job. I was looking forward to earning my own money, to having a credit card, to being a grown woman in my own right." Sylvia understood at that moment how far she was from those dreams. "When you know all those things exist for other people but not for you, sometimes it's very hard to endure the not having."

The second thing Sheehan accomplished was a detailed behind-the-scenes view of life in a mental hospital. Remarkably, the director of Creedmoor had wel-comed her and encouraged her to spend twenty-four hours a day there, to talk to everyone, and to attend all their meetings: "[L]et the public know how bad things are here," he said, "and perhaps they will get better." Sheehan weaved together the perspectives of Sylvia and her family, as well as the doctors, aides, and hospital administrators with whom Sylvia crossed paths. The portrait that emerged was heartbreaking. I finished the series three hours later, feeling electrified, saddened, and angry. *Surely we can do better than this*, I thought.

THE TWO-SYNDROME HYPOTHESIS

Sadly, Sylvia Frumkin's story—a life of abject misery spent cycling through psy-chotic breaks, hospitalizations and often unhelpful treatments, discharge, and relapse—was not unique. But as I lay there at four in the morning, absorbing what I'd just read, I was unaware of the fact that research would soon be under way that would make it possible for us to significantly improve upon the treatment that Sylvia and others were then receiving—and that I would play an integral part.

A number of challenges had so far prevented us from optimizing the treatment of schizophrenia. Aside from a lack of infrastructure (hospital beds, clinics, residential facilities, and a well-trained workforce), there was also a theoretical impediment: the widely held neurodevelopmental theory, which offered a bleak prognosis for schizophrenia sufferers, dampened clinicians' motivation, and lowered expectations for the effectiveness treatment. The other major factor was the notorious heterogeneity of schizophrenia. The homeless man you see on the street corner proclaiming he's the Messiah and your colleague sitting calmly across from you at work could both suffer from schizophrenia. The symptoms that people with the illness experience can vary in their content, combinations, and intensity; they also change over time, with some dominant in the early stages of the illness and others more prevalent later. The age of onset of symptoms, response to treatment, ability to function, number of relapses, and ultimate outcomes all differ among individuals. While in some people the illness plateaus as they grow older, and their symptoms become less disruptive, others continue to deteriorate, often landing in the back wards of state mental hospitals.

Some of the most dramatic differences we see among patients are between the newly ill and those who've been sick for decades. Over the years, it has been a sobering and distressing experience for me to see first-episode patients, still well groomed and high functioning, turn gradually into disheveled and disorganized mental invalids. Were these markedly divergent states bookends of the same disease? Or were they distinct forms of schizophrenia?

This conundrum was addressed in 1982 when British psychiatrist Timothy Crow, working at Northwick Park Hospital, proposed a "two-syndrome" hypothesis of schizophrenia. Type I was characterized by acute episodes with mostly positive symptoms, and minimal negative and cognitive symptoms; it showed excessive dopamine activity and responded well to antipsychotic treatment. Type II was typified by prominent negative and cognitive symptoms, as well as positive symptoms, poor response to antipsychotic treatment, and evidence of structural brain abnormalities. A key feature of Crow's hypothesis was the unidirectional progression of the illness. Type I could progress to Type II, but not vice versa.

Crow's model created a counterpoint to the neurodevelopmental theory that had been postulated two years earlier. Despite my inexperience at the time, I intuitively questioned the neurodevelopmental theory. Later, along with Richard

Wyatt, psychiatrist Lynn DeLisi, and other early dissenters, I would propose an alternative: the neurodegenerative theory, which posited that while schizophrenia might arise from a genetically mediated neurodevelopmental process, once it had begun, it transformed into a progressive, degenerative condition, albeit one we hoped that treatment could arrest.

Until Crow's two-syndrome hypothesis, the longitudinal course of schizophrenia that Kraepelin had emphasized a century before as the illness's cardinal feature had been largely forgotten, as psychiatrists focused on symptoms, psychological conflicts, and genes. But with Crow's theory, the concept of progression began to gain traction.

In 1988 Dr. Thomas McGlashan published a comprehensive review of studies tracking the course of patients' lives both before and after the onset of their illness, which indisputably documented the clinical deterioration in people with schizophrenia and showed that the first five to ten years of the illness were the period of greatest decline. McGlashan's paper was followed in 1991 by Wyatt's seminal review (discussed in chapter 14), which showed that the longer a person had psychotic symptoms before receiving treatment, the poorer his or her response to treatment and prognosis. The upshot of these findings was that psychosis is harmful to the brain in a way that is similar to how the oxygen deprivation associated with strokes is toxic to the brain or the blockage of coronary arteries that limits oxygen supply can damage the heart. (While strokes and heart attacks cause injury in minutes to hours, psychosis is a slower process, producing its damaging effects over weeks, months, and years.) The longer the psychosis lasts and/or the more times it recurs, the greater its potential to induce irreversible chemical and structural changes in the brain.

This dynamic conception of the progressive nature of schizophrenia was quite different from the neurodevelopmental theory, which would not have indicated as much change over time. The irony was that the two theories were not mutually exclusive. Genes that affected brain development could give rise to schizophrenia, which could then become progressive as a result of the underactivity of GABA interneurons and overactivity of glutamate and dopamine and an erosion of dendrites and synapses.

PROVING PROGRESSION

In 1987 I received a grant from the NIMH for a study that would map the course of schizophrenia using clinical and biological assessments over the early stage of the illness. The idea for this study had started with my disquiet at the callous comments of my supervisor ("You just have to let some patients suffer and learn the hard way") and grown when I suspected the inability of the neurodevelopmental theory to explain adequately the clinical course of the illness. The study design was to follow patients for five years, or as long as they would remain in the study, beginning with their first episode of illness. During this time, we would evaluate their response to treatment, the course of their illness (in remission, stable with symptoms, relapsing), and changes in brain structure as measured by MRI. If the neurodevelopmental theory fully explained their illness, then their symptoms, response to treatment, and brain structure would not change much over time. However, if the illness was progressive, then the three variables we were tracking *would* change in relation to people's pretreatment duration of untreated pychosis (DUP) and subsequent relapses.

We collected data from seventy patients with an average age of 24.3 years and an average duration of fifty-two weeks of untreated symptoms. The first findings from the study revealed that 76 percent of the patients achieved symptom remission from their first psychotic episode and that longer DUP was associated with a longer response time to treatment and lower likelihood of symptom remission. This was the first prospective demonstration of this key element in the treatment of schizophrenia.

While the high rate of response was encouraging for patients' prognoses, the fact that 80 percent of these patients relapsed at least once over the next five years was a sobering counterpoint. Moreover, patients' responses to retreatment weakened following each relapse. Perhaps the most dramatic finding was that brain structures changed in relation to clinical course: the longer patients had psychotic symptoms and the more recurrences they had, the greater both the increase in ventricular volume and the decrease in temporal and frontal lobe gray matter. Thus, the results of the study, specifically with regard to treatment response and brain volume, supported our hypotheses.

These results were replicated by other researchers, most emphatically in a series of studies by psychiatrist René Kahn's group at the University of Utrecht in the Netherlands, to the point that progressive brain atrophy became accepted as a standard feature of schizophrenia. Numerous studies had also demonstrated the effectiveness of continuous antipsychotic drug treatment in preventing relapse following symptom remission. What hadn't been shown definitively yet, though, was whether treatment that prevented psychotic relapses halted progression and slowed or averted brain atrophy. Given what we'd learned, however—that medication alleviates acute psychosis and prevents its recurrence, and that psychotic relapses contribute to brain volume loss—it was reasonable to expect that medication had a mitigating effect on brain volume loss. This inference was confirmed by Kahn's team when patients were examined with MRI over a five-year period and their treatment adherence assessed. Those who continued their medication showed less brain volume reduction than those who received less medication.

Reducing the Duration of Untreated Psychosis

Following the seminal articles by Crow, McGlashan, and Wyatt, and beginning with our results published in 1992, evidence accumulated supporting the association between longer duration of untreated psychosis (DUP) and poorer treatment outcomes. This evidence challenged the nihilistic sense of inevitability that surrounded the illness, and, perhaps most importantly, introduced a new sense of urgency about diagnosing and treating people with schizophrenia as early in their illness as possible.

The implication of these findings was that timely treatment could limit or prevent the damaging effects of schizophrenia—something that would be of enormous public health significance. Each year, 1.5 million people developed schizophrenia worldwide, 100,000 of them in the United States. The average time that elapsed from their onset of psychotic symptoms to their first treatment was more than a year. In developing nations, the lag was twice as long. If reducing DUP could limit the disability caused by schizophrenia and improve patients' chances for recovery, then efforts to shorten the time to diagnosis and treatment could bring enormous returns.

While this convergence of theory and data was encouraging, it still didn't *prove* that psychosis was toxic in schizophrenia. To demonstrate the effects definitively would require studies showing that reducing the length of untreated psychosis and preventing relapses improved the outcomes of patients and mitigated their loss of brain volume.

The Treatment and Intervention in Psychosis (TIPS) early-detection study addressed this challenge head-on. The TIPS study, carried out in collaboration with the public mental health systems of specific counties in Norway and Denmark between 1997 and 2007, looked at how the course of schizophrenia and patient outcomes would be affected if DUP was reduced. The study was implemented in four health care sectors. Two in Rogaland County, Norway, were designated early-detection areas, and two in Oslo County, Norway, and Roskilde County, Denmark, were designated usual-detection areas.

In the early-detection regions, a program was implemented that consisted of two main components: information campaigns directed at the general population, schools, and first-line health care workers; and the presence of easily accessible early-detection clinics and dedicated teams capable of rapid assessment and triage. The information campaigns aimed to counteract the stigmatization of people with severe mental disorders and to change help-seeking behavior by making people aware of the resources available and the possibilities for a positive outcome. Households in the early-detection regions all received a free brochure with information on psychotic disorders, which explained the aim of the project and included the message that for someone with a psychiatric disorder, the chance of getting well increased with early treatment. The brochures included the telephone number for the "low-threshold" detection teams and photos of the staff. Public service advertisements were broadcast regularly in key local media, and commercials were run in local cinemas.

At the same time, health care professionals—including general practitioners—were offered tailored educational workshops on recognizing and treating early psychosis, and were taught to use a rating scale of psychotic signs and symptoms. The area's high schools were visited twice each semester and offered educational sessions on early psychosis, with an emphasis on active help seeking and advice on contacting the detection teams.

No such public information campaigns or roving clinical assessment teams operated in the usual-care regions. People in all four regions received the same treatment when diagnosed with schizophrenia, which included antipsychotic medication, supportive psychotherapy, and multifamily psychoeducation (informing the patient and family about the disease and what to expect in the future). Over the course of the study, 281 people with first-episode schizophrenia, schizophreniform disorder, and schizoaffective disorder enrolled. Assessments were carried out when patients first were enrolled in the study and then at three months, and at intervals of one, two, five, and ten years. Treatment was specified for the first two years in which patients were followed. After that, patients availed themselves of whatever treatment they wanted or were offered, or had none at all.

Prior to the study, the median amount of time that passed between the diagnosis and treatment of people with psychotic disorders was twenty-six weeks; for people with schizophrenia, it was fifty-four weeks. The early-detection program had an immediate effect, with an increased number of referrals to the early-detection teams coinciding with each public outreach campaign, and the median time in these regions from onset of symptoms to diagnosis and treatment fell to five weeks. (Interestingly, the median also fell in the comparison usual-detection sectors to sixteen weeks, likely a carryover effect of information leakage from the adjacent early-detection regions.)

At three months, people in the early-detection group showed fewer symptoms and better functioning. At two years, despite the fact that there were no differences between the two groups in the treatment they received, the early-detection group still had fewer symptoms. This was the first evidence we had that proactively reducing DUP was feasible and that it was associated with a lessening of symptoms and better long-term outcomes.

The same pattern of results was found at the five-year mark. However, after ten years, the difference between the two groups was less noticeable. While a significantly higher number of early-detection patients fulfilled overall "recovery" criteria (30.7 percent versus 15.1 percent), which the study defined as requiring "both stable symptomatic remission and intact functional capacity," symptom remission rates showed less of a difference (52.5 percent in early-detection areas and 47.9 percent in usual-detection areas). The study's investigators suggested that the decrease in the difference in symptom remission between the regions could be due to selective attrition—meaning that sicker patients with higher levels of symptoms were more likely to drop out in the usual-detection areas, and that early detection and intervention, along with standard treatments, conferred a lasting benefit for patients with first-episode psychosis.

ESTABLISHING A NEW PARADIGM

The TIPS study showed that it was possible to treat patients sooner to achieve better outcomes. But there was still the challenge of getting patients to stick to their treatment programs. Young patients tend to discontinue treatment prematurely following recovery from the first episode of illness. They often do not understand that the psychotic episode they experienced for the first time signaled the onset of a lifelong, recurrent illness with the potential for causing irreversible harm. They are also uncomfortable with the stigma of mental illness and understandably dislike the side effects of antipsychotic medication. Across demographic groups, there are also social and cultural differences in how mental illness is regarded, disparities in access to health care, and varying levels of trust and confidence in institutional authority and Western medicine. Racial and cultural prejudices, as well as differences in socioeconomic status and educational levels, create a massive implementation challenge. Complicating the picture further, denial (or lack of awareness, called anosognosia) of illness often accompanies schizophrenia, and the disease frequently strikes young people—as a group, somewhat prone to a sense of invulnerability. Consequently, too many people stricken with a first episode of psychosis learn the harsh realities of their illness the hard way, and often after it is too late.

To address the question of whether first-episode patients could be retained in treatment more successfully and, as a result, experience better outcomes, the NIMH proposed an ambitious research project in 2008 called Recovery After an Initial Schizophrenia Episode (RAISE). The groundwork for RAISE had been laid over the previous two decades, beginning with scholarly efforts to establish evidence-based practices. Until the early 1990s, many, or even most, treatment decisions in medicine were made by clinicians without the benefit of systematic syntheses of scientific data about effectiveness and cost. To remedy this, the federal government's Agency for Healthcare Research and Quality (then the Agency for Health Care Policy and Research) began funding Patient Outcomes Research Teams (PORTs). The first PORT study to address mental illness focused on schizophrenia. From 1992 to 2010, systematic reviews of clinical studies on the uses, types, and dosages of antipsychotics and the effectiveness of psychosocial treatments were conducted by groups of experts under the leadership of Anthony Lehman and colleagues at the University of Maryland, including Lisa Dixon, who would play a formative role in establishing a new standard of care for schizophrenia patients. The published treatment recommendations were developed from empirical evidence in the scientific literature rather than expert opinion. The care standard established by the PORT studies consisted of a combination of evidence-based pharmacologic, psychologic, supportive, and rehabilitative treatments that ultimately would contribute to a multidisciplinary team–based treatment model called Coordinated Specialty Care, or CSC. (In other medical specialties this model of care is called "disease management.")

In the meantime, research groups in northern Europe, the United Kingdom, and Australia had already begun testing combined treatment models of care, specifically applying them to patients in the early stages of their illness. The idea of providing care soon after the onset of psychosis emulated similar approaches to other medical disorders and reflected the growing belief that early intervention would limit the chronic disability associated with schizophrenia. In addition, a number of the national health care systems in those countries began investing in this model of care even as it was still being developed, and studies of its effectiveness were being carried out.

America, however, went in the opposite direction, largely because of political pressure. The catastrophic outcome of deinstitutionalization, which displaced hundreds of thousands of mentally ill and disabled patients from state hospitals to the streets, nursing homes, and prisons (largely for petty, nonviolent crimes), had provoked stinging critiques of the government agencies responsible—particularly the Alcohol Drug Abuse Mental Health Administration (ADAMHA), the NIMH, and the Substance Abuse and Mental Health Services Administration (SAMHSA)—for failing to provide the community mental health care services needed to support the deinstitutionalized patients. The criticism forced these agencies to emphasize development of community support services and policy reforms aimed at people with long histories of illness and many relapses who were already significantly impaired. Strategies to support treatment adherence ranged from long-acting injectable medications, to Assertive Community Treatment (ACT), a team-based treatment model that provides multidisciplinary, intensive case management for people at high risk of repeated hospitalization. Ironically, first-episode patients, who stood to gain so much from early treatment, were thought to need only minimal aftercare—little or nothing beyond occasional doctor visits for prescription refills or adjustments to medication. The logic of this was backward, as younger patients had the most to lose; sadly, older, chronic patients had already sustained the ravages of the illness.

Adding to the misguided nature of this policy was the fact that, because of a catch-22 policy, patients with early-stage schizophrenia were not even eligible for the psychosocial and community support services offered to chronic patients. The majority of people experiencing onset of the illness were adolescents or young adults. To be eligible for Medicaid, which would presumably pay for treatment services, they had to qualify for Supplemental Security Income (SSI), which required prior or current disability. As the purpose of providing young new-onset patients with these services was to prevent them from becoming disabled, a policy that required them to be disabled to avail themselves of the services was clearly illogical and self-defeating. Patients with private insurance were also disadvantaged because of the limited coverage for the full array of therapeutic services.

While multidisciplinary support services for chronically ill, functionally impaired patients were certainly needed, the policies focusing resources on them inadvertently diverted resources and attention away from new, younger patients. This policy could be justified by the neurodevelopmental theory, which saw no reason to focus treatment on the newly ill, as the illness was going to do its damage anyway.

CONNECTING THE DOTS: THE RAISE INITIATIVE

By the 2000s, studies carried out largely in Europe, the United Kingdom, and Australia demonstrating the feasibility of multidisciplinary treatment models for first-episode psychosis had been completed. US investigators funded by the NIMH had produced the evidence that formed the rationale for this treatment strategy but hadn't put the pieces together into a treatment model. In 2008 the NIMH was finally ready to proceed with the RAISE project and create its own model that could be translated to clinical practice, complete with a policy, infrastructure, and financing framework specific to the United States.

Bob Heinssen, the director of the Mental Health Services and Interventions Division of the NIMH, was tasked with organizing this initiative. Heinssen was particularly interested in schizophrenia and laid the bureaucratic groundwork for the project. The RAISE initiative was intended to develop and test a model of coordinated specialty care (CSC) for young people with recent-onset psychosis that would consist of a team of specialists (with expertise in psychotherapy, medication management, family education, substance abuse treatment, case management, and support for employment or education) that would tailor a treatment plan based on each patient's needs. The idea was to provide wraparound services to patients. The model of care also promoted shared decision-making and involved family members as much as possible. The RAISE project sought nothing less than to fundamentally alter the trajectory and prognosis of schizophrenia.

Along with Susan Essock at Columbia and Lisa Dixon and Howard Goldman at the University of Maryland, I organized a large multidisciplinary team of researchers to design a study on the impact of early intervention on first-episode schizophrenia patients, and we submitted our grant application in 2008. Normally, regardless of the number of applicants, only one award is made. But in the wake of the financial crisis and the Obama administration's American Recovery and Reinvestment Act, the NIMH was flush with new money and funded two applications, with the idea that their different experimental designs provided two chances for success. My team received one of the awards. Our plan was to collaborate with the state mental health systems of Maryland and New York and implement the model of care we were proposing at clinics under their licensing authority. We called it the RAISE Connection Program, a multisite trial in which individual patients were assigned randomly either to the experimental CSC intervention or to usual care. The CSC we devised included medication, supported employment and education, family psychoeducation, case management, skills training based on cognitive behavioral methods, substance abuse treatment, and suicide prevention.

The other study funded, led by John Kane, Nina Schooler, and Delbert Robinson, was called the RAISE Early Treatment Program (RAISE-ETP) and involved thirty-four community mental health centers in twenty-one states. Half the sites were assigned to deliver the CSC intervention (called NAVIGATE), while the other half would provide usual care. The four key components of the NAVIGATE CSC were psychopharmacology; individual resilience therapy; family therapy/psychoeducation; and supportive employment/education.

For projects of this magnitude (my team's award was $22 million over five years, and it involved more than one hundred staff and four hundred patients at multiple sites), huge effort goes into its organization and laying the groundwork. We needed to train the staff, standardize the assessments we would use, and orient the participating sites. Two years into the project, we were enrolling patients and had established a smooth research operation when I received notification that our funding was being terminated—apparently because of budget shortfalls. This was devastating news, as I felt our study would have contributed significantly to our knowledge about forestalling the disability associated with schizophrenia.

RAISE-ETP proceeded as planned and was successfully completed. The results demonstrated a favorable effect for the NAVIGATE CSC treatment, but the margin of superiority was modest: the median duration of treatment engagement was twenty-three months for NAVIGATE versus seventeen months in usual care; and patients had slightly higher quality-of-life ratings (a scale measuring general categories such as physical well-being, social interactions, and recreational activities), and marginally lower rates of rehospitalization for recurrent symptoms (34 percent for the NAVIGATE group and 37 percent for usual care).

The real story, it turned out, was in the secondary analysis. The criteria for inclusion in the RAISE-ETP study did not limit the length of time that patients could have been ill prior to study entry, but it did stipulate that they could not have received more than six months of antipsychotic drug treatment. The average duration of untreated psychosis was 3.4 years for the patients receiving the NAVI-GATE CSC treatment and slightly more than 4 years for the patients undergoing usual care. The duration of untreated psychosis turned out to be a strong factor in the relative effectiveness of the two types of treatment: people who had been ill for shorter periods (less than seventy-four weeks) derived substantially greater benefit from the NAVIGATE CSC approach than those with longer durations of symptoms did. This suggested that when someone becomes ill, there is a limited window if you are to achieve the greatest therapeutic response and prevent the persistent and disabling effects of schizophrenia.

MAKING LEMONADE OUT OF LEMONS

After our own RAISE Connection study was terminated, we had proposed to the NIMH that with the residual funds that had been awarded (about one-third of the original grant) we carry out a demonstration project utilizing the CSC-Connection treatment approach to verify its feasibility—an exercise in what is known as "implementation science." In order to do this, we had to assume that this treatment model for early-stage schizophrenia was effective and should be adopted as the standard of care. Even without conducting our version of the RAISE study, and before anyone learned the results of the other team's study, based on our clinical experience and the results of the European and Australian studies, we believed in the effectiveness of this model of care. The question was whether mental health care policy makers and administrators would buy it.

Heinssen and the NIMH program officers agreed readily to our proposal, as did the commissioners of the New York and Maryland State Mental Health Systems. In the wake of our project's abrupt transition, I felt that a change in leadership was in order. My colleague Lisa Dixon was better suited to steer it than I was. Dixon had paid her dues working in the trenches of public mental health care, determining which services and treatments really made a difference to patients. She lived and breathed public mental health from both the providers' and advocates' perspectives—she had a personal stake in the issue, as her brother had schizophrenia and had been hospitalized at the Pilgrim Psychiatric Center.

The personal experience of having a family member affected by serious mental illness is a powerful motivator for many mental health care providers. Mike Hogan, New York's commissioner of mental health, decided to pursue a career in the field largely because his sister suffered from schizophrenia. A native New Yorker, Hogan had become the preeminent public mental health administrator in the United States over the course of his career and had been appointed by President George W. Bush to chair the newly established New Freedom Commission on Mental Health in 2002.

Working with Hogan and his staff, Dixon established the paradigm of CSC for first-episode schizophrenia that would become OnTrackNY. New York State, at Hogan's urging, agreed to support the costs. OnTrack has been a historical milestone in mental health care, and CSC programs have facilitated the recovery of countless young people.

I'M A PERSON WHO STILL HAS DREAMS

To be eligible for this innovative, evidence-based treatment program, a young person needs to be experiencing unusual thoughts, hallucinations, or disorganized thinking, or exhibiting strange behaviors that have lasted at least a week but less than two years. Patients who enter the program work closely with a team for two years, on average. The team consists of a care coordinator, a psychiatrist, a primary clinician, a supported education/employment specialist, a peer specialist (a former patient with lived experience), and a nurse, all of whom are trained to work with families. A staff person trained in co-occurring substance use disorders is available as needed. While OnTrack was conceptualized as a time-limited treatment program, many of us involved envisioned that the care could ultimately be offered indefinitely, even for life.

OnTrackNY has now served more than 2,000 people, with about 730 enrolled at any given time, and has expanded to twenty-three clinical programs across New York State, a number set to rise to forty. Using the data acquired from the RAISE NAVIGATE intervention, and the proof of concept demonstrated in the New York and Maryland OnTrack programs, the NIMH moved to establish the OnTrack model as the new standard of care and expand its availability under the umbrella of OnTrackUSA. There are now more than 360 early-psychosis clinics based on the OnTrack model or variations of the CSC model located in all fifty states and

US territories. Evidence for the effectiveness of CSC has continued to accrue. In 2018 a study of 325 OnTrack participants who were followed for a year showed that hospitalization rates dropped from 70 percent to 10 percent by month three, while employment and education enrollment rates rose from 40 percent to 80 percent by month six.

A young psychiatrist named Ilana Nossel was named director of the inaugural OnTrack program in 2013. Nossel's interests had tilted toward community-based psychiatry and, specifically, working with schizophrenia patients, which made her an ideal choice. As the OnTrackNY first-episode clinics began to proliferate in 2016, she became the medical director of the OnTrackNY network, a position she still holds. Nossel has remained a passionate advocate for the OnTrack approach and believes firmly that it provides superior care and produces better outcomes than patients would enjoy otherwise. "Being able to talk to a young person with recent-onset psychosis about 'recovery' is a profound change within the mental health system," she observes. I agree. It's light-years away from the conversations we had with patients and families when I was a young doctor in the 1980s, and a schizophrenia diagnosis was akin to a life sentence of chronic disability.

People come to OnTrack via referrals from physicians, psychologists, and social workers, but OnTrack teams also carry out community outreach to educate the public about psychosis and coordinated specialty care. Because the program is state funded, it's open to anyone, regardless of income or insurance status. The value, in humanitarian and economic terms, of such a program is enormous and begs the question of why broader government support for high-quality, innovative mental health care programs has not been made available. The rationale is compelling. As Nossel points out, schizophrenia is an incredibly expensive illness—between emergency room visits, hospitalizations, imprisonment, and lost wages—and therefore making the early-intervention programs that can prevent worsening of the illness widely accessible is a wise investment. Most importantly, it gives people a chance to take back their lives and realize their dreams.

"The system was very oriented toward treating symptoms," Nossel says, "but the whole concept of recovery is about what a meaningful life looks like to someone. Treating symptoms is part of that, but it's only a small part. The larger part is figuring out what someone's goals are, then supporting them with the services they need to meet those goals." Although most of the participants in OnTrack are on medication, that's not a requirement for being in the program. OnTrack uses a shared decision-making model around medication, as it does around other aspects of treatment. Families are hugely important, as we've learned in recent decades how critical their involvement is to patient outcomes.

Another change is around the concept of insight. In the past, the idea was that patients could make progress only if they had insight into their illness—that is, an understanding of schizophrenia that was essentially medical. Often people with recent-onset psychosis might not think they are mentally ill or in need of treatment. But they often say they want help finding a job. The team can engage with them on that goal first—and certain treatment steps may become part of achieving it. (Nossel also points out that insight into one's mental illness can stir up negative or even suicidal thoughts, especially shortly after a diagnosis. "Insight," she says, "isn't the be-all and end-all.")

Those who work at programs like OnTrack have innovative ways of keeping patients engaged. In traditional mental health services, if someone misses three appointments, you might send a letter and close the case. OnTrack uses an approach called assertive engagement. "You call or text," Nossel explains, "but if you don't hear back, you might show up at their home with a pie. Rather than *tsk-tsk*, it's an expression of concern, welcome, warmth. The real emphasis is on relationships."

One young person who has come through the OnTrack program is Drew, who was diagnosed with schizophrenia when he was twenty-one. A first-generation immigrant whose parents are from Sierra Leone, Drew grew up in New York, raised by a single mother. He was studying media and film at Bronx Community College when he began hearing voices and thinking that people were talking about him. When he told his mother and sister, they had no awareness of mental illness and assumed that Drew was just a young man going through changes and trying to figure things out.

Around that time, his mother, who works for the United Nations, was transferred to Nigeria. Since Drew couldn't be left on his own in the city, he accompanied her to Lagos, where he got a job with a nongovernmental organization (NGO) that mobilized youth voters. It was then that he had his first psychotic break. "Every day, I woke up and I didn't know what my brain was going to do," Drew recalls. "Your brain is the only thing you own, so it was scary."

He was hospitalized, diagnosed with schizophrenia, and treated with antipsychotics. His mother and sister worried for him: With this illness, what kind of life would he have? Drew had no idea, of course. "I don't think anybody looks at what schizophrenia is like for people unless they know someone who has it. So you think of serial killers and things like that."

After two weeks in the hospital, Drew's family decided that the best treatment was in the United States. So Drew went back to New York City to live in Harlem with his uncle, who took him to a community clinic. A social worker there referred him to the OnTrack program. Recovery came slowly. In the beginning, Drew was afraid to even go outside. He would try to play basketball or go to the movies, but everything was scary or difficult.

Drew says the OnTrack staff met him where he was. "That was the best part," he reflects. "Shared decision-making was really important, too. I was able to guide my own recovery. I had input into how I was going to be treated." He still experiences symptoms—differentiating between what's real and what isn't is sometimes hard—but he's able to take a step back and get some perspective.

When I asked him what the system could have done better for him, he talks about the language and attitudes of doctors. Drew went to predominantly white schools growing up, and says he knows how to talk to white doctors—how to "code switch." But he has seen people of color, or people from poor backgrounds, who get frustrated and abandon treatment. "There are all these big terms being thrown at you, you feel drummed out, can't hold a conversation, and you just agree to what they're saying because you don't want to be a bother."

The most helpful thing has been the "human element," he says. "The best treatment is when you find someone you have a connection with." Drew has taken that knowledge with him into his work as a peer specialist. While at OnTrack, he got a job as a security guard, but hated it. When his own peer specialist suggested he train to be a peer, he enrolled at Howie the Harp Advocacy Center, which runs a highly respected peer-training program. (The center is named after the late Howard Geld, a powerful advocate in the early patient-rights movement who had spent time in mental institutions as a young man. While hospitalized, Geld couldn't sleep, and a night attendant taught him to play the harmonica. He later became a regular on the streets of Greenwich Village, playing his harmonica to earn money, hence the name Howie the Harp.) What Drew learned in the classroom—that the mental health system sometimes undermines those it's supposed to be serving—was reassuring to hear. "So it wasn't just me, thinking I'm feeling this because I'm crazy."

After six months of classroom work and a twelve-week internship at a hospital (on a team headed by a doctor who had once admitted him to that same hospital), Drew began paid peer work at OnTrack and the New York Crossroads clinic.

He works with a team just like the one who helped him when he entered the OnTrack program: a nurse, a social worker, an education/employment specialist, and a doctor. "My job is establishing connections with people," he explains. He talks to them about what they like to do, what their goals are, and helps with everything from buying MetroCards to access public transportation, to getting into homeless shelters. "It's given me a different perspective on life in New York City. I see the things in my life that I've always taken for granted."

In 2021 Drew also began working with two other peers and a nurse on a podcast from the black peer perspective. He says the hardest part of being a peer specialist is helping people to believe they are going to get better when they can't see it. There was a time he couldn't see a future for himself. "But one of best things I've learned is I'm more than my diagnosis," he says. "I'm a person who still has dreams."

IDENTIFYING WHO IS AT RISK

Three decades of research, culminating in the RAISE studies, inspired a paradigm shift both in the philosophy and practice of the treatment of schizophrenia. It catalyzed a policy change that enabled a new standard of care offering the possibility not just of recovery but also of modifying or even preempting the devastating consequences of schizophrenia. This is how progress in medicine works. Research evolves to the point where it can be translated into clinical practice. Treatment of schizophrenia began with the discovery of chlorpromazine and the subsequent proliferation of antipsychotics, followed by the introduction of clozapine and the incrementally improved second-generation antipsychotic drugs. Psychosocial treatments were developed, validated, and applied in parallel. But it was the disruptive insight of the importance of early detection and intervention that spurred the combining of these treatments and their application to early-stage patients that has transformed care for this most malignant of mental maladies. After centuries of suffering, it was now possible to believe that we could not only quell the symptoms of the illness but also actually treat patients in a way that prevented schizophrenia's notorious clinical deterioration and destructive effects on the brain. These were statements that could not be made yet about other progressive brain disorders, such as Alzheimer's, Parkinson's, or Huntington's disease.

With these developments, psychiatry was "on a roll," and there were possibilities for further progress. Once we understood that the critical determinant of patients' responses to treatment and outcomes was prompt intervention with state-of-the-art treatments, it didn't take long to realize that, since the illness usually comes on gradually over weeks and months, a strategy of "preventive intervention" could be extended to patients in the pre-syndromal, or prodromal, stage of illness.

When invoking the P-word (prevention), an explanation is required of the different forms of prevention in medicine—primary, secondary, and tertiary—and which we claim to be capable of in psychiatry. Primary prevention prevents disease before it occurs, through correcting potential causes or providing protections. Examples include using diet, exercise, and cholesterol-lowering drugs to prevent heart disease; immunization against infectious diseases; and gene therapy to rescue people from the effects of pathological genetic mutations. Secondary prevention reduces the impact of a disease following its onset by halting it or slowing its progress—like routine mammograms to detect early signs of breast cancer; or aspirin, diet, and exercise programs to prevent heart attacks or strokes in patients with atherosclerosis. Tertiary prevention is essentially palliative treatment that aims to limit the impact of an ongoing illness, as in rehabilitation therapy after joint replacement or orthopedic surgery.

By these definitions, schizophrenia treatments have achieved secondary and tertiary levels of prevention. We clearly aspire to identify vulnerable people early in life and prevent them from developing schizophrenia, but this is well beyond our current capability. What we can do is prevent the illness from worsening by treating people who have been diagnosed and are still in their incipient stages. And what we are on the cusp of doing is developing methods to apply this approach to patients in their prodromal stage, prior to the formal onset of illness.

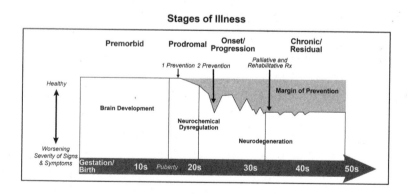

The Natural History and Clinical Course of Schizophrenia: Gestation/Birth: The seeds of the illness are planted at conception in terms of genes that confer risk of schizophrenia. Environmental factors in the form of fetal exposure to trauma during gestation and birth, exposure to toxins, infection, and starvation can augment genetic risk. Premorbid Stage: Minimal or no manifestation of symptoms. Prodromal Stage: During adolescence attenuated symptoms begin to emerge gradually or intermittently. These are nonspecific, mild, and not of clear diagnostic significance in nature. Onset/Progression Stage: Symptoms intensify and persist, causing distress and impairing function. If the first episode of psychosis is not treated or subsequently recurs in the form of psychotic relapses, the illness can progress. Symptoms worsen and respond less well to treatment, causing a decline in intellectual and functional capacity. Chronic/Residual Stage: Residual symptoms and impaired intellectual and functional capacity persist despite treatment. Treatment of Schizophrenia: There are three levels of treatment. Early detection and intervention are the form of primary prevention that can treat the disease before its full onset occurs. Maintenance treatment is a form of secondary prevention that reduces the impact of a disease following its onset by halting or slowing its progress. Palliative and rehabilitative treatment limits the impact of an ongoing illness and seeks to restore function through regenerative treatment and/or rehabilitation therapy.

Our current approach is to identify people who are considered at clinical high risk (CHR) for developing a psychotic disorder. CHR is defined by a series of nonspecific symptoms and behavior changes, including:

- exhibiting attenuated and not overt psychosis-like symptoms;
- being easily distressed (for example, by social interactions, or the behavior of family members);
- becoming interested in a new religion or turning over a new philosophical leaf;
- becoming intolerant and complaining of things that are commonplace;
- withdrawing from old friends and hanging out with a new crowd, or isolating oneself from social interactions;
- wanting to be more independent and not trusting or relying on his or her family;
- having unusual beliefs or strange or suspicious thoughts but lacking conviction about them and remaining able to engage in "reality testing";
- experiencing common cognitive complaints, such as a patient feeling like his or her brain freezes up when spoken to, or that the demands of daily life have become overwhelming.

Analogous conditions relative to other diseases might be people who are mildly obese and have occasional mildly elevated blood glucose levels and a family history of diabetes. Or a person who has high blood pressure or atrial fibrillation and is at risk for a stroke.

While there are appropriate treatments that can prevent or delay the symptoms of diabetes and cardiovascular disease, the same is not true for Alzheimer's disease or schizophrenia. The idea of treating high-risk patients before the illness fully takes hold is not yet ready for prime time. Only about a third of people who meet the criteria for CHR eventually develop schizophrenia. This means that a person who is considered to be at clinically high risk can be confirmed as having been in the prodromal stage only after his or her symptoms have worsened and met criteria for a diagnosis of schizophrenia.

The study of CHR in schizophrenia and the methods for detecting and treating it in the prodromal stage is a distinct field of research. Though it's still a work in progress, early-detection and intervention strategies for schizophrenia have been embraced with enormous enthusiasm, reflected in the growth of organizations and programs dedicated to its research and dissemination.

I was invited to speak at the first meeting of what would become the International Early Psychosis Association (IEPA), held in Melbourne, Australia, in 1996. It was organized by Patrick McGorry, a psychiatrist at the University of Melbourne. If Thomas McGlashan and Richard Wyatt were the fathers of the DUP and first-episode-psychosis strategy, McGorry is the patron saint of the CHR movement.

McGorry is a soft-spoken Aussie with a sly wit, charismatic presence, and fiercely competitive spirit. In 1998 he formally established the IEPA to raise awareness about the benefits of early intervention for psychosis. Over the next decade, he must have logged a million miles journeying from Australia to every international meeting and visiting every center that expressed interest in early psychosis, in order to spread his gospel of early detection and intervention during the prodromal stage of schizophrenia. His efforts are reflected in the explosive growth in the last three decades of programs pursuing research in CHR and offering clinical services to CHR populations. Of the multitude of CHR or prodromal clinics now in existence around the world, some of the best-known are in Melbourne, the United Kingdom, Denmark, Germany, Hong Kong, and Mexico City, as well as in numerous locations throughout the United States. In recognition of his accomplishments, McGorry was selected by his country's federal government as the Australian of the Year in 2010.

Over time, criteria have developed for identifying those at high risk. One is age of onset: people are generally considered CHR only if their attenuated positive symptoms develop between the ages of about fourteen and thirty. The other concerns the time course of symptoms. The prodrome is a very dynamic period when symptoms develop and progress relatively quickly to schizophrenia. Therefore, only people with attenuated positive symptoms that are new or have worsened in the previous year can be considered clinically high risk.

The CHR criteria could identify people at heightened risk for schizophrenia. The next challenge was to improve the capacity to predict who among this population would develop the illness. In 2015 the North American Prodrome Longitudinal Study (NAPLS) published data on seven hundred CHR subjects who were followed for two years or until they met criteria for a syndromal psychotic disorder (most likely schizophrenia or schizoaffective disorder). NAPLS was the brainchild of the NIMH's Bob Heinssen and was led by Ty Cannon, a psychologist at UCLA. It was the largest study to date of a CHR population. NAPLS revealed that very few of the symptoms manifested by CHR patients and measured at baseline predicted later outcome. The specific symptoms that best differentiated those who transitioned to psychosis included unusual thought content and disorganized communication. Perceptual abnormalities, one of the most frequent symptoms at baseline, did not relate at all to later outcome.

EXAMPLES OF
HIGH-RISK SYMPTOMS INCLUDE:

- Feeling like things are unreal
- Ideas or preoccupations others find difficult to understand
- Changes in perception (such as hearing or seeing things others do not)
- Feeling suspicious or mistrustful of others
- Withdrawing from friends and family
- Problems in school or at work
- Loss of interest or lack of motivation
- Changes in sleeping or eating patterns
- Decreased concern with appearance or clothes
- Confusion, trouble thinking clearly
- Changes in personality

These findings were consistent with data from international CHR research groups and were replicated by our Center of Prevention and Evaluation (COPE) of the New York State Psychiatric Institute at Columbia University. COPE is an outpatient research and treatment program focused on teenagers and young adults experiencing prodromal or high-risk symptoms. For two years, COPE researchers monitored symptom progression in two hundred people who had been deemed CHR according to current diagnostic criteria. Thirty percent of the study participants progressed to psychosis, with an average time to conversion of eleven months. The majority of those developed schizophrenia or schizoaffective disorder. The 70 percent of CHR patients who never developed psychosis had varying outcomes. Some exhibited persistent, attenuated positive symptoms that warranted diagnoses of schizoid, schizotypal, paranoid, or borderline personality disorder; others had mood or anxiety symptoms. Some number of patients recovered completely and had no further symptoms.

If we are to extend early identification and intervention as a standard of care to the prodromal phase, two things must happen. First, criteria for a CHR diagnosis must improve so that the false positive rate—which refers to individuals diagnosed with CHR who never develop schizophrenia—of 70 percent can be reduced markedly. This will require a validated diagnostic test, most likely using imaging, genetics, blood tests, or electrophysiological methods. Second, a treatment must be developed that is effective in alleviating prodromal symptoms and preventing the conversion to schizophrenia.

Currently, once someone is diagnosed as CHR or prodromal, the approach is to treat his or her symptoms, such as anxiety and depression, as one would normally. If and when patients have positive symptoms that come closer to meeting the full criteria for psychosis, many physicians will prescribe antipsychotic medications prophylactically. These medications can often help prevent agitation and can enhance the effect of other medications. However, while antipsychotic medications are very effective for syndromal schizophrenia, it is not clear if they are effective or warranted for attenuated symptoms in the prodromal stage. We don't want to treat people unnecessarily with antipsychotics. Moreover, it's possible that the prodromal stage of illness may require or respond better to a different kind of treatment with fewer side effects.

Numerous treatments have been tried on CHR individuals, including antidepressants, benzodiazepine anxiolytics, lithium, and nutraceuticals (nutrients or food supplements used as therapeutic agents) such as omega-3 fatty acids, fish oil, and antioxidants, but none has proven effective. Knowledge of the complexity of the glutamate synapse (see chapter 15) has revealed numerous molecular targets for agents that can modify glutamate activity—including agents that modulate the activity of NMDA receptors that are stimulated by glutamate; those that stimulate receptors located on the presynaptic neuron, which inhibit glutamate release when activated; and others that influence the metabolic enzymes that inactivate and recycle glutamate. Psychosocial treatments such as supportive problem-oriented psychotherapy, cognitive behavioral therapy (CBT), and family therapy can be effective in alleviating CHR symptoms by reducing stress and/or simply allowing time to pass so that the undefined condition can declare itself. This cautious watch-and-wait approach embodies the physicians' dictum *primum non nocere*: first, do no harm.

CROSSING INTO PSYCHOSIS

CHR clinics such as COPE are trying to understand how people progress from their premorbid stage of relatively normal functioning to experiencing their first psychotic episode. This entails examining the nature of CHR symptoms, including how they change over time; their relationship to a range of clinical and biological features (including family history, substance use or abuse, stressful life events, and the structure and function of the brain); and whether certain symptoms or patterns can help us predict who will eventually develop a full disorder. Many clinics support developing more specific and targeted treatments to reduce CHR symptoms with the ultimate aim of preventing the development of psychiatric disorders in people at highest risk. At COPE, treatment is provided for about two years and can include psychotherapy, family support and education, and medication. Anyone participating in research (for example, incorporating MRIs, and various tests and questionnaires) receives clinical services for free.

The incidence of CHR is estimated at about one in ten thousand. In order to connect with some of those people, COPE does a lot of community outreach. They go to high schools and colleges and talk to teachers, students, and mental health counselors, educating them about warning signs. (Maybe someone they know has stopped bathing or started saying strange things.) They're acutely conscious of the fact that they are dealing with people at a critical moment. There is only one prodromal period, and it can make or break a person, not only in terms of disease progression but also in how he or she internalizes stigma and relates to the illness.

Once someone comes to COPE, he or she is given a Structured Interview for Psychosis-Risk Syndromes, or SIPS, which assesses for three psychosis-risk syndromes: (1) attenuated positive symptom psychosis-risk syndrome, (2) genetic risk and deterioration psychosis-risk syndrome, and (3) brief intermittent psychotic psychosis-risk syndrome. The key indicators for high-risk status are based on the scoring of positive symptoms according to their level of severity, frequency, degree of conviction, and behavioral impact. (The scale also includes negative, disorganized, and general/affective symptoms.) The five CHR indicators are: (1) unusual thought content/delusions, (2) suspicious ideas/paranoia, (3) grandiose ideas, (4) perceptual abnormalities/hallucinations, and (5) disorganized communication.

In the absence of a precise and completely reliable biomarker that will tell us who is at high risk, or who among a high-risk group will transition to schizophrenia, good clinicians learn to recognize patterns and pick up on clues instinctively, just as doctors in any field of medicine do. What seems like nascent paranoia, for instance, may be a context-appropriate response to difficulties at home, at school, or in the neighborhood. A story that sounds highly unlikely or a sign of grandiose delusions may turn out to be true. When Elyn Saks told her therapist on 9/11 that planes were flying into towers in New York City, the therapist, unaware of what was happening, assumed she was psychotic. No one wants to be the doctor who carelessly dismisses what a patient says.

Context is important. We have to avoid pathologizing "magical thinking" that aligns with someone's culture or faith. If the idea that you have a direct line to God is acceptable within your traditions, then perhaps it doesn't signal a problem; if a dialogue with God runs counter to your culture or faith, alarm bells ring. There is also the question of how a "symptom" is affecting someone's life. Is he talking to God and walking out into traffic, or talking to God and becoming a humanitarian? Illness impairs, and implicit in the idea of a mental illness is that it harms the person who has it. In other words, we have to look at how the whole picture the person is presenting holds together—or doesn't.

The onset of schizophrenia seems to involve a very rapid multiplication or intensification of the indicators the SIPS picks up on, to the point where disparate symptoms begin to feed into one another in a way that, for the patient, makes sense. If someone is having a hallucinatory experience of hearing footsteps, it's easier for her to believe she's being followed. The delusion supports the hallucination, and what others might view as a breakdown, the person experiences as a break*through*—a eureka moment when everything suddenly makes sense, and he has full conviction in his delusions and is most resistant to the idea that he is ill. Never mind that the pieces don't line up. The person will persist in trying to tie it all into a coherent narrative—an impulse common to all human beings—which can be like watching someone reason himself into illness. One young man I knew described it to me as though he were "waking up to reality for the first time; like someone had yanked me out of *The Matrix*."

Ragy Girgis, the director of COPE, recalls his early days working with prodromal patients in the program. It was an eye-opening experience, even for someone steeped in the study of schizophrenia who had always taken the existence of the prodromal phase for granted. "There are still researchers who doubt the reality of the prodrome, but having worked with it constantly now for eight years, I can tell you it's very real, extremely dynamic, and uniquely disturbing," he says. "There is nothing that will help you better understand schizophrenia like watching someone traverse that boundary from premorbid, to prodromal, to syndromal psychosis."

To receive a diagnosis of schizophrenia or to learn that you're at clinical high risk of psychosis is difficult. Often the first reaction is to blame everyone or everything else. But it can also be the period when someone learns that a belief he or she had held—that schizophrenia is a psychiatric death sentence that leaves sufferers without any chance of meaningful lives—isn't valid. Evaluation by an early-psychosis clinic means that there is a receptive and supportive haven for someone should he be found to be CHR and then go on to develop more serious symptoms. If he does have a first episode of psychosis, he is cared for immediately and, in the case of COPE, offered the opportunity to transition to the OnTrackNY clinic. If he doesn't progress to psychosis, and things clear up, he can resume life without the specter of schizophrenia hanging over him.

Chapter 19

How We (Should)
Treat Schizophrenia

How many times it thundered before Franklin took the hint! How many apples
fell on Newton's head before he took the hint! Nature is always hinting at us. It
hints over and over again. And suddenly we take the hint.

—Robert Frost, poet (1874–1963)

The Humble Art of Common Sense

I attended my first meeting of the American College of Neuropsychopharmacology in 1983. The ACNP was the elite scientific organization of psychiatric research,
and its annual meeting was the highlight of the scientific year. With the vast array
of disciplines being brought to bear on the study of human disease and mental
disorders—molecular and structural biology, genetics, biochemistry, neuroimaging, and so on—the ACNP attested to pharmacology's role as the key discipline
that opened the door to understanding mental illness.

I was a young researcher just beginning my career, and the meeting was an exciting opportunity to be in the company of luminaries. Among the highlights of the
week was the lecture by an eminent NIH scientist who had won the Nobel Prize in
1976 for his discovery of an exotic spongiform encephalopathy (an aggressive form of
degenerative brain disease) caused by a novel pathogenic microorganism. Carleton
Gajdusek was born to Hungarian and Slovakian immigrant parents in Yonkers, New
York, and earned his MD from Harvard Medical School. He became interested in
infectious diseases suffered by remote tribes around the world, and traveled to the
Amazon, the Hindu Kush, Papua New Guinea, and elsewhere in search of them.

In 1957, while in New Guinea, Gajdusek learned of a disease called kuru (meaning "to shiver," reflecting the neurological symptoms of its victims) that was rampant among the indigenous Fore tribe. The victims of kuru had all participated in funerary cannibalism, the ritualistic practice of eating the brains of dead family members, which had been suppressed in the 1940s by missionaries and the Australian authorities.

Gajdusek hypothesized a connection between the practice and the illness, and once back at the National Institutes of Health, he initiated a series of experiments to demonstrate that the disease could be transmitted between animals, injecting small amounts of brain tissue from infected monkeys into the brains of healthy monkeys. It was known that all bacteria, viruses, and parasites that caused disease did so within days or weeks, but for two years, the healthy monkeys showed no sign of illness. Finally, kuru emerged. That so much time passed between exposure to the illness and the manifestation of symptoms suggested that a slow-moving virus or some other unknown infectious agent was responsible.

Kuru resembled a fatal disease that had long been seen in goats and sheep called scrapie. Then, in the 1980s a disease whose symptoms looked similar to both kuru and scrapie broke out in cows in Britain: bovine spongiform encephalopathy (BSE), or mad cow disease. When the illness turned up in humans in the mid-1990s (as variant Creutzfeldt-Jakob disease, or vCJD), the source was traced to British beef. It was eventually determined that the contaminated cattle had been fed meat and bone meal from livestock. Cattle are natural herbivores but were subjected to an industrialized form of cannibalism comparable to the ritualized practices that were the cause of kuru. To prevent further outbreaks, a ban on feeding meal to animals derived from the body parts of common species was enacted in Britain and elsewhere, but hundreds of people have died from vCJD.

Gajdusek's lecture reviewed the story of kuru, as well as neurologist-biochemist Dr. Stanley Prusiner's subsequent discovery of "prions": the infectious particles that are the source of kuru and variants of CJD. It was a fascinating tale, but what struck me most forcefully was something he said during the discussion that followed. Gajdusek explained that although the microbiology and neuropathology that had made his discoveries possible were marvelous testaments to scientific progress, the reality was that, over the course of human history, as many, if not more, people had benefited from simple, practical applications of common sense than from high-tech discoveries: quarantine during plagues, citrus fruits to relieve scurvy, antiseptic practices for surgery, garbage collection, sewage drainage, clean water, and, more recently, cardiopulmonary resuscitation (CPR), the Heimlich maneuver, antismoking laws, the standardization of medical records, and the humble Band-Aid. The treatment for kuru, he added, had been legal, not medical: a ban against funerary cannibalism. With that, Gajdusek concluded his talk and stalked off the stage. (Though Gadjusek's work still stands, his reputation was permanently tarnished after he was convicted of child molestation in the mid-1990s.)

It would be many years before I was able to say that the point Gajdusek made applied to schizophrenia. But over the last couple of decades, we have seen advances in treatments for this illness that, in their commonsense and relatively low-tech ways, are akin to those humble but lifesaving breakthroughs Gajdusek mentioned. Without learning anything more about the complex causes or underlying pathology of schizophrenia, we have the means today to provide life-changing and life-saving care.

THE KEYS TO TREATMENT

Since the advent of antipsychotic medication, a massive body of evidence has accrued demonstrating their effectiveness when used alongside psychosocial and rehabilitation therapies. Over the last couple of decades, this evidence has been formulated into treatment guidelines, algorithms, and databases that health care organizations have made available. We know what the best treatments are and have confirmation to back that up. The latest support for this claim comes from the results of studies of the early-detection and intervention strategy, used in conjunction with coordinated specialty care. Now any person experiencing what appear to be symptoms suggestive of schizophrenia can expect to receive comprehensive, specialized first-episode care that will support recovery and the resumption of his or her education or work. The problem is that this approach isn't being utilized fully or effectively implemented, which is inexcusable, as coordinated specialty care offers the best chance for maximal recovery and for limiting future consequences from the illness. If CSC lives up to its predicted potential, schizophrenia will cease to produce the personal distress and disability from which so many have suffered, as well as the social pathologies that have plagued our society as a result of untreated mental illness.

In the pages that follow, I describe the keys to successful treatment, factors that complicate the treatment of schizophrenia (such as substance abuse), and why, even when patients have been ill for a long period, they can still have meaningful lives if they have the proper support. Finally, I look at innovations on the treatment horizon, including precision medicine, gene therapy, and neuromodulation.

There are three ways to measure treatment effectiveness. We can relieve symptoms without changing the course of the illness, as L-dopa does for Parkinson's sufferers or cholinesterase inhibitors do for those with Alzheimer's. We can prevent or mitigate the progression of the illness, as glatiramer and interferon do in the case of multiple sclerosis. Finally, we can prevent or cure the disease, as through surgical procedures for tumors or vaccines for infectious diseases. In the case of schizophrenia, the long-term aspirations are, on the one hand, to be able to identify people genetically or constitutionally at risk and preempt the possibility of their developing the illness, and, on the other, to rescue those in the chronic stages of illness using regenerative therapies.

Schizophrenia is a low-incidence but high-prevalence disease, meaning that relatively few people develop it each year (15.9 per 100,000 people) but once you develop it, you have it for life (the lifetime prevalence is 4.3 per 1,000). The illness isn't something you contract and get over, like meningitis or pneumonia. It is more like diabetes, hypertension, or epilepsy, a condition that doesn't go away but that you can live with if you have appropriate treatment. Treating schizophrenia is complicated by its heterogeneity (as well as the existence of conditions that imitate it) and by the need to intervene early. The window for intervening and preventing the illness from progressing varies for each person but is limited roughly to the first two to five years of illness, including the prodromal stage. When that window has closed, it's not that there is no point in treating people—in fact, their need for services may increase. But the goals and expectations of treatment have to be adjusted. We shouldn't encourage patients to set goals that are too low, but we have to be realistic and work with them to achieve a newly imagined and meaningful life.

There are five key elements of treatment that offer patients the best possibility of symptom relief, avoiding the illness's disabling effects, and achieving recovery:

1. **The Sooner, the Better.** Act early if you suspect symptoms. Err on the side of caution and seek professional help as soon as possible.

2. **Antipsychotic Medication Is Essential.** It will be needed at the onset of the illness and likely long after the acute symptoms have subsided.

3. **Medication Alone Is Not Sufficient.** Psychosocial therapies and support services will be necessary, ideally in the context of coordinated specialty care.

4. **A Stable Residence.** Recovery requires a safe living arrangement in the community, whether with family or friends or in a supervised residential facility.

5. **A Reliable and Caring Significant Other.** Every person affected by schizophrenia needs a family member, friend, or provider who is consistent, stable, and dedicated to supporting his or her recovery.

The First Step: Seeking Care

The first thing that anyone who has a loved one affected by the illness should do is inform herself—both to understand the nature of the illness and to be aware of the optimal treatments that do exist. Most people know very little about schizophrenia or its symptoms or course. As you would do with a diagnosis of cancer, be proactive: search online for the best treatments, treatment centers, and doctors. It is important to bear in mind that very few mental health centers are equipped to offer comprehensive care, so you may have to piece together a treatment program yourself and actively monitor and manage its implementation. This book is intended to help inform families, but there are many excellent additional resources. The best, in my opinion, is still *Surviving Schizophrenia*, by E. Fuller Torrey, now in its seventh edition.

Begin by getting a referral to a good psychiatrist with specific expertise in schizophrenia and psychotic disorders, either from your primary care physician or by contacting the best medical school or teaching hospital in your community. This is not easy or always feasible for large segments of the population, such as people living in remote or rural areas and small towns, underserved minority communities, and people outside of the mainstream economy. However, the increasing use of telemedicine and mental health paraprofessionals (nurse practitioners, psychologists, social workers, and mental health counselors) is beginning to mitigate this problem—but this, of course, requires technological savvy, an expanded workforce, and resources. Whichever mental health care professional you consult with should review the patient's complete history (as described in chapter 17) before reaching a diagnosis or formulating a treatment plan. This includes understanding what the patient's level of function was before he became ill, how long he has been ill, his treatment history, and the number of relapses he has suffered.

MEDICATIONS

COMPARING ANTIPSYCHOTIC DRUGS

Once someone has been diagnosed with schizophrenia, how do you or the doctor know which antipsychotic drug would be most beneficial? Generally, the best way to determine the relative benefit of drugs is through comparative effectiveness studies, in which all drugs, or a representative selection, are compared. In the United States, the nonprofit Consumer Reports is dedicated to such unbiased testing of consumer products, but no equivalent exists for medicines. After a drug is approved by the FDA, there is no process for tracking how it stacks up against other medications currently in use.

The first (and only) comparative effectiveness studies undertaken by the NIMH were launched in 1999. President George H. W. Bush had declared the 1990s the Decade of the Brain, which triggered legislation that brought increased funding for biomedical research. Simultaneously, the NIMH director at the time, Steve Hyman, was under pressure from mental illness advocacy groups to fund more clinical research relevant to patient care. I was on the faculty of the University of North Carolina at the time and, along with a team of colleagues, was awarded a grant for what became the largest study ever funded by the NIMH: the Clinical Antipsychotic Trials of Intervention Effectiveness (CATIE) study.

The study was led by Scott Stroup, now at Columbia University, and me. The goal was to determine the long-term effectiveness of antipsychotic drugs and to establish whether the new (patent-protected and more expensive) second-generation drugs were superior to the older and cheaper generic antipsychotics. Were they worth the extra cost?

Fifteen hundred patients received one of five medications under double-blind conditions. We followed them for eighteen months or until either the patient or his or her doctor felt the treatment wasn't working. If patients did not respond well to treatment, they could be reassigned to another medication, one of which was clozapine. By the end of the study, more than half the patients had opted to change drugs. Because the medications were being compared against one another rather than against an inactive placebo, this desire to switch drugs shouldn't be read as an indication that the medications were ineffective; rather, patients were still hoping for something with fewer side effects or even greater efficacy.

While there were differences in efficacy between the old and new medications, and among the newer medications themselves, the biggest differences were in their side effects. Clozapine was the most effective medication, followed by olanzapine (Zyprexa). Apart from these two, the older medications did just as well as the newer ones. These findings were replicated in studies in the United Kingdom, Germany, and elsewhere. These rankings are approximate, but they are as good as we can provide without performing large comparative effectiveness studies for each newly approved drug. One cruel irony that has emerged from the research is that the more effective a drug is, the more side effects it has.

When the results of the CATIE study were published in the *New England Journal of Medicine* in 2005, they caused a firestorm of controversy. The pharmaceutical companies disputed the findings. Many of my peers, who had staked their reputations on the superiority of the new drugs, found ways to criticize the study, not because of methodological flaws but because its results jeopardized their financial interests. But as the editorial in the *NEJM* noted, the CATIE study had provided solid evidence to help clinicians and their patients make decisions about drug treatments. The *New York Times* ran a polemical editorial titled, "Comparing Schizophrenia Drugs," which noted that CATIE presented the strongest evidence yet that the system for approving and promoting drugs was "badly out of whack," and that the United States was wasting billions on heavily marketed drugs that hadn't proven themselves more effective than the cheaper competitors. It would make more sense, the editorial concluded, to compel manufacturers to test their drugs not just against placebos but also against the drugs they sought to displace. "And surely it would be cost effective for the government to sponsor large studies comparing a slew of expensive drugs with their cheaper alternatives."

Surely it would, but despite the widespread understanding of the importance of the comparative effectiveness studies, none was extended or renewed. In 2010 Congress did, however, authorize the Patient-Centered Outcomes Research Institute (PCORI), an independent, nongovernmental organization mandated to improve the quality and relevance of evidence available to better inform the decisions of patients, caregivers, clinicians, insurers, and policy makers. The problem is that PCORI has been underfunded and poorly administered, and has not come close to fulfilling its mandate.

Choosing a Medication

Studies of first-episode patients have found that about 85 percent will respond to antipsychotic drug treatment, with substantial or complete remission of symptoms. Patients who've been ill for many years and have had multiple psychotic episodes don't fare as well, but about 50 percent still experience symptom reduction if treated with antipsychotics.

Currently, there are close to thirty antipsychotic drugs on the market worldwide. (See the table in appendix 7.) The lack of comparative information about these drugs means that doctors and patients often have to go through a trial-and-error process to find out which antipsychotic will work best. You aren't flying totally blind, though. And this is where a thorough history is critical, especially if someone has been on antipsychotics before. The doctor will need to find out which medications a patient has received, the doses and duration of treatment, and how effective they were—not always a straightforward process. Sometimes a patient will tell me that a certain medication didn't work, but on delving deeper, I discover that the dose was too low or that the patient discontinued the drug after only a few days, meaning it wasn't given a real chance to work. Other times, people will say a drug gave them terrible side effects, and I'll find out that the medication was prescribed at a higher dose than was needed.

When prescribing a drug, more is not necessarily better. We aim for the minimum effective dose, the margin—or "therapeutic index"—within which a drug is most beneficial but induces the fewest or mildest distressing side effects. A doctor will usually start the medication at a low dose and gradually raise it to a target therapeutic range, while monitoring the patient's response in terms of improvement and side effects. Patients don't respond immediately to antipsychotics (as people do to pain or sleep medications); it takes some number of days or a few weeks. So, doctors, patients, and family members must refrain from raising the dose or switching medications too soon. Any side effects should be managed by lowering the dose or adding medications to counteract them—usually anticholinergic antiparkinsonian drugs for neurologic effects, and metformin or topiramate to combat weight gain and other metabolic effects.

All antipsychotics available today target the D-2 dopamine receptor, but they vary in important ways, including their action at the receptor; their potency (reflected by the affinity for the D-2 receptor); how long they adhere to the receptor; and whether they have affinities for other neurotransmitter receptors (such as norepinephrine or serotonin) in addition to the D-2—actions that are often the basis of the drug's side effects. Drugs also differ in their half-life, or how long they remain active before the body metabolizes and eliminates them.

While the D-2 receptor has been the holy grail for antipsychotic drug development, pharmaceutical companies and researchers have tried to formulate drugs with novel mechanisms of action, until recently with limited success. The newest drugs, not yet FDA approved for general use, are the first effective antipsychotic medications that do not directly target the D-2 receptor. (They do influence dopamine neurotransmission and exert their therapeutic effects by modulating the dopamine synapse.) As discussed in chapters 15 and 18, drugs targeting glutamate neurotransmission may be effective for people in the early stages of the illness.

Given that all antipsychotics act on the D-2 receptor, it's not surprising that there are few marked differences in their therapeutic effects. As we found in the CATIE study, they differ more in their side effects, with first-generation drugs generally causing neurologic side effects that mimic the symptoms of Parkinson's disease (tremor, stiffness, slowness of movement), while second-generation drugs cause weight gain and elevated blood glucose and lipids (cholesterol being one type) but have relatively few neurological effects. But there is a paradoxical phenomenon known to clinicians in which, despite the fundamental similarities between antipsychotic drugs, a patient can respond very well to one of those drugs after having not responded well to the others. It's a kind of selective responsivity, and it is not predictable or fully understood by doctors. It is therefore worth trying different medications in search of greater effectiveness.

Elyn Saks, a professor of law, psychology, and psychiatry and the behavioral sciences at the University of Southern California (USC), speaks eloquently to the patient's dilemma regarding medication in her memoir *The Center Cannot Hold*. Saks was diagnosed with schizophrenia while studying at Oxford University on a prestigious Marshall Scholarship. Despite being very symptomatic at times, and even requiring hospitalization, she went on to get her JD degree from Yale Law

School. She recounts how, after a dozen years on thiothixene (one of the older first-generation drugs, marketed as Navane), which was clearly helping to manage her symptoms, she began to be troubled by its side effects, namely sedation and a tenfold elevation in her level of prolactin, the hormone that induces milk production in new mothers. The drowsiness she combated with a lot of black coffee, but her gynecologist believed that the heightened prolactin production increased her risk of breast cancer.

Her doctor at the time suggested olanzapine. Saks was wary of it, as it had come on the market only recently, but the side effects of thiothixene left her little choice. The change was dramatic. She had fewer side effects on olanzapine (Zyprexa); she felt alert, energetic, and rested rather than groggy, as she had on thiothixene. And she stopped experiencing what we call breakthrough symptoms: fleeting psychotic thoughts that she'd been visited by many times a day. "I could take a break, go off duty, relax a little. I couldn't deceive myself—the illness was still there—but it wasn't pushing me around as much as it once did," she writes. "Finally, I could focus on the task at hand, unencumbered by the threat of lurking demons."

But the most profound effect of olanzapine, she writes, was to finally convince her that she actually had a real illness, something she'd struggled to accept for years. "The clarity that Zyprexa gave me knocked down my last remaining argument," she acknowledges. Elyn had also struggled with the "crutch" of medications, for "to use them meant I was weak of will, weak of character. But now I began to question my own absoluteness. For instance, if I'd had a broken leg, and a crutch was required, I'd have used it without even thinking twice. Was my brain not worth tending to at least as much as my leg? The fact was, I had a condition that required medicine. If I didn't use it, I got sick; if I used it, I got better. I don't know why I had to keep learning that the hard way, but . . . it was a necessary stage of development that I needed to go through to become my full-fledged self. It was the only way I could come to terms with the illness."

CLOZAPINE

The next best thing to comparative effectiveness studies are statistically assisted reviews called meta-analyses, which allow treatments to be ranked according to their therapeutic efficacy based on data from multiple studies. Such reviews, along with the few comparative studies carried out (for instance, CATIE), show that clozapine is indisputably the most effective drug. However, clozapine can cause serious, even life-threatening, adverse effects, including agranulocytosis (an insufficiency of a type of white blood cell needed to fight infections) and myocarditis (inflammation of the heart). It is therefore the treatment of choice only for patients who haven't responded sufficiently to or can't tolerate other medications. These adverse effects are relatively rare (about 1 in 150 people) and are reversible and manageable if detected in time. Anyone on clozapine has to have regular blood tests to monitor his or her white blood cell count.

Clozapine has been life changing for countless people. But it almost disappeared before it had a chance to be widely used. Interestingly, in early rodent studies in the 1950s, the drug was considered unpromising, as it didn't produce the slowness and stiffness of movement thought to be necessary for a drug to have antipsychotic effect. However, human trials found it to be highly effective—and without causing neurologic side effects. But in the 1970s eight patients in Finland died of agranulocytosis as a result of clozapine. More cases of the blood disorder occurred in other countries, and clozapine use was abruptly terminated.

Too many patients had already benefited from it, though, and when they were taken off clozapine and then experienced a severe recurrence of their symptoms, a plea for compassionate use was made to Sandoz Laboratories (which owned the patent) and the regulatory agencies, which was granted. As the number of requests for compassionate use grew, the company met with leading researchers in Europe and the United States, and a strategy began to take shape.

Sandoz approached John Kane, director of research at the Hillside Hospital of Long Island Jewish Medical Center, and Herbert Meltzer at Cleveland's Case Western Reserve School of Medicine about becoming sites for referral of patients pleading for access to clozapine. It was my good fortune, as a young researcher, to have been recruited to Hillside Hospital in 1983, just before this program began. I asked to be added to the protocol so that I might take care of some of the patients who were to be treated with clozapine. The work gave me extensive experience in administering the drug and managing its potentially lethal side effects, and had the added benefit of enhancing my knowledge of hematology.

Having now seen the dramatic effects of clozapine on a significant number of patients, Kane and Meltzer persuaded Sandoz (which is now Novartis) to coordinate a formal clinical trial that would provide the evidence necessary to gain FDA approval. That study would mark the most significant advance in the pharmacologic treatment of schizophrenia since chlorpromazine. Researchers randomly assigned 268 schizophrenia patients to receive six weeks of either clozapine or chlorpromazine. All had been ill for more than five years and hadn't responded to numerous previous treatments. Viewing the results in a blind study, where you don't know which participants are receiving which drug, is always a white-knuckle moment—you can be elated or devastated by what you find. In this case, the results were cause for celebration. Clozapine had proved vastly superior.

The paper reporting the trial results was published in the journal *Archives of General Psychiatry* and instantly became a classic of scientific literature. Clozapine was approved by the FDA in 1989 and marketed for clinical use in 1990. But since then, despite its unique efficacy, the drug has been grossly underutilized in the United States. There are a few reasons for this. Doctors may be reticent to expose their patients to what they see as unwarranted risk, or they may simply want to avoid exposing themselves to liability should adverse events occur. And patients may be reluctant to undergo the necessary blood tests to monitor for dangerous side effects. None of these reasons justify the underuse of a potentially life-changing treatment. But as it stands, while 40 percent of patients with persistent symptoms (despite treatment with other antipsychotic drugs) could benefit from clozapine, it accounts for less than 5 percent of prescriptions in this country. If you do the math, you see that almost a million people who could benefit from it aren't receiving it. The underuse of clozapine is one of the most significant failures in clinical practice in the treatment of schizophrenia.

POLYPHARMACY

A common practice to enhance treatment response is polypharmacy: combining multiple medications. Despite its widespread prevalence, there is limited rationale for this strategy. If the multiple drugs being prescribed are all antipsychotics, and all the therapeutic effects of antipsychotic medication come from action at the D-2 receptor, why would adding a second drug be better than increasing the dose of the first drug? There are some exceptions, though. A comprehensive review found the combination of clozapine and the atypical antipsychotic aripiprazole superior to other drugs, including clozapine on its own. Polypharmacy can allow a doctor to avoid raising the dose of a drug that is working but causing side effects and instead add another antipsychotic that doesn't cause the same side effects.

There is also the possibility of supplementing a long-acting injectable (LAI) medication with an orally administered drug—either the same one or another.

On the other hand, it's entirely warranted to add different psychotropic drugs to antipsychotics to treat co-occurring symptoms. Many people with schizophrenia experience post-psychotic depression, which can be treated with antidepressant medication. Anxiety symptoms can be treated with benzodiazepines. A less well known but frequent practice involves the use of lithium, which is not a drug but rather a naturally occurring element that is highly effective for treating bipolar disorder. In researching its mechanism of action, a NIMH researcher found that lithium had neurotrophic effects, meaning that it stimulates cell growth and increases neuronal connections. It has been suggested that this neurotrophic property could be protective against degenerative processes, mitigating the progressive damage caused by schizophrenia.

Another important principle in drug treatment that is, alarmingly, too often forgotten, is parsimony. As new medication(s) are added to a patient's regimen, doctors often neglect to discontinue those that haven't been effective. As a result, the number of medications a patient is taking can grow to unwieldy and dangerous numbers.

The Challenge of Treatment Adherence

One of the biggest challenges in treating schizophrenia is patients not adhering to treatment, especially taking medication. Any number of reasons contribute to this: denial, cognitive impairment, a perception or experience of being stigmatized, a lapse in prescriptions or insurance coverage, disorganization leading to missed appointments. The most common consequences of interrupting or discontinuing treatment are relapse and hospitalization, sometimes leading to the revolving door.

The extent of the problem is staggering, with 40 percent to 50 percent of schizophrenia patients partially or wholly nonadherent to their prescribed medications and psychosocial treatments such as therapy. Unfortunately, the rates of treatment adherence are no better in patients who have recovered from their first episode of schizophrenia, which is especially tragic, as they have the most to lose by risking relapse and incurring progression of the illness.

Assertive Community Treatment (ACT) is an integrated, team-based approach to delivering mental health care in a community setting to people who are at risk for psychiatric crises, hospitalization, or involvement in the criminal justice system. ACT uses the same proactive approach that Ilana Nossel described as part of the OnTrack ethos. By ensuring continuity of treatment and promoting patient engagement, ACT diminishes the likelihood of nonadherence.

ACT was developed in 1975 and has repeatedly proven effective. Yet forty-five years later, it is still in short supply, and not because it has been replaced by something better. Due to its limited availability, various groups, including family members of people with schizophrenia, began to advocate in the 1980s for a legal mechanism to combat nonadherence. Assisted Outpatient Treatment, or AOT, was the result. AOT involves courts ordering people with severe mental illness and a history of medication nonadherence or dangerousness to comply with a treatment plan while remaining in the community. If patients fail to follow the court-ordered terms of this outpatient commitment, they can be hospitalized for treatment. Currently, every state except Connecticut, Maryland, and Massachusetts permits the use of AOT.

Outpatient commitment has been the major statutory change since the decisions on civil commitment in the 1970s, and the AOT law that was established in New York State in 1999 has served as a model for programs around the country. Kendra's Law was a direct result of the sort of tragedy that can occur due to untreated mental illness. A young woman named Kendra Webdale, standing on a Manhattan subway platform, was abruptly pushed in front of an oncoming subway train by Andrew Goldstein, a stranger who had schizophrenia and had stopped taking his medication. The resulting Kendra's Law created mechanisms and criteria for identifying at-risk individuals who—in light of their treatment history, circumstances, and past unwillingness to take medication—were likely to have difficulty living safely in the community without close monitoring and mandatory treatment. It also enabled courts to mandate the mental health system to provide the treatment and to prioritize access to services for people with court orders.

AOT is not without its critics. Racial disparities have been detected (a 2005 study showed that in New York State, black people were almost five times as likely as white people to be subjected to the law), and some say the programs expose highly vulnerable patients to legal proceedings after the mental health system has failed them. Even those who regard AOT as an essentially positive development (I'm one of them) point out that it lacks teeth. Most states that have adopted AOT laws have not provided additional funding for carrying out their mandates. Mental health systems that are already overwhelmed are given the additional burden of keeping track of and treating people who don't want to be treated—when they likely have long lists of people who *do* want to be treated. Moreover, most people know that if they don't comply with an AOT court order, the most that will likely happen to them is that they'll be picked up and brought to an emergency room. AOT has therefore had less effect than it might have had we funded it properly and put in place enforcement mechanisms. This is unfortunate, as studies have shown that even in its limited capacity, AOT has provided an incentive for many mentally ill people to stay in treatment, and has reduced homelessness, suicide, hospitalizations, and incarcerations.

It is worth noting that when Andrew Goldstein was released from prison in 2018 at the age of forty-nine and transferred to another state agency, he said he hoped he would be sent to Creedmoor Psychiatric Center. He admitted that he could not be trusted to maintain treatment on his own and would feel safer if someone was there to make sure he took his medication.

The advent of long-acting injectable medications gave psychiatrists another means to reduce nonadherence. LAIs are highly effective at controlling symptoms, and last from two to twelve weeks, depending on the formulation. Beyond preventing relapses that can come with going off medication, they have a number of advantages over oral drugs. (People not taking medication are estimated to be five times more likely to relapse within the first five years after diagnosis than those who are on medication.) Because of the slow release of an LAI, there is a steadier concentration of the drug in the brain than with daily oral medication, where levels rise and fall in relation to the dosing schedule. Additionally, with oral medication, a clinical team may not know that someone has stopped taking his or her medication until it's too late, and the person has seriously deteriorated; but with long-acting injectables, doctors know as soon as someone misses an injection appointment. LAIs also enable doctors to know *why* someone has relapsed. The question of whether a relapse is due to someone stopping oral medication or has occurred in spite of the medication is rendered moot: with LAIs, we know it's the latter. LAIs help families, too, eliminating the awkward feeling that one member of the family is being "policed" by the others.

Historically, long-acting injectables have been reserved almost exclusively for people who are chronically ill, but recent studies have shown their advantage in first-episode patients. Given the high rate of nonadherence to treatment in first-episode patients, and the fact that LAIs have been found superior to oral medications in reducing relapse, LAIs offer an important treatment option. Despite this, LAIs remain underutilized, with their prevalence generally lower than 30 percent, even among patients with a history of nonadherence. Doctors may be reluctant to prescribe them, assuming mistakenly that because a patient is adherent today, adherence will never be an issue; or feeling that if they suggest LAIs, they're telling a patient that they don't trust him. In turn, a physician's hesitancy may undermine patients' comfort with LAIs. But just as nonadherence should be destigmatized, so should LAIs—they aren't a punishment for misbehavior but a way of relieving patients of certain burdens common to all medications, such as remembering to fill the prescription and to take the drug daily.

Psychosocial Treatments

The recognition of the importance of psychosocial treatments—therapies and support services that are neither medications nor physical procedures (such as electroconvulsive therapy)—dramatically increased as the limitations of antipsychotic drugs became clear and the crisis of deinstitutionalization unfolded.

Therapeutic Communities

Necessity, as we know, has a habit of spurring invention. The psychosocial treatments we have today, which are grounded in evidence-based approaches to improving cognitive and functional capacities, had their predecessors in the therapeutic community and an outpatient approach called the clubhouse.

The therapeutic community applies "milieu therapy," which was an outgrowth of Philippe Pinel's moral treatment, and aims to foster an environment conducive to trust and learning new coping skills. (One example is a drug rehab facility.) It takes a participatory, group-based approach to mentally ill patients in long-term institutional and residential settings. It began following World War II and was popularized by Maxwell Jones, a British psychiatrist who took a position at the Maudsley Hospital in London just as the war began. The Maudsley was the leading research and training mental hospital in the United Kingdom, and when the war ended, the British government asked the Maudsley to staff a nearby hospital that would be used for rehabilitating and reintegrating the most mentally disturbed

British prisoners of war. Jones ended up heading a three-hundred-bed unit in this hospital.

In this communal therapeutic setting, the men were reoriented to social and behavioral norms and trained for part-time jobs in the community. In group therapy sessions with staff, they talked about their difficulties (negative self-image, lack of confidence, suspiciousness, fears of intimate relationships, and so on). At community meetings, they discussed practical and governance matters: rules about tidiness and recreation time—bed-making, room cleaning, smoking, television access—resolved disagreements between patients, and expressed complaints about staff.

From 1947 to 1959, Jones worked in what he called a "no-man's land" between the disciplines of medicine, social psychology, and economics. The patients were a heterogeneous group, but they shared a lack of social and emotional development. The overriding goal was to foster maturation. To do this, the community endeavored to create a congenial and informal environment, with no locked doors and a democratic social structure. Patients were referred to as clients, and staff wore street clothes and were called by their first names. The use of medications was limited, first because there were no effective drugs and then, after the discovery of antipsychotics in the 1950s, because psychoanalytic theories of causation still predominated.

This model of care spread rapidly and became a standard feature of inpatient units—it was what I encountered during my psychiatric training. Vestiges of the therapeutic community can still be found on inpatient units of long-term or state mental hospitals, but such communities aren't feasible at acute-care hospitals, as patients' lengths of stay have now been shortened so much in order to keep costs down.

The clubhouse model of care, an outpatient approach to social rehabilitation for people with chronic mental illness, originated in 1943 at Rockland Psychiatric Center, a state mental hospital in Orange County, New York. Patients and staff at Rockland realized that when patients were discharged, they benefited from remaining in contact with one another. Patients who had been released eventually formed an organization called We Are Not Alone (WANA). With the support of charitable groups and family members, WANA was able to incorporate as a nonprofit and purchase a townhouse in New York City, which they christened Fountain House. Over time, professional staff were hired, and the activities there were formalized into a clubhouse model of care. Clubhouses began to proliferate in the United States and internationally. In 1977 the NIMH provided funding for a National Clubhouse Training Program. By 1990, an International Clubhouse Network was established, with standards for accreditation, and the effort to sustain and expand clubhouses remains active.

While there has been little research done on how the experience of attending a clubhouse affects symptoms, relapse rates, levels of function, and recovery, the main purpose of clubhouses—socialization—is important. People with mental illness have very specific needs, but some of what they need doesn't differ from what anyone needs: a sense of community and belonging, social interaction, a feeling of being protected and supported. Even if frequenting a clubhouse doesn't help someone to progress in his or her functional capacity, the clubhouse remains a place where people feel welcomed, without fear of judgment by staff or other attendees.

PSYCHIATRIC REHABILITATION AND PSYCHOSOCIAL THERAPIES

Psychiatric rehabilitation was sparked by the glaring failure of deinstitutionalization and has built on the foundations established by the therapeutic community and the clubhouse. Its mission was to improve the functioning of people with long-term disabilities due to mental illness by developing certain skills. Over time, this approach has produced an array of psychosocial therapies that target specific functional deficits. Despite the original intention that they be used for chronic patients, the innovative application of these therapies to first-episode patients in the context of CSC has been the conceptual leap that will have the biggest impact on future generations, saving people who develop schizophrenia from its devastating effects.

Psychosocial therapies have now been integrated into mental health services and innovative models of multidisciplinary specialty care. (See the table in appendix 8.) They include supportive and problem-oriented psychotherapy (as opposed to psychodynamic insight-oriented therapy), cognitive behavioral therapy, family psychoeducation and support, family therapy, social skills training, vocational rehabilitation, supported employment and education, case management, cognitive remediation, substance abuse treatment, suicide prevention, and peer support. The innovative models combined treatments such as ACT, critical time intervention (CTI) and mobile crisis intervention, collaborative care (integrated mental and primary health care), and, most recently, coordinated specialty care. (See the table in appendix 9.)

Psychosocial therapies are largely intended to be used in combination with medication, but mostly after patients have been stabilized from an acute psychotic episode. They can be thought of in two ways: as rehabilitative treatments to recover functions and skills that have been affected by an acute illness, and as mental "prosthetics" (or coping techniques) augmenting cognitive functions damaged or impaired by the illness. People with schizophrenia suffer from a range of functional deficits, but which ones predominate and the degree of impairment vary. Hence the need to individually tailor the program of psychosocial treatments. These treatment choices are most effective when made jointly with the patient, fostering patient understanding and encouraging motivation.

The progress achieved through psychosocial therapies is gradual. While it can be measured by setting short-term goals of incremental improvement, the course of treatment is long term, extending over months or years.

TARGETING COGNITION

Schizophrenia manifests in three ways: psychotic symptoms, negative symptoms, and cognitive impairments. All three affect a person's ability to perform the fundamental tasks of living in order to function effectively in daily life. But a seminal paper published in 1996 by UCLA psychologist Michael Green demonstrated that it was the cognitive deficits—in memory, information processing, executive functions, problem solving, and so on—that were principally responsible for the enduring functional difficulties experienced by people with schizophrenia. These problems relate to such basic life management skills as personal hygiene, scheduling and planning, social interactions, relationships, financial management, and education and work.

Many people don't realize that while antipsychotic drugs alleviate psychotic symptoms relatively rapidly, usually within two to eight weeks, it takes longer for patients to recover their cognitive functions following an acute psychotic episode. Negative symptoms, which are largely emotional and motivational, don't really improve; regrettably, there is very little we can do for them. But we do have effective treatments to improve cognitive functions, and these in turn improve functional capacity. These specialized, labor-intensive therapies take longer to achieve their effects than it takes medication to quell psychosis. And the degree to which they're able to restore cognitive function depends, of course, on what a person's capabilities were prior to the onset of illness.

THE NEAR MODEL

Alice Medalia is a psychologist who has bridged the disciplines of cognitive neuroscience and psychiatric rehabilitation to devise approaches for treating even the most chronically impaired schizophrenia patients. Her career reflects the spirit of the recovery movement and the belief that no patient should be viewed as hopeless. After receiving her doctorate in neuropsychology from the City University of New York in the early 1980s, Medalia worked in the New York State Office of Mental Health at Rockland Psychiatric Center, then joined the faculty of the Albert Einstein College of Medicine. While most neuropsychologists she worked with spoke of test scores and specific forms of cognition (working memory, attention, information processing), Medalia was more functionally oriented. She wanted to know: Could someone live independently? Did they have friends? Could they keep a schedule? At the same time, she had a neuropsychologist's knowledge of anatomy and the corresponding mental functions.

In the mid-2000s, when I became chair of Psychiatry at Columbia, I could see that we needed someone with expertise in psychiatric rehabilitation, and I recruited Medalia. She began working with us in 2007, and the following year published the culmination of her research to date in the form of the Neuropsychological Educational Approach to Cognitive Remediation (NEAR). The NEAR model is an individualized, web-based program where people work at their own pace using commercially available products such as 21 Questions, Luminosity, and BrainHQ. It isn't simply a matter of assigning homework; therapists interact with patients in NEAR, helping them to better understand their cognitive abilities and needs.

"No one is taught how schizophrenia affects cognition," says Medalia, whose team wrote a handbook for families on cognitive function. Helping families to understand the illness is important, as the family is usually the context in which people are trying to recover and gain independence. "Hallucinations and delusions are very dramatic; forgetfulness and inattentiveness less so. But if you understand that someone with schizophrenia has problems with attention, memory, and so on, it may change the way you view them."

It is essential that what is learned in NEAR is transferable and applicable to the individual's real world; it isn't just getting the brain to perform better on neurocognitive tests in a therapeutic environment but generalizing those improvements in ways that enable people to do the things they want to do in life. Medalia has seen how cognitive remediation improves the negative symptoms that have been so resistant to medication: social withdrawal, lack of motivation, and so on. "If you are able to pay better attention to something, then you can remain in a conversation, which means you can have meaningful interactions with your friends or family."

Studies back up what Medalia has witnessed in practice. People with schizophrenia who are engaged in cognitive remediation show significant clinical, neurocognitive, and functional improvements; progress is greater in early-course patients compared with chronic patients. While the conceptual framework for this treatment model is guided by neuroscience, its effectiveness is measured by how well someone is functioning. Can the patient travel to and from the clinic alone? Is he looking after his personal hygiene? How is she interacting with others? Can the person perform tasks related to school or work commitments? Studies are examining neurobiological correlates of cognitive training that will further validate the model, but these are secondary in importance to the observed improvement in a person's ability to function in life.

Sadly, very few places have cognitive remediation programs and the personnel trained to run them. And insurance, for the most part, will not cover the cost—either because insurers insist that the evidence of their efficacy is inadequate or because cognitive remediation treatments aren't sufficiently standardized. Of course, not many people can afford to pay out of pocket.

The timing of Medalia's arrival at Columbia was fortuitous. I was treating Janice Lieber at the time, the patient described in chapter 16, and I brought Medalia onto the treatment team. In the course of mapping out Janice's treatment plan, Medalia developed a close relationship with Janice's parents, Connie and Steve. The care plan that she devised produced striking and continuing improvement in Janice. The Liebers were both impressed and grateful, so much so that they began to wonder how many other mentally ill people were able to access this form of treatment—the sort of question that was characteristic of the Liebers. When we told them very few, Connie and Steve said, "Well, we must do something about that."

The Lieber Rehabilitation and Recovery Clinic formally opened in 2006, with Medalia as its inaugural director. Donations from Connie and Steve Lieber (and from their foundation, following their deaths) have since subsidized the cost of the program so that more people could benefit. The clinic provides outpatient treatment for adults diagnosed with debilitating psychiatric illnesses. Its tailored, recovery-oriented program focuses on treating the cognitive deficits associated with psychotic disorders, as well as on managing psychotic symptoms. Tiffany Herlands, associate director of the clinic, describes how they try to move away from diagnostic labels and focus instead on individual goals. Like Nossel at OnTrack, she says that a lack of insight into the illness—something people with schizophrenia often suffer—is not necessarily a barrier to treatment. "The more insight you have, the easier it is to buy in," she says. "But if you can partner around other things, it's not absolutely necessary to have insight. If the goal is to get back to work, for example, then people can be motivated for treatment."

Much of the treatment at Lieber takes place in groups of four to eight people, though patients also work individually with their psychiatrist. A typical treatment plan could include cognitive skills training, work on social cognition (examples include reading facial expressions and nonverbal cues), support in managing daily activities (commuting, structuring leisure time, managing finances), psychoeducation and support for families, and CBT or dialectical behavioral therapy (DBT) adapted for psychosis. (DBT is a form of therapy that helps patients to balance their emotions, understand and manage symptoms, and stay grounded in reality. The exercises and principles enable patients to gain self-awareness, help them navigate stressful situations, and interact with others more effectively.)

A patient in CBT is taught three Cs: catch the thought, check it, and change it. A skills coach could go out with a patient for a cup of coffee, a situation that might ordinarily be a trigger for psychotic symptoms, and when paranoid thoughts arise—*Another customer is staring at me and looks angry*—the patient is helped to think the situation through. If there are other possible explanations (maybe the customer has received bad news that accounts for the unfriendly expression), then a spiral into paranoia, or a confrontation with the stranger, might be avoided.

This kind of reality testing in CBT can help patients manage delusions and hallucinations, reducing the associated distress and the level of conviction and preoccupation with delusional beliefs, which in turn reduces the degree to which the symptoms interfere with everyday functioning. It also enables greater insight into psychotic experiences. Indeed, CBT might be the only psychosocial treatment proven effective against psychotic symptoms. Psychiatrist Aaron Beck, the inventor of CBT, adapted the therapy to treat negative symptoms. Beck surmised that each negative symptom is associated with certain negative thoughts. In the case of avolition (the absence of drive or desire), for example, a patient may have low expectations of success or enjoyment and therefore see no point in trying something. Beck's team would conduct exercises with the patient that enabled him to see that his predicted level of pleasure or proficiency was often much lower than what he actually experienced when undertaking the activity. CBT treatment is pragmatically oriented but also labor intensive and protracted; it can take a year or more for results to be seen. The arduous and long-term nature of the therapy is likely the main reason it hasn't been widely used in treating negative symptoms.

A ROOM OF ONE'S OWN

The most effective treatment in the world won't work if a person doesn't have a place to live. Sadly, the lack of safe and affordable housing for those with mental illness is one of the biggest barriers to recovery. When people with schizophrenia are discharged from a hospital, they often have nowhere to go. They may be estranged from their families. The place they lived before their hospitalization may not have been held for them, and new living arrangements are hard to come by. Housing is frequently the most difficult part of post-discharge planning that psychiatric social workers are faced with. Homelessness, or even the lack of a stable, safe, and consistent residence, places the discharged person at risk for relapse and readmission, eroding whatever gains were made during hospitalization.

Everyone is aware of this problem—we see it on city streets every day in the form of homeless people with mental illness—but there is too little being done to address it. There have been some heroic efforts, however. Rosanne Haggerty is a housing and community development leader, of great renown, who creates housing for the homeless and most vulnerable citizens. She founded Common Ground, an organization that develops supportive housing and assists communities in solving housing problems. Haggerty, an Amherst College graduate and the recipient of a MacArthur "Genius Grant," gained acclaim for transforming the Times Square Hotel in New York City from a vermin-infested dumping ground for vagrants into a model of subsidized supportive housing with on-site health care and vocational training. She went on to found Community Solutions, a national organization, and launch the 100,000 Homes and Built for Zero campaigns. Haggerty's very impressive accomplishments are a drop in the bucket, but they offer a model for how we can meet the housing needs of those mentally ill people who can live independently and within a community if they have the right support.

Critical time intervention (CTI) grew out of the effort to prevent homelessness in mentally ill people who lacked a stable residence after their discharge from hospitals, shelters, and prisons. It provides evidence-based and time-limited case management for the transitional period when people are struggling to establish themselves in stable housing and to access needed supports. CTI was conceived in the 1980s, when the mental health team at a large men's shelter in the Bronx saw that many of the men who were placed in housing soon became homeless again, lacking the support they needed to navigate the complicated systems involved in their care. CTI teams maintain continuity of care during the initial months of transition to housing, helping the person to establish connections with long-term support services, and gradually handing responsibility for case management over to those community supports. CTI programs can be incredibly important to people in transition, but their success depends, of course, on whether there is a sufficient number of high-quality community services available to those who need them.

A SIGNIFICANT OTHER

Pat Deegan is one of the leaders of the recovery movement. As a teenager in the 1970s, Deegan was diagnosed with schizophrenia and told she would be sick for the rest of her life. She initially refused to believe that it was more than a temporary setback, but when she found herself "drugged and stiff in the hallways of a mental hospital," she began to doubt. By the time she was eighteen, she'd been hospitalized three times. The future appeared barren, while the present was a numbing succession of meaningless days. The simplest tasks were overwhelming. For months, Pat sat in her family's living room, smoking cigarettes to pass the time until eight in the evening, when she could go back to bed.

In despair, she gave up. Giving up wasn't a problem in her eyes, it was the solution to her predicament. If she didn't want anything, nothing more could be taken away; if she didn't try to do anything, there was no possibility of failure. But there were others who didn't give up on her. They didn't overwhelm her with optimistic plans, but they did keep inviting her to participate in life. One day, for no reason that she can recall, she said yes when asked to help with the food shopping. It was a start.

"I began in little ways, with small triumphs and simple acts of courage . . . I rode in the car, I shopped on Wednesdays, and I talked to a friend for a few minutes." In time, these small steps enabled her to shift from merely surviving to becoming an active participant in her own recovery process.

In addition to medications and the range of CSC services, there is one additional factor in supporting someone with schizophrenia whose importance can't be overstated: the consistent presence of another person (or people)—family member, friend, or guardian—dedicated to his or her care and well-being. Part of that dedication can involve both parties knowing when space and independence are needed, a process I saw playing out within a family who were neighbors of mine in Manhattan in the 1990s and with whom I've kept in touch. Laura and Greg had two children, Susan and Eric, both of them bright, happy, outgoing. Eric had tested at the genius level but was also deeply empathetic, instinctively reaching out to children who were excluded or needed help. But in the fourth grade, Eric was diagnosed with ADHD. It was crippling. Despite medications, his problems escalated. By the time he was in high school, he wasn't able to keep track of his assignments or remember to go to class. He also gained weight and was losing friends. Then he went through an anorexic period. All things of concern but not beyond the range of what you could see in a teenager having a tumultuous adolescence. A psychologist told Laura unhelpfully, "If you're living with a teenager, you're living with a psychotic!"

Then the 9/11 attacks happened. Friends of Eric's saw the bodies being brought out of the Towers. Laura remembers how the city smelled of death. Eric hated it. He begged to go to Simon's Rock, a part of Bard College geared toward students who want to enroll early to college. The campus was woodsy and green, and it was what Eric wanted. Laura and Greg thought it was worth a try.

It was there that Eric had his first psychotic break. The next several years were a painful struggle for the family, as Eric got worse. At one point, when his parents had become the focus of his paranoia, he called the police and told them that Laura and Greg had killed children and buried them in the backyard. And then he ran away. When the police picked him up, they brought him to the hospital. By that time, I had moved to Columbia and suggested to Laura that we admit their son to our research program. Eric stayed at Columbia for several months. Gradually he began speaking to his parents again, and his bizarre beliefs disappeared. But things deteriorated again after Eric left the program. He stopped taking his medication, ended up in the Bronx Psychiatric Center, then was homeless for a while. There were at least two suicide attempts.

Fast-forward to the present. Eric is now stable and in a supportive independent living residence in New York City. He has a peer group. The service coordinators and therapists who work with him are his contemporaries; he feels like an equal, in partnership with them. He talks to his parents every evening but also has his own life, much of which he manages independently. The transition out of his parents' home was fraught. Both Laura and Greg have been incredibly devoted to Eric—sticking by him through the terrible accusations he made, continuing to see behind the veil of mental illness the qualities of kindness and thoughtfulness that he'd always had. But when Eric was in his late twenties, Laura knew that he needed more independence; he needed professionals advising and helping him rather than her. (Sadly, when she said this to Eric's psychiatrist, he accused her of wanting to throw her son out of the house.) This is a big question for parents: When does a son or daughter need greater independence? And when is it essential that the family remain more closely involved? Eric was a young man, desperately needing some autonomy. His sense of being trapped, Laura believes, actually helped to precipitate his final, full-blown crisis.

I asked Laura if there was one thing she would change about how the mental health care system operates, and she said, "Keep the family involved. When Eric was young, we were involved, but once he got older, if he didn't give permission, we were excluded." The flip side of that is a doctor who keeps in touch, and Laura says that being kept in the loop has been the most helpful thing for them in navigating Eric's illness. As policy makers, health care providers, and the public consider issues around patient privacy (discussed in chapter 20), we need to bear in mind that someone with schizophrenia requires consistent support from at least one other person, and that we need to find ways to include that person in the treatment and recovery process.

Elyn Saks had been supported by her family, even while she was at a distance. Saks was also fortunate to have two psychiatrists who were near-constant presences for almost twenty years. One of them, Joseph White, was a senior psychoanalyst at Yale. Psychoanalysis is highly unusual for someone with schizophrenia and generally thought to be contraindicated, due to its invasive and unstructured nature. But White's dedication, support, and empathy overcame any of its potentially deleterious effects. White wasn't just a doctor/therapist but also a stable, reliable touchstone for Saks—a surrogate parent with extensive knowledge and good judgment who encouraged her to take medication, accommodated her erratic schedule, and saw her multiple times a week; he no doubt played a critical role in enabling Saks to complete law school.

When Elyn moved to California, she started seeing Steven Kaplan, a psychoanalyst and psychiatrist who adopted a nontraditional proactive approach to their analytic treatment, from which Saks benefited greatly. But after thirteen years, Saks stopped seeing Kaplan; although she knew how much he had helped her, he'd failed to adhere to what has since become a tenet of the current standard of care introduced into psychiatry by the recovery movement: shared decision-making between the health care provider and the patient. This principle wasn't the norm at the time Kaplan was treating Elyn, but she knew nonetheless that Kaplan's increasingly "restrictive" behavior didn't sit well with her. During their sessions, Saks had a habit of moving around the office when she talked to him and covering her face with her hands, something she'd done with all her analysts to help her feel safe and contained. Kaplan objected to these habits and told her that if things didn't change, he was going to "terminate" her, something Saks found "brutal." He was, she wrote, "unpredictable, mercurial, even angry."

She made a list of things she knew needed to change—from her perspective— if she was going to stay with Kaplan: he had to stop saying they weren't getting anywhere, stop threatening termination, and lessen the physical restrictions he'd imposed.

He categorically refused her requests, at which point she announced that she would stop seeing him. She was clear in her decision but grief stricken. "Dr. Kaplan probably helped me more than anyone else in my life, and I love him today as much as I have ever loved anyone. For a long time, I carried inside me a palpable sense of loss. The decision to leave him was so awful, but I couldn't see any way around it."

Saks's other support has come from her husband, Will Vinet, whom she met while he was a librarian at the USC Law School. "He had, in short, the curious, insatiable soul of an artist, and something in that soul had made a decision to care for me." Elyn and Will married in 2001. I've become friends with Elyn and have spent time with her and Will on several occasions. While she is fully functioning and tremendously accomplished, I noticed some of the same caring qualities in Will that I had noticed in Penny Frese and Alicia Nash.

I had met John and Alicia Nash in 2007 at a meeting of the National Association for Research in Schizophrenia and Affective Disorders (now Brain & Behavior Research Foundation) in Sarasota, Florida, where both John and I were speaking.

At dinner that night, I was struck by how, even as she was eating and chatting with others, Alicia kept watch on her husband, anticipated his needs, and came to his aid if he grew confused. I went away thinking that he couldn't have survived and functioned at the level he did if not for Alicia. Elyn's husband has a similar air, hovering in the background, but attentive to Elyn's behavior and ready to provide support as needed. It is touching and inspiring to watch.

SUBSTANCE ABUSE AND SUICIDE

A number of factors complicate the treatment of schizophrenia. People with schizophrenia are at increased risk of substance abuse and suicide—the latter, in almost all cases, attributable to symptoms of the illness. They smoke cigarettes at several times the rate of people without the illness (as high as 90 percent versus 14 percent). This tendency is thought to be, in part, an effort at self-medication, as nicotine may have mitigating effects on symptoms, although studies of drugs that stimulated nicotine receptors in the brain haven't shown any benefit in reducing symptoms. Smoking is likely a major reason for the shortened life spans of people with schizophrenia.

Recreational drug use is also higher for those with schizophrenia, including alcohol, marijuana, stimulants, opiates, psychedelics, and dissociatives such as phencyclidine (PCP) and ketamine. Not all of these drugs are equally harmful. For people at risk of psychosis or who are already ill, the dissociatives are the most dangerous and should be avoided at all costs, along with stimulants such as amphetamine, methamphetamine, MDMA (ecstasy), and cocaine. Both types of drugs pose a serious risk of exacerbating symptoms and worsening the course of schizophrenia. As discussed in chapter 14, products containing THC can also be harmful, provoking the onset of schizophrenia in people with a family history or other indicators of susceptibility, or worsening the illness in those who already have it. Interestingly, psychedelics (LSD, psilocybin, mescaline) pose little risk with regard to schizophrenia, and the same is true of alcohol and opiates.

Suicide is one of the biggest contributors to lower life expectancy for people with schizophrenia—they die by suicide at a rate that is twelve times higher than that of the general population. Following recovery from a first or early episode of psychosis, patients may experience a post-psychotic depression or may become demoralized as the reality of what they've experienced sinks in, and they struggle to reconcile themselves with what it means for their future. The first five years of the illness are therefore the period of highest risk. Other risk factors include unemployment, living alone, being well educated and having a high level of functioning prior to becoming ill, being male, and having access to firearms. The depression can be partially treated with antidepressants, but the process of reckoning with a diagnosis of schizophrenia or an early relapse requires psychosocial therapies, starting with supportive psychotherapy.

Another cause of suicide and suicidal ideation is the experience of command hallucinations: voices instructing people to self-harm. Someone in the throes of such intense hallucinations may not necessarily want to die; he or she may simply feel compelled to follow the command. The treatment for suicidal ideation and suicide risk is better control of symptoms, usually through adjusting medication and cognitive behavioral therapy for psychotic symptoms. Clozapine, in particular, has been shown to reduce suicide risk, so if dose adjustments or adjunctive treatments aren't effective in suppressing psychotic symptoms, it should be used without hesitation. A recent study has also linked long-acting injectables with lower mortality and fewer suicide attempts among patients who switched from oral antipsychotics to LAIs. The effect was particularly striking within the initial two years of treatment: those who switched to LAIs within two years of first beginning oral medications experienced a 47 percent reduction in the risk of dying from suicide.

SCHIZOPHRENIA AND VIOLENCE

Schizophrenia is not a major cause of violent crime. In fact, people with mental illness account for less than 4 percent of overall violent crime in our society. But unlike the majority of crimes, in which some motive ties the perpetrator to the victim(s), in violent incidents involving people with schizophrenia, the motive is often indiscernible. The seeming disconnect is because the perpetrator is impelled by his or her psychotic symptoms (such as paranoid delusions or command hallucinations) or impulsive anger disconnected from reality. A tragic example of this is Troy Hill's stabbing of his brothers while in the throes of paranoid delusions, described in chapter 17.

The risk of violent behavior in people with schizophrenia fluctuates over time and recedes as people grow older. In almost all cases, the risk is greatest when the person is not taking medication or is actively symptomatic despite medication, is abusing intoxicants, or is in the midst of a mental health crisis: patients seen in psychiatric emergency departments, those who have been involuntarily hospitalized, or those experiencing their first episode of psychosis.

While complete strangers can be the victims of irrational violence driven by psychosis, it is more common for family members and those trying to help to be on the receiving end. This includes psychiatrists and other mental health care providers. I've been the target of threats by people with schizophrenia and have experienced a few assaults. The most horrific instance of this occupational hazard, which I remember as clearly as if it happened yesterday, was the murder of my good friend and close colleague Wayne Fenton.

One Monday morning in September 2006, I had just stepped into my office at Columbia when I received a call from Ellen Stover, a senior staffer at the NIMH, telling me that Wayne had been killed by one of his patients.

I froze in stunned disbelief. Wayne and I first met at a conference in 1984, and over the subsequent decades, I had come to think of him as one of the best people I knew. We had spoken only a couple of weeks before.

At the time of his death, Wayne was serving as associate director at the NIMH. But despite this prominent position, he'd remained a compassionate, down-to-earth, committed clinician, known for his willingness to take on complex cases and to go the extra mile to help patients in need. On the Sunday he died, he was seeing a nineteen-year-old patient named Vitali Davydov, who was floridly psychotic. Davydov's father, desperate for help, had pleaded with Wayne to meet his son. Wayne agreed, telling the father that he would encourage Vitali to take medication and would suggest to him that he take a long-acting injectable.

Vitali's father dropped off his son at the office complex in Bethesda, Maryland, where Wayne saw patients and watched as he entered the glass-and-steel building. When he returned to pick up his son, he was greeted by a horrible sight: Vitaly wandering around outside the building in a daze, blood on his hands, pants, and shirt. Paramedics found Wayne lying in his office. Vitali had beaten Wayne to death with his fists.

Terrifying and traumatic incidents of mass violence—especially those that appear to be senseless, random acts directed at strangers in public places—tend to provoke a repetitive set of responses. Political leaders often invoke mental illness as the cause, a narrative that resonates with the widespread public belief that mentally ill individuals pose a danger to others. Since it is difficult to imagine that a "mentally healthy" person would deliberately kill multiple strangers, it is commonly assumed that all perpetrators of mass violence must be mentally ill.

The conclusion that follows from this assumption is that to solve the problem of mass violence, we must restrict the liberty of people with mental illnesses—even removing them from the community. Mental health advocates, on the other hand, tend to react defensively, anxious to reject attitudes that risk lumping the nonviolent mentally ill in with perpetrators of terrible crimes.

Both of these responses are misguided. On the one hand, many different social and psychological factors motivate perpetrators of mass violence that have nothing to do with mental illness. On the other, many people are surprised to learn that people with schizophrenia are less violent in general than non-ill persons. However, if untreated, they *are* more prone to commit acts of mass violence when driven by their psychotic symptoms. Many of these people have become household names in this country: John Hinckley, would-be assassin of President Reagan; Seung-Hui Cho, who gunned down thirty-two students and teachers at Virginia Tech in 2007; Jared Loughner, who shot and severely wounded Arizona congresswoman Gabrielle Giffords and killed six others in 2011; and James Holmes, who killed twelve moviegoers in a Colorado cinema the following year.

Usually, when we hear about an incident such as those above, we tend to shudder and move on, rationalizing what happened as the sort of freak, unpredictable event over which we have no control. Indeed, my own initial reaction to my friend's death was to think that Wayne was simply in the wrong place at the wrong time; that it was just very bad luck. But these acts of violence aren't random anomalies we're helpless to prevent; they are the predictable consequence of systemic social forces and failed policies. In chapter 20 I'll discuss policy changes we can put in place to help protect the public from harm while respecting the rights of the mentally ill.

It's Never Too Late

While the combination of the best treatments is vital to patients at all stages of the illness, it's important to understand that the longer someone has been ill, and the more psychotic episodes he's had, the less responsive to treatment he will generally be. Even if we optimize drug therapy and apply various rehabilitative therapies, we cannot reverse the progressive effects of the illness. The person may improve and gain better functioning, but only to a degree. We see similar limitations in recovery in the cases of some stroke victims who, despite arduous and painstaking rehabilitation, may not regain all their lost functioning. But just because someone has missed that optimal window for early intervention doesn't mean we write them off as untreatable. Goals may need to be adjusted, but comprehensive care can achieve results in all stages of schizophrenia. (The OnTrack program discussed earlier is geared toward those in the early stages of illness, but we should also think in terms of an OnTrack program for life.) Even someone with multiple relapses and hospitalizations can live a meaningful life, provided he or she has coordinated support and a stable living environment. I have witnessed firsthand the truth of this, most notably in a former patient of mine named Rona, who has been a part of my life for more than thirty years.

Rona Gottfried is an only child, born in 1962 in New York City to a middle-class Jewish couple whose forebears had fled persecution in Eastern Europe. Her parents, Henry and Claire, had both grown up poor during the Depression and knew the meaning of hard work and the value of a dollar. By the early 1960s, they had formed their own company; they made posters for Broadway plays and feature films, which adorned billboards and the sides of buses. They had found their niche among the corporate behemoths of the rough-and-tumble advertising industry, and life was good. The only thing lacking was children.

Henry and Claire were still of modest enough means when Rona was born, but she wanted for nothing. She went to private schools, attended birthday parties and bar and bat mitzvahs, and was pampered by her parents. She was social, popular, and intelligent. Her parents doted on her and looked forward to her marrying and giving them grandchildren.

Rona enrolled at Hofstra University in 1980. It was during her sophomore year that the first symptoms of schizophrenia appeared. She began thinking her roommates were scheming against her, hearing their voices saying nasty things about her even if she was alone. She isolated herself and was unable to go to classes.

She told her parents, who requested a medical leave and brought her home. Initially, they did nothing, hoping the strangeness would pass. During the day, Rona would go to their office and sit reading magazines, trying to fend off the voices. Eventually, when she didn't improve, her parents brought her to the Payne Whitney Clinic in Manhattan, where she was admitted to the psychiatric ward. Rona doesn't remember it as therapeutic; at one point, she tried to commit suicide while hospitalized. In her own words, "I didn't know where I was, I was scared, and I just fell apart."

Rona responded to antipsychotic medication but experienced severe side effects in the form of shaking, grimacing, and shuffling. Given what Rona was suffering, neither she nor her parents wanted her to be exposed to medication any longer than was necessary, and once she had been stabilized and discharged, her doctor began tapering off her medication in time for her to return to school. This was a mistake. Predictably, three months later, Rona relapsed.

Thus began the repetitive cycles of treatment, symptom reduction or remission, discharge, stopping medication, and subsequent relapse. After her fourth relapse, the medication to which she had previously responded hardly had any effect on her symptoms. Various other medications were tried, but her symptoms persisted undiminished in intensity.

Having run out of treatment options and no longer able to maintain her at home, the Gottfrieds were forced to choose between a private stand-alone psychiatric hospital or a state mental institution, Creedmoor Psychiatric Center. Neither would do much other than provide custodial care. The former would be preferable but would cost a fortune, as Rona had already reached her lifetime maximum inpatient care coverage. Her parents opted for Creedmoor, not because they were stingy, but because they were pragmatists who didn't see the point of paying exorbitant sums when the outcome was going to be the same either way.

At the time, I was working at the Long Island Jewish Medical Center (LIJ) and on the faculty of the Albert Einstein College of Medicine. I had wanted a position at LIJ because of its connection to Hillside Hospital, where seminal studies of psychotropic medications had been carried out by some of the pioneers of biologically oriented psychiatry, which had transformed the field of psychopharmacology in the 1960s and 1970s. We were currently conducting a study of clozapine in patients for whom other antipsychotics hadn't worked; these were people desperate for anything that might spare them from persistent symptoms and possible long-term institutionalization.

Rona's mother read in a National Alliance on Mental Illness newsletter about our research and called us in desperation to see if we could help her daughter. I made the short drive from the Hillside complex to Creedmoor and found my way through the maze of buildings to Rona's unit. I reviewed her medical records and interviewed her, confirming her diagnosis of schizophrenia and her lack of response to repeated trials of numerous medications. She met the criteria for clozapine treatment, and, at Claire's insistence, we arranged to transfer her to Hillside, where she was enrolled in our clozapine study.

On clozapine, Rona quickly improved and within four weeks showed signs of the "awakening" that we had seen in other patients. Her speech became more coherent, and she began to interact with the other patients and staff and participate in the various activities and therapies. She experienced significant relief from the tormenting voices and the terrifying thoughts that had plagued her. Her other symptoms and disabilities were reduced substantially. She did suffer some of the characteristic side effects of clozapine (sedation, excess production of saliva, and urinary incontinence), but overall, clozapine's effects were profound, and Rona's parents were overjoyed and full of gratitude.

Over time, Rona's symptoms waxed and waned, usually in relation to stressful life events. A new set of symptoms also developed. Although Rona was fun-loving, she had always been cautious and careful. But after several months on clozapine, she worried excessively and sometimes asked questions repeatedly. Rona exhibited repetitive behaviors such as starting to walk, then stopping and taking a few steps back, only to start again. She developed a habit of touching herself in different spots several times in succession. These were classic symptoms of obsessive-compulsive disorder, something Rona had no prior history of. We had observed this in other patients taking clozapine and considered it a side effect syndrome caused by the drug. We lowered her dose and added an antidepressant medication to treat the OCD.

Despite her considerable improvement, Rona's ability to function on her own was still limited. She wasn't going to be able to simply pick up her life where she'd left off. A period of recovery and rehabilitation was needed for relearning social skills, recovering her cognitive functions, and reacquainting herself with the tasks of daily living. When someone suffers a stroke or a spinal cord injury, after corrective treatment, he or she requires care in a residential rehabilitation facility. The equivalent for people recovering from schizophrenia simply doesn't exist, which is a glaring deficiency in the US mental health system.

As the time for Rona's discharge neared, her parents scoured the landscape for residential treatment programs and found Gould Farm, a healing community for people with schizophrenia and other severe mental disorders. Set on a seven-hundred-acre working farm in the Berkshire hills in western Massachusetts, Gould Farm was the first residential therapeutic community in the United States dedicated to moving people from illness to recovery and eventual independent living. It was the Cadillac of rehabilitation programs. Next to clozapine, Gould Farm was the best thing that could have happened to Rona.

I wouldn't be involved in Rona's care, as I had just accepted a position at the University of North Carolina, but I helped Rona's mother identify a psychiatrist skilled in psychopharmacology at McLean Hospital, outside of Boston, one of the leading psychiatric hospitals in the country. At that point, I thought, *Mission accomplished.* My part in Rona's care and in the lives of the Gottfrieds was over.

After my move to North Carolina, Claire kept me informed of her daughter's progress by letter or phone call every few months. Rona's recovery was going well. She was "stepping down" through Gould's decreasing-intensity levels of care, which involved moving from the countryside to the Boston suburbs and eventually graduating to a private apartment with a roommate and twice-weekly visits from a Gould staff member. She also attended their Clubhouse at Fellside, frequented the highly acclaimed Boston University Center for Psychiatric Rehabilitation, and saw her McLean psychiatrist every other week.

Ten years later, in 2004, I was back in New York City, having accepted the chair at Columbia. It was shortly after my return that Claire casually dropped the guardian question. Before I'd even had time to think about it, I received a call from an estates and trusts attorney at a law firm in the city informing me that Claire and Henry had asked that a will be drawn up naming me as Rona's guardian in the event of their deaths. The attorney had actually advised them against this because of the potential for conflicts of interest. I wasn't keen on the idea, either. But the Gottfrieds were insistent. Claire and Henry told me they had no family and didn't want to entrust such an important responsibility to friends with no knowledge of mental illness. I wondered then if Claire had been grooming me for this from the earliest stages of our relationship. Over the years, she had made a point of getting to know my family, always remembering our birthdays, sending gifts for my sons' bar mitzvahs, and offering us theater tickets whenever we visited from North Carolina. It was calculating, but I could hardly blame her. She was facing the fear that torments every parent of a child with schizophrenia: *What will happen when we're gone?*

I discussed it with my wife and with an attorney, and ultimately agreed to their request. At the time, Claire and Henry were in their seventies, but both were robust, active, and healthy. Any guardian duties seemed a long way off. But within a few years, Rona's father suffered a heart attack, and her mother was diagnosed with cancer. They died within months of each other in 2012.

The loss of both parents in such quick succession would have been difficult for anyone, but Rona had a support network—her care team from Gould, her boyfriend Eric, her roommate Grant—and she weathered the losses impressively. (Rona met Eric years ago while waiting for the subway. Eric recognized her from the rehab center at Boston University and asked for her number; they've been together since.) My relationship with Rona continues to this day. She is not fully independent and still suffers some symptoms. But she is coherent, intelligent, responsible, and thoughtful. She has a part-time job as an office assistant at the Boston University Center for Psychiatric Rehabilitation, where she also attends psychosocial classes and a peer support group. She volunteers at Newton-Wellesley Hospital, sorting mail and delivering packages. "It keeps me busy," she says. "My confidence level goes up when I work."

She leads an active social life. She and Eric go to the movies and the Museum of Fine Arts. She loves sports and goes to Celtics and Red Sox games, and every chance she gets, she likes to attend rock concerts. The last time I met her in Boston, before the pandemic, she had recently taken a weekend trip to New York City with Eric (a former staff member from Gould Farm who was living in the city was there to support them) and had been to a Who concert at Fenway Park with Eric and another friend.

Besides Eric, the person closest to Rona in Boston is Grant, with whom she's shared an apartment for about fifteen years. (This was arranged by Rona's mother.) Grant also has schizophrenia. He and Rona met at a clubhouse. Like Rona, Grant is an only child, and the two of them have a rapport like that of close siblings. Rona's nickname for Grant is "Pipsqueak," which makes him smile. When one of them is away, the other's symptoms tend to worsen.

Grant's childhood was much tougher than Rona's had been. His problems started as a teenager, when the boy next door shot himself, and Grant began hearing voices blaming him for the suicide. His parents were Christian Scientists who didn't take him to doctors, and physical and psychological problems went untreated for years. He suffered violent bullying in school, and his mother had an undiagnosed psychiatric condition that resulted in her refusing to come out of her room or eat at the table with Grant and his father.

Grant had numerous breakdowns and hospitalizations, and has attempted suicide at least three times. After various medications, including the antipsychotics Thorazine and Haldol, Grant was treated with clozapine in 1993. Both he and Rona say that in terms of improving their lives, the latter drug is the most helpful treatment they have ever received.

Grant attends the Center Club, the oldest clubhouse in New England for people with psychiatric disabilities, which provides comprehensive support through programs based on principles of empowerment, self-help, and peer support. He performs chores at the club and finds that the voices are less present when he's there, because he's working and because of the social interactions. The club has been the second most helpful thing for him, he says. He also spends time with a peer from the Massachusetts Department of Mental Health program called Adult Clinical Community Services.

Rona and Grant have been able to live comfortably despite the severity of their infirmities in large part because Rona's mother cobbled together a network of services and spent the money necessary to incentivize providers. Claire donated each year to the Boston University program, gave generous gratuities to staff, and paid Grant's share of the apartment rent. She also paid for my services from time to time when Grant was in crisis. When Henry and Claire died, and my wife and I found ourselves becoming surrogate parents, we were able to retain the services of a clinical psychologist, Dr. Trudy Good. She and Stephanie Branca, a Gould Farm staff member, have been tremendous sources of support for Rona.

Rona is now sixty, and Grant, fifty-seven. Neither of them is symptom free. As they have gotten older, they have needed more attention. Rona is troubled by voices and obsessions; Grant, by voices and delusional thoughts. They both say that the voices take away their self-esteem. "They make you feel worthless," Rona explains. "They tell you not to get dressed, not to leave the house, that others are talking about you." Rona doesn't like to take the subway for this reason. "I think everybody else's life is perfect," she says. "They're all well and having good times, and I'm suffering from schizophrenia."

It takes courage, but she and Grant both push through, supporting each other. Rona also has Eric, who she says is always there for her when she's struggling. "Feelings will rise and fall," she says wisely, "unless you attach danger to them." Sometimes she instructs herself to "bear the discomfort until comfort comes." Other times she tells the voices off. I say, "Shut up! Leave me alone! I don't want to hear it anymore!" And it works.

Rona and Grant have both suffered terribly from schizophrenia, and Grant has additional trauma from his childhood to contend with. Had they received state-of-the-art care in the earliest phase of their illness, I have no doubt they would both be in a better place. But their lives are also a testament to the fact that just because early intervention leads to the best outcomes, we should never give up supporting people who missed that chance. This is something the recovery movement, discussed in chapter 21, has helped us to understand: that although a life may look different from the one once imagined, that doesn't mean that it can't be a life with friendship, love, work, and meaning.

The quality of life Rona and Grant enjoy has been possible not only because they availed themselves of existing treatments and services that for many people are not easy to find or to afford, but also because they had someone—Rona's mother—who was dedicated to establishing for them a treatment regimen, a stable residence, and a support network. If we had appropriate supports in place throughout the mental health care system, people from any socioeconomic group, and at any stage of the illness, would be able to live fuller and safer lives.

TREATMENT DISPARITIES

Racial, ethnic, and cultural disparities have been described in various aspects of the clinical care of patients with schizophrenia. The area of treatment is no exception. There are numerous instances of minority and economically disadvantaged patients receiving inferior treatments. These include higher (than necessary) doses of antipsychotic medications, being more likely to receive older first-generation and generic drugs versus second-generation newer medications, greater rates of polypharmacy, and lower frequency of receiving psychosocial and rehabilitative treatments. In essence, the inadequacies of society's attention to mental illness and mental health are reified in their application and availability to underserved and disadvantaged minority groups in our population by limitations in resources and discrimination.

TREATMENT IN THE NOT-TOO-DISTANT FUTURE

I hope that in the coming five to ten years, we will take full advantage of the therapeutic possibilities offered by antipsychotic and other psychotropic drugs, psychosocial therapies, early detection and intervention, and coordinated specialty care. At the same time, I look forward to discoveries that will improve clinical care. These innovations are most likely to come in the form of diagnostic and prognostic biomarkers, and novel personalized treatments. Future treatments will evolve in three ways: the targeting of specific stages of schizophrenia; the advent of new drugs; and the use of neuromodulation devices or brain stimulation to modify neural circuits and cell populations.

A diagnostic test for mental illness is the holy grail for psychiatric researchers, and much effort has gone into identifying biomarkers that are predictive of schizophrenia. We already use such tests (X-rays, EKG and EEG, blood tests, colonoscopies) to identify other disorders and diseases. For the foreseeable future, the most promising candidate technologies with regard to schizophrenia are brain imaging (MRI, PET), genetics, and a form of EEG measuring evoked potentials. EEGs measure electrical activity in the brain, and evoked potentials are forms of brain activity elicited by administering a sensory stimulus. This method cuts down on the "noise" and enhances our ability to detect signals, offering a more refined way of assessing brain function.

In addition to being able to confirm diagnoses or predict treatment response, illness course, and outcome, the information derived from these tests can be combined into profiles that yield probability scores, such as the risk scores we can now obtain for cardiovascular disease, prostate cancer, and staging for other cancers. In a process called deep phenotyping, a person's genotype can be combined with imaging results, electrophysiological and biochemical information, and clinical characteristics to arrive at a more precise diagnostic picture.

A newer technology that holds great potential involves the use of induced pluripotent stem cells (iPSCs), and their elaboration into artificially grown organs, or organoids. iPSCs are derived from skin or blood cells that have been reprogrammed, using molecular biologic techniques, back to their original state—like the generic cells of embryos in the very early stage of pregnancy, before they have differentiated into specific tissue or organ types. These stem cells can then be biologically directed to become neurons that reflect the individual genetic characteristics of the person from whom they were derived. Defects in the structure and function of the neurons can thus be observed. In addition, researchers can incubate the cells in drug substances, allowing them to test their effects and determine which drugs are most likely to be effective.

The initial rationale for the use of iPSCs was for degenerative diseases, and they have so far been used to treat macular degeneration and spinal cord injuries. Because iPSCs can be reprogrammed as any type of human cell and can provide an unlimited source of cells needed for therapeutic purposes, they are also being explored as treatments for a range of other conditions, including diabetes and leukemia, and neuropsychiatric disorders such as Parkinson's, autism, and schizophrenia.

The organoids that are created with iPSCs are tiny, self-organized three-dimensional tissue cultures that can proliferate when placed in a nourishing gel-like substance. Given sufficient time, these iPSC-derived neurons begin to develop the complexity and shape of the brain—in essence, an in vitro (external) personalized mini-brain that has the characteristics of an individual's brain cells and circuitry. We can observe in organoids the structure and function of cells and circuits, and test the ability of drugs to influence these cells and circuits and to correct any dysfunction.

Personalized or precision medicine is an outgrowth of genotyping, the initial function of which was diagnostic. It will be particularly helpful for people with schizophrenia who have rare penetrant mutations of genes and may be treated with existing drugs not normally considered for psychiatric purposes.

With many diseases, the treatments used depend on the stage of the illness. We see this in arteriosclerotic heart disease. In my case, I have a family history of coronary artery disease. My paternal grandfather and only paternal uncle died of heart attacks in their fifties. Knowing this, I began early in life to watch my weight and exercise. But my cholesterol level was high, so I began to take a statin drug to lower it. I also had genetic testing for genes associated with high blood cholesterol (hypercholesterolemia). Thankfully, my resting EKG and exercise stress tests have been good, so I haven't needed further treatment. If I do become symptomatic with chest pain indicative of coronary artery blockage, I would likely be treated with anticoagulants or have a stent inserted into the blocked coronary artery. If multiple blood vessels are blocked, I might undergo a coronary artery bypass graft surgery. If I developed an arrhythmia, I could take medication and, if necessary, a pacemaker could be installed or an electrophysiologic ablation performed. We should think of the treatment of schizophrenia in similar terms, rather than slavishly following a one-size-fits-all philosophy.

Evidence is accruing for drugs that target the glutamate synapse as potential treatments for patients in the prodromal phase of schizophrenia—assuming that they can be reliably identified. For people like Rona and Grant, who are at advanced stages of their illness, what is needed are therapies to enable them to recover what they've lost, whether in the form of stem cells, trophic agents (substances that stimulate growth), or other regenerative agents.

There are many novel treatments born of molecular biology and genetic technologies that have yet to be applied to mental disorders but have been used to treat cancer and autoimmune conditions. RNA interference (RNAi) is a biological process in which RNA molecules are involved in sequence-specific suppression of gene expression. Antisense oligonucleotides (ASOs) are a new class of drugs consisting of specially designed, short, single-stranded molecules that can alter RNA and reduce, restore, or modify protein expression through several distinct mechanisms.

Drugs typically act at the margins of cells, on proteins embedded in the surrounding membrane. RNAi and ASOs act instead at the level of DNA in the cell nucleus, altering the messages emitted by the DNA in order to correct for either under- or overactivity of the gene and the protein that would normally be produced. Researchers are actively exploring the application of this technology to treatment development for schizophrenia and other mental illnesses, but there are currently no drugs of this kind ready for clinical use.

The most widely anticipated therapeutic modality is gene therapy, which will undoubtedly impact every area of medicine, including the treatment of brain disorders such as schizophrenia. The initial approach of gene therapy was the replacement or disruption of defective genes, and scientists focused on diseases caused by single genes, such as cystic fibrosis, Huntington's disease, muscular dystrophy, and sickle cell anemia. A section of DNA with the corrected gene sequence of bases is administered intravenously or directly into the organ of interest, enters the affected cells, and either expresses or inhibits the protein produced by the disease-causing gene. Various methods to deliver the rescue gene have been tried, including viruses, which have been used as a vector (vehicle) by which to penetrate cells and deliver the DNA into the chromosome.

Recent innovations have refined this technology, enabling more precise gene editing than inserting a healthy gene to replace a defective one. As our understanding has increased of how enzymes shape genes and regulate their expression, we have developed techniques that leverage DNA repair mechanisms within the cell to alter a person's genome for therapeutic purposes. This approach involves removing cells from a patient, editing a chromosome, and returning the transformed cells to the patient.

In 2020 the Nobel Prize in Chemistry was awarded for the first time in history to two women, Emmanuelle Charpentier and Jennifer Doudna, who developed a method for gene editing—CRISPR-Cas9—that offers miraculous possibilities. (CRISPR is a memorable acronym for clustered regularly interspaced short palindromic repeats.) Gene-editing technology allows scientists to change an organism's DNA, so that genetic material can be added, removed, or altered at specific locations in the genome. With the CRISPR-Cas9 system, researchers create a small piece of modified RNA with a short "guide" sequence that binds to a particular target sequence of DNA. The Cas9 enzyme cuts the DNA at that targeted location. Once this cut has been made, scientists can use the cell's own DNA repair mechanisms to add or delete pieces of genetic material, or to replace an existing segment with a customized DNA sequence.

It may be unrealistic at present to expect this technology to be applicable to highly polygenic conditions like hypertension, type II diabetes, or schizophrenia, but the rare penetrant mutations of schizophrenia could clearly be candidates for CRISPR-Cas9.

Another technology that would seem ideally suited to the treatment of schizophrenia is neuromodulation. Unlike disorders that are concentrated in a single anatomic location—strokes, seizures, Parkinson's, or Alzheimer's (with its senile plaques and neurofibrillary tangles)—schizophrenia is distributed throughout the brain and linked to circuit dysfunction. Electroconvulsive therapy is known to be an effective treatment and, if not for the advent of less invasive antipsychotic drugs, would be used more often.

Neuromodulation techniques include the less invasive options of repetitive transcranial magnetic stimulation (rTMS) and transcranial direct current stimulation (tDCS). The major problem with these methods is that they are inhibited by the skull, which impedes penetration of the intracranial cavity and causes a smearing effect on any externally applied energy sources, diffusing and diminishing the impact of the neuromodulation. If this can be circumvented, then applications of electrical stimulation or magnetic impulse could target the regions and neural circuits believed to be affected.

Two of the more invasive techniques are deep brain stimulation (DBS) and focused ultrasound (FUS). DBS requires drilling through the skull and threading an electrode as noninvasively as possible to the target location(s) in the brain; the external end of the electrode is attached to a pacemaker-like device implanted in the chest wall. This neurostimulator is controlled via a mobile device that can adjust the frequency of electrical impulses transmitted through the electrodes—which can in turn either decrease or increase the activity of the target cells and circuits. DBS is currently approved for the treatment of movement disorders (Parkinson's disease, idiopathic torsion dystonia), seizure disorders, and OCD. It is being used experimentally for many other brain conditions, including depression and Alzheimer's disease. In schizophrenia, there are two potential target locations: (1) the ventral region of the corpus striatum acting on the meso-limbic dopamine circuit and (2) the CA-1 region of the hippocampus acting on glutamate neurons. Clearly, candidates for such invasive procedures would be people with severe schizophrenia and treatment-refractory symptoms.

All of these innovative technologies are amazing scientific developments, and they promise undreamed-of relief from so many painful and debilitating disorders, including schizophrenia and other mental illnesses. But we shouldn't allow them to blind us to what we have already to treat schizophrenia. To go back to the story of Dr. Carleton Gajdusek, with which I began the chapter, we may wish for and work toward stunning medical advances—but solutions can also be humbler and simpler, and they can be right on our doorstep, if only we recognize them. In terms of medication, simply increasing the use of clozapine and long-acting injectables would significantly improve the quality of care and reduce the burden of illness on patients with schizophrenia. We know already that psychosocial treatments and coordinated specialty care work. What we don't know is how profoundly all of our lives—as patients, family members, citizens—could be changed for the better were these treatments to be properly funded and staffed. How long before we do the right thing? It's long past time.

Chapter 20

SCHIZOPHRENIA AND SOCIETY: DO THE RIGHT THING

People know what they do; frequently they know why they do what they do;
but what they don't know is what what they do does.

—Michel Foucault,
Madness and Civilization: A History of Insanity in the Age of Reason

WHO IS RESPONSIBLE?

Wendell Williamson was a twenty-five-year-old law student at the University of North Carolina (UNC) in 1994, when he became delusional. He had disrupted a class, insisting he had telepathic powers. A law school dean persuaded him to go to UNC's student health service, where Williamson was seen by Myron Liptzin, then the director of psychiatric services. Liptzin learned that this wasn't the first time Williamson had experienced psychiatric problems. The young man had been involuntarily committed to a psychiatric unit two years before when campus police picked him up for screaming at students and hitting himself repeatedly in the face. Williamson had told doctors that he heard voices and was tormented by grotesque images. He also told them he owned a gun. The primary diagnosis was "rule/out schizophrenia," meaning essentially that schizophrenia is assumed until proven otherwise.

Williamson refused medication and did not want to remain at the hospital. As per state law, his case underwent a legal review, and a judge ordered that he be released, despite his delusions and hallucinations, and the fact that he kept a gun in his apartment.

In his sessions with Liptzin in 1994, Williamson talked about being "the world's first telepath," and described how other people, using only their thoughts, could inflict excruciating pain on him. But he denied any urge to harm himself or others, and so was not hospitalized. He refused treatment initially, but when a law school dean informed him that he might not be recommended as a candidate for the bar exam without it, he relented. Liptzin's diagnosis was not schizophrenia, but he did diagnose Williamson with a psychotic disorder—"delusional disorder grandiose"—and prescribed the antipsychotic Navane. Williamson began to improve. He was no longer hearing voices, and his telepathy delusion had disappeared. He attended all his classes, sat for his exams, and told Liptzin that friends had said he seemed "more like his old self."

But Williamson stopped taking his medication while at home with his family that summer. He would say later that Dr. Liptzin had given him the impression that he could do that, provided he informed someone he trusted. His mother said later, "The parents aren't in control of a grown man with a delusional mental illness. All we had to go on was what he told us." She also said that neither Liptzin nor anyone else ever told her or her husband the details of their son's problems. It's worth noting that this conundrum still exists today. While the advent of psycho-education has provided a vehicle for informing patients and their families about the nature of an illness, doctors don't always take the time, either because of a lingering reticence left over from the days when psychiatrists didn't discuss diagnoses with patients and families, or because they simply don't take the initiative. We are also constrained by privacy laws from communicating with the parents of a patient who is no longer a minor.

In the fall, Williamson returned to Chapel Hill. He kept up with his course work, passed all his classes, and performed his daily activities, though a professor of his commented later to a forensic psychiatrist involved in the case that Wendell's answer to an exam essay question was incomprehensible to the point that it was like someone "stamped a title on a sack of flour." He did not go back to the student health service or contact Liptzin. His hallucinations returned, and in January he quickly deteriorated and started living out of his car. Then he acquired a semi-automatic M-1 rifle and hundreds of rounds of ammunition. On January 26, eight months after he last saw Liptzin, Williamson killed two people in broad daylight in downtown Chapel Hill. His confession: he did it to save the world.

Williamson was charged with two counts of first-degree murder but found not guilty by reason of insanity and committed to the forensic unit at Dorothea Dix State

Mental Hospital outside of Raleigh, North Carolina. In 1997 he sued Dr. Liptzin, whom he contended had not made a correct diagnosis and had significantly understated his problems, failing to explain how seriously ill he was. Liptzin said that while Williamson did exhibit some symptoms of schizophrenia, he had decided to record a more "generous" diagnosis, so as not to deprive him of the chance to practice law; he also said his treatment for the two conditions would have been identical.

Expert witnesses called by Williamson's lawyer testified that his deterioration, if not specific acts of violence, was foreseeable, and that had he been correctly diagnosed and properly treated, his delusions could have been kept under control. They also noted that Williamson exhibited risk factors for dangerous behavior: he was a young male who lived alone and had access to a gun. The jury agreed that Liptzin had been negligent, and the trial court ordered him to pay $500,000 to Williamson.

The psychiatrist appealed the decision, however, and won. It was noted that Williamson wasn't a candidate for involuntary commitment, and that North Carolina's policy on the mentally ill promotes less restrictive methods of treatment and greater patient autonomy. Most importantly, the judges ruled that Liptzin could not have foreseen what would happen to Williamson, as his behavior had in no way indicated that he would become violent.

As Liptzin said, "How can I be responsible for something that is not predictable?"

In 1996 I joined the faculty of UNC's School of Medicine as vice chair for research and academic affairs. My responsibilities included overseeing clinical research at Dorothea Dix Hospital, where Williamson was a patient. Some time after my arrival, I was asked to evaluate him to determine if his symptoms had resolved with treatment and he could be released from the hospital. Patients found not guilty by reason of insanity were, by definition, mentally ill when they committed the crime, and presumably compelled by their symptoms. Instead of going to prison, they were remanded to a mental hospital for treatment. If their symptoms improved to the point where they were no longer a threat to society and were otherwise able to be discharged, doctors had the authority to release them—in fact, they had the moral duty to not keep them in the hospital if they neither needed nor wanted to be there.

When I interviewed Williamson, he had been receiving medication and was perfectly lucid and utterly shattered by what had happened. His memory of that horrific day was hazy, like an Ambien-fueled episode of sleepwalking. He told me that his delusional thoughts and hallucinations of what people were saying and doing had been so intense and all-encompassing that he wasn't able to distinguish the inner experience of his perceptions from the external reality of the world. In my opinion, Williamson had improved to the point where he was not psychotic, and, if he remained in treatment and on medication, he would no longer be a danger to society. Therefore, he could be discharged.

However, as of 2021, Williamson is still in a state hospital in North Carolina, despite being in symptom remission and receiving antipsychotic drug treatment, because North Carolina does not have a "conditional release" policy. This is a legal mechanism by which a patient can be discharged to live in the community under specific conditions, including the requirement that he or she adheres to psychiatric treatment as an outpatient. (If patients comply satisfactorily with the terms, they can be granted "unconditional release" status, in which they are no longer under restrictions or judicial oversight; if they don't comply, they can be forcibly returned to the hospital.) Without this mechanism in place, prosecutors and law enforcement officers often sow doubt in the minds of doctors and judges about releasing patients who have committed crimes, claiming it's too risky.

All of this could have been averted if Williamson had continued in treatment or had been required by the UNC health service to remain in treatment and take his medication. Two innocent people would almost certainly be alive today. Instead, despite the fact that he suffered from psychotic delusions and was prescribed antipsychotics to relieve them, the law placed his right as an individual to refuse, and later to stop, treatment—in other words, his right to relapse—above the rights of the public, who deserve to be protected from violence.

It is cases such as Williamson's on which I've consulted, along with the countless patients I've treated who have never engaged in violence, that have shaped my views of mental health policy over the years. In the following pages, I discuss the three interconnected facets of mental health policy—civil commitment laws and patient rights; mental illness and the criminal justice system; and mental health legislation—and set out a series of recommendations that I believe should be put in place if we want to better serve both people who suffer from mental illness and society. We need to reform civil commitment and patient rights laws to more readily enable care of severely impaired people (even over their objection); divert greater numbers of mentally ill people away from the criminal justice system and into treatment; and develop legislation that mandates and funds adequate facilities and personnel to provide state-of-the-art mental health care.

Civil Commitment and the Right to (Refuse) Treatment

The Fruits of Bad Policy

Over the centuries, as civilization progressed and our knowledge of medicine and disease increased, a consensus emerged that health care should be available to citizens to the extent that medical capacity allowed. In general, limitations on care have been determined by the level of knowledge we have about an illness, the effectiveness of treatments, and people's access to services. Whether governments should provide some or all of the health care people need is a question answered differently in different countries, but what is hardly debatable is the notion that governments should not institute policies that inhibit or undermine the care of the sick. Sadly, although it is not intentional, that's the situation we have in the United States when it comes to mental illness. In the case of people with schizophrenia, the limiting factor is not our level of knowledge—our understanding of the illness is admittedly imperfect, but it has not prevented us from developing effective treatments—but access to high-quality care and the policies governing health care financing.

In the past, when mentally ill people were viewed as pariahs and considered a nuisance to society, the policy and preferred form of treatment was confining them to prisons, almshouses, or asylums—and laws facilitated this. But when the appalling conditions in the asylums and the lack of effective treatment offered eventually gave rise to public outrage, policies changed, limiting the circumstances under which patients could be put in institutions.

If Wendell Williamson had developed schizophrenia sixty years earlier, he would have been subject to a different set of laws, which may have led to a different outcome. But changes in mental health policy afforded him the freedom to terminate treatment, permitting his symptoms to recur, which compelled him to murder two people. Sadly, Williamson's story—one of untreated mental illness that resulted in violent tragedy—is not unique. Untreated, symptomatic schizophrenia patients are at increased risk of violence or harm to themselves or others. Mental health advocates point out valiantly that mentally ill people are no more dangerous than the general population. While it is true that less than 4 percent of all violent crime in the United States is committed by the mentally ill, this figure includes both people who are being treated and those who aren't. If we consider only mass violence incidents (usually defined as involving four or more victims), between 20 percent and 30 percent are perpetrated by people with mental illness. Almost every mentally ill perpetrator of mass violence has been symptomatic and untreated for lengthy periods prior to his crime, either because he (or his family) did not seek treatment or because the ill person refused it. Even in cases where family members or doctors invoked civil commitment procedures, patients could be released within seventy-two hours—without a requirement in place that they continue treatment—if mental health lawyers convinced a judge they weren't dangerous.

But violence is only one problem that arises from untreated mental illness. Our prisons, homeless shelters, and streets are filled with the untreated mentally ill, and function as our de facto mental institutions. The mentally ill make up an estimated 25 percent of our country's homeless population, and one in five people in US prisons (approximately 383,000 people) suffers from a serious mental illness. Today it is exceedingly rare to find a patient who has been in a mental institution for more than a year, but mentally ill people are routinely imprisoned for years or decades. Many are nonviolent offenders convicted either of drug possession or survival crimes such as panhandling, petty theft, and trespassing for shelter.

And then there is the cost. The annual cost of schizophrenia in the United States in 2020 was $281.6 billion—$62 billion in direct costs, incurred chiefly through health care, housing, homelessness, and incarceration; and the rest in indirect costs, many of which are related to caregiver unpaid wages, and nonemployment or reduced wages for the mentally ill. It is estimated that for each person diagnosed with schizophrenia at age twenty-five, the annual cost is $92,000. Finally, there is the hidden human misery and lost potential that no statistic can capture.

How did we arrive at a point where we are treating people so poorly and at such great expense? How can we do better for those who are suffering and for those whose judgment is so impaired by their illness that they refuse the treatment that can help them? To understand why our system is failing us, we should first recall how we got here.

THE END OF *PARENS PATRIAE*

From the time the first hospitals were built in the United States until the 1960s, our rationale and criteria for civil commitment were based on the need for treatment.

If a physician believed it necessary to confine someone to a mental institution against his or her will, the doctor needed merely to declare the person mentally ill and in need of treatment. All mental patients were presumed incapable of making decisions. Under the principle of *parens patriae* (Latin for "parent of the country"), the state had a moral obligation, and a legal right, to act as guardian for those unable to care for themselves. It also allowed family members and physicians to seek treatment on behalf of people who they believed were ill, even over a person's objection. There was little distinction between voluntary and involuntary admissions to psychiatric facilities.

Between the opening of the first private mental asylum in 1817 and the mid-twentieth century, commitment to an asylum consisted, at best, of custodial care, and at worst of chains, beatings, and relentless degradation. The *parens patriae* doctrine, while philosophically well intended, undeniably allowed for possible abuse.

The potential for abuse wasn't limited to the way people were treated in mental institutions. The vagueness of the "need for treatment" criterion allowed unscrupulous family members and doctors to railroad people into mental hospitals for nefarious reasons. The practice was common enough that it even became a plot device. In the film *Suddenly Last Summer*, based on a Tennessee Williams play, Katharine Hepburn plays a wealthy dowager who has institutionalized her niece (Elizabeth Taylor) and encourages the newly arrived neurosurgeon (Montgomery Clift) to perform a lobotomy. The popular term "gaslighting," derived from the 1944 film *Gaslight*, is also based on this premise. Ingrid Bergman won the Academy Award for her role as the wife of a fortune-hunting gigolo (Charles Boyer), who schemes to convince her she is going insane so he can have her institutionalized.

Compounding the potential for abuse was the fact that captive populations such as mental patients had few civil protections and were therefore convenient subjects for medical experiments. Tens of thousands would be sterilized under horrific eugenics policies during the twentieth century (peaking in the 1930s and 1940s but continuing for decades after), with explicit approval from the US Supreme Court.

As we entered the 1900s, the demand for more institutions to house the mentally ill grew, and the proportion of public to private care increased dramatically— to where public institutions were often the largest item in state budgets. Facing constant pressure to reduce spending, these institutions found themselves perpetually underfunded, which exacerbated the appalling living conditions. But patients continued to pour into the asylums (peaking in the United States in 1955 at 559,000) for one simple reason: there were no effective treatments for severe mental illness and thus no alternatives to institutionalization.

Then, in the 1950s a number of forces began to converge that would bring about major changes in our country's thinking about the treatment and confinement of the mentally ill: condemnation of the inhumane conditions of state mental hospitals; a suspicion of the psychiatric establishment; the availability of new antipsychotic medications; and a community treatment ethos that had emerged from World War II, where US Army Medical Corps psychiatrists treated soldiers right behind front lines instead of sending them to hospitals far removed from their combat units or shipping them home.

These forces together gave rise to the deinstitutionalization movement discussed in chapter 9, in which severely mentally ill people were released en masse from hospitals with the assumption that community-based programs would care for them. Deinstitutionalization turned out to be a disaster for many people who needed hospital care or who could have flourished in the community with adequate support, and a slow-rolling fiasco for state budgets. The cost of running state mental hospitals was merely redistributed to other agencies and institutions for managing the displaced patients: Medicaid, homeless shelters, disability payments, emergency services, nursing homes, and prisons.

Along with the push for deinstitutionalization was a growing focus on individual rights, including the civil rights of the mentally ill, which would lead to a reorientation of constitutional law in the 1970s. In addition to concerns about the quality of care in state mental institutions, the courts saw the commitment laws as too vague or broad, and open to either inadvertent misuse or exploitation, as in cases where people had family members committed in order to take control of their wealth. A series of key decisions in the Supreme Court and lower courts ushered in a new generation of much narrower commitment laws, and by the end of the 1970s, every state had changed from a need-for-treatment standard to one based on dangerousness. It was a seismic shift, one whose repercussions we're still wrestling with today. At the heart of our current dilemma sits the individual's right to refuse treatment, a right predicated on deep-rooted cultural respect for personal autonomy and free will. These are noble and necessary values. But in the case of a psychotic illness, the question necessarily arises: What if someone's will is not truly free?

THE RIGHT TO TREATMENT—OR TO REFUSE IT

In 1960 the physician-attorney Morton Birnbaum published a journal article titled "The Right to Treatment," which advanced the then-revolutionary argument that every mental patient had a legal right to treatment that would offer "a realistic opportunity to be cured or improve his mental condition." Failing the delivery of such treatment, Birnbaum argued, the patient should be able to "obtain his release at will in spite of the existence or severity of his mental illness." Birnbaum wanted to reform the asylums, not empty them, and he felt the potential for untreated mentally ill people being released into the community would compel hospitals to provide proper treatment and thus serve as an enforcement mechanism.

Birnbaum's thesis was taken up by an Alabama attorney named George Dean, who was representing the plaintiffs in *Wyatt v. Stickney*, a case in which it was being argued that psychiatric patients' treatment had suffered as a result of lay-offs at a hospital in Tuscaloosa. Birnbaum became cocounsel. But another lawyer with a very different agenda also joined the team. Bruce Ennis, who would later become national legal director of the American Civil Liberties Union (ACLU), was much younger than Birnbaum, part of a new generation of mental health advocates who supported abolishing or severely limiting involuntary commitment of mental patients.

Ennis had been working on a three-year investigation for the ACLU on legal issues affecting mental patients in state hospitals. When he began, he expected to uncover abuses within the system. But what he discovered was far worse than he'd ever imagined. He concluded that the system itself was irreparable, and drastic action was needed. He began to argue that involuntary hospitalization was an unjustifiable form of coercion aimed at ridding the community of troublesome and unproductive eccentrics.

"I think if it were put to a popular referendum," he said, "the people in this country would favor massive custodial warehouses where people are swept off the streets and kept for the rest of their lives and drugged, tranquilized, shocked, whatever is necessary to keep them off the streets. . . . [T]he only thing that makes sense is to talk about a 'right to refuse treatment.' In other words, I don't really believe in the 'right to treatment' concept."

Ennis knew that successfully arguing the case on the basis of a right to treatment would help to legitimize involuntary confinement. But he saw in that argument potential for *Wyatt v. Stickney* to open a back door to deinstitutionalization:

if hospitals were unable to provide treatment at court-determined standards, they would have no choice but to discharge many of their patients. Winning the right to treatment, Ennis reasoned, might therefore offer "the best method for deinstitutionalizing thousands of persons."

Ennis was right. In 1972 the judge in *Wyatt* ruled that failing to provide adequate treatment to those confined violated due process and mandated the state of Alabama to implement specific changes related to staffing ratios and various other criteria. The state failed to achieve these benchmarks, both because of budget and because of the difficulty of attracting professionals to Alabama. The population of state psychiatric hospitals in Alabama was reduced by almost two-thirds between 1970 and 1975. The right-to-refuse lobby had won out over those who advocated for a right to treatment. Similar litigation followed around the country, and rather than face costly court-ordered overhauls or attempt to meet sometimes impossible standards, states emptied their hospitals—more often than not into communities unprepared to receive them.

A CURTAILMENT OF LIBERTY

At the same time that *Wyatt v. Stickney* was unfolding, another pivotal case, taking place in Wisconsin, further transformed mental health law by drastically limiting the state's power to commit patients on *parens patriae* grounds. In the 1972 *Lessard v. Schmidt* ruling, a federal district court in Milwaukee struck down the state's broad commitment law as unconstitutional, stating that involuntary commitment was permissible only when "there is an extreme likelihood that if the person is not confined, he will do immediate harm to himself or others."

In the years after the *Lessard* decision, state after state followed Wisconsin in sharply constricting, or all but abandoning, the traditional *parens patriae* principle. But *Lessard* unfortunately shared certain anti-psychiatric assumptions prevalent at the time—namely, that psychiatry had no effective treatments and that commitment seriously damaged an individual, so that, in most cases, people were better off foregoing treatment altogether than being hospitalized for it. The judges in *Lessard* stressed the "massive curtailment of liberty" that commitment represented, failing to recognize that a disease process had already curtailed that liberty and that treatment might be needed to restore a meaningful level of autonomy.

Lessard required, for the first time, that commitment proceedings provide the mentally ill with the protections accorded a criminal suspect: among them a right to counsel, a right to remain silent, exclusion of hearsay evidence, and a standard of proof beyond a reasonable doubt. Involuntary civil commitment ceased to be viewed as a primarily medical decision (authorized by a court) and came to be seen as a quasi-criminal proceeding, with power shifted from medical professionals to judges and magistrates. It was a dramatic repudiation of the notion that a society had a responsibility to care for those citizens who could not care for themselves as well as a vote of no confidence in psychiatry's ability to effectively treat and care for the mentally ill.

The Duty to Protect

As civil commitment laws were narrowing to a criterion of dangerousness, clinicians saw their own responsibilities expanded. In the summer of 1969, a University of California at Berkeley graduate student, Prosenjit Poddar, began receiving treatment from a psychologist named Lawrence Moore. During his seventh and final session, Poddar confessed that he planned to kill fellow student Tatiana Tarasoff. Poddar was obsessed with Tarasoff and enraged that she had rejected his advances. Moore diagnosed Poddar with an acute and severe "paranoid schizophrenic reaction." He and two physicians determined that Poddar should be committed to a psychiatric hospital for observation and they contacted the police. The police detained Poddar but released him when he promised to stay away from Tarasoff. Although Moore and the other doctors who examined Poddar had informed the police, they never notified the young woman or her family about Poddar's threats. On October 27 Poddar went to Tarasoff's home, shot her with a pellet gun, then chased her into the street with a kitchen knife and stabbed her seventeen times, killing her.

Poddar was found guilty of second-degree murder and served five years before his lawyer successfully appealed, and Poddar was released and deported to India. Tarasoff's parents sued the clinicians and the police who were involved in the case, and the suit resulted in what is known as the Tarasoff rule, which states that when therapists determine that a patient presents a serious danger of violence to another, they incur an "obligation to use reasonable care to protect the intended victim against such danger." The challenge then for therapists and psychiatrists became identifying the point at which "dangerousness" outweighed confidentiality.

The Hazards of Freedom

The dangerousness criterion for commitment was legally formalized in a US Supreme Court case concerning Kenneth Donaldson, a Philadelphia man in his midthirties. In 1956 Donaldson was visiting his parents in Florida and mentioned that a neighbor in Philadelphia might be poisoning his food. His father thought he was experiencing paranoid delusions and initiated an involuntary commitment. (Donaldson had been hospitalized previously, voluntarily checking himself into a psychiatric facility in Pennsylvania in 1943, where he received electroconvulsive therapy. In the years since, his behavior may have been erratic—he changed his name, then changed it back; he moved repeatedly; he showed signs of paranoia— but he held down a job, supported his family, and was never violent.) After hearings before a county judge in Florida, Donaldson was diagnosed with paranoid schizophrenia and confined to the state hospital. For the next fifteen years, he remained there, while repeatedly demanding his release on the basis that he was dangerous to no one, was not mentally ill, and that the hospital was, in any case, not providing treatment for his supposed illness. (During those years, Donaldson said he was seen for no more than a total of three hours by a psychiatrist.) Finally, in 1971 Donaldson brought a lawsuit in Florida's district court claiming that the hospital superintendent had intentionally and maliciously deprived him of his constitutional right to liberty.

Court testimony demonstrated that Donaldson had posed no danger to others during his confinement or, indeed, at any point in his life. Nor was there evidence that he had ever been suicidal or likely to engage in self-harm. His frequent requests for release had been supported by reliable people who were willing to assume responsibility for him, but the requests were all refused; the superintendent believed Donaldson would be unable to make a "successful adjustment outside the institution." For long periods, he was simply kept in a large room with sixty other patients, many of whom were under criminal commitment.

The jury found in Donaldson's favor, and the case of *O'Connor v. Donaldson* subsequently made its way to the Supreme Court, where Donaldson's chief lawyer was Bruce Ennis of the ACLU, who had worked on *Wyatt v. Stickney*. In 1975 the court ruled unanimously that mental illness alone "cannot justify a State's locking a person up against his will and keeping him indefinitely in simple custodial confinement," and that there was no constitutional basis for confining the mentally ill involuntarily "if they are dangerous to no one and can live safely in freedom."

In shifting the criteria for commitment from need-for-treatment to dangerousness, the system was now asking psychiatrists to do something they weren't necessarily good at (not many people are): predict dangerousness. And it was making it more difficult for them to do what they *are* trained to do, which is determine whether someone has a severe mental illness that is in need of a level of treatment that can be provided only in a hospital.

Following *Donaldson*, if you were not a danger to yourself or others, you had the right to refuse treatment. The ruling didn't define dangerousness in any detail or specify how such dangerousness (or imminent dangerousness) was to be established. It did state, in a footnote, that the concept of danger to self included "helpless to avoid the hazards of freedom."

For the seriously mentally ill, the hazards of freedom are often significant. Many mental health experts have argued since the *Donaldson* case that in trying to protect people from needless and merely custodial care, we have allowed the pendulum to swing too far in the other direction: that a respect for rights has sadly become an excuse for neglect. Paul Stavis, former counsel to the New York Commission on Quality of Care for the Mentally Disabled, remarked that by living "safely in freedom," the court did not have in mind rummaging in garbage cans for food or lying in the street in one's own waste. It's the sort of situation that prompted Dr. Darold Treffert, a Wisconsin psychiatrist, to remark ruefully that people who were seriously psychiatrically disabled too often "died with their rights on."

Why People Refuse Treatment

People do have the legal right to refuse treatment for other illnesses, as well as to engage in manifestly unhealthy behaviors. Christian Scientists may decline medical treatments on religious grounds. People may choose naturopathic remedies over recommended medical procedures or prescribed drugs. Others smoke, drink, and eat to excess, leading to lung cancer, cirrhosis of the liver, heart disease, diabetes, and other illnesses. But there are two differences between these examples and cases of serious mental illness: the health and safety of the wider public, and the matter of insight. As to the first, the state is entitled to write statutes for the benefit of society at large, even when this may restrict the liberties of certain individuals. This principle is clear in the case of dangerous criminals or drunk drivers, but it also operates in medicine. In many states, schools and colleges require students to have vaccinations (and the US requires numerous vaccinations for immigrants) because unvaccinated individuals can present a risk to public health. Some states require people to share their HIV status with sex or injection partners. And we can think of the Covid-19 pandemic and the various statutes such as mask mandates and travel restrictions that prioritized public safety over individual rights.

The second thing to consider with regard to serious mental illness is whether someone has insight into his or her predicament. To refuse treatment when one is of sound mind (or at least able to distinguish between reality and delusion) is one thing; to refuse treatment when one is fully convinced that an alien abduction is underway or that the CIA is sending messages through the television is quite another. This lack of insight into one's illness—not being aware or believing that one is sick, or understanding the benefits of treatment—occurs commonly in schizophrenia, and we need to take it into account when legislating for civil commitment.

There is another brain disease that we treat routinely without the full understanding or sometimes even the consent of those afflicted. People with Alzheimer's disease very often "wander," which can be dangerous to them; they occasionally become agitated and even violent. We don't want our loved ones walking barefoot around the neighborhood in the middle of the night or sleeping on city streets. (Many people with Alzheimer's make advance directives early in their illness to plan for the time when they become medically incompetent.) When their capacity deteriorates to the point where they may not always understand why they're taking medication, we don't stop medicating them. And when they are in facilities for people with Alzheimer's and they say repeatedly that they want to go home, if no one at home is able to care for them, or they wouldn't be safe there, we don't just release them.

In the case of people with Alzheimer's, we're thinking almost entirely of the safety of the person who is ill, because even if people with Alzheimer's become violent, they are incapable of committing mass violence. With regard to schizophrenia or other psychoses, we need to think not only of patient safety and wellbeing but also of public safety. Therefore, it seems that the case for appropriate civil commitment and medication over objection would be stronger, not weaker, for schizophrenia, especially when we take into account that while both diseases are progressive, the deterioration associated with untreated schizophrenia can be ameliorated by effective treatment, enabling people to return to the community and live productive and meaningful lives—a prospect that currently does not exist for anyone suffering from Alzheimer's.

No analogy is airtight, but it is worth thinking about why we view these situations so differently. Is it because we still don't really believe that schizophrenia is a brain disease in the way that we have fully accepted that fact about Alzheimer's? Is it because of the stigma we still attach to schizophrenia? Is it because Alzheimer's strikes primarily older adults, and we view their freedoms as somehow less important than we do the freedoms of young people? Or, conversely, are we *more* caring of vulnerable older adults than we are of the young? What would we think of ourselves as a society if our streets and prisons were filled with old people suffering the terrors and indignities of untreated dementia? It may be that we see it as a question of effective treatments, which is ironic, as there are no truly effective treatments for Alzheimer's disease, but there are for schizophrenia.

REVISING COMMITMENT STANDARDS

The changes in inpatient commitment standards effected in the 1970s are essentially still with us, though commitment law now has additional components. These newer criteria are welcome, especially those that recognize the cumulative long-term effects of leaving someone untreated.

1. The bedrock requirement for commitment remains a serious mental illness (for example, substantial disorder of thought or mood that grossly impairs judgment and behavior, and usually excluding substance use disorders, intellectual disabilities, and dementia) that is in need of treatment.

2. The dangerousness standard remains in nearly every state but in most states is no longer an exclusive criterion. All but a few states have explicitly adopted a standard of "grave disability," defined generally as the inability of someone with untreated serious mental illness to provide for his or her basic needs.

3. The criterion of "serious deterioration" appears in some form in about half of US states—either as a distinct standard or as part of the definition of "grave disability." It refers to protecting someone from the brain damage that results when a serious mental illness goes untreated for extended periods.

It must be shown that someone is (a) at risk for suffering such deterioration if untreated and (b) that they are unable to recognize that need themselves, and so are unlikely to seek treatment voluntarily.

4. Most states require that commitment aligns with the principle of providing care in the least restrictive setting.

Civil commitment laws are just one aspect of caring for the mentally ill, but they are a critical piece of the puzzle, and right now they aren't serving either those who are ill or their families and communities. When thinking about legislating for commitment and medication over objection, we need to bear past abuses in mind; but those abuses should be lessons learned rather than reasons to stay mired in a situation that often does more harm than good. We need to employ alternatives to the old methods, emphasizing supportive engagement, mutual respect, and shared decision-making for people with mental illness who lack competence or pose risks.

I've had numerous discussions on this subject with Elyn Saks, who herself experienced involuntary commitment, including forcible restraint and injection, and was motivated to pursue mental health law. For years, Elyn vigorously opposed forced treatment. In her memoir *The Center Cannot Hold*, she describes being bound hand and foot in painful restraints, with a net pulled tight over her from her neck to her ankles, which made her feel as though she couldn't breathe. She also recalls being told by one doctor how restraints helped patients "feel safe, more in control." Had anyone asked her how she felt being in restraints, those were definitely not the words she would have used.

I come to the situation as a clinician. For forty years, I have witnessed the ravages of untreated psychosis and the damage that our overly restrictive commitment and treatment laws can result in. Though Elyn and I approach the dilemma from different perspectives and have had many animated but cordial discussions over the years, we agree there must be a better way of helping people in crisis, supporting their loved ones, and protecting the public. The combination of a less heavy-handed form of civil commitment and a more proactive approach to treatment—through, for instance, psychiatric advance directives (PADs) as early in the course of illness as possible—can help to ensure appropriate care without imposing it forcibly.

PADs are a mechanism that allow people, when in their right mind, to contemplate situations in which they may become incompetent or psychotic and to enter into an agreement about what treatment they will receive should they become ill. They are legal contracts akin to living wills, and they preclude the possibility that, in the event of relapse, someone's symptoms might cause them to refuse treatment. Though relatively new, PADs are allowed in most of the states, half of which have adopted statutes related specifically to them. At Columbia, we're working to develop the legal mechanism that will allow us to help patients draw up PADs.

When I think about PADs, I recall a particularly powerful scene in Susannah Cahalan's memoir *Brain on Fire*, where she recounts the experience of watching a hospital video of herself taken while she was in the throes of psychosis:

> I have never seen myself so unhinged and unguarded before, and it frightens me. The raw panic makes me uncomfortable, but the thing that truly unsettles me is the realization that emotions I once felt so profoundly, so viscerally, have now completely vanished. That petrified person is as foreign to me as a stranger, and it's impossible for me to imagine what it must have been like to be her. Without this electronic evidence, I could never have imagined myself capable of such madness and misery.

When people are in active psychosis or otherwise seriously mentally ill, they don't have the necessary distance from or understanding of their situation to make decisions in their own best interests. The idea of PADs is to engage the countless people who now fall through the cracks; those who *would* want treatment if they were making the choice in the full of their health. Once someone agrees to future treatment, it becomes possible to admit her at a point in her illness that she chooses rather than waiting until she's a danger to herself or to others—a day that might never come or that might come too suddenly for anyone to intervene before the violent event occurs.

PADs are one very specific remedy, but we need broader and more overarching reform: a reexamination of the whole right-to-refuse policy in order to protect both those who are ill and the communities in which they live. In the absence of a PAD, we need to be able to commit people early, if needed, in their illness so that we can provide compassionate care at a less restrictive level and can proactively prevent the cascade of negative consequences that results from untreated mental illness. Civil commitment criteria should be amended to permit treatment to be provided without consent to a mentally ill person if:

1. it can be reasonably held by an independent authority that the person lacks the capacity to consent to the proposed treatment;

2. it can be reasonably held by an independent authority that the person will gain substantial benefit from the proposed treatment or, alternatively, that a proxy decision-maker believes that the person would have consented to the treatment had he or she the capacity to do so; and

3. the treatment is provided in the least restrictive environment practicable.

Where my views differ from existing statutes lies more in the implementation of the law than in the substance, and in the return to a greater emphasis on the principle of *parens patriae*. Dangerousness and deterioration are determined subjectively, and the tendency of most health care providers and judicial officials is to err on the side of a very narrow interpretation of these terms, thus limiting who is treated. We can think of the analogy of head trauma. Someone who has sustained an injury but is exhibiting no apparent consequences requiring treatment would still be admitted for observation and tests—and to protect him from any additional possible harm. But in the case of mental illness, the person in need of treatment may not even be admitted in the first place.

Involuntary civil commitment and "medication over objection" are two separate issues, and meeting the criteria for the former doesn't automatically establish the correctness of the latter. If a doctor is going to medicate someone over objection in a nonemergency situation and in the absence of a PAD or surrogate decision-maker, a number of things should be established: that appropriate efforts have been made to engage the person voluntarily; that such efforts have failed and are unlikely to succeed in the near future; and that there is clear and convincing evidence (say, a medical diagnosis, or proven drug efficacy) that the medication is appropriate for the condition. It should also be shown that the person lacks the capacity to make the medication decision, and that the medication is likely to prevent him or her from deteriorating to the point where emergency intervention would be needed. (Emergency medication over objection is widely available; the idea is to enable medication *before* someone is in an emergency situation.) Ideally, the issues of commitment and medication should be addressed by a single legal process involving a trained mediator or mental health–friendly judicial mechanism, one that is not so cumbersome that it discourages use.

Care models and legal mechanisms other than civil commitment exist that facilitate treatment and encourage adherence, including the use of long-acting injectable medications and outpatient commitment or Assisted Outpatient Treatment. LAIs and AOT have been shown to improve treatment engagement and to reduce relapse, hospitalization, and violent behavior. However, as discussed in chapter 19, they are both underutilized for a number of reasons, including the stigma attached to LAIs, and practical and financial challenges related to fully implementing AOT.

The Equitas Foundation Legislation Committee, in which I participated along with a group of lawyers, judges, and mental health providers, all experts in their field, has developed model legislation with new recommendations governing the process of civil commitment and treatment over objection and new pathways from the criminal justice system to the civil justice system. The Report and Recommendations have been endorsed by the Conference of Chief Justices (CCJ) and the Conference of State Court Administrators (COSCA) National Judicial Task Force to Examine State Courts' Response to Mental Illness and will be submitted to various federal and state governments for their consideration and possible adoption in 2023 and 2024.

Mental Illness and Criminal Justice

How Did Mental Illness Become a Crime?

I have worked with many patients over the years who have had run-ins with the police or been arrested or jailed. People with mental health issues are sixteen times more likely to be killed by police than those without mental illness. (Other groups are also, of course, at increased risk of being killed by police, including people of color.) The less bad outcome sees those desperately needing hospitalization and mental health care arrested and entering the maw of the criminal justice system, sometimes becoming stuck there.

The police were never meant to be first responders to people in mental health emergencies. But they ended up in that role through a kind of mission creep, called out to deal with volatile situations involving people with psychosis and other psychiatric disturbances because too many of the mentally ill are inadequately treated or completely untreated, and we have too few mobile Crisis Intervention Teams. If we expect police to respond to these crises—and they may be needed when someone is armed or dangerous—they should be carefully trained and/or accompanied by a mental health expert. Responding to someone in the midst of a psychotic break is very different from apprehending a person who is perfectly sane and committing a crime, and it shouldn't surprise us that when we send armed law enforcement into a volatile situation involving someone in the throes of psychosis, tragedy may result.

Over the last several decades, through ill-conceived policies, underfunding of services, and inadequate community-based resources, we have taken a public health problem—mental illness—and handed it over to the criminal justice system. In the 1980s about 5 percent of inmates in jails and prisons were mentally ill. Now it is estimated that 20 percent to 25 percent of the more than two million people incarcerated in the US each year are mentally ill. As mentioned previously, the largest mental health care facilities in the country are Chicago's Cook County Jail and Los Angeles County Jail, with Rikers Island not far behind. The vast majority of mentally ill inmates aren't violent criminals, and about three-quarters have drug and alcohol problems. Most have not yet gone to trial or are serving short sentences.

Once someone with a mental illness becomes involved with the criminal justice system, the consequences depend on various factors: a family's capacity to navigate the system, race (racial and ethnic minority youth with behavioral health issues are referred more readily to the juvenile justice system than to specialty primary care, compared with white youth), whether the county has good services in place to divert the mentally ill away from incarceration and into treatment, and so on. What we know is that mentally ill inmates suffer worse outcomes once incarcerated than inmates without mental illness. Many don't receive the treatment they need, and the environment of incarceration adds to their deterioration. (An estimated 83 percent of jail inmates with a mental illness do not have access to treatment.) They tend to remain incarcerated for four to eight times longer for the same offenses, and are more likely to have difficulties with prison staff and other people in prison. They are also more likely to be victimized while incarcerated. Once released, they often have no access to health care or assistance finding it, and commonly wind up once again homeless or in emergency rooms or rearrested, a common cycle of unrelieved suffering and wasted resources.

The long-standing explanation for the high incarceration rate of the mentally ill has been that the dramatic drop in psychiatric beds following deinstitutionalization, coupled with the failure of community mental health centers to provide appropriate services, has resulted in our jails becoming de facto mental institutions. While it is true that rising inmate numbers paralleled the emptying out of psychiatric hospitals, the picture is more nuanced. The rise in incarceration rates among the mentally ill has been part of a general increase in incarceration linked to "tough on crime" policies such as the war on drugs and "three strikes" laws. The mentally ill were swept up in this. Recent data suggest that only a small proportion of criminal behavior by people with mental illness is driven directly by the symptoms of their disorder; the rest appears to be motivated by structural risk factors related to mental illness, such as homelessness, poverty, unemployment, and substance use—in other words, the same factors that are related to criminality in people without mental illness. So, we should be careful about overemphasizing mental illness as a causal factor in the criminalization of the mentally ill and think instead in terms of the complex relationship between (untreated) mental illness, social, racial, and economic factors, and systemic shortcomings. It's also impossible to discuss the criminal justice system and rising incarceration rates without also noting the major role systemic racism plays in these tragedies. The connection between, for instance, the war on drugs, racial targeting, and the incarceration of black people has been more fully discussed elsewhere, but it also has a part in the incarceration of mentally ill people—and, in particular, which mentally ill people are more likely to end up in prison.

Paul Appelbaum, who has written extensively on psychiatry and the law, likens the situation to the one in which water flows down channels of least resistance: if a police officer picks up a mentally ill person who is causing a public disturbance and takes him or her to the ER, the officer will have to wait until the person is seen, sometimes for hours. If the officer takes him or her to jail, however, they can quickly book the person and get on with other duties. We have created a system in which it's often easier to incarcerate the mentally ill than to treat them.

DIVERSION: TREATMENT OVER INCARCERATION

It's a tragic irony that the deinstitutionalization activists and patient advocates of the 1970s helped bring about the very thing they were trying to eliminate: the long-term incarceration of the mentally ill on a vast scale. If we're to prevent nonviolent mentally ill people from becoming needlessly enmeshed in the criminal justice system and enable them to live safely in the community, the first thing we need is a full continuum of integrated community mental health services that make effective, recovery-oriented treatments accessible and affordable. We must also address larger social factors that drive criminality in general, such as poverty.

Diversion programs, a key development over the past two decades, bring together mental health systems, law enforcement, and courts to coordinate on behalf of people who need treatment more than they need punishment. These programs are divided broadly into pre- and post-arrest, and, ideally, diversion occurs before someone enters the criminal justice system, by identifying people at risk of psychiatric disorders and providing them with mental health services rather than arresting them. Given what we know about how people with mental illnesses tend to deteriorate once in the criminal justice system, pre-arrest or prebooking strategies should be provided to anyone for whom a voluntary mental health treatment plan is a reasonable alternative to criminal prosecution.

Pre-arrest diversion strategies focus on the police officers who are likely to be the first point of contact. They aim to educate police about mental illness—recognizing the signs and learning how to deescalate crises. Crisis Intervention Teams (CITs) are formal partnerships among police departments and mental health providers that ensure that responders are educated about mental health crisis situations. The CIT model was developed in Memphis, where the police department established the first CIT in 1988. There are now 2,954 CITs active in forty-six states. CITs reduce arrest rates and the number of injuries to responding officers and increase the use of diversion programs. More broadly, diversion programs that are well designed and implemented reduce arrests, recidivism, and time spent in jail for mentally ill people accused of misdemeanor crimes, and they decrease criminal justice costs.

Filing criminal charges against people with mental illnesses should be the last resort after other reasonable efforts at diversion have been exhausted. This is where mental health courts come in, a form of postbooking diversion. Mental health courts are similar to other specialized court systems (drug courts, for instance) and align with current moves to reduce incarceration across the board for minor offenses. The first mental health court was established in 1997, and more than three hundred now operate in the United States. Mental health courts convene attorneys and mental health providers or advocates to reroute mentally ill defendants out of the system and into treatment. The decision as to who is admitted to a mental health court is made according to certain medical and legal criteria (such as the nature of someone's illness and the nature of the offense), and involves representatives from various parties, including judges, prosecutors, defense attorneys, clinicians, victims, clients, and so on.

One of the pioneers of the effort to align the criminal justice and judicial systems with the mentally ill more effectively is Judge Steven Leifman. When Leifman was elected to the bench in Florida, he had no idea that he was also becoming the gatekeeper to the largest psychiatric facility in the state: the Miami-Dade County Jail. Miami-Dade has the largest percentage of people with serious mental illnesses of any urban community in the United States: a rate two to three times that of the national average. Only about 1 percent of these people receive treatment in the community mental health system, leaving the justice system to deal with the rest.

The issue goes way back for Leifman. In 1973, he was seventeen and working as an intern for a Miami legislator when he was sent to check on the son of a constituent being held at the state hospital. He found the bloated young man tied to a bed, while hospital staff injected him with the antipsychotic Thorazine. (As it turned out, the man was autistic, not psychotic.) An advocate then led Leifman on a tour of the hospital, down a dark hallway to a metal cage, where a guard was hosing feces off several naked men.

"Those are the men I see in my courtroom now," Leifman has said.

In 2000, by which time Leifman was a judge with the Criminal Division of Florida's Eleventh Circuit, he created one of the most admired diversion programs in the country: the Criminal Mental Health Project. CMHP has a prebooking component of crisis intervention to minimize arrests. From 2010 to 2017, there were only 149 arrests out of about 83,000 mental health–related calls to Miami and Miami-Dade police departments, a lower rate than that of arrests for all calls during that period. People charged with low-level offenses can choose between treatment and jail. About 80 percent choose treatment—not surprising, perhaps, but what *is* surprising is how many people stay out of the system afterward. Early analysis showed that the recidivism rate one year later among participants who had completed the program was only 20 percent; in comparison, 72 percent of people who didn't enter the program were back in jail within a year of their release.

Leifman's current project is the ambitious Miami Center for Mental Health and Recovery, a 208-bed facility scheduled to open in 2023 that will be the first of its kind in the country. The center will target those with serious mental illness who have long histories of chronic homelessness and hospitalizations and who have had repeated involvement with the justice system or are at risk of becoming involved. It will offer transitional housing, addiction treatment, primary care, vocational training, reentry support, and space for the courts and social service agencies. Leifman's vision is a facility that can offer comprehensive services in one place, thereby eliminating many of the difficulties of navigating traditional community mental health and social services, gently reintegrate people once they're stable, and break the pattern in which the acutely ill keep cycling through the justice system.

PARITY IN MENTAL HEALTH COVERAGE

THE BIRTH OF A QUAGMIRE

In the spring of 2019 I came across an article about a woman named Jill Williams, a special education teacher in Granite Bay, California. The previous year, Jill had taken her twenty-five-year-old son, Austin, to the emergency room at Sutter Roseville Medical Center. Austin suffers from schizophrenia, and he'd become agitated and verbally unresponsive. Late that night, Jill left the hospital to get some sleep and asked that someone let her know before her son was released. A few hours later, a nurse called her to say that Austin was being discharged.

Jill returned to the hospital immediately. She recalled that when she arrived, her son was standing outside wearing no shoes—despite it being a cold winter morning—and was surrounded by security guards. He suddenly took off at a sprint and threw himself off the third floor of a parking structure. Austin landed on the ground in front of the entrance to the ER. Jill saw a doctor rush to attend to him. A triage unit quickly loaded him onto a gurney, and Austin was rushed back inside the hospital and admitted for treatment. He survived.

It is hard to imagine a more overt display of the contrast between how our systems respond to mental and physical crises. Jill was shocked. "It was just profound—and so sad."

The article also contained an interview with Seong Brown, whose daughter, Elizabeth, had taken her own life. The teenager had been in and out of psychiatric care, and Seong felt the medical system had failed her daughter "at every turn." She referred to an email sent to her husband from a colleague, which detailed the comprehensive treatment his wife was receiving from the health maintenance organization Kaiser Permanente for her cancer: a team of oncologists, nurses, social workers, grief counselors, and other outside specialists. The Browns, by contrast, had to battle (often unsuccessfully) for access to more intensive services for Elizabeth and had incurred tens of thousands of dollars in out-of-pocket expenses.

The stories of these two families epitomize so many things about our systemic failures: the disparity in the way we treat mental and physical illnesses; the barriers we've allowed insurance companies to erect to coverage for mental illness; how people slip through the cracks of our commitment laws and wind up worse off; the helplessness parents feel, especially when their children are older than eighteen.

How did we land ourselves in such a quagmire? Whose responsibility is it to provide mental health care, and who is responsible for figuring out how to obtain it? One of the signs of a humane society is equal access to health care for everyone, regardless of gender, race, ethnicity, or ability to pay. Most people in the United States now profess to believe that health care is a basic human right, but the debate over how it should be financed continues to rage.

Striving for Parity

The historic stigma toward mental illness and reluctance of people to self-disclose their illness, along with the fact that the mentally ill do not coalesce easily into powerful lobbies or voting blocs, have enabled private insurance companies to get away with offering meager and inequitable benefits for mental health care.

Until World War II, mental health care was a responsibility of the states. When employer-sponsored health insurance became available in the postwar period, policies tended to either exclude mental health coverage or offer extremely limited benefits—an omission that was the forerunner to the carveouts that would emerge in the 1990s with the advent of managed care mechanisms used by private insurers to contain costs.

With the advent of Medicare and Medicaid in 1965, limits were set on facilities in which mental health care was provided. The IMD (institutions for mental diseases) exclusion prohibited the use of federal Medicaid funds in residential psychiatric facilities or general hospitals with sixteen or more beds. The intent was to support the emptying of the asylums initiated by the Community Mental Health Act and ensure that states continued to fund state mental hospitals, as they had done for more than a hundred years. These policies drove a differentiation between physical and mental health care, and righting this wrong has been one of the biggest legislative battles of recent decades.

In the early 1990s two senators came together to try to remedy the lack of parity in coverage for mental and physical illnesses. Paul Wellstone was a progressive

Democrat from Minnesota, and Republican Pete Domenici of New Mexico was a fiscal and social conservative. Wellstone called them "the odd couple." Whatever their political differences, their common cause was born out of personal experience. Domenici's daughter Clare had dropped out of Wake Forest University several years before, after experiencing symptoms of what would later be diagnosed as atypical schizophrenia. Domenici would admit later that if it weren't for that experience, mental health care would likely have not become part of his legislative agenda: "I don't believe the subject ever would have come up."

Wellstone's awakening had come at a much earlier age. At ten years old, he'd visited his older brother in a state mental hospital. His brother had suffered a breakdown, and Wellstone's parents had gone into serious debt trying to keep their son in a private clinic once their insurance ran out. Wellstone described the public hospital as a "snake pit," and said his energy on the issue of care for the mentally ill was fired by "tremendous indignation."

Together the duo introduced and orchestrated the passage of the Mental Health Parity Act of 1996. The bill mandated equal annual and lifetime dollar limits for mental and physical benefits. (Those for mental illness coverage had been capped at about $125,000, compared with about $1 million in benefits for physical disorders; in some instances, benefits for the latter were unlimited.) But the act was too narrow in its effects, and Domenici referred to it as "mental illness coverage lite."

In 2008 the senators reprised their first effort with the Mental Health Parity and Addiction Equity Act, which built on the provisions of the earlier law by requiring parity in health insurance benefits for psychiatric and nonpsychiatric medical services; it was also the first national law to require parity for substance use disorders. However, the 2008 act did not mandate that a plan provide either mental health or substance abuse benefits—it stated only that if a plan did provide such benefits, they must be comparable to medical benefits. Neither did the requirement apply to health insurance policies held by employers with fifty or fewer employees or to individual policies. Finally, the legislation did not create a mechanism to regularly monitor and enforce its implementation. It didn't help that the bill came into being just as the Great Recession hit the country, an economic downturn that would accelerate the ongoing decline in mental health spending. The law was strengthened in 2010, when the Affordable Care Act listed mental health as an essential health benefit that insurance companies were required to provide, but between 2009 and 2012, state legislatures cut nearly $4.5 billion in services for the mentally ill.

Despite the fact that parity is now enshrined in law, the reality on the ground tells a different story. In 2018 the Kennedy Forum, a national advocacy organization for mental health care and addiction founded by former congressman Patrick Kennedy, and several other organizations recognized the ten-year anniversary of the Parity Act by releasing a report that graded every state's parity statutes. Thirty-two states received an F.

Much of the problem lies with the resistance of private insurers, who can create onerous review processes to limit benefits or apply de facto criteria that take the place of the medical necessity standards and can preclude approval for ongoing hospitalizations. For instance, health plans can require reauthorization every five days for hospitalizations for mental health or substance abuse treatment—even for evidence-based durations of care that last longer.

Since the passage of the Parity Act, there have been a few legislative advances, including the Affordable Care Act and its expansion of Medicaid, the largest insurer of mental health services. Whatever their shortcomings, recent statutes have begun to reflect what we've learned about early intervention in psychosis and to prioritize early treatments. In 2014 H.R. 3547 was signed into law, which provided the Substance Abuse and Mental Health Services Administration, for the first time, with funding authority for the specified purpose of supporting the implementation of evidence-based treatment programs for early psychosis. Two years later saw the passage of the 21st Century Cures Act, the most significant mental health legislation since the Parity Act of 2008. It pushes states to provide evidence-based early treatment for psychosis, generally requiring them to use at least 10 percent of their block grants for mental health on early intervention and coordinated specialty care. Importantly, it created a new position, assistant secretary for mental health and substance use, the first cabinet-level position related to mental health; the secretary oversees SAMHSA and disseminates information about the most successful approaches to treating mental illness to community-based mental health facilities and providers.

THE BIG FIX: RECOMMENDATIONS FOR BETTER CARE

APPLYING THE TOOLS WE HAVE

Every year—every day, perhaps—someone in my field can be heard calling for an overhaul of the mental health system. I will add my voice to the chorus. To lack treatment for an illness is an unmet clinical need. To have effective treatments and not provide them to specific segments of the population is a health care disparity. To have such treatments and not make them accessible, affordable, and available to those who need them is a social injustice.

The history of medicine has its share of cautionary tales, a few of which remind us that we should never allow arrogance or dogmatism to prevent us from using the tools at our disposal. Ignaz Philipp Semmelweis was a Hungarian physician working in a Vienna hospital in the mid-nineteenth century, a time when many women were dying of puerperal fever due to infection contracted during childbirth. Semmelweis noticed something alarming: the mortality rate in mothers attended by physicians and medical students was several times higher than in the mothers attended by midwives (13 percent to 18 percent versus 2 percent). After studying the problem, he realized that doctors were going straight from autopsies, where they'd handled corpses (including some of patients who had died from infections), to the delivery room, with no sterilizing procedures in between. Midwives, on the other hand, didn't perform autopsies. Semmelweis initiated a mandatory hand-washing policy for physicians in his hospital, using chlorinated water, and the mortality rate fell to 2 percent, on par with the midwives. When the policy extended to washing medical instruments, it fell to 1 percent.

Surprisingly, Semmelweis's findings were rejected by the medical establishment. Apparently, his colleagues didn't want to hear that they'd been responsible for killing their patients, or that mothers had been safer in the hands of midwives. Undeterred, he continued to present his theory but was widely ridiculed, as many in his field clung to the prevailing "miasma" theory of infection, which held that infectious diseases were caused by pollution or noxious air, which is now obsolete.

Semmelweis finally became so enraged by his colleagues' resistance to adopting the practice of hand washing, even as lives continued to be lost unnecessarily, that he began publicly haranguing his superiors and wrote defamatory letters to prominent European doctors—even calling them murderers.

In 1865, nearly twenty years after his breakthrough discovery, Semmelweis was committed to a mental asylum, where he died of sepsis from an infected wound—possibly incurred during a beating by attendants. It was only when Louis Pasteur presented his germ theory of disease in 1861, which explained Semmelweis's findings, that they finally gained acceptance.

Semmelweis's story is sadly relevant to the treatment of schizophrenia, in that we have effective treatments but aren't using them at nearly the level we could and should be—either because people don't believe they work or because we, as a society, aren't willing to pay for them. Perhaps both. Instead, we prefer to wait for the miraculous breakthrough: the gene, the hidden cause, the cure. Modern scientific and technological advances—the MRI and PET scans that probe the living brain, genetic mapping that can predict a person's medical future, the altering of brain circuits with bioengineering and neuromodulation, and designer drugs that target specific brain proteins and neural circuits—all bode well for eventually curtailing the distressing and disabling effects of the illness. But they shouldn't prevent us from applying the knowledge we already have.

There are a number of steps that could readily be taken to greatly improve the mental health care system, enhancing the quality, quantity, and cost-effectiveness of care. I describe these on the pages that follow.

COMPREHENSIVE CARE IN THE COMMUNITY

The most vexing aspect of schizophrenia treatment is the fact that it's near impossible to find all the therapies you need to manage the illness most effectively in one clinical setting. And if by some chance you were able to assemble a regimen of treatments, it's unlikely they would be affordable or covered by health insurance. This situation is worse for chronic patients. What exists in terms of mental health care for the majority of schizophrenia patients is a woefully deficient and disconnected mosaic of mental health resources. As a result, 40 percent of people with schizophrenia in the United States receive *no mental health care*, and the rate is above 50 percent for people of color.

The starting point for improving mental health care for people with schizophrenia doesn't require something completely new so much as it requires correcting what we previously failed to do. The idea guiding the Community Mental Health Act in 1963—that wherever you lived, there would be a single point of access for outpatient treatment, emergency evaluation, social services, and so on—was a good one. Most people who were in hospitals prior to deinstitutionalization could have lived successfully in the community *if they were able to access consistent services*. We have the chance to rethink how we provide mental health services in the community, drawing on what we've learned over the last several decades about evidence-based treatments for schizophrenia and identifying people early who are at high risk of psychosis. Only when we have solid systems in place for delivering mental health care in the community will we have a clearer picture of what the need is for psychiatric beds in general hospitals and mental institutions.

LEVERAGING HOSPITALS AND MEDICAL CENTERS

Our current mental health system is a patchwork of services strewn across our community landscapes: a hodgepodge of public, nonprofit, private for-profit, and academic facilities within a network of individual and group practice providers. Who does what where, and for which disorders, can be fragmented and arbitrary. As a result of this scattering of services, patients and their families must shop around, hoping to find what they need. Instead of continuing this haphazard approach to service provision, why not use the regulatory authority of the states to set standards for which types of services medical institutions must provide? Left to their own devices, health care institutions are often tempted to game the system and prioritize what is most profitable and convenient (such as procedural and surgical services) rather than what their patient populations actually need. As is, each health care facility that receives government funding, starting with Medicaid and Medicare, must be licensed by the state in which it operates. This requirement could be used to mandate which health care services, including mental health, must be offered to the patient population of the surrounding area that the facility serves, helping to ensure adequate distribution of services.

MATCHING CLINICAL CARE TO SCIENTIFIC KNOWLEDGE

In our current system, mental health services, diagnoses, and treatments are too often inconsistent. Treatment guidelines and algorithms would help to address this problem. The standards of care for schizophrenia have accrued over time from research and clinical practice, and they change as our knowledge increases. To save doctors from having to stay abreast of the burgeoning scientific literature and best standards of care, treatment guidelines for specific diseases, such as those I worked on for the American Psychiatric Association regarding schizophrenia, are developed by professional associations and scientific organizations. Algorithms are decision trees that operationalize the guidelines in order to consistently achieve the best treatment responses and outcomes, whatever the clinical context. If a patient doesn't respond well to the initial medication or develops intolerable side effects, the treatment algorithm suggests the next logical, evidence-based step.

Currently, use of and adherence to these instruments is voluntary, but if institutions monitored physicians' compliance with treatment guidelines or recommended algorithms, they could hold doctors accountable for deviations and poor outcomes. Such oversight would not initially be welcomed by doctors, but the more favorable results it produced in terms of quality care and effective treatment would justify the imposition.

CONTROLLING FORMULARIES

Annual health care expenditure in the United States, which was nearly $4 trillion in 2020, is projected to exceed $6 trillion by 2028. Medication expenditures in 2020 accounted for more than 13 percent of total health care costs and is one of the fastest-growing segments of health care spending. A major contributor to these costs is the preferential use of new, patent-protected medications that are more expensive than older drugs available in generic forms; in addition, doctors often prescribe multiple medications simultaneously to treat the same illness. One way to rein in these wasteful and potentially harmful practices is to institute structured formularies. A formulary is an approved list of medicines that may be prescribed by a health care provider. If Medicaid and other third-party payers were to align their formularies with existing evidence about comparative effectiveness and treatment guidelines, tremendous cost savings would be achieved—and drugs that are underprescribed, such as clozapine and long-acting injectable medications, would be more widely used. Pharmaceutical companies would lobby against this idea. Doctors and consumers might complain of lack of choice. But organizing drug formularies in tiers of preference and requiring prior approval to prescribe more expensive drugs that haven't been proved superior would not disadvantage patients and would likely result in better and more cost-effective treatment.

ADDRESSING RACIAL AND ECONOMIC DISPARITIES

People with lower incomes and from certain racial and ethnic minority groups are less likely than their more affluent or white counterparts to receive mental health care. While their rates of disorders may not differ significantly from the general population, black and Latinx populations tend to have less access to mental health and substance abuse treatment services. There are a number of reasons for mental health care disparities: the effects of structural racism and variations in the level of stigma attached to mental illness, the high cost of services, and a general lack of trust in institutions arising from a history of discrimination and specific abuses in the field of medicine. (Importantly, a belief that mental health services wouldn't help does not seem to be driving reluctance. Inadequate insurance coverage is the most frequently cited reason for not using services.) We need to improve our efforts to increase awareness and access to care for people of color in culturally sensitive ways, and not just in medical institutional settings but in their own communities. New models of care developed in New York City have involved outreach in churches, barbershops, community centers, and public parks. The key is to engage people where they are rather than expecting that they will find you. Such an approach requires a diverse workforce that understands cultural norms in a given community and can work effectively within them.

EXPANDING THE MENTAL HEALTH CARE WORKFORCE

The US Department of Health and Human Services projects that by 2025, there will be a shortage of 250,000 mental health providers, including psychiatrists, psychologists, psychiatric social workers, nurse practitioners, and counselors. These critical deficiencies in the mental health workforce vary by geographic region, and by the ethnic, racial, and age groups they serve. Any efforts to address workforce shortages should be informed by the new model of team-based care. Mental health care doesn't have to be physician-centric and can utilize allied mental health professionals as "physician extenders." While the diagnostic evaluation and the treatment plan are developed with the psychiatrist, components of care are delegated to the team members and overseen by the psychiatrist. Some procedures and complex cases with medical comorbidities certainly call for psychiatrists, but medically trained nurse practitioners and physician assistants can fulfill some of the same functions as physicians and are permitted to carry these out in states that grant them authority to practice independently.

COLLABORATIVE CARE

Approximately 60 percent to 80 percent of all primary care visits include a mental or behavioral health component, but many primary care clinicians feel unable to meet their patients' needs in these areas. At the same time, patients with schizophrenia do not receive adequate primary health care, which contributes to their shortened life expectancy. A proven solution to both of these unmet clinical needs is what is called collaborative care. Simply stated, collaborative care means locating mental health providers in primary care settings and primary care providers in mental health care settings. Such integrated services facilitate earlier intervention and also reduce stigma and decrease barriers to accessing care.

HOW PRIVACY LAWS CAN HURT PATIENT CARE

Current legislation through the 1996 Health Insurance Portability and Accountability Act, better known as HIPAA, inhibits doctors from sharing vital information with other health providers, and, in the case of patients who are eighteen and older, from sharing information with their families without the patient's permission. For someone with a serious mental illness, these restrictions are often more harmful than helpful. Many patients with schizophrenia depend on their families for care, even if they are estranged from them, especially in cases when they don't recognize that they are sick or need help. A body of research shows that families play a crucial role in recovery from serious mental illness. But families can't facilitate care or provide support if they're kept in the dark.

Many health care providers don't understand what information HIPAA allows them to share and thus tend to err on the side of caution. (Others find it convenient to hide behind HIPAA: it gives an excuse to lazy practitioners who don't want to deal with distressed family members.) Hospital administrators are inclined to prioritize the avoidance of liability. But between 2003, when the privacy rule was enacted, and 2016, the Department of Health and Human Services has fined health providers only thirty times, and none of the infractions involved people with mental illness or those caring for them.

Doctors must understand patient concerns about sharing information and the family dynamics involved, and remember that people can change their minds and become open to family involvement. A reluctance to permit sharing information may arise from a wish not to burden loved ones, and it is often possible to persuade patients to involve their families, especially when treating them early in their illness and if they understand that they need help. We need to support legislative efforts to amend HIPAA regulations to allow providers to disclose the diagnosis, treatment plan, appointment schedule, and medications to a responsible caregiver for a patient with a serious mental illness under the following conditions: if withholding the information would contribute to the worsening of someone's condition, or if the patient has diminished capacity to follow a treatment plan that would prevent that worsening. This would create an exception to the privacy rule when someone's mental health would suffer without the involvement of their families.

Mental Health Parity and Insurance Coverage

Psychiatry has the highest proportion in all medical specialties of doctors that don't accept insurance. The main reason for this is that government and private insurers' reimbursement rates are too low to compensate psychiatrists for the time and effort needed to treat someone. Just 62 percent of psychiatrists take commercial insurance or Medicare, and only 35 percent accept Medicaid. (This is compared with 90 percent of all providers who accept private insurance and 71 percent who see Medicaid patients.) In 2019 reimbursement rates for primary care physicians were almost 24 percent higher than for psychiatrists, and in eleven states, the difference was more than 50 percent. We need to establish insurance benefits and reimbursement rates commensurate with the effort and services required to provide state-of-the-art treatment. Cost-based reimbursement is a fee-for-service reimbursement method based on the costs incurred in providing services that advocates are promoting, which would help to facilitate provision of care. The Affordable Care Act, which made insurance obtainable and affordable for far more people than was previously the case, in combination with the Mental Health Parity and Addiction Equity Act, requires equivalence between mental health and medical benefits.

We need to expand and enforce our parity laws. All "medical necessity" determinations in health plans should be fully consistent with generally accepted standards of care for mental health treatment. Caps that government payers put on mental health services (the 190-day Medicare inpatient limit and Medicaid coverage limits for certain facility-base care, to cite examples) should be eliminated. Special Medicaid eligibility coverage should be established for young people with early psychosis and youth involved in the juvenile justice system. And all mental health providers, including peers (persons with lived mental illness experience who act as mental health providers), should be paid on par with comparable health care providers.

REFORM AT THE HIGHEST LEVEL

Over the last several decades, individuals and organizations in the United States have made heroic efforts to fill the gaps in the mental health care system. These innovative bottom-up and usually one-off initiatives have come from the combination of compassionate and civic-minded people who wanted to help those who were suffering and the patient/consumer movement that demanded better and more humane treatment from mental health providers. The famous Fountain House initiated the clubhouse model of care, while Community Access's Howie the Harp Advocacy Center provided person-centered services and patient advocacy. Comprehensive and holistic residential care systems now exist: Gould Farm in Massachusetts, CooperRiis in North Carolina, and Skyland Trail in Atlanta. Steve Leifman's Miami Center for Mental Health and Recovery will fill certain gaps, and OneFifteen in Ohio is providing state-of-the-art treatment for opioid addiction. In Cook County, Illinois, police officers are voluntarily becoming certified in critical time intervention (CTI) to intervene in what Cook County sheriff Thomas Dart told me was the revolving door of mentally ill inmates. The program is working well, and I'm sure has spared some mentally ill Chicagoans from being assaulted or killed. But the program, like all of those above, is a drop in the bucket of needed mental health services.

Even valuable initiatives at the level of municipal, county, or state governments rarely have adequate support or can scale sufficiently to be transformative. The OnTrackNY program for first-episode psychosis, initiated by the state's visionary commissioner of mental health, Mike Hogan, was groundbreaking, but New York State's bureaucracy and the fragmentation across mental health care systems has stifled other initiatives. New York is certainly not unique in having systems that fail to facilitate best practices or the delivery of state-of-the-art treatment.

In the 1980s I began to participate in annual visits to Capitol Hill to lobby for funding for mental health care and research on mental illness at the national level. I learned which government leaders were sympathetic to our efforts. The roll call of members of Congress who have worked valiantly to pass sensible and compassionate mental health care legislation includes Senators Pete Domenici, Daniel Patrick Moynihan, Arlen Specter, Paul Wellstone, Ted Kennedy, and Gordon Smith, and Congressmen John Porter, Silvio Conte, Jim Ramstad, and, of course, Patrick Kennedy. What these advocates have in common is that they all had a personal knowledge of mental illness—either through family members or because they themselves struggled with substance abuse or depression. Smith's son committed suicide. Domenici's daughter developed schizophrenia. Ramstad, who was alcoholic, became Patrick Kennedy's sponsor in Alcoholics Anonymous.

There have also been presidential initiatives dating back to the 1960s, with JFK's support for the Community Mental Health Act. Jimmy Carter created the first-ever presidential commission to address the mental health system. George W. Bush was prompted by the increased frequency of mass violence to establish the New Freedom Commission on Mental Health. All of these efforts raised the visibility of mental illness and temporarily increased public awareness, but they did little to improve care of the mentally ill, either through increased funding for services or advances from research.

As I write, President Joe Biden has just announced his appointment to the first-ever cabinet-level position, created under the previous administration, dedicated to mental health, the assistant secretary for mental health and substance use. Like the mental health advocates in government that have preceded him, President Biden is personally acquainted with tragedy (his first wife and daughter were killed in a car crash, and his adult son Beau died of brain cancer), and he understands the pain of substance abuse through his son Hunter's struggles with addiction. I met then–vice president Biden in 2013 at the fiftieth-anniversary commemoration of JFK's Community Mental Health Act. I was president of the APA at the time and invited him to be the keynote speaker at our next annual meeting. Six months later, I found myself introducing the vice president to sixteen thousand psychiatrists and mental health professionals at the Jacob K. Javits Convention Center in New York City. He spoke sincerely, from the heart. His empathy was genuine. He clearly understood the complexities of mental illness at the personal and societal levels, and the urgent need to do better by those affected by it.

As I listened to the vice president, I felt hopeful in the way I often do when hearing someone speak who clearly wants what I want—better care for the mentally ill—and who has the sort of power that might enable us to move closer to that goal. But I also realized that if we want to affect major systemic change at the national level, we cannot rely on the goodwill of individuals motivated by personal experience. Mental illness affects all of us, directly or indirectly, because it is one of the forces that shapes our society—whether through the homelessness that is rampant in our cities, the social costs of addiction, or the mass violence that might have been avoided with proper treatment. What we need are policies that recognize the fact that virtually nothing in our society is unaffected by our failure to treat mental illness, and to embrace mental health care reform as an urgent national priority.

Just as we cannot rely on sympathetic individuals in Congress, or even in the White House—personnel changes, after all—neither can we continue to attempt to address mental health care needs through the patchwork of programs created by pioneers such as Steve Leifman, however innovative and amazing the programs may be. We need comprehensive reform from the top down—policy driven from the federal level that will consolidate, standardize, and scale up the full range of care and services indicated for the treatment of schizophrenia. The federal government has to be all in if we are to finally properly address mental illness and its signature disorder, schizophrenia.

The newly appointed assistant secretary for mental health, Dr. Miriam Delphin-Rittmon, should be charged to chair a commission to develop a national plan for mental health care, including its structure, funding, workforce, and scope and rollout of services. The commission must be fully cognizant of how and where mental illness overlaps with substance abuse, developmental disabilities, and social and economic factors such as education, employment, housing, and poverty. Its work must serve as a catalyst for breaking down the silos and bureaucratic fragmentation that for too long have impeded care and exacerbated suffering. Only by taking such a big-picture approach to mental illness and the many social problems and intimate tragedies it creates will we be able to deliver—equitably and affordably—the state-of-the-art treatments now available for schizophrenia to all those who need them.

Chapter 21

OWNING RECOVERY

I dwell in possibility . . .

—Emily Dickinson

CLOZAPINE AND CHIMPANZEES

When Brandon Staglin was first hospitalized and told he had a serious mental illness, he was outraged. Brandon, discussed in chapter 12, was a student at Dartmouth and had ambitious plans for his life. Now his parents were insisting that he take medications that produced unpleasant side effects. Navane made him feel as though thunder and lightning were going on in his head. The antipsychotic Stelazine made him drool. Another medication prompted a seizure.

Faced with a suddenly uncertain future, Brandon sank into depression. What pulled him out after that first episode were clozapine and chimpanzees. Brandon had gone back to the hospital for two weeks in the fall of 1990, and his medication had been switched to clozapine. Not long after, his mother heard him singing in his room. Over the next months, while seeing a psychiatrist and continuing to take his medication, Brandon audited classes at UC Berkeley and volunteered to work on a chimp study at the Oakland Zoo. He was still depressed, though, and at one point suicidal. But he felt conflicted: Did he really want to die? It occurred to him that he still hadn't seen a certain chimp at the zoo enact a dominance display. What a spectacle that would be to see firsthand, he thought. "And by extension, I thought of all the other experiences that were waiting for me in life," he reflects. "And so I decided it was worth living."

Within six months, Brandon was back at Dartmouth. He stayed on his medication and continued to see a psychiatrist. He was still struggling with strange thoughts and irrational fears, but he was determined, and in 1993 he graduated with honors with degrees in engineering and anthropology. He got a job in Palo Alto, California, designing communications panels for satellites. It was the kind of work he'd long dreamed of doing, and he loved it.

Brandon began planning for a graduate degree and was accepted to programs at MIT and Stanford. There was one problem: he knew he'd never be able to keep up with his studies if he was sleeping nine hours a night—which clozapine caused him to do. Without consulting his doctor, he began to cut back on his medication. The hallucinations returned, now accompanied by obsessive-compulsive behaviors. He began acting erratically. He resigned from his job and wound up back in the hospital.

Brandon's second recovery was harder. He was living by himself in an apartment in San Francisco, lacking the motivation to do anything. For someone who had been driven all his life, this apathy was a new and awful twist. What helped to get him back on his feet was a clinical trial run by Dr. Sophia Vinogradov at the San Francisco VA Medical Center. The trial used cognitive training to strengthen neural pathways in the brain, specifically those circuits weakened or damaged by schizophrenia. Brandon practiced the training five days a week for ten weeks, playing computer games that required him to differentiate among various auditory tones. He began to regain his conversational skills and his ability to respond appropriately to what others said. His desire to get on with his life returned.

Brandon was now stable, but he needed to reimagine his future. Powering his way into a career as an astronautical engineer was going to be too stressful. In 1999 he began to work at his parents' vineyard as webmaster.

Shari and Garen, meanwhile, had been on their own learning curve. When Brandon's trouble started, they knew next to nothing about schizophrenia, although Shari had studied psychology in college. "I learned that it was a horrible disease, a no-hope kind of thing, and that it was caused by the mother." She and Garen worried that they'd pushed Brandon too hard. They read E. Fuller Torrey's book *Surviving Schizophrenia*, but still shied away from the word "schizophrenia." It seemed such an ugly word, and they didn't want the stigma.

But Shari and Garen are people who, when confronted by a problem, set about finding a solution—or, in this case, a way to rise to the challenge. Their recent experience of the mental health system had taught them a few things: that the biological causes of schizophrenia were still not well understood, that finding the right medication could be an agonizing trial-and-error process, and that accessing optimal care was exhausting and costly—if you could even find it. They decided that the best thing they could do to help people like their son was to support funding for research. In 1995, five years after Brandon's diagnosis, they launched what would become the annual Music Festival for Brain Health, a weekend to raise funds and awareness that draws scientists and donors from around the world.

Brandon still hung back. He felt resentful of his parents for having started a nonprofit because of *his* condition. But one day, a director was at the vineyard filming a documentary about wine, and he happened to ask Garen and Shari what had inspired them to start the music festival. Seeing an opportunity, Brandon said, "I'll tell you about that." The act of talking to a stranger about his illness was liberating, and he began to speak more openly about schizophrenia.

It was around this time that another big change occurred: Brandon's doctor switched him to Abilify, a newer atypical antipsychotic. Though he'd remained stable for a number of years, he hadn't felt particularly happy; he had struggled with his weight and was still short of motivation. On Abilify, he initially felt restless and anxious, but what he also noticed was that his emotional range was coming back. He wanted to socialize. He hadn't dated since his second psychotic episode, but he now began seeing Nancy, the sister of the vineyard's manager, whom he'd met at a harvest party. They married in 2009, the year after the Staglins launched the nonprofit that is today One Mind.

One Mind has raised and leveraged millions each year, supporting cutting-edge research into diagnosis, prevention, and treatment for psychiatric illnesses and traumatic brain injuries. The Staglins advocate against stigma and discrimination. Any discomfort the family once felt about their son's diagnosis is gone. Brandon, meanwhile, is thriving. He's now director of marketing communications for the vineyard, and president of One Mind. He sometimes feels an "undercurrent of anxiety" that his health might be fragile, but he has tools on top of his medication. He exercises, eats well, gets enough sleep, meditates, and maintains relationships with family and friends—the same things many of us do to feel well. In 2018 he completed a Master of Science in Healthcare Administration and Interpersonal Leadership program at the University of California, San Francisco. He did worry that the stress of a degree program might lead to another break, but work gives him a sense of purpose; the anxiety, he says, can even be helpful, driving him to advocate for better health care for others.

A number of things that helped him recover are incorporated into coordinated specialty care, for which Brandon is a big advocate. He had high-quality medical care and medication management, supported employment, and the involvement of his family. He also began treatment immediately after his first psychotic break. Early on, he had a psychiatrist he trusted and who persevered until they found the medication that worked best for him. Medication, Brandon feels, has been necessary but not sufficient for his recovery. Recovery isn't just about admitting you have a medical condition, he explains, or even being symptom free. It's about getting your life back, being able to do the things you care about. For recovery, he needed to reclaim agency. "The patient has to lead the definition of recovery," he says. "And you have to be active and try to live again."

What Is Recovery?

As our understanding and treatment of mental illness have evolved over the last several decades, so has our conception of recovery. Doctors traditionally defined it objectively: according to symptoms, impairments, and relapses. Symptoms lead to diagnosis and treatment, upon which they improve or remit, and you have few or no residual impairments. But a more enlightened conception of recovery emerged from the chaos of deinstitutionalization. It borrowed from the twelve-step philosophy, long used by those recovering from addiction, and shares its ethos of accepting the reality of a lifelong condition from which one is always recovering but is never fully recovered.

In *The Center Cannot Hold*, Elyn Saks writes: "My good fortune is not that I've recovered from mental illness. I have not, nor will I ever. My good fortune lies in having found my life." Brandon Staglin marks his having read Saks's memoir as a turning point in his life and the beginning of his own recovery. Elyn's ability to accept and live with her condition inspired Brandon to accept his own illness, which allowed him to turn his attention to other things and begin to build a life for himself that included schizophrenia.

Recovery is a continuous process; a challenge to be faced and navigated over the course of one's life. It goes beyond symptom reduction and enables full participation in mainstream society despite continued infirmity. SAMHSA, the lead federal agency implementing recovery approaches to mental health treatment, cites four major dimensions that support recovery—health, home, purpose, and community—and offers specific guiding principles that include hope, peer support, and the need to address trauma.

The psychiatrist Anthony Lehman at the University of Maryland observed that the word "recovery" had both radical and mainstream meanings. He saw "recovery" as a loaded word that conveyed, on the one hand, an optimistic message about the possibility of leading healthy fulfilling lives, but implied, on the other hand, that patients were victims of an oppressive mental health system from which they were seeking freedom.

THE ROOTS OF A MOVEMENT

Over the previous half century, our attitude as a society toward the idea of recovery for people with schizophrenia has evolved from an impossibility to the point where a degree of recovery is regarded as achievable and even expected. The advent of the early-detection and intervention strategy has made substantial, even full, recovery a more realistic goal. Research on developing diagnostic measures and treatments for people in the premorbid or prodromal stages of schizophrenia offers the future possibility of prevention.

This evolution in attitude and possibility has been due as much to the recovery movement as to progress in research. While the movement's origins are generally attributed to the reforms of the eighteenth and nineteenth centuries led by Philippe Pinel, William Tuke, and others, the contemporary concept of recovery has come from patients who were the consumers of mental health care rather than from physicians and institutional providers.

The first stirrings of the recovery movement arose out of the travails of Clifford Beers. Born into a prominent Connecticut family in 1876, he was educated at elite prep schools before going on to study at Yale. In 1900, three years after graduating, he suffered the first of several mental breakdowns and was hospitalized for three years. The experience prompted Beers to publish his autobiography, *A Mind That Found Itself*, in which he described the demeaning treatment and physical abuse he suffered in the asylum. Beers acknowledged the seriousness of his condition but condemned the brutality to which he and his fellow patients were subjected. The book's balanced voice and candid descriptions had a powerful impact on readers.

Beers subsequently joined with psychiatrist Adolf Meyer, physician William Welch, and the philosopher William James to establish the Connecticut Society for Mental Hygiene. The society advocated for the improvement of mental health care and the prevention of mental illness. But it was the third aim of the organization—working to correct the misapprehension that *one cannot recover from mental illness*—that represented what may have been the first vision of recovery from the patients' perspective.

Beers's efforts represented a conceptual milestone and attracted much attention but did not lead to substantive reform or sweeping changes in the plight of patients. For this to occur, mental health advocates would have to wait for more conducive social conditions.

The cultural upheaval of the 1960s fundamentally altered the relationship between institutional authority and individual citizens. This disruptive zeitgeist dovetailed with the dissatisfactions with psychiatry and the mental health system that had been growing over the twentieth century. Now people with mental illnesses, who referred to themselves as "survivors" (that is, of neglect and abuse at the hands of the system) joined other groups in the larger civil rights movement—women, people of color, gay people, people with disabilities—to demand change.

Various constituencies in society reacted differently to the growing unhappiness with psychiatry. The general public, now broadly aware of the profession's long-standing failure to deliver effective treatments and the inhumane conditions in state mental institutions, lost confidence in the mental health care system. The anti-psychiatry movement, in its critiques of its legitimacy, claimed that its treatments were ineffective, and even challenged whether mental illness was real. Another coalition, composed of former patients and mental health care providers who were sympathetic to their discontent, declared their independence from mainstream psychiatry—aiming to carve a middle way between the psychoanalytic contingent and biological psychiatry, which was just learning how to use the new antipsychotic medications and sometimes erred on the side of devaluing any approaches to treating mental illness other than pharmacological. This alliance, which would quickly coalesce into the recovery movement, said, *Enough is enough.* After centuries of vilification, neglect, mistreatment, and stigmatization, people suffering from schizophrenia and other mental illnesses began to take matters into their own hands. If they couldn't rely on doctors and the mental health care system to help them, they would determine for themselves how best to facilitate their recovery from mental illness. They might be ill, and suffering symptoms and limitations in their functioning (sometimes despite ostensibly effective treatments), but they could still lead meaningful lives. This empowering and revolutionary concept launched the recovery movement.

Among the first groups to emerge from this ethos was the Insane Liberation Front, formed in Portland, Oregon, in 1970, followed the next year by the Mental Patients Liberation Project in New York City and the Mental Patients Liberation Front in Boston. In 1972 the Network Against Psychiatric Assault formed in San Francisco. These groups often protested at psychiatric hospitals and at APA conferences. They communicated with one another by way of national newsletters and conferences of their own. *Madness Network News*, published for more than ten years, provided an outlet for people to share their stories and political positions. The first annual Conference on Human Rights and Against Psychiatric Oppression was held in Detroit in 1972. Many of those attending would have been surviving on Social Security disability payments, but they found a way to get there—hitching, or by bus or in packed cars—as these gatherings were among the few opportunities people had to network and share their experiences.

While the diagnoses and circumstances of those who joined the patients' rights groups varied, all shared a feeling of being dehumanized and written off. One of the landmark books of the movement was Judi Chamberlin's *On Our Own: Patient-Controlled Alternatives to the Mental Health System* (1978). In her subsequent writings, Chamberlin highlighted a key tenet that the recovery movement shared with other civil rights movements: "Among the major organizing principles of these movements were self-definition and self-determination. Black people felt that white people could not understand their experiences; women felt similarly about men; homosexuals similarly about heterosexuals. . . . To mental patients who began to organize, these principles seemed equally valid."

This spirit of change would eventually encourage former mental patients to adopt the mantra of the disability rights movement—"Nothing about us without us"—to fight against forced treatment, stigma, and discrimination, and to promote peer-run services as an alternative to the traditional top-down structures of the mental health system. Unlike mental health services based on the medical model, peer-run services were based on the principle that individuals who have shared similar experiences can engage in self-help and mutual support. The recovery movement also focused on the importance of rehabilitation programs—things such as vocational, art, and drama therapy—provided in less medicalized settings than people were used to. These programs gave patients a friendly place to congregate, and they would serve as the basis for what evolved later into evidence-based psychosocial therapies.

In the 1980s the federal government began to take notice of the groups led by former patients and the successful programs that they were operating without outside support. Suddenly, previously disenfranchised leaders of the recovery movement were invited to join policy-making committees of government agencies, and groups received an influx of funding from the NIMH and SAMHSA.

Meanwhile, psychiatric rehabilitation centers were gaining ground and would be critical in solidifying the recovery movement. These clinical programs focused on helping people relearn the necessary skills for independent living. They were the closest thing patients had to a safe haven, and, apart from their therapeutic role, they served to empower people to adopt the recovery philosophy. Instead of blaming them or abusing them in the name of treatment, rehabilitation centers empathized with patients, welcoming them with all their symptoms and making them feel supported.

One of the pioneers of psychiatric rehabilitation was psychologist William Anthony, who founded the Center for Psychiatric Rehabilitation at Boston University in 1979. Dr. Anthony defined recovery in 1993 as "a deeply personal, unique process of changing one's attitudes, values, feelings, goals, skills and/or roles. It is a way of living a satisfying, hopeful, and contributing life even with limitations caused by the illness." Anthony makes clear that the process is called recovery but its essence is a form of cognitive reframing—that is, reconfiguring the criteria by which we define recovery.

This movement was fortuitously punctuated by the passage of the Americans with Disabilities Act in 1990. The ADA redefined serious mental illnesses as disabilities and extended to the mentally ill the rights and opportunities that the physically disabled possessed, including a range of accommodations that enabled them, for example, to live in their own homes, attend school, and work. By the end of the decade, the US surgeon general, David Satcher, had explicitly mandated recovery-based care for mental illnesses, stating in his 1999 report: "[T]he goal of services must not be limited to symptom reduction but should strive for restoration of a meaningful and productive life."

As these developments were taking place, new research seemed to provide evidence supporting the plausibility of recovery from schizophrenia. Studies examining middle-aged or older patients who had been ill for many years reported finding that most of them had improved compared to the earlier stages of their illness. They were still symptomatic, but they managed their symptoms and were functional. Some studies noted that up to two-thirds of people diagnosed with schizophrenia experienced significant improvement over time, while many recovered completely. These findings extended the concept of the long-standing "rule of thirds," which originated at a time when diagnoses of psychotic disorders were far less precise and before the advent of antipsychotic medications. This rule stated that a third of people diagnosed with schizophrenia would completely recover; a third would experience periodic relapse but be able to live a relatively normal life; and a third would continue to deteriorate over the course of their lives. In other words, there was considerable variation in people's outcomes, and not everyone exhibited the inevitable decline described by Emil Kraepelin. (The rule of thirds doesn't accurately reflect the course of the illness in the modern age: we now have more rigorous and reliable diagnostic techniques, and patients have access to effective treatments.)

I regard the interpretations of these studies as interesting but unconvincing—and overly optimistic. Of the thousands of people with schizophrenia I have seen or treated over four decades, I have never known anyone to spontaneously recover completely and require no further treatment. Experience tells me that such instances are either extremely rare or nonexistent. What I have seen very often is the well-documented fluctuating and evolving course of the illness: patients exhibit discrete florid psychotic episodes in the early stages, and, as they get older and the illness progresses, their psychotic symptoms diminish in intensity, and negative symptoms become more prominent.

The other source of evidence now cited for the possibility of recovery is the early-intervention psychosis research (described in chapter 18) focusing on disease-modifying treatments. These studies I *do* view as confirming recovery, but the recovery-promoting effects, both biological and functional, of early-intervention strategies apply only to younger patients. The rest—the long-term ill—can benefit from treatments, but as discussed in the previous chapter, we don't have treatments that enable them to return to their pre-illness condition.

The upshot of the recovery movement—which began in earnest with breakaway groups that called out psychiatry for its failings—has been the coming together of patients and mental health care providers in a kinder, gentler model of care that respects the wishes and input of patients. Of course, there are still bad apples in psychiatry and medical care generally, but on the whole, psychiatry has responded constructively to the demands of patient groups. In learning to listen to patients, we became more empathic and attuned to those factors contributing to recovery that are not always easy to measure.

Pat Deegan, whom we met in chapter 19, has spoken of the spark of hope that drives recovery, a phenomenon that "all of the polemic and technology of psychia-try, psychology, social work, and science cannot account for." It's also a feeling she insists must be followed by a willingness to act. Deegan took responsibility for managing her life and illness. She continued to take her medications, got a part-time job, and eventually earned a PhD in clinical psychology. She has subsequently dedicated herself to helping others in their recovery and to helping clinicians bet-ter understand how to support recovery. She is one of the most well-known faces of the modern recovery movement.

The episodic nature of severe mental illness enables significant recovery to occur even without complete symptom relief. Parallels can be seen with physi-cal illnesses that might be episodic (rheumatoid arthritis, multiple sclerosis, and others) but that don't prevent people from living full or meaningful lives. But a psychotic episode or a diagnosis of serious mental illness can shatter a person's sense of self in a way few physical illnesses do; in mental illness, the engine of recovery—the brain—is also the organ affected. One feels stigmatized. Lifelong goals seem suddenly out of reach.

Clinicians, friends, and family can help the patient to regain selfhood by rec-ognizing which roles and activities still enable him or her to experience a sense of agency. We should take care in how we interpret behaviors. Just because someone with schizophrenia is quiet, withdrawn, or passive, we should not infantilize him by making decisions for him, doing things to him without asking, or explaining to him what is happening and why. Find out the person's pleasures and interests—the sense of meaning and purpose that has kept him alive. Agency can be encouraged and supported at the most granular levels, but it's also relevant to community life. The notion of full citizenship is important to recovery—enabling participation for everyone in a context of rights, responsibilities, and a sense of belonging. All of these principles have come to us in the field of psychiatry through the recovery movement, and we owe a great debt to our patients for teaching us, finally, how to listen to them.

MEASURING RECOVERY

While individuals with mental illness may refer to recovery as a personal journey, clinicians want also to refer to measurable outcomes. One of the conundrums of recovery is that, like so much about schizophrenia and other serious mental illnesses, it can't be measured easily or quantitatively, and it doesn't mean the same thing to every person who is ill. I have seen the frustration with this imprecision change the career paths of young students and trainee doctors.

Standard medical and psychiatric language cannot completely encapsulate the recovery process. Part of the challenge is that people with schizophrenia vary in each category of recovery (cognitive functioning, vocational functioning, and so on), and the various categories are themselves relatively independent of one another. It often makes more sense to define recovery in terms of improvements in specific domains rather than globally.

The approach to care from a recovery perspective is also different from the traditional hierarchical medical model, in which doctors were the omniscient experts and decision-makers, intent mainly on alleviating symptoms and restoring functional capacity. The philosophy of the recovery movement values and seeks the input of people with mental illness and their loved ones. Decision-making is shared rather than imposed, and the patient retains a sense of control and responsibility.

There is divergence within the recovery movement about how such decision-making might play out in the case of someone who is very disabled. Elyn Saks has spent much of her career attempting to understand and measure capacity. She has argued that if someone lacks even a low level of capacity—for instance, he or she believes that taking a medication will cause a nuclear explosion—then the recovery-model principle of self-determination should not apply. But if the person *does* have low-level capacity, he should be able to decide what is in his best interests, even if a medical professional views the choice as irrational or substandard.

Ideally, the predominantly subjective and politically oriented recovery model can work in tandem with a more objective, scientific approach. Medical and mental health professionals, while continuing to utilize clinical examinations and diagnostic tests, and to measure treatment response, can also evolve along the path of patient-centered and recovery-oriented care that emphasizes shared decision-making.

None of this means that the clinician is denying or downplaying someone's illness. Rather, it's an attempt to meet individuals where they are—building relationships based on their understanding of their predicament—rather than requiring them to meet us on our terms. This strategy can be most helpful to people who haven't found a biomedical explanation of their difficulties. For instance, if someone doesn't accept that he or she has a mental illness, a clinician can focus on aspects of the condition that the patient finds most troubling or disruptive. (This element of recovery-based care was discussed in the context of CSC and insight in chapter 18.) The doctor might note that harassing voices leave the patient feeling unsafe, and explore ways to mitigate those fears without taking the additional step of explaining that such experiences are part of a serious mental illness called schizophrenia. It's also possible to suggest medications or other interventions or coping strategies to help address these experiences without necessarily labeling them "psychotic"—in other words, remaining within patients' frames of reference as much as possible, while introducing new information that could help them with their immediate and pressing concerns, rather than asking them to believe in the usefulness of a diagnostic label that may mean little to them or overwhelm them with negative connotations.

The Right Resources

People who struggle with mental disorders, Elyn Saks has said, "can lead full, happy, productive lives, if we have the right resources." The "right resources" is the key phrase. Systemic changes should promote services that foster financial, residential, and personal independence, along with the roles all of us tend to seek out and enjoy, such as employment and social connectedness. Coordinated specialty care programs such as those discussed in chapter 18 aim to support people in building such lives for themselves, and they adhere to the sort of shared-decision-making ethos that is a pillar of the recovery movement.

Recovery, as Pat Deegan writes, isn't a perfectly linear process. There are periods of rapid gains, and there are disappointing setbacks; there are periods of quiet, rest, and regrouping. This means that everyone involved in someone's treatment and recovery should accept that failure and setbacks will be part of the process. But many rehabilitation programs are designed in a linear manner, requiring people to move through a series of steps, with failure at any point returning them to square one. Deegan wants those of us working with the mentally ill to think about what we're asking someone to risk when we ask him or her to try or to care about something. Failure is painful, but rehabilitation programs can nurture recovery if they are structured in a way that accepts the "try/fail dynamic" at the heart of the recovery process. People are more likely to thrive in a program when they can return after a setback and pick up where they left off instead of having the "failure" compounded by penalties.

Deegan raises the interesting point that much of our programming in the United States is based on the traditional values of "rugged individualism, competition, personal achievement, and self-sufficiency," to the exclusion of other possibilities. For some people with psychiatric disorders, such values can be oppressive, and programs built on them are invitations to failure. Independent living, for example, can mean a lonely room in a boarding house rather than a sense of empowerment. What if the focus was shifted to more cooperative group efforts or living situations? Instead of competitive vocational training based on individual achievement, Deegan suggests a more cooperative work setting that stresses group achievement.

It is essential to recognize how important connection to fellow human beings is for people with mental illness, as it is for everyone. Peer support is a critical element of comprehensive care and recovery. Grant, Rona's roommate in Boston, told me that the voices are tamped down when he's with others at Center Club. People who are recovering also talk about those who believed in them when they had no self-belief, who encouraged their recovery without trying to force it, and who tried to listen and understand when nothing was making sense. Brandon recalls how even when his family was very scared, they were always supportive. "There was a time I was really depressed," he says. "I remember walking into the dining room, and my father saying, 'There's a lot of love here, Brandon.' I couldn't feel love at that time, but hearing him say that inspired me to want to get better." Increasingly, peers play a part in this support. In order to serve as a role model, someone need not be fully recovered. In fact, the person who is only a few steps ahead can often be a more effective peer support than one whose achievements seem out of reach to the person on the receiving end.

DOING THE SIMPLE THINGS

Despite the scarcity of adequate treatment facilities, I know many people who have been able to avail themselves of the resources and care they needed, and have taken the steps to regain their footing and bolster their own recovery.

Daniel was twenty-four years old when I met him, a full-time student at a prominent university in New York City, on track for graduate school. But there was a time when delusions were his whole life. "It was like reading a book with no plot," he says now. He became convinced that his dorm was an insane asylum and that he was being secretly drugged. There were cameras in his room, and everything he did, his most private moments, were "on blast" to the world. Everyone was out to get him; people were going to tie him up and torture him. He didn't feel safe sleeping at home, and imagined his parents were attacking him in his sleep.

Because he didn't trust anyone, Daniel tried to keep what was going on to himself as much as possible, sharing just enough so that he could "gain information" about what people were doing. He did wonder once if he might have paranoid schizophrenia—he'd looked up the definition. But then he thought: *No, I can't have that, because the things I'm thinking aren't delusions, they're true. And if they're true, they aren't crazy.*

Somewhere in this first dark period of his illness, there was insight. Daniel's mother remembers that when his trouble began, he told her, "Either everyone I love is out to get me, or I'm mentally ill."

Daniel's life until his second year in college had not been unusual. The son of two professional parents, he'd had his ups and downs. There were years he studied hard and was among the top few students in his class, and years when he was lax. He loved the math club and was a nationally rated fencer. The transition to high school had been hard; he was very shy, and, for the first two years, he was teased and bullied. Then he shot up to six foot three before his junior year. The bullying ended. He studied harder and was accepted to a college in California—far from his family home in New York.

Away at college, Daniel began to drink heavily. He wasn't studying at all, and halfway through his second semester, in danger of flunking out, he withdrew and came back to New York City. At home, he regrouped—got a part-time job and started to get physically fit. But he wanted a degree and the opportunities that went with that, and so he returned to school in California, this time to a community college, where he studied hard and fell for a classmate. Her name was Jessica, and though she became a friend, she didn't return his affections. Daniel transferred to a university in New York City in the fall of 2017. Jessica, meanwhile, had gone back to her home in the United Kingdom.

That winter, Daniel went with a mutual friend to visit Jessica. His drinking was out of hand again, and when he came home, he says, he "just tanked emotionally." He wrote Jessica a letter, full of paranoia and conspiracy theories. He was convinced his feelings for her were a running joke among all their friends; at the same time, he believed that Jessica was in love with him and that she was secretly in New York arranging to surprise him. He thought everyone who spoke to him was conversing in metaphors about Jessica.

Things quickly got worse. Daniel withdrew from school again. His sleep was disrupted; sometimes he was up for forty hours straight. He came to believe he was being held secretly in a mental asylum. "It was taking up so much of my cognitive faculties, I collapsed on the floor. I was hyperventilating. I got really scared then because I knew there was a problem."

Daniel was already in therapy, and his therapist insisted he see a psychiatrist. The psychiatrist, whom he saw only once, prescribed olanzapine and aripiprazole (Abilify). That was March 2018. Within a week of Daniel's going on medication, his parents enrolled him at the Lieber Rehabilitation and Recovery Clinic.

He describes his relationship to treatment at the time as compliant but resistant. "I was letting them try things out, but it was to appease them, not because I thought I needed it. I was doing it for my reward." The reward was, first of all, Jessica. Daniel imagined that all of this was a test, and if he passed, he'd get to marry her. And there was the belief that he was being recruited to run for president. "I was very arrogant," he admits, "overly fond of my own intelligence. I felt the simple exercises the group was doing were beneath me. Why should I challenge my thoughts if I'm right? I thought I was a genius—apparently not an uncommon delusion."

At the Lieber Clinic, he was switched to quetiapine (brand name, Seroquel), which helped to regulate his sleep patterns, and he began group therapy. When an addiction specialist came to talk to Daniel about his drinking, she wanted to get him into a rehab facility immediately. Daniel wished at all costs to avoid any kind of institutionalization. He signed a contract saying that if he drank again, he'd be institutionalized. "I knew I was done," he says. He's been sober since then and attending AA.

Meanwhile, he continued with various clinic groups: like DBT and CBT for psychosis. His goals were to return to school and pursue his longer-term academic interests. After some months, though Daniel wasn't free of delusions, he felt well enough to go on a cruise ship to Antarctica with his father. The Lieber Clinic staff advised against the trip, but Daniel is strong willed—a trait, he says, that has helped with his resilience but has sometimes led him to return to things prematurely.

The trip went well. But when he returned to New York, he experienced what he describes as "whiplash"—going from the peace and calm of the ship to the intense bustle of the city. He got worse. His psychiatrist upped his dose of Seroquel, but Daniel hated the side effects, which he describes as "I felt like I had a blanket over my mind." The Seroquel had made sense, he says, when he was trying to get his sleep regulated, but increasing it wasn't the solution now.

Eventually Daniel switched to Risperdal. That was spring of 2019, and it was a turning point. On Risperdal, Daniel began to feel like himself again. He was much less delusional, and his thinking about his illness changed, too. He accepted that doing less for the time being was the best thing for him. "That was a big moment for me, and very against my nature. I'd always been hard on myself, and I felt like going easier was a cop-out." But he did it, took time off from school, and began to take his treatment more seriously; he learned zazen meditation, which he describes as life changing. "And doing the simple things, like cleaning up my room. That was me taking things into my own hands, developing a long-term plan."

Giving up caffeine helped significantly, too. "When you're delusional," Daniel says, "you want these big solutions that will radically change things. But it's the small, simple steps that can really help. I don't mean simple as in easy. But steps that might not have a dramatic effect on a nonmentally ill person can have a huge impact."

Daniel returned to his university in New York City in the fall of 2019 and finished his degree, maintaining a 3.7 GPA. As I write this in 2021, he is preparing to enter a clinical PsyD program, to which he's been offered a merit scholarship. Two years ago, he started playing the piano. He describes himself as more relationship oriented than he used to be.

Daniel's recovery has much in common with Brandon's, a reminder of the key aspects in optimal treatment. He received comprehensive treatment early. He has supportive parents. He didn't give up on medication, despite a period of trial and error. He took ownership of the recovery process, but also knew that he needed to be open to things doctors and therapists were suggesting. In a patient-doctor relationship, Daniel says, sometimes the doctor knows better, and sometimes the patient does. "Who's the right person to trust at the right time?" And he made the decision to commit to getting back out into the community. "Being a functioning member of society, getting jobs, which gave me an identity outside of treatment. Seeing that I could do things even if I still had some delusions." Like Brandon, Daniel is using his experience to help others. He finished a course in peer-to-peer counseling with the Academy of Peer Services (APS) and will begin supporting others with mental illness. (The APS is a private nonprofit collaboration between the Rutgers University Department of Psychiatric Rehabilitation, the New York

Association of Psychiatric Rehabilitation Services, and a network of Community Collaborators with funding from the New York State Office of Mental Health. It offers online, self-directed training using interactive media courses for persons with mental illness seeking certification as peer specialists to work in mental health care settings.)

He still has to check his thoughts. "If it's too good to be true," he says, "then it's probably all in my head. I have to be attuned to when I get slightly off, because it could be warning of something bigger. This is an integral part of who I am. It's like alcoholism. You'll never be free of thoughts of drinking, but there's a difference between passing thoughts and strong cravings. Same with delusions. Now they're more like thoughts than cravings. I recognize what's happening, and they don't have the same sway over me."

Daniel is the sort of patient who keeps Alice Medalia, the cognitive psychologist, motivated. She admits that being diagnosed can be very scary. "Any illness is hard, and schizophrenia is very difficult. But there's no need to be scared. You can lead a productive life," she stresses. "People with schizophrenia work really hard to get back on track. And it's a pleasure to be with people who are trying so hard."

Alice recalls that when she first went into the field, schizophrenia had connotations of hopelessness. "Colleagues looked at me and said, 'Why would you want to go into schizophrenia? There's nothing you can do.'" She told me that she wanted to prove them wrong. Her experience is reminiscent of my own, back when I was a young doctor and asked my supervisor how I could help my patient Jonah escape the cycle of relapse and hospitalization: "You just have to let some patients suffer and learn the hard way." Like Alice, my instincts told me we could do better than that for the people who looked to us for treatment. Time has borne out our intuitions. No one with schizophrenia should now have to go untreated, suffer multiple relapses, or endure the inexorable decline of their mental faculties. We have effective treatments, and we see our patients recovering.

Epilogue

> Of all the forms of inequality, injustice in health is the most
> shocking and inhumane.
>
> —Martin Luther King Jr., speech to
> Medical Committee for Human Rights (1966)

Quo Vadis?

In the religious school I attended as a boy, the rabbi told us a story that has stuck with me ever since: the "Parable of the Long Spoons." In this story, a man dreams that he has died and is met at the gates of the afterlife by God, who offers him a choice between heaven and hell. The man asks what each is like. First, God leads him to a great hall, where a banquet table is laid with a magnificent feast: bowls of fragrant soups, succulent roasts, aromatic loaves of bread, fresh fruit, the finest of wines, and a dazzling array of sweet desserts. But the scene is one of pain and anguish. Around the table, seated skeletal forms writhe from hunger and thirst. When the dreamer asks why the diners are so unhappy, God points to the long spoons fastened like splints to their arms. The handles are so long that the diners cannot bring the food or drink to their mouths.

"This is hell," says God. "Anger and misery amid plenty."

God then leads the man to another great hall, where they find a second banquet table, covered with a similarly sumptuous spread of food and drink. Here, however, they hear the sounds of laughter and gaiety, as the happy diners enjoy the bounty before them. The man notices that they, too, have long spoons fastened to their arms, but instead of struggling futilely to feed themselves, the diners at the second banquet are feeding one another.

"And this," God says, "is heaven."

Over the course of my career, I have come to appreciate the relevance of the parable to the circumstances of the mentally ill. We as a society, and those among us who are afflicted with severe mental illnesses, resemble the figures at the first table: continuing to suffer despite the fact that we possess the means to alleviate our agonies.

The answer to the question of what lies ahead for mental health care depends on whether we decide to make full use of the treatments we currently have and that we know work, even while awaiting a major scientific breakthrough; or if we continue to underfund and underutilize existing therapies, focusing all of our energies on the search for a silver bullet. We shouldn't have to choose between the two, but we seem to have turned it into a zero-sum game.

The treatments and services I've described in the preceding chapters, such as coordinated specialty care, community support services, cognitive remediation, and medication, involve relatively little really new and are relatively low-tech, but when combined effectively with the right models of service delivery, they improve the quality of mental health care and the lives of people with schizophrenia enormously. And yet we aren't making them widely available enough. Nor are we doing sufficient research on improving current pharmacological and psychosocial treatments or developing new ones.

Virtually all of the funding for research on schizophrenia currently comes from the federal government through the NIMH. (The National Institute on Drug Abuse and the National Institute on Alcohol Abuse and Alcoholism fund substance abuse research.) Treatment research is supported largely by pharmaceutical, biotechnology, and medical device companies in the private sector. Over the past twenty-five years, the amount of funding from both sources for clinical research and treatment development has declined drastically.

Previously, the NIMH maintained a research portfolio that was relatively evenly split between basic (nonhuman) laboratory research for studying mechanisms of disease and developing novel treatments, and clinical research in humans aimed at improving care for the mentally ill. In the twenty-first century, the latter tranche has dropped to less than 10 percent of the agency's total $1.8 billion budget, the potential findings from clinical research were increasingly regarded as less important than eagerly awaited big genetic or neuroscience breakthroughs. This shift in funding priorities in the NIMH research portfolio occurred largely under the aegis of Tom Insel, who was director of the NIMH from 2002 to 2015.

After Insel left the NIMH for a position with Verily Life Sciences, a Google subsidiary using data-driven approaches to improve health care, he issued a mea culpa. In an interview with *Wired* magazine in 2017, Insel voiced regret about the fact that the money spent during his tenure hadn't led to commensurate improvements in patient outcomes. "I spent thirteen years at NIMH really pushing on the neuroscience and genetics of mental disorders," he said, "and when I look back on that, I realize that while I think I succeeded at getting lots of really cool papers published by cool scientists at fairly large costs—I think twenty billion dollars—I don't think we moved the needle in reducing suicide, reducing hospitalizations, improving recovery for the tens of millions of people who have mental illness. I hold myself accountable for that."

Insel had even gone so far as to say to audiences, "You'll think that I probably ought to be fired, and I can certainly understand that."

Such comments were unsettling and disheartening for the mental illness community to hear and particularly to me, who had known and been friends with Insel for many years.

Speaking to the *Atlantic*, Insel recalled how he'd once been giving a talk outlining the amazing things the NIMH was learning about the brain, when someone in the audience said, "You don't get it."

"Excuse me?" Insel asked. "I don't get what?"

"Our *house* is on fire," the man said, "and you're telling us about the chemistry of the paint. We need someone to focus on the fire."

Insel knew that what the man said was true. "It's not just that we don't know enough," he reflected. "The gap between what we know and what we do is unacceptable."

The current NIMH director, Joshua Gordon, is under pressure from the National Alliance on Mental Illness, the Treatment Advocacy Center, and other mental illness advocacy organizations to address this imbalance, but unless the amount of funds allocated to the NIH by the president and Congress is increased, it remains a zero-sum game.

At the same time, the private sector has substantially decreased its investment in research to develop new drugs for mental illness, including schizophrenia. In recent years, numerous companies have reduced or eliminated their drug development programs for mental disorders, shifting resources to treatments for conditions such as cancer, autoimmune disorders, and infectious and cardiovascular diseases, which they see as more scientifically tractable and financially profitable. Some companies have stayed the course, and new, smaller companies are working on drugs for mental illness, but their investments represent only a fraction of the total previously being spent.

Making the proven treatments that we already have at our disposal more available and improving their utilization requires increased funding to expand and train the workforce. Essentially, it's a matter of social and political will. The major agencies that have the authority and means to fund research and support care for people with serious mental illness are primarily the NIH, the Centers for Medicare and Medicaid Services (CMS), SAMHSA, and the US Department of Veterans Affairs (VA). Currently, the infrastructure and workforce needed to provide the scope and quality of mental health care to which we aspire and are capable of are woefully insufficient. But if the treatments and services needed were approved for reimbursement and funded by CMS, SAMHSA, and the VA, and training programs expanded, mental health services could rapidly be scaled up to the population's needs. To paraphrase the line from the movie *Field of Dreams*, "If you fund it, they will come."

We have the right to expect that the government agencies responsible for providing mental health care use the tools we have now to reduce the burden of schizophrenia and other mental disorders. For development of new, innovative, and better treatments, shouldn't the resources invested in biomedical research be organized like an investment portfolio—with the expectation of short-term, intermediate, and long-term returns? As psychiatrist and advocate E. Fuller Torrey has often argued, the emphasis on basic neuroscience and genetics *will* yield informative (and eventually transformative) results, but it will likely be a decade or more before any of these will be translated into anything that improves the plight of patients. This is not to understate the enormous value of basic research but to recognize that while we wait for it to inform our clinical practice, we should be investing money and effort into things that will help people now.

If improving the care for people with schizophrenia became an urgent national priority, we could see rapid transformation both in services and in people's lives. I was an intern at St. Vincent's Hospital in Greenwich Village when the first AIDS patients appeared. People were coming into the ER with terrible infections and no white blood cells, and we had no idea why they were sick or how to treat them. The mystery alone was enough to stigmatize the illness, but the fact that its victims were primarily gay men and intravenous drug users left those affected virtual pariahs. But as we know, an incredibly effective lobbying campaign commenced, with AIDS activists pressuring the government to fund intensive research. The US Centers for Disease Control and Prevention (CDC) recorded the first AIDS case in 1981. By 1984, the human immunodeficiency virus (HIV) had been identified as the cause of AIDS. By 1987, the first treatment, AZT, was introduced. In 1996 Dr. David Ho and his colleagues at the Aaron Diamond AIDS Research Center created the treatment regimen of giving three drugs simultaneously to patients, thereby trapping the virus, preventing its mutation, and giving rise to the HAART (highly active antiretroviral therapy) treatment for AIDS. In a short period of time, HIV/AIDS went from a fatal disease we were completely ignorant about to a chronic illness that can be managed effectively, allowing people to live normal lives. In some cases, it can even be cured now, with antiretroviral and protease inhibitor drugs.

But we don't even need to look that far back. In late December 2019 word spread of a mysterious viral outbreak in China. By early January 2020, the coronavirus genome had been mapped and the genome sequence shared with the world. The first known death from the virus had also been reported. Soon the number of cases and deaths was rising exponentially around the world, overwhelming health care systems and shutting down whole economies—but also creating an unprecedented level of motivation to find a vaccine for this virus. Which we did. In December 2020 the FDA issued its first emergency use authorization for a Covid-19 vaccine. Vaccines are normally years in development, and even people in the medical field were astonished at the speed with which scientists had been able to create a safe and effective Covid vaccine. This is the sort of thing that can happen when scientists are galvanized to act collectively and governments are committed to real financial support.

I am not naive and not requesting special favors for mental illness—only what the number of people affected and the burden on our society warrant. I know that schizophrenia doesn't resonate with most people the way cancer and heart disease do, or present us with the same dire emergency that Covid did. But as I marveled at the vaccine news, I was reminded of the medical response to AIDS, and felt—for the thousandth time since I was a young doctor and recalled my former supervisor callously advising me to allow my young patient to relapse—that we are failing people with schizophrenia. We used to fail them because we had little to offer by way of treatment. Now we're failing them because we do have effective treatments, but ensuring that they are affordable to everyone who needs them, and accessible in a single clinical setting, simply isn't a priority for our government or our health care system.

Discoveries, breakthroughs, and serendipity are not fully under our control. What we do have control over is whether we will use our existing knowledge effectively, while research generates new information, and commit ourselves as a society to taking full advantage of the currently available treatments for schizophrenia. That we have so far failed to do so means either that we don't believe they work or that we don't care about the people they could help. I cannot believe it's the latter. I think our failures are due to skepticism about the effectiveness of treatments—a lack of confidence we see reflected in government health care policies and in the funding practices of the NIH.

Unless we eliminate this biased perception and these discriminatory policies, we will not close the unacceptable gap between what we know and what we do. We will be stuck in the nightmare of the long spoons: the optimal treatments as the feast, the long spoons our reticence, skepticism, and stigma, and our will and commitment determining whether we help and nourish one another or not. My fervent dream is that we finally stop denying people the care they deserve and use the resources we have worked so long and hard to develop to relieve and prevent the suffering of people with schizophrenia.

ACKNOWLEDGMENTS

I am deeply grateful to the many people who contributed to and enabled me to write this book. This group includes the patients, family members, teachers, colleagues, public figures, and advocates whom I have known and learned from throughout my career; many of these people have worked to enhance public awareness and improve the treatment of schizophrenia. Some of their stories are told in this book. Others such as Elyn Saks, JD; Kay Jamison, PhD; and Andrew Solomon, PhD, have written brilliant first-person accounts of their mental illnesses and professional success, dramatically demonstrating the possibility of recovery from serious mental illness. Sylvia Nasar wrote a brilliant biography of a genius whose mind was laid waste by schizophrenia. Patrick Kennedy's heroic efforts in fighting for parity in services and insurance benefits for mental illness and addiction and to eliminate stigma have inspired me.

Special thanks goes to the Staglin and Lieber families, whose courage, candor, and leadership allowed me to share their stories. They have contributed importantly to advancing the awareness and treatment of schizophrenia. I am especially grateful to the Juman family, and to Martin Juman in particular, for recounting his son Michael's painful story of adoption, illness, and death.

I must thank my agent, Gail Ross, who convinced me that there would be interest in this topic and encouraged me to write the book, and who introduced me to Molly McCloskey, whose skill as a writer and experience with a mentally ill family member provided invaluable help shaping the narrative and polishing my prose when I lapsed into turgid academic style. Molly and Gabriella Dishy, an ever-helpful, multi-talented graduate student, researched numerous threads of schizophrenia's history, bringing a richness to the story that otherwise would have been lacking. Gabriella logged the numerous references and formatted the photos and figures. Amy Wachs was the most thorough and efficient genealogist I could ever have hoped to find. She provided detailed multigenerational pedigrees of families with full documentation of birth, death, and marriage certificates, prison and hospital records, ship manifests, and news items. Iris Delgado, my übercompetent administrative assistant, effectively managed my schedule throughout, enabling me to devote sufficient time to the project and acting as my liaison to the many people involved.

I am grateful to Scribner for their enthusiastic interest, beginning with their glorious publisher, Nan Graham; Valerie Steiker, who acquired the book; and Sally Howe, the chief editor, who orchestrated the development and editorial process, all the while showing great patience with the numerous delays caused by the Covid-19 pandemic, and guided the book to the finish line. Thank you, too, to Liese Mayer, whose revisions sharpened and elucidated the book's content, and to Philip Bashe for his meticulous copyediting.

Numerous colleagues generously provided valuable input during the book's development. Alan Breier, Lisa Dixon, Michael First, Ragy Girgis, Don Goff, Dan Javitt, Alice Medalia, Ilana Nossel, and Linda Rosenberg advised on many aspects of schizophrenia treatment and policy and on the OnTrackNY and NEAR treatment programs. Anthony Zoghbi explained the complexities of molecular genetics, Jonathan Javitch shared his experience in the Snyder Laboratory and his knowledge of dopamine, and Paul Appelbaum clarified aspects of the legal system with regard to mental illness. William Harris, the Shepherd Professor of History at Columbia, generously advised me on the ancient history of mental illness. Cherished colleagues Anissa Abi Dargham, Anthony Grace, and Judith Wilcox allowed me to include vignettes from their careers, and Susannah Cahalan's comments and books revealed important information about her clinical experience and a dark chapter in psychiatry's history. E. Fuller Torrey, a modern-day Dorothea Dix, offered advice and inspiration through his early readings of parts of the manuscript and his example as a prolific and impactful author with personal and professional experience with schizophrenia. Most important, thank you to the many patients who allowed me to tell their stories here, and to all those who may not appear by name but whose lives, struggles, and perseverance have informed my work and enriched my life.

I must thank my mother, whose contributions to what I have become and accomplished defy description and whose revelations about my own family history helped enormously in the writing of this book. Finally, I am most grateful to my wife for her unwavering love and support.

APPENDICES

Prologue

APPENDIX 1: TIMELINE OF HISTORICAL MILESTONES OF SCHIZOPHRENIA

ANCIENT WORLD – MIDDLE AGES

Pre-HX — Mental Illness Caused by Supernatural or Spiritual Entities

400 BC — Early Scientific Theories of Mental Illness
- **400 BC** — Humoral theory of mental illness: result of an imbalance in the body's four fluids, or humors
- **AD 100-200** — Brain-based theory of mental disturbances: association of brain with mental functions and behavior

1563 — Mental Illness Caused by Spirits, Moral Deviance, Religious Heresy
Moral, social, and religious causes of mental illness

1628 — Foundation of Medical Biology
First detailed description of the circulatory system: heart, blood vessels, and blood being pumped to organs including the brain

18TH – 19TH CENTURIES

1778 — Prescientific Theories of Mental Illness
Conceptualized mental illness as naturally occurring condition
- **1778** — Animal magnetism theory of mental illness
- **1789** — Phrenology theory of brain anatomy and function

1792 — Asylum Movement and Moral Treatment

1840 — 1840 United States Census: First Assessment of Frequency of Mental Illness

1861 — Postmortem Studies of Brain Anatomy and Neuropathology
- **1861** — Mapped the brain's anatomy
- **1892** — Described fronto-temporal dementia (Pick's disease)
- **1906** — Identified the senile plaques and neurofibrillary tangles, now known as the hallmarks of Alzheimer's disease

Foundation of Modern Neuroscience — **1873**
- Development of Golgi stains — **1873**
- Development of the neuron doctrine — **1888**

- **1909** — Established a cartography of the brain into functional anatomical regions
- **1915** — Described pathomorphology in postmortem brains of schizophrenia: found structural pathology in 90% of schizophrenia cases

1891 — Definition of Dementia Praecox
Identified illness now called schizophrenia and creation of a nosology of mental illness

Catamnestic Studies of Schizophrenia — **1896**
Described the different trajectories of the natural history of schizophrenia

20TH – 21ST CENTURIES

1908 — Dementia Praecox Redefined as Schizophrenia

Discovered Cause of General Paresis of — **1913**
the Insane
Isolated the spirochete that caused neurosyphilis in postmortem brain tissue

1916 — Early Theories of Schizophrenia
- **1916** — Genetic theory of schizophrenia
- **1962** — High emotional expression in the family
- **1962** — Stress-Diathesis Model

Somatic Treatments of Schizophrenia — **1918**
- Malaria therapy — **1918**
- Psychosurgery — **1936**
- Development of electroconvulsive therapy — **1939**

1927 — In-Vivo Structural Brain Abnormalities
- **1976** — First CT study of schizophrenia showing ventricular enlargement
- **1989** — First MRI study of temporal lobe volume abnormalities in schizophrenia
- **1990** — MRI studies demonstrated gray matter volume abnormalities in schizophrenia
- **1990** — In-vivo imaging demonstration of reduced size of the hippocampus

Environmental Effects on Risk of Schizophrenia — **1934**
- Obstetrical complications — **1934**
- Social environment/ethnicity/migration — **1965**
- Paternal age — **1983**
- Drug abuse — **1987**
- Infections/pathogens — **1988**
- Maternal stress — **1998**
- Nutritional effects — **2011**

Neurophysiologic Manifestations of — **1938**
Schizophrenia
- Eye-tracking studies demonstrated (epiphenomenal) — **1973** biologic features
- Mismatch negativity: demonstrated biologic features — **1991** in high-risk individuals
- Decreased neuronal synchrony and gamma-band activity — **2000**

1938 — Epidemiologic Genetic Studies
- **1938** — Schizophrenia more frequent in family members of patients
- **1946** — Twin studies show increased concordance for schizophrenia among monozygotic compared to dizygotic twins
- **1966** — Adoption studies of offspring of people with schizophrenia found genes had greater effect than environment
- **1967** — Polygenic theory of schizophrenia by Gottesman and Shields
- **1987** — Sporadic vs. familial schizophrenia

Clubhouse Movement Established in the — **1943**
United States

1949 — Pharmacologic Treatments of Schizophrenia
- **1949** — Discovery of chlorpromazine: development of antipsychotic drugs
- **1952** — First demonstrations of efficacy of chlorpromazine

Psychosocial Treatments for Schizophrenia — **1952**

Cognitive behavioral therapy — 1952
Social skills training — 1976
Case management — 1978
Psychoeducation — 1980
Cognitive remediation — 1993
Supportive employment — 1994

Drug-Induced Schizophrenia — 1958
Chronic psychostimulant use induces sustained schizophrenia — 1958
Chronic PCP use induces sustained schizophrenia — 1992

Dopamine Hypothesis — 1974
First scientifically credible pathophysiological theory of schizophrenia

Cognitive Impairments — 1977
Identified attentional disturbances in schizophrenia as symptom of the illness — 1977
Impairment of cognitive functions as a core pathologic dimension of schizophrenia — 1978
Demonstrated relationship between cognitive impairment and functional capacity — 1996
Demonstrated severe dementia in elderly chronically ill schizophrenia patients — 1999

Models of Care — 1980
Assertive community treatment — 1980
Early intervention — 1992
Assisted outpatient treatment — 2000
Coordinated specialty care of first-episode psychosis — 2015

Schizophrenia Subtypes — 1982
Two syndrome topology of schizophrenia — 1982
Kraepelinian schizophrenia subtype: defined based on symptoms, course, and biologic features (e.g., brain morphology, frontal blood flow) — 1987

Neuropathology of Schizophrenia — 1984
Reduced volume of the hippocampus — 1985
Absence of neurodegeneration and neural injury in postmortem brains — 1998
Reduced cortical dendritic length and spine density — 1998
GABA dysfunction of interneurons in hippocampus and frontal cortex — 1999
Neuropil hypothesis of schizophrenia: reduction in focal cortical volume due to neuropil not cell bodies — 1999

Neurodegenerative Hypothesis of Schizophrenia — 1991
Pathophysiological theory of schizophrenia based on clinical neuroimaging studies of the progressive course of the illness, inspiring early detection and intervention research

Autoimmune Encephalitis — 2001
Autoimmune disorders affecting brain function can mimic schizophrenia

1971 — First use of long-acting injectable antipsychotic medicine: reduction in nonadherence and relapse
1974 — Clozapine, first atypical antipsychotic drug: studies of efficacy and safety
1975 — Discovery of clozapine's serious adverse effects (agranulocytosis, myocarditis)
1988 — Study showed clozapine's superior efficacy in treatment-refractory patients
1991 — Introduction of second-generation (atypical) antipsychotics
2020 — First non-D2 receptor targeted drug treatments: SEP363856 (TAAR-1 agonist) and xanomeline/trospium (M1M4 agonist)

1963 — **Community Mental Health Act Passed**
Legislation that stimulated deinstitutionalization

1972 — **Formulation of Operational Criteria for Diagnosis of Mental and Substance Use Disorders**
1980 — Diagnostic and Statistical Manual of Mental Disorders, 3rd edition: formal codification by American Psychiatric Association for clinical use and alignment with International Classification of Diseases (ICD)

1974 — **Functional Brain Abnormalities in Schizophrenia**
1974 — Hypofrontality: reduced cerebral blood flow in frontal cortex resting state
1984 — Hypoactivation of frontal cortex on Wisconsin Card Sort activation
1986 — PET studies determined D2 occupancy levels of antipsychotics at therapeutic dosing
1996 — SPECT and PET demonstrated dopamine dysregulation: first direct in vivo confirmation of the dopamine hypothesis (found excess striatal dopamine release)
1996 — Functional imaging studies demonstrated increased neural activity in CA1 region of the hippocampal formation in schizophrenia
2001 — fMRI studies demonstrated working memory/executive function deficits
2014 — fMRI/resting state & connectivity: identified network abnormalities within the frontoparietal control network

1980 — **Longitudinal Brain Abnormalities**
1991 — MRI studies show progressive brain morphologic changes over the course of schizophrenia

1981 — **Treatment Outcomes of First-Episode Psychosis**
Prospective studies of early stages of schizophrenia demonstrated good treatment response, reduction in duration of untreated psychosis, and feasability and efficacy of specialized treatment programs

1982 — **Neurodevelopmental Hypotheses of Schizophrenia**
1983 — Synaptic pruning hypothesis
1987 — Neurodevelopmental hypothesis

1984 — **Epidemiologic Studies of Schizophrenia**
1984 — World Health Organization study of population frequencies of schizophrenia: epidemiologic studies in ten countries utilizing objective diagnostic criteria
1994 — Epidemiologic Catchment Area Study: epidemiologic study rates of mental illness in the United States

1987 — **Glutamate Hypothesis**
Pathophysiological theory of schizophrenia
1990 — Integration of dopamine and glutamate theories
1991 — PCP model of schizophrenia implicates NMDA receptor hypofunction correction
1998 — NMDA antagonism increases synaptic glutamate

1997 — **Reduced Life Expectancy of Schizophrenia Patients**
1997 — Due to medical comorbidities and suicide
2007 — Associated with lack of antipsychotic medication treatment

2008 — **Molecular Genetics**
2008 — Rare chromosomal deletions and duplications increase risk of schizophrenia
2009 — First evidence of schizophrenia polygenes
2012 — Genomewide Association Study (GWAS) on schizophrenia uses Genomewide Complex Trait Analysis to infer presence of polygenes
2012 — Copy number variation (CNV) in psychiatric genetics
2014 — Polygenic burden of rare disruptive mutations in schizophrenia

Chapter 4: Medical Specialization

APPENDIX 2: ACADEMIC PEDIGREE

Pedigree of Post-Enlightenment Brain Doctors

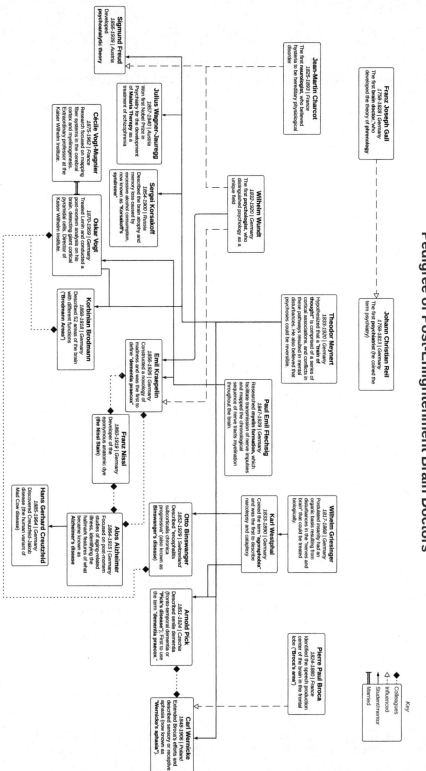

Franz Joseph Gall
1758-1828 | Germany
The first **brain doctor,** who developed the theory of **phrenology**

Johann Christian Reil
1759-1813 | Germany
The first **psychiatrist** (he coined the term psychiatry)

Jean-Martin Charcot
1825-1893 | France
The first **neurologist,** who believed hysteria to be hereditary physiological disorder

Sigmund Freud
1856-1939 | Austria
Developed **psychoanalytic theory**

Julius Wagner-Jauregg
1857-1940 | Austria
Won first Nobel Prize in Psychiatry for the development of **Malaria Therapy** as a treatment of schizophrenia

Cécile Vogt-Mugnier
1875-1962 | France
Research focused on mapping fiber systems in the cerebral cortex and myelinogenesis. Extraordinary professor at the Kaiser Wilhelm Institute.

Sergei Korsakoff
1854-1900 | Russia
Described the brain atrophy and memory loss caused by excessive alcohol consumption, now known as **"Korsakoff's syndrome"**

Wilhelm Wundt
1832-1920 | Germany
The first psychologist, who distinguished psychology as a unique field

Oskar Vogt
1870-1959 | Germany
Treated Lenin and conducted a post-mortem analysis on his brain, detecting giant cortical pyramidal cells. Director of Kaiser Wilhelm Institute.

Korbinian Brodmann
1868-1918 | Germany
Described 52 areas of the brain with different functions (**Brodmann Areas**)

Theodor Meynert
1833-1920 | Germany
Hypothesized that a **"train of thought"** is comprised of a series of cortical associations, and conflicts in these pathways resulted in mental disturbances. He also believed that psychoses could be reversible.

Paul Emil Flechsig
1847-1929 | Germany
Researched **myelin formation,** which facilitate transmission of nerve impulses and mapped the chronological sequence of nerve tracts myelination throughout the brain.

Emil Kraepelin
1856-1926 | Germany
Constructed a nosology of madness and was the first to define **"dementia praecox"**

Franz Nissl
1860-1919 | Germany
Developer of the eponymous anatomic dye (**the Nissl Stain**)

Karl Westphal
1833-1890 | Germany
Coined the term **"agoraphobia"** and was the first to describe narcolepsy and cataplexy

Wilhelm Griesinger
1817-1868 | Germany
Postulated that insanity had an organic basis resulting from disturbances in the "nerves and brain" that could be treated biologically.

Otto Binswanger
1852-1929 | Switzerland
Described "encephalitis subcorticalis chronica progressiva" (also known as Binswanger's disease)

Alois Alzheimer
1864-1915 | Germany
Focused on post-mortem studies of aging-related illness, identifying the hallmark features of what became known as **Alzheimer's disease**

Hans Gerhard Creutzfeld
1885-1964 | Germany
Discovered Creutzfeld-Jakob disease (the human variant of Mad Cow disease)

Arnold Pick
1851-1924 | Czechia
Described senile dementia (fronto-temporal dementia or **"Pick's disease"**). First to use the term **"dementia praecox."**

Pierre Paul Broca
1824-1880 | France
Identified the speech production center of the brain in the frontal lobe (**"Broca's area"**)

Carl Wernicke
1848-1906 | Poland
Extended Broca's efforts and described sensory or receptive aphasia (now known as **"Wernicke's aphasia"**).

Key

◆ Colleagues
◁--- Influenced
⊢⊣ Student/mentor
⊨ Married

Chapter 10: The Taxonomist of Mental Illness
APPENDIX 3: *DSM-II*: DEFINITION OF SCHIZOPHRENIA*

The second edition of the *DSM* was the operative system until 1980. Contrast the criteria for schizophrenia in the *DSM-II* to the more detailed, explicit criteria in *DSM-III* that follows. The current edition is the *DSM-5*, published in 2013.

295 Schizophrenia

This large category includes a group of disorders manifested by characteristic disturbances of thinking, mood and behavior. Disturbances in thinking are marked by alterations of concept formation which may lead to misinterpretation of reality and sometimes to delusions and hallucinations, which frequently appear psychologically self-protective. Corollary mood changes include ambivalent, constricted and inappropriate emotional responsiveness and loss of empathy with others. Behavior may be withdrawn, regressive and bizarre. The schizophrenias, in which the mental status is attributable primarily to a *thought* disorder, are to be distinguished from the *Major affective illnesses* (q.v.) which are dominated by a *mood* disorder. The *Paranoid states* (q.v.) are distinguished from schizophrenia by the narrowness of their distortions of reality and by the absence of other psychotic symptoms.

295.0 Schizophrenia, simple type

This psychosis is characterized chiefly by a slow and insidious reduction of external attachments and interests and by apathy and indifference leading to impoverishment of interpersonal relations, mental deterioration, and adjustment on a lower level of functioning.

295.1 Schizophrenia, hebephrenic type

This psychosis is characterized by disorganized thinking, shallow and inappropriate affect, unpredictable giggling, silly and regressive behavior and mannerisms, and frequent hypochondriacal complaints.

295.2   Schizophrenia, catatonic type
295.23   Schizophrenia, catatonic type, excited
295.24   Schizophrenia, catatonic type, withdrawn

It is frequently possible and useful to distinguish two subtypes of catatonic schizophrenia. One is marked by excessive and sometimes violent motor activity and excitement and the other by generalized inhibition manifested by stupor, mutism, negativism, or waxy flexibility.

---

* Reprinted with permission from the *Diagnostic and Statistical Manual of Mental Disorders*, Second Edition (Copyright © 1968). American Psychiatric Association. All Rights Reserved.

295.3 Schizophrenia, paranoid type

This type of schizophrenia is characterized primarily by the presence of perse-cutory or grandiose delusions, often associated with hallucinations. Excessive religiosity is sometimes seen. The patient's attitude is frequently hostile and aggressive, and his behavior tends to be consistent with his delusions.

295.4 Acute schizophrenic episode

This diagnosis does not apply to acute episodes of schizophrenic disorders de-scribed elsewhere. This condition is distinguished by the acute onset of schizo-phrenic symptoms, often associated with confusion, perplexity, ideas of reference, emotional turmoil, dreamlike dissociation, and excitement, depression, or fear. The acute onset distinguishes this condition from simple schizophrenia. In time these patients may take on the characteristics of catatonic, hebephrenic or para-noid schizophrenia, in which case their diagnosis should be changed accordingly. In many cases the patient recovers within weeks, but sometimes his disorganiza-tion becomes progressive. More frequently remission is followed by recurrence.

295.5 Schizophrenia, latent type

This category is for patients having clear symptoms of schizophrenia but no history of a psychotic schizophrenic episode. Disorders sometimes designated as incipient, pre-psychotic, pseudoneurotic, pseudopsychopathic, or border-line schizophrenia are categorized here.

295.6 Schizophrenia, residual type

This category is for patients showing signs of schizophrenia but who, follow-ing a psychotic schizophrenic episode, are no longer psychotic.

295.7 Schizophrenia, schizo-affective type

This category is for patients showing a mixture of schizophrenic symptoms and pronounced elation or depression. Within this category it may be useful to distinguish excited from depressed types as follows:

295.73 Schizophrenia, schizo-affective type, excited
295.74 Schizophrenia, schizo-affective type, depressed
295.8 Schizophrenia, childhood type

This category is for cases in which schizophrenic symptoms appear before puberty. This condition may be manifested by autistic, atypical, and withdrawn behavior; failure to develop identity separate from the mother's; and general un-evenness, gross immaturity and inadequacy in development. These developmental defects may result in mental retardation, which should also be diagnosed.

295.90   Schizophrenia, chronic undifferentiated type

This category is for patients who show mixed schizophrenic symptoms and who present definite schizophrenic thought, affect and behavior not classifiable under the other types of schizophrenia.

295.99   Schizophrenia, other [and unspecified] types

This category is for any type of schizophrenia not previously described. (In DSM-I "Schizophrenic reaction, chronic undifferentiated type" included this category and also what is now called *Schizophrenia, latent type* and *Schizophrenia, chronic undifferentiated type.*)

APPENDIX 4: *DSM-III*: DIAGNOSTIC CRITERIA FOR A SCHIZOPHRENIC DISORDER*

A.   At least one of the following during a phase of the illness:

    (1)   Bizarre delusions (content is patently absurd and has *no* possible basis in fact), such as delusions of being controlled, thought broadcasting, thought insertion, or thought withdrawal

    (2)   somatic, grandiose, religious, nihilistic, or other delusions without persecutory or jealous content

    (3)   delusions with persecutory or jealous content if accompanied by hallucinations of any type

    (4)   auditory hallucinations in which either a voice keeps up a running commentary on the individual's behavior or thoughts, or two or more voices converse with each other

    (5)   auditory hallucinations on several occasions with content of more than one or two words, having no apparent relation to depression or elation

    (6)   incoherence, marked loosening of associations, markedly illogical thinking, or marked poverty of content of speech if associated with at least one of the following:

        (a) blunted, flat, or inappropriate affect

        (b) delusions or hallucinations

        (c) catatonic or other grossly disorganized behavior

B.   Deterioration from a previous level of functioning in such areas as work, social relations, and self-care

---

C. **Duration: Continuous signs of the illness for at least six months at some time during the person's life, with some signs of the illness at present. The six-month period must include an active phase during which there were symptoms from A, with or without a prodromal or residual phase, as defined below:**

Prodromal phase: A clear deterioration in functioning before the active phase of the illness not due to a disturbance in mood or to a Substance Use Disorder and involving at least *two* of the symptoms noted below.

Residual phase: Persistence, following the active phase of the illness, of at least *two* of the symptoms noted below, not due to a disturbance in mood or to a Substance Use Disorder.

Prodromal or Residual Symptoms:

(1) social isolation or withdrawal

(2) marked impairment in role functioning as wage-earner, student, or homemaker

(3) markedly peculiar behavior (e.g., collecting garbage, talking to self in public, or hoarding food)

(4) marked impairment in personal hygiene and grooming

(5) blunted, flat, or inappropriate affect

(6) digressive, vague, overelaborate, circumstantial, or metaphorical speech

(7) odd or bizarre ideation, or magical thinking, e.g., superstitiousness, clairvoyance, telepathy, "sixth sense," "others can feel my feelings," over-valued ideas, ideas of reference

(8) unusual perceptual experiences, e.g., recurrent illusions, sensing the presence of a force or person not actually present

Examples: Six months of prodromal symptoms with one week of symptoms from A; no prodromal symptoms with six months of symptoms from A; no prodromal symptoms with two weeks of symptoms from A and six months of residual symptoms; six months of symptoms from A, apparently followed by several years of complete remission, with one week of symptoms in A in current episode

D. **The full depressive or manic syndrome (criteria A and B of major depressive or manic episode), if present, developed after any psychotic symptoms, or was brief in duration relative to the duration of the psychotic symptoms in A.**

E. **Onset of prodromal or active phase of the illness before age 45.**

F. **Not due to any Organic Mental Disorder or Mental Retardation.**

Chapter 12: Am I My Genes?
APPENDIX 5: STAGLIN FAMILY PEDIGREE

Please see the author's website, **https://jeffreyliebermanmd.com**, for the maternal and paternal Staglin family pedigrees.

Chapter 16: Peeling the Onion
APPENDIX 6: CLINICAL EVALUATION AND DIAGNOSIS

I. **In assessing the PPHx the following information should be obtained:**

- What was the nature and consistency of symptoms and diagnoses over the course of the illness?

- What was the frequency and circumstances of previous relapses?

- Were previous relapses due to . . .

    i) interruption of maintenance treatment?

    ii) breakthrough of symptoms while on maintenance medication?

    iii) precipitating event (traumatic experience, substance abuse)?

- What intercurrent complications has the patient experienced, such as depression, suicidal behavior, substance abuse, or medical comorbidities?

- What treatments were received, for how long, and at what doses? Were they effective, did they cause side effects? Were they adherent to treatment?

II. **Following the clinical histories the next step in the clinical evaluation is to review the Developmental and Social Histories.**

A. DEVELOPMENTAL HISTORY

- Is patient adopted or biologic offspring? If the latter, how old were the parents?

- Was the conception natural or assisted? If the latter, in-vitro or fertility?

- Was the pregnancy complicated by . . .

    i) eclampsia?

    ii) maternal drug use?

    iii) fetal exposure to toxins or infectious pathogens?

- Were there any birth complications?

    i) prematurity

    ii) breech position

    iii) birth trauma (e.g., high forceps delivery)

    iv) hypoxia (e.g., umbilical cord wrapped around neck)

    v) low Apgar scores

    vi) Did newborn go to NICU?

    vii) Did the newborn go home with the mother?

- Postnatal period, infancy, childhood, adolescence:

    i) What was the baby's temperament?

    ii) Was baby breast fed?

    iii) Did baby grow normally?

    iv) Did baby reach developmental milestones on schedule (e.g., walk, talk, toilet train)?

    v) Any history of bed wetting, night terrors, separation anxiety, and/or school phobias?

    vi) How was their academic performance in school?

    vii) Were there any behavioral or learning difficulties?

B. SOCIAL HISTORY

- Did the patient relate well to people?
- How is their relationship with family?
    - ◆) How often do they see them?
- Do they have many friends?
    - ◆) Did they have a best friend?
- Do they have romantic relationships?
    - ◆) Are they or have they ever been married?
- Do they have children?
- Do they have recreational activities?
    - ◆) What are they?
- Were they athletic and liked sports?
- Have they ever used/are they currently using recreational drugs?
    - ◆) What type?
        - ◆) Did they have a euphoric or dysphoric effect?
        - ◆) At what age did they start?
    - ◆) How long has it continued?
    - ◆) What amounts and frequencies?
    - ◆) Were they dependent?
- What was their educational and employment history?
    - ◆) Were they good students?
    - ◆) How far did they get in school?
    - ◆) Are they employed? If so, where and for how long have they worked at current and prior job?
- Did they ever get in trouble with the law?
- Were there any abrupt changes in the pattern of above social activities?

III. MENTAL STATUS EXAM

- **Level of Consciousness**

    a) Is the patient alert, attentive, distracted, responsive, obtunded?

    b) Orientation in person, place, and time

- **Appearance and General Behavior**

    a) Do they appear neatly dressed, well groomed, calm, cooperative or undernourished, disheveled, distracted, inattentive, agitated, aggressive, have poor hygiene and significant body odor?

- **Motor Activity**

    a) Manifestations associated with schizophrenia are infrequent

    b) Can exhibit rigid and bizarre postures, or unusual mannerisms

- **Speech**

    a) Coherence, syntax, rate, hesitancy, and volume. Depression may cause a patient to speak slowly and softly; with mania, to speak rapidly and loudly; and with schizophrenia, to speak in a rambling illogical way that is difficult to follow and at times incoherent.

    b) There are some forms of speech that are characteristic of schizophrenia. Clang associations refers to using rhyming words in a nonsensical fashion. In severe cases of illness speech can be so incoherent that their speech is characterized as word salad.

- **Affect and Mood**

    a) Can be assessed by asking patients to describe how they have been feeling. The patient's tone of voice, posture, body movements and facial expressions are all considered. Mood (emotional state reported by the patient) and affect (patient's expression of emotional state as observed by the interviewer) should be assessed. Affect and its range (i.e., full, constricted, flat) should be noted as well as the appropriateness of affect to thought content (e.g., patient smiling while discussing a tragic event).

    b) Patients with schizophrenia often exhibit flat and/or inappropriate affect

- **Thought Organization and Content**

    a) Questions are asked to draw the patient out and then observe the organization and content of their answers.

    b) Thought organization is reflected by the patient's speech, whether it's coherent, logical, consistent and orderly in syntax and content. Characteristics of schizophrenia are rambling speech on loosely associated or disconnected topics.

    c) Abnormal content may take the form of the following:

        i) Ideas of reference (notions that everyday occurrences have special meaning or significance personally intended for or directed to the patient). These are usually a precursor to delusions.

        ii) Ideation: over-valued ideas, obsessions (recurrent, persistent, unwanted, intrusive thoughts but that patient knows are not true or realistic), delusions (false, fixed beliefs) which can be conventional (my wife is cheating on me, everyone in the office is against me) or bizarre (aliens have abducted me and removed my brain).

- **Perception**

    a) Patients are often self-referential perceiving random events to be specific to them. For example, thinking people on television are talking to them directly, or walking in the street thinking that the passersby are looking or talking about them. Patients with paranoid delusions are likely to perceive things in a paranoid way, perceiving people as conspiring against or wanting to hurt them.

    b) The more extreme perceptual abnormalities are illusions and hallucinations:

    i) *Illusions* are perceiving real stimuli in a distorted and self-referential way (e.g., hearing someone shouting and thinking they are calling your name or saying something about you)

    ii) *Hallucinations* are perceiving sensory stimuli that are not real. These can occur in any sensory modality (hearing, seeing, feeling, smelling, tasting) but most commonly are auditory in the form of voices commenting on the person. The most ominous form are command hallucinations where the voices are directing the person to do things including possibly violent acts.

- **Insight and Judgment**

    i) *Insight* refers to a patient's understanding of their illness. Patients often lack or have limited insight as they believe their symptoms are real despite all evidence to the contrary.

    ii) *Judgment* is often linked to insight and refers to a patient's ability to make good decisions. For example, patients that repeat the same mistakes over and over or refuse to take medications show poor judgment.

- **Cognition**

    a) *Attention*: Assess by asking patient to spell a word forward and backward, or count backward from 70 by 7's.

    b) Memory subdivides into many forms:

    i) *Immediate recall*: Repeat a string of numbers

    ii) *Delayed recall*: Ask patient to remember three objects and then recall them at the end of the interview

    iii) *Recent memory*: Ask patient what they had for breakfast today

    iv) *Long-term memory*: Ask patient about past events in their life like "what high school they attended" or "what was the name of their pet."

v) *Abstraction* (refers to patient's ability to understand meaning and concepts): Can assess by asking similarity of objects (apple and orange are fruit) or meaning of proverbs (people in glass houses shouldn't throw stones).

- **Further assessment of cognition can be aided by the use of the two most common bedside instruments that require about 10 to 15 minutes to administer:**

    a) Montreal Cognitive Assessment (MoCA)

    b) Mini-Mental State Examination

IV. ADDITIONAL TESTS

STANDARD LABORATORY TESTS OF BLOOD AND URINE

- CBC with differential
- Erythrocyte sedimentation rate
- Electrolytes
- Renal function tests (BUN, creatinine)
- Glucose
- Liver function tests (ALT, AST, Bilirubin, Albumin, GGT)
- Calcium, phosphorous
- Thyroid function test (TSH; if abnormal T3/T4)
- C-reactive protein
- Sedimentation rate
- Anti-nuclear antibody
- Thyroid peroxidase antibody
- Globulin level: albumin/globulin ratio
- Syphilis (Fluorescent Treponemal Antibody)
- HIV
- Hepatitis
- Serum vitamin levels (Vitamin A, B3, B12, D)
- Serum copper and Ceruloplasmin
- Urinalysis
- Urine toxicology screen

DIAGNOSTIC PROCEDURES

- EKG
- Chest X-ray
- EEG
- MRI

TESTS FOR AUTOIMMUNITY AND SPONGIFORM ENCEPHALOPATHIES

- Antibody screening should be performed in young people presenting with psychosis, seizures and cognitive disturbance
- Serum antibody testing is 75%–97% sensitive/specific; CSF antibody testing is 100% sensitive/specific
- NMDA receptor antibodies present in 6.5% of first episode psychosis cases

- Test for Hashimoto's encephalitis (HE), also known as SREAAT (steroid responsive encephalopathy associated with autoimmune thyroiditis). Psychosis is present in less than 25% of HE cases.
- Anti-thyroid antibodies are present in less than 10% of cases of schizophrenia
- Brain biopsies are rarely done

SPECIAL TESTS TO INFORM THE DIAGNOSIS OF SCHIZOPHRENIA

- MRI
- PET scan
- Genotyping: Exome or whole genome sequencing

Chapter 19: How We (Should) Treat Schizophrenia

APPENDIX 7: LIST OF ANTIPSYCHOTIC DRUGS CLINICALLY IN USE

First Generation		Second Generation		Third Generation		International
1957	Chlorpromazine	1989	Clozapine	2012	Aripiprazole	Amisulpride
1957	Perphenazine	1993	Risperidone*	2015	Brexpiprazole	Sulpiride
1959	Trifluoperazine	1996	Olanzapine*	2015	Cariprazine	Zotepine
1960	Fluphenazine*	1997	Quetiapine	2020	Lumateperone	Sertindole
1962	Thioridazine	2001	Ziprasidone	2020	Xanomeline (M1, M4 agonist)	Blonanserin
1967	Haloperidol*	2006	Paliperidone*			Zuclopenthixol
1967	Thiothixene	2009	Iloperidone	2022	SEP-363856 (TAAR-1 agonist)	Clopenthixol
1974	Molindone	2009	Asenapine			Levomepromazine
1975	Loxapine	2010	Lurasidone			Penfluridol
1984	Pimozide					

*indicates drug comes in long-acting form

APPENDIX 8: PSYCHOSOCIAL THERAPIES

Psychosocial Treatment	Indication (what are they used for)	Brief Description
Case Management	A collaborative process that connects patients who require intensive levels of care to the services they need	Case management achieves patient wellness and autonomy through five core functions: assessment, planning, advocacy, service linkage, and evaluation. Case manager uses a needs-based approach to connect patients to the appropriate providers and resources through a continuum of health care resources. Some models of case management also include coping skills and family education, crisis intervention, and vocational activities.
Cognitive Behavioral Therapy (CBT)	Reduction of positive and negative symptoms	In CBT, the therapist works within the patient's framework of reality and instructs patients to examine the evidence for their distressing beliefs. The goal is to encourage patients to reality test and dispel fears and thoughts for which there is no objective evidence.
Cognitive Remediation	Enhance executive functioning and social cognition to improve interpersonal relationships and vocational functioning	Cognitive remediation utilizes cognitive training and exercises to teach and enhance basic cognitive functions using computer-based programs and paper-based tasks.
Family Therapy	Serves multiple purposes including: Educating the family and patient about the nature of the illness; resolving intra-family conflict and stressful emotional tone of family interactions; and providing coping strategies and support to family members who are caregivers to patients.	Mental health provider meets with family members with or without the patient to address one or more of the indicated purposes of the therapy.

Peer Support	Peers are patients whose lived experience enables them to provide unique assistance to patients to enhance their engagement, acceptance and response to treatment. Among the various goals that peer support can address is to enhance patients' knowledge, skills, confidence, and attitudes for managing health and treatment to improve patients' health, better quality of life (QOL), engage in more health care practices, and increase treatment satisfaction.	Peer support refers to the help and support that people with lived experience of mental illness can provide to one another. To do so they must undergo a transition from patient to provider with appropriate instruction and training. While the evidence for efficacy is limited, there is a subjective benefit and no adverse effects or consequences associated with peer support.
Psychoeducation	Providing didactic information to patients and families about the nature of their illness. This is needed given the limited awareness of people about mental illness.	Used as an adjunct to other interventions, the treatment team provides the patient (and often the family as well) information regarding schizophrenia, its treatment, management of behaviors, problem-solving, coping skills, and community resources.
Social Skills Training	Improve psychosocial functioning through communication abilities to better equip patients with the skills needed to achieve their interpersonal and vocational goals, and to deal with stressful life events	Social skills training utilizes behavioral therapy principles and techniques to teach individuals how to communicate their emotions thereby improving their interpersonal relationships and ability to live independently. Some of the learning-based procedures used include problem identification (identifying barriers to personal goals), role playing social interactions, social modeling (a therapist or peer demonstrating desired behaviors), and homework assignments to motivate patients to enact their skills in real-life scenarios.

Substance Abuse Treatment	For individuals with comorbid substance abuse	Various strategies are used to address substance abuse in individuals with schizophrenia and should be identified and administered according to the patient's needs. Strategies include family intervention, skills training, cognitive therapy, motivational interventions, lifestyle changes, and development of substance refusal. Notably, though 12-step approaches are commonly used, they do not have an integrated approach to disorders, have inflexible goals, and sometimes even oppose medication, thus making them less effective for many patients.
Suicide Prevention	To prevent suicide in individuals with schizophrenia, careful management of psychotic symptoms, comorbid depression, and substance use disorders is essential. Additional risk factors include younger age, male sex, being unemployed, and being well-educated.	The best suicide prevention method is the provision of and compliance with comprehensive treatment. Prevention efforts should focus on delivering the best possible therapy to manage psychotic symptoms and comorbid depression and/or substance misuse, alongside educating health care providers about suicide prevention strategies. Additional efforts should focus on enhancing medication compliance, as studies suggest that antipsychotics and antidepressants reduce suicide risk.
Supported Education	Aims to provide individuals with assistance to develop and achieve academic goals in community-based educational settings.	Similar to supported employment, supported education provides students with schizophrenia the skills and support needed to achieve academic success. There are three models of supported education: 1. *Self-contained classrooms*, in which young adults attend classes in a postsecondary school setting but are not integrated into regular classes. While they may or may not receive credit, they receive

		support from special program staff and can utilize the educational institution's resources. Eventually they typically move into integrated classrooms. 2. *On-site support*: Students attend and receive credit for regular classes while receiving support from the educational institution, usually from disability or college counseling services. 3. *Mobile support*: Similar to on-site support, students attend and receive credit for regular classes but receive support from community-based mental health services. These services can be provided either on or off site.
Supported Employment	Based on the philosophy that anyone can gain competitive employment, supported employment aims to help individuals with schizophrenia who want to work develop realistic goals and seek and maintain employment	Supported employment begins with high-quality vocational rehabilitation (see below), which includes an assessment of the patient's needs and the provision of a structured work skills training program. Subsequently, the patient is placed in an already-established network of employers willing to accept patients for work. Throughout their employment, individuals receive support to maintain their job.
Supportive and Problem-Oriented Psychotherapy	Aims to assist individuals in maintaining their existing situation or with their coping abilities.	Considered the "treatment of choice" for most people with mental illness, individuals receiving supported therapy receive general support rather than specific forms of psychotherapy (such as CBT), in which the provider will listen to the concerns of the patient, provide encouragement, and assist with basic daily living tasks.

	Aims to enhance the work capacities of individuals living with schizophrenia.	Vocational rehabilitation provides individuals with the skills and support needed to obtain competitive employment by teaching them job-related skills and facilitating the acquisition of a job (paid or volunteer). These programs can be found in hospitals, sheltered workshops, assertive case management, psychosocial rehabilitation (for example, prevocational training or transitional employment), supported employment, and counseling and education.
Vocational Rehabilitation		

APPENDIX 9: INNOVATIVE MODELS OF CARE

Psychosocial Treatment	Indication (what they are used for)	Brief Description
Assertive Community Treatment (ACT)	For those who have transferred out of inpatient care but still require the same level of care and may be noncompliant or nonadherent to treatment, or are at high risk of relapse.	ACT integrates pharmacotherapy, rehabilitation, and social services, and is delivered directly in the community by a multidisciplinary team of mental health professionals. Additional features of ACT include assertive community outreach to maintain treatment engagement, continuous responsibility and staff continuity, frequent albeit brief contacts with the patient, and a high staff-to-client caseload.

Collaborative Care	For individuals with comorbid physical and mental health conditions.	Collaborative care refers to the integration of primary care and specialist health care (forming a mental health treatment team), in which a patient's treatment team works together in a collaborative effort to meet both the physical and mental health needs of the patient.
Coordinated Specialty Care (CSC)	For youth, adolescents, and young adults in the early stages of psychosis.	A community-based and recovery-oriented approach, CSC employs a multidisciplinary treatment team and combines individual and family therapy, case management, supportive employment and education services, psychoeducation, and collaborative care.
Crisis Intervention Models	For patients in crisis (experiencing acute psychotic symptoms, for example) in order to prevent hospitalization (if possible) and further symptom deterioration.	Crisis intervention is a twenty-four-hour service that can be provided either at home by a mobile unit or in a community setting (such as a hospital or residential care facility). Using a multidisciplinary team, crisis intervention models may employ a combination of drug treatment, psychotherapy, and psychoeducation to stabilize a patient.
Critical Time Intervention (CTI)	For those who are in a critical transitional period, such as transitioning from homelessness, prison, or a psychiatric hospital and back into the community.	With similarities to ACT and case management, CTI is a time-limited approach that connects patients to community services, fosters a community support network, and assists them in developing independent living skills. The primary goal of CTI is to set up a secure and independently functioning support network.

APPENDIX 10: NOTES

DSM-II: Definition of Schizophrenia: American Psychiatric Association, *Diagnostic and Statistical Manual of Mental Disorders*, 2nd ed. (Washington, DC: American Psychiatric Association, 1968), 33–35.

DSM-III: Diagnostic Criteria for a Schizophrenic Disorder: American Psychiatric Association, *Diagnostic and Statistical Manual of Mental Disorders*, 3rd ed. (Washington, DC: American Psychiatric Association, 1980), 188–90.

Staglin Family Pedigree: Amy Wachs, "Staglin Genealogy Research" (unpublished report, February 21, 2021), PDF file.

Case Management: Yvonne Lidberg and Bo Liljenberg, "Two-Year Outcome of Team-Based Intensive Case Management for Patients with Schizophrenia," *Psychiatric Services* 46, no. 12 (December 1995): 1263–66; see also Jack E. Scott and Lisa B. Dixon, "Assertive Community Treatment and Case Management for Schizophrenia," *Schizophrenia Bulletin* 21, no. 4 (January 1995): 657–68.

Cognitive Behavioral Therapy (CBT): Aaron T. Beck, "Successful Outpatient Psychotherapy of a Chronic Schizophrenic with a Delusion Based on Borrowed Guilt," *Psychiatry* 15, no. 3 (August 1952): 305–12; see also Wai Tong Chien et al., "Current Approaches to Treatments for Schizophrenia Spectrum Disorders, Part II: Psychosocial Interventions and Patient-Focused Perspectives in Psychiatric Care," *Neuropsychiatric Disease and Treatment* 9, no. 9 (September 2013): 1463–81.

Cognitive Remediation: Alice Medalia and Jimmy Choi, "Cognitive Remediation in Schizophrenia," *Neuropsychology Review* 19, no. 3 (September 2009): 353–64.

Family Therapy: Chien et al., "Current Approaches to Treatments."

Peer Support: Reham A. Hameed Shalaby and Vincent I. O. Agyapong, "Peer Support in Mental Health: Literature Review," *JMIR Mental Health* 7, no. 6 (June 2020): e15572.

Psychoeducation: Carol M. Anderson, "A Psychoeducational Model of Family Treatment for Schizophrenia," in *Psychosocial Intervention in Schizophrenia*, eds. Helm Stierlin, Lyman C. Wynne, and Michael Wirsching (Springer: Berlin, 1983), 227–23.

Social Skills Training: Alex Kopelowicz, Robert Paul Liberman, and Roberto Zarate, "Recent Advances in Social Skills Training for Schizophrenia," *Schizophrenia Bulletin* 32 (October 2006): S12–S23; see also Chien et al., "Current Approaches to Treatments."

Substance Abuse Treatment: Bernadette Winklbaur et al., "Substance Abuse in Patients with Schizophrenia," *Dialogues in Clinical Neuroscience* 8, no. 1 (March 2006): 37–43; see also David J. Kavanagh et al., "Substance Misuse in Patients with Schizophrenia," *Drugs* 62, no. 5 (April 2002): 743–55.

Suicide Prevention: Leo Sher and René S. Kahn, "Suicide in Schizophrenia: An Educational Overview," *Medicina* 55, no. 7 (July 2019): 361.

Supported Employment: Matthew Modini et al., "Supported Employment for People with Severe Mental Illness: Systematic Review and Meta-Analysis of the International Evidence," *British Journal of Psychiatry* 209, no. 1 (July 2016): 14–22.

Supported Education: William A. Anthony and Karen V. Unger, "Supported Education: An Additional Program Resource for Young Adults with Long Term Mental Illness," *Community Mental Health Journal* 27, no. 2 (April 1991): 145–56.

Supportive and Problem-Oriented Psychotherapy: Lucy A. Buckley et al., "Supportive Therapy for Schizophrenia," *Cochrane Database of Systematic Reviews*, no. 4 (April 2015).

Vocational Rehabilitation: Elizabeth W. Twamley, Dilip V. Jeste, and Anthony F. Lehman, "Vocational Rehabilitation in Schizophrenia and Other Psychotic Disorders: A Literature Review and Meta-Analysis of Randomized Controlled Trials," *Journal of Nervous and Mental Disease* 191, no. 8 (August 2003): 515–23.

Assertive Community Treatment (ACT): Gary R. Bond et al., "Assertive Community Treatment for People with Severe Mental Illness," *Disease Management and Health Outcomes* 9, no. 3 (March 2001): 141–59; see also Jack E. Scott and Lisa B. Dixon, "Assertive Community Treatment and Case Management for Schizophrenia," *Schizophrenia Bulletin* 21, no. 4 (January 1995): 657–68.

Collaborative Care: Siobhan Reilly et al., "Collaborative Care Approaches for People with Severe Mental Illness," *Cochrane Database of Systematic Reviews*, no. 11 (November 2013).

Coordinated Specialty Care (CSC): Robert K. Heinssen, Amy B. Goldstein, and Susan T. Azrin, *Evidence-Based Treatments for First Episode Psychosis: Components of Coordinated Specialty Care*, Recovery After an Initial Schizophrenia Episode (RA1SE) (Bethesda, MD: National Institute of Mental Health online, April 14, 2014), https://www.nimh.nih.gov/health/topics/schizophrenia/raise/nimh-white-paper-csc-for-fep_147096.pdf.

Crisis Intervention Models: Suzanne Murphy et al., "Crisis Intervention for People with Severe Mental Illnesses," *Cochrane Database of Systematic Reviews*, no. 5 (May 2012).

Critical Time Intervention (CTI): "CTI Model," Center for Advancement of Critical Time Intervention, Silberman School of Social Work, Hunter College online, accessed March 31, 2021, https://www.criticaltime.org/cti-model/.

Notes

Prologue

1   *priests whose lineage*: "Hebrew Bible: Jewish Sacred Writings," *Encyclopaedia Britannica* online, last modified May 20, 2020, https://www.britannica.com/topic/Hebrew -Bible.

4   *leading causes of disability*: Spencer L. James et al., "Global, Regional, and National Incidence, Prevalence, and Years Lived with Disability for 354 Diseases and Injuries for 195 Countries and Territories, 1990–2017: A Systematic Analysis for the Global Burden of Disease Study 2017," *Lancet* 392, no. 10159 (November 2018): 1789–858.

4   *lifetime prevalence*: Sukanta Saha et al., "A Systematic Review of the Prevalence of Schizophrenia," *PLOS Medicine* 2, no. 5 (May 2005): e141; see also Berta Moreno-Küstner, Carlos Martin, and Loly Pastor, "Prevalence of Psychotic Disorders and Its Association with Methodological Issues. A Systematic Review and Meta-Analyses," *PloS One* 13, no. 4 (April 2018): e0195687.

5   *Since the advent of gene-sequencing*: Stephan Ripke et al., "Biological Insights from 108 Schizophrenia-Associated Genetic Loci," *Nature* 511, no. 7510 (July 2014): 421–27.

5   *Environmental factors that impact*: Sandra L. Matheson et al., "A Systematic Meta-Review Grading the Evidence for Non-Genetic Risk Factors and Putative Antecedents of Schizophrenia," *Schizophrenia Research* 133, no. 1–3 (December 2011): 133–42; see also Mark Opler et al., "Environmental Risk Factors and Schizophrenia," *International Journal of Mental Health* 42, no. 1 (December 2013): 23–32.

5   *Certain recreational drugs*: Robert A. Power et al., "Genetic Predisposition to Schizophrenia Associated with Increased Use of Cannabis," *Molecular Psychiatry* 19, no. 11 (November 2014): 1201–4.

5   *Despite its relative frequency*: Pooja R. Desai et al., "Estimating the Direct and Indirect Costs for Community-Dwelling Patients with Schizophrenia," *Journal of Pharmaceutical Health Services Research* 4, no. 4 (July 2013): 187–94.

6   *"Schizophrenia terrifies"*: Esmé Weijun Wang, *The Collected Schizophrenias* (Minneapolis: Graywolf Press, 2019), 3.

6   *"a perfectly rational response"*: Sean O'Hagan, "Kingsley Hall: R.D. Laing's Experiment in Anti-Psychiatry," *Guardian* (US edition) online, last modified September 1, 2012, https://www.theguardian.com/books/2012/sep/02/rd-laing-mental -health-sanity.

7   *One such character*: Derek Krueger, *Symeon the Holy Fool: Leontius's Life and the Tate Antique City*, vol. 25 (Berkeley: University of California Press, 1996); see also Fernando Espí Forcén and Carlos Espí Forcén, "Symeon the Holy Fool: Patron of the Mentally Ill," *British Journal of Psychiatry* 205, no. 2 (August 2014): 94.

7   *Built in 1855*: Jessica Carmosino, "The Cleveland State Hospital," Cleveland Histori-
        cal, last modified September 12, 2019, https://clevelandhistorical.org/items
        /show/576.

10   *This neurodevelopmental theory*: Robin M. Murray and Shôn W. Lewis, "Is Schizo-
        phrenia a Neurodevelopmental Disorder?," *British Medical Journal* 295, no. 6600
        (September 1987): 681–82; see also Daniel R. Weinberger, "Implications of Normal
        Brain Development for the Pathogenesis of Schizophrenia," *Archives of General
        Psychiatry* 44, no. 7 (July 1987): 660–69.

10   *"doomed from the womb"*: Robin M. Murray, Colm McDonald, and Elvira Bramon,
        "Neurodevelopmental Impairment, Dopamine Sensitisation, and Social Adversity in
        Schizophrenia," *World Psychiatry* 1, no. 3 (October 2002): 137.

11   *From these studies*: Jeffrey Lieberman et al., "Time Course and Biologic Correlates of
        Treatment Response in First-Episode Schizophrenia," *Archives of General Psychiatry* 50,
        no. 5 (May 1993): 369–76; see also Jeffrey Lieberman et al., "Treatment Outcome of First
        Episode Schizophrenia," *Psychopharmacology Bulletin* 25, no. 1 (January 1989): 92.

11   *What the studies also*: Diana O. Perkins et al., "Relationship Between Duration of Un-
        treated Psychosis and Outcome in First-Episode Schizophrenia: A Critical Review
        and Meta-Analysis," *American Journal of Psychiatry* 162, no. 10 (October 2005):
        1785–804.

12   *The reality is that*: Alkomiet Hasan et al., "World Federation of Societies of Biologi-
        cal Psychiatry (WFSBP) Guidelines for Biological Treatment of Schizophrenia—A
        Short Version for Primary Care," *International Journal of Psychiatry in Clinical
        Practice* 21, no. 2 (June 2017): 82–90.

CHAPTER 1: FROM THE ANCIENT WORLD
TO FATHER AMORTH

18   *"It's a physiological state"*: William Friedkin, "The Devil and Father Amorth: Witness-
        ing 'the Vatican Exorcist' at Work," *Vanity Fair* online, last modified October 31,
        2016, https://www.vanityfair.com/hollywood/2016/10/father-amorth-the-vatican
        -exorcist.

18   *We settled in to watch*: These scenes can be seen in Friedkin's documentary film *The
        Devil and Father Amorth* (2018).

20   *The most common antecedent*: Jean M. Goodwin and Roberta G. Sachs, "Child Abuse
        in the Etiology of Dissociative Disorders," chap. 5 in *Handbook of Dissociation*, ed.
        Larry K. Michelson and William J. Ray (Boston: Springer, 1996), 91–105.

20   *Medicine and religion have been*: Richard P. Sloan, *Blind Faith: The Unholy Alliance of
        Religion and Medicine* (New York: St. Martin's Press, 2006), 16.

21   *"The melancholy character"*: Susan Sontag, *Illness as Metaphor* (New York: Farrar,
        Straus & Giroux, 1978), 32–33.

22   *"If it is still difficult to imagine"*: Ibid., 35.

23   *The "Book of Hearts"*: "Ebers Papyrus," New World Encyclopedia, last modified April
        20, 2011, https://www.newworldencyclopedia.org/entry/Ebers_Papyrus; see also

Ahmed Okasha, "Mental Health in the Middle East: An Egyptian Perspective," *Clinical Psychology Review* 19, no. 8 (December 1999): 917–33.

23   *The Hindu Vedas*: Daisy Yuhas, "Evolution of Schizophrenia," *Scientific American Mind* 24, no. 1 (March/April 2013): 62–67; see also Theocharis C. Kyziridis, "Notes on the History of Schizophrenia," *German Journal of Psychiatry* (September 2005): 42–48.

23   *One of the earliest biographical*: Andrew Scull, *Madness in Civilization: A Cultural History of Insanity, from the Bible to Freud, from the Madhouse to Modern Medicine* (Princeton, NJ: Princeton University Press, 2015), 17–18.

23   *"But the Spirit of the LORD"*: 1 Samuel 16:14, 23 (King James Version).

23   *"eat grass as oxen"*: Daniel 4:33 (KJV).

24   *In ancient societies*: Sloan, *Blind Faith*, 17.

24   *As medical historian Andrew Scull*: Scull, *Madness in Civilization*, 17, 19.

24   *"sending madness upon him"*: E. E. G., *The Makers of Hellas: A Critical Inquiry into the Philosophy and Religion of Ancient Greece*, ed. Frank Byron Jevons (London: Charles Griffin, 1903), 437.

24   *"Zeus robbed me"*: Homer, *The Iliad*, trans. A. T. Murray, vol. 2 (Cambridge, MA: Harvard University Press, 1925), 347.

25   *The Hippocratics were*: Scull, *Madness in Civilization*, 27.

25   *"Men ought to know"*: Hippocrates, "The Sacred Disease XVII," in *Prognostic. Regimen in Acute Diseases. The Sacred Disease. The Art. Breaths. Law. Decorum. Physician (Ch. 1). Dentition*, ed. and trans. W. H. S. Jones, Loeb Classical Library 148 (Cambridge, MA: Harvard University Press, 1923), 175.

25   *Hippocratic physicians made sport*: Scull, *Madness in Civilization*, 31–33.

25   *A key Hippocratic text*: Hippocrates, "Sacred Disease II," in *Prognostic. Regimen in Acute Diseases: The Sacred Disease. The Art. Breaths. Law. Decorum. Physician (Ch. 1). Dentition*, ed. and trans. W. H. S. Jones, Loeb Classical Library 148 (Cambridge, MA: Harvard University Press, 1923), 141.

25   *"reason is disturbed"*: Hippocrates, "Glands 12," in *Places in Man. Glands. Fleshes. Prorrhetic 1–2. Physician. Use of Liquids. Ulcers. Haemorrhoids and Fistulas*, ed. and trans. Paul Potter, Loeb Classical Library 482 (Cambridge, MA: Harvard University Press, 1995), 119.

25   *"hunt in the empty"*: Hippocrates, "Prognostic 4," in *Prognostic. Regimen in Acute Diseases. The Sacred Disease. The Art. Breaths. Law. Decorum. Physician (Ch. 1). Dentition*, ed. and trans. W. H. S. Jones, Loeb Classical Library 148 (Cambridge, MA: Harvard University Press, 1923), 15.

25   *Medical explanations of what*: William V. Harris, "Greek and Roman Hallucinations," in *Mental Disorders in the Classical World*, ed. William V. Harris (Leiden, Neth.: Brill, 2013), 304.

25   *Celsus (25 BC–AD 50)*: Katie Evans, John McGrath, and Robert Milns, "Searching for Schizophrenia in Ancient Greek and Roman Literature: A Systematic Review," *Acta Psychiatrica Scandinavica* 107, no. 5 (May 2003): 323–30.

25   *"duped . . . by phantoms"*: Celsus, "Volume I: Book III," in *De Medicina*, ed. and trans. W. G. Spencer, Loeb Classical Library 292 (Cambridge, MA: Harvard University Press, 1935), 295, 301.

26   *Celsus also held that*: Celsus, "Volume I: Book II," in *De Medicina*, ed. and trans.
        W. G. Spencer, Loeb Classical Library 292 (Cambridge, MA: Harvard University
        Press, 1935), 127.

26   *He believed that all*: Vivian Nutton, "Galenic Madness," in Harris, *Mental Disorders in
        the Classical World*, 123–24.

26   *When he served as physician*: Symeon Missios, "Hippocrates, Galen, and the Uses of Trepa-
        nation in the Ancient Classical World," *Neurosurgical Focus* 23, no. 1 (July 2007): 5.

26   *Galen describes a patient*: Nutton, "Galenic Madness," 125.

27   The Digest *(AD 530)*: Peter Toohey, "Madness in the Digest," in Harris, *Mental Disor-
        ders in the Classical World*, 441–59.

CHAPTER 2: MADNESS IN THE MIDDLE AGES

28   *In Europe, the centuries*: Scull, *Madness in Civilization*, 69–70.

28   *In Christianity, illness*: Sloan, *Blind Faith*, 5.

28   *"some other spirit"*: Saint Augustine, *De Genesi Ad Litteram* (AD 401–415), 12.12.25;
        quoted in Harris, "Greek and Roman Hallucinations," 305.

28   *"the return to high intellectual"*: Harris, "Greek and Roman Hallucinations," 305.

29   *"a lively young man"*: Valerie Martin, *Salvation: Scenes from the Life of St. Francis* (New
        York: Random House, 2002), 5.

29   *At the age of twenty*: "St. Francis of Assisi," *Encyclopaedia Britannica* online, last modi-
        fied December 2, 2019, https://www.britannica.com/biography/Saint-Francis-of
        -Assisi.

29   *In the ensuing years*: Adrian House, *Francis of Assisi: A Revolutionary Life* (Mahwah,
        NJ: HiddenSpring/Paulist Press, 2003), cited in: Geoffrey Moorhouse, "The Patron
        Saint of Greenies," *New York Times* online, March 11, 2001, https://www.nytimes
        .com/2001/03/11/books/the-patron-saint-of-greenies.html.

29   *"As the vision disappeared"*: "St. Francis of Assisi," *Encyclopaedia Britannica* online.

31   *Sometime in the 1430s*: Lynn Staley, introduction in *The Book of Margery Kempe*, ed.
        Lynn Staley (Kalamazoo, MI: Medieval Institute Publications, 1996).

31   *"owt of hir mende"*: Margery Kempe, *The Book of Margery Kempe*, ed. Lynn Staley
        (Kalamazoo, MI: Medieval Institute Publications, 1996), 59.

31   *"And in this time she saw"*: Margery Kempe, *The Book of Margery Kempe*, ed. and trans.
        Barry Windeatt (New York: Penguin Books, 1994), 41.

31   *As a result of her agitated*: Alison Torn, "Margery Kempe: Madwoman or Mystic—A
        Narrative Approach to the Representation of Madness and Mysticism in Medieval
        England," chap. 9 in *Narrative and Fiction: An Interdisciplinary Approach*, ed. David
        Robinson (Huddersfield, UK: University of Huddersfield Press, 2008), 80.

31   *"In lyknesse of a man"*: Kempe, *Book of Margery Kempe* (1996), 1.

31   *She describes conversations*: Corinne Saunders and Charles Fernyhough, "Reading Mar-
        gery Kempe's Inner Voices," *Postmedieval: A Journal of Medieval Cultural Studies* 8,
        no. 2 (June 2017): 209–17.

31   *"a good cawdel"*: Kempe, *Book of Margery Kempe* (1996), 81.

31   *She has auditory hallucinations*: Ibid., 124.

32   *She experienced God*: Saunders and Fernyhough, "Kempe's Inner Voices," 209–17.

32   *"horybyl syghtys and abhominabyl"*: Kempe, *Book of Margery Kempe* (1996), 59.

32   *Many rejected*: Alison Torn, "Looking Back: Medieval Mysticism or Psychosis?," *Psychologist*, October 2011, 788–90.

32   *She certainly didn't comply*: Liz Herbert McAvoy, "Motherhood: The Book of Margery Kempe," *Medieval Feminist Newsletter* 24, no. 1 (Fall 1997); see also Johanna Luthman, "The Paradox of Margery Kempe," *Oxford University Press Blog*, July 24, 2017, https://blog.oup.com/2017/07/margery-kempe-paradox/.

32   *"a truly embodied spiritual"*: Torn, "Looking Back," 788–90.

33   *Religious, political, and economic*: Scull, *Madness in Civilization*, 86.

33   *the witch hunts of Europe*: Neel Burton, "A Brief History of Psychiatry," *Psychology Today*, June 2, 2012, https://www.psychologytoday.com/sg/blog/hide-and-seek/201206/brief-history-psychiatry?amp; see also Jonathan L. Pearl, "Reviewed Work: On Witchcraft: An Abridged Translation of Johann Weyer's De Praestigiis Daemonum by Johann Weyer, Benjamin G. Kohl, H. C. Erik Midelfort, John Shea," *Sixteenth Century Journal* 31, no. 3 (Autumn 2000): 882–83.

33   *"Lunatics were placed"*: Scull, *Madness in Civilization*, 77.

33   *Geel still draws those*: Angus Chen, "For Centuries, a Small Town Has Embraced Strangers with Mental Illness," National Public Radio (NPR) online, last modified July 1, 2016, https://www.npr.org/sections/health-shots/2016/07/01/484083305/for-centuries-a-small-town-has-embraced-strangers-with-mental-illness.

33   *"The drama of an exorcism"*: Scull, *Madness in Civilization*, 77.

34   *Doctors reinterpreted*: Torn, "Looking Back," 788–90.

34   *While studying in Austria*: Scull, *Madness in Civilization*, 182.

34   *he was asked to give*: Burkhard Peter, "Gassner's Exorcism—Not Mesmer's Magnetism—Is the Real Predecessor of Modern Hypnosis," *International Journal of Clinical and Experimental Hypnosis* 53, no. 1 (January 2005): 1–12.

34   *The belief that physical*: Scull, *Madness in Civilization*, 177–81.

35   *Patients (usually women)*: Ibid., 186.

35   *Mesmer disappeared for*: Frederick L. Burwick, "Inchbald: Animal Magnetism and Medical Quackery," in *The New Science and Women's Literary Discourse: Prefiguring Frankenstein*, ed. Judy A. Hayden (New York: Palgrave Macmillan, 2011), 165–81.

35   *following allegations of quackery*: Scull, *Madness in Civilization*, 186.

35   *As for Gassner*: Ibid., 180.

37   *Munchausen by proxy*: Herbert Scheirer, "Munchausen by Proxy Defined," *Pediatrics* 110, no. 5 (November 2002): 985–88.

CHAPTER 3: THROUGH A GLASS, DARKLY

40   *As the mad were*: Scull, *Madness in Civilization*, 122–23.

40   *The eighteenth century saw*: Ibid., 129, 238.

40   *Conditions inside these facilities*: Evelyn A. Woods and Eric T. Carlson, "The Psychia-

try of Philippe Pinel," *Bulletin of the History of Medicine* 35, no. 1 (January/February 1961): 14–25.

41   *his descriptions in 1809*: Yuhas, "Evolution of Schizophrenia," 62–67.

41   *Pinel had seen*: Philippe Pinel, *A Treatise on Insanity*, trans. D. D. Davis (Sheffield, UK: Cadell & Davies, 1806), 52–53; see also Mohammad Shaiyan Rahman, "A Treatise on Insanity," *British Medical Journal* 342, no. 7806 (May 2011): 1089.

41   *he rose to head the Paris*: Woods and Carlson, "Psychiatry of Philippe Pinel," 14–25.

41   *Others in Europe*: Others included Joseph Daquin in France, Vincenzo Chiarugi in Italy, Samuel Tuke in England, and Benjamin Rush in Pennsylvania; see also Woods and Carlson, "Psychiatry of Philippe Pinel," 14–25.

41   *unchaining asylum inmates*: Unfortunately, the shackling of mental hospital patients still continues globally to this day; see also Kriti Sharma, *Living in Chains: Shackling of People with Psychosocial Disabilities Worldwide* (New York: Human Rights Watch, 2020), https://www.hrw.org/report/2020/10/06/living-chains/shackling-people-psychosocial-disabilities-worldwide.

41   *"well-timed variety"*: William Battie, *A Treatise on Madness* (London: J. Whiston and B. White, 1758), 69.

42   *Other institutions*: Jarvis, *Insanity and Insane Asylums*, 16, 21–22; see also Pliny Earle, "Historical and Descriptive Account of the Bloomingdale Asylum for the Insane," *American Journal of Insanity* 2, no. 1 (July 1845): 1–13; see also Edward Shorter, *A History of Psychiatry: From the Era of the Asylum to the Age of Prozac* (New York: John Wiley & Sons, 1997), 255.

43   *appreciated by some states*: Examples include Massachusetts Lunatic Hospital in 1833, Ohio Lunatic Asylum in 1838 (see also Jarvis, *Insanity and Insane Asylums*, 20–21), New York State Lunatic Asylum in 1843 (see also T. H. Hubbard et al., *Annual Report of the Managers of the State Lunatic Asylum* [Albany, NY: Carroll and Cook, 1844]), and Augusta Mental Health Institute in Maine, 1840 (see also William H. Nelson and William A. Brennan, "Augusta Mental Health Institute, 1840–2004," *American Journal of Psychiatry* 162, no. 10 [October 2005]: 1823).

43   *the majority of mentally ill*: David Rothman, *The Discovery of the Asylum: Social Order and Disorder in the New Republic*, rev. ed. (New York: Aldine de Gruyter, 2002), 130.

44   *Dorothea Dix was born*: Manon S. Parry, "Dorothea Dix (1802–1887)," *American Journal of Public Health* 96, no. 4 (April 2006): 624–25.

44   *Her biographer*: David Gollaher, *Voice for the Mad: The Life of Dorothea Dix* (New York: Free Press, 1995), 91–106.

44   *Her doctor encouraged her*: Parry, "Dorothea Dix (1802–1887)," 624–25.

44   *Upon returning to Boston*: Jessica Citronberg, "TBT: Dorothea Dix Visits East Cambridge Jail for the First Time," *Boston* online, March 29, 2018, https://www.boston magazine.com/news/2018/03/29/dorothea-dix-tbt/.

44   *She began to investigate*: Scull, *Madness in Civilization*, 196–99.

44   *The 1840 census*: Albert Deutsch, "The First U.S. Census of the Insane (1840) and Its Use as Pro-Slavery Propaganda," *Bulletin of the History of Medicine* 15, no. 5 (May 1944): 469–82.

44 *in 1855, Dix founded*: Aaron Levin, "History of St. Elizabeths Parallels U.S. Psychiatry's," *Psychiatric News* online, last modified June 17, 2005, https://doi.org/10.1176/pn.40.12.00400017.

45 *Her own declining years*: Scull, *Madness in Civilization*, 198.

45 *The hospital had been named*: Penny Colman, *Breaking the Chains: The Crusade of Dorothea Lynde Dix* (Lincoln, NE: ASJA Press, 2007), 73. With Dorothea Dix's permission, the hospital was originally named Dix Hill, in memory of her grandfather.

CHAPTER 4: MEDICAL SPECIALIZATION

49 *enabled the medical field*: The Enlightenment brought about a more humane and rational way of viewing people afflicted by madness. This was presaged in the eighteenth century, when the British physician Thomas Willis, known for his studies of brain vasculature and the eponymous "circle of Willis," wrote *De Anima Brutorum*, a work describing psychological states in terms of brain function. Some years after, another British physician, William Battie, published *A Treatise on Madness*, which recommended treatments for asylum inmates. At the turn of the nineteenth century, Benjamin Rush published the first American textbook of mental illness, *Medical Inquiries and Observations upon Diseases of the Mind*.

49 *specialties began in France*: George Weisz, "The Emergence of Medical Specialization in the Nineteenth Century," *Bulletin of the History of Medicine* (Fall 2003): 536–75.

50 *As a consequence of these*: Ibid.

50 *The earliest indication*: Maximilian Schochow and Florian Steger, "Johann Christian Reil (1759–1813): Pioneer of Psychiatry, City Physician, and Advocate of Public Medical Care," *American Journal of Psychiatry* 171, no. 4 (April 2014): 403; see also *OED Online*, Oxford University Press, under the word "psychiatry (*n.*)," last modified September 2021, https://www.oed.com/view/Entry/153856?rskey=ruTslr&result=1.

50 *While we now think of psychiatry*: M. Jeanne Peterson, *The Medical Profession in Mid-Victorian London* (Berkeley: University of California Press, 1978), 267; see also Walter E. Barton, *The History and Influence of the American Psychiatric Association* (Washington, DC: American Psychiatric Press, 1987), 38–39; see also Christopher G. Goetz, Teresa A. Chmura, and Douglas Lanska, "Part 1: The History of 19th Century Neurology and the American Neurological Association," *Annals of Neurology* 53, no. S4 (April 2003): S2–S26.

51 *Gall became interested*: John Van Wyhe, "The Authority of Human Nature: The Schädellehre of Franz Joseph Gall," *British Journal for the History of Science* 35, no. 1 (March 2002): 17–42.

51 *When Gall moved*: Scull, *Madness in Civilization*, 213.

51 *Such observations laid*: Ibid., 213–17; see also Donald Simpson, "Phrenology and the Neurosciences: Contributions of F. J. Gall and J. G. Spurzheim," *ANZ Journal of Surgery* 75, no. 6 (June 2005): 475–82.

51 *phrenology offered visual representation of deviance*: Nicole Hahn Rafter, *Creating Born Criminals* (Urbana: University of Illinois Press, 1997).

53 *Arnold Pick*: Josef Spatt, "Arnold Pick's Concept of Dementia," *Cortex* 39, no. 3 (June 2003): 525–31.

53 *Alois Alzheimer*: Hanns Hippius and Gabriele Neundörfer, "The Discovery of Alzheimer's Disease," *Dialogues in Clinical Neuroscience* 5, no. 1 (2003): 101.

53 *Sergei Korsakoff*: S. A. Ovsyannikov and A. S. Ovsyannikov, "Sergey S. Korsakov and the Beginning of Russian Psychiatry," *Journal of the History of the Neurosciences* 16, no. 1/2 (February 2007): 58–64.

53 *Karl Wernicke and Paul Broca*: Juergen Tesak and Chris Code, *Milestones in the History of Aphasia: Theories and Protagonists*, 1st ed. (London: Psychology Press, 2008), 67–109, 207–22.

53 *Korbinian Brodmann's monograph*: Korbinian Brodmann, *Vergleichende Lokalisationslehre Der Großhirnrinde* (Leipzig, Ger.: Johann Ambrosius Barth, 1909); see also Korbinian Brodmann, *Brodmann's Localisation in the Cerebral Cortex*, ed. and trans. Laurence J. Garey (London: Springer, 1994).

53 *The fifty-two anatomic areas*: Michael Strotzer, "One Century of Brain Mapping Using Brodmann Areas," *Clinical Neuroradiology* 19, no. 3 (July 2009): 179–86.

53 *templates still used today*: For example, see Jean Talairach and Pierre Tournoux, *Co-Planar Stereotaxic Atlas of the Human Brain*, trans. Mark Rayport (Stuttgart, Ger.: Thieme, 1988).

54 *human remains from the brutality of war and violence*: Deirdre Cooper Owen, *Medical Bondage: Race, Gender, and the Origins of American Gynecology* (Athens: University of Georgia Press, 2017).

54 *gave rise to radical theories of racial differences*: Jim Downs, *Maladies of Empire: How Colonialism, Slavery, and War Transformed Medicine* (Cambridge, MA: Belknap Press of Harvard University, 2021).

54 *black people were not susceptible to mental illness*: Wendy Gonaver, *The Peculiar Institution and the Making of Modern Psychiatry, 1840–1880* (Chapel Hill: University of North Carolina Press, 2019).

55 *Silas Weir Mitchell*: Mitchell and his "rest cure" came in for harsh condemnation from writers Virginia Woolf and Charlotte Perkins Gilman, both of whom he treated; see also Ellen L. Bassuk, "The Rest Cure: Repetition or Resolution of Victorian Women's Conflicts?," *Poetics Today* 6, no. 1/2 (1985): 245–57.

55 *"to take away from neurology"*: Siang Y. Tan and Daito Shigaki, "Jean-Martin Charcot (1825–1893): Pathologist Who Shaped Modern Neurology," *Singapore Medical Journal* 48, no. 5 (2007): 383–84.

56 *His first position was*: Venita Jay, "The Legacy of Jean-Martin Charcot," *Archives of Pathology & Laboratory Medicine* 124, no. 1 (January 2000): 10–11; see also David R. Kumar et al., "Jean-Martin Charcot: The Father of Neurology," *Clinical Medicine & Research* 9, no. 1 (March 2011): 46–49; see also Asti Hustvedt, *Medical Muses: Hysteria in Nineteenth-Century Paris* (New York: W. W. Norton, 2011).

56 *As professor of pathological*: Kumar et al., "Jean-Martin Charcot," 46–49.

56   *"great neurosis"*: Mark S. Micale, "On the 'Disappearance' of Hysteria: A Study in the
      Clinical Deconstruction of a Diagnosis," *Isis* 84, no. 3 (September 1993): 503.

57   *The people confined to insane asylums*: Daniel Yohanna, "Deinstitutionalization of
      People with Mental Illness: Causes and Consequences," *AMA Journal of Ethics* 15,
      no. 10 (October 2013): 886–91.

57   *he'd grown frustrated*: Hannah S. Decker, "How Kraepelinian Was Kraepelin? How
      Kraepelinian Are the Neo-Kraepelinians?—from Emil Kraepelin to DSM-III," *History of Psychiatry* 18, no. 3 (September 2007): 337–60.

57   *Kraepelin initially approached*: Scull, *Madness in Civilization*, 263.

57   *He kept stacks of note cards*: Decker, "How Kraepelinian Was Kraepelin?," 337–60.

57   *Kraepelin defined three types*: See lectures I, II, and III in Emil Kraepelin, *Lectures on
      Clinical Psychiatry*, ed. and trans. Thomas Johnstone (London: Bailliere, Tindall and
      Cox, 1904).

58   *"Delusions, either transitory or permanent"*: Emil Kraepelin, *Dementia Praecox and
      Paraphrenia*, ed. George M. Robertson, trans. R. Mary Barclay (Edinburgh:
      E & S Livingstone, 1919), 26–27, 123.

58   *Swiss psychiatrist Eugen Bleuler*: Eugen Bleuler, *Dementia Praecox: Or the Group of
      Schizophrenias* (New York: International Universities Press, 1911).

59   *Bleuler's shift of emphasis*: Andrew Moskowitz and Gerhard Heim, "Eugen Bleuler's
      Dementia Praecox or the Group of Schizophrenias (1911): A Centenary Appreciation and Reconsideration," *Schizophrenia Bulletin* 37, no. 3 (May 2011): 471–79; see
      also Ahbishekh Hulegar Ashok, John Baugh, and Vikram K. Yeragani, "Paul Eugen
      Bleuler and the Origin of the Term Schizophrenia (Schizopreniegruppe)," *Indian
      Journal of Psychiatry* 54, no. 1 (January–March 2012): 95.

59   *a typology that was*: American Psychiatric Association, *Diagnostic and Statistical
      Manual of Mental Disorders*, 3rd ed. (Washington, DC: American Psychiatric Association, 1980), 190–93.

60   *During his academic training*: Eric J. Engstrom and Kenneth S. Kendler, "Emil Kraepelin:
      Icon and Reality," *American Journal of Psychiatry* 172, no. 12 (December 2015): 1190–96.

60   *Wundt was an aspiring*: Edward B. Titchener, "Wilhelm Wundt," *American Journal of
      Psychology* 32, no. 2 (April 1921): 161–78.

60   *In his 1874 book*: Wilhelm Wundt, *Principles of Physiological Psychology*, trans.
      Edward B. Titchener, 5th ed. (London: Swan Sonnenschein, 1902), 2–5; see also
      Thomas Hardy Leahey, *A History of Psychology: Main Currents in Psychological
      Thought*, 5th ed. (Upper Saddle River, NJ: Prentice Hall, 2000), 250–51.

60   *Titchener conceived of psychology's*: Leahey, *History of Psychology*, 260–62, 338–45.

60   *James regarded the scientific*: William James, *The Principles of Psychology*, vol. 1 (New
      York: Henry Holt, 1918), 349.

CHAPTER 5: THE FREUDIANS

62 *Freud was enormously*: Joseph Aguayo, "Charcot and Freud: Some Implications of Late 19th Century French Psychiatry and Politics for the Origins of Psychoanalysis," *Psychoanalysis and Contemporary Thought* 9, no. 2 (1986): 223–60.

62 *Freud subsequently studied*: Peter Gay, *Freud: A Life for Our Time* (New York: W. W. Norton, 1998), 65; see also Josef Breuer and Sigmund Freud, "Fräulein Anna O.," in *The Standard Edition of the Complete Psychological Works of Sigmund Freud*, ed. James Strachey et al., trans. James Strachey (London: Hogarth Press, 1955), 21–47.

62 *Freud understood mental disorders*: Sigmund Freud, *The Standard Edition of the Complete Psychological Works of Sigmund Freud*, vol. 19, *(1923–1925): The Ego and the Id and Other Works*, ed. and trans. James Strachey (London: Hogarth Press and the Institute of Psychoanalysis, 1964), 3–5, 17–39.

62 *Freud's view of the precise*: Ping-Nie Pao, "Notes on Freud's Theory of Schizophrenia," *International Journal of Psycho-Analysis* 54 (1973): 469–76; see also William N. Goldstein, "Toward an Integrated Theory of Schizophrenia," *Schizophrenia Bulletin* 4, no. 3 (January 1978): 426.

63 *comments by Kraepelin*: Kraepelin, *Dementia Praecox and Paraphrenia*, 251.

63 *Freud made his first and only visit*: Rand B. Evans and William A. Koelsch, "Psychoanalysis Arrives in America: The 1909 Psychology Conference at Clark University," *American Psychologist* 40, no. 8 (August 1985): 942.

63 *In America, one of those*: Richard Skues, "Clark Revisited: Reappraising Freud in America," chap. 2 in *After Freud Left: A Century of Psychoanalysis in America*, ed. John Burnham (Chicago: University Press of Chicago, 2012), 73–74.

63 *Despite his warm reception*: Howard L. Kaye, "Why Freud Hated America," *Wilson Quarterly* 17, no. 2 (Spring 1993): 118–25; see also Dale Harley, "Sigmund Freud Hated America: 5 Reasons Why," *Psychology Today*, January 9, 2018, https://www.psychologytoday.com/us/blog/machiavellians-gulling-the-rubes/201801/sigmund-freud-hated-america-5-reasons-why.

64 *Hitler specifically denounced*: Daniel Goleman, "Psychotherapy and the Nazis," *New York Times* online, July 3, 1984, https://www.nytimes.com/1984/07/03/science/psychotherapy-and-the-nazis.html.

64 *A psychiatry resident*: Shorter, *History of Psychiatry*, 177–78.

65 *With psychiatry's embrace*: Tamar Lewin, "The Seriously Ill and the 'Worried Well,'" *New York Times* online, December 18, 1988, 7, https://www.nytimes.com/1988/12/18/books/the-seriously-ill-and-the-worried-well.html.

65 *Freud differentiated among*: Glen O. Gabbard and Bonnie E. Litowitz, "Through Scopes Broad and Narrow," in *Textbook of Psychoanalysis*, ed. Bonnie E. Litowitz, Glen O. Gabbard, and Paul Williams (Arlington, VA: American Psychiatric Publishing, 2011), 163–65; see also Sigmund Freud, "Introduction to Psycho-Analysis and the War Neuroses (1919)," in *The Standard Edition of the Complete Psychological Works of Sigmund Freud*, ed. and trans. James Strachey (London: Hogarth Press, 1955), 205–16; see also Sigmund Freud, "An Autobiographical Study (1925)," in *The*

Standard Edition of the Complete Psychological Works of Sigmund Freud, ed. and trans. James Strachey (London: Hogarth Press, 1959), 1–74.

65   *American psychoanalyst Leo Stone*: Leo Stone, "The Widening Scope of Indications for Psychoanalysis," *Journal of the American Psychoanalytic Association* 2, no. 4 (1954): 567–94.

66   *In 1917 only 8 percent*: Nathan G. Hale Jr., "From Berggasse XIX to Central Park West: The Americanization of Psychoanalysis, 1919–1940," *Journal of the History of the Behavioral Sciences* 14, no. 4 (October 1978): 313n15.

67   *Freud had clearly proscribed*: Gabbard and Litowitz, "Through Scopes," 163–65.

67   *In 1942 Freud's colleague Helene Deutsch*: Helene Deutsch, "Some Forms of Emotional Disturbance and Their Relationship to Schizophrenia," *Psychoanalytic Quarterly* 11, no. 3 (1942): 301–21.

67   *In 1949 Paul Hoch and*: Michael H. Stone, *The Fate of Borderline Patients: Successful Outcome and Psychiatric Practice* (New York: Guilford Press, 1990), 3; see also Paul Hoch and Phillip Polatin, "Pseudoneurotic Forms of Schizophrenia," *Psychiatric Quarterly* 23, no. 2 (April 1949): 248–76; see also Paul H. Hoch et al., "The Course and Outcome of Pseudoneurotic Schizophrenia," *American Journal of Psychiatry* 119, no. 2 (August 1962): 106–15.

67   *The proliferation of these*: John G. Gunderson, "Borderline Personality Disorder: Ontogeny of a Diagnosis," *American Journal of Psychiatry* 166, no. 5 (May 2009): 530–39.

67   *American psychoanalyst Harry Stack Sullivan*: George Makari, *Revolution in Mind: The Creation of Psychoanalysis* (New York: HarperCollins, 2009), 481.

68   *"schizophrenogenic mother"*: Frieda Fromm-Reichmann, "Notes on the Development of Treatment of Schizophrenics by Psychoanalytic Psychotherapy," *Psychiatry* 11, no. 3 (August 1948): 265.

68   *This label, which would*: Fritz B. Simon, Helm Stierlin, and Lyman C. Wynne, *The Language of Family Therapy: A Systemic Vocabulary and Sourcebook* (New York: Family Process Press, 1985), 311.

68   *She believed that schizophrenia*: Frieda Fromm-Reichmann, "Remarks on the Philosophy of Mental Disorder," *Psychiatry* 9, no. 4 (November 1946): 293–308.

68   *at one point, it was said*: Robert Kolker, *Hidden Valley Road: Inside the Mind of an American Family* (New York: Doubleday, 2020), 33.

68   *She was immortalized*: Joanne Greenberg, *I Never Promised You a Rose Garden* (New York: Holt Paperbacks, 1989).

68   *Fromm-Reichmann could be a*: Robert A. Cohen, "Notes on the Life and Work of Frieda Fromm-Reichmann," *Psychiatry: Interpersonal and Biological Processes* 73, no. 3 (Fall 2010): 217.

68   *"mutual enterprise"*: Frieda Fromm-Reichmann, *Principles of Intensive Psychotherapy* (Chicago: University of Chicago Press, 1950), 45.

68   *The "schizophrenogenic mother"*: John Neill, "Whatever Became of the Schizophrenogenic Mother?," *American Journal of Psychotherapy* 44, no. 4 (October 1990): 499–505.

68   *Riffing on this*: Kolker, *Hidden Valley Road*, 36.

68   *Bateson, an anthropologist*: Gregory Bateson et al., "Toward a Theory of Schizophrenia," *Behavioral Science* 1, no. 4 (January 1956): 251–64; see also Matthijs Koop-

mans, "From Double Bind to N-Bind: Toward a New Theory of Schizophrenia and Family Interaction," *Nonlinear Dynamics, Psychology, and Life Sciences* 5, no. 4 (October 2001): 289–323.

69   *Searles developed a form*: Harold F. Searles, "Oedipal Love in the Counter Transference," *International Journal of Psychoanalysis* 40 (May–August 1959): 180–90; see also Adele Tutter, "The Erotics of Knowing: A Neglected Contribution to Analytic Erotism," *Journal of the American Psychoanalytic Association* 66, no. 3 (June 2018): 407–41.

69   *"loving sacrifice of his"*: Harold F. Searles, *Collected Papers on Schizophrenia and Related Subjects* (London: Karnac Books, 1986), 220.

69   *Searles traced the conflict*: Ibid., 221–26.

69   *Videos of Searles's patient*: "Dr. Harold F. Searles—Case Study—Interview 1973," YouTube video, 1:23:08, https://youtu.be/8R4xDwLF9UE.

70   *Vladimir Nabokov, who famously*: Vladimir Nabokov, *Strong Opinions* (New York: Vintage Books, 1990), 23–24, 47.

70   *The hegemony that psychoanalytic*: *The Psychiatrist: His Training and Development. Report of the 1952 Conference on Psychiatric Education Held at Cornell University, Ithaca, New York, June 19–25, 1952*, organized and conducted by the American Psychiatric Association and the Association of American Medical Colleges (Washington, DC, 1953), 22–48, 91–100; see also Shorter, *History of Psychiatry*, 173.

70   *Recently, I asked psychiatrist Darrell Kirch*: Darrell Kirch (former president of the Association of American Medical Colleges), in discussion with the author, 2014.

CHAPTER 6: DESPERATE MEASURES

71   *In 1904 there were*: Bicentennial Edition: Historical Statistics of the United States, Colonial Times to 1970, Department of Commerce and Bureau of the Census (Washington, DC: GPO, 1975), 84, table B 423–427, https://www2.census.gov/library /publications/1975/compendia/hist_stats_colonial-1970/hist_stats_colonial -1970p1-chB.pdf.

71   *By 1955, the number*: E. Fuller Torrey, *Out of the Shadows: Confronting America's Mental Illness Crisis* (New York: John Wiley & Sons, 1997), 8.

71   *Pilgrim State Hospital*: "Pilgrim Psychiatric Center," New York State Office of Mental Health online, accessed October 12, 2020, https://omh.ny.gov/omhweb/facilities /pgpc/.

71   *In 1946 a former patient*: Mary Jane Ward, *The Snake Pit* (New York: Random House, 1946).

71   *One of the most famous*: Vaslav Nijinsky, introduction in *The Diary of Vaslav Nijinsky*, ed. Joan Acocella, trans. Kyril Fitzlyon (New York: Farrar, Straus & Giroux, 1995).

72   *His brother, Stanislav*: Emilio Fernandez-Egea, "One Hundred Years Ago: Nijinsky and the Origins of Schizophrenia," *Brain* 142, no. 1 (January 2019): 220–26; see also Nijinsky, introduction in *Diary of Nijinsky*, xii–xvi.

72   *It was not long*: Nijinsky, introduction in *Diary of Nijinsky*, xvii–xx.

72   *Romola consulted a doctor*: Peter Ostwald, *Vaslav Nijinsky: A Leap into Madness* (New York: Carol, 1991), 196–98; see also Nijinsky, introduction in *Diary of Nijinsky*, xxi–xxxiv.

73   *"One feels a frantic struggle"*: Nijinsky, introduction in *Diary of Nijinsky*, xxiv–xxv.

73   *"I am standing in front"*: Ibid., xxv.

73   *"God is fire in the head"*: Nijinsky, *Diary of Nijinsky*, 106.

74   *"My soul is sick"*: Ibid., 145.

74   *In the latter half*: Thomas A. Ban, "Pharmacotherapy of Mental Illness—A Historical Analysis," *Progress in Neuro-Psychopharmacology and Biological Psychiatry* 25, no. 4 (May 2001): 709–27.

74   *it also created addicts*: Shorter, *History of Psychiatry*, 197–99.

74   *Chloral hydrate followed*: James A. Inciardi, "The Changing Life of Mickey Finn: Some Notes on Chloral Hydrate Down Through the Ages," *Journal of Popular Culture* 11, no. 3 (Winter 1977): 591–96.

74   *Scottish psychiatrist Neil Macleod*: Neil Macleod, "The Bromide Sleep: A New Departure in the Treatment of Acute Mania," *British Medical Journal* 1, no. 2038 (January 1900): 134; see also Shorter, *History of Psychiatry*, 200–202.

74   *Manfred Sakel, an Austrian*: Edward Shorter, "Sakel Versus Meduna: Different Strokes, Different Styles of Scientific Discovery," *Journal of ECT* 25, no. 1 (March 2009): 12–14; see also Kingsley Jones, "Insulin Coma Therapy in Schizophrenia," *Journal of the Royal Society of Medicine* 93, no. 3 (March 2000): 147–49.

75   *"loss of tension and hostility"*: Eugene Revitch, "Observations on Organic Brain Damage and Clinical Improvement Following Protracted Insulin Coma," *Psychiatric Quarterly* 28, no. 1–4 (January 1954): 91.

75   *In 1917 a Viennese professor*: Shorter, *History of Psychiatry*, 192–94.

76   *Wagner-Jauregg and other*: Ibid., 194–95.

76   *For his pioneering work*: Magda Whitrow, "Wagner-Jauregg and Fever Therapy," *Medical History* 34, no. 3 (July 1990): 294–310; see also Edward Shorter, *A Historical Dictionary of Psychiatry* (New York: Oxford University Press, 2005), 299. According to Shorter, Wagner-Jauregg "blighted his historical reputation by permitting himself to be enrolled in the Nazi Party after the union of Austria with Hitler's Germany in 1938."

77   *In 1935 Moniz attended*: Glenn Frankel, "D.C. Neurosurgeon Pioneered 'Operation Icepick' Technique," *Washington Post* online, April 7, 1980, https://www.washington post.com/archive/politics/1980/04/07/dc-neurosurgeon-pioneered-operation-icepick-technique/d861181c-3af5-4779-96c3-f514b3a7f6cd/.

77   *Moniz would say later*: Siang Yong Tan and Angela Yip, "António Egas Moniz (1874–1955): Lobotomy Pioneer and Nobel Laureate," *Singapore Medical Journal* 55, no. 4 (April 2014): 175; see also "Moniz Develops Lobotomy for Mental Illness, 1935," PBS online, accessed September 22, 2020, https://www.pbs.org/wgbh/aso/databank/entries/dh35lo.html.

78   *In 1936 Moniz and Lima*: Egas Moniz, *Tentatives Opératoires Dans Le Traitement De Certaines Psychoses* (*Tentative Methods in the Treatment of Certain Psychoses*) (Paris: Masson et Cie, 1936); see also Egas Moniz, "Prefrontal Leucotomy in the Treatment of Mental Disorders," *American Journal of Psychiatry* 93, no. 6 (June 1937): 1379–85.

78   *In 1939 Moniz himself was*: Marco Artico et al., "Egas Moniz: 90 Years (1927–2017) from Cerebral Angiography," *Frontiers in Neuroanatomy* 11 (September 2017): 81.

78   *The Nobel Prize committee*: Mark C. Preul and T. Forcht Dagi, "London 1935: The Frontal Lobe, Insanity, and a Brain Surgery," *Journal of Neurosurgery* 43, no. 5 (September 2017): E5.

78   *Walter Freeman*: Frankel, "D.C. Neurosurgeon."

78   *The inaugural patient*: Walter Freeman and James W. Watts, *Psychosurgery: Intelligence, Emotion, and Social Behavior Following Prefrontal Lobotomy for Mental Disorders* (Springfield, IL: Charles C. Thomas, 1942), 117–18.

79   *Of their first 623 cases*: Frankel, "D.C. Neurosurgeon."

79   *"It will be a hell"*: Howard Dully and Charles Fleming, *My Lobotomy: A Memoir* (New York: Three Rivers Press, 2008), 68.

79   *Watts described the miraculous*: Frankel, "D.C. Neurosurgeon."

79   *The nurse on the scene*: Kate Clifford Larson, *Rosemary: The Hidden Kennedy Daughter* (New York: Houghton Mifflin Harcourt, 2015), 2–4.

79   *Rosemary seemed like a physically*: Ibid., 40–45.

80   *The experts the family*: E. Fuller Torrey, *American Psychosis: How the Federal Government Destroyed the Mental Illness Treatment System* (New York: Oxford University Press, 2013), 4–10.

80   *In 1938, when Rosemary*: Ibid., 2–5.

80   *When World War II broke out*: Ibid., 6–10.

80   *"up and down the halls"*: Doris Kearns Goodwin, *The Fitzgeralds and the Kennedys* (New York: Simon & Schuster, 1987), 640.

80   *At one point, she attacked*: Torrey, *American Psychosis*, 8–9.

80   *She shuttled from*: Meryl Gordon, " 'Rosemary: The Hidden Kennedy Daughter,' by Kate Clifford Larson," review of *Rosemary: The Hidden Kennedy Daughter*, by Kate Clifford Larson, *New York Times* online, October 6, 2015, https://www.nytimes.com/2015/10/11/books/review/rosemary-the-hidden-kennedy-daughter-by-kate-clifford-larson.html.

80   *Rosemary took to sneaking out*: Larson, *Rosemary*, 158–59.

80   *As E. Fuller Torrey*: Torrey, *American Psychosis*, 9–10.

80   *Desperate for a solution*: Ronald Kessler, *The Sins of the Father: Joseph P. Kennedy and the Dynasty He Founded* (New York: Warner Books, 1997), 238–45.

81   *The lobotomy was a disaster*: Torrey, *American Psychosis*, 10–15; see also Kessler, *Sins of the Father*, 245–47.

81   *According to David Nasaw's*: David Nasaw, *The Patriarch: The Remarkable Life and Turbulent Times of Joseph P. Kennedy* (New York: Penguin Books, 2013), 629.

81   *In later years*: Larson, *Rosemary*, 217–31.

81   *"silent on the question"*: Jack El-Hai, *The Lobotomist: A Maverick Medical Genius and His Tragic Quest to Rid the World of Mental Illness* (Hoboken, NJ: John Wiley & Sons, 2005), 174.

81   *There had also been*: Torrey, *American Psychosis*, 3–4.

81   *"A neurological disturbance"*: Rose F. Kennedy, *Times to Remember* (Garden City, NY: Doubleday, 1974), 286.

81 *numerous studies have reported*: Vera A. Morgan et al., "Intellectual Disability Co-Occurring with Schizophrenia and Other Psychiatric Illness: Population-Based Study," *British Journal of Psychiatry* 193, no. 5 (November 2008): 364–72; see also Per Nettelbladt et al., "Risk of Mental Disorders in Subjects with Intellectual Disability in the Lundby Cohort 1947–97," *Nordic Journal of Psychiatry* 63, no. 4 (February 2009): 316–21.

82 *"I would do anything"*: Larson, *Rosemary*, 75.

82 *"our love was, and is"*: Tennessee Williams, *Memoirs* (Garden City, NY: Doubleday, 1975), 120.

82 *"Her heart broke, then"*: Ibid., 125.

82 *"The house is wretched"*: Tennessee Williams, *Notebooks*, ed. Margaret Rose Thornton (New Haven, CT: Yale University Press, 2006), 59.

82 *"We have had no deaths"*: Ibid., 73.

82 *A medical report from 1939*: Ibid., 176–77.

82 *In 1943 Rose's parents*: Steve Baker, "Rose Williams, Sister of Late Playwright Tennessee Williams, Dies," Associated Press, September 6, 1996, https://apnews.com/article/6f8df007f6bafb5d0ec3d7d9e45a82e9.

82 *"A cord breaking"*: Williams, *Notebooks*, 361.

83 *"I've had a great deal"*: Colm Tóibín, *New Ways to Kill Your Mother: Writers and Their Families* (New York: Scribner, 2012), 273–74.

83 *Instead, as writer Colm Tóibín*: Colm Tóibín, "The Shadow of Rose," *New York Review of Books*, December 20, 2007, https://www.nybooks.com/articles/2007/12/20/the-shadow-of-rose/. Writer Colm Tóibín has eloquently described how Rose's fate weighed on her brother: "As he worked with fierce determination on his plays, as he traveled the world like a maniac, as he sought new sexual partners, as he drank and took pills and went to parties, there was always the sense, made clear in many notebook entries, that he was in flight from what was done to his sister. He lived in the shadow of her suffering, and there were times when he seemed to seek pleasure and experience enough for two of them."

83 *In 1945 Freeman parted ways*: Howard Dully, "Howard Dully Talks About 'My Lobotomy,'" interview by Neal Conan, National Public Radio, 2005, https://www.npr.org/transcripts/5016775; see also Elizabeth Day, "He Was Bad, So They Put an Ice Pick in His Brain . . . ," *Guardian* (US edition) online, last modified January 13, 2008, https://www.theguardian.com/science/2008/jan/13/neuroscience.medicalscience.

84 *It could, Freeman insisted*: Walter Freeman and James W. Watts, *Psychosurgery: In the Treatment of Mental Disorders and Intractable Pain*, 2nd ed. (Oxford: Blackwell Scientific, 1950), 407; see also James P. Caruso and Jason P. Sheehan, "Psychosurgery, Ethics, and Media: A History of Walter Freeman and the Lobotomy," *Journal of Neurosurgery* 43, no. 3 (September 2017): E6.

84 *Freeman demonstrated this*: "A Lobotomy Timeline," National Public Radio (NPR), November 16, 2005, https://www.npr.org/templates/story/story.php?storyId=5014576&ps=rs.

84 *While the lobotomy had*: Frankel, "D.C. Neurosurgeon."

85 *In 1967 Freeman performed*: "A Lobotomy Timeline," NPR online; see also Elliot S.

Valenstein, *Great and Desperate Cures: The Rise and Decline of Psychosurgery and Other Radical Treatments for Mental Illness* (New York: Basic Books, 1986), 274; see also Lewis P. Rowland, "Walter Freeman's Psychosurgery and Biological Psychiatry: A Cautionary Tale," *Neurology Today*, April 2005, 70–72.

85   *performed nearly 3,500 lobotomies*: Jack El-Hai, *The Lobotomist: A Maverick Medical Genius and His Tragic Quest to Rid the World of Mental Illness* (Hoboken, NJ: John Wiley & Sons, 2005).

85   *evidence to the contrary*: Kara Rogers, "Walter Jackson Freeman II," *Encyclopedia Britannica*, May 27, 2022.

Chapter 7: Laborit's Drug

88   *a spectrum called the endogenous psychoses*: M. Dominic Beer, "The Endogenous Psychoses: A Conceptual History," *History of Psychiatry* 7, no. 25 (March 1, 1996): 1–29.

88   *"With faint hope"*: Max Fink, "Meduna and the Origins of Convulsive Therapy," *American Journal of Psychiatry* 141, no. 9 (September 1984): 1035.

88   *"My legs suddenly"*: Ibid., 1035–36.

88   *After five camphor-induced*: Ibid., 1036.

88   *Meduna went on*: Ibid.

89   *In 1939 a study was*: Phillip Polatin et al., "Vertebral Fractures Produced by Metrazol-Induced Convulsions: In the Treatment of Psychiatric Disorders," *Journal of the American Medical Association* 112, no. 17 (April 1939): 1684–87.

89   *In the mid-1930s*: Stefano Pallanti, "Ugo Cerletti 1877–1963," *American Journal of Psychiatry* 156, no. 4 (April 1999): 630.

89   *"submitting a man"*: Ugo Cerletti, "Electroshock Therapy," in *The Great Physiodynamic Therapies in Psychiatry: An Historical Reappraisal*, ed. Arthur M. Sackler et al. (New York: Hoeber-Harper, 1956), 92.

90   *In April 1938*: Konstantina Kotsaki, Aristidis Diamantis, and Emmanouil Magiorkinis, "Ugo Cerletti (1877–1963): An Early Italian Father of Electroshock and a Pioneer in Many Other Ways," *Neuroscientist* 27, no. 5 (October 2020): 454–62; see also George Mora, "Ugo Cerletti, Md: (1877–1963)," *American Journal of Psychiatry* 120, no. 6 (December 1963): 620–22.

90   *The results were dramatic*: Fink, "Meduna," 1036–37.

90   *By the mid-1940s*: Lara Rzesnitzek, " 'A Berlin Psychiatrist with an American Passport': Lothar Kalinowsky, Electroconvulsive Therapy, and International Exchange in the Mid-Twentieth Century," *History of Psychiatry* 26, no. 4 (November 2015): 433–51.

91   *The German-born psychiatrist*: Ibid.

92   *The introduction of ECT*: Fink, "Meduna," 1038–39.

93   *The American Psychiatric Association*: William McDonald and Laura Fochtmann, "What Is Electroconvulsive Therapy (ECT)?," American Psychiatric Association, updated July 2019, https://www.psychiatry.org/patients-families/ect; see also "Brain

Stimulation Therapies," National Institute of Mental Health, updated June 2016, https://www.nimh.nih.gov/health/topics/brain-stimulation-therapies/brain -stimulation-therapies.shtml#part_152877.

93   *In the 1940s Henri Laborit*: Anne E. Caldwell, "History of Psychopharmacology," in *Principles of Psychopharmacology*, ed. William G. Clark and Joseph del Giudice (New York: Academic Press, 1978), 23–33; see also Thomas A. Ban, "The Role of Serendipity in Drug Discovery," *Dialogues in Clinical Neuroscience* 8, no. 3 (September 2006): 335–44; see also Francisco López-Muñoz et al., "History of the Discovery and Clinical Introduction of Chlorpromazine," *Annals of Clinical Psychiatry* 17, no. 3 (July–September 2005): 113–35.

94   *"Laborit's drug"*: López-Muñoz et al., "History of the Discovery," 113–35.

94   *But Laborit recognized*: Thomas A. Ban, "Fifty Years Chlorpromazine: A Historical Perspective," *Neuropsychiatric Disease and Treatment* 3, no. 4 (August 2007): 495–500.

94   *Outraged over this ad hoc*: López-Muñoz et al., "History of the Discovery," 113–35.

94   *While dining in the canteen*: Thomas Hager, *Ten Drugs: How Plants, Powders, and Pills Have Shaped the History of Medicine* (New York: Abrams Press, 2019), 104.

94   *On January 19, 1952*: Ban, "Fifty Years Chlorpromazine," 495–500.

94   *"resume normal life"*: Ibid., 496.

94   *Soon they were publishing*: Ibid., 496–500; see also Marc Zanello et al., "History of Psychosurgery at Sainte-Anne Hospital, Paris, France, Through Translational Interactions Between Psychiatrists and Neurosurgeons," *Neurological Focus* 43, no. 3 (September 2017): E9.

94   *The following year, chlorpromazine*: Heinz E. Lehmann, "William E. Bunney's Interview of Heinz E. Lehmann," *Neuropsychopharmacology in Historical Perspective*, December 12, 1994.

95   *As Lehmann has told it*: Joel Gold and Ian Gold, *Suspicious Minds: How Culture Shapes Madness* (New York: Free Press, 2014), 46.

95   *"had to live [her] whole"*: Sidney Katz, "The New Wonder Drugs That Fight Insanity," *Maclean's*, November 12, 1955, 114.

95   *The drug's effects were*: Gold and Gold, *Suspicious Minds*, 47.

95   *chlorpromazine was the first*: Shorter, *History of Psychiatry*, 255.

95   *Lehmann published his findings*: Ban, "Fifty Years Chlorpromazine," 495–500.

96   *The Elkeses reported*: Joel Elkes and Charmian Elkes, "Effect of Chlorpromazine on the Behaviour of Chronically Overactive Psychotic Patients," *British Medical Journal* 2, no. 4887 (January 1954): 560–65.

96   *"in no case was"*: Ibid.

96   *SmithKline, which had licensed*: Ban, "Fifty Years Chlorpromazine," 495–500.

96   *If state-funded mental institutions*: Michael Rosenbloom, "Chlorpromazine and the Psychopharmacologic Revolution," *Journal of the American Medical Association* 287, no. 14 (April 2002): 1860–61.

97   *"The ivory-tower critics"*: "Medicine: Pills for the Mind," *Time*, March 7, 1955, 63–64.

97   *"reemergence or exacerbation"*: Harold L. Blackburn and J. L. Allen, "Behavioral Effects of Interrupting and Resuming Tranquilizing Medication Among Schizophrenics," *Journal of Nervous and Mental Disease* 133, no. 4 (October 1961): 303–8.

97   *well-designed, placebo-controlled*: Leon S. Diamond and John B. Marks, "Discontinuance of Tranquilizers Among Chronic Schizophrenic Patients Receiving Maintenance Dosage," *Journal of Nervous and Mental Disease* 131, no. 3 (September 1960): 247–51; see also W. W. Good, Mac Sterling, and Wayne H. Holtzman, "Termination of Chlorpromazine with Schizophrenic Patients," *American Journal of Psychiatry* 115, no. 5 (November 1958): 443–48; see also Burtrum C. Schiele, Norris D. Vestre, and Kenneth E. Stein, "A Comparison of Thioridazine, Trifluoperazine, Chlorpromazine, and Placebo: A Double-Blind Controlled Study on the Treatment of Chronic, Hospitalized, Schizophrenic Patients," *Journal of Clinical and Experimental Psychopathology & Quarterly Review of Psychiatry and Neurology* 22 (July–September 1961): 151–62; see also John R. Shawver et al., "Comparison of Chlorpromazine and Reserpine in Maintenance Drug Therapy," *Diseases of the Nervous System* 20 (October 1959): 452–57; see also David M. Engelhardt et al., "Prevention of Psychiatric Hospitalization with Use of Psychopharmacological Agents," *Journal of the American Medical Association* 173, no. 2 (May 1960): 147–49; see also Martin Gross et al., "Discontinuation of Treatment with Ataractic Drugs: A Preliminary Report," *American Journal of Psychiatry* 116, no. 10 (April 1960): 931–32.

97   *"to achieve ego reorganization"*: Robert F. Prien, Jonathan O. Cole, and Naomi F. Belkin, "Relapse in Chronic Schizophrenics Following Abrupt Withdrawal of Tranquilizing Medication," *British Journal of Psychiatry* 115, no. 523 (June 1969): 680.

97   *He acknowledged the major*: David Healey, *The Psychopharmacologists: Interviews by David Healey* (London: Arnold, 2001), 171.

CHAPTER 8: THE ANTI-PSYCHIATRY MOVEMENT

98   *"no more a person"*: W. H. Auden, "In Memory of Sigmund Freud," in *W. H. Auden: Collected Poems*, ed. Edward Mendelson (New York: Vintage International, 1991), 273–76.

98   *Freud's influence also led psychiatry*: Edward Shorter, *A History of Psychiatry: From the Era of the Asylum to the Age of Prozac* (New York: John Wiley & Sons, 1998).

99   *French philosopher and historian*: Pat Bracken, "On Madness and Civilisation: A History of Insanity in the Age of Reason (1961), by Michel Foucault," *British Journal of Psychiatry* 207, no. 5 (November 2015): 434.

99   *"total institutions"*: Erving Goffman, *Asylums: Essays on the Social Situation of Mental Patients and Other Inmates* (Garden City, NY: Anchor Books, 1961), 4–5.

99   *"no rigorous and explicit"*: Thomas J. Scheff, *Being Mentally Ill: A Sociological Theory*, 3rd ed. (Hawthorne, NY: Aldine de Gruyter, 1999), 2.

99   *While there was unquestionably*: Douglas G. Altman and J. Martin Bland, "Statistics Notes: Absence of Evidence Is Not Evidence of Absence," *British Medical Journal* 311, no. 7003 (August 1995): 485.

100   *Chief among these contrarians*: Ned Stafford, "Thomas Szasz," *British Medical Journal* 345 (October 2012).

100   *Szasz argued that*: Thomas Szasz, "The Myth of Mental Illness," *American Psychologist* 14 (February 1960): 17, 113.

100   *"pseudoscience"*: Thomas Szasz, *The Myth of Mental Illness: Foundations of a Theory of Personal Conduct*, rev. ed. (New York: Hoeber-Harper, 1961), 1.

100   *In a later book*: Thomas Szasz, *Schizophrenia: The Sacred Symbol of Psychiatry*, repr. (Syracuse, NY: Syracuse University Press, 1988), 67, 72, 102, 136.

100   *Szasz's final betrayal*: Hannah S. Decker, *The Making of DSM-III: A Diagnostic Manual's Conquest of American Psychiatry* (New York: Oxford University Press, 2013), 17; see also Matthew Charcet, "The Citizens Commission on Human Rights and Scientology's War Against Psychiatry," in *Handbook of Scientology*, ed. James R. Lewis and Kjersti Hellesøy (Leiden, Neth.: Brill, 2017); see also "Real Disease Vs. Mental 'Disorder,'" Citizens Commission on Human Rights (CCHR) online, accessed August 20, 2020, https://www.cchr.org/quick-facts/real-disease-vs-mental -disorder.html.

101   *"one of the forms"*: R. D. Laing, *The Politics of Experience and the Bird of Paradise*, repr. (Middlesex, UK: Penguin Books, 1967), 107.

101   *"We are all murderers"*: Ibid., 11.

101   *Laing suggested that*: R. D. Laing, *The Divided Self*, repr. (London: Penguin Books, 1990), 34, 38.

101   *Laing applied his radical*: Cheryl McGeachan, "'The World Is Full of Big Bad Wolves': Investigating the Experimental Therapeutic Spaces of R. D. Laing and Aaron Esterson," *History of Psychiatry* 25, no. 3 (September 2014): 283–98.

101   *The basic premise was*: Alex Mar, "Breakdown Palace," Topic, last modified April 2019, https://www.topic.com/breakdown-palace; see also Laing, *Politics of Experience*, 97.

101   *At least two people*: O'Hagan, "Kingsley Hall."

102   *One of the visitors to*: Jeanne Lenzer, "Loren Mosher," *British Medical Journal* 329, no. 7463 (August 2004): 463; see also Leon Redler, "Loren Mosher: U.S. Psychiatrist Whose Non-Drug Treatments Helped His Patients," *Guardian* (US edition) online, last modified July 27, 2004, https://www.theguardian.com/news/2004/jul/28/guard ianobituaries.obituaries.

102   *"a concept of schizophrenia"*: William T. Carpenter Jr. and Robert W. Buchanan, "Commentary on the Soteria Project: Misguided Therapeutics," *Schizophrenia Bulletin* 28, no. 4 (January 2002): 577–81.

102   *By the 1980s*: Lenzer, "Loren Mosher," 463; see also Adam Bernstein, "Contrarian Psychiatrist Loren Mosher, 70," *Washington Post* online, July 20, 2004, B6, https://www .washingtonpost.com/wp-dyn/articles/A63107-2004Jul19.html.

102   *Szasz quotes John Clay*: Thomas Szasz, "The Cure of Souls in the Therapeutic State," *Psychoanalytic Review*, no. 1 (February 2003): 45–62.

103   *"It was a double bind"*: Elizabeth Day and Graham Keeley, "My Father, R. D. Laing: 'He Solved Other People's—but Not His Own,'" *Guardian*, last modified May 13, 2008, https://www.theguardian.com/books/2008/jun/01/mentalhealth.society.

104   *Torrey knew all about*: E. Fuller Torrey, "What Shaped My Career," *Psychiatric Services* 70, no. 10 (October 2019): 961–62.

104   *"When the blame wasn't"*: E. Fuller Torrey, in discussion with the author, July 3, 2019.

104   *In 1977 Torrey published*: E. Fuller Torrey, "A Fantasy Trial About a Real Issue," *Psychology Today*, March 1977, 22.

CHAPTER 9: THE COST OF GOOD INTENTIONS

106   *Rose was designated*: Amy Wachs, "Rose Lieberman" (unpublished report, January 3, 2020), PDF file; see also Committee on Statistics of the American Medico-Psychological Association, *Statistical Manual for the Use of Institutions for the Insane* (New York: Bureau of Statistics of the National Committee for Mental Health, 1918).

107   *On May 6, 1946*: Albert Q. Maisel, "Bedlam 1946: Most U.S. Mental Hospitals Are a Shame and a Disgrace," *Life*, May 6, 1946, 102–18.

107   *Maisel had written about*: University of Montana–Missoula and Office of University Relations, "Albert Q. Maisel to Teach Article Writing at Annual Writers' Conference," news release, June 11, 1958, https://scholarworks.umt.edu/cgi/viewcontent.cgi?article=1251&context=newsreleases.

107   *Deinstitutionalization was a*: Bernard E. Harcourt, "Reducing Mass Incarceration: Lessons from the Deinstitutionalization of Mental Hospitals in the 1960s," *Ohio State Journal of Criminal Law* 9 (January 2011): 53; see also Deanna Pan, "Timeline: Deinstitutionalization and Its Consequences," *Mother Jones* online, last modified April 29, 2013, https://www.motherjones.com/politics/2013/04/timeline-mental-health-america/; see also Deanna Pan, "Map: Which States Have Cut Treatment for the Mentally Ill the Most?," *Mother Jones* online, last modified September 29, 2013, https://www.motherjones.com/politics/2013/04/map-states-cut-treatment-for-mentally-ill/.

108   *"brutality was commonly practiced"*: Maisel, "Bedlam 1946," 106.

108   *Nellie Bly, whose real name*: Nellie Bly [Elizabeth Cochran], *Ten Days in a Mad-House* (New York: Norman L. Munro, 1887).

108   *"Nellie practices insanity"*: Ibid., 7.

108   *More than three decades*: Hannah Karena Jones, *Byberry State Hospital* (Charleston, SC: Arcadia, 2013), 46.

109   *By then, Americans had*: Agence France-Presse (AFP), "How the World Discovered the Nazi Death Camps," *Times of Israel* online, January 14, 2020, https://www.timesofisrael.com/how-the-world-discovered-the-nazi-death-camps/#gs.f7q8jg; see also "Bedlam 1946," American Experience, Public Broadcasting Service (PBS), accessed September 1, 2020, https://www.pbs.org/wgbh/americanexperience/features/lobotomist-bedlam-1946/.

109   *The preceding few decades*: E. Fuller Torrey and Judy Miller, *The Invisible Plague: The Rise of Mental Illness from 1750 to the Present* (New Brunswick, NJ: Rutgers University Press, 2001), 284; see also Alexandra Minna Stern, "That Time the United States Sterilized 60,000 of Its Citizens," *Huffington Post*, last modified January 6, 2016, https://www.huffpost.com/entry/sterilization-united-states_n_568f35f2e4b0c8beacf68713.

109 *This number would grow*: Compulsory sterilization continues to this day in some parts of the United States. See Bill Chappell, "California's Prison Sterilizations Reportedly Echo Eugenics Era," NPR online, last modified July 9, 2013, https://www.npr.org/sections/thetwo-way/2013/07/09/200444613/californias-prison-sterilizations-reportedly-echoes-eugenics-era; see also Erin McCormick, "Survivors of California's Forced Sterilizations: 'It's Like My Life Wasn't Worth Anything,'" *Guardian* (US edition) online, last modified July 19, 2021, https://www.theguardian.com/us-news/2021/jul/19/california-forced-sterilization-prison-survivors-reparations.

109 *"dreary, dilapidated excuses"*: Maisel, "Bedlam 1946," 103.

110 *community-based care*: Gerald N. Grob, *From Asylum to Community: Mental Health Policy in Modern America* (Princeton, NJ: Princeton University Press, 1991).

110 *Its report, published in 1961*: Joint Commission on Mental Illness and Health, *Action for Mental Health: Final Report of the Joint Commission on Mental Illness and Health* (New York: Basic Books, 1961).

110 *community-based treatment*: Donald G. Langsley, "The Community Mental Health Center: Does It Treat Patients?," *Psychiatric Services* 31, no. 12 (1980): 815–19.

110 *Two years later, President Lyndon Johnson*: Torrey, *American Psychosis*, 72–73; see also Alison Mitchell, *Medicaid's Institutions for Mental Disease (IMD) Exclusion*, Congressional Research Service (July 2019).

110 *so-called IMD*: "Reflecting on JFK's Legacy of Community-based Care," Substance Abuse and Mental Health Services Administration, https://www.samhsa.gov/homelessness-programs-resources/hpr-resources/jfks-legacy-community-based-care.

111 *"Having gotten them"*: Michelle R. Smith, "Kennedy's Vision for Mental Health Never Realized," Associated Press News, October 20, 2013.

111 *severe mental illness*: Paul J. Fink and Stephen P. Weinstein, "Whatever Happened to Psychiatry? The Deprofessionalization of Community Mental Health Centers," *American Journal of Psychiatry* 136, no. 4A (1979): 406–9.

111 *patients simply stopped*: Torrey, *American Psychosis*, 44–45.

111 *Around three quarters of people*: Gerald N. Grob, "Public Policy and Mental Illnesses: Jimmy Carter's Presidential Commission on Mental Health," *Milbank Quarterly* 83, no. 3 (September 2005): 425–56.

112 *while the total number of staff*: Walter W. Winslow, "The Changing Role of Psychiatrists in Community Mental Health Centers," *American Journal of Psychiatry* 136, no. 1 (January 1979): 25.

112 *known as transinstitutionalization*: Torrey, *American Psychosis*, 96–113.

112 *mentally ill persons in prisons, nursing homes, and on the streets*: Bernard E. Harcourt, "Reducing Mass Incarceration: Lessons from the Deinstitutionalization of Mental Hospitals in the 1960s" (John M. Olin Program in Law and Economics Working Paper No. 542, 2011); see also Anne E. Parsons, *From Asylum to Prison: Deinstitutionalization and the Rise of Mass Incarceration after 1945* (Chapel Hill: University of North Carolina Press, 2018).

112 *Between 1955 and 1994*: Torrey, *Out of the Shadows*, 8.

112 *The number of long-term*: E. Fuller Torrey, "A Dearth of Psychiatric Beds," *Psychiatric Times* 33, no. 2 (February 2016).

112   *when Ronald Reagan was elected president*: Smith, "Kennedy's Vision."

112   *when state budgets*: Paul Appelbaum (Elizabeth K. Dollard Professor of Psychiatry, Medicine and Law, and Director, Division of Law, Ethics and Psychiatry at Columbia University Department of Psychiatry), in discussion with the author, March 16, 2021.

113   *By the 1990s*: *Psychiatry and Homeless Mentally Ill Persons. Report of the Task Force on the Homeless Mentally Ill* (Washington, DC: American Psychiatric Association, 1990); see also *Deinstitutionalization of the Mentally Ill*, 106th S., S8296 (1999) (statement of Daniel Patrick Moynihan).

113   *These numbers steadily increased*: Social Security Income (SSI), passed in 1972, provided supplemental benefits to anyone sixty-five or older and to people of any age who had specific disabilities. In 1975 the proportion of SSI recipients who were disabled, as opposed to elderly, was 42 percent. By 1994, this number had risen to 67 percent—yet another reflection of the effects of deinstitutionalization. See *Statement Before the Subcommittee on Social Security of the Committee on Ways and Means*, 106th S. (2000) (statement of Edward D. Berkowitz, PhD, Professor and Chair, Department of History, George Washington University).

113   *in May 1994, Moynihan opened*: *Deinstitutionalization, Mental Illness, and Medications: Hearings before the Committee on Finance*, 103rd S., 2–3 (1994) (statement of Daniel Patrick Moynihan, chairman of the committee).

113   *Reading Moynihan's statement*: Ibid.

113   *"Then a generation went by"*: *Deinstitutionalization*, 3 (1994) (statement of Moynihan).

113   *By the mid-2000s*: E. Fuller Torrey et al., *More Mentally Ill Persons Are in Jails and Prisons Than Hospitals: A Survey of the States* (Arlington, VA: Treatment Advocacy Center, May 2010).

113   *In 2014, there were*: Treatment Advocacy Center, *SMI Prevalence in Jails and Prisons*.

113   *Today the three largest*: Jerry Davich, "Confession: My Compassion for Prison Inmates Has Been Incarcerated for Life," Chicago Tribune (Post-Tribune) online, March 16, 2021, https://www.chicagotribune.com/suburbs/post-tribune/opinion/ct-ptb -davich-no-compassion-for-prisoners-st-0317-20210316-l74rzrotj5gxhdz lixly3abr3q-story.html; see also Laura Sullivan, "Nation's Jails Struggle with Mentally Ill Prisoners," September 4, 2011, in *All Things Considered*, podcast, 11:11.

113   *federal entitlements like Medicare and Medicaid*: David Mechanic and David A. Rochefort, "Deinstitutionalization: An Appraisal of Reform," *Annual Review of Sociology* 16 (1990): 301–27.

114   *The high cost of good intentions indeed*: Ibid.

CHAPTER 10: THE TAXONOMIST OF MENTAL ILLNESS

115   *Bible-o'-Madness*: Wang, *Collected Schizophrenias*, 21.

116   *The study, conducted*: John E. Cooper et al., "Cross-National Study of Diagnosis of the Mental Disorders: Some Results from the First Comparative Investigation," *American Journal of Psychiatry* 125, no. 10S (April 1969): 21–29.

116   *Americans applied the diagnosis*: Robert Evan Kendell et al., "Diagnostic Criteria of
       American and British Psychiatrists," *Archives of General Psychiatry* 25, no. 2 (August
       1971): 123–30.

116   *The author was David Rosenhan*: David L. Rosenhan, "On Being Sane in Insane
       Places," *Science* 179, no. 4070 (January 1973): 250–58.

117   *proposed a second*: Rosenhan, Ibid.

117   *"Compared to other types"*: Quoted in Mitchell Wilson, "DSM-III and the Transforma-
       tion of American Psychiatry: A History," *American Journal of Psychiatry* 150, no. 3
       (March 1993): 403.

118   *"a sword plunged"*: Robert L. Spitzer, Scott O. Lilienfeld, and Michael B. Miller, "Rosen-
       han Revisited: The Scientific Credibility of Lauren Slater's Pseudopatient Diagno-
       sis Study," *Journal of Nervous and Mental Disease* 193, no. 11 (November 2005):
       734–39.

118   *Spitzer composed a detailed*: Robert L. Spitzer, "On Pseudoscience in Science, Logic in
       Remission, and Psychiatric Diagnosis: A Critique of Robert Rosenhan's 'On Being
       Sane in Insane Places,'" *Journal of Abnormal Psychiatry* 85, no. 5 (October 1975):
       442–52.

118   *Spitzer was tapped*: Susannah Cahalan, *The Great Pretender: The Undercover Mission
       That Changed Our Understanding of Madness* (New York: Grand Central, 2019),
       172, 177.

118   *The changes Spitzer oversaw*: Decker, *Making of DSM-III*, 35.

118   *As Hannah S. Decker describes*: Ibid., 84–87; see also Alix Spiegel, "The Man Behind
       Psychiatry's Diagnostic Manual," August 18, 2003, in *All Things Considered*, podcast,
       12:43, https://www.npr.org/templates/story/story.php?storyId=1400925.

118   *As a teenager, Spitzer*: Decker, *Making of DSM-III*, 89–90.

118   *"full orgastic potency"*: Wilhelm Reich, *The Function of the Orgasm*, trans. Vincent R.
       Carfagno (New York: Farrar, Straus and Giroux, 1973), 130, 268.

119   *Spitzer's early desire*: Cahalan, *Great Pretender*, 18, 176.

119   *"translating feelings"*: Spiegel, "Psychiatry's Diagnostic Manual."

119   *He also became determined*: Robert L. Spitzer, "Wilhelm Reich and Orgone Therapy:
       The Story of Robert L. Spitzer's Paper, 'An Examination of Wilhelm Reich's Dem-
       onstrations of Orgone Energy,'" *Scientific Review of Mental Health Practice* 4, no. 1
       (Spring/Summer 2005): 9.

119   *Spitzer graduated from*: Jack Drescher, "An Interview with Robert L. Spitzer, MD,"
       chap. 6 in *American Psychiatry and Homosexuality: An Oral History*, ed. Jack
       Drescher and Joseph P. Merlino (New York: Routledge, 2012), 97.

119   *By the time he'd finished*: Decker, *Making of DSM-III*, 92–96; see also Drescher, "Inter-
       view with Spitzer," 99.

120   *"sexual deviations"*: American Psychiatric Association, *Diagnostic and Statistical
       Manual of Mental Disorders*, 2nd ed. (Washington, DC: American Psychiatric As-
       sociation, 1968), 44.

120   *Spitzer didn't know any*: Drescher, "Interview with Spitzer," 99–104; see also Decker,
       Making of DSM-III, 32–33.

121   *Spitzer resolved the dilemma*: Drescher, "Interview with Spitzer," 101–3, and Decker,
       Making of DSM-III, 150–61.

121   *The APA voted*: See footnote 20 in Drescher, "Interview with Spitzer," 102, 109.

121   *In 1987 the latter*: Jack Drescher, "Out of DSM: Depathologizing Homosexuality," *Behavioral Sciences* 5, no. 4 (December 2015): 565–75.

121   *The change was officially*: Rick Mayes and Allan V. Horwitz, "DSM-III and the Revolution in the Classification of Mental Illness," *Journal of the History of the Behavioral Sciences* 41, no. 3 (June 2005): 249–67.

121   *Spitzer's adroit handling*: Drescher, "Interview with Spitzer," 98; see also Decker, *Making of DSM-III*, 96.

122   *He quickly proposed*: Decker, *Making of DSM-III*, 143; see also Ronald Bayer and Robert L. Spitzer, "Neurosis, Psychodynamics, and DSM-III: A History of the Controversy," *Archives of General Psychiatry* 42, no. 2 (March 1985): 187–96; see also Alina Surís, Ryan Holliday, and Carol S. North, "The Evolution of the Classification of Psychiatric Disorders," *Behavioral Sciences* 6, no. 1 (March 2016): 5.

122   *"Chinese menu"*: Richard J. Haier, "The Diagnosis of Schizophrenia: A Review of Recent Developments," *Schizophrenia Bulletin* 6, no. 3 (January 1980): 421.

123   *"clinical judgment is of paramount"*: Decker, *Making of DSM-III*, 298.

124   *That came in 2019*: Cahalan, *Great Pretender*; see also Jennifer Szalai, "Investigating a Famous Study About the Line Between Sanity and Madness," review of *The Great Pretender*, by Susannah Cahalan, *New York Times* online, November 27, 2019, https://www.nytimes.com/2019/11/27/books/review-great-pretender-susannah -cahalan.html; see also Emily Eakin, "Her Illness Was Misdiagnosed as Madness. Now Susannah Cahalan Takes on Madness in Medicine," *New York Times* online, November 2, 2019, https://www.nytimes.com/2019/11/02/books/susannah -cahalan-great-pretender.html.

CHAPTER 11: THE ENCHANTED LOOM

127   *"Schizophrenia is the graveyard"*: G. W. Roberts and C. J. Bruton, "Notes from the Graveyard: Neuropathology and Schizophrenia," *Neuropathology and Applied Neurobiology* 16, no. 1 (February 1990): 3–16.

129   *Looking at the brain's exterior*: Cornelia I. Bargmann and Jeffrey A. Lieberman, "What the BRAIN Initiative Means for Psychiatry," *American Journal of Psychiatry* 171, no. 10 (October 2014): 1038–40.

129   *The chemical conduit*: Dale Purves et al., "Neurotransmitters," chap. 6 in *Neuroscience*, ed. Dale Purves et al. (Sunderland, MA: Sinauer, 2001).

130   *Antonie van Leeuwenhoek was*: "Antonie Van Leeuwenhoek," in *The Britannica Guide to the World's Most Influential People*, ed. Philip Wolny, Virginia Forte, and Kevin Geller (Britannica Digital Learning, 2017).

130   *In 1873 the Italian pathologist*: Francisco López-Muñoz, Jesús Boya, and Cecilio Alamo, "Neuron Theory, the Cornerstone of Neuroscience, on the Centenary of the Nobel Prize Award to Santiago Ramón y Cajal," *Brain Research Bulletin* 70, no. 4–6 (October 2006): 391–405.

131 *He was prone to*: Stanley Finger, *Minds Behind the Brain: A History of the Pioneers and Their Discoveries* (New York: Oxford University Press, 2000), 207.

131 *"saw in the cadaver"*: Santiago Ramón y Cajal, *Recollections of My Life* [*Recuerdos de mi vida*], trans. E. Horne Craigie and Juan Cano, 3rd ed. (Cambridge, MA: MIT Press, 1996), 169.

131 *Cajal made a series*: Marina Bentivoglio, "Life and Discoveries of Santiago Ramón y Cajal," NobelPrize.org., last modified April 20, 1998, Nobel Prize Outreach AB 2021, https://www.nobelprize.org/prizes/medicine/1906/cajal/article/; see also Susana Martinez-Conde, "Santiago Ramón y Cajal, the Young Artist Who Grew up to Invent Neuroscience," *Scientific American*, March 30, 2018; see also Finger, *Minds Behind the Brain*, 197–216.

132 *The X-ray, invented in 1895*: Daniel J. Nolan, "100 Years of X Rays," *British Medical Journal* 310 (March 1995).

133 *Godfrey Hounsfield*: "The Nobel Prize in Physiology or Medicine 1979," news release, October 11, 1979, NobelPrize.org, Nobel Prize Outreach AB 2021, https://www.nobelprize.org/prizes/medicine/1979/press-release/.

133 *The first CT scan*: Eve C. Johnstone et al., "Cerebral Ventricular Size and Cognitive Impairment in Chronic Schizophrenia," *Lancet* 308, no. 7992 (October 1976): 924–26.

133 *The ventricular enlargement*: Daniel Goleman, "Brain Structure Differences Linked to Schizophrenia in Study of Twins," *New York Times* online, March 22, 1990, https://www.nytimes.com/1990/03/22/us/health-psychiatry-brain-structure-differences-linked-schizophrenia-study-twins.html.

134 *In 1982 a little-known*: Irwin Feinberg, "Schizophrenia: Caused by a Fault in Programmed Synaptic Elimination During Adolescence?," *Journal of Psychiatric Research* 17, no. 4 (1982): 319–34.

135 *Sleep was what*: Irwin Feinberg et al., "Sleep Electroencephalographic and Eye-Movement Patterns in Schizophrenic Patients," *Journal of Psychiatric Research* 5, no. 1 (February 1964): 44–53; see also Irwin Feinberg, Richard L. Koresko, and Naomi Heller, "EEG Sleep Patterns as a Function of Normal and Pathological Aging in Man," *Journal of Psychiatric Research* 5, no. 2 (June 1967): 107–44; see also Irwin Feinberg et al., "Stage 4 Sleep in Schizophrenia," *Archives of General Psychiatry* 21, no. 3 (September 1969): 262–66.

135 *Colleagues of Feinberg's*: Seymour S. Kety, "Human Cerebral Blood Flow and Oxygen Consumption as Related to Aging," *Journal of Chronic Diseases* 3, no. 5 (May 1956): 478–86.

135 *Then, in 1979 a pediatric*: Peter R. Huttenlocher, "Synaptic Density in Human Frontal Cortex—Developmental Changes and Effects of Aging," *Brain Research* 163, no. 2 (March 1979): 195–205.

136 *he proposed a novel*: Feinberg, "Schizophrenia: Caused by a Fault."

137 *volume reductions*: Bernhard Bogerts et al., "Reduced Temporal Limbic Structure Volumes on Magnetic Resonance Images in First Episode Schizophrenia," *Psychiatry Research: Neuroimaging* 35, no. 1 (April 1990): 1–13; see also Bernhard Bogerts et al., "Hippocampus-Amygdala Volumes and Psychopathology in Chronic Schizo-

phrenia," *Biological Psychiatry* 33, no. 4 (February 1993): 236–46; see also Martha E. Shenton et al., "Abnormalities of the Left Temporal Lobe and Thought Disorder in Schizophrenia: A Quantitative Magnetic Resonance Imaging Study," *New England Journal of Medicine* 327, no. 9 (August 1992): 604–12; see also Matcheri S. Keshavan et al., "Decreased Caudate Volume in Neuroleptic-Naive Psychotic Patients," *American Journal of Psychiatry* 155, no. 6 (June 1998): 774–78.

137   *increased volume*: Gustav Degreef et al., "Volumes of Ventricular System Subdivisions Measured from Magnetic Resonance Images in First-Episode Schizophrenic Patients," *Archives of General Psychiatry* 49, no. 7 (July 1992): 531–37.

137   *physiologic differences*: Marek Kubicki, Robert W. McCarley, and Martha E. Shenton, "Evidence for White Matter Abnormalities in Schizophrenia," *Current Opinion in Psychiatry* 18, no. 2 (March 2005): 121.

137   *In 1915 Elmer Ernest Southard*: Elmer Ernest Southard, "On the Topographical Distribution of Cortex Lesions and Anomalies in Dementia Praecox, with Some Account of Their Functional Significance," *American Journal of Insanity* 71, no. 3 (January 1915): 603–71.

138   *In March 1990*: Richard L. Suddath et al., "Anatomical Abnormalities in the Brains of Monozygotic Twins Discordant for Schizophrenia," *New England Journal of Medicine* 322, no. 12 (March 1990): 789–94.

139   *"Almost all the drop in stigma"*: Torrey, in discussion with the author.

140   *With the advent of MRI*: Timothea Toulopoulou et al., "The Relationship Between Volumetric Brain Changes and Cognitive Function: A Family Study on Schizophrenia," *Biological Psychiatry* 56, no. 6 (September 2004): 447–53; see also Geartsje Boonstra et al., "Brain Volume Changes After Withdrawal of Atypical Antipsychotics in Patients with First-Episode Schizophrenia," *Journal of Clinical Psychopharmacology* 31, no. 2 (April 2011): 146–53; see also Sander V. Haijma et al., "Brain Volumes in Schizophrenia: A Meta-Analysis in over 18,000 Subjects," *Schizophrenia Bulletin* 39, no. 5 (September 2013): 1129–38.

140   *In one five-year study*: Neeltje E. M. van Haren et al., "Focal Gray Matter Changes in Schizophrenia Across the Course of the Illness: A 5-Year Follow-up Study," *Neuropsychopharmacology* 32, no. 10 (October 2007): 2057–66.

140   *The main evidence for medication*: Karl-Anton Dorph-Petersen et al., "The Influence of Chronic Exposure to Antipsychotic Medications on Brain Size Before and After Tissue Fixation: A Comparison of Haloperidol and Olanzapine in Macaque Monkeys," *Neuropsychopharmacology* 30, no. 9 (September 2005): 1649–61; see also Glenn T. Konopaske et al., "Effect of Chronic Exposure to Antipsychotic Medication on Cell Numbers in the Parietal Cortex of Macaque Monkeys," *Neuropsychopharmacology* 32, no. 6 (June 2007): 1216–23.

141   *Insights from Developments in Imaging*: For this section, I am grateful for the help of Dr. Frank Provenzano, Assistant Professor of Neurological Sciences, Taub Institute for Research on Alzheimer's Disease and the Aging Brain in the Department of Neurology at Columbia University.

141   *Magnetic resonance spectroscopy (MRS)*: Sachin K. Gujar et al., "Magnetic Resonance Spectroscopy," *Journal of Neuro-Ophthalmology* 25, no. 3 (September 2005): 217–26; see also Stephen R. Dager et al., "Research Applications of Magnetic Reso-

nance Spectroscopy (MRS) to Investigate Psychiatric Disorders," *Topics in Magnetic Resonance Imaging* 19, no. 2 (April 2008): 81–96.

141   *Functional magnetic resonance imaging (fMRI)*: Edgar A. DeYoe et al., "Functional Magnetic Resonance Imaging (fMRI) of the Human Brain," *Journal of Neuroscience Methods* 54, no. 2 (October 1994): 171–87; see also Nina V. Kraguljac, Annusha Srivastava, and Adrienne C. Lahti, "Memory Deficits in Schizophrenia: A Selective Review of Functional Magnetic Resonance Imaging (fMRI) Studies," *Behavioral Sciences* 3, no. 3 (September 2013): 330–47.

142   *Diffusion tensor imaging (DTI)*: Andrew L. Alexander et al., "Diffusion Tensor Imaging of the Brain," *Neurotherapeutics* 4, no. 3 (July 2007): 316–29; see also Marek Kubicki et al., "A Review of Diffusion Tensor Imaging Studies in Schizophrenia," *Journal of Psychiatric Research* 41, no. 1/2 (January/February 2007): 15–30.

142   *PET imaging relies*: Yen F. Tai and Paola Piccini, "Applications of Positron Emission Tomography (PET) in Neurology," *Journal of Neurology, Neurosurgery & Psychiatry* 75, no. 5 (April 2004): 669–76; see also Ramin V. Parsey and J. John Mann, "Applications of Positron Emission Tomography in Psychiatry," *Seminars in Nuclear Medicine* 33, no. 2 (April 2003): 129–35.

142   *PET findings in schizophrenia*: Provenzano added: "There have not been consistent findings with this technique, and they vary depending on the severity of illness and medication."

142   *James Robertson, the engineer*: US Department of Energy and Office of Biological Environmental Research, *A Vital Legacy: Biological and Environmental Research in the Atomic Age*, Ernest Orlando Lawrence Berkeley National Laboratory (September 1997), 25–26.

143   *Interneurons serve two*: Leonid S. Krimer and Patricia S. Goldman-Rakic, "Prefrontal Microcircuits: Membrane Properties and Excitatory Input of Local, Medium, and Wide Arbor Interneurons," *Journal of Neuroscience* 21, no. 11 (June 2001): 3788–96; see also Enrico Cherubini and Fiorenzo Conti, "Generating Diversity at GABAergic Synapses," *Trends in Neurosciences* 24, no. 3 (March 2001): 155–62.

143   *Benes looking in the medial temporal lobe*: Francine M. Benes et al., "A Reduction of Nonpyramidal Cells in Sector CA2 of Schizophrenics and Manic Depressives," *Biological Psychiatry* 44, no. 2 (July 1988): 88–97.

143   *Lewis in the frontal lobes*: David A. Lewis, "GABAergic Local Circuit Neurons and Prefrontal Cortical Dysfunction in Schizophrenia Brain Research," *Brain Research Reviews* 31, no. 2/3 (March 2000): 270–76.

143   *Stereological counting involves*: D. S. Woodruff-Pak, "Memory and Aging, Neural Basis Of," in *Encyclopedia of Behavioral Neuroscience*, ed. George F. Koob, Michel Le Moal, and Richard F. Thompson (Oxford, UK: Academic Press, 2010), 200–205.

143   *Their findings confirmed*: They would have been the first but for a prior report of reduced neuronal number in the thalamus (medial dorsal nucleus) that has not been consistently replicated. See Bente Pakkenberg, "Pronounced Reduction of Total Neuron Number in Mediodorsal Thalamic Nucleus and Nucleus Accumbens in Schizophrenics," *Archives of General Psychiatry* 47, no. 11 (November 1990): 1023–28.

144   *Goldman-Rakic had attended*: Mark Henderson, "Patricia Goldman-Rakic," *Lancet* 362, no. 9392 (October 2003): 1337.

144   *Goldman-Rakic's research on*: Patricia S. Goldman-Rakic, "The Relevance of the Dopamine-D1 Receptor in the Cognitive Symptoms of Schizophrenia," *Neuropsychopharmacology* 21, no. 2 (December 1999): S170–S80.

144   *What Selemon found*: Lynn D. Selemon and Patricia S. Goldman-Rakic, "The Reduced Neuropil Hypothesis: A Circuit Based Model of Schizophrenia," *Biological Psychiatry* 45, no. 1 (January 1999): 17–25.

145   *They were quickly extended*: Leisa A. Glantz and David A. Lewis, "Decreased Dendritic Spine Density on Prefrontal Cortical Pyramidal Neurons in Schizophrenia," *Archives of General Psychiatry* 57, no. 1 (January 2000): 65–73.

145   *Subsequent work by*: Joseph N. Pierri et al., "Decreased Somal Size of Deep Layer 3 Pyramidal Neurons in the Prefrontal Cortex of Subjects with Schizophrenia," *Archives of General Psychiatry* 58, no. 5 (May 2001): 466–73; see also Nutan Kolluri et al., "Lamina-Specific Reductions in Dendritic Spine Density in the Prefrontal Cortex of Subjects with Schizophrenia," *American Journal of Psychiatry* 162, no. 6 (June 2005): 1200–1202; see also Kevin Broadbelt, William Byne, and Liesl B. Jones, "Evidence for a Decrease in Basilar Dendrites of Pyramidal Cells in Schizophrenic Medial Prefrontal Cortex," *Schizophrenia Research* 58, no. 1 (November 2002): 75–81.

145   *"make it in a man's world"*: "Patricia Goldman-Rakic," Connecticut Women's Hall of Fame, accessed May 4, 2021, https://www.cwhf.org/inductees/patricia-goldman -rakic; see also Amy F. T. Arnsten, "Patricia Goldman-Rakic: A Remembrance," *Neuron* 40, no. 3 (October 2003): 465–70.

146   *We're able to go beyond*: Isobel Ronai and Paul E. Griffiths, "The Case for Basic Biological Research," *Trends in Molecular Medicine: CellPress* 25, no. 2 (Feburary 2019): 65–69.

146   *Neuroscience has generated*: Bargmann and Lieberman, "BRAIN Initiative."

CHAPTER 12: AM I MY GENES?

149   *Brandon Staglin was about*: Brandon Staglin, in discussion with the author, November 15, 2019.

150   *A family history going back*: Amy Wachs, "Staglin Genealogy Research" (unpublished report, February 21, 2021), PDF file.

151   *basic model of genetic heritability*: Siddhartha Mukherjee, *The Gene: An Intimate History* (New York: Scribner, 2016), 47–63.

151   *In France, the psychiatrist*: Kelly Hurley, "Hereditary Taint and Cultural Contagion: The Social Etiology of Fin-De-Siècle Degeneration Theory," *Nineteenth Century Contexts* 14, no. 2 (1990): 193–214; see also Ernest L. Abel, "Benedict-Augustin Morel (1809–1873)," *American Journal of Psychiatry* 161, no. 12 (December 2004): 2185.

151   *The term "eugenics"*: Andrea DenHoead, "The Forgotten Lessons of the American Eugenics Movement," *New Yorker* online, last modified April 27, 2016, https://www .newyorker.com/books/page-turner/the-forgotten-lessons-of-the-american-eugen ics-movement; see also Peter J. Bowler, *Evolution: The History of an Idea*, 3rd ed.

(Los Angeles: University of California Press, 2003), 309–10; see also Mukherjee, *The Gene*, 64–76.

151   *Charles Davenport expanded*: Joshua A. Krisch, "When Racism Was a Science," *New York Times* online, October 13, 2014, https://www.nytimes.com/2014/10/14/sci ence/haunted-files-the-eugenics-record-office-recreates-a-dark-time-in-a-laborato rys-past.html; see also Stefan Kühl, *The Nazi Connection: Eugenics, American Racism, and German National Socialism* (New York: Oxford University Press, 1994), 14–21, 68–70; see also Mukherjee, *The Gene*, 76–77.

152   *In 1927 the practice*: *Buck v. Bell* (274 U.S. 1927).

152   *More than thirty US states*: Torrey and Miller, *Invisible Plague*, 284; see also Stern, "United States Sterilized 60,000."

153   *Dawkins's book took*: Richard Dawkins, *The Selfish Gene*, 2nd ed. (New York: Oxford University Press, 1989), ix, 11.

153   *Each of us has around*: Cassandra Willyard, "New Human Gene Tally Reignites Debate," *Nature* 558, no. 7710 (June 2018): 354–56; see also J. Craig Venter et al., "The Sequence of the Human Genome," *Science* 291, no. 5507 (February 2001): 1304–51.

154   *What we term "negative selection"*: Matthew Avila, Gunvant Thaker, and Helene Adami, "Genetic Epidemiology and Schizophrenia: A Study of Reproductive Fitness," *Schizophrenia Research* 47, no. 2/3 (March 2001): 233–41.

154   *In the 1940s and 1950s*: Stephen F. Schaffner and Pardis C. Sabeti, "Evolutionary Adaptation in the Human Lineage," *Nature Education* 1, no. 1 (2008): 14; see also Pardis C. Sabeti, "Natural Selection: Uncovering Mechanisms of Evolutionary Adaptation to Infectious Disease," *Nature Education* 1, no. 1 (2008): 13.

154   *Since sickle cell disease*: Anthony Clifford Allison, "Protection Afforded by Sickle-Cell Trait Against Subtertian Malarial Infection," *British Medical Journal* 1, no. 4857 (February 1954): 290–94.

154   *It was found that the*: Lucio Luzzatto, "Sickle Cell Anaemia and Malaria," *Mediterranean Journal of Hematology and Infectious Diseases* 4, no. 1 (October 2012): e2012065; see also Allison, "Protection Afforded by Sickle-Cell Trait."

155   *Add to this list*: Jari Tiihonen et al., "Effectiveness of Antipsychotic Treatments in a Nationwide Cohort of Patients in Community Care After First Hospitalisation Due to Schizophrenia and Schizoaffective Disorder: Observational Follow-up Study," *British Medical Journal* 333, no. 7561 (July 2006): 224; see also World Health Organization (WHO), *Excess Mortality in Persons with Severe Mental Disorders* (Geneva: WHO, November 2015); see also Mark Olfson et al., "Premature Mortality Among Adults with Schizophrenia in the United States," *JAMA Psychiatry* 72, no. 12 (December 2015): 1172–81; see also Jari Tiihonen, Antti Tanskanen, and Heidi Taipale, "20-Year Nationwide Follow-up Study on Discontinuation of Antipsychotic Treatment in First-Episode Schizophrenia," *American Journal of Psychiatry* 175, no. 8 (August 2018): 765–73; see also Mark Olfson et al., "Suicide Risk in Medicare Patients with Schizophrenia Across the Life Span," *JAMA Psychiatry* 78, no. 8 (May 2021): 876–85.

155   *Females with schizophrenia have*: Susana Ochoa et al., "Gender Differences in Schizophrenia and First-Episode Psychosis: A Comprehensive Literature Review," *Schizophrenia Research and Treatment* 2012 (April 2012).

157   *"the experience and behaviour"*: Laing, *Politics of Experience*, 95.

157   *"the nature and origins"*: Theodore Lidz, *The Origin & Treatment of Schizophrenic Disorders* (New York: Basic Books, 1973), 12.

157   *He began working with*: Philip S. Holzman, "Seymour S. Kety and the Genetics of Schizophrenia," *Neuropsychopharmacology* 25, no. 3 (September 2001): 299–304.

157   *Kety and his colleagues knew*: Seymour S. Kety et al., "Mental Illness in the Biological and Adoptive Families of Adopted Individuals Who Have Become Schizophrenic," *Behavior Genetics* 6, no. 3 (July 1976): 219–25; see also Irving I. Gottesman and Dorothea Wolfgram, *Schizophrenia Genesis: The Origins of Madness* (New York: W. H. Freeman, 1991), 95–97.

158   *Kety examined children*: Seymour S. Kety, "Schizophrenic Illness in the Families of Schizophrenic Adoptees: Findings from the Danish National Sample," *Schizophrenia Bulletin* 14, no. 2 (January 1988): 217–22.

159   *In My Heart*: I am indebted to Martin Juman for helping me to recall and clarify many details of Michael's story, both in our meetings of November 18 and 19, 2019, and in his unpublished written account of Michael's life.

161   *Michael was hospitalized*: Lisa Belkin, "What the Jumans Didn't Know About Michael," *New York Times*, March 14, 1999, 6.

161   *Michael's previous psychiatrist*: Letter from Michael Juman's former psychiatrist to author (December 18, 1989). Supplied by Martin Juman.

162   *During the year he*: Discharge note from High Point hospital in Port Chester, NY (October 18, 1988).

163   *He would later say*: From a recording of a phone message from Michael in: "Secrets & Lies (Adoption)," *60 Minutes*, aired July 5, 1998, on CBS.

164   *His comment was based on*: Donald W. Black, Giles Warrack, and George Winokur, "The Iowa Record-Linkage Study: I. Suicides and Accidental Deaths Among Psychiatric Patients," *Archives of General Psychiatry* 42, no. 1 (January 1985): 71–75; see also J. B. Copas and Ashley Robin, "Suicide in Psychiatric In-Patients," *British Journal of Psychiatry* 141, no. 5 (November 1982): 503–11.

165   *The social worker at Louise Wise*: Belkin, "What the Jumans Didn't Know," 6.

165   *"Florence had difficulty"*: Ibid.

165   *The case went to trial*: *Juman v. Louise Wise Services*, 159 Misc. 2d 314, 608 N.Y.S.2d 612 (N.Y. Sup. Ct. 1994); see also *Juman v. Louise Wise Services*, 211 A.D.2d 446, 620 N.Y.S.2d 371 (N.Y. App. Div. 1995); see also *Juman v. Louise Wise Services*, 174 Misc. 2d 49, 663 N.Y.S. 2d 483 (N.Y. Sup. Ct. 1997); see also *Juman v. Louise Wise Services*, 254 A.D.2d 72, 678 N.Y.S.2d 611 (N.Y. App. Div. 1998); see also *Juman v. Louise Wise Services*, 3 A.D.3d 309, 770 N.Y.S.2d 305 (N.Y. App. Div. 2004); see also Paul Appelbaum, in discussion with the author, January 8, 2021; see also Amy Wachs, "Adoption Practices" (unpublished report, March 8, 2021), PDF file.

165   *Similar legal questions have*: Wachs, "Adoption Practices"; see also *Norman Et Al. v. Xytex Corporation Et Al.*, 310 Ga. 127 (Ga. Sup. Ct. 2020); see also Ross Williams, "Georgia Supreme Court Allows Couple to Pursue Case of Sperm Donor 'Fraud,'" *Georgia Recorder* online, September 28, 2020, https://georgiarecorder .com/2020/09/28/georgia-supreme-court-allows-couple-to-pursue-case-of-sperm

-donor-fraud/; see also Kate Brumback, "Georgia Court Allows Lawsuit Against Sperm Bank to Proceed," *Washington Post*, September 20, 2020.

166   *"They put Michael in my arms"*: Martin Juman, email message to author, July 12, 2021.

166   *a detailed family history*: Amy Wachs, "Dayboch Report" (unpublished report, June 26, 2020), PDF file.

167   *Brandon's background suggests*: Wachs, "Staglin Genealogy Research."

167   *One well-known case*: J. Alexander Bodkin et al., "Targeted Treatment of Individuals with Psychosis Carrying a Copy Number Variant Containing a Genomic Triplication of the Glycine Decarboxylase Gene," *Biological Psychiatry* 86, no. 7 (October 2019): 523–35.

168   *"like giving insulin"*: Thomas Insel, "Post by Former NIMH Director Thomas Insel: Celebrating Science," National Institute of Mental Health, March 21, 2014, https://www.nimh.nih.gov/about/directors/thomas-insel/blog/2014/celebrating-science.

169   *In a 1988 publication*: Robin Sherrington et al., "Localization of a Susceptibility Locus for Schizophrenia on Chromosome 5," *Nature* 336, no. 6195 (November 1988): 164–67.

169   *The* New York Times *trumpeted*: Harold M. Schmeck Jr., "Schizophrenia Study Finds Strong Signs of Hereditary Cause," *New York Times*, November 10, 1988, A1.

169   *In 2003 the Human Genome Project*: International Human Genome Sequencing Consortium, "Finishing the Euchromatic Sequence of the Human Genome," *Nature* 431, no. 7011 (October 2004): 931–45; see also National Human Genome Research Institute, "Human Genome Project Results," updated November 12, 2018, https://www.genome.gov/human-genome-project/results; see also National Human Genome Research Institute, "What Is the Human Genome Project?," updated October 28, 2018, https://www.genome.gov/human-genome-project/What.

170   *But perhaps the bigger surprise*: Another surprise was the fact that only 1 percent of the human genome are genes that code for proteins (called exons). The other 99 percent of noncoding DNA ("junk" DNA) contains regulatory sequences signaling enzymes and transcription factors about where to activate or silence the expression of coding genes. See also Wojciech Makalowski, "Not Junk After All," *Science* 300, no. 5623 (May 2003): 1246–47.

170   *less than 1 percent*: National Institutes of Health and Biological Sciences Curriculum Study, *Understanding Human Genetic Variation*, NIH Curriculum Supplement Series (Bethesda, MD: National Institutes of Health, 2007), https://www.ncbi.nlm.nih.gov/books/NBK20363/.

170   *Through further study of*: Stylianos E. Antonarakis and David N. Cooper, "Human Gene Mutation: Mechanisms and Consequences," in *Vogel and Motulsky's Human Genetics: Problems and Approaches*, ed. Michael R. Speicher, Arno G. Motulsky, and Stylianos E. Antonarakis (New York: Springer, 2009).

171   *Michael Wigler pioneered*: Robert Lucito et al., "Representational Oligonucleotide Microarray Analysis: A High-Resolution Method to Detect Genome Copy Number Variation," *Genome Research* 13, no. 10 (October 2003): 2291–305.

171   *An oligonucleotide is a*: National Human Genome Research Institute, "Human Genome Project Results."

171   *Wigler's primary focus*: Virginia Hughes, "Michael Wigler: Applying Simple Logic to

Complex Genetics," *Spectrum News*, September 18, 2009, https://www.spectrumnews
.org/news/profiles/michael-wigler-applying-simple-logic-to-complex-genetics/.

171 *Wigler and Sebat found*: Jonathan Sebat et al., "Strong Association of De Novo Copy
Number Mutations with Autism," *Science* 316, no. 5823 (April 2007): 445–49; see
also Jonathan Sebat et al., "Large-Scale Copy Number Polymorphism in the Human
Genome," *Science* 305, no. 5683 (July 2004): 525–28; see also Tom Walsh et al., "Rare
Structural Variants Disrupt Multiple Genes in Neurodevelopmental Pathways in
Schizophrenia," *Science* 320, no. 5875 (April 2008): 539–43; see also Jonathan Sebat,
Deborah L. Levy, and Shane E. McCarthy, "Rare Structural Variants in Schizophre-
nia: One Disorder, Multiple Mutations; One Mutation, Multiple Disorders," *Trends
in Genetics* 25, no. 12 (December 2009): 528–35.

172 *But molecular genetic studies*: Michael Ronemus et al., "The Role of De Novo Mutations in the Genetics of Autism Spectrum Disorders," *Nature Reviews Genetics* 15,
no. 2 (February 2014): 133–41; see also Ivan Iossifov et al., "The Contribution of
De Novo Coding Mutations to Autism Spectrum Disorder," *Nature* 515, no. 7526
(November 2014): 216–21.

172 *Women who became pregnant*: Carl Zimmer, "The Famine Ended 70 Years Ago, but
Dutch Genes Still Bear Scars," *New York Times* online, January 13, 2018, https://
www.nytimes.com/2018/01/31/science/dutch-famine-genes.html.

172 *Prenatal exposure to influenza*: Alan S. Brown et al., "Serologic Evidence of Prenatal
Influenza in the Etiology of Schizophrenia," *Archives of General Psychiatry* 61, no. 8
(August 2004): 774–80; see also Alan S. Brown, "Prenatal Infection as a Risk Factor
for Schizophrenia," *Schizophrenia Bulletin* 32, no. 2 (April 2006): 200–202.

172 *certain drugs taken during*: M. A. Honein, L. J. Paulozzi, and J. D. Erickson, "Continued Occurrence of Accutane-Exposed Pregnancies," *Teratology* 64, no. 3 (August
2001): 142–47; see also James E. Crandall et al., "Retinoic Acid Influences Neuronal
Migration from the Ganglionic Eminence to the Cerebral Cortex," *Journal of Neurochemistry* 119, no. 4 (November 2011): 723–35.

173 *The third advance*: National Human Genome Research Institute, "Genome-Wide Association Studies Fact Sheet," updated August 17, 2020, https://www.genome.gov
/about-genomics/fact-sheets/Genome-Wide-Association-Studies-Fact-Sheet.

173 *Most of the genes*: Dimitrios Avramopoulos, "Recent Advances in the Genetics of
Schizophrenia," *Molecular Neuropsychiatry* 4, no. 1 (June 2018): 35–51.

173 *GWAS have shed additional*: Daniel J. M. Crouch and Walter F. Bodmer, "Polygenic
Inheritance, GWAS, Polygenic Risk Scores, and the Search for Functional Variants,"
Proceedings of the National Academy of Sciences 117, no. 32 (August 2020): 18924–33.

173 *The "common disease–common variant" form*: Nicholas J. Schork et al., "Common
Vs. Rare Allele Hypotheses for Complex Diseases," *Current Opinion in Genetics &
Development* 19, no. 3 (June 2009): 212–19.

174 *DiGeorge syndrome*: Donna M. McDonald-McGinn and Kathleen E. Sullivan,
"Chromosome 22q11.2 Deletion Syndrome (Digeorge Syndrome/Velocardiofacial
Syndrome)," *Medicine* 90, no. 1 (January 2011): 1–18; see also Stephen Monks et al.,
"Further Evidence for High Rates of Schizophrenia in 22q11.2 Deletion Syndrome,"
Schizophrenia Research 153, no. 1–3 (March 2014): 231–36.

175 *There is another factor*: Cecilia Heyes, "New Thinking: The Evolution of Human Cog-

nition," *Philosophical Transactions of the Royal Society B: Biological Sciences* 367, no. 1599 (August 2012).

CHAPTER 13: PSYCHOSIS, PSYCHEDELICS, AND THE SEROTONIN THEORY

177   *The first drug*: Albert Hofmann, *LSD, My Problem Child: Reflections on Sacred Drugs, Mysticism, and Science*, trans. Jonathan Ott (New York: McGraw-Hill, 1980), 5–11; see also Sean J. Belouin and Jack E. Henningfield, "Psychedelics: Where We Are Now, Why We Got Here, What We Must Do," *Neuropharmacology* 142 (November 2018): 7–19.

178   *"strange feeling"*: Albert Hofmann, interview by Stanislav Grof, Multidisciplinary Association for Psychedelic Studies (MAPS), 1984, https://maps.org/news-letters /v11n2/11222gro.pdf.

178   *While preparing a batch*: Martin Lee and Bruce Shlain, *Acid Dreams: The Complete Social History of LSD: The CIA, the Sixties, and Beyond* (New York: Grove Press, 1992), xviii.

178   *"I had the impression"*: Ibid.

178   *"a malevolent, insidious"*: Hofmann, *LSD, My Problem Child*, 13.

178   *"Kaleidoscopic, fantastic images"*: Ibid., 14.

178   *"Everything glistened"*: Ibid.

178   *The events of what came*: Lee and Shlain, *Acid Dreams*, xviii–xix; see also Paolo Fusar-Poli and Stefan Borgwardt, "Albert Hofmann, the Father of LSD (1906–2008)," *Neuropsychobiology* 58, no. 1 (September 2008): 53–54.

179   *In 1947 LSD was*: Ben Sessa, "A Brief History of Psychedelics in Medical Practices: Psychedelic Medical History 'Before the Hiatus,'" chap. 2 in *The Psychedelic Policy Quagmire: Health, Law, Freedom, and Society*, ed. Harold J. Ellens and Thomas B. Roberts (Santa Barbara, CA: Praeger, 2015), 38–44.

179   *It was tested initially*: Walter N. Pahnke et al., "The Experimental Use of Psychedelic (LSD) Psychotherapy," *Journal of the American Medical Association* 212, no. 11 (June 1970): 1856–63; see also Juan José Fuentes et al., "Therapeutic Use of LSD in Psychiatry: A Systematic Review of Randomized-Controlled Clinical Trials," *Frontiers in Psychiatry* 10 (January 2020): 943.

179   *LSD showed such*: Sessa, "Brief History of Psychedelics," 38–44.

179   *By the mid-1960s*: Mo Costandi, "A Brief History of Psychedelic Psychiatry," *Guardian* (US edition) online, last modified September 2, 2014, https://www.theguardian .com/science/neurophilosophy/2014/sep/02/psychedelic-psychiatry.

181   *endotoxin theory of schizophrenia*: M. L. Throne and C. W. Gowdey, "A Critical Review of Endogenous Psychotoxins as a Cause of Schizophrenia," *Canadian Psychiatric Association Journal* 12, no. 2 (April 1967): 159–74; see also Lewis Brodsky, "A Biochemical Survey of Schizophrenia," *Canadian Psychiatric Association Journal* 15, no. 4 (August 1970): 375–88.

181   *Bodily fluids were chemically*: William T. Carpenter Jr. et al., "The Therapeutic Efficacy

of Hemodialysis in Schizophrenia," *New England Journal of Medicine* 308, no. 12 (March 1983): 669–75; see also Alan A. Boulton and Carol A. Felton, "The 'Pink Spot' and Schizophrenia," *Nature* 211, no. 5056 (September 1966): 1404–5.

181   *It was true*: Max Rinkel et al., "Experimental Schizophrenia-Like Symptoms," *American Journal of Psychiatry* 108, no. 8 (February 1952): 572–78; see also Leo E. Hollister, *Chemical Psychoses: LSD and Related Drugs* (Springfield, IL: Charles C. Thomas, 1968).

182   *researchers taped interviews*: A. Hoffer, "Studies with Niacin and LSD," in *Lysergic Acid Diethylamide and Mescaline in Experimental Psychiatry*, ed. L. Cholden (New York: Grune & Stratton, 1956), 44–45, cited in Lawrence G. Fischman, "Dreams, Hallucinogenic Drug States, and Schizophrenia: A Psychological and Biological Comparison," *Schizophrenia Bulletin* 9, no. 1 (January 1983): 73–94.

182   *Another dispute arose*: Fischman, "Dreams, Hallucinogenic Drug States, and Schizophrenia," 73–94.

182   *From 1953 until*: Nicholas M. Horrock, "80 Institutions Used in C.I.A. Mind Studies," *New York Times*, August 4, 1977, 17.

182   *Ken Kesey*: John Marks, *The Search for the "Manchurian Candidate": The CIA and Mind Control* (New York: Times Books, 1978), 120–21; see also Kinzer Stephen, "The CIA's Secret Quest for Mind Control: Torture, LSD and a 'Poisoner in Chief,'" interview by Terry Gross, *Fresh Air*, NPR, 2019, https://www.npr.org/transcripts/758989641.

182   *Harold Abramson*: Marks, *"Manchurian Candidate,"* 59–62; see also Robert Polner, "P&S Prof Conducted LSD Tests," *Columbia Spectator*, May 16, 1979.

183   *It was Abramson*: Marks, *"Manchurian Candidate,"* 73–86; see also A. O. Scott, "Review: 'Wormwood' Confirms That Errol Morris Is Our Great Cinematic Sleuth," review of *Wormwood*, directed by Errol Morris, *New York Times* online, December 14, 2017, https://www.nytimes.com/2017/12/14/movies/wormwood-review-errol-morris-peter-sarsgaard.html; see also *Project Mkultra, the CIA's Program of Research in Behavioral Modification*, 95th S., 74–80 (1977) (statement of Daniel Patrick Moynihan, chairman of the committee).

183   *Questions have persisted*: Olson v. United States, Civil Action No. 2012-1924 (2013). The family of Frank Olson had a second autopsy performed in 1994, and a forensics team found injuries on the body that had likely occurred before the fall.

183   *In 1969 Diane, the twenty-year-old*: William J. Ryczek, *The Sixties in the News: How an Era Unfolded in American Newspapers, 1959–1973* (Jefferson, NC: McFarland, 2021), 137–38.

183   *By 1970, LSD*: David E. Nichols, "Psychedelics," *Pharmacological Reviews* 68, no. 2 (April 2016): 264–355.

184   *As Michael Pollan wrote*: Michael Pollan, *How to Change Your Mind: What the New Science of Psychedelics Teaches Us About Consciousness, Dying, Addiction, Depression, and Transcendence* (New York: Penguin Press, 2018), 5, 216.

184   *It turned out that LSD's*: Steven A. Barker, "N, N-Dimethyltryptamine (DMT), an Endogenous Hallucinogen: Past, Present, and Future Research to Determine Its Role and Function," *Frontiers in Neuroscience* 12 (August 2018): 536.

184   *These substances all brought on*: Javier González-Maeso et al., "Hallucinogens Recruit Specific Cortical 5-HT2A Receptor-Mediated Signaling Pathways to Affect Behavior," *Neuron* 53, no. 3 (February 2007): 439–52.

184   *While the mental states*: Malcolm B. Bowers and Daniel X. Freedman, "Psychedelic Experiences in Acute Psychoses," *Archives of General Psychiatry* 15, no. 3 (September 1966): 240–48; see also Hollister, *Chemical Psychoses.*

184   *And the similarities seemed*: Fischman, "Dreams, Hallucinogenic Drug States, and Schizophrenia," 73–94.

CHAPTER 14: DOPAMINE: THE WIND IN THE PSYCHOTIC FIRE

185   *could induce a toxic psychosis*: David S. Bell, "The Experimental Reproduction of Amphetamine Psychosis," *Archives of General Psychiatry* 29, no. 1 (July 1973): 35–40.

185   *In such instances*: Malcolm B. Bowers, "Acute Psychosis Induced by Psychotomimetic Drug Abuse: I. Clinical Findings," *Archives of General Psychiatry* 27, no. 4 (October 1972): 437–40.

188   *Within a decade*: Frank J. Ayd, "Chlorpromazine: Ten Years' Experience," *Journal of the American Medical Association* (*JAMA*) 184, no. 1 (April 1963): 51–54.

188   *Chemical communication between*: Kathleen A. Montagu, "Catechol Compounds in Rat Tissues and in Brains of Different Animals," *Nature* 180, no. 4579 (August 1957): 244–45.

188   *Dopamine is the transmitter*: Paul Bernard Foley, "Dopamine in Psychiatry: A Historical Perspective," *Journal of Neural Transmission* 126 (February 2019): 473–79; see also Arvid Carlsson, "The Occurrence, Distribution and Physiological Role of Catecholamines in the Nervous System," *Pharmacological Reviews* 11, no. 2 (June 1959): 490–93.

189   *In the 1960s*: Arvid Carlsson, "Does Dopamine Play a Role in Schizophrenia?," *Psychological Medicine* 7, no. 4 (November 1963): 583–97; see also Arvid Carlsson, "A Half-Century of Neurotransmitter Research: Impact on Neurology and Psychiatry. Nobel Lecture," *Bioscience Reports* 21, no. 6 (December 2001): 691–710.

189   *One of them*: Vikram K. Yeragani et al., "Arvid Carlsson, and the Story of Dopamine," *Indian Journal of Psychiatry* 52, no. 1 (January–March 2010): 87–88.

189   *Dutch pharmacologist*: Jacques van Rossum, "The Significance of Dopamine-Receptor Blockade for the Mechanism of Action of Neuroleptic Drugs," *Archives Internationales de Pharmacodynamie et de Therapie* 160, no. 2 (April 1966): 492–94.

189   *Subsequent studies in the early 1970s*: Alan S. Horn and Solomon H. Snyder, "Chlorpromazine and Dopamine: Conformational Similarities That Correlate with the Antischizophrenic Activity of Phenothiazine Drugs," *Proceedings of the National Academy of Sciences* 68, no. 10 (October 1971): 2325–28; see also Philip Seeman et al., "Brain Receptors for Antipsychotic Drugs and Dopamine: Direct Binding Assays," *Proceedings of the National Academy of Sciences* 72, no. 11 (November 1975): 4376–80; see also Philip Seeman and T. Lee, "Antipsychotic Drugs: Direct Correlation Between Clinical Potency and Presynaptic Action on Dopamine Neurons," *Science* 188, no. 4194 (June 1975): 1217–19; see also Ian Creese, David R. Burt, and Solomon H. Snyder, "Dopamine Receptor Binding Predicts Clinical and Pharmaco-

logical Potencies of Antischizophrenic Drugs," *Science* 192, no. 4238 (April 1976): 481–83; see also Philip Seeman et al., "Antipsychotic Drug Doses and Neuroleptic /Dopamine Receptors," *Nature* 261, no. 5562 (June 1976): 717–19.

189   *went on to trace the route*: Anders Björklund and Stephen B. Dunnett, "Dopamine Neuron Systems in the Brain: An Update," *Trends in Neurosciences* 30, no. 5 (May 2007): 194–202; see also O. Pogarell et al., "Dopaminergic Neurotransmission in Patients with Schizophrenia in Relation to Positive and Negative Symptoms," *Pharmacopsychiatry* 45, no. S1 (May 2012): S36–S41.

191   *The first stimulant*: William J. Panenka et al., "Methamphetamine Use: A Comprehensive Review of Molecular, Preclinical and Clinical Findings," *Drug and Alcohol Dependence* 129, no. 3 (May 2013): 167–79.

191   *But it wasn't until 1938*: Lukasz Kamienski, *Shooting Up: A Short History of Drugs and War* (New York: Oxford University Press, 2016), 110–11; see also Ray J. Defalque and Amos J. Wright, "Methamphetamine for Hitler's Germany: 1937 to 1945," *Bulletin of Anesthesia History* 29, no. 2 (April 2011): 21–24, 32.

191   *For most soldiers*: Kamienski, *Shooting Up*, 111–12.

191   *In January 1942*: Andreas Ulrich, "The Nazi Death Machine: Hitler's Drugged Soldiers," *Spiegel International* online, last modified May 6, 2005, https://www.spiegel .de/international/the-nazi-death-machine-hitler-s-drugged-soldiers-a-354606.html.

191   *The military leadership*: Kamienski, *Shooting Up*, 112–13.

191   *Japanese military leaders began*: Bert Edström, "The Forgotten Success Story: Japan and the Methamphetamine Problem," *Japan Forum* 27, no. 4 (2015): 522; see also Masaaki Kato, "An Epidemiological Analysis of the Fluctuation of Drug Dependence in Japan," *International Journal of the Addictions* 4, no. 4 (December 1969): 592.

192   *Substantial quantities of the*: Akihiko Sato, "Methamphetamine Use in Japan After the Second World War: Transformation of Narratives," *Contemporary Drug Problems* 35, no. 4 (Winter 2008): 720.

192   *By the late 1940s*: Edström, "Forgotten Success Story," 521–22; see also Sato, "Methamphetamine Use in Japan," 721; see also Kamienski, *Shooting Up*, 128.

192   *The Japanese economy*: Jim Impoco, "Life After the Bubble: How Japan Lost a Decade," *New York Times* online, October 18, 2008, https://www.nytimes.com/2008/10/19 /weekinreview/19impoco.html.

192   *It is estimated that*: M. Douglas Anglin et al., "History of the Methamphetamine Problem," *Journal of Psychoactive Drugs* 32, no. 2 (April–June 2000): 137–41.

192   *Some of them*: Sato, "Methamphetamine Use in Japan."

193   *Initially, it was believed*: David S. Bell, "Comparison of Amphetamine Psychosis and Schizophrenia," *British Journal of Psychiatry* 111, no. 477 (August 1965): 701–7; see also Burton Angrist et al., "Amphetamine Psychosis: Behavioral and Biochemical Aspects," *Journal of Psychiatric Research* 11 (1975): 13–23; see also Carol L. M. Caton et al., "Differences Between Early-Phase Primary Psychotic Disorders with Concurrent Substance Use and Substance-Induced Psychoses," *Archives of General Psychiatry* 62, no. 2 (February 2005): 137–45; see also Rebecca McKetin, "Methamphetamine Psychosis: Insights from the Past," *Addiction* 113, no. 8 (March 2018): 1522–27.

193   *Japanese psychiatrist Mitsumoto Sato*: Mitsumoto Sato, "A Lasting Vulnerability to

Psychosis in Patients with Previous Methamphetamine Psychosis," *Annals of the New York Academy of Sciences* 654, no. 1 (June 1992): 165–66.

193   *The Australian researcher*: Bell, "Amphetamine Psychosis and Schizophrenia," 704. This case was first described by English psychiatrist Philip H. Connell in the book, *Amphetamine Psychosis*, Maudsley Monograph, No. 5 (1958).

194   *In the late 1960s*: Bell, "Experimental Reproduction of Amphetamine Psychosis," 35–40.

194   *Bell's experiment replicated*: Bell, "Amphetamine Psychosis and Schizophrenia," 704.

194   *Burt Angrist, a researcher*: Burt Angrist, John Rotrosen, and Samuel Gershon, "Responses to Apomorphine, Amphetamine, and Neuroleptics in Schizophrenic Subjects," *Psychopharmacology (Berlin)* 67, no. 1 (January 1980): 31–38; see also Burt Angrist, John Rotrosen, and Samuel Gershon, "Differential Effects of Amphetamine and Neuroleptics on Negative Vs. Positive Symptoms in Schizophrenia," *Psychopharmacology* 72, no. 1 (December 1980): 17–19.

195   *The dopamine theory of schizophrenia*: Solomon H. Snyder, "The Dopamine Hypothesis of Schizophrenia: Focus on the Dopamine Receptor," *American Journal of Psychiatry* 133, no. 2 (February 1976): 197–202.

195   *People who took antipsychotics*: William T. Carpenter and J. M. Davis, "Another View of the History of Antipsychotic Drug Discovery and Development," *Molecular Psychiatry* 17, no. 12 (August 2012): 1168–73.

196   *The results of the study*: Jeffrey A. Lieberman et al., "Methylphenidate Challenge as a Predictor of Relapse in Schizophrenia," *American Journal of Psychiatry* 141, no. 5 (May 1984): 633–38.

196   *I then came across a study*: David S. Janowsky and John M. Davis, "Methylphenidate, Dextroamphetamine, and Levamfetamine: Effects on Schizophrenic Symptoms," *Archives of General Psychiatry* 33, no. 3 (March 1976): 304–8.

197   *L-dopa was made famous*: Oliver Sacks, *Awakenings*, repr. (New York: Vintage Books, 1976), 28–55.

197   *"I was seeing such things"*: Oliver Sacks, foreword in *Awakenings*, repr. (New York: HarperPerennial, 1990), xxix.

198   *and yet studies had shown*: Gerard E. Hogarty and Richard F. Ulrich, "Temporal Effects of Drug and Placebo in Delaying Relapse in Schizophrenic Outpatients," *Archives of General Psychiatry* 34, no. 3 (March 1977): 297–301; see also Timothy J. Crow et al., "The Northwick Park Study of First Episodes of Schizophrenia: II. A Randomised Controlled Trial of Prophylactic Neuroleptic Treatment," *British Journal of Psychiatry* 148, no. 2 (February 1986): 120–27.

198   *Thirty-four patients completed*: Jeffrey A. Lieberman et al., "Prediction of Relapse in Schizophrenia," *Archives of General Psychiatry* 44, no. 7 (July 1987): 597–603.

199   *challenge tests*: William T. Carpenter, "The Schizophrenia Ketamine Challenge Study Debate," *Biological Psychiatry* 46, no. 8 (1999): 1081–91; see also "Precision Medicine," U.S. Food and Drug Administration, September 27, 2018, https://www.fda.gov/medical-devices/in-vitro-diagnostics/precision-medicine.

200   *Researchers launched an*: J. Kornhuber et al., "Dopamine D2-Receptors in Post-Mortem Human Brains from Schizophrenic Patients," in *From Neuron to Action: An Appraisal of Fundamental and Clinical Research*, ed. Lüder Deecke, John C.

Eccles, and Vernon B. Mountcastle (New York: Springer-Verlag, 1990), 507–13; see also F. Owen et al., "Dopamine-Mediated Behaviour and 3H-Spiperone Binding to Striatal Membranes in Rats After Nine Months Haloperidol Administration," *Life Sciences* 26, no. 1 (January 1980): 55–59; see also Robert G. Mackenzie and Michael J. Zigmond, "Chronic Neuroleptic Treatment Increases D-2 but Not D-1 Receptors in Rat Striatum," *European Journal of Pharmacology* 113, no. 2 (July 1985): 159–65; see also Philip Seeman et al., "Human Brain D_1 and D_2 Dopamine Receptors in Schizophrenia, Alzheimer's, Parkinson's, and Huntington's Diseases," *Neuropsychopharmacology* 1, no. 1 (December 1987): 5–15.

201   *While they did indeed*: Philip Seeman and Shitij Kapur, "Schizophrenia: More Dopamine, More D2 Receptors," *Proceedings of the National Academy of Sciences* 97, no. 14 (July 2000): 7673–75.

202   *Laruelle and Abi-Dargham performed*: Marc Laruelle et al., "Single Photon Emission Computerized Tomography Imaging of Amphetamine-Induced Dopamine Release in Drug-Free Schizophrenic Subjects," *Proceedings of the National Academy of Sciences* 93, no. 17 (August 1996): 9235–40.

202   *Other laboratories replicated their findings*: Alan Breier et al., "Schizophrenia Is Associated with Elevated Amphetamine-Induced Synaptic Dopamine Concentrations: Evidence from a Novel Positron Emission Tomography Method," *Proceedings of the National Academy of Sciences* 94, no. 6 (March 1997): 2569–74.

203   *But a seminal paper*: C. J. Pycock, R. W. Kerwin, and C. J. Carter, "Effect of Lesion of Cortical Dopamine Terminals on Subcortical Dopamine Receptors in Rats," *Nature* 286, no. 5768 (July 1980): 74–77.

203   *The work prompted an important*: Weinberger, "Implications of Normal Brain Development," 660–69; see also Kenneth L. Davis et al., "Dopamine in Schizophrenia: A Review and Reconceptualization," *American Journal of Psychiatry* 148, no. 11 (November 1991): 1474–86.

204   *The prevailing neurodevelopmental theory*: Murray and Lewis, "Is Schizophrenia a Neurodevelopmental Disorder?," 681–82; see also Antonia Najas-García, Sílvia Rufián, and Emilio Rojo, "Neurodevelopment or Neurodegeneration: Review of Theories of Schizophrenia," *Actas Españolas de Psiquiatría* 42, no. 4 (July/August 2014): 185–95.

205   *Moreover, the theory didn't*: Jeffrey A. Lieberman, B. B. Sheitman, and B. J. Kinon, "Neurochemical Sensitization in the Pathophysiology of Schizophrenia: Deficits and Dysfunction in Neuronal Regulation and Plasticity," *Neuropsychopharmacology* 17, no. 4 (October 1997): 205–29.

205   *because his family*: Eric Kandel, *In Search of Memory: The Emergence of a New Science of Mind* (New York: W. W. Norton, 2006), 12–32.

205   *Kandel's research had*: Eric Kandel, "Eric R. Kandel—Biographical," NobelPrize.org, Nobel Prize Outreach AN 2021, accessed April 24, 2021, https://www.nobelprize .org/prizes/medicine/2000/kandel/biographical/.

206   *Studies had demonstrated*: Marina E. Wolf et al., "Differential Development of Autoreceptor Subsensitivity and Enhanced Dopamine Release During Amphetamine Sensitization," *Journal of Pharmacology and Experimental Therapeutics* 264, no. 1 (January 1993): 249–55; see also Marina E. Wolf and Michael Jeziorski, "Coadminis-

tration of MK-801 with Amphetamine, Cocaine or Morphine Prevents Rather Than Transiently Masks the Development of Behavioral Sensitization," *Brain Research* 613, no. 2 (June 1993): 291–94.

206   *Moreover, once this sensitized*: Amphetamine sensitization has been demonstrated in humans and observed to persist for at least one year following as few as three doses forty-eight hours apart. See: Isabelle Boileau et al., "Modeling Sensitization to Stimulants in Humans: An [11c]Raclopride/Positron Emission Tomography Study in Healthy Men," *Archives of General Psychiatry* 63, no. 12 (December 2006): 1386–95.

207   *Then he decided to*: Richard Jed Wyatt, "Neuroleptics and the Natural Course of Schizophrenia," *Schizophrenia Bulletin* 17, no. 2 (January 1991): 325–51.

207   *The results of the studies*: Ibid.; see also Jeffrey A. Lieberman et al., "Psychobiologic Correlates of Treatment Response in Schizophrenia," *Neuropsychopharmacology* 14, no. 3 (March 1996): S13–S21; see also Antony Loebel et al., "Time to Treatment Response in Successive Episodes of Early Onset Schizophrenia," *Schizophrenia Research* 1, no. 15 (1995): 158; see also Elizabeth Spencer, Max Birchwood, and Dermot McGovern, "Management of First-Episode Psychosis," *Advances in Psychiatric Treatment* 7, no. 2 (March 2001): 133–40.

207   *We concluded that acute*: Antony D. Loebel et al., "Duration of Psychosis and Outcome in First-Episode Schizophrenia," *American Journal of Psychiatry* 149, no. 9 (September 1992): 1183–88.

208   *Shitij Kapur developed*: Shitij Kapur, "Psychosis as a State of Aberrant Salience: A Framework Linking Biology, Phenomenology, and Pharmacology in Schizophrenia," *American Journal of Psychiatry* 160, no. 1 (January 2003): 13–23.

210   *The aberrant salience caused*: Ibid.

210   *But from the late 1980s*: David M. Fergusson et al., "Cannabis and Psychosis," *British Medical Journal* 332, no. 7534 (January 2006): 172–75.

210   *The first of these*: Sven Andréasson et al., "Cannabis and Schizophrenia: A Longitudinal Study of Swedish Conscripts," *Lancet* 330, no. 8574 (December 1987): 1483–86.

210   *At that time, cannabis*: Ian Hamilton, "Cannabis, Psychosis and Schizophrenia: Unravelling a Complex Interaction," *Addiction* 112, no. 9 (September 2017): 1653–57.

211   *The conscription registry showed*: Andréasson et al., "Cannabis and Schizophrenia"; see also Hamilton, "Cannabis, Psychosis and Schizophrenia."

211   *Endocannabinoid transmission*: Marc Steffens et al., "Cannabinoid CB1 Receptor-Mediated Modulation of Evoked Dopamine Release and of Adenylyl Cyclase Activity in the Human Neocortex," *British Journal of Pharmacology* 141, no. 7 (April 2004): 1193–203; see also Joseph F. Cheer et al., "Cannabinoids Enhance Subsecond Dopamine Release in the Nucleus Accumbens of Awake Rats," *Journal of Neuroscience* 24, no. 18 (May 2004): 4393–400.

211   *Avshalom Caspi and Terrie Moffitt*: Douglas Starr, "Two Psychologists Followed 1,000 New Zealanders for Decades. Here's What They Found About How Childhood Shapes Later Life," *Science*, February 1, 2018, https://www.sciencemag.org/news /2018/02/two-psychologists-followed-1000-new-zealanders-decades-here-s-what -they-found-about-how.

212   *The Dunedin Study*: Richie Poulton, Terrie E. Moffitt, and Phil A. Silva, "The Dunedin Multidisciplinary Health and Development Study: Overview of the First 40 Years,

with an Eye to the Future," *Social Psychiatry and Psychiatric Epidemiology* 50, no. 5 (April 2015): 679–93.

212   *The Dunedin Study results*: Richie Poulton et al., "Patterns of Recreational Cannabis Use in Aotearoa-New Zealand and Their Consequences: Evidence to Inform Voters in the 2020 Referendum," *Journal of the Royal Society of New Zealand* 50, no. 2 (May 2020): 348–65.

212   *The increased risk*: Louise Arseneault et al., "Causal Association Between Cannabis and Psychosis: Examination of the Evidence," *British Journal of Psychiatry* 184, no. 2 (February 2004): 110–17; see also Hannelore Ehrenreich et al., "Specific Attentional Dysfunction in Adults Following Early Start of Cannabis Use," *Psychopharmacology* 142, no. 3 (March 1999): 295–301; see also Marco Pistis et al., "Adolescent Exposure to Cannabinoids Induces Long-Lasting Changes in the Response to Drugs of Abuse of Rat Midbrain Dopamine Neurons," *Biological Psychiatry* 56, no. 2 (July 2004): 86–94; see also Harrison G. Pope Jr. et al., "Early-Onset Cannabis Use and Cognitive Deficits: What Is the Nature of the Association?," *Drug and Alcohol Dependence* 69, no. 3 (April 2003): 303–10.

212   *The results of the Swedish*: Wendy Swift et al., "Adolescent Cannabis Users at 24 Years: Trajectories to Regular Weekly Use and Dependence in Young Adulthood," *Addiction* 103, no. 8 (August 2008): 1361–70; see also Hans-Ulrich Wittchen et al., "Cannabis Use and Cannabis Use Disorders and Their Relationship to Mental Disorders: A 10-Year Prospective-Longitudinal Community Study in Adolescents," *Drug and Alcohol Dependence* 88 (April 2007): S60–S70; see also Jim Van Os et al., "Cannabis Use and Psychosis: A Longitudinal Population-Based Study," *American Journal of Epidemiology* 156, no. 4 (August 2002): 319–27.

212   *What the studies also*: Cécile Henquet et al., "Prospective Cohort Study of Cannabis Use, Predisposition for Psychosis, and Psychotic Symptoms in Young People," *British Medical Journal* 330, no. 7481 (December 2004): 11.

212   *Because of the dopamine-stimulating*: Michael A. P. Bloomfield et al., "The Effects of Δ 9-Tetrahydrocannabinol on the Dopamine System," *Nature* 539, no. 7629 (November 2016): 369–77; see also Lee Ellis, David P. Farrington, and Anthony W. Hoskin, "Biological Factors," chap. 7 in *Handbook of Crime Correlates*, eds. Lee Ellis, David P. Farrington, and Anthony W. Hoskin (Cambridge, MA: Academic Press, 2019), 307–87.

212   *They had three reasons*: Gunvant K. Thaker and William T. Carpenter, "Advances in Schizophrenia," *Nature Medicine* 7, no. 6 (June 2001): 667–71.

212   *Caspi and Moffitt's team*: Avshalom Caspi et al., "Moderation of the Effect of Adolescent-Onset Cannabis Use on Adult Psychosis by a Functional Polymorphism in the Catechol-O-Methyltransferase Gene: Longitudinal Evidence of a Gene X Environment Interaction," *Biological Psychiatry* 57, no. 10 (May 2005): 1117–27.

213   *Subsequent studies have*: Michael Wainberg et al., "Cannabis, Schizophrenia Genetic Risk, and Psychotic Experiences: A Cross-Sectional Study of 109,308 Participants from the UK Biobank," *Translational Psychiatry* 11, no. 1 (April 2021); see also Cécile Henquet et al., "Gene-Environment Interplay Between Cannabis and Psychosis," *Schizophrenia Bulletin* 34, no. 6 (November 2008): 1111–21; see also Centre for Addiction and Mental Health, "Genetic Predisposition to Schizophrenia May

Increase Risk of Psychosis from Cannabis Use," news release, April 13, 2021, https://www.eurekalert.org/pub_releases/2021-04/cfaa-gpt041321.php.

213   *Depending on the frequency*: Gurbakhsh S. Chopra and James W. Smith, "Psychotic Reactions Following Cannabis Use in East Indians," *Archives of General Psychiatry* 30, no. 1 (1974): 24–27; see also Hinderk M. Emrich, F. Markus Leweke, and Udo Schneider, "Towards a Cannabinoid Hypothesis of Schizophrenia: Cognitive Impairments Due to Dysregulation of the Endogenous Cannabinoid System," *Pharmacology Biochemistry and Behavior* 56, no. 4 (April 1997): 803–7; see also Andrew Johns, "Psychiatric Effects of Cannabis," *British Journal of Psychiatry* 178, no. 2 (February 2001): 116–22; see also Deepak Cyril D'Souza et al., "The Psychotomimetic Effects of Intravenous Delta-9-Tetrahydrocannabinol in Healthy Individuals: Implications for Psychosis," *Neuropsychopharmacology* 29, no. 8 (June 2004): 1558–72.

213   *Cannabis can also exacerbate*: Darold A. Treffert, "Marihuana Use in Schizophrenia: A Clear Hazard," *American Journal of Psychiatry* 135, no. 10 (October 1978): 1213–15; see also Don H. Linszen, Peter M. Dingemans, and Marie E. Lenior, "Cannabis Abuse and the Course of Recent-Onset Schizophrenic Disorders," *Archives of General Psychiatry* 51, no. 4 (April 1994): 273–79; see also Lakshmi Voruganti et al., "Cannabis Induced Dopamine Release: An In-Vivo SPECT Study," *Psychiatry Research: Neuroimaging* 107, no. 3 (October 2001): 173–77; see also Deepak Cyril D'Souza et al., "Delta-9-Tetrahydrocannabinol Effects in Schizophrenia: Implications for Cognition, Psychosis, and Addiction," *Biological Psychiatry* 57, no. 6 (March 2005): 594–608.

213   *The use of cannabis may*: Andréasson et al., "Cannabis and Schizophrenia"; see also P. Miller et al., "Genetic Liability, Illicit Drug Use, Life Stress and Psychotic Symptoms: Preliminary Findings from the Edinburgh Study of People at High Risk for Schizophrenia," *Social Psychiatry and Psychiatric Epidemiology* 36, no. 7 (July 2001): 338–42.

213   *overactivity in this system*: Emrich, Leweke, and Schneider, "Towards a Cannabinoid Hypothesis of Schizophrenia, 803–7; see also S. R. Laviolette and A. A. Grace, "The Roles of Cannabinoid and Dopamine Receptor Systems in Neural Emotional Learning Circuits: Implications for Schizophrenia and Addiction," *Cellular and Molecular Life Sciences (CMLS)* 63, no. 14 (July 2006): 1597–613.

213   *It is thought that cannabis*: William A. Devane et al., "Determination and Characterization of a Cannabinoid Receptor in Rat Brain," *Molecular Pharmacology* 34, no. 5 (November 1988): 605–13; see also Miles Herkenham et al., "Characterization and Localization of Cannabinoid Receptors in Rat Brain: A Quantitative In Vitro Autoradiographic Study," *Journal of Neuroscience* 11, no. 2 (February 1991): 563–83; see also Tamas F. Freund, Istvan Katona, and Daniele Piomelli, "Role of Endogenous Cannabinoids in Synaptic Signaling," *Physiological Reviews* 83, no. 3 (July 2003): 1017–66; see also Pál Pacher, Sándor Bátkai, and George Kunos, "The Endocannabinoid System as an Emerging Target of Pharmacotherapy," *Pharmacological Reviews* 58, no. 3 (September 2006): 389–462; see also Roger G. Pertwee, "Ligands That Target Cannabinoid Receptors in the Brain: From THC to Anandamide and Beyond," *Addiction Biology* 13, no. 2 (June 2008): 147–59.

213   *A recent meta-analysis*: Matthew Large et al., "Cannabis Use and Earlier Onset of Psy-

chosis: A Systematic Meta-Analysis," *Archives of General Psychiatry* 68, no. 6 (June 2011): 555–61.

CHAPTER 15: GLUTAMATE AND GABA: THE ACCELERATOR AND THE BRAKE

216   *The dopamine hypothesis*: Daniel C. Javitt and Stephen R. Zukin, "Recent Advances in the Phencyclidine Model of Schizophrenia," *American Journal of Psychiatry* 148, no. 10 (October 1991): 1301–8; see also Oliver Howes, Rob McCutcheon, and James Stone, "Glutamate and Dopamine in Schizophrenia: An Update for the 21st Century," *Journal of Psychopharmacology* 29, no. 2 (February 2015): 97–115.

216   *Many patients didn't*: Bita Moghaddam and Daniel Javitt, "From Revolution to Evolution: The Glutamate Hypothesis of Schizophrenia and Its Implication for Treatment," *Neuropsychopharmacology* 37, no. 1 (January 2012): 4–15; see also Daniel C. Javitt et al., "Has an Angel Shown the Way? Etiological and Therapeutic Implications of the PCP/NMDA Model of Schizophrenia," *Schizophrenia Bulletin* 38, no. 5 (September 2012): 958–66.

217   *PCP had debuted*: "'Angel Dust' Use in Capital Said to Reach Epidemic Proportions," *New York Times* online, December 9, 1984, https://www.nytimes.com/1984/12/09/us/angel-dust-use-in-capital-said-to-reach-epidemic-proportions.html.

217   *Although its powerful effects*: Steven Lerner, "So Much for Cocaine and LSD—Angel Dust Is America's Most Dangerous New Drug," interview by Sue Ellen Jares, *People*, no. 10, September 4, 1978, https://people.com/archive/so-much-for-cocaine-and-lsd-angel-dust-is-americas-most-dangerous-new-drug-vol-10-no-10/.

217   *Initially, doctors in New York*: Daniel C. Javitt (professor of psychiatry, Columbia University College of Physicians and Surgeons; director of Division of Experimental Therapeutics at Columbia University Department of Psychiatry; director of schizophrenia research at the Nathan Kline Institute), in discussion with the author, July 24, 2020.

217   *In Washington, DC*: Yota Uno and Joseph T. Coyle, "Glutamate Hypothesis in Schizophrenia," *Psychiatry and Clinical Neurosciences* 73, no. 5 (May 2019): 204–15.

217   *Though synthesized in 1926*: George M. Beschner and Harvey W. Feldman, "Introduction," chap. 1 in *Angel Dust: An Ethnographic Study of PCP Users*, eds. Harvey W. Feldman, Michael H. Agar, and George M. Beschner (Lexington, MA: Lexington-Books, 1979), 8–10; see also Edward F. Domino and Elliot D. Luby, "Phencyclidine/Schizophrenia: One View Toward the Past, the Other to the Future," *Schizophrenia Bulletin* 38, no. 5 (September 2012): 914–19.

217   *FDA approval in 1957*: Hamilton Morris and Jason Wallach, "From PCP to MXE: A Comprehensive Review of the Non-Medical Use of Dissociative Drugs," *Drug Testing and Analysis* 6, no. 7/8 (July 2014): 614–32.

217   *Edward Domino*: Nicholas Denomme, "The Domino Effect: Ed Domino's Early Studies of Psychoactive Drugs," *Journal of Psychoactive Drugs* 50, no. 4 (August 2018): 298–305.

217   *Domino joined a group*: Domino and Luby, "Phencyclidine/Schizophrenia."

218   *"We had come to respect"*: Ibid., 916.

219   *"its extremely poor ratio"*: Shaila K. Dewan, "A Drug Feared in the '70s Is Tied to Suspect in Killings," *New York Times* online, April 6, 2003, https://www.nytimes.com/2003/04/06/nyregion/a-drug-feared-in-the-70-s-is-tied-to-suspect-in-killings.html.

219   *Fortunately, Parke-Davis hadn't*: David Lodge and M. S. Mercier, "Ketamine and Phencyclidine: The Good, the Bad, and the Unexpected," *British Journal of Pharmacology* 172, no. 17 (September 2015): 4254–76; see also Denomme, "Domino Effect."

219   *clinical trials on prison volunteers*: Experimentation on inmates remains controversial, as there have been egregious abuses of prisoners and other vulnerable populations, often racially motivated. But until the 1970s, much pharmaceutical research was conducted in prisons. See Dina Fine Maron, "Should Prisoners Be Used in Medical Experiments?," *Scientific American* online, last modified July 2, 2014, https://www.scientificamerican.com/article/should-prisoners-be-used-in-medical-experiments/; see also Anna Charles et al., "Prisoners as Research Participants: Current Practice and Attitudes in the UK," *Journal of Medical Ethics* 42, no. 4 (April 2016): 246–52.

219   *this was necessary for two reasons*: Saul Krugman, "The Willowbrook Hepatitis Studies Revisited: Ethical Aspects," *Reviews of Infectious Diseases* 8, no. 1 (January–February 1986): 157–62. See also Centers of Excellence, Bioethics Center, Tuskegee University, "About the USPHS Syphilis Study," https://www.tuskegee.edu/about-us/centers-of-excellence/bioethics-center/about-the-usphs-syphilis-study.

219   *National Commission for the Protection of Human Subjects of Biomedical and Behavioral Research*: Margaret R. Moon, "The History and Role of Institutional Review Boards: A Useful Tension," *Virtual Mentor* 11, no. 4 (2009): 311–16.

219   *Belmont Report*: Office for Human Research Protection, U.S. Department of Health & Human Services, "The Belmont Report: Ethical Principles and Guidelines for the Protection of Human Subjects of Research," April 18, 1979, https://www.hhs.gov/ohrp/regulations-and-policy/belmont-report/index.html.

220   *Domino's study commenced*: Edward F. Domino and David S. Warner, "Taming the Ketamine Tiger," *Journal of the American Society of Anesthesiologists* 113, no. 3 (September 2010): 678–84.

220   *In 1970 ketamine was*: Parke-Davis, "Ketamine Hydrochloride (Ketalar)," *Clinical Pharmacology & Therapeutics* 11, no. 5 (September 1970): 777–80; see also Lodge and Mercier, "Ketamine and Phencyclidine."

220   *It has been used widely*: Madhuri S. Kurdi, Kaushic A. Theerth, and Radhika S. Deva, "Ketamine: Current Applications in Anesthesia, Pain, and Critical Care," *Anesthesia, Essays and Researches* 8, no. 3 (September 2014): 283; see also Gaël De Rocquigny et al., "Use of Ketamine for Prehospital Pain Control on the Battlefield: A Systematic Review," *Journal of Trauma and Acute Care Surgery* 88, no. 1 (January 2020): 180–85; see also US Food and Drug Administration, "FDA Approves New Nasal Spray Medication for Treatment-Resistant Depression; Available Only at a Certified Doctor's Office or Clinic," news release, March 5, 2019, https://www.fda.gov/news-events/press-announcements/fda-approves-new-nasal-spray-medication-treat-ment-resistant-depression-available-only-certified.

221   *non-mainstream medical practices*: Andrew Weil, *The Natural Mind: An Investigation of Drugs and the Higher Consciousness* (New York: Houghton Mifflin, 1972).

223   *Snyder was focused*: Solomon H. Snyder, "Solomon H. Snyder," in *The History of Neuroscience in Autobiography*, ed. Larry R. Squire (New York: Oxford University Press, 2009).

223   *cadre of talented protégés*: Snyder's protégés included Joe Coyle, Robbie Schwarcz, Sam Enna, Candace Pert, Rob Zaczek, Michael Kuhar, and Steve Zukin.

223   *The first time glutamate*: J. S. Kim et al., "Low Cerebrospinal Fluid Glutamate in Schizophrenic Patients and a New Hypothesis on Schizophrenia," *Neuroscience Letters* 20, no. 3 (December 1980): 379–82.

224   *But it was only when*: Solomon H. Snyder, "Phencyclidine," *Nature* 285, no. 5764 (June 1980): 355–56.

224   *Together the Zukins*: Stephen R. Zukin and R. Suzanne Zukin, "Specific [3H] Phencyclidine Binding in Rat Central Nervous System," *Proceedings of the National Academy of Sciences* 76, no. 10 (October 1979): 5372–76.

224   *What makes glutamate*: David L. Hunt and Pablo E. Castillo, "Synaptic Plasticity of NMDA Receptors: Mechanisms and Functional Implications," *Current Opinion in Neurobiology* 22, no. 3 (June 2012): 496–508.

226   *In the mid-1980s*: Javitt, in discussion with the author.

226   *In an influential paper*: Javitt and Zukin, "Phencyclidine Model of Schizophrenia."

227   *Unfortunately, although glycine*: Daniel C. Javitt et al., "Amelioration of Negative Symptoms in Schizophrenia by Glycine," *American Journal of Psychiatry* 151, no. 8 (August 1994): 1234–36.

227   *"Until 1994"*: Javitt, in discussion with the author.

228   *Born in Iran, Moghaddam*: Bruce Steele, "Neuroscience Department Lures Yale Prof," *University Times* online, December 3, 2003, https://www.utimes.pitt.edu/archives/?p=43058.

228   *began a series of glutamate*: Bita Moghaddam et al., "Activation of Glutamatergic Neurotransmission by Ketamine: A Novel Step in the Pathway from NMDA Receptor Blockade to Dopaminergic and Cognitive Disruptions Associated with the Prefrontal Cortex," *Journal of Neuroscience* 17, no. 8 (April 1997): 2921–27.

228   *From these experiments*: Moghaddam and Javitt, "From Revolution to Evolution."

228   *It is now believed*: Bita Moghaddam, "Bringing Order to the Glutamate Chaos in Schizophrenia," *Neuron* 40, no. 5 (December 2003): 881–84; see also Javitt et al., "Has an Angel Shown the Way?"

228   *synaptic glutamate levels*: Studies performed by other investigators added support to Javitt and Moghaddam's revised glutamate theory. See John H. Krystal et al., "Subanesthetic Effects of the Noncompetitive NMDA Antagonist, Ketamine, in Humans: Psychotomimetic, Perceptual, Cognitive, and Neuroendocrine Responses," *Archives of General Psychiatry* 51, no. 3 (March 1994): 199–214; see also John H. Krystal et al., "Preliminary Evidence of Attenuation of the Disruptive Effects of the NMDA Glutamate Receptor Antagonist, Ketamine, on Working Memory by Pretreatment with the Group II Metabotropic Glutamate Receptor Agonist, Ly354740, in Healthy Human Subjects," *Psychopharmacology* 179, no. 1 (April 2005): 303–9; see also John H. Krystal et al., "Comparative and Interactive Human Psychopharmacologic Effects

of Ketamine and Amphetamine: Implications for Glutamatergic and Dopaminergic Model Psychoses and Cognitive Function," *Archives of General Psychiatry* 62, no. 9 (September 2005): 985–95; see also Adrienne C. Lahti et al., "Subanesthetic Doses of Ketamine Stimulate Psychosis in Schizophrenia," *Neuropsychopharmacology* 13, no. 1 (August 1995): 9–19; see also Anil K. Malhotra et al., "Ketamine-Induced Exacerbation of Psychotic Symptoms and Cognitive Impairment in Neuroleptic-Free Schizophrenics," *Neuropsychopharmacology* 17, no. 3 (September 1997): 141–50; see also Eline M. P. Poels et al., "Glutamatergic Abnormalities in Schizophrenia: A Review of Proton MRS Findings," *Schizophrenia Research* 152, no. 2/3 (February 2014): 325–32.

229   *The glutamate hypothesis has*: Javitt et al., "Has an Angel Shown the Way?"

229   *The two neurotransmitter systems*: Howes, McCutcheon, and Stone, "Glutamate and Dopamine."

230   *This new pathological model*: Maria Carlsson and Arvid Carlsson, "Schizophrenia: A Subcortical Neurotransmitter Imbalance Syndrome?," *Schizophrenia Bulletin* 16, no. 3 (January 1990): 425–32.

230   *In 1997 Moghaddam*: Moghaddam et al., "Activation of Glutamatergic Neurotransmission."

230   *The finding was confirmed*: Alan Breier et al., "Effects of NMDA Antagonism on Striatal Dopamine Release in Healthy Subjects: Application of a Novel PET Approach," *Synapse* 29, no. 2 (June 1998): 142–47.

231   *GABA works mostly*: Yehezkel Ben-Ari, "Excitatory Actions of GABA During Development: The Nature of the Nurture," *Nature Reviews Neuroscience* 3, no. 9 (September 2002): 728–39.

231   *Interestingly, the function*: Pascal Steullet et al., "Oxidative Stress-Driven Parvalbumin Interneuron Impairment as a Common Mechanism in Models of Schizophrenia," *Molecular Psychiatry* 22, no. 7 (July 2017): 936–43.

231   *The deficiency of GABA*: David A. Lewis, Takanori Hashimoto, and David W. Volk, "Cortical Inhibitory Neurons and Schizophrenia," *Nature Reviews Neuroscience* 6, no. 4 (April 2005): 312–24; see also Francine M. Benes and Sabina Berretta, "GABAergic Interneurons: Implications for Understanding Schizophrenia and Bipolar Disorder," *Neuropsychopharmacology* 25, no. 1 (July 2001): 1–27; see also John H. Krystal et al., "Impaired Tuning of Neural Ensembles and the Pathophysiology of Schizophrenia: A Translational and Computational Neuroscience Perspective," *Biological Psychiatry* 81, no. 10 (May 2017): 874–85.

231   *A possible explanation*: Takao K. Hensch, "Critical Period Plasticity in Local Cortical Circuits," *Nature Reviews Neuroscience* 6, no. 11 (November 2005): 877–88.

232   *Working with Bunney*: Anthony A. Grace and Benjamin S. Bunney, "The Control of Firing Pattern in Nigral Dopamine Neurons: Single Spike Firing," *Journal of Neuroscience* 4, no. 11 (November 1984): 2866–76.

233   *"depolarization blockade"*: Anthony A. Grace et al., "Dopamine-Cell Depolarization Block as a Model for the Therapeutic Actions of Antipsychotic Drugs," *Trends in Neurosciences* 20, no. 1 (January 1997): 31–37.

233   *Grace began investigating*: Antonieta Lavin, Holly M. Moore, and Anthony A. Grace, "Prenatal Disruption of Neocortical Development Alters Prefrontal Cortical Neuron

Responses to Dopamine in Adult Rats," *Neuropsychopharmacology* 30, no. 8 (August 2005): 1426–35.

233   *These findings offered*: Daniel J. Lodge and Anthony A. Grace, "The Hippocampus Modulates Dopamine Neuron Responsivity by Regulating the Intensity of Phasic Neuron Activation," *Neuropsychopharmacology* 31, no. 7 (July 2006): 1356–61; see also Daniel J. Lodge and Anthony A. Grace, "Aberrant Hippocampal Activity Underlies the Dopamine Dysregulation in an Animal Model of Schizophrenia," *Journal of Neuroscience* 27, no. 42 (October 2007): 11424–30.

234   *A second strategy*: Harri J. Tuominen, Jari Tiihonen, and Kristian Wahlbeck, "Glutamatergic Drugs for Schizophrenia: A Systematic Review and Meta-Analysis," *Schizophrenia Research* 72, no. 2/3 (January 2005): 225–34.

234   *The initial efforts involved*: Robert W. Buchanan et al., "The Cognitive and Negative Symptoms in Schizophrenia Trial (CONSIST): The Efficacy of Glutamatergic Agents for Negative Symptoms and Cognitive Impairments," *American Journal of Psychiatry* 164, no. 10 (October 2007): 1593–602; see also Donald C. Goff, "Bitopertin: The Good News and Bad News," *JAMA Psychiatry* 71, no. 6 (June 2014): 621–22.

234   *Studies of these drugs*: Joshua T. Kantrowitz et al., "Proof of Mechanism and Target Engagement of Glutamatergic Drugs for the Treatment of Schizophrenia: RCTs of Pomaglumetad and TS-134 on Ketamine-Induced Psychotic Symptoms and PharmacoBOLD in Healthy Volunteers," *Neuropsychopharmacology* 45, no. 11 (October 2020): 1842–50.

Chapter 16: Peeling the Onion

237   *Nico Jacobellis, an Italian immigrant*: Michael Rotman, "Heights Art Theater," Cleveland Historical, updated September 12, 2019, https://clevelandhistorical.org/items /show/436; see also Sven Dubie, "Obscene History in the Heights: The Case of Nico Jacobellis and Les Amants," accessed January 31, 2021, http://www.chhistory.org /FeatureStories.php?Story=ObsceneHistory.

237   *His attorneys appealed the case*: Jacobellis v. Ohio, 378 U.S. 184 (1964).

237   *Justice Potter Stewart's comment*: Jon Lewis, *Hollywood v. Hard Core: How the Struggle over Censorship Created the Modern Film Industry* (New York: NYU Press, 2002), 251.

240   *An example of a genocopy*: Monks et al., "Further Evidence for High Rates of Schizophrenia," 231–36.

240   *In 1913 Hideyo Noguchi*: Hideyo Noguchi and Joseph W. Moore, "A Demonstration of Treponema Pallidum in the Brain in Cases of General Paralysis," *Journal of Experimental Medicine* 17, no. 2 (February 1913): 232.

240   *Other infectious agents*: Keely Cheslack-Postava and Alan S. Brown, "Prenatal Infection and Schizophrenia: A Decade of Further Progress," *Schizophrenia Research* (May 2021); see also Robert H. Yolken and E. Fuller Torrey, "Are Some Cases of Psychosis Caused by Microbial Agents? A Review of the Evidence," *Molecular Psychiatry* 13, no. 5 (February 2008): 470–79.

241   *People with seizure disorders*: Thomas M. Hyde and Daniel R. Weinberger, "Seizures
      and Schizophrenia," *Schizophrenia Bulletin* 23, no. 4 (January 1997): 611–22; see
      also Lynn G. Irwin and Dónal G. Fortune, "Risk Factors for Psychosis Secondary
      to Temporal Lobe Epilepsy: A Systematic Review," *Journal of Neuropsychiatry and
      Clinical Neurosciences* 26, no. 1 (January 2014): 5–23.

242   *psychotic symptoms could occur*: David B. Weiss et al., "Psychiatric Manifestations of
      Autoimmune Disorders," *Current Treatment Options in Neurology* 7, no. 5 (September 2005): 413–17.

242   *Autoimmune encephalitis targeting*: Josep Dalmau et al., "Paraneoplastic Anti–N-
      Methyl-D-Aspartate Receptor Encephalitis Associated with Ovarian Teratoma,"
      Annals of Neurology 61, no. 1 (January 2007): 25–36.

242   *Cahalan recounts her experience*: Susannah Cahalan, *Brain on Fire: My Month of Madness* (New York: Simon & Schuster Paperbacks, 2012), 127–34.

243   *"Education is not for everyone"*: Ibid., 128.

243   *The clock drawing test*: Ibid., 143–60.

243   *Susannah's biopsy showed*: Ibid., 131–34.

243   *Once Najjar had*: Ibid., 162–64.

245   *A number of factors*: Mary Catherine Clarke, Michelle Harley, and Mary Cannon, "The
      Role of Obstetric Events in Schizophrenia," *Schizophrenia Bulletin* 32, no. 1 (January
      2006): 3–8; see also Kimberlie Dean and Robin M. Murray, "Environmental Risk
      Factors for Psychosis," *Dialogues in Clinical Neuroscience* 7, no. 1 (March 2005):
      69–80.

245   *"two-hit hypothesis"*: Alfred G. Knudson, "Mutation and Cancer: Statistical Study of
      Retinoblastoma," *Proceedings of the National Academy of Sciences* 68, no. 4 (April
      1971): 820–23.

245   *1990 by the landmark study*: Richard L. Suddath et al., "Anatomical Abnormalities in
      the Brains of Monozygotic Twins Discordant for Schizophrenia," *New England Journal of Medicine* 322, no. 12 (March 1990): 789–94; see also E. Fuller Torrey et al.,
      *Schizophrenia and Manic-Depressive Disorder: The Biological Roots of Mental Illness
      as Revealed by the Landmark Study of Identical Twins* (New York: Basic Books,
      1995); see also E. Fuller Torrey, "Are We Overestimating the Genetic Contribution
      to Schizophrenia?," *Schizophrenia Bulletin* 18, no. 2 (January 1992): 159–70.

251   *Three days later*: Daniel R. Weinberger, "In Memoriam: Steve Lieber," Lieber Institute
      for Brain Development online, last modified March 31, 2020, https://www.libd.org
      /in-memoriam-steve-lieber/.

252   *The DSM-5 specifies three types*: American Psychiatric Association, "Dissociative Disorders," in *Diagnostic and Statistical Manual of Mental Disorders*, 5th ed. (Washington, DC: American Psychiatric Association, 2013), 291–307.

252   *The typical patient diagnosed*: Paulette Marie Gillig, "Dissociative Identity Disorder: A
      Controversial Diagnosis," *Psychiatry (Edgmont)* 6, no. 3 (March 2009): 24.

255   *An old diagnostic technique*: L. R. Marcos and M. Trujillo, "The Sodium Amytal Interview as a Therapeutic Modality," *Current Psychiatric Therapies* 18 (1978): 129–36.

256   *the alternate mental states*: Gillig, "Dissociative Identity Disorder."

CHAPTER 17: DIAGNOSING SCHIZOPHRENIA

261   *However, in 1942*: Amy Wachs, "Joseph Kohn's History" (unpublished report, November 3, 2020), PDF file.

262   *This inability is different*: Daniel C. Mograbi and Robin G. Morris, "Anosognosia," *Cortex* 103 (June 2018): 385–86.

263   *Growing up, Troy Hill*: Dep. of Troy Hill Sr at 22-32, *Hill v. WPIC*, No. 09-1428 (Pa. Ct. Comm. Pleas 2015); see also Milan Simonich and Tom Birdsong, "Stabbing of Twins, Arrest of Brother Triggers Disbelief," *Pittsburgh Post-Gazette* online, August 30, 2007, https://www.post-gazette.com/local/neighborhoods/2007/08/30 /Stabbing-of-twins-arrest-of-brother-triggers-disbelief/stories/200708300229.

263   *He completed his freshman*: Pl.'S Pre-Trial Summ. Statement at 3–5, 111–122, 181, *Hill v. WPIC*, No. 09-1428 (Pa. Ct. Comm. Pleas 2015).

264   *His family became increasingly*: Pl.'S Pre-Trial Summ. Statement at 4–5, 86–89, 113–117, *Hill v. WPIC*, No. 09-1428 (Pa. Ct. Comm. Pleas 2015); see also Def.'S Pre-Trial Summ. Statement at 5–6, 92–94, 119–121, *Hill v. WPIC*, No. 09-1428 (Pa. Ct. Comm. Pleas 2015); see also Pl.'S Br. Opp'n Mot. Summ. J. at 57–119, *Hill v. WPIC*, No. 09-1428 (Pa. Ct. Comm. Pleas 2015).

265   *tragedy struck*: Pl.'S Pre-Trial Summ. Statement at 4–5, 115–118, 164–168, *Hill v. WPIC*, No. 09-1428 (Pa. Ct. Comm. Pleas 2015).

265   *Two years after*: Pl.'S Praecipe for Writ of Summons in a Civil Action, *Hill v. WPIC*, No. 09-1428 (Pa. Ct. Comm. Pleas 2015); see also Pl.'S Pre-Trial Summ. Statement at 32–33, *Hill v. WPIC*, No. 09-1428 (Pa. Ct. Comm. Pleas 2015); see also Def.'S Pre-Trial Summ. Statement at 15–16, *Hill v. WPIC*, No. 09-1428 (Pa. Ct. Comm. Pleas 2015).

265   *I was asked to be*: Def.'S Suppl. Pretrial Statement at 4–5, *Hill v. WPIC*, No. 09-1428 (Pa. Ct. Comm. Pleas 2015).

265   *The Hill family*: Pl.'S Pet. For Leave to Settle a Death Case at 4, *Hill v. WPIC*, No. 09-1428 (Pa. Ct. Comm. Pleas 2015).

265   *Two years later*: "Family of Man Accused of Stabbing Half-Brothers Settles Suit against Western Psych," *CBS Pittsburgh* online, last modified June 2, 2015, https://pitts burgh.cbslocal.com/2015/06/02/family-of-man-accused-of-stabbing-half-brothers -settles-suit-against-western-psych/.

267   *Hispanic heritage*: Robert C. Schwartz and David M. Blankenship, "Racial Disparities in Psychotic Disorder Diagnosis: A Review of Empirical Literature," *World Journal of Psychiatry* 4, no. 4 (December 22, 2014): 133–40.

267   *Immigration status*: Lasse Brandt et al., "Risk of Psychosis Among Refugees: A Systematic Review and Meta-analysis," *JAMA Psychiatry* 76, no. 11 (2019): 1133–40.

267   *Gender is also an issue*: Howard N. Garb, "Race Bias, Social Class Bias, and Gender Bias in Clinical Judgment," *Clinical Psychology: Science and Practice* 4 (1997): 99–120.

268   *The best way to do*: Anthony J. F. Griffiths et al., "Human Pedigree Analysis," in *Modern Genetic Analysis* (New York: W. H. Freeman, 1999); see also Joanna Spahis, "Human Genetics: Constructing a Family Pedigree," *American Journal of Nursing* 102, no. 7 (July 2002): 44–50.

269   *The mental status examination (MSE)*: Rachel M. Voss and Joe M. Das, "Mental Status Examination," in *StatPearls [Internet]* (Treasure Island, FL: StatPearls, 2020); see also Michael B. First, "Routine Psychiatric Assessment," *Merck Manual Professional Version* online, last modified February 2020, https://www.merckmanuals.com/pro fessional/psychiatric-disorders/approach-to-the-patient-with-mental-symptoms /routine-psychiatric-assessment.

269   *The structure of an MSE*: A more extensive assessment of cognitive functions can be gleaned from a MATRICS exam, a battery of neuropsychologic tests that the family can request but that often provides more detail than is useful or necessary.

269   *Soft neurologic signs*: Silke Bachmann et al., "Neurological Soft Signs in the Clinical Course of Schizophrenia: Results of a Meta-Analysis," *Frontiers in Psychiatry* 5 (December 2014): 185.

270   *PET scanning has yielded*: Marc Laruelle and Anissa Abi-Dargham, "Dopamine as the Wind of the Psychotic Fire: New Evidence from Brain Imaging Studies," *Journal of Psychopharmacology* 13, no. 4 (December 1999): 358–71.

270   *One of the most notorious*: Richard J. Bonnie, John C. Jeffries Jr., and Peter W. Low, *A Case Study in the Insanity Defense: The Trial of John W. Hinckley, Jr.*, 2nd ed. (New York: Foundation Press, 2000), 24–28; see also Natalie Jacewicz, "After Hinckley, States Tightened Use of the Insanity Plea," NPR online, last modified July 18, 2016, https://www.npr.org/sections/health-shots/2016/07/28/486607183/after-hinckley-states-tightened-use-of-the-insanity-plea.

270   *Two psychiatrists*: Bonnie, Jeffries Jr., and Low, *Case Study in Insanity Defense*, 28–29; see also Lincoln Caplan, *The Insanity Defense and the Trial of John W. Hinckley, Jr.* (Boston: David R. Godine, 1984), 75–85; see also Stuart Taylor Jr., "Judge Rebukes Hinckley Witness over CAT Scan," *New York Times* online, May 20, 1982, https://www.nytimes.com/1982/05/20/us/judge-rebukes-hinckley-witness-over-cat-scan .html; see also Stuart Taylor Jr., "CAT Scans Said to Show Shrunken Hinckley Brain," *New York Times* online, June 2, 1982, https://www.nytimes.com/1982/06/02/us/cat -scans-said-to-show-shrunken-hinckley-brain.html.

270   *Ultimately, the jury*: Jacewicz, "After Hinckley"; see also Carrie Johnson, "John Hinckley, Who Shot President Reagan, Wins Unconditional Release," NPR online, last modified September 27, 2021, https://www.npr.org/2021/09/27/1040872498/john -hinckley-unconditional-release.

271   *Given the enormity*: Teri A. Manolio et al., "Finding the Missing Heritability of Complex Diseases," *Nature* 461, no. 7265 (October 2009): 747–53.

271   *Goldstein had proven*: Xiaolin Zhu et al., "A Case-Control Collapsing Analysis Identifies Epilepsy Genes Implicated in Trio Sequencing Studies Focused on De Novo Mutations," *PLoS Genetics* 13, no. 11 (November 2017): e1007104.

271   *This approach of using*: Sarah A. Dugger, Adam Platt, and David B. Goldstein, "Drug Development in the Era of Precision Medicine," *Nature Reviews Drug Discovery* 17, no. 3 (March 2018): 183–96.

272   *As the policy of deinstitutionalization*: Torrey, *Out of the Shadows*, 8; see also *National Mental Health Services Survey (N-MHSS): 2018*, Department of Health and Human Services, Substance Abuse and Mental Health Services Administration (SAMHSA)

(Rockville, MD: October 2019), 58, https://www.samhsa.gov/data/sites/default/files
/cbhsq-reports/NMHSS-2018.pdf.

272   *The center, which opened*: "Pilgrim Psychiatric Center," New York State Office of Mental Health online.

274   *our study of extreme phenotypes*: Anthony W. Zoghbi et al., "High-Impact Rare Genetic Variants in Severe Schizophrenia," *Proceedings of the National Academy of Sciences of the United States of America* 118, no. 51 (December 2021): e2112560118.

CHAPTER 18: THE IMPORTANCE OF EARLY INTERVENTION

275   *It told the story*: Jennifer Gonnerman, "A Beautiful Mind: In *Is There No Place on Earth for Me?*, Susan Sheehan Told the Complete Story of One Woman's Struggles with Schizophrenia," *Columbia Journalism Review*, February 2013, https://archives.cjr .org/second_read/a_beautiful_mind.php.

275   *Shortly after midnight*: Susan Sheehan, "The Patient," *New Yorker* online, last modified May 25, 1981, https://www.newyorker.com/magazine/1981/05/25/the -patient.

276   *Creedmoor, which Sheehan*: Susan Sheehan, *Is There No Place on Earth for Me?* (New York: Vintage Books, 1983), 44.

276   *Sylvia spent weeks*: Gonnerman, "A Beautiful Mind"; see also Sheehan, *Is There No Place on Earth for Me?*, 12–47, 100–101, 153–54.

277   *The third part was*: Susan Sheehan, "The Patient III—Is There No Place on Earth for Me?," *New Yorker* online, last modified June 8, 1981, https://www.newyorker.com/ magazine/1981/06/08/the-patient-iii-is-there-no-place-on-earth-for-me.

277   *The question was*: Gonnerman, "A Beautiful Mind."

277   *Mick Jagger wanted*: Sheehan, *Is There No Place on Earth for Me?*, 104.

277   *"I once thought"*: Ibid., 112.

277   *Remarkably, the director*: Gonnerman, "A Beautiful Mind"; see also Sheehan, *Is There No Place on Earth for Me?*, vii.

278   *This conundrum was*: Timothy J. Crow, A. J. Cross, and Eve C. Johnstone, "Two Syndromes in Schizophrenia and Their Pathogenesis," in *Schizophrenia as a Brain Disease*, ed. F. A. Henn and H. A. Nasrallah (New York: Oxford University Press, 1982), 196–234; see also Timothy J. Crow, "The Two-Syndrome Concept: Origins and Current Status," *Schizophrenia Bulletin* 11, no. 3 (January 1985): 471–88.

278   *A key feature of Crow's*: Jeffrey A. Lieberman, Scott A. Small, and Ragy R. Girgis, "Early Detection and Preventive Intervention in Schizophrenia: From Fantasy to Reality," *American Journal of Psychiatry* 176, no. 10 (October 2019): 794–810.

279   *I would propose an alternative*: Jeffrey A. Lieberman, "Is Schizophrenia a Neurodegenerative Disorder? A Clinical and Neurobiological Perspective," *Biological Psychiatry* 46, no. 6 (September 1999): 729–39.

279   *In 1988 Dr. Thomas McGlashan*: Thomas H. McGlashan, "A Selective Review of Re-

cent North American Long-Term Followup Studies of Schizophrenia," *Schizophrenia Bulletin* 14, no. 4 (January 1988): 515–42.

279 *Wyatt's seminal review*: Wyatt, "Neuroleptics and Natural Course."

279 *In 1987 I received*: Jeffrey A. Lieberman et al., "Prospective Study of Psychobiology in First-Episode Schizophrenia at Hillside Hospital," *Schizophrenia Bulletin* 18, no. 3 (January 1992): 351–71.

281 *This inference was*: W. Cahn et al., "Psychosis and Brain Volume Changes During the First Five Years of Schizophrenia," *European Neuropsychopharmacology* 19, no. 2 (February 2009): 147–51; see also W. Cahn et al., "Brain Volume Changes in the First Year of Illness and 5-Year Outcome of Schizophrenia," *British Journal of Psychiatry* 189, no. 4 (October 2006): 381–82.

281 *Following the seminal*: Loebel et al., "Duration of Psychosis and Outcome," 1183–88; see also Diana O. Perkins et al., "Relationship Between Duration of Untreated Psychosis and Outcome in First-Episode Schizophrenia: A Critical Review and Meta-Analysis," *American Journal of Psychiatry* 162, no. 10 (October 2005): 1785–804.

281 *The average time that*: Perkins et al., "Duration of Untreated Psychosis and Outcome in First-Episode Schizophrenia."

281 *The Treatment and Intervention in Psychosis (TIPS)*: Ingrid Melle et al., "Early Detection of the First Episode of Schizophrenia and Suicidal Behavior," *American Journal of Psychiatry* 163, no. 5 (May 2006): 800–804; see also Inge Joa et al., "Information Campaigns: 10 Years of Experience in the Early Treatment and Intervention in Psychosis (TIPS) Study," *Psychiatric Annals* 38, no. 8 (August 2008).

282 *Prior to the study*: Wenche ten Velden Hegelstad et al., "Long-Term Follow-Up of the TIPS Early Detection in Psychosis Study: Effects on 10-Year Outcome," *American Journal of Psychiatry* 169, no. 4 (April 2012): 374–80.

283 *At three months*: Lieberman, Small, and Girgis, "Early Detection and Preventive Intervention."

283 *The same pattern*: Hegelstad et al., "Long-Term Follow-Up of the TIPS."

284 *To address the question*: Lisa B. Dixon et al., "Transforming the Treatment of Schizophrenia in the United States: The RAISE Initiative," *Annual Review of Clinical Psychology* 14 (May 2018): 237–58.

284 *The first PORT study*: Anthony F. Lehman, Donald M. Steinwachs, and Co-Investigators of the PORT Project, "Translating Research into Practice: The Schizophrenia Patient Outcomes Research Team (PORT) Treatment Recommendations," *Schizophrenia Bulletin* 24, no. 1 (January 1998): 1–10.

284 *The published treatment*: Anthony F. Lehman et al., "The Schizophrenia Patient Outcomes Research Team (PORT): Updated Treatment Recommendations 2003," *Schizophrenia Bulletin* 30, no. 2 (January 2004): 193–217; see also Lisa B. Dixon et al., "The 2009 Schizophrenia PORT Psychosocial Treatment Recommendations and Summary Statements," *Schizophrenia Bulletin* 36, no. 1 (January 2010): 48–70.

284 *In the meantime, research groups*: Vinod H. Srihari, Jai Shah, and Matcheri S. Keshavan, "Is Early Intervention for Psychosis Feasible and Effective?," *Psychiatric Clinics* 35, no. 3 (September 2012): 613–31; see also *The NHS Plan: A Plan for Investment, a Plan for Reform* (London: National Health Service online, July 2000), http://1nj5ms2lli 5hdggbe3mm7ms5.wpengine.netdna-cdn.com/files/2010/03/pnsuk1.pdf.

285   *America, however, went*: Dixon et al., "The RAISE Initiative," 237–58.

285   *Strategies to support treatment*: Mary Ann Test and Leonard I. Stein, "Practical Guide-lines for the Community Treatment of Markedly Impaired Patients," *Community Mental Health Journal* 12, no. 1 (Spring 1976): 72–82.

285   *patients with early-stage*: Dixon et al., "The RAISE Initiative."

286   *US investigators funded*: Ibid.

286   *The RAISE initiative*: Lisa B. Dixon, "Early Psychosis Treatment: How Did We Get Here & Where Are We Going?" (presentation, University of Washington, Department of Psychiatry & Behavioral Sciences, Grand Rounds, November 2017).

287   *We called it the RAISE*: Lisa B. Dixon et al., "Implementing Coordinated Specialty Care for Early Psychosis: The RAISE Connection Program," *Psychiatric Services* 66, no. 7 (July 2015): 691–98.

287   *The other study funded*: John M. Kane et al., "Comprehensive Versus Usual Community Care for First-Episode Psychosis: 2-Year Outcomes from the NIMH RAISE Early Treatment Program," *American Journal of Psychiatry* 173, no. 4 (April 2016): 362–72.

287   *RAISE-ETP proceeded*: Ibid.

288   *My colleague Lisa Dixon was*: Lisa B. Dixon (Edna L. Edison Professor of Psychiatry, Columbia University Vagelos College of Physicians and Surgeons, and director, NewYork-Presbyterian, Division of Behavioral Health Services and Policy Research & Center for Practice Innovations), in discussion with the author, September 4, 2021.

289   *OnTrackNY has now*: Ibid.; see also Ilana Nossel (medical director of OnTrack), in discussion with the author, June 12, 2019.

290   *In 2018 a study of*: Ilana Nossel et al., "Results of a Coordinated Specialty Care Program for Early Psychosis and Predictors of Outcomes," *Psychiatric Services* 69, no. 8 (August 2018): 863–70.

290   *A young psychiatrist named*: Nossel, in discussion with the author.

291   *One young person*: Drew, in discussion with the author, January 2021.

292   *The center is named*: Lawrence van Gelder, "Howard Geld, 42, Advocate for Mentally Ill, Dies," *New York Times* online, February 14, 1995, https://www.nytimes.com/1995/02/14/obituaries/howard-geld-42-advocate-for-mentally-ill-dies.html.

294   *different forms of prevention*: Patrick D. McGorry, Eóin Killackey, and Alison Yung, "Early Intervention in Psychosis: Concepts, Evidence and Future Directions," *World Psychiatry* 7, no. 3 (October 2008): 148–56.

295   *Our current approach*: Paolo Fusar-Poli et al., "The Psychosis High-Risk State: A Comprehensive State-of-the-Art Review," *JAMA Psychiatry* 70, no. 1 (January 2013): 107–20.

296   *Only about a third*: Ibid.; see also Paolo Fusar-Poli et al., "Predicting Psychosis: Meta-Analysis of Transition Outcomes in Individuals at High Clinical Risk," *Archives of General Psychiatry* 69, no. 3 (March 2012): 220–29; and Jordina Tor et al., "Clinical High Risk for Psychosis in Children and Adolescents: A Systematic Review," *European Child & Adolescent Psychiatry* 27, no. 6 (September 2018): 683–700.

296   *In recognition of his*: "Mental Health Expert Is Australian of the Year," *ABC Australia*

online, last modified January 25, 2010, https://www.abc.net.au/news/2010-01-25/mental-health-expert-is-australian-of-the-year/308004.

297   *In 2015 the North American*: Jean Addington et al., "North American Prodrome Longitudinal Study (NAPLS 2): The Prodromal Symptoms," *Journal of Nervous and Mental Disease* 203, no. 5 (May 2015): 328.

297   *Examples of high-risk symptoms*: "Center of Prevention and Evaluation (COPE)," Columbia University Department of Psychiatry online, accessed June 6, 2021, https://www.columbiapsychiatry.org/research-clinics/cope.

298   *COPE researchers monitored*: Gary Brucato et al., "Baseline Demographics, Clinical Features and Predictors of Conversion among 200 Individuals in a Longitudinal Prospective Psychosis-Risk Cohort," *Psychological Medicine* 47, no. 11 (August 2017): 1923–35.

298   *Some number of patients*: When the *DSM-5* was being revised, there was active debate as to whether a diagnostic category of attenuated psychosis syndrome should be included. However, given the lack of evidence for it being a discrete condition and the vagueness of its definition, it was placed in the appendix as a diagnostic construct requiring further research.

298   *Numerous treatments have*: Alice Egerton et al., "Glutamate in Schizophrenia: Neurodevelopmental Perspectives and Drug Development," *Schizophrenia Research* 223 (October 2020): 59–70; see also Naista Zhand, David G. Attwood, and Philip D. Harvey, "Glutamate Modulators for Treatment of Schizophrenia," *Personalized Medicine in Psychiatry* 15–16 (July/August 2019): 1–12; see also Jeffrey Lieberman et al., "Hippocampal Dysfunction in the Pathophysiology of Schizophrenia: A Selective Review and Hypothesis for Early Detection and Intervention," *Molecular Psychiatry* 23, no. 8 (August 2018): 1764–72; see also Daniel C. Javitt, "Glutamate as a Therapeutic Target in Psychiatric Disorders," *Molecular Psychiatry* 9, no. 11 (November 2004): 984–97.

299   *The incidence of CHR*: Jean Addington et al., "North American Prodrome Longitudinal Study: A Collaborative Multisite Approach to Prodromal Schizophrenia Research," *Schizophrenia Bulletin* 33, no. 3 (May 2007): 665–72.

299   *In order to connect with*: Gary Brucato (then–assistant director of the Center of Prevention and Evaluation [COPE]), in discussion with the author, June 2018.

300   *Structured Interview for Psychosis-Risk Syndromes*: Tandy J. Miller et al., "Prodromal Assessment with the Structured Interview for Prodromal Syndromes and the Scale of Prodromal Symptoms: Predictive Validity, Interrater Reliability, and Training to Reliability," *Schizophrenia Bulletin* 29, no. 4 (January 2003): 703–15.

300   *When Elyn Saks told*: Elyn R. Saks, *The Center Cannot Hold: My Journey Through Madness* (New York: Hyperion, 2007), 290.

300   *Context is important*: Brucato, in discussion with the author.

301   *"There are still researchers"*: Ragy R. Girgis, email message to author, February 18, 2021.

301   *Often the first reaction*: Brucato, in discussion with the author.

Chapter 19: How We (Should) Treat Schizophrenia

302   *Carleton Gajdusek*: David M. Asher with Michel B. A. Oldstone, *D. Carleton Gajdusek: A Biographical Memoir* (Washington, DC: National Academy of Sciences, 2013), http://www.nasonline.org/publications/biographical-memoirs/memoir-pdfs/gajdusek-d-carleton.pdf; see also Donald G. McNeil Jr., "D. Carleton Gajdusek, Who Won Nobel for Work on Brain Disease, Is Dead at 85," *New York Times* online, December 15, 2008, https://www.nytimes.com/2008/12/15/science/15gajdusek.html; see also D. Carleton Gajdusek, "D. Carleton Gajdusek—Biographical," Nobel Prize.org, Nobel Prize Outreach AB 2021, accessed April 24, 2021, https://www.nobelprize.org/prizes/medicine/1976/gajdusek/biographical/.

303   *The victims of kuru*: Michael P. Alpers, "The Epidemiology of Kuru: Monitoring the Epidemic from Its Peak to Its End," *Philosophical Transactions of the Royal Society B: Biological Sciences* 363, no. 1510 (November 2008): 3707–13.

303   *Gajdusek hypothesized a connection*: Daniel Carleton Gajdusek, Clarence J. Gibbs Jr., and Michael Alpers, "Experimental Transmission of a Kuril-like Syndrome to Chimpanzees," *Nature* (London) 209 (February 1966): 794–96; see also Clarence J. Gibbs Jr. and D. Carleton Gajdusek, "Attempts to Demonstrate a Transmissible Agent in Kuru, Amyotrophic Lateral Sclerosis, and Other Subacute and Chronic Progressive Nervous System Degenerations of Man," in *Slow, Latent, and Temperate Virus Infections*, ed. D. Carleton Gajdusek, Clarence J. Gibbs Jr., and Michael Alpers (Washington, DC: US Department of Health, Education, and Welfare, National Institute of Neurological Diseases and Blindness, 1965), 39–46.

303   *Then, in the 1980s*: Peter G. Smith and Ray Bradley, "Bovine Spongiform Encephalopathy (BSE) and Its Epidemiology," *British Medical Bulletin* 66, no. 1 (June 2003): 185–98; see also James W. Ironside, "Variant Creutzfeldt-Jakob Disease: An Update," *Folia Neuropathologica* 50, no. 1 (March 2012): 50–56.

303   *Stanley Prusiner's subsequent*: Stanley B. Prusiner, "Prions," *Proceedings of the National Academy of Sciences* 95, no. 23 (November 1998): 13363–83.

304   *this evidence has been*: Around the same time the US government initiated the PORT studies in mental illness, the Cochrane Centre at the University of Oxford began to assemble a collection of databases and systematic reviews that summarized and interpreted the results of medical research. Seeing this, the professional medical associations, such as the APA, followed suit. I was among a group of schizophrenia treatment experts to serve on the APA's inaugural panel to develop practice guidelines for schizophrenia treatment. The process involved a comprehensive review of the massive amount of relevant published studies, pharmacological and psychosocial, and resulted in a detailed compendium on what was then state-of-the-art treatment. See also Marvin I. Herz et al., "Practice Guideline for the Treatment of Patients with Schizophrenia," *American Journal of Psychiatry* 154, no. 4 suppl. (April 1997): 1–63; see also Guideline Writing Group, Systematic Review Group, and Committee on Practice Guidelines, *The American Psychiatric Association Practice*

Guideline for the Treatment of Patients with Schizophrenia, 3rd. ed. (Washington, DC: American Psychiatric Association, 2020).

305   *There are three ways*: Jeffrey A. Lieberman, Scott A. Small, and Ragy R. Girgis, "Early Detection and Preventive Intervention in Schizophrenia: From Fantasy to Reality," *American Journal of Psychiatry* 176, no. 10 (October 2019): 794–810.

305   *Schizophrenia is a low-incidence*: John McGrath et al., "Schizophrenia: A Concise Overview of Incidence, Prevalence, and Mortality," *Epidemiologic Reviews* 30, no. 1 (November 2008): 67–76.

307   *The first (and only)*: Jeffrey A. Lieberman and T. Scott Stroup, "The NIMH-CATIE Schizophrenia Study: What Did We Learn?," *American Journal of Psychiatry* 168, no. 8 (August 2011): 770–75; see also National Institute of Mental Health, "Questions and Answers About the NIMH Clinical Antipsychotic Trials of Intervention Effectiveness Study (CATIE)—Phase 1 Results," news release, September 2005, https://www.nimh.nih.gov/funding/clinical-research/practical/catie/phase1results.

307   *Clinical Antipsychotic Trials of Intervention Effectiveness (CATIE) study*: It was actually two studies. As antipsychotic drugs were used extensively in treating psychotic symptoms and agitation in Alzheimer's disease, one-third of the funds supported a study led by Lon Schneider of the University of Southern California and Pierre Tariot of the University of Rochester.

308   *These findings were replicated*: Peter B. Jones et al., "Randomized Controlled Trial of the Effect on Quality of Life of Second- Vs. First-Generation Antipsychotic Drugs in Schizophrenia: Cost Utility of the Latest Antipsychotic Drugs in Schizophrenia Study (CUtLASS 1)," *Archives of General Psychiatry* 63, no. 10 (October 2006): 1079–87; see also Maximilian Huhn et al., "Comparative Efficacy and Tolerability of 32 Oral Antipsychotics for the Acute Treatment of Adults with Multi-Episode Schizophrenia: A Systematic Review and Network Meta-Analysis," *Focus* 18, no. 4 (October 2020): 443–55.

308   *When the results of the CATIE*: Jeffrey A. Lieberman et al., "Effectiveness of Antipsychotic Drugs in Patients with Chronic Schizophrenia," *New England Journal of Medicine* 353, no. 12 (September 2005): 1209–23; see also Robert Freedman, "The Choice of Antipsychotic Drugs for Schizophrenia," *New England Journal of Medicine* 353, no. 12 (September 2005): 1286–88.

308   *The* New York Times *ran*: "Comparing Schizophrenia Drugs," editorial, *New York Times*, September 21, 2005, 24.

308   *In 2010 Congress did*: Patient Protection and Affordable Care Act, H.R. Rep. No. 111-148, at 727–47 (2010).

309   *Studies of first-episode patients*: Lieberman et al., "Time Course and Biologic Correlates of Treatment Response," 369–76; see also Joseph P. McEvoy et al., "Efficacy and Tolerability of Olanzapine, Quetiapine, and Risperidone in the Treatment of Early Psychosis: A Randomized, Double-Blind 52-Week Comparison," *American Journal of Psychiatry* 164, no. 7 (July 2007): 1050–60; see also Kayvon Salimi, L. Fredrik Jarskog, and Jeffrey A. Lieberman, "Antipsychotic Drugs for First-Episode Schizophrenia," *CNS Drugs* 23, no. 10 (October 2009): 837–55.

310   *While the D-2 receptor*: Seiya Miyamoto et al., "Pharmacological Treatment of Schizo-

phrenia: A Critical Review of the Pharmacology and Clinical Effects of Current and Future Therapeutic Agents," *Molecular Psychiatry* 17, no. 12 (December 2012): 1206–27; see also Kenneth S. Koblan et al., "A Non–D2-Receptor-Binding Drug for the Treatment of Schizophrenia," *New England Journal of Medicine* 382, no. 16 (April 2020): 1497–506; see also Stephen K. Brannan et al., "Muscarinic Cholinergic Receptor Agonist and Peripheral Antagonist for Schizophrenia," *New England Journal of Medicine* 384, no. 8 (February 2021): 717–26.

310   *drugs targeting glutamate*: Bruce J. Kinon et al., "Exploratory Analysis for a Targeted Patient Population Responsive to the Metabotropic Glutamate 2/3 Receptor Agonist Pomaglumetad Methionil in Schizophrenia," *Biological Psychiatry* 78, no. 11 (December 2015): 754–62; see also Kantrowitz et al., "Proof of Mechanism and Target Engagement of Glutamatergic Drugs"; see also Joshua T. Kantrowitz et al., "D-Serine for the Treatment of Negative Symptoms in Individuals at Clinical High Risk of Schizophrenia: A Pilot, Double-Blind, Placebo-Controlled, Randomised Parallel Group Mechanistic Proof-of-Concept Trial," *Lancet Psychiatry* 2, no. 5 (May 2015): 403–12.

311   *She recounts how*: Saks, *Center Cannot Hold*, 282–304.

311   *And she stopped experiencing*: Ibid., 303–4.

311   *Elyn had also struggled*: Ibid., 282.

312   *However, clozapine can*: Pasquale De Fazio et al., "Rare and Very Rare Adverse Effects of Clozapine," *Neuropsychiatric Disease and Treatment* 11 (August 2015): 1995–2003; see also Oliver Freudenreich and Joseph McEvoy, "Guidelines for Prescribing Clozapine in Schizophrenia," UpToDate, last modified September 13, 2021, https://www.uptodate.com/contents/guidelines-for-prescribing-clozapine-in-schizophrenia.

312   *Clozapine has been*: John Crilly, "The History of Clozapine and Its Emergence in the US Market: A Review and Analysis," *History of Psychiatry* 18, no. 1 (March 2007): 39–60.

312   *That study would mark*: John Kane et al., "Clozapine for the Treatment-Resistant Schizophrenic: A Double-Blind Comparison with Chlorpromazine," *Archives of General Psychiatry* 45, no. 9 (1988): 789–96.

313   *A comprehensive review*: Jari Tiihonen et al., "Association of Antipsychotic Polypharmacy Vs Monotherapy with Psychiatric Rehospitalization Among Adults with Schizophrenia," *JAMA Psychiatry* 76, no. 5 (February 2019): 499–507.

314   *In researching its mechanism*: Guang Chen et al., "Enhancement of Hippocampal Neurogenesis by Lithium," *Journal of Neurochemistry* 75, no. 4 (October 2000): 1729–34; see also Gregory J. Moore et al., "Lithium-Induced Increase in Human Brain Grey Matter," *Lancet* 356, no. 9237 (October 2000): 1241–42; see also Husseini K. Manji et al., "Neuroplasticity and Cellular Resilience in Mood Disorders," *Molecular Psychiatry* 5, no. 6 (November 2000): 578–93.

314   *The extent of the problem*: Peter M. Haddad, Cecilia Brain, and Jan Scott, "Nonadherence with Antipsychotic Medication in Schizophrenia: Challenges and Management Strategies," *Patient Related Outcome Measures* 5 (June 2014): 43–62.

314   *the rates of treatment adherence*: Mark Rabinovitch et al., "Early Predictors of Nonadherence to Antipsychotic Therapy in First-Episode Psychosis," *Canadian Journal of Psychiatry* 54, no. 1 (January 2009): 28–35; see also Martin Lambert et al., "Prevalence, Predictors, and Consequences of Long-Term Refusal of Antipsychotic

Treatment in First-Episode Psychosis," *Journal of Clinical Psychopharmacology* 30, no. 5 (October 2010): 565–72; see also Lauren M. Hickling et al., "Non-Adherence to Antipsychotic Medication in First-Episode Psychosis Patients," *Psychiatry Research* 264 (June 2018): 151–54.

315   *ACT was developed in*: Leonard I. Stein, Mary A. Test, and Arnold J. Marx, "Alternative to the Hospital: A Controlled Study," *American Journal of Psychiatry* 132, no. 5 (May 1975): 517–22.

315   *Assisted Outpatient Treatment*: Marvin S. Swartz et al., *New York State Assisted Outpatient Treatment Program Evaluation* (Durham, NC: Duke University School of Medicine, June 2009); see also Marvin S. Swartz et al., "A Randomized Controlled Trial of Outpatient Commitment in North Carolina," *Psychiatric Services* 52, no. 3 (March 2001): 325–29; see also Marvin S. Swartz et al., "Can Involuntary Outpatient Commitment Reduce Hospital Recidivism? Findings from a Randomized Trial with Severely Mentally Ill Individuals," *American Journal of Psychiatry* 156, no. 12 (December 1999): 1968–75.

315   *Outpatient commitment has been*: Appelbaum, in discussion with the author, March 16, 2021.

315   *A young woman named*: National Alliance on Mental Health, Laurie M. Flynn, "The Kendra Webdale–Andrew Goldstein Tragedy: One More Failure in America's Mental Healthcare System," news release, January 7, 1999.

315   *Racial disparities have*: John A. Gresham, *Implementation of "Kendra's Law" Is Severely Biased* (New York: New York Lawyers for the Public Interest, April 7, 2005).

315   *Most states that have*: Appelbaum, in discussion with the author, March 16, 2021.

316   *as studies have shown*: Swartz et al., *NYS AOT Program Evaluation*; see also Swartz et al., "Outpatient Commitment in North Carolina"; see also Swartz et al., "Involuntary Outpatient Commitment"; see also Jeffrey W. Swanson et al., "The Cost of Assisted Outpatient Treatment: Can It Save States Money?," *American Journal of Psychiatry* 170, no. 12 (December 2013): 1423–32.

316   *It is worth noting that*: Ali Watkins, "A Horrific Crime on the Subway Led to Kendra's Law. Years Later, Has It Helped?," *New York Times* online, September 11, 2018, https://www.nytimes.com/2018/09/11/nyregion/kendras-law-andrew-goldstein -subway-murder.html?searchResultPosition=1.

316   *Beyond preventing relapses*: "Benefit of Long-Acting Injectables in Schizophrenia," *Expert Perspectives on Schizophrenia Treatment Approaches and Relapse Prevention-Episode 6*, released December 19, 2018, on AJMC, https://www.youtube.com /watch?v=VkJmjLJeb5w.

316   *Historically, long-acting injectables*: Kenneth L. Subotnik et al., "Long-Acting Injectable Risperidone for Relapse Prevention and Control of Breakthrough Symptoms After a Recent First Episode of Schizophrenia. A Randomized Clinical Trial," *JAMA Psychiatry* 72, no. 8 (August 2015): 822–29.

317   *Despite this, LAIs remain*: Jean-Pierre Lindenmayer et al., "Persistent Barriers to the Use of Long-Acting Injectable Antipsychotics for the Treatment of Schizophrenia," *Journal of Clinical Psychopharmacology* 40, no. 4 (July/August 2020): 346–49; see also Maxine X. Patel et al., "Attitudes of European Physicians Towards the Use of Long-Acting Injectable Antipsychotics," *BMC Psychiatry* 20, no. 1 (March 2020): 123.

317   *Doctors may be reluctant*: "Benefit of LAIs in Schizophrenia," *Episode 6.*

317   *The therapeutic community applies*: T. F. Main, "The Hospital as a Therapeutic Institution," *Bulletin of the Menninger Clinic* 10, no. 3 (May 1946): 66; see also Maxwell Jones, *Social Psychiatry: A Study of Therapeutic Communities* (London: Tavistock, 1952); see also Maxwell Jones, "In Conversation with Maxwell Jones," interview by Brian Barraclough, September 23, 1983, *Bulletin of the Royal College of Psychiatrists,* available at https://www.cambridge.org/core/services/aop-cambridge-core/content /view/4941C60A0028B6313C5CA1474E070D21/S0140078900000213a.pdf/in_con versation_with_maxwell_jones.pdf.

318   *The clubhouse model of care*: John H. Beard, Rudyard N. Propst, and Thomas J. Malamud, "The Fountain House Model of Psychiatric Rehabilitation," *Psychosocial Rehabilitation Journal* 5, no. 1 (January 1982): 47–53; see also Stephen B. Anderson, *We Are Not Alone: Fountain House and the Development of Clubhouse Culture* (New York: Fountain House, 1998); see also Sandra E. Herman et al., "Sense of Community in Clubhouse Programs: Member and Staff Concepts," *American Journal of Community Psychology* 36, no. 34 (December 2005): 343–56.

319   *Its mission was to*: Marianne D. Farkas and William A. Anthony, *Psychiatric Rehabilitation Programs: Putting Theory into Practice* (Baltimore: Johns Hopkins University Press, 1989).

319   *Psychosocial therapies have*: Wai Tong Chien et al., "Current Approaches to Treatments for Schizophrenia Spectrum Disorders, Part II: Psychosocial Interventions and Patient-Focused Perspectives in Psychiatric Care," *Neuropsychiatric Disease and Treatment* 9, no. 9 (September 2013): 1463–81; see also Uta Gühne et al., "Psychosocial Therapies in Severe Mental Illness: Update on Evidence and Recommendations," *Current Opinion in Psychiatry* 33, no. 4 (June 2020): 414–21.

320   *These treatment choices are*: Alan S. Bellack, "Psychosocial Treatment in Schizophrenia," *Dialogues in Clinical Neuroscience* 3, no. 2 (June 2001): 136–37.

320   *But a seminal paper published*: Michael Foster Green, "What Are the Functional Consequences of Neurocognitive Deficits in Schizophrenia?," *American Journal of Psychiatry* 153, no. 3 (March 1996): 321–30.

321   *the following year published*: Alice Medalia and Bryan Freilich, "The Neuropsychological Educational Approach to Cognitive Remediation (NEAR) Model: Practice Principles and Outcome Studies," *American Journal of Psychiatric Rehabilitation* 11, no. 2 (April 2008): 123–43.

321   *"No one is taught how"*: Alice Medalia (clinical director, Cognitive Health Services, New York State Office of Mental Health; director, Lieber Recovery Clinic; and professor of psychology at Columbia University Vagelos College of Physicians and Surgeons, Columbia University Irving Medical Center), in discussion with the author, June 11, 2019.

322   *Studies back up what*: Tamiko Mogami, "Cognitive Remediation for Schizophrenia with Focus on NEAR," *Frontiers in Psychiatry* 8 (January 2018): 304; see also Alice Medalia et al., "Personalised Treatment for Cognitive Dysfunction in Individuals with Schizophrenia Spectrum Disorders," *Neuropsychological Rehabilitation* 28, no. 4 (June 2018): 602–13; see also Giacomo Deste et al., "Effectiveness of Cognitive Remediation in Early Versus Chronic Schizophrenia: A Preliminary Report," *Fron-*

tiers in Psychiatry 10 (April 2019): 236; see also Philip D. Harvey and Christopher R. Bowie, "Cognitive Remediation in Severe Mental Illness," *Innovations in Clinical Neuroscience* 9, no. 4 (April 2012): 27–30.

323   *This kind of reality testing*: Max Birchwood et al., "Cognitive Behaviour Therapy to Prevent Harmful Compliance with Command Hallucinations (Command): A Randomised Controlled Trial," *Lancet Psychiatry* 1, no. 1 (June 2014): 23–33; see also Douglas Turkington, David Kingdon, and Trevor Turner, "Effectiveness of a Brief Cognitive–Behavioural Therapy Intervention in the Treatment of Schizophrenia," *British Journal of Psychiatry* 180, no. 6 (June 2002): 523–27; see also Til Wykes et al., "Cognitive Behavior Therapy for Schizophrenia: Effect Sizes, Clinical Models, and Methodological Rigor," *Schizophrenia Bulletin* 34, no. 3 (May 2008): 523–37.

323   *Psychiatrist Aaron Beck*: Aaron T. Beck, "Successful Outpatient Psychotherapy of a Chronic Schizophrenic with a Delusion Based on Borrowed Guilt," *Psychiatry* 15, no. 3 (August 1952): 305–12; see also Neil A. Rector, Aaron T. Beck, and Neal Stolar, "The Negative Symptoms of Schizophrenia: A Cognitive Perspective," *Canadian Journal of Psychiatry* 50, no. 5 (April 2005): 247–57; see also "Aaron Beck: Reducing Schizophrenia's Negative Symptoms," *Brain & Behavior Research Foundation*, April 1, 2010, https://www.bbrfoundation.org/content/aaron-beck-reducing-schizophrenia%E2%80%99s-negative-symptoms.

324   *Homelessness, or even*: "Finding Stable Housing," National Alliance on Mental Illness online, accessed June 21, 2021, https://www.nami.org/Your-Journey/Individuals-with-Mental-Illness/Finding-Stable-Housing.

325   *Critical time intervention (CTI)*: "CTI Model," Center for Advancement of Critical Time Intervention, Silberman School of Social Work, Hunter College online, accessed March 31, 2021, https://www.criticaltime.org/cti-model/; see also "Background," Center for Advancement of Critical Time Intervention, Silberman School of Social Work, Hunter College online, accessed March 31, 2021, https://www.criticaltime.org/cti-model/background/; see also *Critical Time Intervention: Preventing Homelessness in the Transition from Institution to Community*, Center for Advancement of Critical Time Intervention (New York: Hunter College Silberman School of Social Work, April 2009), https://www.criticaltime.org/wp-content/uploads/2009/04/cti-handout4.pdf.

325   *One of the leaders of*: Patricia E. Deegan, "Recovery: The Lived Experience of Rehabilitation," *Psychosocial Rehabilitation Journal* 11, no. 4 (April 1988): 12–13.

327   *Joseph White, was a*: Saks, *Center Cannot Hold*, 187–246.

328   *When Elyn moved*: Ibid., 243–52, 321–22.

328   *"Dr. Kaplan probably helped"*: Ibid., 324.

328   *"He had, in short"*: Ibid., 307.

329   *People with schizophrenia*: National Institutes of Health, "Severe Mental Illness Tied to Higher Rates of Substance Use," news release, January 3, 2014, https://www.nih.gov/news-events/news-releases/severe-mental-illness-tied-higher-rates-substance-use; see also Sarah M. Hartz et al., "Comorbidity of Severe Psychotic Disorders with Measures of Substance Use," *JAMA Psychiatry* 71, no. 3 (March 2014): 248–54.

329   *They smoke cigarettes*: Monica E. Cornelius et al., "Tobacco Product Use Among Adults—United States, 2019," *Morbidity and Mortality Weekly Report* 69, no. 46

(November 2020): 1736–42; see also NIH State-of-the-Science Panel, "National Institutes of Health State-of-the-Science Conference Statement: Tobacco Use: Prevention, Cessation, and Control," *Annals of Internal Medicine* 145, no. 11 (December 2006): 839–44; see also Faith Dickerson et al., "Cigarette Smoking by Patients with Serious Mental Illness, 1999–2016: An Increasing Disparity," *Psychiatric Services* 69, no. 2 (February 2018): 147–53.

329   *studies of drugs*: Joshua T. Kantrowitz et al., "Double Blind, Two Dose, Randomized, Placebo-Controlled, Cross-over Clinical Trial of the Positive Allosteric Modulator at the Alpha7 Nicotinic Cholinergic Receptor Avl-3288 in Schizophrenia Patients," *Neuropsychopharmacology* 45, no. 8 (July 2020): 1339–45.

329   *Recreational drug use*: Bernadette Winklbaur et al., "Substance Abuse in Patients with Schizophrenia," *Dialogues in Clinical Neuroscience* 8, no. 1 (March 2006): 37–43; see also Glenn E. Hunt et al., "Prevalence of Comorbid Substance Use in Schizophrenia Spectrum Disorders in Community and Clinical Settings, 1990–2017: Systematic Review and Meta-Analysis," *Drug and Alcohol Dependence* 191 (October 2018): 234–58.

329   *Suicide is one of*: Sukanta Saha, David Chant, and John McGrath, "A Systematic Review of Mortality in Schizophrenia: Is the Differential Mortality Gap Worsening Over Time?," *Archives of General Psychiatry* 64, no. 10 (October 2007): 1123–31.

330   *Other risk factors*: Leo Sher and René S. Kahn, "Suicide in Schizophrenia: An Educational Overview," *Medicina* 55, no. 7 (July 2019): 361.

330   *Another cause of suicide*: Jill M. Harkavy-Friedman et al., "Suicide Attempts in Schizophrenia: The Role of Command Auditory Hallucinations for Suicide," *Journal of Clinical Psychiatry* 64, no. 8 (August 2003): 871–74; see also Zerlina Wong et al., "Command Hallucinations and Clinical Characteristics of Suicidality in Patients with Psychotic Spectrum Disorders," *Comprehensive Psychiatry* 54, no. 6 (August 2013): 611–17.

330   *Clozapine, in particular*: Cheng-Yi Huang, Su-Chen Fang, and Yu-Hsuan Joni Shao, "Comparison of Long-Acting Injectable Antipsychotics with Oral Antipsychotics and Suicide and All-Cause Mortality in Patients with Newly Diagnosed Schizophrenia," *JAMA Network Open* 4, no. 5 (May 2021): e218810.

330   *Schizophrenia is not a major cause of violence*: Jonathan M. Metzl and Kenneth T. MacLeish, "Mental Illness, Mass Shootings, and the Politics of American Firearms," *American Journal of Public Health* 105, no. 2 (2015): 240–49.

330   *The risk of violent behavior*: Jeanne Y. Choe, Linda A. Teplin, and Karen M. Abram, "Perpetration of Violence, Violent Victimization, and Severe Mental Illness: Balancing Public Health Concerns," *Psychiatric Services* 59, no. 2 (February 2008): 153–64; see also Matthew M. Large and Olav Nielssen, "Violence in First-Episode Psychosis: A Systematic Review and Meta-Analysis," *Schizophrenia Research* 125, no. 2/3 (February 2011): 209–20; see also Gary Brucato et al., "Prevalence and Phenomenology of Violent Ideation and Behavior Among 200 Young People at Clinical High-Risk for Psychosis: An Emerging Model of Violence and Psychotic Illness," *Neuropsychopharmacology* 44, no. 5 (April 2019): 907–14; see also Katrina Witt, Richard Van Dorn, and Seena Fazel, "Risk Factors for Violence in Psychosis: Systematic Review and Meta-Regression Analysis of 110 Studies," *PloS One* 8, no. 2 (February 2013): e55942.

335   *Gould Farm, a healing community*: "About Us," Gould Farm online, accessed June 24, 2021, https://gouldfarm.net/about-us/.

339   *treatment is no exception*: Els van der Ven et al., "Racial-Ethnic Differences in Service Use Patterns Among Young, Commercially Insured Individuals with Recent-Onset Psychosis," *Psychiatric Services* 71, no. 5 (2020): 433–39; see also Schwartz and Blankenship, "Racial Disparities in Psychotic Disorder Diagnosis."

339   *psychosocial and rehabilitative treatments*: Jennifer I. Manuel, "Racial/Ethnic and Gender Disparities in Health Care Use and Access," *Health Services Research* 53, no. 3 (2018): 1407–29; see also Jean Addington et al., "Duration of Untreated Psychosis in Community Treatment Settings in the United States" *Psychiatric Services* 66, no. 7 (2015): 753–56.

340   *A diagnostic test*: Brett A. Clementz et al., "Identification of Distinct Psychosis Biotypes Using Brain-Based Biomarkers," *American Journal of Psychiatry* 173, no. 4 (April 2016): 373–84; see also Daniela Rodrigues-Amorim et al., "Schizophrenia: A Review of Potential Biomarkers," *Journal of Psychiatric Research* 93 (October 2017): 37–49.

340   *the most promising candidate*: Nina V. Kraguljac et al., "Neuroimaging Biomarkers in Schizophrenia," *American Journal of Psychiatry* 178, no. 6 (June 2021): 509–21; see also Donald C. Goff et al., "Biomarkers for Drug Development in Early Psychosis: Current Issues and Promising Directions," *European Neuropsychopharmacology* 26, no. 6 (June 2016): 923–37; see also Andrea Schmitt et al., "Consensus Paper of the WFSBP Task Force on Biological Markers: Criteria for Biomarkers and Endophenotypes of Schizophrenia Part II: Cognition, Neuroimaging and Genetics," *World Journal of Biological Psychiatry* 17, no. 6 (September 2016): 406–28.

340   *the information derived from*: Leila Jahangiry, Mahdieh Abbasalizad Farhangi, and Fatemeh Rezaei, "Framingham Risk Score for Estimation of 10-Years of Cardiovascular Diseases Risk in Patients with Metabolic Syndrome," *Journal of Health, Population and Nutrition* 36, no. 1 (December 2017): 1–6; see also Felipe Couñago et al., "Clinical Applications of Molecular Biomarkers in Prostate Cancer," *Cancers (Basel)* 12, no. 6 (June 2020): 1550.

340   *A newer technology*: Vimal K. Singh et al., "Induced Pluripotent Stem Cells: Applications in Regenerative Medicine, Disease Modeling, and Drug Discovery," *Frontiers in Cell and Developmental Biology* 3 (February 2015): 2; see also Natalie de Souza, "Organoids," *Nature Methods* 15, no. 1 (January 2018): 23.

340   *The initial rationale*: Riham Mohamed Aly, "Current State of Stem Cell–Based Therapies: An Overview," *Stem Cell Investigation* 7 (2020): 8.

341   *RNA interference (RNAi)*: Ryan L. Setten, John J. Rossi, and Si-ping Han, "The Current State and Future Directions of RNAi-Based Therapeutics," *Nature Reviews Drug Discovery* 18, no. 6 (June 2019): 421–46.

342   *The initial approach of gene therapy*: Thomas Wirth, Nigel Parker, and Seppo Ylä-Herttuala, "History of Gene Therapy," *Gene* 525, no. 2 (August 2013): 162–69; see also I. M. Verma et al., "Gene Therapy: Promises, Problems and Prospects," in *Genes and Resistance to Disease*, eds. V. Boulyjenkov, K. Berg and Y. Christen (Heidelberg, Ger.: Springer, 2000), 147–57.

342   *Recent innovations have*: Fyodor D. Urnov et al., "Genome Editing with Engineered Zinc Finger Nucleases," *Nature Reviews Genetics* 11, no. 9 (September 2010):

636–46; see also Dana Carroll, "Genome Engineering with Zinc-Finger Nucleases," *Genetics* 188, no. 4 (August 2011): 773–82.

342   *In 2020 the Nobel Prize in Chemistry*: Press release: "The Nobel Prize in Chemistry 2020," NobelPrize.org, Nobel Prize Outreach AB 2021, last modified October 7, 2020, https://www.nobelprize.org/prizes/chemistry/2020/press-release/; see also Emmanuelle Charpentier and Jennifer A. Doudna, "Rewriting a Genome," *Nature* 495, no. 7439 (March 2013): 50–51; see also Jennifer A. Doudna and Emmanuelle Charpentier, "The New Frontier of Genome Engineering with CRISPR-Cas9," *Science* 346, no. 6213 (November 2014): 1258096.

343   *Neuromodulation techniques include*: Steven E. Davis and Glen A. Smith, "Transcranial Direct Current Stimulation Use in Warfighting: Benefits, Risks, and Future Prospects," *Frontiers in Human Neuroscience* 13 (April 2019): 114.

343   *Two of the more invasive*: Paul S. Fishman and Victor Frenkel, "Focused Ultrasound: An Emerging Therapeutic Modality for Neurologic Disease," *Neurotherapeutics* 14, no. 2 (April 2017): 393–404; see also A. M. Lozano et al., "A Multicenter Pilot Study of Subcallosal Cingulate Area Deep Brain Stimulation for Treatment-Resistant Depression," *Journal of Neurosurgery* 116, no. 2 (February 2012): 315–22; see also A. W. Laxton and A. M. Lozano, "Deep Brain Stimulation for the Treatment of Alzheimer Disease and Dementias," *World Neurosurgery* 80, no. 3/4 (September/October 2013): S28.e1–8.

CHAPTER 20: SCHIZOPHRENIA AND SOCIETY: DO THE RIGHT THING

345   *Wendell Williamson was*: William Glaberson, "Killer Blames His Therapist, and Jury Agrees," *New York Times*, October 10, 1998, A1.

346   *In his sessions with Liptzin*: Ibid.

346   *"The parents aren't in control"*: Ibid.

346   *"stamped a title"*: Nicole Wolfe (forensic psychiatrist, Central Regional Hospital, Forensic Services), in discussion with the author, September 27, 2021.

347   *In 1997 he sued Dr. Liptzin*: *Williamson v. Liptzin*, 539 S.E.2d 313 (N.C. App. 2000).

347   *"How can I be responsible"*: Glaberson, "Killer Blames Therapist."

348   *However, as of 2021*: Wolfe, in discussion with the author.

349   *While it is true that*: Jeffrey W. Swanson et al., "Mental Illness and Reduction of Gun Violence and Suicide: Bringing Epidemiologic Research to Policy," *Annals of Epidemiology* 25, no. 5 (May 2015): 366–76.

350   *If we consider only mass*: Jennifer Skeem and Edward Mulvey, "What Role Does Serious Mental Illness Play in Mass Shootings, and How Should We Address It?," *Criminology & Public Policy* 19, no. 1 (February 2020): 85–108; see also National Council Medical Director Institute, *Mass Violence in America*, National Council for Mental Wellbeing (August 2019), 14–16.

350   *The mentally ill make up*: HUD 2020 Continuum of Care, *Homeless Assistance Programs, Homeless Populations and Subpopulations*, US Department of Housing and Urban Development (December 15, 2020).

350   *one in five people*: Treatment Advocacy Center, *SMI Prevalence in Jails and Prisons*, 1.

350   *The annual cost of schizophrenia*: *Societal Costs of Schizophrenia & Related Disorders*, Schizophrenia & Psychosis Action Alliance (Alexandria, VA: July 2021), 17–23.

350   *From the time the first*: Appelbaum, in discussion with the author, March 16, 2021; see also George B. Curtis, "The Checkered Career of Parens Patriae: The State as Parent or Tyrant," *DePaul Law Review* 25, no. 4 (Summer 1976): 895–917.

351   *"parent of the country"*: Julia Halloran McLaughlin, "The Fundamental Truth About Best Interest," *Saint Louis University Law Journal* 54, no. 1 (Fall 2009): 120.

351   *Tens of thousands*: Alexandra Stern, "Forced Sterilization Policies in the US Targeted Minorities and Those with Disabilities—and Lasted into the 21st Century," *Conversation*, August 26, 2020; see also Sanjana Manjeshwar, "America's Forgotten History of Forced Sterilization," *Berkeley Political Review*, November 4, 2020; see also Stern, "United States Sterilized 60,000."

352   *peaking in the United States*: Torrey, *Out of the Shadows*, 8.

352   *a community treatment ethos*: Hans Pols and Stephanie Oak, "War & Military Mental Health: The US Psychiatric Response in the 20th Century," *American Journal of Public Health* 97, no. 12 (December 2007): 2132–42; see also Edgar Jones and Simon Wessely, "'Forward Psychiatry'" in the Military: Its Origins and Effectiveness," *Journal of Traumatic Stress* 16, no. 4 (August 2003): 411–19.

352   *Along with the push for*: Appelbaum, in discussion with the author, March 16, 2021.

353   *In 1960 the physician-attorney*: Morton Birnbaum, "The Right to Treatment," *American Bar Association Journal* 46, no. 5 (May 1960): 499–505.

353   *Birnbaum's thesis was taken*: Susan Hatters Friedman, "Raising American Standards in the Treatment of Persons with Mental Illness: Wyatt v. Stickney (1972)," chap. 2 in *From Courtroom to Clinic: Legal Cases That Changed Mental Health Treatment*, ed. Peter Ash (New York: Cambridge University Press, 2019), 9–14.

353   *Ennis had been working*: Ellen Willis, "Prisoners of Psychiatry," *New York Times*, March 4, 1973, 422.

353   *"I think if it were put"*: Leonard Roy Frank, "An Interview with Bruce Ennis," in *Madness Network News Reader*, eds. Sherry Hirsch et al. (San Francisco: Glide Publications, 1974), 162–63.

354   *"the best method for"*: Ibid., 163.

354   *In 1972 the judge in*: *Wyatt v. Stickney*, 344 F. Supp. 373 (M.D. Ala. 1972); see also Friedman, "Raising American Standards," 9–16.

354   *In the 1972* Lessard: *Lessard v. Schmidt*, 349 F. Supp. 1078–1097, 1103–1104 (E.D. Wis. 1972).

354   *"massive curtailment of liberty"*: Ibid., 1093.

355   *In the summer of 1969*: Robert G. Meyer and Christopher M. Weaver, *Law and Mental Health: A Case-Based Approach* (New York: Guilford Press, 2006), 82–84; see also Fillmore Buckner and Marvin Firestone, "'Where the Public Peril Begins': 25 Years After Tarasoff," *Journal of Legal Medicine* 21, no. 2 (June 2000): 187–222.

355   *Poddar was found guilty*: Ibid.

355   *The challenge then*: Ahmad Adi and Mohammad Mathbout, "The Duty to Protect: Four Decades After Tarasoff," *American Journal of Psychiatry Residents' Journal* 13, no. 4 (April 2018): 6–8.

356   *The dangerousness criterion for*: Meyer and Weaver, *Law and Mental Health*, 131–35.

356   *Court testimony demonstrated*: *O'Connor v. Donaldson*, 422 U.S. 565–569 (1975).

356   *In 1975 the court ruled*: Ibid., 575.

357   *In shifting the criteria*: Appelbaum, in discussion with the author, March 16, 2021.

357   *"helpless to avoid the hazards"*: *O'Connor v. Donaldson*, 422 U.S. 578 (1975).

357   *Paul Stavis, former counsel*: Rael Jean Isaac and D. J. Jaffe, "Toward Rational Com-
       mitment Laws: Committed to Help," Mental Illness Policy Organization online,
       January 29, 1996, https://mentalillnesspolicy.org/media/bestmedia/rational-com
       mitment.html.

357   *"died with their rights on"*: Darold A. Treffert, "The Macarthur Coercion Studies: A
       Wisconsin Perspective," *Marquette Law Review* 82, no. 4 (Summer 1999): 775.

357   *In many states, schools*: "State School and Childcare Vaccination Laws," Centers for
       Disease Control and Prevention online, last modified April 28, 2017, https://www
       .cdc.gov/phlp/publications/topic/vaccinations.html.

358   *Some states require people*: "Am I Legally Required to Share My HIV Status with
       Others?," Centers for Disease Control and Prevention online, last modified May 20,
       2021, https://www.cdc.gov/hiv/basics/livingwithhiv/telling-others.html.

358   *This lack of insight*: Douglas S. Lehrer and Jennifer Lorenz, "Anosognosia in Schizo-
       phrenia: Hidden in Plain Sight," *Innovations in Clinical Neuroscience* 11, no. 5–6
       (May 2014): 10–17.

358   *In the case of people*: Victor I. Reus et al., "The American Psychiatric Association
       Practice Guideline on the Use of Antipsychotics to Treat Agitation or Psychosis
       in Patients with Dementia," *American Journal of Psychiatry* 173, no. 5 (May 2016):
       543–46; see also Franz Müller-Spahn, "Behavioral Disturbances in Dementia," *Dia-
       logues in Clinical Neuroscience* 5, no. 1 (March 2003): 49–59.

359   *The changes in inpatient*: Appelbaum, in discussion with the author, March 16, 2021.

359   *The bedrock requirement*: *Civil Commitment and the Mental Health Care Continuum:
       Historical Trends and Principles for Law and Practice*, SAMHSA (Rockville, MD:
       January 2019), 7–12.

360   *In her memoir*: Saks, *Center Cannot Hold*, 145–59.

360   *PADs are a mechanism*: Jeffrey W. Swanson et al., "Psychiatric Advance Directives: A
       Survey of Persons with Schizophrenia, Family Members, and Treatment Providers,"
       International Journal of Forensic Mental Health 2, no. 1 (2003): 73–86.

361   *"I have never seen myself"*: Cahalan, *Brain on Fire*, 175.

362   *Involuntary civil commitment and*: Vincent Atchity et al., "Model Legal Processes to
       Support Clinical Intervention for Persons with Serious Mental Illnesses," Equitas
       Project (unpublished report, November 17, 2021), PDF file.

363   *People with mental health issues*: Doris A. Fuller et al., *Overlooked in the Undercoun-
       ted: The Role of Mental Illness in Fatal Law Enforcement Encounters*, Treatment
       Advocacy Center (Arlington, VA: December 2015), 1, 12.

364   *Over the last several decades*: E. Fuller Torrey, "The Rise and Fall of the Asylum,"
       interview by John Hirschauer, *National Review*, March 5, 2020, https://www.nation
       alreview.com/2020/03/doctor-e-fuller-torrey-unintended-consequences-emptying
       -out-mental-hospitals/; see also "Jailing People with Mental Illness," National Alli-
       ance on Mental Illness, accessed March 11, 2021, https://www.nami.org/Advocacy

/Policy-Priorities/Divert-from-Justice-Involvement/Jailing-People-with-Mental
-Illness.

364   *about three-quarters have*: "Criminal Justice DrugFacts," National Institute on Drug
       Abuse, last modified June 1, 2020, https://www.drugabuse.gov/publications/drug
       facts/criminal-justice.

364   *racial and ethnic minority youth*: Purva Rawal et al., "Racial Differences in the Mental
       Health Needs and Service Utilization of Youth in the Juvenile Justice System,"
       Journal of Behavioral Health Services & Research 31, no. 3 (July/September 2004):
       242–54; see also Elizabeth Spinney et al., "Racial Disparities in Referrals to Mental
       Health and Substance Abuse Services from the Juvenile Justice System: A Review of
       the Literature," *Journal of Crime and Justice* 39, no. 1 (January 2016): 153–73.

364   *An estimated 83 percent*: "Jailing People with Mental Illness," National Alliance on
       Mental Illness, accessed March 11, 2021, https://www.nami.org/Advocacy/Policy
       -Priorities/Divert-from-Justice-Involvement/Jailing-People-with-Mental-Illness.

364   *They tend to remain incarcerated*: "Mental Illness and the Prison Industrial Complex,"
       Amanpour & Company, aired July 24, 2020, on PBS, https://www.pbs.org/wnet
       /amanpour-and-company/video/mental-illness-and-the-prison-industrial-complex/;
       see also Natalie Bonfine, Amy Blank Wilson, and Mark R. Munetz, "Meeting the
       Needs of Justice-Involved People with Serious Mental Illness within Community
       Behavioral Health Systems," *Psychiatric Services* 71, no. 4 (April 2020): 355–63; see
       also Pete Earley, "Mental Illness Is a Health Issue, Not a Police Issue," *Washington
       Post* online, June 15, 2020.

365   *Recent data suggest that*: Jennifer L. Skeem, Sarah Manchak, and Jillian K. Peterson,
       "Correctional Policy for Offenders with Mental Illness: Creating a New Paradigm
       for Recidivism Reduction," *Law and Human Behavior* 35, no. 2 (April 2011):
       110–26; see also Matthew W. Epperson et al., "Envisioning the Next Generation of
       Behavioral Health and Criminal Justice Interventions," *International Journal of Law
       and Psychiatry* 37, no. 5 (September 2014): 427–38; see also Bonfine, Wilson, and
       Munetz, "Meeting the Needs of Justice-Involved People," 355–63.

365   *Paul Appelbaum, who has written*: Appelbaum, in discussion with the author, March
       16, 2021.

366   *Pre-arrest diversion strategies*: Richard Williams, "Addressing Mental Health in the
       Justice System," *National Conference of State Legislatures LegisBriefs* 23, no. 31
       (August 2015); see also Michael T. Compton et al., "The Police-Based Crisis Inter-
       vention Team (CIT) Model: II. Effects on Level of Force and Resolution, Referral,
       and Arrest," *Psychiatric Services* 65, no. 4 (April 2014): 523–29; see also Michael T.
       Compton et al., "A Comprehensive Review of Extant Research on Crisis Interven-
       tion Team (CIT) Programs," *Journal of the American Academy of Psychiatry and the
       Law Online* 36, no. 1 (March 2008): 47–55.

366   *More broadly, diversion programs*: Henry J. Steadman et al., "Effect of Mental Health
       Courts on Arrests and Jail Days: A Multisite Study," *Archives of General Psychiatry*
       68, no. 2 (February 2011): 167–72.

366   *The first mental health court*: Warren A. Reich et al., *Predictors of Program Compli-
       ance and Re-Arrest in the Brooklyn Mental Health Court*, Center for Court Innova-
       tion (New York: June 2014), iii.

366   *The decision as to*: Nancy Wolff, Nicole Fabrikant, and Steven Belenko, "Mental Health Courts and Their Selection Processes: Modeling Variation for Consistency," *Law and Human Behavior* 35, no. 5 (October 2011): 402–12.

367   *Miami-Dade has the largest*: *Miami-Dade County—Mental Health Diversion Facility*, National Association of State Mental Health Program Directors (Alexandria, VA: July 2016), 2.

367   *The issue goes way back*: "Steve Leifman: A Judge on the Mental Health Frontlines in Miami," Stepping Up Initative, accessed April 9, 2021, https://stepuptogether.org /people/steve-leifman; see also John Buntin, "Miami's Model for Decriminalizing Mental Illness in America," *Governing* online, July 29, 2015, https://www.governing .com/archive/gov-miami-mental-health-jail.html.

367   *"Those are the men"*: "Steve Leifman," Stepping Up Initative.

367   *In 2000, by which time*: Stephen Eide, "Keeping the Mentally Ill Out of Jail," *City Journal* online, Autumn 2018, https://www.city-journal.org/miami-dade-criminal -mental-health-project.

367   *About 80 percent*: Buntin, "Miami's Model."

367   *Leifman's current project*: Rachel Looker, "Miami-Dade County Builds Center for Mental Health and Recovery," *National Association of Counties* online, November 7, 2019, https://www.naco.org/articles/miami-dade-county-builds-center-mental -health-and-recovery.

368   *In the spring of 2019*: Jocelyn Wiener, "For Families Across California, a Desperate Struggle to Get Mental Health Care," *CalMatters* online, March 10, 2019, https:// calmatters.org/projects/californians-struggle-to-get-mental-health-care/.

369   *These policies drove*: The IMD law has been modified from its original form to allow for limited reimbursement to hospitals with more than sixteen beds for mental illness, but it still serves to limit psychiatric services in hospitals and acts as an economic disincentive to states to support mental institutions. The net effect of the legislation has been contrary to its original purpose, and the IMD law should be rescinded or, at the very least, revised again.

369   *In the early 1990s*: Deborah Sontag, "When Politics Is Personal," *New York Times Magazine*, September 15, 2002, 90.

370   *Wellstone described the public*: Ibid.

370   *Together the duo*: Ibid.

370   *it was also the first national*: Sarah A. Friedman et al., "The Mental Health Parity and Addiction Equity Act (MHPAEA) Evaluation Study: Did Parity Differentially Affect Substance Use Disorder and Mental Health Benefits Offered by Behavioral Health-care Carve-out and Carve-in Plans?," *Drug and Alcohol Dependence* 190 (September 2018): 151–58.

370   *However, the 2008 act*: *Parity Toolkit for Addiction & Mental Health Consumers, Providers & Advocates* (Washington, DC: Parity Implementation Coalition online, last modified September 2010), https://atforum.com/documents/Parity_Toolkit_Final.pdf.

370   *Finally, the legislation did not*: Ellen Weber, "Equality Standards for Health Insurance Coverage: Will the Mental Health Parity and Addiction Equity Act End the Discrimination?," *Golden Gate University Law Review* 43, no. 2 (April 2013): 179–80, 224–35.

370   *between 2009 and 2012*: Matt Ford, "America's Largest Mental Hospital Is a Jail," *Atlantic* online, last modified June 8, 2015, https://www.theatlantic.com/politics/archive/2015/06/americas-largest-mental-hospital-is-a-jail/395012/.

371   *In 2014 H.R. 3547 was*: Dixon, "Early Psychosis Treatment"; see also "State Health Administrators and Clinics," National Institute of Mental Health, accessed April 6, 2021, https://www.nimh.nih.gov/health/topics/schizophrenia/raise/state-health-administrators-and-clinics.shtml; see also Robert K. Heinssen, Amy B. Goldstein, and Susan T. Azrin, "Evidence-Based Treatments for First Episode Psychosis: Components of Coordinated Specialty Care," National Institute of Mental Health, April 14, 2014, https://www.nimh.nih.gov/health/topics/schizophrenia/raise/evidence-based-treatments-for-first-episode-psychosis-components-of-coordinated-specialty-care.

371   *Two years later*: Liz Szabo, "Senate Approves Landmark Mental Health Bill as Part of 21st Century Cures Act," *Kaiser Health News* online, December 7, 2016, https://khn.org/news/senate-approves-landmark-mental-health-bill-as-part-of-21st-century-cures-act/.

372   *Ignaz Philipp Semmelweis was*: Mark Best and Duncan Neuhauser, "Ignaz Semmelweis and the Birth of Infection Control," *British Medical Journal Quality & Safety* 13, no. 3 (June 2004): 233–34.

372   *Surprisingly, Semmelweis's findings*: Ibid.; see also Hilary J. Lane, Nava Blum, and Elizabeth Fee, "Oliver Wendell Holmes (1809–1894) and Ignaz Philipp Semmelweis (1818–1865): Preventing the Transmission of Puerperal Fever," *American Journal of Public Health* 100, no. 6 (June 2010): 1008–9; see also Meagan Flynn, "The Man Who Discovered That Unwashed Hands Could Kill—and Was Ridiculed for It," *Washington Post* online, March 23, 2020, https://www.washingtonpost.com/nation/2020/03/23/ignaz-semmelweis-handwashing-coronavirus/.

373   *40 percent of people*: Office of Research & Public Affairs, *Serious Mental Illness and Treatment Prevalence*, Treatment Advocacy Center (May 2017); see also SAMHSA, *Racial/Ethnic Differences in Mental Health Service Use Among Adults* (Rockville, MD: Substance Abuse and Mental Health Services Administration [SAMHSA], 2015), 32–39.

373   *Most people who were*: Torrey, "Rise and Fall of the Asylum."

375   *Annual health care expenditure*: "NHE Fact Sheet," Centers for Medicare & Medicaid Services, last modified December 16, 2020, https://www.cms.gov/Research-Statistics-Data-and-Systems/Statistics-Trends-and-Reports/NationalHealthExpendData/NHE-Fact-Sheet; see also Eric M. Tichy et al., "National Trends in Prescription Drug Expenditures and Projections for 2021," *American Journal of Health-System Pharmacy* 78, no. 14 (July 2021): 1294–308.

376   *black and Latinx populations*: SAMHSA reported in 2015 that 69 percent of whites with serious mental illness used mental health services, while only 57 percent of black people and 50 percent of Hispanic people used them. See *Racial/Ethnic Differences in Mental Health Service Use*.

376   *The US Department of Health*: *National Projections of Supply and Demand for Selected Behavioral Health Practitioners: 2013–2025*, US Department of Health and Human Services, Health Resources and Services Administration (Rockville, MD: November 2016), 18–19; see also Stacy Weiner, "Addressing the Escalating Psychiatrist Short-

age," Association of American Medical Colleges, February 12, 2018, https://www
.aamc.org/news-insights/addressing-escalating-psychiatrist-shortage.

377   *Approximately 60 percent to 80*: Tyler Barton et al., *Tackling America's Mental Health and Addiction Crisis through Primary Care Integration*, Bipartisan Policy Center (Washington, DC: March 2021), 67.

377   *At the same time*: Stefan Leucht et al., "Physical Illness and Schizophrenia: A Review of the Literature," *Acta Psychiatrica Scandinavica* 116, no. 5 (November 2007): 317–33.

377   *A proven solution to both*: Jürgen Unützer et al., "The Collaborative Care Model: An Approach for Integrating Physical and Mental Health Care in Medicaid Health Homes," Center for Health Care Strategies, May 2013; see also Bonfine, Wilson, and Munetz, "Meeting the Needs of Justice-Involved People," 355–63.

377   *A body of research*: Kane et al., "Comprehensive Versus Usual Community Care"; see also Camice J. Revier et al., "Ten-Year Outcomes of First-Episode Psychoses in the MRC ÆSOP-10 Study," *Journal of Nervous and Mental Disease* 203, no. 5 (May 2015): 379–86.

377   *But between 2003*: Liz Szabo, "Mental Illness: Families Cut Out of Care," *USA Today* online, March 7, 2016, https://www.usatoday.com/story/news/2016/02/26/privacy-law-harms-care-mentally-ill-families-say/80880880/.

378   *Just 62 percent of psychiatrists*: Jennifer Bresnick, "PCPs, Psychiatrists Much Less Likely to Accept Medicaid," HealthPayerIntelligence, February 6, 2019, https://healthpayer intelligence.com/news/pcps-psychiatrists-much-less-likely-to-accept-medicaid.

378   *In 2019 reimbursement rates*: Judith Warner, "Psychiatry Confronts Its Racist Past, and Tries to Make Amends," *New York Times* online, April 30, 2021, https://www.nytimes.com/2021/04/30/health/psychiatry-racism-black-americans.html.

378   *Cost-based reimbursement*: Louis C. Gapenski and Kristin L. Reiter, *Healthcare Finance: An Introduction to Accounting and Financial Management*, 6th ed. (Chicago: Health Administration Press, 2016), 52.

378   *The Affordable Care Act, which made*: *The Affordable Care Act: A Brief Summary*, National Conference of State Legislatures (Washington, DC: 2011), https://www.ncsl.org/research/health/the-affordable-care-act-brief-summary.aspx.

378   *We need to expand*: *A Unified Vision for Transforming Mental Health and Substance Use Care*, Well Being Trust (Oakland, CA: December 2020), 11–12.

379   *The famous Fountain House*: Anderson, *We Are Not Alone*.

379   *while Community Access's*: Gelder, "Howard Geld."

379   *Steve Leifman's Miami*: Looker, "Miami-Dade County."

379   *OneFifteen in Ohio*: Kaitlin R. Schroeder, "OneFifteen Opens New Apartments for Addiction Recovery," *Dayton Daily News* online, September 19, 2020, https://www.daytondailynews.com/news/onefifteen-opens-new-apartments-for-addiction-recovery/XVVP6QGECNHMVELOH4BPB3CMOM/.

379   *In Cook County, Illinois*: *Mental Health Template*, Cook County Sheriff's Office (Cook County, IL: July 2016), 7–8, https://www.cookcountysheriff.org/mental-health-template/.

380   *The roll call of members*: Rich Daly, "Congress About to Lose Key MH Advocates," *Psychiatric News* online, January 2, 2009, https://doi.org/10.1176/pn.44.1.0001; see also "Former US Rep. Jim Ramstad, Champion of Recovery, Dies at 74," Associated

Press, November 6, 2020, https://apnews.com/article/health-jim-ramstad-mental
-health-minneapolis-minnesota-b1ac699cccde59117322a039d3ad82c5.

380   *Jimmy Carter created*: Grob, "Public Policy and Mental Illnesses."

Chapter 21: Owning Recovery

382   *When Brandon Staglin was first*: Staglin, in discussion with the author.

384   *In 1995, five years after*: "One Mind's Music Festival for Brain Health Surpasses Half Billion Dollars Raised to Date," Business Wire, news release, September 13, 2021, https://www.businesswire.com/news/home/20210913005258/en/.

384   *Brandon still hung back*: Staglin, in discussion with the author.

385   *Doctors traditionally defined*: Larry Davidson, "Let's Talk About Recovery," public lecture, Sydney University, Australia, July 4, 2013, YouTube video, 2:06, https://www.youtube.com/watch?v=8p5l36yNPnY.

385   *"My good fortune is not"*: Saks, *Center Cannot Hold*.

385   *Recovery is a continuous process*: Robert E. Drake and Rob Whitley, "Recovery and Severe Mental Illness: Description and Analysis," *Canadian Journal of Psychiatry* 59, no. 5 (May 2014): 236–42.

385   *SAMHSA, the lead federal agency*: "Recovery and Recovery Support," SAMHSA, last modified April 23, 2020, https://www.samhsa.gov/find-help/recovery; see also *SAMHSA's Working Definition of Recovery*, SAMHSA (Rockville, MD: February 2012), 2–7, https://store.samhsa.gov/sites/default/files/d7/priv/pep12-recdef.pdf.

386   *The psychiatrist Anthony Lehman*: Anthony F. Lehman, "Putting Recovery into Practice: A Commentary on 'What Recovery Means to Us,'" *Community Mental Health Journal* 36, no. 3 (June 2000): 329–33.

386   *Over the previous half century*: Frederick J. Frese III, Edward L. Knight, and Elyn Saks, "Recovery from Schizophrenia: With Views of Psychiatrists, Psychologists, and Others Diagnosed with This Disorder," *Schizophrenia Bulletin* 35, no. 2 (June 2009): 370–80.

386   *The first stirrings of*: Manon Parry, "From a Patient's Perspective: Clifford Whittingham Beers' Work to Reform Mental Health Services," *American Journal of Public Health* 100, no. 12 (December 2010): 2356–57.

386   *Beers subsequently joined*: Ibid.

387   *Various constituencies in*: David J. Rissmiller and Joshua H. Rissmiller, "Open Forum: Evolution of the Antipsychiatry Movement into Mental Health Consumerism," *Psychiatric Services* 57, no. 6 (June 2006): 863–66.

388   *Among the first groups*: Judi Chamberlin, "The Ex-Patients' Movement: Where We've Been and Where We're Going," *Journal of Mind and Behavior* 11, no. 3–4 (Summer and Autumn 1990): 323–36.

388   *The first annual Conference*: Conference on Human Rights and Psychiatric Oppression, "Conference on Psychiatric Oppression to Be Held in Boston," news release, 1976, retrieved from the Digital Public Library of America, https://dp.la/item/3773c e8a84d5725f9d5cbf2820dc3c09.

388   *"Among the major organizing"*: Chamberlin, "Ex-Patients' Movement," 325.

388   *In the 1980s the federal*: Ibid., 328–30; see also Rissmiller and Rissmiller, "Evolution of the Antipsychiatry Movement," 864–66; see also Laysha Ostrow and Neal Adams, "Recovery in the USA: From Politics to Peer Support," *International Review of Psychiatry* 4, no. 1 (February 2012): 70–78.

389   *"a deeply personal, unique"*: William A. Anthony, "Recovery from Mental Illness: The Guiding Vision of the Mental Health Service System in the 1990s," *Psychosocial Rehabilitation Journal* 16, no. 4 (April 1993): 15.

389   *"[T]he goal of services"*: *Mental Health: A Report of the Surgeon General*, US Department of Health and Human Services, Substance Abuse and Mental Health Services Administration, Center for Mental Health Services, National Institutes of Health, National Institute of Mental Health (Pittsburgh, PA: 1999), 455.

389   *Studies examining middle-aged*: John S. Strauss and Alan Breier, "The Vermont Longitudinal Study of Persons with Severe Mental Illness, I: Methodology, Study Sample, and Overall Status 32 Years Later," *American Journal of Psychiatry* 144, no. 6 (June 1987): 718–26; see also Courtenay M. Harding et al., "The Vermont Longitudinal Study of Persons with Severe Mental Illness, II: Long-Term Outcome of Subjects Who Retrospectively Met DSM-III Criteria for Schizophrenia," *American Journal of Psychiatry* 144, no. 6 (June 1987): 727–35.

390   *The upshot of the recovery*: Jeffrey A. Lieberman et al., "Science and Recovery in Schizophrenia," *Psychiatric Services* 59, no. 5 (May 2008): 487–96.

391   *"all of the polemic"*: Deegan, "Recovery: The Lived Experience," 14.

391   *The episodic nature of severe*: Anthony, "Recovery from Mental Illness," 11–23.

391   *Clinicians, friends, and family*: Davidson, "Let's Talk About Recovery."

391   *The notion of full*: Francisco José Eiroa-Orosa and Michael Rowe, "Taking the Concept of Citizenship in Mental Health across Countries. Reflections on Transferring Principles and Practice to Different Sociocultural Contexts," *Frontiers in Psychology* 8 (June 2017): 1020.

391   *While individuals with*: Atul Jaiswal et al., "Essential Elements That Contribute to the Recovery of Persons with Severe Mental Illness: A Systematic Scoping Study," *Frontiers in Psychiatry* 11 (November 2020): 586230.

392   *Standard medical and psychiatric*: Deegan, "Recovery: The Lived Experience," 12; see also Lieberman et al., "Science and Recovery."

392   *The approach to care*: Larry Davidson, "The Recovery Movement: Implications for Mental Health Care and Enabling People to Participate Fully in Life," *Health Affairs* 35, no. 6 (June 2016): 1091–97.

392   *Elyn Saks has spent*: Frese, Knight, and Saks, "Recovery from Schizophrenia."

393   *"can lead full, happy"*: Benedict Carey, "Expert on Mental Illness Reveals Her Own Fight," *New York Times* online, June 23, 2011, https://www.nytimes.com/2011/06/23/health/23lives.html.

393   *Systemic changes should*: Drake and Whitley, "Recovery and Severe Mental Illness."

393   *Recovery, as Pat Deegan writes*: Deegan, "Recovery: The Lived Experience," 16–19; see also Patricia Deegan, "Recovery as a Journey of the Heart," *Psychiatric Rehabilitation Journal* 19, no. 3 (Winter 1996): 91–97.

394   *"rugged individualism"*: Deegan, "Recovery: The Lived Experience," 17.

394   *People who are recovering*: Anthony, "Recovery from Mental Illness," 11–23.

394   *Brandon recalls how*: Staglin, in discussion with the author.

394   *"It was like reading"*: Daniel, in discussion with the author, March 28, 2020, and April 26, 2020.

398   *She admits that*: Medalia, in discussion with the author.

EPILOGUE

400   *Previously, the NIMH maintained*: E. Fuller Torrey et al., "The Continuing Decline of Clinical Research on Serious Mental Illnesses at NIMH," *Psychiatric Services* online, last modified April 6, 2021, https://ps.psychiatryonline.org/doi/10.1176/appi.ps .202000739.

400   *In an interview with*: Adam Rogers, "Star Neuroscientist Tom Insel Leaves the Google-Spawned Verily for . . . a Startup?," *Wired* online, last modified May 11, 2017, https://www.wired.com/2017/05/star-neuroscientist-tom-insel-leaves-google -spawned-verily-startup/.

401   *Insel had even gone*: David Dobbs, "The Smartphone Psychiatrist," *Atlantic*, July/ August 2017, https://www.theatlantic.com/magazine/archive/2017/07/the-smart phone-psychiatrist/528726/.

401   *Speaking to the*: Ibid.

401   *The current NIMH director*: E. Fuller Torrey, Robert H. Yolken, and H. Richard Lamb, "NIMH Drug Trials for Schizophrenia," *Journal of Clinical Psychiatry* 80, no. 1 (January 2019).

401   *At the same time, the private sector*: Jacob Bell, "Big Pharma Backed Away from Brain Drugs. Is a Return in Sight?," BioPharma Dive, last modified January 29, 2020, https://www.biopharmadive.com/news/pharma-neuroscience-retreat-return-brain -drugs/570250/.

402   *The US Centers for Disease Control*: Michael S. Gottlieb et al., "Pneumocystis Pneumonia—Los Angeles," *Morbidity and Mortality Weekly Report (MMWR)* 30, no. 21 (June 1981): 1–3.

403   *In 1996 Dr. David Ho*: David Ho, "HIV Research Overview: Interview with David Ho, MD. Interview by John S. James," *AIDS Treatment News*, no. 282 (November 1997): 1–6.

404   *I think our failures*: Thomas Insel, "Urgent Issues in Mental Health Now: An Expert Interview with Thomas R. Insel, MD," interview by Elizabeth Saenger, *Medscape*, May 16, 2008.

Illustration Credits

INDEX

About the Author

JEFFREY A. LIEBERMAN, MD, is Professor and the Constance and Stephen Lieber Chair in Psychiatry at Columbia University. Over his forty-year career as a physician and scientist, he has treated thousands of patients with mental disorders, and his research has elucidated the pathological basis for schizophrenia and improved treatments for the disease. Lieberman was elected to the National Academy of Medicine in 2000 and served as the president of the American Psychiatric Association from 2013 to 2014. A frequent public spokesperson on mental illness and psychiatry, he has published more than seven hundred articles in leading scientific journals and seventeen books for the scientific and medical communities. His first book for trade audiences was the critically acclaimed *Shrinks: The Untold Story of Psychiatry*, which became the basis for a four-part PBS series titled *Mysteries of Mental Illness*.